PEN, STYLUS, AND CHISEL

An Ancient Egypt Sourcebook

First Edition

Edited by David Miano
Executive Director, Schola Antiquorum

Bassim Hamadeh, CEO and Publisher
Michael Simpson, Vice President of Acquisitions
Jamie Giganti, Managing Editor
Jess Busch, Graphic Design Supervisor
Jessica Knott, Senior Project Editor
Luiz Ferreira, Licensing Associate

First published in the United States of America in 2015 by Cognella, Inc.

Trademark Notice: Product or corporate names may be trademarks or registered trademarks, and are used only for identification and explanation without intent to infringe.

Cover images: David Roberts, Egypt & Nubia: From Drawings Made on the Spot by David Roberts. Copyright in the Public Domain; Copyright © 2009 by Depositphotos/Viktor Zhugin.

Printed in the United States of America

ISBN: 978-1-63189-006-2 (pbk) / 978-1-63189-007-9 (br)

www.cognella.com   800-200-3908

CONTENTS

FIRST INTERMEDIATE PERIOD   37

THIRD INTERMEDIATE PERIOD   263

LATE KINGDOM   287

PERSIAN PERIOD   295

PTOLEMAIC PERIOD   339

Preface

To create a book of this sort was never a part of my planned career path, but the project arose out of a nagging need for something distinctly appropriate to use in my upper-division ancient Egyptian history course, which I offer twice every year. The course itself wasn't even of my own design—it was handed to me by the administration after the previous instructor retired. As an ancient historian, I welcomed the opportunity to teach on the subject and immediately set to work refurbishing the course. One of the challenges I encountered at the outset was locating a suitable anthology of primary sources. Mind you, there are a handful of Egyptian literature anthologies out there, but I don't offer an Egyptian literature course. I do Egyptian history. So my preference would be for a reader that contained some historical documents in addition to the literature. For a time I used William Kelly Simpson's *The Literature of Ancient Egypt*, because it does contain a few historical inscriptions, but there are so many important texts that are absent from that book. Miriam Lichtheim's *Ancient Egyptian Literature* contains a wider selection, but it comes in three volumes and thus is too cumbersome for teaching purposes. So I had no other option than to make an anthology of my own. I'm hoping that my efforts have resulted in something useful for all instructors of ancient Egyptian history.

What makes this book so valuable, I think, is that not only does it provide translations of a broad selection of Egyptian literary works, inscriptions, letters, and legal documents, but also writings by non-Egyptians whose observations of the Egyptians would prove informative to the student of Egyptian history. I mean, what a gap in knowledge we would have without the Amarna Letters or the Histories of Herodotus! No other anthology, so far as I know, offers these sorts of texts.

The translations are not my own but have been selected from other books and articles, quite frequently from the public domain to keep the licensing fees to a minimum. Early translators followed the fashion of rendering ancient Egyptian in King James-style English, which students today find rather confusing, so in prose translations from the public domain I have updated the antiquated English to more modern usage without changing the meaning. I left the poetry as is, and of course, have not touched more recent copyrighted translations.

I would be glad to hear any recommendations for improvement in a subsequent edition of this book, so feel free to email me at dmiano@sdccd.edu.

May your heart be light!

—David Miano

Chronology of Ancient Egypt[1]

Period	Dynasty	Manetho's Dynasty #s	Name	From	To
Early Dynastic (2900–2593)	Menid Dynasty	1st	Narmer / Meni (Menes)	2900	?
			'Aha	?	2870
			Djer	2870	2823
			Djet	2822	2815
			Den	2814	2772
			Anedjib	2771	2764
			Semerkhet	2763	2756
			Qa'a	2755	2732
	Boethid Dynasty	2nd	Hetepsekhemwy Bedjau (Boethos)	2730	?
			Ra'neb	?	2700
			Nynetjer	2700	2660
			Peribsen	2660	2650
			Sekhemib	2650	?
			Sened	?	2610
	Khasekhemwid Dynasty		Khasekhemwy	2610	2593
Old Kingdom (2592–2152)		3rd	Djoser (Tosorthros, Sesorthos)	2592	2566
			Sekhemkhet	2565	2559
			Kha'ba	2559	?
			Nebka	?	?
			Huni	?	2544
		4th	Snefru (Soris)	2543	2510
			Khufu (Cheops)	2509	2483
			Djedefre'	2482	2475
			Bikheris	2474	2473
			Khafre' (Chephren)	2472	2448
			Menkaure' (Mycerinus)	2447	2442
			Shepseskaf	2441	2436
		5th	Userkaf	2435	2429
			Sahure'	2428	2416
			Neferirkare' Kakai	2415	2405
			Neferefre'	2404	2404
			Shepseskare' Izi	2403	2403
			Niuserre' Ini	2402	2374
			Menkauhor	2373	2366
			Djedkare' Izezi	2365	2322
			Unas	2321	2306
		6th	Teti (Othoes)	2305	2279
			Userkare'	?	?
			Pepy I	2276	2228
			Merenre Nemtyemzaf	2227	2217
			Pepy II	2216	2153
			Nemtyemzaef II	2152	2152

---

1   These dates are based on the calculations of Krauss and Warburton (*Ancient Egyptian Chronology* [Leiden: Brill, 2006], pp. 473–495).

Period	Dynasty		King		
1st Intermediate (2151–1980)		8th	Various kings	2150	2127
			Neferkaure'	2126	2113
			Neferkauhor	2122	2120
			Neferirkare'	2119	2118
	?	9th and 10th	Several kings	2118	?
			Merikare	?	?
			Other kings	?	1980
	Mentuhotepid Dynasty	11th	Mentuhotep I	2080	?
			Inyotef I	?	2067
			Inyotef II	2066	2017
			Inyotef III	2016	2009
Middle Kingdom (1980–1661)			Mentuhotep II	2009	1959
			Mentuhotep III	1958	1947
			Mentuhotep IV	1947	1940
	Amenhemid Dynasty	12th	Amenemhet I	1939	1910
			Senusret I (Sesostris I)	1920	1875
			Amenemhet II	1878	1843
			Senusret II	1845	1837
			Senusret III	1837	1819
			Amenemhet III	1818	1773
			Amenemhet IV	1772	1764
			Neferusobek / Sobekneferu	1763	1760
	?	13th	Wegaf	1759	1757
			Amenemhet VII	1753	1748
			Sobekhotep II	1737	1733
			Khendjer	1732	1728
			Sobekhotep III	1725	1722
			Neferhotep I	1721	1710
			Sobekhotep IV	1709	1701
			Sobekhotep V	1700	1695
			Ibiau	1695	1685
			Merneferre' Aya	1684	1661
2nd Intermediate (1660–1539)			Ini I	1660	1659
			Sewadjtu	?	?
			Ined	?	?
			Hori	?	?
			Dedumose I (Tutimaeos)	?	1630
	Dynasty of Khasut	14th	Nehesi	1660	?
			Sekheperenre'	?	?
			Meridjefare	?	?
			Other kings	?	1630
	Hyksos kings	15th	Sheshi (Salitis)	1630	?
			Bnon	?	?
			Khian	?	?
			Auserre Apepi (Apophis)	1575	1540
			Khamudi	?	?
	?	16th	Several kings	?	?
	Theban Dynasty	17th	Rahotep	?	?
			Sobekemsaf I	?	?
			Sobekemsaf II	?	?
			Sekhemre'-Wepmaat Intef	?	?
			Nubkheperre' Intef	?	?
			Senakhtenre' Tao I	?	?
			Sekenenre' Tao II	?	?
			Kamose	?	1540

New Kingdom **(1539–1077)**		18th	'Ahmose I	1539	1515
			Amenhotep I (Amenophis)	1514	1494
			Thutmose I (Tuthmosis)	1493	1483
			Thutmose II	1482	1480
			Hatshepsut	1479	1458
			Thutmose III	1479	1425
			Amenhotep II	1425	1400
			Thutmose IV	1400	1390
			Amenhotep III	1390	1353
			Amenhotep IV / Akhenaten	1353	1336
			Smenkhkare' / Nefernefruaten	1336	1334
			Nefernefruaten	1334	?
			Tut'ankhaten / Tut'ankhamun	?	1324
			Ay	1323	1320
			Horemheb	1319	1292
	Ramessid Dynasty	19th	Ramesses I	1292	1291
			Seti I (Sethos)	1290	1279
			Ramesses II	1279	1213
			Merenptah	1213	1203
			Amenmesses	1202	1200
			Seti II	1202	1198
			Siptah	1197	1193
			Twosret (Thuoris)	1192	1191
	Pseudo- Ramessid Dynasty	20th	Setnakhte	1190	1188
			Ramesses III	1187	1157
			Ramesses IV	1156	1150
			Ramesses V	1149	1146
			Ramesses VI	1145	1139
			Ramesses VII	1138	1131
			Ramesses VIII	1130	1130
			Ramesses IX	1129	1111
			Ramesses X	1110	1107
			Ramesses XI	1106	1077
3rd Intermediate **(1076–723)**	Tanaite Dynasty	21st	Nesbanedbjed (Smendes)	1076	1052
			Pasibkhanu (Psusennes) I	1051	1006
			Neferkare' Amenemnisut	1005	1002
			Amenemope	1102	993
	Meshwesh Libyan Dynasty -		Osorkon (Osochor) the Elder	992	987
			Siamun (Psinaches)	986	968
			Pasibkhanu (Psusennes) II	967	944
	Meshwesh Libyan Dynasty	22nd	Shoshenq I	943	923
			Osorkon I	922	888
			Takelot I	887	874
			Shoshenq II	873	873
			Osorkon II	872	842
			Shoshenq III	841	803
			Shoshenq IIIa	?	790
			Pami	789	784
			Shoshenq V	783	746
		23rd	Various rival kings	845	730
	Saite Dynasty	24th	Tefnakhte I	736	729
			Bakenranef (Bocchoris)	728	723
	Napatan Dynasty	25th	Piye / Pi'ankhi	753	723
Kushite Period **(722–671)**			Shabaka (Sabacos)	722	707
			Shebitku (Sebichos)	698	690
			Taharqa (Tarachos)	690	667
Assyrian Period **(671–656)**	Sargonid Dynasty	-	Esarhaddon	671	669
			Ashurbanipal	669	656

Late Kingdom (656–525)	Saite Dynasty	26th	Psamtik (Psammetichus) I	656	610
			Nekau (Necho) II	610	595
			Psamtik II	595	589
			Haaibre' (Apries)	589	570
			Ahmose (Amasis) II	570	526
			Psamtik III	526	525
Persian Period (525–332)	Achaemenid Dynasty	27th	Cambyses	525	522
			Darius I	521	486
			Xerxes I	486	466
			Artaxerxes I	465	424
			Darius II	424	404
	Saite Dynasty	28th	Amenirdisu (Amyrtaios)	404	399
	-	29th	Nefaarud (Nepherites) I	399	393
	-		Psimut (Psammuthis)	393	393
	Achorid Dynasty		Hakor (Achoris)	393	380
			Nefaarud II	380	380
	Nectanebid Dynasty	30th	Nekhtnebef (Nectanebo) I	380	362
			Djedhor (Teos, Tachos)	365	360
			Nekhtnebef (Nectanebo) II	360	343
	Achaemenid Dynasty	31st	Ochus (Artaxerxes III)	343	338
			Arses	338	336
			Darius III Codomannus	335	332
Hellenistic Period (332–30)	Argead Dynasty	Kings of Macedon	Alexander the Great	332	323
			Philip Arrhidaeus	323	317
			Alexander IV	316	309
	Ptolemaic Dynasty	Ptolemies	Ptolemy I Soter I	309	285
			Ptolemy II Philadelphus	282	246
			Ptolemy III Euergetus I	246	222
			Ptolemy IV Philopator	222	205
			Ptolemy V Epiphanes	205	180
			Ptolemy VI Philometor	180	170
			Ptolemy VI & Ptolemy VIII	170	163
			Ptolemy VI Philometor	163	145
			Ptolemy VII Neos Philopator	145	145
			Ptolemy VIII Euergetes II	145	116
			Cleopatra III & Ptolemy IX Soter II	116	107
			Cleopatra III & Ptolemy X Alexander I	107	88
			Cleopatra III & Ptolemy IX Soter II	88	81
			Cleopatra Berenice	81	80
			Ptolemy XI Alexander II	80	80
			Ptolemy XII Neos Dionysos	80	58
			Berenice IV	58	55
			Ptolemy XII Neos Dionysos	55	51
			Cleopatra VII & Ptolemy XIII	51	47
			Cleopatra VII & Ptolemy XIV	47	44
			Cleopatra VII & Ptolemy XV	44	30

Lower Egypt

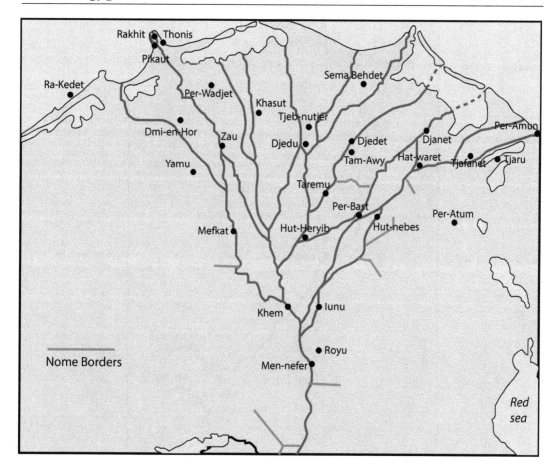

Upper Egypt

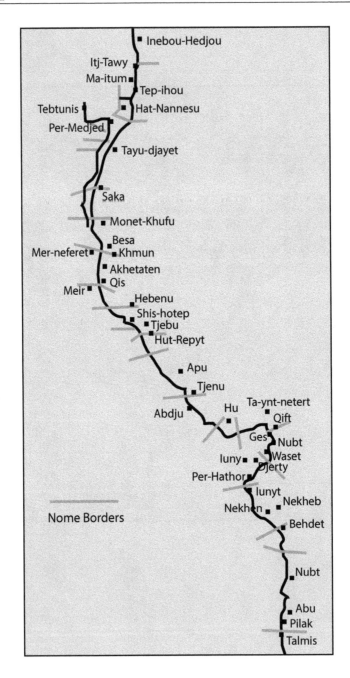

Kush

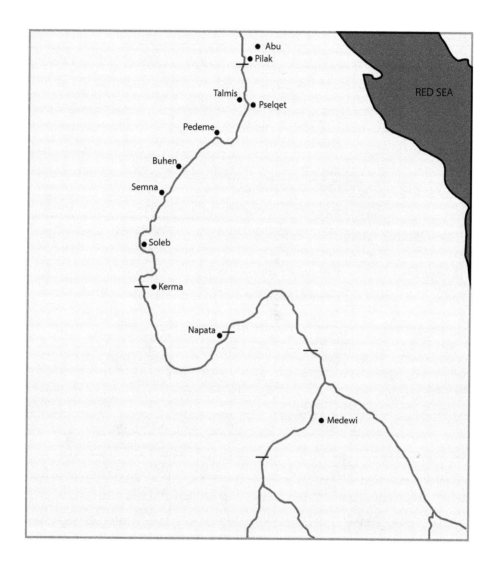

Cities of Ancient Egypt

Upper Egypt		
Egyptian name	*Greek name*	*Modern name*
Abdju	Abydos	Abydos
Abu (or Yebu)	Elephantine	Aswan
Apu (or Ipu) / Kent-min	Khemmis / Panopolis	Akhmim
Behdet	Idfu (or Edfu)	Tell Edfu
Djerty	Touphion	El-Tod
Gebtu	Koptos (or Coptos)	Qift
Ges	Apollonopolis Parva	Qus
Hut-Repyt	Athribis / Tripheion	Wannina
Iuny	Hermonthis	Armant
Iunyt / Ta-senet	Latopolis (or Letopolis)	Esna
Nekheb	Eileithyiaspolis	El-Kab
Nekhen	Hierankopolis	Kom El-Ahmar
Nubt	Ombos	Naqada
Nubt	Ombos	Kom Ombo
Per-Hathor / Inerty	Pathyris / Aphroditopolis	Gebelein
Pilak	Philae	[now under Lake Nasser]
Talmis	Talmis	Kalabsha
Ta-ynt-netert	Tentyra	Dendera
Tjebu / Djew-Qa	Antaeopolis	Qaw el-Kebir
Tjenu	Thinis	Girga
Waset	Thebes	Luxor

Lower Egypt		
Egyptian name	*Greek name*	*Modern name*
Djanet	Tanis	San al-Hagar
Djedet / Anpet	Mendes	Tell el-Ruba
Dmi-en-Hor	Hermopolis Mikra	Damanhur
Hat-waret / Pi-Ramesse	Avaris	Tell-el-Daba / Qantir
Hut-Heryib	Athribis (or Athlibis)	Tell Atrib / Medinet Ashaysh

Inebou-Hedjou / Men-nefer	Memphis	Mit Rahina
Iunu	Heliopolis	Cairo
Khasut (or Khaset)	Xois	Sakha
Khem (or Sekhem)	Letopolis	Ausim
Mefkat	Terenuthis	Kom Abu Billo
Ney-ta-hut	Leontopolis	Tell el-Yahudiya
-	Naukratis	Kom Gieif
Per-Atum (or Pi-Atum)	Heroöpolis	[exact location unknown]
Per-Bast (or Per-Bastet)	Bubastis	Tell Basta
Per-Wadjet	Buto (or Boutos)	Tell al-Farain
Pikaut	Kanopos / Canopus	Aboukir
Ra-Kedet	Rakotis/ Alexandria	Alexandria
Royu (or Troyu)	Troia	Tura
Tam-Awy	Thmuis	Tell el-Timai
Tjeb-nutjer	Sebennytos	Samannud
Zau	Sais	Sa el-Hagar
Shedyet	Crocodilopolis / Arsinoe	Medinet el-Fayum
Taremu	Leontopolis	Tell al-Muqdam
Thonis	Heracleion	Abu Qir Bay [under water]
Tjafanet (or Tahpanhes)	Daphnae	Tell Defenneh

Middle Egypt

Egyptian name	Greek name	Modern name
Akhetaten	-	Tell el-Amarna
Hat-Nennesu	Herakleopolis Magna	Ihnasiya Umm al-Kimam
Hebenu	-	Kom el Ahmar
Itj-Tawy	-	[near El-Lisht but not yet found]
Khmun	Hermopolis Magna	El- Ashmunein
Mer-neferet / Dehenet	Akoris	Tihna al-Gabal
Per-Medjed	Oxyrhynchos	El-Bahnasa
Tayu-djayet	Ankyronpolis	El-Hiba
Zawty	Lykopolis	Asyut

Glossary of Names and Terms

'A'amu
Asiatics (i.e., people from the land of Retenu).

akh (also akhu)
The intellect as a living entity, reanimated after death by the reunification of the ka and ba.

Akhet
1) Season of inundation (also known as Shait);
2) The place where the Egyptians believed a dead person becomes an akh. It is located between the horizon and the underworld.

Alashia (also Alashya, Alasyia)
Cyprus.

Amenlrdls
Wife of the God (High priestess of Amun).

Amenti
Realm of the dead (cf. Duat).

amkhu
An Egyptian award of honor given to soldiers of distinction, which granted that they be buried at the government's expense.

Ammit (also Ammut, Ahemait)
Female demon, part lion, hippo and crocodile, destroyer of the hearts of the dead who were not justified (Greek: Chimera).

Amurru
Region of Syria around the city of Qadesh. Also the name of its inhabitants (sometime called Amorites).

Anhur (also Anhuret, Onuris)
God of war, originally worshipped at Thinis. (Greek: Ares)

ankh (also anch)
Symbol of enduring life: a cross with a handle. Was often worn as an amulet.

Anubis (also Anpu, Khenty-Imentiu, Hermanubis)
Jackal-headed god associated with mummification and the afterlife. Conductor of souls. God of the necropolis.

Apiru
see Hapiru.

Apis (also Hapis)
A bull symbolizing fertility venerated at Memphis.

artaba
A Persian term for a dry measure (about 36 liters in Persian times, about 27 liters under the Ptolemies).

arura (also aroura)
A greek term referring to the ground covered by a yoke of ploughing oxen in one day, about 2700 m².

Atef
Crown worn by Osiris—the white crown with red feathers attached.

Aten

One of Egypt's sun gods. This one was equated with the actual disk of the sun and never depicted in human form.

ba

One of the souls of a person, the one associated with personality and character. Could also be the manifestation of a god. Depicted in tombs as a bird with a human head. The plural form bau is often used to refer to the power of appearance of a deity.

Ba'ah (also Seba-djai)

The planet Venus.

Bast (also Bastet, Ubasti, Pasht)

Cat goddess of the home. Her cultural center was at Bubastis. (Greek: Artemis)

Bat

Cow goddess, who eventually merged with Hathor.

benben

1) the first land to rise from the primordial waters at creation;
2) pyramid-shaped sacred stone at Heliopolis.

Bes (also Bisu)

Dwarf god, protector of households.

byssus

fine linen. (Greek: bussos)

crook

A symbol often carried by kings, which represented his shepherding of the people.

cubit (from Latin)

Unit of linear measurement, the distance between the elbow and tips of the fingers.

deben (also teben)

A unit of weight, commonly used for metals to express their value. From the New Kingdom on about 91 grams. In the Greek period worth 20 silver drachmas, later 20 copper drachmas.

deshret

1) The red crown of Lower Egypt;
2) The red land, i.e. the desert.

Diadochi

"Successors," rival generals, family and friends of Alexander the Great, who fought for the control of Alexander's empire after his death.

Djahi (also Djahy, Tjahi, Zahi)

Southern Canaan.

djed

A pillar-like symbol representing stability. Often carried as an amulet.

djet

Eternity, continuous and linear (cf. neheh).

drachma

Greek monetary unit, the rough equivalent of a skilled worker's daily wage.

Duat

Originally the starry sky, but later the Realm of the Dead, where the gods reside, where the sun travels at night and where the deceased have become stars.

Ennead (from Greek enneas, nine)
>1) a group of nine deities;
>2)all the gods of a locality.

flail
>A symbol often carried by kings, which represented his authority to punish the people. (Egyptian: nekhekh)

Geb (also Keb)
>Earth god.

Gebal (also Gubla, Kubna, Byblos in Greek)
>City in Lebanon.

God's Father
>Middle-ranking priest of Amun.

Great Green
>The Sea, usually the Mediterranean.

Hamamat (also Hammamat)
>A wadi connecting the Nile valley to the Red Sea near Thebes.

Hapi (also Hapy)
>God of the Nile flooding.

Hapiru (also Apiru, Habiru)
>Asiatics of the hill country during the mid-2nd millennium BCE, often considered outlaws.

Harakhte
>Sun god, one of the forms of Horus.

Hathor
>Cow goddess associated with the milky way, love, mirth, beauty, and fertility. (Greek: Aphrodite)

Hatti (also Kheta)
>Great state of Anatolia during the Egyptian New Kingdom.

hat-ya
>The second highest honorific title given to an Egyptian noble. (cf. iry-pat)

Heb-Sed
>Renewal celebration of the kingship after 30 years of a king's rule (and every three years after that). Included a reenactment of creation and a display of the king's physical abilities.

Hedjet (also Nefer-hedjet)
>The white crown of Upper Egypt.

Heh (also Huh, Hah)
>Personification of infinity or eternity.

Heka
>Magic personified.

Heqa
>see crook.

heqat (also hekat)
>Measure of volume similar to a barrel or bushel.

Heqet (also Heqat, Hekt, Hekat, Heket)
>Frog goddess associated with birth.

Her-ka-pet

The planet Saturn.

Heru-deshret

The planet Mars.

Her-ur (also Harwer, Horus the Elder, Haroeris in Greek)

Horus in his final form, as victor over his enemies, husband of Hathor.

Her-wepes-tawy

The planet Jupiter.

heseb

Unit of area measurement: 25 square cubits.

hin (also hinu)

Unit of volume roughly equivalent to a jar.

Horus (also Hor, Heru, Hru)

Falcon god of Hierankopolis, son of Isis and Osiris, associated with the kingship.

iaret

see uraeus.

imakhu

Egyptian term meaning "the privilege of being provided for" or "one who has been provided for." Used in the context of the afterlife.

ipet

A harem.

iry-pat

The highest honorific title given to an Egyptian noble. (cf. hat-ya)

isfet

Egyptian word meaning disorder or chaos, opposite of ma'at.

Isis (also Auset, Aset, Ast)

Goddess of fertility and nature, consort of Osiris (and therefore thought of as consort of any deceased king). (Greek: Demeter or Aphrodite)

iteru

Unit of linear measurement: 20,000 cubits.

ka

One of the souls inhabiting a person (including gods), the one animating the body. "To go to his ka" = to die.

Kadesh

see Qadesh.

Kamutef

An epithet of the gods Amun and Min (particularly when they are considered as one).

Keftiu

An island in the Mediterranean, probably Crete, but perhaps Cyprus or the Cyclades.

Kemet

"The black (land)," the fertile soil of the Nile flood plain, but often used to mean the land of Egypt in general.

kenbet

Judicial commission or court.

khar

A sack, measure of capacity.

kheker

An architectural decoration.

khenty-she

A title used of an attendant of government property, specially appointed by the pharaoh.

khepresh (also kheperesh)

The blue crown (war crown).

Khepri (also Khepra, Chepri)

The dung beetle god (scarab), who rolls the sun across the sky.

khet (also khet-en-nu)

Unit of linear measure, 100 cubits.

Kheta

see Hatti.

Khons (also Khonsu)

The moon god, son of Amun and Mut.

kite (also kit, qite)

Unit of weight measurement, one tenth of a deben.

kohl

Black eyeliner.

Kush

Nubian region south of the second cataract of the Nile.

Libu (also Ribu)

Libyans.

lesonis (Greek)

An elected official in charge of the economic management of a temple.

Ma

see Meshwesh.

maa-kheru

Someone who is truthful, justified. Used for the winning party in a trial or the dead who passed judgment successfully in the afterlife.

ma'at (also mayet)

Egyptian word meaning order, truth, or righteousness. Believed to be a spiritual force regulating and maintaining the world. Sometimes represented as a goddess.

Mafdet (also Maftet)

Goddess symbolizing legal justice, who also protected against snakes and scorpions.

maziqda

Measure of capacity, 38 hin.

Medjay

Kushite (Nubian) mercenaries who were recruited into the Egyptian police force and guarded the tombs of the pharaohs near Thebes.

meh-ta

Unit of area measurement, 100 cubits squared.

Menat

1) Name for the goddess Hathor;

2) An amulet connected with Hathor that was sometimes used as a rattle.

Meskhenet (also Mesenet, Meskhent)
>   1) Goddess of childbirth;
>   2) The two bricks placed under the feet of a woman giving birth.

Meshwesh (also Ma)
>   Libyans living on or near Egyptian soil.

metu
>   The channels that were believed to convey various substances throughout the human body.

Min
>   God of fertility.

Mitanni
>   State run by the Hurrian people living in Naharin during the Egyptian New Kingdom.

Mnevis (also Mer-wer)
>   Bull god of Heliopolis.

Montu (also Mont)
>   War god of Thebes.

Mut
>   1) Mother goddess;
>   2) Deceased person.

Naharin (also Naharina)
>   Region in Syria-Lebanon.

natron (from Spanish, originally Greek)
>   Carbonate salt mixture used in mummification.

nefer
>   1) Beauty, goodness;
>   2) A good luck charm.

neheh
>   Eternity, cyclical (cf. djet).

Nehes
>   see Nubia.

nekhekh
>   see flail.

Nekhbet
>   Goddess of Upper Egypt represented in the form of a vulture.

nemes
>   A striped headcloth worn by the pharaohs.

Nephthys (also Nepthys, Nebt-Het)
>   Goddess, nurse of the Pharaoh, sister of Isis, wife of Seth.

neshmet
>   The barque of Osiris.

nomarch (from Greek nomarches)
>   Governor of a nome.

nome (from Greek nomos)
>   An administrative district or region. (Egyptian: sepat)

nub
>   Gold.

Nubia
Region south of the first cataract.

Nun
Primordial god of water and fertility.

Nut
Sky goddess.

Ogdoad (from Greek ogdoas, eight)
The eight primeval gods of creation worshipped in Hermopolis.

oipe
Measure of capacity, 4 heqat.

Opet
Annual festival held in Thebes in which statues of the gods and kings were carried between the temples of Thebes and Karnak. The festival was thought to rejuvenate the spirits of the king.

Osiris (also Asr, Ausar, Khenty-Imentiu)
God of duat and the dead, consort of Isis. Legendary ancient king of Egypt. Usually depicted as a green-skinned man with a pharaoh's beard. (Greek: Dionysos)

Peleset
One of the Sea Peoples, the Philistines.

Peret (also Pert, Proit)
Growing season (cf. Akhet, Shemu).

Perw-nefer
Egyptian naval base near Memphis.

pesesh-kaf
Ceremonial instrument used in the Opening of the Mouth Ceremony.

pshent
The double crown of Upper and Lower Egypt.

Ptah (also Ptach)
Egyptian craftsman god, who was the patron of god of Memphis and in some myths is credited as creator of the world. (Greek: Hephaestos)

Punt
A region south of Nubia, probably in Somalia or Ethiopia.

qa'a
A high-roofed reception room in Egyptian houses.

Qadesh (also Kedesh, Kadesh)
City of Amurru.

qenbet
see kenbet.

Re (also Ra)
Sun god, originating in Lower Egypt, who became Egypt's state god beginning around Dynasty 5. (Greek: Helios)

remen
1) Unit of linear measurement, five palms;
2) Unit of area measurement, 5,000 sq. cubits.

Retenu (also Retjenu, Rezenu)
The land along the eastern Mediterranean coast (Canaan and Syria).

Rosetau (also Rostau, Rasetjau)
  A dry and arid place in the Afterlife.
Sabgu
  The planet Mercury.
Sah
  The constellation of Orion, associated with Osiris.
sau (also sa)
  An amulet used to ward off evil.
scarab (Egyptian: kheprer)
  1) dung beetle;
  2) amulet in the form of a dung beetle.
Sekhmet (also Sechmet)
  Goddess of love and protection.
Sed
  see Heb-Sed.
senet
  Board game.
seniu
  Unit of weight measurement, one twelfth of a deben.
sepat
  see nome.
Seshat
  Female scribe goddess.
Seth (also Set)
  God of the desert, storms, violence, and disorder. Sometimes considered brother of
  Horus, sometimes brother of Osiris.
setat (also setjat)
  Unit of area measurement, 10,000 square cubits.
setep
  Ceremonial instrument used in the Opening of the Mouth Ceremony.
shabti (also shawabti, ushabti)
  Magical burial figurines designed to perform work in the afterlife for the deceased.
Shemu (also Shammu, Shamu)
  Harvest season (cf. Akhet, Peret).
Shu
  Air god. (Greek: Heracles)
Sopdet (Greek: Sothis)
  A star (and goddess), called Sirius today, the heliacal rising of which marked the begin-
  ning of the Egyptian civil year.
strategos (plural: strategoi)
  Greek term for a military officer serving as a governor in Egypt in the Ptolemaic and Ro-
  man periods.
ta
  Unit of area measurement, 100 square cubits.
talent
  Unit of commercial weight, about 60 lbs.

Ta-netjer (also Ta-nuter)

"God's Land," a term used for foreign regions (usually forested), such as Punt or places in Syria.

Taweret (also Tauret, Tauwret)

Goddess of fertility and childbirth.

Tefnut

Goddess of dew and rain.

Tehenu (also Tehennu, Ta-Seti)

People living in the Sahara desert, Libyans.

Thoth (also Djehuti, Tehuti)

God of knowledge and wisdom and scribes, moon god (Greek: Hermes or Trismegistus).

tyet (also tet)

The Blood of Isis, The Buckle of Isis, an amulet.

uraeus (from Greek *ouraios*)

An image of a rearing cobra worn on the brow of an Egyptian pharaoh. (Egyptian: iaret)

ushabti

see shabti.

Wadjet (also Wedjat, Uzat, Uto, Uat)

1) Goddess of Buto, protector of Lower Egypt (Greek: Leto);

2) Eye of Horus, often used in amulet form to protect from the evil eye;

3) A sceptre symbol representing power and well-being.

Wawat

see Nubia.

Wepwawet (also Upuaut)

Wolf god of war who clears the way for the army.

OLD KINGDOM

1. TOMB DEDICATION INSCRIPTIONS

Among the earliest extant writings from ancient Egypt are inscriptions on the mastaba tombs of Egypt's nobles. They were composed by the sons of the deceased, who made sure to put on record that they paid for the burials of their parents. The following examples are from the Fourth Dynasty.

1. By his eldest son, the chief mortuary priest and scribe, Ptah: "I came that I might do this for him, when he was buried in the beautiful west, according to that which he spoke about it, while he was [alive] upon his two feet."

2. One whose son shall do this for him, when he is in the west, Ikhi, he says: "I did this for my father, when he journeyed to the west upon the beautiful ways, whereon the revered (dead) journey ."

3. By his son, the overseer of the pyramid, "Great-is-Khafre," the king's-confidant, Thethi, who made (this) for his father and his mother, when they mere both buried in the western highland.

4. Revered by the great god, king's-confidante, Henutsen. It was her eldest son, the field-judge, who made (it) for her, to make mortuary offerings to her therein.

2. TOMB INSCRIPTION OF KHAMERERNEBTY II

From Giza comes this inscription from the mastaba tomb of Khamerernebty, one of King Menkaure's wives (later Fourth Dynasty).

The mother of the king of Upper and Lower Egypt, daughter of the god, who sees Horus and Seth, great of affection, great of favor, priest(ess) of Thoth, priest(ess) of Tjasepef, his beloved royal wife, king's daughter of his body, the possessor of *imakhu* in the sight of the Great God, Khamerernebty.

Eldest daughter, who sees Horus and Seth, great of affection, great of favor, priest(ess) of Thoth, priest(ess) of Tjasepef, intimate of Horus, consort of he who is beloved of the Two Ladies, his beloved royal wife, king's daughter of his body, the possessor of *imakhu* in the sight of her father, Khamerernebty.

(1) [Beloved of Anubis is he who shall provide protection]

(2) for the property of another who has gone to [her ka];

(3) I have never done anything evil against [anyone].

(4) With regard to [him who shall do anything] to this (tomb),

(5) [I shall be judged with him by the Great God.

(6) I have] satisfied the craftsmen [who made this for me].

3. TOMB STELA OF NYANKHSEKHMET

The following inscription was found on a limestone stela used as a false door in a mastaba tomb at Saqqara near Memphis, which was built during the reign of Sahure of the Fifth Dynasty. The stela is of much better quality than the rest of the tomb. The reason for this can be ascertained after reading the inscription.

The chief physician, Nyankhsekhmet, spoke before his majesty: "May your person, beloved of Re, command that there be given to me a false door of stone for this my tomb of the cemetery."

His majesty caused that there be brought for him two false doors from Troja of stone, that they be laid in the audience hall of the house (called): "Sahure-Shines-with-Crowns," and that the two high priests of Memphis and the artisans of the [...] be assigned to them, that the work on them might be done in the presence of the king himself. The stone-work went on every day; there was an inspection of that which was done on them in the court daily. His majesty had [color] put on them, and had them painted in blue.

His majesty said to the chief physician Nyankhsekhmet: "As these my nostrils enjoy health, as the gods love me, may you depart into the cemetery at an advanced old age as one revered." I praised the king greatly and lauded every god for Sahure's sake, for he knows the desire of the entire suite. When anything goes forth from the mouth of his majesty, it immediately comes to pass. For the god has given to him knowledge of things that are in the body, because he is more august than any god. If you love Re, you shall praise every god for Sahure's sake, who did this for me. I was his revered one; never did I do anything evil toward any person.

4. TOMB INSCRIPTION OF HETEPHERAKHET

Hetepherakhet was a priest who served at the Sun Temple of Niuserre (Dynasty 5) at Abu Ghurab near Memphis. The following words, directed towards future visitors, were inscribed on his tomb at Saqqara.

Judge, attached to Nekhen, Hetepherakhet; he says: "I have made this tomb as a just possession, and never have I taken a thing belonging to any person. 'Whosoever shall make offering to me therein, I will do (it) for them; I will commend them to the god for it very greatly; I will do this for them, for bread, for beer, for clothing, for ointment, and for grain, in great quantity. Never have I done aught of violence toward any person. As the god loves a true matter, I was in honor with the king.

Judge, eldest of the hall, Hetepherakhet; he says: "I have made this my tomb upon the western arm in a pure place. There was no tomb of any person therein, in order that the possessions of him, who has gone to his *ka*, might be protected. As for any people who shall enter into this tomb as their mortuary property or shall do an evil thing to it, judgment shall be had with them for it, by the great god. I have made this tomb as my shelter; I was honored by the king, who brought for me a sarcophagus."

5. LETTER FROM KING IZEZI TO RESHEPSES

Royal letters from this period are not likely to exist anymore, but fortunately for us, this piece of correspondence from King Djedkaré-Izezi (Dynasty 5) was so valued by its recipient Reshepses that he had it inscribed on his mastaba tomb at Saqqara.

(1) Royal decree for the vizier, overseer of royal document scribes, Reshepses.

(2) My majesty has seen this wonderful letter which you have had brought to me in the palace on this perfect day in which the heart of Izezi is truly pleased (3) with what he truly loves. Seeing this letter of yours is what my majesty desired above all else, for you indeed know how to say what my majesty loves better than anything, and what you say is more pleasing to me than anything else. (4) My majesty knows full well that you desire to say everything which my majesty loves.

(5) O Reshepses: I say to you millions of times: (7) (you are) one whom his lord loves, (8) one whom his lord favors, (9) one who is close to his lord, (10) the keeper of secrets of his lord; (11) truly I know that Re loves me as he has given you to me. (12) As Izezi lives for ever, you should say all your desires to my majesty (13) in your letters immediately this day, and I shall see to it that they are executed immediately.

6. TOMB INSCRIPTION OF SENEDJEMIB

From the mastaba tomb of Senedjemib Inti, a high official under Isesi (Dynasty 5) who was buried at Giza, come several lengthy inscriptions, including some biographical material, which sheds light on the relationship that the king had with his officials. One such text from the tomb is provided here.

(1) The *iry-pat, haty-a*, vizier, overseer of royal document scribes, (2) overseer of all works of the king, overseer of the six Great Mansions, (3) overseer of the two granaries, overseer of the two treasuries, (4) overseer of the two chambers of the royal ornament, overseer of the armory, (5) overseer of every office of the Residence, overseer of the royal children.

(6) (I have spent) five years, four months, and three days now under Izezi.

(7) During (this) time I have been more valuable in the sight of Izezi than any like me in my capacity as keeper of secrets of his majesty and as one who is in the heart of his majesty in every matter (8) which his majesty is desirous of doing. During (this) time his majesty was praising me concerning all the works which his majesty has ordered to be done, as I always acted in accordance with the wishes of his majesty concerning these things.

(9) Izezi gave me a necklace of malachite (?) (perhaps) through the greatness of favor of (?) his majesty when he was in the document office, when it happened that (10) I was in attendance in the grounds (of the palace). His majesty had it tied upon my neck...and his majesty saw to it that I was anointed with unguent (11) and that my skin was cleansed in the presence of his majesty by an inspector of hairdressers of the Great House, a chief of Nekheb and the keeper of the diadem. Never had the like been done in the presence of the king for any man, (12) for I was more valuable, excellent and beloved in the sight of Izezi than any like me.

(13) Izezi made for me a decree which his majesty wrote with his own hand in order to favor me (14) for everything which I had done nobly, perfectly and excellently in relation to his majesty's wish concerning it.

7. PYRAMID TEXTS OF UNAS

On the walls of the pyramid of Unas, last king of the Fifth Dynasty, at Saqqara are found our earliest examples of Pyramid Texts, containing spells to assist the king through his journey in the afterworld. Provided here are some spells written in the antechamber on the east gable and wall intended to revive Unis' spirits after death.

[393] To say: The sky is overcast, the stars are darkened, the bows are agitated, the bones of the earth-gods quake.

[394] The agitations cease after they have seen Unas dawning (as) a *ba*, as a god, who lives on his fathers and feeds on his mothers. Unas is lord of craftiness, whose name his mother knows not.

[395] The honour of Unas is in heaven, his might is in the horizon, like his father, Atum, who begat him. He has begotten him mightier than he.

[396] The *kas* of Unas are behind him, his maid-servants are under his feet, his gods are over him, his uraeus-serpents are upon his brow; the leader-serpent of Unas is on his forehead, she who perceives the soul (of the enemy), (as) a diadem, a flame (?) of fire; the might of Unas is for his protection.

[397] Unas is the bull of heaven, who (once) suffered want and decided (lit. gave in his heart) to live on the being of every god, who ate their entrails (?) when it came (to pass) that their belly was full of magic from the Isle of Flame.

[398] Unas is equipped, he who has incorporated his spirits. Unas dawns as the Great One, lord of those with (ready) hands. He sits, his side towards Geb (the earth).

[399] It is Unas who judges with him whose name is hidden, (on) this day of slaying the eldest (gods). Unas is lord of offerings, who knots the cord, who himself prepares his meal.

[400] Unas is he who eats men and lives on gods, lords of messengers, who distributes orders.

[401] It is "Grasper-of-the-top-knot" who is in *ḫ3.w* who lassoes them for Unas. It is "The serpent with raised head" who watches them (the gods) for Unas, who repels them for him. It is "He who is upon the willows" who binds them for Unas.

[402] It is "Khonsu who slaughters the lords (gods)," in that he beheads them for Unas, and takes out for him what is in their body. He (Khonsu?) is the messenger whom he (Unas) sends forth to punish.

[403] It is *Šsm.w* who cuts them up for Unas, cooking for him a meal of them in his evening cooking-pots.

[404] It is Unas who eats their magic and swallows their spirits; their Great Ones are for his morning meal, their middle-sized ones are for his evening meal, their little ones are for his night meal, their old men and old women are for his incense-burning (or, fire).

[405] It is "The Great Ones in the north side of heaven" who lay for him the fire to the kettles containing them, with the thighs of their eldest (as fuel).

[406] The inhabitants of heaven wait on Unas, when the hearth was constructed for him with (out of) the legs of their women. He has completely encircled the two heavens; he has revolved about the two lands.

[407] Unas is the great mighty one, who has power over the mighty ones. Unas is the *ḫm*-falcon, who surpasses the *ḫm*-falcons—the great falcon. Whom he finds on his way, he eats for himself bit by bit. The respect of Unas is before (first of) all noble ones who are in the horizon.

[408] Unas is a god older than the eldest. Thousands serve him; hundreds make offering to him. A certificate as (of) a mighty, great one is given to him by *Š3ḥ*, father of the gods.

[409] Unas has dawned again in heaven; he is crowned with the Upper Egyptian crown as lord of the horizon. He has smashed the dorsal vertebra; he has carried off the hearts of the gods; he has eaten the red crown, he has swallowed the green one;

[410] Unas feeds on the lungs of the wise ones; he is satisfied by living on hearts as well as their magic.

[411] Unas is disgusted when he licks the emetics which are in the red crown, (but) he is delighted when their magic is in his belly. The dignities of Unas shall not be taken from him, (for) he has swallowed the intelligence of every god.

[412] The lifetime of Unas is eternity, its limit is everlastingness, in this his dignity of "If he wishes he does, if he wishes not he does not," who is within the boundary of the horizon for ever and ever.

[413] Behold, their soul (of the gods) is in the belly of Unas, their spirits are with Unas, as his soup a la ntr.w, cooked for Unas from their bones. Behold, their soul is with Unas, their shadows afe taken away from the hand of those to whom they belong.

[414] Unas is as that which dawns, which dawns, which endures, which endures. The doers of evil shall not be able to destroy the favourite place of Unas among the living in this land for ever and ever.

8. TOMB INSCRIPTION OF HENKU

Henku was nomarch of the Cerastes-Mountain nome in Upper Egypt in the early Sixth Dynasty. On his rock-cut tomb at Deir el-Gabrawi the following inscription was found. It is in terrible condition, but it provides us with a rare glimpse into the affairs of Old Kingdom nomarchs.

O all you people of the Cerastes-Mountain; O you great lords of other nomes, who shall pass by this tomb, I, Henku, tell good things:

I gave bread to all the hungry of the Cerastes-Mountain; I clothed him who was naked therein. I filled its shores with large cattle, and its [lowlands] with small cattle. I satisfied the wolves of the mountain and the fowl of heaven with [flesh] of small cattle . . . . . . I was lord and overseer of southern grain in this nome . . . . I settled the [feeble] towns in this nome with the people of other nomes; those who had been peasant-serfs therein, I made their offices as officials. I never oppressed one in possession of his property, so that he complained of me because of it to the god of my city; (but) I spoke, and told that which was good; never was there one fearing because of one stronger than he, so that he complained because of it to the god.

I arose then to be ruler in the Cerastes-Mountain, together with my brother, the revered, the sole companion, ritual priest, Re-am, I was a benefactor to it (the nome) in the folds of the cattle, in the settlements of the fowlers. I settled its every district with men and cattle - - small cattle indeed.

I speak no lie, for I was one beloved of his father praised of his mother, excellent in character to his brother, and amiable to [his sister]. . . . .

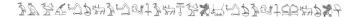

9. TOMB INSCRIPTION OF HERYMERU

Near the pyramid of Unas at Saqqara is the tomb of a priest, Herymeru, who served at the pyramid during the early Sixth Dynasty. The following words appear on the lintel of his tomb.

(1) The priest of the pyramid of Unas, *khenty-she* of the pyramid of Unas, the *imakhu* in the sight of the king of Upper and Lower Egypt, the Golden Horus Wadj, Unas, supervisor of *khenty-she* of the Great House, Herymeru.

(2) An offering which the king and an offering which Anubis, who dwells in the divine tent-shrine, who is in his wrappings, who is on his mountain, lord of the sacred land, give that he might be buried in his tomb of the necropolis as an imakbu who loves the god; may the West stretch out her arms to him as he is one who has done what is satisfactory and who has reached the state of *imakhu*. The sole companion, overseer of the *khenty-she*, Herymeru, whose perfect name is Merery.

(3) May he be united with the land, may he cross the heavens, may he ascend to the Great God, may his ka dwell in the presence of the king, may his ba endure in the presence of the god, may his document be taken by the god to the pure places, as (is done) for one whom his father loves and his mother favors.

(4) An offering which the king and which Osiris give that he may make a perfect journey on the perfect ways on which the imakhu travel, that he may be followed by his ka, that he may be led on the holy ways, that his kas may be excellent in the sight of the king, and that where he resides may be pure in the sight of the god.

(5) An offering which the king and which all the gods of the West give that invocation offerings may be made for him in the Wag festival, the New Year festival, the festival of Sokar, the great festival, the Rekeb festival, the festival of the appearance of Min, the Sadj festival, the monthly and half monthly festivals, and in every perfect daily festival, for the imakhu, (6) supervisor of *khenty-she* of the Great House, Herymeru.

I am an excellent *akh*, one who knows things, a speaker of perfection and a repeater of perfection.

I have never said or done any evil thing in relation to anyone, for I am one who loves Maat in the sight of the perfect god and in the sight of men.

But with regard to any man (7) who shall do anything evil to my tomb, or who shall enter it with the intention of stealing,

I shall seize his neck like a bird's, and I shall be judged with him in the court of the Great God.

However, with regard to any person who shall make invocation offerings or shall pour water, they shall be pure like the pureness of god, and I shall protect him in the necropolis.

10. PYRAMID TEXTS OF TETI

The pyramid of Teti at Saqqara (early Sixth Dynasty) contains more extensive pyramid texts than those of Unas, but also less well preserved. Provided here are examples of spells written on the east wall of the burial chamber to help the king leave the duat (the starry night sky in the east where the spirits of the dead reside) and spells written on the west wall of the antechamber to help him enter the akhet (the horizon where one becomes an akh).

Utterance 356.

[575] To say: O Osiris Teti, Horus has come that he may seek thee. He has caused that Thot turn back for thee the Followers of Set and that he bring them to thee all together.

[576] He has made the heart of Set timid. Thou art greater (or, elder) than he; thou didst come forth (from the womb) before him; thy qualifications are better than his. Geb has seen thy qualifications; he has put thee in thy place.

[577] Geb has brought to thee thy two sisters, to thy side, Isis and Nephthys. Horus has caused the gods to unite with thee, to fraternize with thee in thy name of "He of the two *śnw.t*-palaces," but not to reject thee in thy name of "He of the two *'itr.t* palaces."

[578] He has caused the gods to avenge thee. Geb has put the sole of his foot on the head of thine enemy, who is afraid of thee.

[579] Thy son Horus has smitten him; he has snatched back his eye from him; he has given it to thee, that thou mayest become glorious thereby, that thou mayest become mighty before the spirits. Horus has caused thee to seize thine enemy, that there should be none escaping among them from thee.

[580] Horus was indeed ingenious in that he recognized in thee his father, in thy name of *b3-'iti-rp.t*. Nut has established thee as god, in spite of Set, in thy name of "god"; thy mother Nut has spread herself over thee in her name of "She of *Št-p.t*."

[581] Horus has seized Set; he has placed him under thee, that he may carry thee and that he may quake under thee like the quaking of the earth, for thou art more exalted than he, in thy name of "He of the exalted land."

[582] Horus has caused that thou recognize him (Set) in himself without his getting away from thee; he has caused that thou seize him with thy hand without his escaping from thee. O Osiris Teti, Horus has avenged thee; he has done (it) for his *ka* in thee, that thou mayest be satisfied in thy name of "Satisfied *ka*."

Utterance 357

[583] To say by Horus: May Geb make an offering to Osiris Teti O Osiris Teti, Geb has given to thee thy two eyes that thou mayest be satisfied. Take in thee the two eyes of this Great One. Geb has caused Horus to give them to thee that thou mayest be satisfied with them.

[584] Isis and Nephthys have seen thee; they have found thee. Horus has taken care of thee; Horus has caused Isis and Nephthys to protect thee. They have given thee to Horus that he may be satisfied with thee.

[585] It is pleasing to Horus (to be) with thee in thy name of "He of the horizon, whence Re' goes forth," in thine arms in thy name of "He from within the palace." Thou hast closed thine arms about him, about him, so that his bones stretch and he become proud.

[586] O Osiris Teti, betake thyself to Horus, approach thyself to him, do not go far from him.

[587] Horus has come, he recognizes thee; he has smitten (and) bound Set for thee, for thou art his *ka*. Horus has made him afraid of thee, for thou art greater than he; he swims under thee; he carries in thee one greater than he.

[588] His followers have noticed thee how thy strength is greater so that they dare not resist thee. than his,

[589] Horus comes; he recognizes his father in thee, for thou art young in thy name of "He of the fresh water." Horus has opened for thee thy mouth.

[590] O Osiris Teti, be not in distress, groan not. Geb has brought Horus to thee, that he may count for thee their hearts. He has brought to thee all the gods together; there is not one among them who escapes him.

[591] Horus has avenged thee; it was not long till he avenged thee. Horus has snatched back his eye from Set; he has given it to thee. This his eye, the sweet one, cause it to stay with thee, reclaim it for thyself. O may it be pleasing to thee.

[592] Isis has taken care of thee. The heart of Horus is glad because of thee in thy name of "He who is First of the Westerners." It is Horus who will avenge what Set has done to thee.

Utterance 364.

[609] To say: O Osiris Teti, arise. Horus comes; he reclaims thee from the gods. Horns has loved thee, he has equipped thee with his eye; Horns has adapted to thee his eye.

[610] Horns has opened for thee thine eye that thou mayest see with it. The gods have bound to thee thy face; they have loved thee. Isis and Nephthys have healed thee. Horus is not far from thee; thou art his *ka*.

[611] Thy face is gracious unto him; hasten, accept the word of Horus and be satisfied with it. Hearken unto Horus, it will not be harmful to thee; he has caused the gods to follow thee.

[612] Osiris Teti, awake. Geb has brought Horus to thee, and he recognizes thee; Horus has found thee; he rejoices over thee.

[613] Horus has caused the gods to ascend to thee; he has given them to thee that they may illuminate thy face (cheer thee). Horus has placed thee at the head of the gods; he has caused thee to take the double crown, the lady. Horus has accustomed himself to thee; he cannot part from thee.

[614] Horus has caused thee to live in this thy name of *'nd.ti*. Horus has given thee his eye, the hard (one); (he) has placed it to thee (i.e. in thy hand), that thou mayest be strong, and that all thine enemies may fear thee. Horus has completely filled thee with his eye, in this its name of "Fullness of god."

[615] Horus has corralled the gods for thee, so that they cannot get away from thee, from the place where thou hast gone. Horus has counted the gods for thee, so that they cannot get away from thee, from the place where thou wast drowned.

[616] Nephthys has assembled for thee all thy limbs, in her name of "*Šš3.t*, lady of builders." She has made them well for thee. Thou art given over to thy mother Nut, in her name of "Grave"; she has embraced thee, in her name of "Grave"; thou art brought to her, in her name of Mataba."

[617] Horus has united for thee thy limbs and does not allow thee to be sick; he has put thee together, so that there is no disorder in thee (or, without anything being disordered in thee). Horus has set thee up without staggering.

[618] O Osiris Teti, let thy heart be glad for him (Horus); thy heart is great, thy mouth is opened. Horus has avenged thee; it was not long till he avenged thee.

[619] O Osiris Teti, thou art the mightiest god; there is no god like thee. Horus has given to thee his children, that they may carry thee;

[620] he has given to thee all gods that they may follow thee and that thou mayest have power over them. Horus has set thee up, in his name of "*Hnw*-boat"; he carries thee, in thy name of "Seker."

[621] Thou livest; thou movest every day; thou art glorious, in thy name of "Horizon whence Re' goes forth"; thou art honoured, thou art pre-eminent, thou art a soul, thou art mighty for ever and ever.

11. TOMB INSCRIPTIONS OF HEZI

Hezi was a vizier under Teti (early Sixth Dynasty), who had served also as an official under the previous two kings Isesi and Unas. Hezi's tomb is located near Teti's pyramid at Saqqara and contains several inscriptions, including the following.

(1) He speaks: I was a judge and scribe of the time of Izezi; I was a judge and inspector of scribes of the time of Unas; it was Teti my lord who appointed me judge and boundary official (2) and who appointed me first under the king.

His majesty permitted that (this) be done for me as his majesty knew my name from when I took the (office of) scribe from his hands, as there was no helper whom he recalled and of whom it was said that he was a wise man. (3) I carried out the role of a scribe in the presence of his majesty actually at the forefront of the scribes, and I carried out the role of an official in the presence of his majesty actually at the forefront of the officials.

(4) His majesty regularly had me go down to the barque to carry out guard duty, and had me to come to the ways, and had gifts prepared for me as is normally done for a chamberlain or a first under the king, even though I was (only) a judge and boundary official, with the like not being done for any of my equals.

Because of my efficiency, his majesty used to ask my advice (5) among the officials, even though I was only a judge and inspector of scribes, for he knew my name was valued more highly than that of any other servant.

𓀀𓏏𓄿𓅓𓂋𓏤𓈖𓀁𓏏𓄿𓅓𓂋𓏏𓄿𓅓𓂋𓏏𓄿𓈖𓏏𓅓𓂋𓏏𓄿𓈖𓏏

12. TOMB INSCRIPTIONS OF NEKHEBU

Biographical inscriptions from the tomb of Ankhmeryremeryptah Nekhebu in the Western Cemetery at Giza reveal something of the life of an official who organized labor for king Pepi I's building projects (Dynasty 6). Originally they appeared on either side of a doorway in the tomb. Nekhebu appears to have been related to Senedjemib Inti (see reading #6).

Boston Text (MFA 13.4331)

(1) The sole companion, royal master <builder (?)>, Ankhmeryremeryptah, speaks:

(2) I was a worker of Meryre, my lord. His majesty sent me [to direct all the works of the king, and I acted] to the satisfaction of his majesty in Lower and Upper Egypt.

His majesty sent me to direct the construction (3) of soul chapels for his majesty in Lower Egypt, the *ges-per* of the mansion, my northern limit being in the City of the Pools in the Akhbit of Horus, and my southern limit being at the pyramid of Pepy I. I came back only when I had finished. (4) I [erected (?)] the soul chapels there, built the hall, and I placed wood on it composed of timber felled in Lower Egypt. I came back only when it had been finished through my efforts, and his majesty favored me for it (5) right in the presence of the officials. His majesty gave me nub-ankh amulets and bread and beer in large amounts, and his majesty had one of the divisions of the Residence come to me with it until they reached my gate. (6) (This all happened) as I was more excellent in his sight than any other royal master <builder (?)> whom his majesty had (previously) sent to deal with a ges-per of the royal estate.

His majesty sent me to lay out a canal in the Akhbit of Horus and to excavate it. (7) I excavated it in a period of three months, so that when I came back to the Residence it was already full of water. For this his majesty favored me, and his majesty gave me *nub-ankh* amulets and bread and beer, as I was one whom his majesty favored highly with regard to what he had sent me to do, (8) having done everything which I was sent to do.

His majesty sent me to Kis to excavate his canal (?) for Hathor-in-Kis. I acted (9) and excavated it so that his majesty favored me for it. Then I came back to the Residence and his majesty favored me highly, and gave me nub-ankh amulets and bread and beer.

Cairo Text (JE 44608)

(1) [The sole companion, the royal master <builder (?)>, Ankhmeryremeryptah,] speaks:

(2) [I was a worker of] Meryre, my lord. His majesty sent me to direct work on his monuments in Heliopolis, and I acted to the satisfaction of his majesty. I spent six years there directing work, and whenever I came to the Residence his majesty favored me for it. Everything I did came about through the vigilance I practiced... (3)... there in accord with what I myself know.

His majesty found me (originally) just as one of many builders, and his majesty appointed (me) as inspector of builders, overseer of builders and the leader of a phyle; (then) his majesty appointed me as royal master builder and first under the king and royal master builder; (then) his majesty appointed me to be sole companion and royal master builder in the two houses. His majesty acted above all through the greatness of his favor for me.

(4) I am the beloved one of his father and the favored one of his mother.

I never gave them reason to punish me on any matter until they went to their tomb of the necropolis.

I am one favored of his siblings. Now I was working with my brother, the overseer of works (name lost) [When he did (something or other, possibly his first promotion?)] I wrote, I carried his palette. When he was appointed as inspector of builders, I carried his measuring rod (?). (5) When he was appointed as overseer of builders, I was his companion (?). When he was appointed royal master builder, I was in charge of his town for him, and I did everything excellently for him. When he was appointed as sole companion and royal master builder in the two houses, I took charge of all his property for him, as there was more in his house than that of any noble. When (6) he was promoted to overseer of works, I followed up on all of his commands to his satisfaction in these matters. I looked after matters for him in his funerary estate for a period of more than twenty years.

Never did I beat any man there so that he fell as a result of my action; never did I enslave anyone therein. With regard to anyone therein (7) with whom I dealt, I am he who propitiated them; I never slept in a state of anger with anyone. I it was who gave clothing, bread, and beer to everyone who was naked and hungry there. I am the beloved one of everyone; I never said anything evil against any man to a king or someone in power.

I am one favored of his father and mother and of the noble ones in the necropolis (8) for making invocation offerings for them and for conducting all the festivals for them in the Wag festival, the festival of Sokar, the first of the year festival, the festival of Thoth, the festival of opening the year, the first of the month festival and the last of the month festival, and in every perfect festival made at every season of the year.

O soul priests of the *imakhu*: do you wish that the king favor you and that you shall be in the state of *imakhu* in the sight of your lords and fathers in the necropolis? (Then) you shall make invocation offerings (9) of bread and beer as I have done for your fathers themselves. Since you wish that I intercede on your behalf in the necropolis, then teach your children the words of making invocation offerings for me on the day of my passing there. I am an excellent *akh*; I know everything through which I may become transfigured in the necropolis.

O you who live on earth and shall pass by this tomb, if you wish that the king might favor you and that you may be imakhu in the sight of the Great God, (10) [then do not] enter this tomb as you are tainted...on account of your impurity. With regard to any man who shall enter therein in a hostile manner after this (I have said), I shall be judged with him by the Great God; I shall destroy their descendants and their doorways on earth. O you who live on earth and who shall pass by this tomb, do you desire that the king favor you and that you be imakhu in he sight of the Great God? Then you shall say "a thousand of bread and a thousand of beer for Nekhebu, the *imakhu*." You shall not destroy anything in this tomb, for I am an [excellent] and prepared akh. With regard to any man who shall destroy anything in this tomb, I shall be judged with them by the Great God. For I am speaker of perfection and a repeater of perfection. I never spoke anything evil against any man.

13. PYRAMID TEXTS OF PEPI I

The most extensive of all Old Kingdom pyramid texts, amounting to 2,263 columns and lines, are those of Pepi I in his pyramid at Saqqara. Here is a selection of spells for entering the womb of Nut in the midst of the duat *(from the burial chamber), for entering the* akhet *and for the spirit's rebirth (from the antechamber), and for proceeding into the sky (from the corridor).*

Utterance 422.

[752] To say: O Pepi, thou art departed that thou mayest become a spirit, that thou mayest become mighty as a god, an enthroned one like Osiris,

[753] since thou hast thy soul in thy body, since thou hast thy might behind thee, since thou hast thy double-crown on thy head, since thou hast thy *misw.t*-crown before thee (at hand). Thy face is before thee, thy homage is before thee;

[754] the followers of a god are behind thee, the nobles of a god are before thee; they recite: "A god comes, a god comes, Pepi comes (who shall be) on the throne of Osiris, that spirit comes who is in *Ndi.t*, that power which is in the Thinite nome."

[755] Isis speaks to thee; Nephthys laments for thee. The spirits come to thee, bowing down; they kiss the earth at thy feet, because the terror of thee, Pepi, is in the cities of *Śi3*.

[756] Thou ascendest to thy mother Nut; she lays hold of thine arm; she shows thee the way to the horizon, to the place where Re‘ is. The double doors of heaven are opened for thee, the double doors of *ḳbḥ.w* are opened for thee.

[757] Thou findest Reʻ standing, while he waits for thee. He lays hold of thy hand, he leads thee into the double ʻitr.t-palace of heaven, he places thee on the throne of Osiris.

[758] O Pepi, the eye of Horus comes to thee, it addresses thee: "Thy soul which is among the gods comes to thee; thy might which is among the spirits comes to thee. A son has avenged his father; Horus has avenged Osiris." Horus has avenged Pepi on his enemies.

[759] Thou standest, Pepi, avenged, equipped as a god, endued with the form of Osiris; on the throne of him who is First of the Westerners, and doest what he was accustomed to do among the spirits, the imperishable stars.

[760] Thy son stands on thy throne endued with thy for,m, he does what thou wast accustomed to do formerly at the head of the living by the command of Reʻ, the Great God.

[761] He tills barley, he tills spelt, that he may present thee therewith.

[762] O Pepi, all life and health are given to thee, eternity is thine, saith Reʻ to thee, that thou thyself mayest speak after thou hast taken the form of a god, wherewith thou shalt be great among the gods who are over the lake.

[763] O Pepi, thy soul stands among the gods, among the spirits, it is thus that thy fear is in their hearts. O Pepi, Pepi stands upon thy throne at the head of the living, it is thus that thy terror is in their hearts.

[764] Thy name which is upon the earth lives; thy name which is upon the earth endures; thou wilt not perish; thou wilt not pass away for ever and ever.

Utterance 468.

[894] To say: A Great One is awake beside his *ka*, after this Great One had fallen asleep by his *ka*; Pepi is awake beside his *ka*, after this Pepi had fallen asleep by his *ka*; this Great One is awake; Pepi is awake; the gods are awake, awakened are the mighty ones.

[895] O Pepi, raise thyself up, stand up. The Great Ennead, who are in Heliopolis, have assigned thee to thy great position, that thou mayest sit, Pepi, at the head of the Ennead, like Geb, the hereditary prince of the gods, like Osiris at the head of the mighty ones, as Horus lord of men and gods.

[896] O Pepi, who keeps secret his form like Anubis, take to thee thy face as jackal. The keeper, who presides in the two ʻitr.t-palaces, stands up before thee, as before Anubis, who presides in *sh-nṯr*.

[897] Thou causest the Followers of Horus to be satisfied. Horus avenges thee, Pepi; Horus causes thee to be satisfied, Pepi, with the offering which he bath, that thy heart, Pepi, may be satisfied with it, on the feast of the month and on the feast of the half-month. The joyful rejoices for thee, as for Anubis, who presides in *sh-nṯr*.

[898] Isis laments for thee, Nephthys bemoans thee, as Horus who avenged his father, Osiris. A son who avenged his father, Horus has avenged Pepi

[899] Osiris lives, the spirit who is in *Ndi.t* lives, Pepi lives. O Pepi, thy name lives among the living; thou wilt be a spirit, Pepi, among the spirits; thou wilt mighty among the mighty.

[900] O Pepi, thy fear (i.e. the fear of thee) is the sound eye Horus, that white crown, (which is) the *wt.t*-uraeus, which is el-Kab. She puts thy fear, Pepi, in the eyes of all gods, in the eyes of the spirits, the imperishable stars, those of secret places, in the eyes of all things (beings), who will see thee and who will hear thy name.

[901] O Pepi, equip thyself with the red eye of Horus, the red crown, which is great in fame (spirits), which is rich in appearances (beings), that it may protect thee, Pepi, as it protected Horus.

[902] It gives thee fame, Pepi, among the Two Enneads, through the two *wt.t*-uraeuses, which are on thy forehead. They lift thee up, Pepi; they lead thee to thy mother Nut; it (the uraeus of the North) lays hold of thine arm,

[903] that thou be not in need, that thou mayest not moan (like a cedar) , that thou perish not. Horus has caused thee to be a spirit at the head of the spirits, that thou mayest be mighty at the head of the living. How beautiful is that which Horus has done for Pepi, for this spirit, who was conceived by a god, who was conceived by two gods!

[904] O Pepi, thou wilt be a soul like the Souls of Heliopolis; thou wilt be a soul like the Souls of Hierakonpolis; thou wilt be a soul like the Souls of Buto; thou wilt be a soul like the star of life, which is at the head of his brothers.

[905] O Pepi, I am Thot. May the king give an offering: Thy bread and thy beer are given to thee; these are thy two *p3d*-cakes, which are delivered by Horus, which are in the broad-hall, that he may cause thy heart to be satisfied thereby, Pepi, for ever and ever.

Utterance 510.

[1128] To say: It is certainly not Pepi who asks to see thee in the form which has become thine; Osiris asks to see thee in the form which has become thine;

[1129] it is thy son who asks to see thee in the form which has become thine; it is Horus who asks to see thee in the form which has become thine.

[1130] When thou sayest, "statues", in respect to these stones, which are like fledglings of swallows under the river-bank; when thou sayest, "his beloved son is coming," in the form which had become that of "his beloved son";

[1131] they (the "statues") transport Horus; they row Horus over, as Horus ascends (lit. in the ascent of Horus) in the *Mḥ.t-wr.t*-cow.

[1132] The double doors of heaven are open, the double doors of *ḳbḥ.w* are open for Horus of the East, at daybreak, that he may descend and purify himself in the Marsh of Reeds.

[1133] The double doors of heaven are open, the double doors of *ḳbḥ.w* are open for Pepi, at daybreak, that Pepi may descend and purify himself in the Marsh of Reeds.

[1134] The double doors of heaven are open, the double doors of *ḳbḥ.w* are open for Horus of the *D3.t*, at daybreak, that he may descend and purify himself in the Marsh of Reeds.

[1135] The double doors of heaven are open, the double doors of *ḳbḥ.w* are open for Pepi, at daybreak, that he may descend and purify himself in the Marsh of Reeds.

[1136] The double doors of heaven are open, the double doors of *ḳbḥ.w* are open for Horus of the Sism.t-land, at daybreak, that he may descend and purify himself in the Marsh of Reeds.

[1137] The double doors of heaven are open, the double doors of *ḳbḥ.w* are open for Pepi, at daybreak, that Pepi may descend and purify himself in the Marsh of Reeds.

[1138] The ground is hoed for him; the *wdn.t*-offering is made for him when he dawns as king and takes charge of his throne. He ferries over the *ptr.ti*-sea; he traverses the Winding Watercourse.

[1139] *'Imt.t* lays hold of the arm of Pepi, beginning with her chapel, beginning with her hidden place, which the god made for her, for Pepi is pure (a priest), the son of a pure one (a priest).

[1140] Pepi is purified with these four *nmś.t*-jars, filled at the divine-lake in *Ntr.w*; (he is dried) by the wind of the great Isis, together with (which) the great Isis dried (him) like Horus.

[1141] Let him come, he is pure, so said the priest of Reʿ concerning Pepi to the door-keeper of *kbh.w* (who) was to announce him to these four gods, who are over the lake of *Kns.t*.

[1142] They recite: "How just is Pepi to his father, Geb!" They recite: "How just is Pepi to Reʿ!" His frontiers exist not; his boundary stones are not to be found. Also, Geb, whose (one) arm (reaches) to heaven, whose (other) arm is on earth, announces Pepi to Reʿ.

[1143] Pepi leads the gods; Pepi directs the divine boat; Pepi seizes heaven, its pillars and its stars.

[1144] The gods come to him bowing; the spirits escort Pepi to his *ba*; they reckon (gather up) their war-clubs; they destroy their weapons;

[1145] for behold Pepi is a great one, the son of a great one, whom Nut has borne; the power of Pepi is the power of Set of Ombos, his Pepi is the great wild-bull, who comes forth like *Ḫnti-ʾimnti.w*.

[1146] Pepi is the pouring down of rain; he came forth as the coming into being of water; for he is the *Nḥb-k3.w*-serpent with the many coils; Pepi is the scribe of the divine book, who says what is and causes to exist what is not;

[1147] Pepi is the red bandage, who comes forth from the great *ʾIḥ.t*; Pepi is that eye of Horns, stronger than men, mightier than the gods.

[1148] Horns carries Pepi, Set lifts him up. Let Pepi make an offering which a star gives; he satisfies the two gods, let them be satisfied; he satisfies the two gods, and so they are satisfied.

Utterance 511.

[1149] To say: Geb laughs, Nut smiles before him, (when) Pepi ascends to heaven.

[1150] Heaven rejoices for him; the earth quakes for him; the tempest roars (lit. drives) for him. He howls (or, roars) like Set;

[1151] the guardians of the parts (?) of heaven open the doors of heaven for him. He stands on Shu, he upholds the stars, in the shadow of the wails of god.

[1152] He crosses the sky like *Swnt*; the third (with him) is Sothis of the pure places, for he purifies himself in the lakes of the *Dw3.t*.

[1153] The *nmt-š*-cow will make his ways pleasant; she will guide him to the great seat, which the gods made, which Horns made, which Thot begat.

[1154] Isis will conceive him; Nephthys will bear him. Then he will take his seat on the great throne which the gods made.

[1155] *Dw3.w* in jubilation and the gods in homage will come to him; the gods of the horizon will come to him on their face, and the imperishable stars, bowing.

[1156] He takes the offering table; he directs the mouth of the gods; he supports the sky in life; he sustains the earth in joy; his right arm, it supports the sky in satisfaction (might ?); his left arm, it sustains the earth in joy.

[1157] He finds *Štt*, the crier, the door-keeper of Osiris. His abomination is ferrying over without doing *ʾisnw.t*.

[1158] He receives the wind of life, he breathes joy, and he abounds in divine offerings; he inhales wind and breathes out the wind of the North; he prospers among the gods.

[1159] He is sharp like the great: *Špd*; he advances towards the two *'itr.t*-palaces; he strikes with the *'b3*-sceptre and directs with the *'i33.t*-sceptre.

[1160] He puts his record among men, and his love among the gods, saying: "Say what is; do not say what is not; the abomination of a god is a deceitful word."

[1161] Let him be tested! Thou shalt not speak (thus of) him. This Pepi is thy son; this Pepi is thine heir.

Utterance 535.

[1280] To say by Isis and Nephthys: The *h3.t*-bird comes, the kite comes; they are Isis and Nephthys. They are come in search of their brother Osiris; (They are come) in search of their brother Pepi

[1281] Thou who art (here), thou who art (there), weep for thy brother; Isis, weep for thy brother; Nephthys, weep for thy brother. Isis sits, her hands upon her head;

[1282] Nephthys has indeed seized the tip of (her) two breasts because of her brother, Pepi; Anubis being on his belly; Osiris being wounded; Anubis being before the fist (?).

[1283] Thy putrefaction, Pepi, is not; thy sweat, Pepi, is not; thy outflowing, Pepi, is not; thy dust, Pepi, is not.

[1284] *H3.ti* son of *H3.ti* (is) at *Mnii* coming as *Mn.ti* to divide in three these your four days and your eight nights.

[1285] The stars follow thy beloved *Kbh.wt*, who is chief of thy *nmh* (attendants); thou art chief of those who are chief of the *nmh.w* (attendants); thou hast made *nmh* the *nmh.w*. Loose Horus from his bonds, that he may punish the Followers of Set; that he may seize them; that he may remove their heads; that he may take off their legs.

[1286] Cut thou them up, take thou out their hearts; drink thou of their blood; count their hearts, in this thy name of "Anubis counter of hearts."

[1287] Thy two eyes have been given to thee as thy two uraeusserpents, for thou art like Wepwawet on his standard, Anubis who presides in *sh-ntr*.

[1288] O Pepi, the houses of the great who are in Heliopolis make thee "first"; the spirits and even the imperishable stars fear thee. The dead fall on their face before thee; the blessed dead(?) care for thee.

[1289] "Eldest (son), *'Im3h*, is for Pepi," say the Souls of Heliopolis, who furnish thee with life and satisfaction. He lives with the living as Seker lives with the living; he lives with the living as Pepi lives with the living.

[1290] O Pepi, come, live thy life there, in thy name, in thy time, in these years, which are to be peaceful, according to (?) thy wish.

Utterance 606.

[1683] To say: Arise for me, father; stand up for me, Osiris Pepi. It is I; I am thy son; I am Horus.

[1684] I have come to thee, that I may purify thee, that I may cleanse thee, that I may revivify thee, that I may assemble for thee thy bones, that I may collect for thee thy flesh, that I may assemble for thee thy dismembered limbs,

[1685] for I am as Horus his avenger, I have smitten for thee him who smote thee; I have avenged thee, father Osiris Pepi, on him who did thee evil.

[1686] I have come to thee by order of *Ḥrw*; (for) he has appointed thee, father Osiris Pepi, (to be) upon the throne of Re'-Atum, that thou mayest lead the blessed dead(?).

[1687] Thou shalt embark into the boat of Re', in which the gods love to ascend, in which the gods love to descend, in which Re' is rowed to the horizon; Pepi shall embark into it, like Re'.

[1688] Thou shalt seat thyself upon this throne of Re', that thou mayest command the gods, for thou art indeed Re', who comes forth from Nut, who gives birth to Re' every day. Pepi is born every day like Re'.

[1689] Take to thyself the heritage of thy father Geb before the corporation of the Ennead in Heliopolis. "Who is equal to him?", say the Two great and mighty Enneads who are at the head of the Souls of Heliopolis.

[1690] These two great and mighty gods have appointed thee those who are chiefs of the Marsh of Reeds upon the throne of *Ḥrw*, as their eldest son;

[1691] they placed Shu at thy left (east side), Tefnut at thy right (west side), Nun before thee (at thy south side), Nnt behind thee (at thy north side);

[1692] they lead thee to these their places, beautiful and pure, which they made for Re' when they placed him upon their thrones (his throne).

[1693] Pepi, they make thee live, so that thou mayest surpass the years of Horus of the horizon, when they make thy (for "his") name, "Withdraw not thyself from the gods."

[1694] They recite for thee this chapter, which they recited for Re'-Atum who shines every day; they have appointed Pepi to their thrones (his throne) at the head of every Ennead, as Re' and as his deputy.

[1695] They cause Pepi to come into being as Re', in this his name of "Khepri." Thou mountest to them as Re', in this his name of "Re', thou turnest back again from their face as Re', in this his name of "Atum."

[1696] The Two Enneads shall rejoice, O father; when thou approachest, O father, Osiris Pepi, they say: "Our brother is come to us."

[1697] The Two Enneads say to Osiris Pepi: "King, Osiris Pepi, one of us is come to us."

[1698] The Two Enneads say to thee: "King, Osiris Pepi, the eldest son of his father is come to us." The Two Enneads say to thee: "King, Osiris Pepi, he is the eldest son of his mother."

[1699] The Two Enneads say to thee: "King, Osiris Pepi, he to whom evil was done by his brother Set comes to us." The Two Enneads say: "And we shall not permit that Set be delivered from carrying thee for ever, king, Osiris Pepi"

[1700] The Two Enneads say to thee:"King, Osiris Pepi, raise thyself up, king, Osiris Pepi; thou livest."

14. LETTER TO THE DEAD

A linen from the tomb of a nobleman, Sankhenptah, at Saqqara (Dynasty 6) contains a petition to Sankhenptah written jointly by the deceased's sister and son. It is the oldest example of this kind of writing.

(1) A sister addresses her brother, and a son addresses his father. Your condition is like that of he who lives a million times! May Ha, lord of the West, and Anubis, lord of burial, act for you in the way she (wife) and he (son) desire!

(2) This (letter) is a reminder of the fact that the agent of Behezti came for (some) leather when I was sitting by your head when Irti's son Iy was summoned (3) to vouch for the agent of Behezti, and that you said "keep him hidden for fear of the elder Iy. May the wood (4) of this bed beneath me rot (?) if a man's son is barred from his household property."

But now, look, Wabut has come (5) along with Izezy; they have devastated your house, and they have seized everything which was in it with the specific aim of enriching Izezy. (5) They wished to ruin your son while enriching the son of Izezy. She has taken Iazet, Iti, and Anankhi away from you; (7) she is taking away your personal attendants after taking everything which was in your house.

(8) Can your heart be calm about this? I wish you would bring (me) to you so that I might be there at your side in preference to seeing your son dependent on the son (9) of Izezy. Wake up your father Iy against Behezti! Rouse yourself and make haste against him! (10) You know that I come to you here on the matter of litigation with Behezti and Aai's son Anankhi. Rouse yourself against them, (11) along with your ancestors and brothers and your friends so that you might overthrow Behezti and Aai's son Anankhi.

(12) Remember what you said to Ireti's son Iy: "the houses of the ancestors should be protected" when you (also) said "a son's house is (his) son's house." May your son set up your house in the way you set up the house of your father!

(13) O Sankhenptah my father, may it please you to have Ini summoned to you to seize the house of Anankhi born to Wabut!

𓂝𓃀𓅓𓂋𓏏𓈖𓏏𓅱𓂋𓏛𓈖𓂋𓏏𓅓𓏏𓈖𓅓𓏏𓂋𓏏𓅓𓈖𓏏𓂋𓅱𓂋𓏏𓈖𓏏𓅱𓂋

15. AUTOBIOGRAPHY OF WENI THE ELDER

Probably our most important historical inscription from the Old Kingdom is the lengthy autobiography of Weni (sometimes referred to as Uni) written on his mastaba tomb at Abydos in Upper Egypt. His long career under the pharaohs Teti, Pepi I, and Merenre saw him rise from a minor official to a nomarch of Upper Egypt. He provides us with these details in his narrative, which is reproduced in full here. The spellings of some of the names in the original translation have been revised.

Introduction

[Royal offering to Osiris the lord of Busiris] in order that there may be given to him a revenue in bread and liquors, at every festival and each day, with an abundance [of everything, a thousand loaves], a thousand cups of beer, a thousand oxen, a thousand geese, a thousand ducks, a thousand fowls, a thousand birds, a thousand cloths, a thousand [pieces of linen, for] the prefect of the country of the south, the guardian of Nekhen, the dictator of Nekhabit, sole friend, feudal vassal of Osiris-Khonta-mentit, [Weni;] [He says:]

Career under Teti

[I was bom under the Majesty of Unas. I was still a youth] wearing the fillet under the Majesty of Teti, and employed as superintendent of the treasury, when I was promoted to the inspectorship of the irrigated lands ot Pharaoh.

Career under Pepi I

When I was chief of the secret chamber under the Majesty of Pepi, his Majesty confers on me the dignity of Friend (and) controlling prophet of his pyramid; then when [I held this office] his Majesty made me Sabu, guardian of Nekhen, [for his heart] was satisfied with me above any other of his servants. I heard then all that happened, I alone with a Sabu, clerk to the Porte, in every secret affair, [and I executed all the writings] which had to be executed in the name of the king whether for the harem of the king or for the residence of the Six, so that I satisfied the heart of the king more than any other of his peers, (or) of his mamelouk nobles, more than any other of his servants.

[An order was also issued] by the Majesty of my lord that a sarcophagus of white stone should be brought to me from Royu. His Majesty sent a temple-slave in a boat with the soldiers [the hewers of the stone and the artisans] with orders to convey this sarcophagus to me from Royu; and this sarcophagus comes with a temple-slave in a large pontoon from the royal administration, as well as its lid, a stele in the form of a gate, (to wit) the frame, the two middle blocks, and the threshold; never had anything like it been made for any other servant whatever; but it happened that my wisdom pleased his Majesty and that also my zeal pleased his Majesty and that also the heart of his Majesty was satisfied with me.

Also from my being Sabu, guardian of Nekhen, his Majesty made me sole Friend, superintendent of the irrigated lands of the Pharaoh over the superintendents of the cultivated lands who are there, and I acted to the satisfaction of his Majesty, both when I had to keep guard behind the Pharaoh and (when I had) to settle the royal itinerary, or to arrange the peers, and I acted in all this to the satisfaction of his Majesty above everything. When moreover one went to the royal harem to inform against the great royal wife Amitsi, secretly, his Majesty made me alone descend into it in order to listen to business, no Sabu clerk of the Porte being there, nor any peer except myself alone, because of (my) wisdom and my zeal which pleased his Majesty, because the heart of his Majesty was satisfied with me; it was I who wrote everything down, I alone with a Sabu guardian of Nekhni. Now my employment was that of superintendent of the irrigated lands of the Pharaoh, and there never had been any of this rank who had heard the secrets of the royal harem, in former days, excepting me, when his Majesty made me hear (them), because my wisdom pleased his Majesty more than any other of his peers, more than any other of his mamelouks, more than any other of his servants.

When his Majesty carried war to the district of the nomad Hirushau, and when his Majesty formed an army of several myriads, levied throughout the entire South, southward starting from Elephantine, northward starting from the Letopolitan nome, in the country of the north, in the two confines in their entirety, in each station between the fortified stations of the desert, in Jrtjet a country of the Nubians, in Medja a country of the Nubians, in Aamu a country of the Nubians, in Wawet a country of the Nubians, in Qaau a country of the Nubians, in Temehu a country of the Nubians; his Majesty sent me at the head of this army. There were generals in it, there were mamelouks of the king of Lower Egypt in it, there were sole Friends of the Pharaoh in it, there were in it dictators and princes of the south and of the land of the north, Golden Friends and superintendents of the prophets of the south and of the land of the north, prefects of the confines at the head of the militia of the south" and of the land of the north, cities and boroughs which they governed, as well as Nubians from the regions mentioned (above), and nevertheless it was I who laid down the law for them—although my employment was that of superintendent of the irrigated lands of the Pharaoh with the title belonging to my office—so that each of them obeyed like all the rest, and each of them took with him what he needed as regards bread and sandals for the journey, and each of them took beer from every town, and each of them took every kind of small cattle from every individual. I led them to the gateway of I(m)hotep, the plateau of Horneb-maat;[1] then being in this locality [I marshalled them, I regulated] everything and I counted the number of this army which no servant had ever counted (before). This army marched prosperously; it shattered the country of the Hirushau. This army marched prosperously; it destroyed the country of the Hirushau. This army marched prosperously; it conquered their fortresses. This army marched prosperously; it cut down their fig-trees and their vines. This army marched prosperously; it set fire to the [houses of] the inhabitants. This army marched prosperously; it slew their soldiers by myriads. This army marched in peace; it led away captive a very great number of the inhabitants of the country, and his Majesty praised me because of this above everything. His Majesty sent me to lead this army five times, in order to penetrate into the country of the Hirushau, as often as they revolted against this army, and I acted to the satisfaction of his Majesty in this above everything. Then as it was said that there were rebels among those barbarians who extended as far as towards Tiba, I sailed in ships with this army, I attacked the coasts of this country to the north of the country of the Hirushau; then this army being on the march, I went and overthrew them all, and I slew all the rebels among them.

Career under Merenre

When I was at the great House with the right of carrying the wand and the sandals, the Pharaoh Merenre made me governor-general of the South, southward starting from Elephantine (and) north-ward as far as the Letopolitan nome, because my wisdom pleased his Majesty, because my zeal pleased his Majesty, because the heart of his Majesty was satisfied with me: when then I was invested with the right of carrying the wand and the sandals, his Majesty favoured me therefore (giving me part of) the cattle intended for the palace; when I was in my place I was above all his peers, and all his mamelouks and all his servants, and this dignity had never been conferred on any servant whatever before. I filled to the satisfaction of the king my part of superintendent of the South, so as to be allowed to stand at

---

1   For these places, I follow the reading of Simpson in *LAE*.

his side second (in rank) to him, accomplishing all the duties of an engineer, judging all causes that there were to judge for the royal administration in this south of Egypt, as second judge, at every hour appointed for judgment for the royal administration in this south of Egypt as second judge; regulating as governor all there was to do in this south of Egypt, and never had anything like (this) taken place in this south of Egypt before; and I did all this to the satisfaction of his Majesty accordingly.

His Majesty sent me to Ibhat, to bring back the sarcophagus (called) the Coffer of the Living, with its lid, as well as the true and precious pyramidion of the pyramid (called) "Khanefer-mistress-of-Merenre." His Majesty sent me to Elephantine to bring a stele in the form of a false door, together with its base of granite, as well as the portcullis and the framework of granite [for the passage of the pyramid], (and) to bring back the gates and the thresholds of the exterior chapel of the pyramid "Khanefer-mistress-of-Merenre." I returned with them to the pyramid Khanefer of Merenre in six galliots, three pontoons, three barges, (and) a man of war,—never had there been a man of war at Ibhat or at Elephantine; so all things that his Majesty had ordered me (to do) were accomplished fully as his Majesty had ordered them.

His Majesty sent me to Hatnub to transport a large table of offerings of alabaster. I brought this table of offerings down [from the mountain]: as it was impossible in Hatnub to despatch (it) along the course of the current in this galliot, I cut a galliot out of the wood of the acacia-sont, 60 cubits long and 30 cubits broad; I embarked the 17th day of the third month of Shomu, and although there was no water over the sand-banks of the river I reached the pyramid Khanefer of Merenre prosperously; I was there with [the table of offerings] without fail according to the order which the majesty of my lord had deigned to command me.

His Majesty sent me to excavate five docks (?) in the South and to construct three galliots and four pontoons of acacia-sont of Wawet; now the Nubian princes of the countries of Jrtjet, Wawet, Aamu, (and) Medja felled the wood for that purpose, and I accomplished it all in only one year, the transportation to the water and the loading of large quantities of granite for the pyramid Khanefer of Merenre; and moreover I caused a palace to be constructed for each of these five docks (?), because I venerate, because I exalt, because I adore above all the gods, the souls of the king Merenre, living for ever, because I have been (raised) above everything according to the order of which his double lias given unto me, even to me who am the beloved of his father, the lauded of his mother, the magnate in his city, the delighter of his brethren, the governor in actual command of the South, the vassal of Osiris, Weni.

16. AUTOBIOGRAPHY OF HARKHUF

Another long autobiography appears on a rock-cut tomb found at Qubbet al-Hawa near Aswan. Like Weni (see previous reading), the owner of the tomb, Harkhuf, was a nomarch of Upper Egypt in the reign of Merenre (Dynasty 6). He also was an overseer of caravans and led several trade expeditions into lands to the south of Egypt. His autobiographical narrative is reproduced here in full.

I came today from my city, I descended from my nome, I built a house, I set up the doors. I dug a lake, and I planted trees. The king praised me. My father made a will for me, (for) I was excellent—[one beloved] of his father, praised of his mother, whom all his brothers lobed. I gave bread to the hungry, clothing to the naked, I ferried him who had no boat.

O you living, who are upon earth, [who shall pass by this tomb whether] going down-stream or going up-stream, who shall say: "A thousand loaves, a thousand jars of beer for the owner of this tomb;" I will [...] for their sakes in the nether world. I am an excellent, equipped spirit, a ritual priest, whose mouth knows.

As for any man who shall enter into [this] tomb [as his mortuary possession, I will seize] him like a wild fowl; he shall be judged for it by the great god.

I was one saying good things and repeating what was loved. Never did I say aught evil, to a powerful one against any people, (for) I desired that it might be well with me in the great god's presence. Never did I [judge two brothers] in such a way that a son was deprived of his paternal possession.

Introduction

Count, sole companion, ritual priest, chamber-attendant, judge attached to Nekhen, lord of Nekheb, wearer of the royal seal, caravan-conductor, privy councilor of all affairs of the South, favorite of his lord, Harkhuf, ... who brings the products of all the countries to his lord, who brings the tribute of the royal ornaments, governor of all countries of the South, who sets the terror of Horus among the countries, who does that which his lord praises, ... the revered by Ptah-Sokar, Harkhuf.

First Journey

He says: The majesty of Mernere, my lord, sent me, together with my father, the sole companion, and ritual priest, Iri, to Yam, in order to explore a road to this country. I did it in only seven month, and I brought all (kinds of) gifts from it [...]. I was very greatly praised for it.

Second Journey

His majesty sent me a second time alone; I went forth upon the Elephantine road, and I descended from Irthet, Mekher, Tereres, Irtheth, being an affair of eight months. When I descended I brought gifts from this country in very great quantity. Never before was the like brought to this land. I descended from the dwelling of the chief of Sethu and Irthet, after I had explored these countries. Never had any companion or caravan-conductor who went forth to Yam before this, done (it).

Third Journey

His majesty now sent me a third time to Yam; I went forth from [...] upon the Uhet road, and I found the chief of Yam going to the land of Temeh to smite Temeh as far as the western corner of heaven. I went forth after him to the land of Temeh, and I pacified him, until he praised all the gods for the king's sake.

Yam who followed [...] in order to inform the majesty of Mernere, my lord, ... after the chief of Yam. Now when I had pacified that chief of Yam below Irthet and above Sethu, I found the chief of Irthet, Sethu, and Wawat .....[...].

I descended with 300 asses laden with incense, ebony, heknu, grain, panthers, [...] , ivory, [throwsticks], and every good product. Now when the chief of Irthet, Sethu, and Wawat saw how strong and numerous was the troop of Yam, which descended with me to the court, and the soldiers who had been sent with me, (then) this [chief] brought and gave to me bulls and small cattle, and conducted me to the roads of the highlands of Irthet, because I was more excellent, vigilant, and [...] than any count, companion or caravan-conductor, who had been sent to Yam before. Now, when the servant there was descending to the court, one sent the [...], sole companion, the master of the bath, Khuni, up-stream with a vessel laden with date-wine, [cakes], bread, and beer. The count, wearer of the royal seal, sole companion, ritual priest, treasurer of the god, privy councilor of decrees, the revered, Harkhuf.

Letter of Pepi II (Fourth Journey)

Royal seal, year 2, third month of the first season, (third month), day 15.

Royal decree (to) the sole companion, the ritual priest and caravan-conductor, Harkhuf.

I have noted the matter of your letter, which you have sent to the king, to the palace, in order that one might know that you have descended in safety from Yam with the army which was with you. You have said [in] your letter, that you have brought all great and beautiful gifts, which Hathor, mistress of Imu has given to the *ka* of the king of Upper and Lower Egypt Neferkere,[2] who lives forever and ever. You have said in your letter that you have brought a dancing dwarf of the god from the land of spirits, like the dwarf which the treasurer of the god Burded brought from Punt in the time of Isesi. You have said to my majesty: "Never before has one like him been brought by any other who has visited Yam."

Each year [...] you doing that which your lord desires and praises; you spend day and night [with the caravan] in doing that which your lord desires, praises and commands. His majesty will make your many excellent honors to be an ornament for the son of your son forever, so that all people will say when they hear what my majesty does for you: "Is there anything like this which was done for the sole companion, Harkhuf, when he descended from Yam, because of the vigilance which he showed, to do that which his lord desired, praised and commanded!"

Come northward to the court immediately; [...] you shall bring this dwarf with you, which you bring living, prosperous and healthy from the land of spirits, for the dances of the god, to rejoice and [gladden] the heart of the king of Upper and Lower Egypt, Neferkere, who lives forever. When he goes down with you into the vessel, appoint excellent people, who shall be beside him on each side of the vessel; take care lest he fall into the water. When [he] sleeps at night appoint excellent people, who shall sleep beside him in his tent; inspect ten times a night. My majesty desires to see this dwarf more than the gifts of Sinai and of Punt. If you arrive at court this dwarf being with you alive, prosperous and healthy, my majesty will do for you a greater thing than that which was done

---

2   Pepi II's throne name.

for the treasurer of the god, Burded in the time of Isesi, according to the heart's desire of my majesty to see this dwarf.

Commands have been sent to the chief of the New towns, the companion, and superior prophet, to command that sustenance be taken from him in every store-city and every temple, without stinting therein.

17. AUTOBIOGRAPHY OF PEPINAKHT

Pepinakht was an official who served under Pepi II (Dynasty 6). His rock cut tomb, containing his autobiography, is also at Qubbet al-Hawa near Aswan. In it he describes several successful military expeditions he led on behalf of Pepi.

Pepinakht's Character

I was one who said that which was good, and repeated that which was loved. Never did I say anything evil to a powerful one against any people, (for) I desired that it be well with me in the great god's presence. I gave bread to the hungry, and clothing to the naked. Never did I judge two brothers in such a way that a son was deprived of his paternal possession. I was one beloved of his father, praised of his mother, whom his brothers and sisters loved.

First Nubian Expedition

The majesty of my lord sent me, to hack up Wawat and Irthet. I did so that my lord praised me. I slew a great number there consisting of chiefs' children and excellent commanders of [...]. I brought a great number of them to the court as living prisoners, while I was at the head of many mighty soldiers as a hero. The heart of my lord was satisfied with me in every commission with which he sent me.

Second Nubian Expedition

Now, the majesty of my lord sent me to pacify these countries. I did so that my lord praised me exceedingly, above everything. I brought the two chiefs of these countries to the court in safety, bulls and live [goats] which they [...] to the court, together with chiefs' children, and the two commanders of [..], who were with them. [...] that which the lords of the South do, because I was excellent in watchfulness and because I did that which my lord desired.

Expedition against Asiatics

Now the majesty af my lord sent me to the country of the Asiatics to bring for him the sole companion, [commander] of the sailors, the caravan-conductor, Enenkhet, who was building a ship there for Punt, when the Asiatics belonging to the Sand-dwellers slew him, together with a troop of the army which was with him ....

𓈖𓏏𓆑𓉐𓈖𓂧𓏏𓇯𓏤𓈖𓐍𓏏𓊃𓏤𓈖𓂋𓏏𓇯𓈖𓏏𓆑𓉐𓈖𓂧𓏏𓇯𓏤

18. LEGAL TEXT CONCERNING AN INHERITANCE DISPUTE

A papyrus document (Berlin 9010) found at Aswan and dating to the Old Kingdom contains a judgment rendered by a court in a lawsuit between a man named Sebekhotep and another man named Tjau.

Part of the Submissions Made by the Parties

(1) ... the aforementioned Sebekhotep has brought a document relating the words of the royal noble and overseer of foreigners User, that he should carry out his task for (2) his (User's) wife and his children, whereby all his property is in his control until all the children (3) of the aforementioned User are satisfied therewith-the older one according to his greater (age), the younger one according to his younger (age).

The aforementioned Tjau has said that this is not the case, (4) that his father has in no way done it (made such an agreement).

The Verdict of the Court

If the aforementioned Sebekhotep can bring three excellent witnesses who are convincing on this matter (5) and who shall make (this oath) "May your might be against him, O god" in relation to this document which is in agreement with that which the aforementioned User said on the matter, (6) then matters will remain in the hands of Sebekhotep, for he has brought these three witnesses who say on this matter in their presence (7) "The aforementioned Sebekhotep is the beneficiary." If he does not bring these three witnesses to speak on this matter (8) in their presence, then everything belonging to the aforementioned User shall not remain with him but (rather) remain with his son, the royal noble and overseer of foreigners, Tjau.

𓈖𓏏𓆑𓉐𓈖𓂧𓏏𓇯𓏤𓈖𓐍𓏏𓊃𓏤𓈖𓂋𓏏𓇯𓈖𓏏𓆑𓉐𓈖𓂧𓏏𓇯𓏤

19. THE PRECEPTS OF PTAHHOTEP

This work, known also as the Instruction of Ptahhotep and the Maxims of Ptahhotep, is a well-preserved Egyptian text of the "Instructions in Wisdom" genre (known as sebayt in Egyptian) containing ethical teachings. As with most texts from this genre, the "instructions" are presented by a father to his son. In this case the father purports to be Ptahhotep, a vizier who had worked under the pharaoh Isesi from the Fifth Dynasty. It is more likely that it is pseudepigraphal and was written in the late Sixth Dynasty, when the Instructions in Wisdom texts are more likely to have first appeared. It now exists in several versions with some slight differences between them. The oldest is in the Prisse Papyrus, which dates to the Twelfth Dynasty of the Middle Kingdom. It is also the only complete surviving copy of the text. The Precepts are presented here in their entirety.

PRECEPTS OF THE PREFECT, THE LORD PTAH-HOTEP, UNDER THE MAJESTY OF THE KING OF THE SOUTH AND NORTH, ISESI, LIVING ETERNALLY FOREVER.

1. The prefect, the feudal lord Ptah-hotep, says: O Ptah with the two crocodiles, my lord, the progress of age changes into senility. Decay falls upon man and decline takes the place of youth. A vexation weighs upon him every day; sight fails, the ear becomes deaf; his strength dissolves without ceasing. The mouth is silent, speech fails him; the mind decays, remembering not the day before. The whole body suffers. That which is good becomes evil; taste completely disappears. Old age makes a man altogether miserable; the nose is stopped up, breathing no more from exhaustion. Standing or sitting there is here a condition of ... Who will cause me to have authority to speak, that I may declare to him the words of those who have heard the counsels of former days? And the counsels heard of the gods, who will give me authority to declare them? Cause that it be so and that evil be removed from those that are enlightened; send the double ... The majesty of this god says: Instruct him in the sayings of former days. It is this which constitutes the merit of the children of the great. All that which makes the soul equal penetrates him who hears it, and that which it says produces no satiety.

2. Beginning of the arrangement of the good sayings, spoken by the noble lord, the divine father, beloved of Ptah, the son of the king, the first-born of his race, the prefect and feudal lord Ptah-hotep, so as to instruct the ignorant in the knowledge of the arguments of the good sayings. It is profitable for him who hears them, it is a loss to him who shall transgress them. He says to his son:

3. Be not arrogant because of that which you know; deal with the ignorant as with the learned; for the barriers of art are not closed, no artist being in possession of the perfection to which he should aspire. But good words are more difficult to find than the emerald, for it is by slaves that that is discovered among the rocks of pegmatite.

4. If you find a disputant while he is hot, and if he is superior to you in ability, lower the hands, bend the back, do not get into a passion with him. As he will not let you destroy his words, it is utterly wrong to interrupt him; that proclaims that you are incapable of keeping yourself calm, when you are contradicted. If then you have to do with a disputant while he is hot, imitate one who does not stir. You have the advantage over him if you keep silence when he is uttering evil words. "The better of the two is he who is impassive," say the bystanders, and you are right in the opinion of the great.

5. If you find a disputant while he is hot, do not despise him because you are not of the same opinion. Be not angry against him when he is wrong; away with such a thing. He fights against himself; require him not further to flatter your feelings. Do not amuse yourself with the spectacle which you have before you; it is odious, it is mean, it is the part of a despicable soul so to do. As soon as you let yourself be moved by your feelings, combat this desire as a thing that is reproved by the great.

6. If you have, as leader, to decide on the conduct of a great number of men, seek the most perfect manner of doing so that your own conduct may be without reproach. Justice is great, invariable, and assured; it has not been disturbed since the age of Ptah. To throw obstacles in the way of the laws is to open the way before violence. Shall that which is below gain the upper hand, if the unjust does not attain to the place of justice? Even he who says: I take for myself, of my own free-will; but says not: I take by virtue of my authority. The limitations of justice are invariable; such is the instruction which every man receives from his father.

7. Inspire not men with fear, else Ptah will fight against you in the same manner. If any one asserts that he lives by such means, Ptah will take away the bread from his mouth; if any one asserts that he enriches himself thereby, Ptah says: I may take those riches to myself. If any one asserts that he beats others, Ptah will end by reducing him to impotence. Let no one inspire men with fear; this is the will of Ptah. Let one provide sustenance for them in the lap of peace; it will then be that they will freely give what has been torn from them by terror.

8. If you are among the persons seated at meat in the house of a greater man than yourself, take that which he gives you, bowing to the ground. Regard that which is placed before you, but point not at it; regard it not frequently; he is a blameworthy person who departs from this rule. Speak not to the great man more than he requires, for one knows not what may be displeasing to him. Speak when he invites you and your worth will be pleasing. As for the great man who has plenty of means of existence, his conduct is as he himself wishes. He does that which pleases him; if he desires to repose, he realizes his intention. The great man stretching forth his hand does that to which other men do not attain. But as the means of existence are under the will of Ptah, one can not rebel against it.

9. If you are one of those who bring the messages of one great man to another, conform yourself exactly to that wherewith he has charged you; perform for him the commission as he has enjoined you. Beware of altering in speaking the offensive words which one great person addresses to another; he who perverts the trustfulness of his way, in order to repeat only what produces pleasure in the words of every man, great or small, is a detestable person.

10. If you are a farmer, gather the crops in the field which the great Ptah has given you, do not boast in the house of your neighbors; it is better to make oneself dreaded by one's deeds. As for him who, master of his own way of acting, being all-powerful, seizes the goods of others like a crocodile in the midst even of watchment, his children are an object of malediction, of scorn, and of hatred on account of it, while his father is grievously distressed, and as for the mother who has borne him, happy is another rather than herself. But a man becomes a god when he is chief of a tribe which has confidence in following him.

11. If you abase yourself in obeying a superior, your conduct is entirely good before Ptah. Knowing who you ought to obey and who you ought to command, do not lift up your heart against him. As you know that in him is authority, be respectful toward him as belonging to him. Wealth

comes only at Ptah's own good-will, and his caprice only is the law; as for him who ... Ptah, who has created his superiority, turns himself from him and he is overthrown.

12. Be active during the time of your existence, do no more than is commanded. Do not spoil the time of your activity; he is a blameworthy person who makes a bad use of his moments. Do not lose the daily opportunity of increasing that which your house possesses. Activity produces riches, and riches do not endure when it slackens.

13. If you are a wise man, bring up a son who shall be pleasing to Ptah. If he conforms his conduct to your way and occupies himself with your affairs as is right, do to him all the good you can; he is your son, a person attached to you whom your own self has begotten. Separate not your heart from him. ... But if he conducts himself ill and transgresses your wish, if he rejects all counsel, if his mouth goes according to the evil word, strike him on the mouth in return. Give orders without hesitation to those who do wrong, to him whose temper is turbulent; and he will not deviate from the straight path, and there will be no obstacle to interrupt the way.

14. If you are employed in the larit, stand or sit rather than walk about. Lay down rules for yourself from the first: not to absent yourself even when weariness overtakes you. Keep an eye on him who enters announcing that what he asks is secret; what is entrusted to you is above appreciation, and all contrary argument is a matter to be rejected. He is a god who penetrates into a place where no relaxation of the rules is made for the privileged.

15. If you are with people who display for you an extreme affection, saying:"Aspiration of my heart, aspiration of my heart, where there is no remedy! That which is said in your heart, let it be realized by springing up spontaneously. Sovereign master, I give myself to your opinion. Your name is approved without speaking. Your body is full of vigor, your face is above your neighbors." If then you are accustomed to this excess of flattery, and there be an obstacle to you in your desires, then your impulse is to obey your passion. But he who ... according to his caprice, his soul is ... , his body is ... While the man who is master of his soul is superior to those whom Ptah has loaded with his gifts; the man who obeys his passion is under the power of his wife.

16. Declare your line of conduct without reticence; give your opinion in the council of your lord; while there are people who turn back upon their own words when they speak, so as not to offend him who has put forward a statement, and answer not in this fashion:"He is the great man who will recognize the error of another; and when he shall raise his voice to oppose the other about it he will keep silence after what I have said."

17. If you are a leader, setting forward your plans according to that which you decide, perform perfect actions which posterity may remember, without letting the words prevail with you which multiply flattery, which excite pride and produce vanity.

18. If you are a leader of peace, listen to the discourse of the petitioner. Be not abrupt with him; that would trouble him. Say not to him:"You have already recounted this." Indulgence will encourage him to accomplish the object of his coming. As for being abrupt with the complainant because he described what passed when the injury was done, instead of complaining of the injury itself let it not be! The way to obtain a clear explanation is to listen with kindness.

19. If you desire to excite respect within the house you enter, for example the house of a superior, a friend, or any person of consideration, in short everywhere where you enter, keep yourself from making advances to a woman, for there is nothing good in so doing. There is no prudence in taking part in it, and thousands of men destroy themselves in order to enjoy a moment, brief as a dream,

while they gain death, so as to know it. It is a villainous intention, that of a man who thus excites himself; if he goes on to carry it out, his mind abandons him. For as for him who is without repugnance for such an act, there is no good sense at all in him.

20. If you desire that your conduct should be good and preserved from all evil, keep yourself from every attack of bad humor. It is a fatal malady which leads to discord, and there is no longer any existence for him who gives way to it. For it introduces discord between fathers and mothers, as well as between brothers and sisters; it causes the wife and the husband to hate each other; it contains all kinds of wickedness, it embodies all kinds of wrong. When a man has established his just equilibrium and walks in this path, there where he makes his dwelling, there is no room for bad humor.

21. Be not of an irritable temper as regards that which happens at your side; grumble not over your own affairs. Be not of an irritable temper in regard to your neighbors; better is a compliment to that which displeases than rudeness. It is wrong to get into a passion with one's neighbors, to be no longer master of one's words. When there is only a little irritation, one creates for oneself an affliction for the time when one will again be cool.

22. If you are wise, look after your house; love your wife without alloy. Fill her stomach, clothe her back; these are the cares to be bestowed on her person. Caress her, fulfil her desires during the time of her existence; it is a kindness which does honor to its possessor. Be not brutal; tact will influence her better than violence; her ... behold to what she aspires, at what she aims, what she regards. It is that which fixes her in your house; if you repel her, it is an abyss. Open your arms for her, respond to her arms; call her, display to her your love.

23. Treat your dependents well, in so far as it belongs to you to do so; and it belongs to those whom Ptah has favored. If any one fails in treating his dependents well it is said: "He is a person ..." As we do not know the events which may happen tomorrow, he is a wise person by whom one is well treated. When there comes the necessity of showing zeal, it will then be the dependents themselves who say: "Come on, come on," if good treatment has not quitted the place; if it has quitted it, the dependents are defaulters.

24. Do not repeat any extravagance of language; do not listen to it; it is a thing which has escaped from a hasty mouth. If it is repeated, look, without hearing it, toward the earth; say nothing in regard to it. Cause him who speaks to you to know what is just, even him who provokes to injustice; cause that which is just to be done, cause it to triumph. As for that which is hateful according to the law, condemn it by unveiling it.

25. If you are a wise man, sitting in the council of your lord, direct your thought toward that which is wise. Be silent rather than scatter your words. When you speak, know that which can be brought against you. To speak in the council is an art, and speech is criticized more than any other labor; it is contradiction which puts it to the proof.

26. If you are powerful, respect knowledge and calmness of language. Command only to direct; to be absolute is to run into evil. Let not your heart be haughty, neither let it be mean. Do not let your orders remain unsaid and cause your answers to penetrate; but speak without heat, assume a serious countenance. As for the vivacity of an ardent heart, temper it; the gentle man penetrates all obstacles. He who agitates himself all the day long has not a good moment; and he who amuses himself all the day long keeps not his fortune. Aim at fulness like pilots; once one is seated another works, and seeks to obey one's orders.

27. Disturb not a great man; weaken not the attention of him who is occupied. His care is to embrace his task, and he strips his person through the love which he puts into it. That transports men to Ptah, even the love for the work which they accomplish. Compose then your face even in trouble, that peace may be with you, when agitation is with ... These are the people who succeed in what they desire.

28. Teach others to render homage to a great man. If you gather the crop for him among men, cause it to return fully to its owner, at whose hands is your subsistence. But the gift of affection is worth more than the provisions with which your back is covered. For that which the great man receives from you will enable your house to live, without speaking of the maintenance you enjoy, which you desire to preserve; it is thereby that he extends a beneficent hand, and that in your home good things are added to good things. Let your love pass into the heart of those who love you; cause those about you to be loving and obedient.

29. If you are a son of the guardians deputed to watch over the public tranquillity, execute your commission without knowing its meaning, and speak with firmness. Substitute not for that which the instructor has said what you believe to be his intention; the great use words as it suits them. Your part is to transmit rather than to comment upon.

30. If you are annoyed at a thing, if you are tormented by someone who is acting within his right, get out of his sight, and remember him no more when he has ceased to address you.

31. If you have become great after having been little, if you have become rich after having been poor, when you are at the head of the city, know how not to take advantage of the fact that you have reached the first rank, harden not your heart because of your elevation; you are become only the administrator, the prefect, of the provisions which belong to Ptah. Put not behind you the neighbor who is like you; be unto him as a companion.

32. Bend your back before your superior. You are attached to the palace of the king; your house is established in its fortune, and your profits are as is fitting. Yet a man is annoyed at having an authority above himself, and passes the period of life in being vexed thereat. Although that hurts not your ... Do not plunder the house of your neighbors, seize not by force the goods which are beside you. Exclaim not then against that which you hear, and do not feel humiliated. It is necessary to reflect when one is hindered by it that the pressure of authority is felt also by one's neighbor.

33. Do not make ... you know that there are obstacles to the water which comes to its hinder part, and that there is no trickling of that which is in its bosom. Let it not ... after having corrupted his heart.

34. If you aim at polished manners, call not him whom you accost. Converse with him especially in such a way as not to annoy him. Enter on a discussion with him only after having left him time to saturate his mind with the subject of the conversation. If he lets his ignorance display itself, and if he gives you all opportunity to disgrace him, treat him with courtesy rather; proceed not to drive him into a corner; do not ... the word to him; answer not in a crushing manner; crush him not; worry him not; in order that in his turn he may not return to the subject, but depart to the profit of your conversation.

35. Let your countenance be cheerful during the time of your existence. When we see one departing from the storehouse who has entered in order to bring his share of provision, with his face contracted, it shows that his stomach is empty and that authority is offensive to him. Let not that happen to you; it is ...

36. Know those who are faithful to you when you are in low estate. Your merit then is worth more than those who did you honor. His ... , behold that which a man possesses completely. That

is of more importance than his high rank; for this is a matter which passes from one to another. The merit of one's son is advantageous to the father, and that which he really is, is worth more than the remembrance of his father's rank.

37. Distinguish the superintendent who directs from the workman, for manual labor is little elevated; the inaction of the hands is honorable. If a man is not in the evil way, that which places him there is the want of subordination to authority.

38. If you take a wife, do not … Let her be more contented than any of her fellow-citizens. She will be attached to you doubly, if her chain is pleasant. Do not repel her; grant that which pleases her; it is to her contentment that she appreciates your work.

39. If you hear those things which I have said to you, your wisdom will be fully advanced. Although they are the means which are suitable for arriving at the maat, and it is that which makes them precious, their memory would recede from the mouth of men. But thanks to the beauty of their arrangement in rhythm all their words will now be carried without alteration over this earth eternally. That will create a canvass to be embellished, whereof the great will speak, in order to instruct men in its sayings. After having listened to them the pupil will become a master, even he who shall have properly listened to the sayings because he shall have heard them. Let him win success by placing himself in the first rank; that is for him a position perfect and durable, and he has nothing further to desire forever. By knowledge his path is assured, and he is made happy by it on the earth. The wise man is satiated by knowledge; he is a great man through his own merits. His tongue is in accord with his mind; just are his lips when he speaks, his eyes when he gazes, his ears when he hears. The advantage of his son is to do that which is just without deceiving himself.

40. To attend therefore profits the son of him who has attended. To attend is the result of the fact that one has attended. A teachable auditor is formed, because I have attended. Good when he has attended, good when he speaks, he who has attended has profited, and it is profitable to attend to him who has attended. To attend is worth more than anything else, for it produces love, the good thing that is twice good. The son who accepts the instruction of his father will grow old on that account. What Ptah loves is that one should attend; if one attends not, it is abhorrent to Ptah. The heart makes itself its own master when it attends and when it does not attend; but if it attends, then his heart is a beneficent master to a man. In attending to instruction, a man loves what he attends to, and to do that which is prescribed is pleasant. When a son attends to his father, it is a twofold joy for both; when wise things are prescribed to him, the son is gentle toward his master. Attending to him who has attended when such things have been prescribed to him, he engraves upon his heart that which is approved by his father; and the recollection of it is preserved in the mouth of the living who exist upon this earth.

41. When a son receives the instruction of his father there is no error in all his plans. Train your son to be a teachable man whose wisdom is agreeable to the great. Let him direct his mouth according to that which has been said to him; in the docility of a son is discovered his wisdom. His conduct is perfect while error carries away the unteachable. Tomorrow knowledge will support him, while the ignorant will be destroyed.

42. As for the man without experience who listens not, he effects nothing whatsoever. He sees knowledge in ignorance, profit in loss; he commits all kinds of error, always accordingly choosing the contrary of what is praiseworthy. He lives on that which is mortal, in this fashion. His food is evil words, whereat he is filled with astonishment. That which the great know to be mortal he lives

upon every day, flying from that which would be profitable to him, because of the multitude of errors which present themselves before him every day.

43. A son who attends is like a follower of Horus; he is happy after having attended. He becomes great, he arrives at dignity, he gives the same lesson to his children. Let none innovate upon the precepts of his father; let the same precepts form his lessons to his children. "Verily," will his children say to him, "to accomplish what you say works marvels." Cause therefore that to flourish which is just, in order to nourish your children with it. If the teachers allow themselves to be led toward evil principles, verily the people who understand them not will speak accordingly, and that being said to those who are docile they will act accordingly. Then all the world considers them as masters and they inspire confidence in the public; but their glory endures not so long as would please them. Take not away then a word from the ancient teaching, and add not one; put not one thing in place of another; beware of uncovering the rebellious ideas which arise in you; but teach according to the words of the wise. Attend if you wish to dwell in the mouth of those who shall attend to your words, when you have entered upon the office of master, that your words may be upon our lips … and that there may be a chair from which to deliver your arguments.

44. Let your thoughts be abundant, but let your mouth be under restraint, and you shall argue with the great. Put yourself in unison with the ways of your master; cause him to say: "He is my son," so that those who shall hear it shall say "Praise be to her who has borne him to him!" Apply yourself while you speak; speak only of perfect things; and let the great who shall hear you say: "Twice good is that which issues from his mouth!"

45. Do that which your master bids you. Twice good is the precept of his father, from whom he has issued, from his flesh. What he tells us, let it be fixed in our heart; to satisfy him greatly let us do for him more than he has prescribed. Verily a good son is one of the gifts of Ptah, a son who does even better than he has been told to do. For his master he does what is satisfactory, putting himself with all his heart on the part of right. So I shall bring it about that your body shall be healthful, that the Pharaoh shall be satisfied with you in all circumstances and that you shall obtain years of life without default. It has caused me on earth to obtain one hundred and ten years of life, along with the gift of the favor of the Pharoah among the first of those whom their works have ennobled, satisfying the Pharaoh in a place of dignity.

46. It is finished, from its beginning to its end, according to that which is found in writing.

FIRST INTERMEDIATE PERIOD

20. INSCRIPTIONS OF HEMIRE

The following inscriptions appear on a false door from the tomb of Hemire, priestess of Hathor, at Busiris. It dates probably to the Eighth Dynasty or a little later.

Outer Jambs, Left

(1) An offering which the king gives by Osiris, lord of Busiris (for) bread, beer and everything pure which should be put (literally "goes forth") on the offering slab of Osiris in Busiris for the *imakhu* Hemire whose perfect name is the royal acquaintance, priestess of Hathor, Hemi.

(2) O you who live on earth and who shall pass by on this path, (are) you who shall say: "It is the pure bread of Osiris (and) it is for the *imakhu* Hemi."

Outer Jambs, Right

(1) [An offering which the king and which] Anubis, who dwells in the divine tent-shrine, who is in his wrappings, lord of the sacred land give that invocation offerings may be made in the Wag festival and the festival of Thoth for the *imakhu* Hemire whose perfect name is Hemi.

(2) [I am one who makes] peace and who attains the state of *imakhu*, the favored one of her father and beloved one of her [mother], the *imakhu* of Hathor mistress of Busiris, Hemire whose perfect name is Hemi.

Inner Jambs, Left

(1) May she travel on the perfect ways of the necropolis as an *imakhu* of the Great God, Hemire whose perfect name is Hemi.

(2) With regard to any scribe who shall pass by this tomb of mine, he it is who shall say "bread and beer for the mistress of this tomb, the *imakhu* Hemi."

Inner Jambs, Right

(1) I am she who gives bread to the hungry and clothes to the naked, one favored of her husband, Hemire. (2) With regard to any man who shall say "bread and beer for Hemi in this her tomb!" I am an excellent *akh* and I will not allow that evil (happen) to them.

21. AUTOBIOGRAPHY OF ANKHTIFY

Ankhtify was a nomarch of Hierankopolis in Upper Egypt. His autobiography, found in his rock-cut tomb at El-Mo'alla, describes his conquest of Edfu and conflict with Thebes. Ankhtify apparently was loyal to the pharaoh Neferkare of Herakleopolis, but whether this Neferkare ruled during the Ninth or Tenth Dynasty is unclear. Here is a portion of Ankhtify's autobiography.

(1) The Prince, Count, Royal Seal-bearer, Sole Companion, Lector-priest, General, Chief of scouts, Chief of foreign regions, Great Chief of the nomes of Edfu and Hieraconpolis, Ankhtifi, says:

(2) Horus brought me to the nome of Edfu for life, prosperity, health, to reestablish it, and I did (it). For Horus wished it to be reestablished, because he brought me to it to reestablish it.

I found the House of Khuu inundated like a marsh, abandoned by him who belonged to it, in the grip of a rebel, under the control of a wretch. I made a man embrace the slayer of his father, the slayer of his brother, so as to reestablish the nome of Edfu. How happy was the day on which I found well-being in this nome! No power in whom there is the heat of strife will be accepted, now that all forms of evil which people hate have been suppressed.

(3) I am the vanguard of men and the rearguard of men. One who finds the solution where it is lacking. A leader of the land through active conduct. Strong in speech, collected in thought, on the day of joining the three nomes. For I am a champion without peer, who spoke out when the people were silent, on the day of fear when Upper Egypt was silent.

(4) As to everyone on whom I placed my hand, no misfortune ever befell him, because my heart was sealed and my counsel excellent. But as to any fool, any wretch, who stands up in opposition—I shall give according as he gives. "O woe," will be said of one who is accused by me. His *w'r* will take water like a boat. For I am a champion without peer!

22. INSCRIPTION OF KHETY II

Wakhare Khety II was a nomarch of Lycopolis (modern Asyut) in Upper Egypt during the reign of Merikare of the Tenth Dynasty, who ruled from Herakleopolis. In Khety's rock cut tomb was found this inscription, in which he describes his loyalty to King Merikare.

Khety's Lineage

[Heir] of a ruler, ruler of rulers, son of a ruler, son of the daughter of a ruler, an ancient stock ...... [son of the daughter] of a ruler, [...] of the beginning, a noble [without] an equal........ for you have put [fear] in the land, you have chastised Middle Egypt for his sake alone.

Services for the King

You did convey him up-river, the heaven cleared for him, the whole land was with him, the counts of Middle Egypt, and the great ones of Heracleopolis, the district [of] the queen of the land, who came to repel the evil-doer. The land trembled, Middle Egypt [feared], all the people were in terror, the villages in [panic], fear entered into their limbs. The officials of Pharaoh were (a prey) to fear, the favorites to the terror of Heracleopolis. The land burned in its flame........... Never was the front of a fleet brought into Sheshotep, while its rear was still at .... They descended by water and landed at Heracleopolis. The city came, rejoicing over [her] lord, the son of her lord; women mingled with men, old men and children.

Old Age

The ruler's son, he reached his city, entering into the house of his father. He saw the [approach] to their house, his sarcophagus, his old age. When a man is in his place (his tomb), the city [...] of eternity [...].

Building the Temple

Your city-god loves you, Tefibi's son, Kheti. He has [presented] you, that he might look to the future in order to restore his temple, in order to raise the ancient walls, the original places of offering, to [...] the venerable ground, [...] which Ptah built with his fingers, which Thoth founded, for Upwawet, lord of Siut, [by] command of the king, the ruler of the Two Lands, the king of Upper and Lower Egypt, Merikere, to make a monument for the souls of Anubis, the great god; that he (the king) might spend for him (the god) millions of years, that he might repeat Sed Jubilees; under the leadership of the confidant of the king, Tefibi's son, Kheti, great lord of Middle Egypt. Behold, your name shall be forever in the temple of Upwawet, your memory shall be beautiful in the colonnade. Some shall communicate it to other, [...] the future [...] in years, one hundred after another hundred, of added life upon earth; you shalt (still) be among them that dwell on [earth.] ....

Peaceful Rule

How beautiful is that which happens in your time, the city is satisfied with you. That which was concealed from the people, you have done it [openly], in order to make gifts to Siut, [...] by your plan alone. Every [official] was at his post, there was no one fighting, nor any shooting an arrow. The child was not smitten beside his mother, (nor) the citizen beside his wife. There was no evil-doer in [...]; nor anyone doing violence against his house [...]. Your city-god, your father who loves you, [leads] you.

23. THE TEACHING FOR MERIKARE

This work of the sebayt *genre is addressed to the pharaoh Merikare of the Tenth Dynasty by his father. Whether Merikare's father really authored the work is questionable, considering the commonly pseudepigraphical nature of this genre of literature, but the work is usually dated by scholars to the First Intermediate Period. The oldest copy is found on the Leningrad Papyrus 1116 and was transcribed by the scribe Khamwese during the Middle Kingdom.*

"[THE INSTRUCTION WHICH THE KING OF UPPER AND LOWER EGYPT......... MADE] FOR HIS SON (KING) MERY-KE-RE."

§ 1. The cardinal virtue.

"(2) .... mild in a case [deserving].........., but punish (3).................. them (?) in every word. It is the first principle(?) of (4) [kingship(??)]."

§ 2. On rebellions.

"[If you find(?) a city(??), whose ....] has happened, suppress the rebels (5) ....with .... (6) .... As for him who makes report ....(7).................. After your word has taken place ...... (8) ....(9)......... If(?) he makes half of it in(?) life........., then (10).........................my dependents, (11)..............seem (?) to you many, you err on the way (12).................. You should slay .... (13)......... if(?) you know dependents of his who love him."

§ 3. On the treatment of unruly vassals.

"If [you] find ....[who] is a ....of a city, a possessor (14) [of] clansmen, order him to yourself, that he(?) may not..................(15)......... Often (??) when a man violates the law .... (16)........the Great Halls (of Justice) .... (17) ....he [appeals to(??)] the clansmen. Beware lest ....

§ 4. (Subject obscure.)

".........(18)...beware... living. When (?) a month has passed (?) .... (19)......... his own ...... He speaks his thought (?) and recalls ....(20) ....[be reconciled (??)] to him, your heart being appeased ....(21).........those who are [reconciled (??)]."

§ 5. More advice concerning unruly vassals.

"[If] you [find a ......] like a god ...., whose neighbours are [evil(?)], whom (22) the city....... whose dependents are many in sum(??).............. whose...... enters in (?)............(23), and he is pleasant in the sight of his serfs......—a man who talks much(?) is a mischief-maker (??)—suppress him, slay <him>, (24) wipe out his name, [destroy(?)] his kinsfolk, suppress his memory, and(?) his dependents who(?) love him."

§ 6. On turbulent vassals.

"The turbulent man is confusion (25) to a city. He creates two factions among the young genera-tion. If then you find (26) one who belongs to a ...... city, [and] his doings are passed beyond you, cite him before the nobles, and suppress [him]. He is a rebel (27) moreover. A man who talks much(?) is a mischief-maker (??) for a city. Bend (?) the multitude, suppress its ardour. There is none who.............. rebellion (28) with(?) the poor man. He [is(?)] made to rebel."

§ 7. On the avoidance of passion.

"A subject (?) ....when (?) the soldiers are (?) in confusion .... Make (29) its end as................. (When) many rage, let them (??) be placed in the magazine (?). Mild .... you punish (30) ...., [the citizens(??)] are in joy. Make yourself innocent before God.[1] Let the people say [in] spite of(?) you (31) that you punish in accordance with your (?)........ A good disposition is a man's heaven; the blaspheming of the pass[ionate] man (?) is baneful."

§ 8. On the value of cleverness in speech.

"(32) Be skilful in speech, in order that you may prevail. The tongue is a ......and(?) a sword (?) to a [king(?)]. Speech is more powerful than any fighting. None can circumvent (33) him who is clever.......... A wise (king) is a [school (??)] to the nobles; they do not thwart him (34) who know (the measure of) his knowledge. No [falsehood (?)] draws near to him. Truth comes to him in pure essence like the sayings of the Ancestors (35)."

§ 9. Seek ancient models.

"Copy your fathers who have gone before you. ....is achieved by knowledge. Behold, their words are recorded in writing. (36) Open and read and copy him who knows (?). Thus he who is skilled becomes one who is instructed. Be not evil; good is willingness of heart. (37) Make a lasting monument for yourself in the love of you. Multiply ...., show kindness (?) to the city. God will praise you for reward; .... will [give] you (38) praises for your goodness, will wish for your health henceforward (??)."

§ 10. Look to the future.

"Show consideration to the nobles and prosper your people. Make firm your boundaries (39) and your borders(??). Good it is to work for the future. Respect a life of energy(?), for self-content will make a wretched man. Let men ....(40) through your good disposition. Weak it is to bind to oneself the land .... A fool is he who is greedy when others possess. [Life] (41) upon earth passes; it is not long. Fortunate is he who is remembered(?) in it. (The possession of [?]) a million men avails not the Lord of the Two Lands. The [good man (?)] shall be (42) living for ever. He who has passed with Osiris (??) departs, even as he who was pleasant to himself(?) is dissolved (?)."

---

1 "God" here refers to Re (Ra).

§ 11. Magnify your nobles.

"Magnify your nobles, that they may do (43) your ordinances. He who is wealthy in his house does not deal partially; he is rich and does not want. The poor man does not speak (44) according to his truth. He who says "I desire" is not fair. He is partial to him whom he loves; he inclines towards the possessor of rewards. Great is the Great One, when his great ones are great. Strong (45) is the King who possesses courtiers. Exalted is he who is wealthy in nobles. Speak Truth in your house, that the nobles (46) who are upon earth may fear you. Uprightness of heart beseems the Sovereign. The inside (of a house) inspires the outside with fear."

§ 12. Act justly.

"Do (47) Justice, that you may endure upon earth. Calm the weeper. Oppress not the widow. Expel no man from the possessions of his father. Degrade not (48) magistrates from their posts. Take heed lest you punish wrongfully. Slaughter not, for it does not profit you. But punish with beatings (49) and imprisonment, for thus shall this land prosper. Excepting only (?) the rebel who has devised his plans, for God knows the froward, (50) and God requites his sins in blood. It is the lenient man who .... lifetime. (Yet) slay not a man, when you know his good qualities, (51) with whom you once did rehearse (your) letters, and recite (?)............ God. Advance boldly in difficult places. (52) The soul comes to the place that it knows; it mistakes not its paths of yesterday. No magic can restrain it, but it hastens towards them who (53) give it water."

§ 13. Remember the Day of Judgment.

"(As for) the Magistrates who judge sinners, mark that they will not be lenient on that day of judging miserable (54) (men), in the hour of performing (their) function. Woe is him who is accused as one conscious (of sin [?]). Put not your faith in length of years, (55) (for) they regard a lifetime as (but) an hour. A man remains over after (reaching) the haven (of) Death. His deeds are laid beside him for (all) treasure. (56) Eternal is the existence yonder. A fool is he who has made light of (?) it. But he who has reached it without wrongdoing, shall continue yonder like a God, (57) stepping forward boldly like the Lords of Eternity."

§ 14. On the recruiting of soldiers.

"Raise up your young troops, that the Residence may love you. Multiply your dependents as henchmen (??). (58) Behold, your city is full of fresh recruits. Twenty years it is, (that) the young generation is happy in following its heart. (Afterwards), henchmen (?) (59) come forth again; the head of a family (?) enters in with(?) children...... (Thus) does antiquity fight for us, (60) whence I raised (troops) when I arose (as King). Exalt your great ones, advance your [warriors (?)]. Increase the young generation of (61) your followers, (that they may be) equipped with possessions, endowed with fields, rewarded with cattle."

§ 15. Recognize merit. Perform religious duties.

"Distinguish not between the son of a noble and him (62) of lowly birth. Take to yourself a man because of his capacity. All crafts are done according to .... the Lord of Valour. Protect (?) your boundary, (63) and raise up your monuments. Profitable are gangs of workmen to their lord. Make [beautiful] monuments for the God; that causes to live the name of him who does it. A man does (64) what is profitable to his soul, (even) the monthly service of priest, and wearing the white sandals. Frequent the shrine. Be discreet concerning the mysteries, enter into (65) the sanctuary. Eat bread in the temple."

§ 16. Religious institutions and the making of monuments.

"Replenish the table of offerings, increase the loaves. Add to the daily sacrifices, (66) for it is profitable to him who does so. Make firm your monuments according as you are rich. For a single day gives for eternity, an hour makes (67) beautiful for futurity. God knows him who works for him. Bring your statues from a distant land, nor let them(?) reckon the total (68) thereof. For miserable is he that is free <from(?)> enmity; never is the enemy still in the midst of Egypt."

§ 17. Occurrences in the neighbourhood of Thinis.

"Troops (69) shall subdue (?) troops, as (runs) the prophecy of the Ancestors concerning it. Egypt fights (70) in the Necropolis. Injure not the tombs with deeds of injury (?); for even so I did and even so it did occur, even as should be(??) done to (71) one who has transgressed in this way(?) with(?) the god. Deal not evilly with the Southern land, for you know the prophecy of the Residence concerning it. (72) That (?) shall (?) happen even as this did happen. They did not transgress, according as they said .... I speak of(??) Thinis ...... (73) ......, its southern boundary at Taut(?). I captured it like a flood of water. King (74) Mer (?) ......, the deceased, did not do it. Be lenient concerning it .... (75) There is no ......which causes it(?)self to lie hid. It is good to work for the future."

§ 18. Present relations with the South.

"You stand well with the South; the bearers (76) of loads come to you with gifts. I did the same as the Ancestors; there was none who had corn that he should give it. Be indulgent (?) (77) for(?) their weaknesses towards you(?). Be satisfied with your bread and your beer. The red granite comes to you (78) without expeditions (??). Harm not the monument of another, but quarry stone in Royu. Build not (79) your tomb out of that which has been overturned, (making) what once was made into what is yet to make(?). Behold the King <is one(?)> full of joy of heart. You are indolent (80) and sleep through my (??) strength; <you(?)> follow your heart through what I have done. There is no enemy within (81) your border."

§ 19. The subjugation of the North-West.

"When any ruler arose in a city(??), his heart was oppressed by reason of the North-land, (from) Hat-shenu to S(?)beka, (82) its southern boundary to Khawey (?). I pacified the entire West, as far as the stretches(?) of the Fayûm. It works (83) for itself(??), and it yields............ The East is one rich <in(??)> foreigners, (84) their produce .... islands in the midst (?), every man within it. The estates (?) say, 'Greatly revered are you(??)' concerning me."

§ 20. The subjugation of the North-East.

"Behold [the land] which they destroyed is made into districts. Every great city...... The principality of one (86) is in the hand of ten men. The magistrate (?)...... with all manner of tax which exists. The priest is entrusted(with fields. (They) work for you like (87) a single gang (of labourers). How comes it that rebels are not made? (Because) the Nile does not fail you by not coming. Produce (88) is in your hand from the North-land. Behold, I drove in my(?) mooring-post in the region(?) which I made(?) on the East, from (??) the boundaries of Hebenu to (89) the Horus-Way, equipped with cities, filled with people of the best of the entire land, so as to repel (90) their attacks. Let(?) me see a brave man who shall (?) copy it, and add to what I have done ......from(?) a (91) cowardly heir."

§ 21. Characterization of the Aamu.

"Speak thus moreover to the barbarian. Behold the wretched Aamu, toilsome is the land wherein he is, (a land) troubled <with> (92) water, (made) difficult by many trees, its ways (made) toilsome by reason of the mountains. He dwells not in a single place, but (93) his legs are (ever) driven wandering(??). He is fighting (ever) since the time of Horus. He conquers not, nor yet is he conquered. (94) He announces not a day in fighting, like one who undertakes (??) the suppression (?) of conspirators."

§ 22. The defeat of the barbarians.

".....(95) whilst I existed (??), these barbarians were as a battle-axe in a fortress (??) .... (96) I caused the North-land to smite them, I carried captive their inhabitants, I plundered their cattle. (97) An abomination (??) is the Aamu unto(??) Egypt. Do not trouble yourself concerning him. He is an Aamu ...., he ...... on (98) his coast. He plunders a lonely settlement(?) but he will not attack a populous city."

§ 23. Fortifications are to be made.

"Dig a (99) dyke(?) against [half(??)] of it, and flood half of it, (even) Kem-wey. Behold it is the navel-string of the desert-people; (100) its walls and its warriors are many, and subjects are in it able to......, the pure (101) ... of the region of Dad-esut. It counts ten thousand men as citizens, free(?) and without imposts. (102) There are magistrates in it since the time of the Residence. Established are(?) <its(?)> boundaries, strong its garrison (??), northerners (103) many(??). Inundate them (??). The North-land gives (?) produce (?) in corn in freedom (?). It is to ...... (104) ...... of him who does it. Behold it is the handle (?) of the North-land. They have made a dyke against (105) Herakleopolis. Suitable (??) is a populous city. Beware lest you be(??) surrounded by subjects of an enemy (106), for prisoners (??) ...... old(?) a year."

§ 24. Build castles in the North-land.

"When your boundary is troubled towards the South, it is the barbarians (107) who take the girdle (?). Build castles in the North-land. A man's name is surely not small (108) through that which he does. A well-provided town is not harmed. Build castles......, for the enemy (109) loves him who is destructive(?), whose deed is evil (?). King Akhthoi the deceased foretold (?) in (giving) instruction (?): (110) 'He who is(??) quiet shall be(??) violent .... God thwarts(?) the rebel ...... home.'"

§ 25. Exhortation to be industrious.

"There comes one...(111) who(?) shall do it. He shall be wise in what he has decreed (?) ....
, on that day of (112) <his> coming. Enrich the tables of offerings. Revere the god, and say not he is weak. Let not your arms be slack, (113) but work joyfully (??). Satiety (?) is the violation of heaven (?). Death (?) is a monument in the opinion of(?) an enemy. (114) He does not diminish it(?) though desire that what he has done may be embellished by one who comes after him. There is none without an (115) enemy. Full of knowledge is the <ruler> of the two lands. Not ignorant is the King who possesses nobles. He is wise at (116) his going forth from the womb; <the god(??)> exalted him from among a million men(?)."

§ 26. The responsibilities of Kingship.

"A goodly office is that of King; (117) it has no son, nor has it a brother who is made to endure upon its monuments. One brings honour to another. A man works for [him who] (118) (went) before him, through the desire that what he has done may be embellished by him who comes after him. (119) Behold a calamity happened in my time; the regions of (120) Thinis were violated. It happened in truth through that which I had done; I knew (121) it after it was done. Behold my recompense(?) (followed) from what I had done. No, but weak is he, and no good man, (122) who restores what he has destroyed, and demolishes what he has built, and improves what he has made beautiful. Take heed (123) concerning it. A blow is rewarded with the like thereof; that is the consequence (??) of all that is done."

§ 27. God, even when hidden, exacts piety from men.

"A generation of men passes, (124) and God, who discerns characters, has hidden himself. (Yet) there is none that can oppose the possessor of a hand (?); he is one who thwarts (?) (even [?]) what is (125) seen by the eyes. Reverence must(?) be shown to God upon his path. (Men) work in precious stones, and carve(?) [out of] bronze. The mud-flat(?) is (126) replaced by a flood. There is no river that suffers itself to be concealed; but it loosens the dam(?) by(?) which (127) it lay hid. (Even so) also the soul comes to the place that it knows. Make stately your castle in the West, adorn your place (128) in the Necropolis; even as one who is just, as one who does Right. This is that whereon men's hearts repose. More acceptable (129) is the nature of one just of heart than the ox of him who does iniquity. Work for God, that he may work for you the like; with offerings (130) to replenish the offering-tables, and with carved inscription--it is what points out your name. God is cognizant of (the man) who works for him."

§ 28. God the creator of all.

"Command (131) men, the flocks of God. He made heaven and earth at their desire. He checked the greed of the waters, and made the air to give life (132) to their nostrils. They are his own images proceeding from his flesh. He arises in heaven at their desire. He made (133) for them grass and cattle, fowl and fish to nourish them. He slew his enemies and destroyed his own children (134) because of their plots in making rebellion. He makes the dawn at their desire. He sails by(??) in order to see them. He has raised (135) a shrine behind them. When they weep, he hears. He made for them rulers in the egg, a supporter(?) (136) to support(??) the back of the weak. He made for them magic as weapons to ward off (137) (evil) events; dreams (also) by night and day. How has he slain the froward of heart? Even as a man (138) smites his son for his brother's sake. For God knows every name."

§ 29. Conclusion.

"Do not do anything(?) which my mouth ...., when(?) it gives (139) any laws concerning the King. Direct (?) your face straight forward (?), and ...... as a man. O that you may reach me, without (finding) your accuser. Slay not (140) any that is near to you; the god who knows him commends him to you. He who is happy upon earth is one of them; gods are they (141) who serve the King. Instill the love of yourself in all the land. A good character is (for a) remembrance (??) ...... It was said (142) concerning you (?), 'Perished is the time of the weak' by those at the back in the house of (143) Akhthoi, in foretelling its(?) coming today. Behold I have spoken to you (144) the best of my inner thoughts; set them stedfastly before your face."

𓏏𓆼𓏤𓎛𓏛𓊪𓂝𓈖𓐍𓏏𓆓𓂋𓅓𓏏𓀀𓈖𓏏𓐍𓏏𓆓𓏤𓊪𓂋𓅓𓏏𓀀𓊪𓂋𓅓

24. LETTER TO A DECEASED WIFE

This letter was written on a stela by a certain Merirtyfy and deposited in the tomb of his wife.

A communication by Merirtyfy to Nebetiotef:

How are you? Is the West taking care of you [according to] your desire? Now since I am your beloved upon earth, fight on my behalf and intercede on behalf of my name. I did not garble [a spell] in your presence when I perpetuated your name upon earth. Remove the infirmity of my body! Please become a spirit for me [before] my eyes so that I may see you in a dream fighting on my behalf. I will then deposit offerings for you [as soon as] the sun has risen and outfit your offering slab for you.

A communication by Khuau to his sister:

I have not garbled a spell in your presence nor have I withdrawn offerings from you. Rather I have emptied out(?) [for you my coffers(?)]. Fight on my behalf, and fight on behalf of my wife and children.

𓏏𓆼𓏤𓎛𓏛𓊪𓂝𓈖𓐍𓏏𓆓𓂋𓅓𓏏𓀀𓈖𓏏𓐍𓏏𓆓𓏤𓊪𓂋𓅓𓏏𓀀𓊪𓂋𓅓

25. TJETJI STELA

This autobiography was written by Tjetji, the chief treasurer under kings Intef I and Intef II during the early Eleventh Dynasty, and inscribed on a stela that was put in his tomb near Thebes. It provides us with valuable historical information about the domain of the Theban rulers of this period.

Introduction

[Live] Horus: Wahenekh; King of Upper and Lower Egypt, Son of Re, Intef (I), fashioner of beauty, living like Re forever.

Tjetji's Titles

His real and favorite servant, having an advanced seat in the house of his lord, great and favorite official, knowing the private affairs of his lord, following him at all his goings, [great] hearted — in very truth, head of the grandees of the palace, in charge of the seal in the privy office, one whom his lord trusted more than the grandees, who delighted the heart of Horus (the king) with that which he desired, favorite of his lord, his beloved, chief treasurer, in charge of the privy office which his lord loved, chief, treasurer, first under the king, the revered, Tjetji, says:

Career under Intef I

I was one beloved of his lord, his favorite every day. I passed a long period of years under the majesty of my lord, Horus, Wahenekh, King of Upper and Lower Egypt, Son of Re, Intef, this land being under his authority up-river as far as [This] and down-river as far as Thinis; while I was his servant, his subject, his real subordinate. He made me great, he advanced my seat, he set me in his confidential office, in his palace because of [...]; the treasury was put in my charge, under my seal-ring, as one chosen for the sake of every good thing brought to the majesty of my lord, from South and from North at every [accounting]; for the sake of pleasing (the king) with the tribute of this whole land; because of his apprehension lest this land diminish that which was brought to the majesty of my lord from the sheiks who are in the Red Land; and because of his apprehension lest the highlands diminish. Then he gave this (office) to me, recognizing the excellence of my ability. Then I reported it to him; never was anything lacking therein [...] because of my great wisdom.

I was one who was a real favorite of his lord, a great and favorite official, the coolness and the warmth in the house of his lord, [to whom] the arms were drooped (in respect) among the grandees, I did not [...] behind the two [...], for which men are hated. I was one loving good, and hating evil, a character beloved in the house of his lord, attending to every procedure according to the [...] of the desire of my lord. Now, at every procedure on account of which he (the king) commanded me to arise.......... I did not exceed the number which he commanded me; I did not put one thing in the place of another [....] I did not take a thing from a legacy, (but) every procedure was attended to. Now, as for all royal food which the majesty of my lord commanded to give to him, I made for it a list of all that his *ka* desired; then I rendered it to him; I carried out successfully all their administration; never was a thing lacking therein, because of my great wisdom.

Death of Intef I

I made a barge for the city, and a boat for following my lord. I was counted with the grandees at every time of [...], while I was honored and great. I supplied [myself] with my own things, which the majesty of my lord gave to me because he so greatly loved me, (even) Horus, Wahenekh, King of Upper and Lower Egypt, Son of Re, Intef (I), living like Re, forever; until he journeyed to his horizon (tomb).

Career under Intef II

Then, when his son assumed his place, (even) Horus, Nakhtneb-Tepnefer, King of Upper and Lower Egypt, Son of Re, Intef (II), fashioner of beauty, living like Re, forever, I followed him to all his good seats of pleasure. Never did he [...] therein, because of my great wisdom. He gave me the function which I had in the time of his father, making it to prosper under his majesty, without anything being lacking therein. I passed all my time on earth, as first under the king, his subject; being mighty and great under his majesty. I was one fulfilling his character, whom his lord praised every day.

26. THE INTEF HARPER'S SONG

Harpers' songs are believed to have been performed at funerary feasts. This one comes from the reign of Intef (Antef) II of Dynasty 11, though our earliest version is from a tomb in the reign of Akhenaten (Dynasty 18) and our earliest complete copy is on Papyris Harris 500 from Dynasty 19. Harper's songs are rather diverse in their content, and this one is notable for its scepticism about survival in the afterlife.

(2) Song which is in the house of King Antef the justified
(And) which is in front of the (3) harpist.
Flourishing indeed is this good lord!
A kindly fate has come to pass.
(One) generation passes away
And others (4) remain (in its place)
Since the time of the ancestors.
The gods that were aforetime
Rest in their pyramids;
Nobles (5) and glorified likewise
Are buried in their pyramids.
They that built houses,
Their places are no more;
What (6) has been done with them?
I have heard the sayings of Imhotep and Djedefhor

With whose words men (still) speak (7) so much;
What are their places?
Their walls have crumbled,
Their places are no more,
As if they had never (8) been.
None cometh from thence
That he might tell their circumstances,
That he might tell their needs
And content our heart
Until we have reached (9) the place
Whither they have gone.
May thy heart be cheerful
To permit the heart to forget
The making of (funerary) services for thee.
Follow thy desire while thou livest!
(10) Put myrrh upon thy head,
Clothe thyself in fine linen,
Anoint thee with the genuine wonders
(11) Which are the god's own.
Increase yet more thy happiness,
And let not thy heart languish;
Follow thy desire and thy good,
(12) Fashion thine affairs on earth
After the command of thy heart.
That day of lamentation will come to thee,
When the Still (1) of Heart does not hear their lamentation,
And mourning does not deliver a man from the netherworld.
Refrain: (2) Make holiday!
Do not weary thereof!
Lo, none is allowed to take his goods with him,
Lo, none that has gone has (3) come back!
death treats kings and commoners alike; for both "lie buried in their pyramids."

MIDDLE KINGDOM

27. INSCRIPTION OF HENU

This inscription was cut on a rock in the Wadi Hammat in the eastern desert near Thebes, where the Egyptians quarried for stone. It was composed by a man named Henu, an official of Mentuhotep III (Dynasty 11), who led an expedition to Punt on behalf of the pharaoh.

Introduction

Year 8, first month of the third season (ninth month), day 3; his real favorite servant, who does all that he praises every day, wearer of the royal seal, [sole] com[panion], —overseer of that which is and that which is not, overseer of the temples, overseer of the granary and White House, overseer of horn and hoof, chief of the six courts of justice, high-voiced in proclaiming the name of the king on the day of warding off [...] who judges the prisoner according to his desert.................. Satisfying the heart of the king as keeper of the Door of the South; over the administration of the nomes of the South, chief treasurer.............. who quells the Haunebu, to whom the Two Lands come bowing down, to whom every office reports; wearer of the royal seal, sole companion, the steward, Henu says:

Preparation for the Expedition

[My lord—life, prosperity], health—sent me to dispatch a ship to Punt to bring for him fresh myrrh from the sheiks over the Red Land, by reason of the fear of him in the highlands. Then I went forth from Koptos upon the road, which his majesty commanded me. There was with me an army of the South from [...] of the Oxyrrhyncus nome, the beginning thereof as far as Gebelen; the end thereof as far as [...]; every office of the king's house, those who were in town and field, united, came after me. The army [...] cleared the way before, overthrowing those hostile toward the king, the hunters and the children of the highlands were posted as the protection of my limbs. Every official body of his majesty was placed under my authority. They reported messengers to me, as one alone commanding, to whom many hearken.

Departure and Provisions

I went forth with an army of 3,000 men. I made the road a river, and the Red Land (desert) a stretch of field, for I gave a leathern bottle, a carrying pole, jars of water and 20 loaves to each one among them every day. The asses were laden with sandals [...].

Wells Dug

Now, I made 12 wells in the bush, and two wells in Idehet, [square] cubits in one, and [square] cubits in the other. I made another in Iheteb, 20 by 20 cubits on each side [...].

Ship Built and Sent

Then I reached the (Red) Sea; then I made this ship, and I dispatched it with everything, when I had made for it a great oblation of cattle, bulls and ibexes.

Return and Quarrying at Hammamat

Now, after my return from the (Red) Sea, I executed the command of his majesty, and I brought for him all the gifts, which I had found in the regions of God's-Land. I returned through the [valley] of Hammamat, I brought for him august blocks for statues belonging to the temple. Never was brought down the like thereof for the king's court; never was done the like of this by any king's-confidant sent out since the time of the god. I did this for the majesty of my lord because he so much loved me............

28. LETTER OF HEKANAKHT

This is one of three papyrus letters from Thebes written by the mortuary priest Hekanakht, who served under Mentuhotep III (Dynasty 11). The letters appear to indicate that Hekanakht was able to make a considerable amount of money by renting (not buying) farmland, hiring workers to cultivate it, and then selling the produce for a profit.

It is a son who speaks to his mother, namely, the mortuary priest Hekanakht to his mother Ipi and to Hetepe: How are you both? Are you alive, prospering, and healthy? In the favor of Montu, lord of the Theban nome!

And to the entire household: How are you? Are you alive, prospering, and healthy? Don't worry about me, for I'm healthy and alive. Now you are the case of the one who ate until he was sated having gotten so hungry that his eyes had become glassy white. Whereas the whole land has died off, [you] haven't hungered; for when I came south to where you are, I fixed your food allowance in good measure. Isn't the Nile inundation very [low]? Since [our] food allowance has been fixed for us according to the nature of the Nile inundation, bear patiently, each of you, for I have succeeded so far among you in keeping you alive.

Record of food rations for the household:

Ipi and her maidservant	8 hekat-measures
Hetepe and her maidservant	8 hekat-measures
Hety's son Nakht and his dependents	8 hekat-measures
Merisu and his dependents	8 hekat-measures
Sihathor	8 hekat-measures
Sinebniut	7 hekat-measures
Anup	4 hekat-measures
Snefru	4 hekat-measures
Siinut	4 hekat-measures
My's daughter Hetepe	5 hekat-measures
Nofre	3.5 hekat-measures

Sitwere	2 hekat-measures

Total: 6 (text: 7) khar-measures, 9.5 hekat-measures (of barley).

(Note): It is from his northern barley that rations should be meted out to Sinebniut; and until he leaves for Perhaa, they (the rations) should be at his disposal.

Lest you be angry about this, look here, the entire household is just like [my] children, and I'm responsible for everything so that it should be said, "To be half alive is better than dying outright." Now it is only real hunger that should be termed hunger since they have started eating people here, and none are given such rations anywhere else. Until I come back home to you, you should comport yourselves with stout hearts, for I shall be spending the third season here.

Communication by the mortuary priest Hekanakht to Merisu and to Hety's son Nakht, who is subordinate: Only as long as my people keep on working shall you give them these rations. Take great care! Hoe every field of mine, keep sieving (the seed grain), and hack with your noses in the work! Now if they are assiduous, you shall be thanked so that I will not have to make it miserable for you. On the first day of the month of Khentykhetyperty one shall start distributing the rations about which I have written for the new first day of the month.

Don't be unmindful then of the 10 arouras of land which are in the neighborhood and which were given to Ip Junior's son Khentykhe and hoe them. Be very assiduous since you are consuming my food.

Now as for any chattel belonging to Anup which is in your possession, give it back to him! As for what is lost, reimburse him for it. Don't make me write you about this again since I've already written you about this twice.

Now if, as you say, Snefru wants to be in charge of the bulls, you should put him in charge of them. He neither wants to be with you plowing, going up and down, nor does he want to come here to be with me. Whatever else he may want, it is with what he wants that you should make him happy.

Now as for whoever of the women or men may reject these rations, he should come to me here to be with me just to live as I live.

Now when I came to where you are, didn't I warn you not to keep a companion of Hetepe's from her, be it her hairdresser or her domestic? Take great care of her! If only you would persevere in everything accordingly. But since, as you say, you don't want her around, you should have Iutenhab (Hekanakht's new wife?) brought to me.

As this man lives for me—it's Ip I'm referring to—whoever shall make any sexual advance against my new(?) wife, he is against me and I against him.

Since this is my new(?) wife and it is known how a man's new(?) wife should be helped, so as for whoever shall help her, it's the same as helping me. Would even one of you be patient if his wife has been denounced to him? So should I be patient! How can I remain with you in the same community if you won't respect my new(?) wife for my sake?

Now I have sent to you by Sihathor 24 copper debens for the renting of land. Have then 20 arouras of land cultivated for us on lease in Perhaa next to Hau Junior's (paying) in copper, in clothing, in northern barley, or [in] any[thing] else, but only if you shall have gotten a good value there for oil or for whatever else. Take great care! Be very assiduous and be vigilant, [since] you are on good irrigated land of the region of Khepesheyet.

Address: What the mortuary priest Hekanakht sends to his household of the village of Nebeseyet.

ॐ ... (hieroglyphs)

29. THE COMMANDER'S TABLET

Like that of Henu (reading #27), there are other inscriptions cut onto the rock walls at the Wadi Hammamat, including several from the reign of Mentuhotep IV, last king of the Eleventh Dynasty. We are told in one of them that the king sent his vizier Amenhemet (future founder of the Twelfth Dynasty) to the quarry to get a large stone block to make for the king a sarcophagus. At the quarry, Amenhemet recorded his achievement:

Date and Introduction

Year 2, second month of the first season, day 15. Royal commission, executed by the hereditary prince, count, governor of the city, chief judge, favorite of the king, chief of works, distinguished in his office, great in his rank, with advanced place in the house of his lord, commanding the official body, chief of the six courts of justice, judging the people and the inhabitants, and hearing [causes]; to whom the great come bowing down, and the whole land, prone upon the belly; whose offices his lord advanced; his favorite, as keeper of the Door of the South; conducting for him millions of the inhabitants to do for him the desire of his heart toward his monuments, enduring on earth; magnate of the King of Upper Egypt, great one of the King of Lower Egypt, conductor of the palace, [...] in stretching the measuring-cord; judging without partiality, governor of the whole South, to whom is reported that which is and that which is not; conducting the administration of the Lord of the Two Lands; [zealous] of heart upon a royal commission; commander of those that command, conductor of overseers; the vizier of the king, at his audiences, Amenemhet, says:

Choice of Amenemhet

My lord, the king of Upper and Lower Egypt, Nibtowere (Mentuhotep IV) living forever, sent me, as one sending, in whom are divine members; to establish his monument in this land. He chose me before his city, I was preferred before his court.

Personnel of Expedition

Now, his majesty commanded that there go forth to this august highland an army with me, men of the choicest of the whole land: miners, artificers, quarrymen, artists, draughtsmen, stonecutters, gold [workers], treasurers of Pharaoh, of every department of the White House, and every office of the king's-house, united behind me. I made the highlands a river, and the upper valleys a water-way.

Return with Sarcophagus

I brought for him a sarcophagus, an eternal memorial, an everlasting reminder. Never descended its like in this highland since the time of the god. My soldiers descended without loss; not a man perished, not a troop was missing, not an ass died, not a workman was enfeebled. It happened for the majesty of my lord as a distinction, which Min wrought for him because he so much loved him, that his ka might endure upon the great throne in the kingdom of the two regions of Horus. [He made (it) as something greater than it.] I am his favorite servant, who does all that he praises every day.

𓀀𓏤𓋴𓈖𓏏𓅱𓏤𓂋𓏏𓏤𓋴𓈖𓏏𓅱𓏤𓂋𓏏𓏤𓋴𓈖𓏏𓅱𓏤𓂋𓏏

30. THE PROPHECIES OF NEFERTY

One of the works found on the Leningrad Papyrus 1116 is a narrative work we call The Prophecies of Neferty. *The legend is set in the time of King Snefru of the Fourth Dynasty but is in fact a piece of propaganda from the reign of Amenhemet I, founder of the Twelfth Dynasty. The tale suggests that Amenhemet's glorious rule was predicted in advance.*

Now it happened when King Snofru the deceased was beneficent King throughout the land; in one (2) of those days it happened that the magistrates of the Residence entered the Great House to perform their duty. And they (3) went forth again in order that they might perform their duty according to their daily observance.

Said His Majesty to the chancellor (4) who was at his side: "Haste and bring to me the magistrates of the Residence who have gone forth hence in order to perform their duty on this day." Audience was given to them (5) forthwith, and they lay on their bellies in the Presence of His Majesty a second time.

Said His Majesty to them: "My friends, (6) I have caused you to be summoned in order that you may seek out for me from your sons one who has understanding, or from your brothers one who excels, (7) or from your friends one who has achieved some noble deed, that he may speak to me some beauteous words, choice (8) speeches in the hearing of which My Majesty may find diversion."

Thereupon they laid <themselves> on their bellies in the Presence of His Majesty yet again, (9) and spoke before His Majesty: "There is a Great Lector of Ubast, O King our Lord, whose name (10) is Neferrohu, a commoner valiant with his arm, a scribe excellent with his fingers, a wealthy man great of possessions (11) beyond all his equals. Would it [might be vouchsafed to] him to see your (?) Majesty."

Said His Majesty: "Haste and bring him to me," and audience (12) was given to him forthwith, and he lay on his belly in the Presence of His Majesty.

Said His Majesty: "Come now, Neferrohu (13) my friend, and speak to me some beauteous words, choice speeches in the hearing of which My Majesty may (14) find diversion."

Said the Lector Neferrohu: "Shall it be of things past or of things future, O King my Lord?"

(15) Said his Majesty: "Nay, of things future; today (a thing) happens and is past (?)." Thereupon he stretched forth his hand to the box holding the (16) writing materials, and took him a scroll and a reed, and put (what was spoken) in writing.

What was spoken by the Lector (17) Neferrohu, that wise man of the East, who belongs to Ubast at her rising, that native of the Heliopolitan nome, as he (18) was brooding over what should come to pass in the land, and conjuring up the condition of the East, when the Asiatics approach in their might (19) and their hearts rage against those who are gathering in the harvest, and they take away (their) kine from the ploughing. (20) And he said:

"Up, my heart, and bewail this land from where you sprung. He who is silent is a transgressor(??). Behold, that exists whereof men spoke (21) as a thing to be dreaded (??). Behold the great one is fallen <in the land> from where you sprung. Be not weary. Behold, these things are before you; (22) rise up against what is in your presence. Behold, princes hold sway in the land, things made are as though they had never been made. Day begins in falsehood(??). (23) The land is utterly perished, and nought remains; never did a finger-nail complete .... (??).

(24) Perished is this land, none there is who meditates upon it; none speaks, none acts. You weeper(?), how fares this land? The sun is veiled (25) and shines not <in> the sight of men. None can live, <when the sun(??)> is veiled <by(??)> clouds(?)9. The sight of all is dulled(?) (26) through the want of it.

I will speak of what is before me. I prophesy not that which is not yet come.

The river is dry, (even the river) of Egypt. Men cross over (27) the water on foot. Men shall need water for the ships and for the sailings thereof. Their course is become a sand-bank. And the sand-bank (28) shall be stream .... The South wind shall blow against the North wind, the sky shall not have (29) one wind alone. A fearsome bird shall be born in the swamps of the Delta; it makes a nest on (30) either side; the people have caused it to approach through want of it.

Perished are those good things (of yore), the ponds of those(?) (31) who slit fish, teeming with fish and fowl. All good things are passed away. The earth is (32) fallen into misery for the sake of yonder food of the Beduins who pervade the land. For foes (33) are in the East, and Asiatics shall (?) descend into Egypt ....is in want, though (?) another is beside him; no protector hears. (34) Men shall delay...... in the night. Men shall enter the strongholds(?), sleep shall be banished (?) from my eyes, (35) (so that) I pass the night wakeful.

The beasts of the desert shall drink from the rivers (36) of Egypt, and take their ease on their sand-banks in the lack of (any) to scare them away(?). (37) For this land shall be(?) in perturbation (?); none knows the issue that shall be. Hidden (?) ....(38) seeing (?), hearing (?). Men are deaf(?), silence is before (men's) faces (?).

I show you the land upside down, (39) happened that which never (yet) had happened. Men shall take weapons of warfare; the land lives in (40) uproar.

Men shall fashion arrows of bronze; they crave for the bread (41) of blood. Men laugh with the laughter of pain. None there is who weeps because of death. (42) None spends the night hungry because of death. (Every) man's heart cares for his own self. No dishevelled (?) locks are made (43) today. Hearts are entirely......... A man sits in his corner (44) careless(?) while one slays another. I show you the son as enemy, the brother as foe, a man (45) slaying his father.

Every mouth is full of 'Love me!' All good things have departed. Destruction(?) (46) of the land, laws are decreed concerning it. There is a paucity (?) of things done; men are bereft of what was found (existent); things made are (47) as though they had never been made. Men take a man's possessions from him; they are given to him who is a stranger. I show you the possessor as one needy (?), while the stranger is satisfied. (48) He who never was one who filled for himself is one who is empty. Men [regard (?)] fellow-citizens(?) as to be hated, so as(?) to silence the mouth that speaks. A word is answered, and (49) an arm goes forth with a stick; people speak, 'Slay him not!'

The discourse of speech in (men's) hearts is as a fire. (50) No utterance of the mouth is tolerated. The land is minished, its rulers are multiplied. Lacking is any rich in his produce(?). Little is the corn, (51) great the corn-measure; (yet) it is measured to overflowing. Re removes himself from men. (If) he shines, it is (but) an hour(?). None (52) knows that midday is there; his shadow is not discerned. Not dazzled is the sight when he is beheld; the eyes are not moist (53) with water. He is in the sky like the Moon; his accustomed(?) season fails not, for in truth (54) his rays are in (men's) faces after his former wise.

I show you the land upside down; the man weak of arm is (now) the possessor of an arm; men (55) do the bidding of him who (once) did (other men's) bidding. I show you the undermost uppermost .... Men live in the Necropolis. (56) The poor man will make (his) hoard .... The pauper eats (57) offering-bread. Servants are......... The nome of Heliopolis will not be the land of birth (?) of any god.

There is a (58) King who shall come from the South, whose name is Ameny, son of a Nubian woman, (59) a child of Chen-khon. He shall receive the White Crown; he shall assume the Red Crown; (60) he shall unite the Two Powerful Ones; he shall propitiate Horus and Seth with what they love, the "Surrounder of fields" in (61) his grasp, the oar.............. The people of his time shall rejoice, (this) man of noble birth (62) shall make his name for ever and ever. Those who turn to mischief, who devise rebellion (63) shall subdue their mouthings through fear of him. The Asiatics shall fall by his sword, the Libyans (64) shall fall before his flame, and the rebels before his wrath, and the froward before (65) his majesty. The Uraeus that dwells in front shall pacify for him the froward.

(66) There shall be built the 'Wall of the Prince,' so as not to allow the Asiatics to go down (67) into Egypt, that they may beg for water after (their) wonted wise, (68) so as to give their cattle to drink. And Right shall come into its place, (69) and Iniquity be cast(?) forth. He will rejoice who shall behold (70) and who shall serve the King. And he that is prudent shall (71) pour to me libation when he sees fulfilled what I have spoken.

It has come to a successful end. (Written) by the scribe [Mahu].

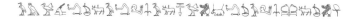

31. HELIOPOLIS TEMPLE INSCRIPTION

Of several obelisks erected at the great temple of Heliopolis, only one remains, and on it is an inscription by Senusret I, second pharaoh of the Twelfth Dynasty, written on the occasion of his Heb-Sed festival.

The year 3, month Athor, of the reign of the King of Upper and Lower Egypt, Kheperkare, the Son of the Sun, Senusret, may he triumph and live for ever!

The King was crowned with the double crown, there was a sitting in the hall, a council of his attendants. the counsellors of Pharaoh, may he live! and the great ones for the place of the foundations.

"Come, let my Majesty order the works, let me think duly of the glories.

Henceforth I will make monuments and erect carved columns to the Double Harmachis,

He created me to do what becomes him, to fulfil what he ordered to do.

He made me overcome this country, he took note and inclined (?), he bestowed on me his protection, illustrating what is in the eyes (?). Let me do the same in his love,

I am king of his making; a monarch long-living, not by the father(?). I occupied as a mere child, not yet worshipped, in the egg already I was a superior of the road of Anubis. He exalted me as lord of both parts, as an infant not yet gone forth.

He anointed my forehead as lord of men, creating me as chief of mortals. He placed me into the palace, as youth not yet come forth from my mother's womb.

He gave me his length and his width, and I have a name in his being victorious. He gave me the land, I am its lord, and I penetrated unto the souls in the heights of heaven,

Let me do good deeds to him who made me, let me conciliate the god by offerings to him. his son

He ordered me to occupy what he had occupied. I come, O Horus, examiner of the body.

I established the offerings of the gods, and I shall make works in the house of father Tum, May he give increase as he made me begin (?).

I shall fill his altar upon earth, and I shall build, while I abide.

There will be a remembrance of my benefits in his house,

Let my name be the temple, my monument the lake. Immortality is a glorious deed.

There is no calculating a king of age out of his works, they will not know (how) to name him, (?) unless his name be engraved.

There is no desolation by the effect of time, the works will last, it is a striving for glories; it is an enterprise of a perfect name; it is the watching over an eternal work."

𓂝𓏤𓆓𓈖𓏏𓀀𓈖𓏏𓆑𓀭𓈖𓏏𓊪𓏤𓈖𓆓𓏏𓀀𓈖𓊪𓏤𓈖𓏏𓆓𓂝𓏤

32. AUTOBIOGRAPHY OF AMENI

Ameni was a nomarch of the Oryx nome in Middle Egypt. He was buried along with several other members of his family at Beni Hasan. On the jambs of a doorway in his cliff-tomb is his autobiography, which among other matters tells of several expeditions he led into Nubia on behalf of his king, Senusret I (Dynasty 12).

Year 43 under the majesty of Sesostris I, living forever and ever; corresponding to year 25 in the Oryx nome with the hereditary prince, count, […] Amen[emhet], triumphant. Year 43, second month of the first season, day 15. O ye who love life and hate death, say ye, 1,000 loaves and beer, 1,000 oxen and geese for the *ka* of the hereditary prince, count, […], great lord of the Oryx nome, […], attached to Nekhen, lord of Nekhbet, chief of prophets, Ameni, triumphant.

First Expedition

I followed my lord when he sailed southward to overthrow his enemies among the four barbarians. I sailed southward, as the son of a count, wearer of the royal seal, and commander in chief of the troops of the Oryx nome, as a man represents his old father, according to [his] favor in the palace and his love in the court. I passed Kush, sailing southward, I advanced the boundary of the land, I brought all gifts; my praise, it reached heaven. Then his majesty returned in safety, having overthrown his enemies in Kush the vile. I returned, following him, with ready face. There was no loss among my soldiers.

Second Expedition

I sailed southward, to bring gold ore for the majesty of the King of Upper and Lower Egypt, Kheperkere (Sesostris I), living forever and ever. I sailed southward together with the hereditary prince, count, oldest son of the king, of his body, Ameni. I sailed southward, with a number, 400 of all the choicest of my troops, who returned in safety, having suffered no loss. I brought the gold exacted of me; I was praised for it in the palace; the king's-son praised god for me.

Third Expedition

Then I sailed southward to bring ore, to the city of Coptos, together with the hereditary prince, count, governor of the city and vizier, Sesostris. I sailed southward with a number, 600 of all the bravest of the Oryx nome. I returned in safety, my soldiers uninjured; having done all that had been told me.

Ameni's Able Administration

I was amiable, and greatly loved, a ruler beloved of his city. Now, I passed years as ruler in the Oryx nome. All the imposts of the king's house passed through my hand. The gang-overseers of the crown possessions of the shepherds of the Oryx nome gave to mea 3,000 bulls in their yokes. I was praised on account of it in the palace each year of the loan-herds. I carried all their dues to the king's house; there were no arrears against me in any office of his. The entire Oryx nome labored for me in [...].

Ameni's Impartiality and Benevolence

There was no citizen's daughter whom I misused, there was no widow whom I oppressed, there was no [peasant] whom I repulsed, there was no shepherd whom I repelled, there was no overseer of serf-laborers whose people I took for (unpaid) imposts, there was none wretched in my community, there was none hungry in my time. When years of famine came I plowed all the fields of the Oryx nome, as far as its southern and northern boundary, preserving its people alive and furnishing its food so that there was none hungry therein. I gave to the widow as (to) her who had a husband; I did not exalt the great above the small in all that I gave. Then came great Niles, possessors of grain and all things, (but) I did not collect the arrears of the field.

𓂀𓏤𓇋𓅓𓂋𓏤𓈖𓏏𓏤𓇋𓏏𓊪𓈖𓆓𓏏𓄿𓈖𓏏𓇋𓅱𓏏𓈖𓆑

33. THE TALE OF SINUHE

This narrative work, reproduced here in full, recounts the story of Sinuhe (probably a fictional character), an official under Senusret I (Dynasty 12). Although the earliest extant version of the story is from the reign of Amenhemet III from the same dynasty, it is generally believed that it was composed shortly after the time of its setting. The tale is regarded by many as one of the finest works of Egyptian literature.

1. The hereditary prince and count, governor of the domains of the Sovereign in the lands of the Setiu, true acquaintance of the king, beloved of him, the henchman Sinuhe; he says: —

2. I was a henchman who followed his lord, a servant of the Royal *harîm* attending on the hereditary princess, the highly-praised Royal Consort of Sesostris in the Pyramid-town of Khnem-esut, the Royal Daughter of Amenemmes in the Pyramid town of Ka nofru, even Nofru, the revered.

3. In year 30, third month of Inundation, day 7, the god attained his horizon, the King of Upper and Lower Egypt Sehetepebre (Amenhemet I). He flew to heaven and was united with the sun's disk; the flesh of the god was merged in him who made him. Then was the Residence hushed; hearts were filled with mourning; the Great Portals were closed; the courtiers crouched head on lap; the people grieved.

4. Now His Majesty had despatched an army to the land of the Temhi, and his eldest son was the captain thereof, the good god Sesostris (Senusret I). Even now he was returning, having carried away captives of the Tehenu and cattle of all kinds beyond number. And the Companions of the Royal Palace sent to the western border to acquaint the king's son with the matters that had come to pass at the Court. And the messengers met him on the road, they reached him at time of night. Not a moment did he wait; the Falcon flew away with his henchmen, not suffering it to be known to his army. Howbeit, message had been sent to the Royal Children who were with him in this army, and one of them had been summoned. And lo, I stood and heard his voice as he was speaking, being a little distance aloof; and my heart became distraught, my arms spread apart, trembling having fallen on all my limbs. Leaping I betook myself thence to seek me a hiding-place, and placed me between two brambles so as to sunder the road from its traveller.

5. I set out southward, yet purposed not to approach the Residence; for I thought there would be strife, and I had no mind to live after him. I crossed the waters of Mewoti hard by the Sycamore, and arrived in Island-of-Snofru. I tarried there in the open fields, and was afoot early, when it was day. I met a man who rose up in, my path; he showed dismay of me and feared. When the time of supper came, I drew nigh to the town of Gu.

6. I ferried over in a barge without a rudder, by the help of a western breeze; and passed on by the East of the quarry in the district Mistress-of-the-Red-Mountain. I gave a road to my feet northward and, attained the Wall of the Prince, which was made to repel the Setiu and to crush the Sandfarers. I bowed me down in a thicket through fear lest the watcher on the wall for the day might see.

7. I went on at time of night, and when it dawned I reached Petni. I halted at the Island-of-Kemwer. An attack of thirst overtook me; I was parched, my throat burned, and I said: This is the taste of death. Then I lifted my heart, and gathered up my body. I heard the sound of the lowing of cattle, and espied men of the Setiu.

8. A sheikh among them, who was aforetime in Egypt, recognised me, and gave me water; he boiled for me milk. I went , with him to his tribe, and they entreated me kindly .

9. Land gave me to land. I set forth to Byblos, I pushed on to Kedme. I spent half a year there; then Enshi son of Amu, prince of Upper Retenu, took me and said to me: "You fare well with me, for you hear the tongue of Egypt." This he said, for that he had become aware, of my qualities, he had heard of my wisdom; Egyptian folk, who were there with him, had testified concerning me. And he said to me: "Why have you come here? Has anything happened at the Residence?" And I said to him: "Sehetepebre is departed to the horizon, and none knows what has happened in this matter." And I spoke again dissembling: "I came from the expedition to the land of the Temhi, and report was made to me, and my understanding reeled, my heart was no longer in my body; it carried me away on the path of the wastes. Yet none had spoken evil of me, none had spat in my face. I had heard no reviling word, my name had not been heard in the mouth of the herald. I know not what brought me to this country. It was like the dispensation of God."

10. Then said he to me: "How shall yonder land fare without him, the beneficent god, the fear of whom was throughout the lands like Sakhmet in a year of plague?" I spoke to him and answered him: "Of a truth his son has entered the Palace and has taken the inheritance of his father. A god is he without a peer; none other surpasses him. A master of .prudence is he, excellent in counsel, efficacious in decrees. Goings and comings are at his command. It is he who subdued the foreign lands while his father was within his Palace, and reported to him what was ordered him to do. Valiant is he, achieving with his strong, arm; active, and none is like to him, when he is seen charging down on Ro-pedtiu, or approaching the melee. A curber of horns is he, a weakener of hands; his enemies cannot marshal their ranks. Vengeful is he, a splasher of foreheads; none can stand in his neighbourhood. Long of stride is he, destroying the fugitive; there is no ending for any that turns his back to him. Stout of heart is he when he sees a multitude; he suffers not sloth to encompass his heart. Headlong is he when he falls upon the Easterners; his joy is to plunder the Ro-pedtiu. He seizes the buckler, he tramples under foot; he repeats not his blow in order to kill. None can turn his shaft or bend his bow. The Pedtiu flee before him as before the might of the Great Goddess. He fights without end; he spares not and there is no remnant. He is a master of grace, great in sweetness; he conquers through love. His city loves him more than itself, it rejoices over him more than over its god. Men and women pass by in exultation concerning him, now that he is king. He conquered while yet in the egg; his face has been set toward kingship ever since he was born. He is one who multiplies those who were born with him. He is unique, god-given. This land that he rules rejoices. He is one who enlarges his borders. He will conquer the southern lands, but he heeds not the northern lands. He was made to smite the Setiu, and to crush the Sandfarers. Send to him, let him know thy name. Utter no curse against His Majesty: He fails not to do good to the land that is loyal to him."

11. He said to me: "Of a truth Egypt is happy, since it knows that he prospers. But you, behold, you are here; you shall dwell with me, and I will treat you kindly."

12. And he placed me even before his children, and mated me with his eldest daughter. He caused me to choose for myself of his country, of the best that belonged to him on his border to another country. It was a goodly land called Yaa. Figs were in it and grapes, and its wine was more abundant than its water. Plentiful was its honey, many were its olives; all manner of fruits were upon its trees. Wheat was in it and spelt, and limitless cattle of all kinds. Great also was that which fell to my portion by reason of the love bestowed on me. He made me ruler of a tribe of the best of his country.

Food was provided me for my daily fare, and wine for my daily portion, cooked meat and roast fowl, over and above the animals of the desert; for men hunted and laid before me in addition to the quarry of my clogs. And there were made for me many dainties, and milk prepared in every way.

13. I spent many years, and my children grew up as mighty men, each one controlling his tribe. The messenger who fared, north, or south to the Residence, tarried with me, for I caused all men to tarry. I gave water to the thirsty, and set upon the road him who was strayed; I rescued him who was plundered. When the Setiu waxed insolent to oppose the chieftains of the deserts, I counselled their movements; for this prince of Retenu caused me to pass many years as commander of his host. Every country against which I marched, when I made my assault it was driven from its pastures and wells. I spoiled its cattle, I made captive its inhabitants, I took away their food, I slew people in it; by my strong arm, by my bow, by my movements and by my excellent counsels. I found favour in his heart and he loved me, he marked my bravery and placed me even before his children, when he had seen that my hands prevailed.

14. There came a mighty man of Retenu and flaunted me in my tent. He was a champion without a peer, and had subdued the whole of Retenu. He vowed that he would fight with me, he planned to rob me, he plotted, to spoil my cattle, by the counsel of his tribesfolk. The prince communed with me and I said: "I know him not, indeed I am no confederate of his, nor one who strode about his encampment. Yet have I ever opened his door, or overthrown his fence? Nay, it is envy because he sees me doing your behest. Assuredly, I am like a wandering bull in the midst of a strange herd, and the steer of those cattle charges him, a long-horn attacks him. Is there a humble man who is beloved in the condition of a master? There is no Pedti that makes cause with a man of the Delta. What can fasten the papyrus to the rock? Does a bull love combat and shall then a stronger bull wish to sound the retreat through dread lest that one might equal him? If his heart be toward fighting, let him speak his will. Does God ignore what is ordained for him, or knows he how the matter stands?"

15. At night-time I strung my bow, and tried my arrows. I drew out my dagger, and polished my weapons. Day dawned and Retenu was already come; it had stirred up its tribes and had assembled the countries of a half of it, it had planned this fight. Forth he came against me where I stood, and I posted myself near him. Every heart burned for me. Women and men jabbered. Every heart was sore for me, saying: "Is there another mighty man who can fight against him?" Then his shield, his battle-axe and his armful of javelins fell, when I had escaped from his weapons and had caused his arrows to pass by me, uselessly sped; while one approached the other, I shot him, my arrow sticking in his neck. He cried, aloud, and fell on his nose. I laid him low with his own battle-axe, and raised my shout of victory over his back. Every 'A'am shrieked. I gave thanks to Montu, but his serfs mourned for him. This prince Enshi, son of Amu, took me to his embrace. Then carried I off his possessions, and spoiled his cattle. What he had devised to do to me, that I did to him. I seized what was in his tent, I ransacked his encampment.

16. I became great thereby, I grew large in my riches, I became abundant in my flocks. Thus God has done, so as to show mercy to him whom he had condemned, whom he had made wander to another land. For today is his heart satisfied. A fugitive fled in his season; now the report of me is in the Residence. A laggard lagged because of hunger; now I give bread to my neighbour. A man left his country because of nakedness; but I am clad in white raiment and linen. A man sped for lack of one whom he should send; but I am a plenteous owner of slaves. Beautiful is my house, wide my dwelling-place; the remembrance of me is in the Palace.

17. O God, whoever you are that did ordain this flight, show mercy and bring me to the Residence! Peradventure you will grant me to see the place where my heart dwells. What matter is greater than that my corpse should be buried in the land wherein I was born? Come to my aid! A happy event has befallen. I have caused God to be merciful. May he do the like again so as to ennoble the end of him whom he had abased, his heart grieving for him whom he had compelled to live abroad. If it so be that today he is merciful, may he hear the prayer of one afar off, may he restore him whom he had stricken to the place where he took him.

18. O may the King of Egypt show mercy to me, that I may live by his mercy. May I salute the Lady of the Land who is in his Palace. May I hear the behests of her children. O let my flesh grow young again, for old age has befallen, feebleness has overtaken me, my eyes are heavy, my hands are weak, my legs refuse to follow, my heart is weary, and death approaches me, when they shall bear me to the city of Eternity. Let me serve my Sovereign Lady. O let her discourse to me of her children's beauty. May she spend an eternity over me!

19. Now it was told the King of Upper and Lower Egypt Kheperkere (Senusret I) concerning this pass wherein I was. Thereupon His Majesty sent to me with gifts of the Royal bounty, and gladdened the heart of this his servant, as it had been the prince of any foreign country. And the Royal Children who were within his Palace caused me to hear their behests.

Copy of the Decree which was Brought to this Humble Servant Concerning his Return to Egypt

20. "Horus, Life-of-Births; Two Goddesses, Life-of-Births; King of Upper and Lower Egypt, Kheperkere; Son of Re, Sesostris, living for ever and ever.

21. "A Royal decree to the henchman Sinuhe. Behold, this decree of the King is brought to you to instruct you as following:—You have traversed the foreign lands and are gone forth from Kedme to Retenu; land gave you to land, self-counselled by your own heart. What have you done, that anything should be done against you? You have not blasphemed, that your words should be reproved. You have not spoken in the council of the nobles, that your utterances should be banned. This determination, it seized your own heart, it was not in my heart against you. This your Heaven, who is in the Palace, is established and prospers daily; she has her part in the kingship of the land, her children are at the Court.

22. "May you long enjoy the goodly things that they shall give you; may you live by their bounty. Come to Egypt, that you may see the Residence where you did grow, that you may kiss the earth at the Great Portals and have your lot among the Companions. For today already you have begun to be old, your manhood is spent. Be mindful of the day of burial, the passing into beatitude: how that the night shall be devoted to you with ointments, with bandages from the hands of Tayt; and a funeral procession shall be made for you on the day of joining the earth; the mummy-shell of gold, with head of lazuli; and a heaven above you; and you placed upon the hearse, oxen dragging you, musicians in front of you; and there shall be performed the dance of the Muu at the door of your tomb; and the offering-list shall be invoked for you and slaughterings made beside your stele; your columns being shapen of white stone amid the tombs of the Royal Children. Thus shall you not die abroad. 'A'amu shall not escort you. You shall not be placed in a sheep-skin, when your mound is made. Yes, all these things shall fall to the ground. Wherefore think of your corpse, and come."

23. This decree reached me as I stood in the midst of my tribesfolk. It was read aloud to me, and I laid me on my belly and touched the soil, I strewed it on my hair. And I went about my encampment rejoicing, and saying: "How should such things be done to a servant whom his heart led astray to barbarous lands? Fair in truth is the graciousness which delivers me from death; inasmuch as your *ka* will grant me to accomplish the ending of my body at home."

Copy of the Acknowledgement of this Decree

24. "The servant of the *harîm* Sinuhe says: — Fair hail! Discerned is this flight that your servant made in his witlessness, yes even by your *ka*, good god, lord of the two lands, whom Re loves and Montu, lord of Thebes, praises. Amun lord of Karnak, Sobk, Re, Horus, Hathor, Atum with his Ennead, Sopdu, Neferbaiu, Semseru, Horus of the East, the Lady of Imet who rests on your head, the Conclave upon the waters, Min in the midst of the deserts, Wereret lady of Punt, Har-uer-re, and all the gods of Ti-muri and of the islands of the sea: they give life and strength to your nose, they endue you with their gifts, they give to you eternity illimitable, time without bourn; the fear of you is bruited abroad in corn-lands and desert-hills, you have subdued all the circuit of the sun.

25. "This your servant's prayer to his lord to rescue him in the West, the lord of Perception, who perceives lowly folk, he perceived it in his noble Palace. Your servant feared to speak it; now it is like some grave circumstance to repeat it. Great god, peer of Re in giving discretion to one toiling for himself this your servant is in the hand of a good counsellor to his advantage; truly I am placed beneath his guidance. For Your Majesty is the victorious Horus, your hands are strong against all lands.

26. "Let now Your Majesty cause to be brought Maki from Kedme, Khentiaush from Khentkesh, Menus from the lands of the Fenkhu. They are renowned princes, who have grown up in love of you, albeit unremembered. Retenu is yours, just like your hounds.

27. "But regarding this your servant's flight, I planned it not, it was not in my heart, I conceived it not, I know not what sundered me from my place. It was the manner of a dream, as when a Delta-man sees himself in Elephantine, a man of the marshes in Ta-seti. I had not feared. None had pursued after me. I had heard no reviling word. My name had not been heard in the mouth of the herald. No, but my body quivered, my feet began to scurry, my heart directed me, the god who ordained this flight drew me away. Yet am I not stiff-backed, inasmuch as suffering the fear of a man that knows his land: For Re has set the fear of you throughout the land, the dread of you in every foreign country. Whether I be at home or whether I be in this place, it is you that can obscure yonder horizon. The sun rises at your pleasure, the water in the rivers is drunk at your will, the air in heaven is breathed at your word. Your servant will hand over the viziership which your servant has held in this place. But let Your Majesty, do as pleases you. Men live by the breath that you give. Re, Horus and Hathor love this your august nose; which Montu, lord of Thebes, wills shall live eternally."

28. Envoys came to this servant, and I was suffered to spend a day in Yaa to hand over my possessions to my children, my eldest son taking charge of my tribe, all my possessions being in his hand, my serfs and all my cattle, my fruit and every pleasant tree of mine. Then came this humble servant southward and halted at Paths-of-Horus. The commander who was there in charge of the frontier-patrol sent, a message to the Residence to bear tidings. And His Majesty sent a trusty head-fowler

of the Palace, having with him ships laden with presents of the Royal bounty for the Setiu that were come with me to conduct me to Paths-of-Horus. And I named each several one of them by his name. Brewers kneaded and strained in my presence, and every serving-man made busy with his task.

29. Then I set out and sailed, until I reached the town of Ithtoue. And when the land was lightened and it was morning there came men to summon me, ten coming and ten going to convey me to the Palace. And I pressed my forehead to the ground between the sphinxes, the Royal Children standing in the gateway against my coming. The Companions that had been ushered into the Forecourt showed me the way to the Hall of Audience. And I found His Majesty on a throne in a gateway of gold; and I stretched myself on my belly and my wit forsook me in his presence, albeit this god greeted me joyously. Yes, I was like a man caught in the dusk; my soul fled, my flesh quaked, and my heart was not in my body, that I should know life from death.

30. Thereupon His Majesty said to one of those Companions: "Raise him up, let him speak to me." And His Majesty said: "Lo, you have come, you have trodden the deserts, you have traversed the wastes; eld has prevailed against you, you have reached old age. It is no small matter that your corpse should be buried without escort of Pedtiu. But do not do that, do not do that, staying ever speechless, when your name is pronounced."

31. But truly I feared punishment, and answered him with the answer of one afraid: "What speaks my lord to me? Would I might answer it, and may not. Lo, it is the hand of God, yes the dread that is in my body, like that which caused this fateful flight, Behold, I am in your presence. Yours is life; may Your Majesty do as pleases you."

32. The Royal Children were, caused, to be ushered in. Then His Majesty said to the Royal Consort: "Behold Sinuhe, who is come as an 'A'am, an offspring of Setiu-folk." She gave a great cry, and the Royal Children shrieked out all together. And they said to His Majesty: "It is not really he, O Sovereign, my lord." And His Majesty said: "Yes, it is really he."

33. Then they brought their necklaces, their rattles and their sistra, and presented them to His Majesty: — "Your hands be on the Beauteous one, O enduring King, on the ornament of the Lady of Heaven. May Nub give life to your nose, may the Lady of the Stars join herself to you. Let the goddess of Upper Egypt fare north, and the goddess of Lower Egypt fare south, united and conjoined in the name of Your Majesty. May the Uraeus be set upon your brow. You have delivered your subjects out of evil. May Re, lord of the lands, show you grace. Hail to you, and also to our Sovereign Lady. The horn of your bow is slacked, your arrow loosened. Give breath to one that is stifled, and grant us our goodly guerdon in the person of this sheikh Si-mehyt, the Pedti born in Ti-muri. He fled through fear of you; he left this land through dread of you. But as for the face of him who sees Your Majesty, it blenches not; as for the eye that regards you, it fears not."

34. Then said His Majesty: "No, but he shall not fear, he shall not dread. For he shall be a Companion among the magistrates, he -shall be set in the midst of the nobles. Get you gone to the Chamber of Adornment to wait upon him."

35. So when I was gone forth from the Hall of Audience, the Royal Children giving me their hands, we went together to the Great Portals, and I was placed in the house of a Royal Son. There was noble equipment in it, a bathroom and painted devices of the horizon; costly things of the Treasury, were in it. Garments of Royal stuff were in every chamber, unguent and the fine oil of the King and of the courtiers whom he loves; and every serving-man made busy with his task. Years were caused to pass away from my flesh, I was shaved and my hair was combed. A burden was given

over to the desert and clothing to the Sandfarers. And I was clad in soft linen, and anointed with fine oil; by night I lay upon a bed. I gave up the sand to them that dwell therein, and oil of wood to him who smears himself with it. There was given to me the house of a provincial governor, such as a Companion may possess; many artificers built it, and all its woodwork was new appointed. And meals were brought to me from the Palace three times, yes four times, a day, over and above that which the Royal Children gave, without remiss.

36. And there was constructed for me a tomb of stone in the midst of the tombs; the masons that hew tombs marked out its ground-plan; the master-draughtsmen designed in it; the master-sculptors carved in it; and the master-architects who are in the Necropolis bestowed their care upon it. And all the gear that is placed in a tomb-shaft went to its equipment. And ka-servants were given to me, and there was made for me a sepulchral garden, in which were fields, in front of my abode, even as is done for a chief Companion. And my statue was overlaid with gold, and its apron was of real gold. It was His Majesty caused it to be made.

37. There is no poor man for whom the like has been done; and I enjoyed the favours of the Royal bounty until the day of death came.

𓂝𓏤𓆓𓅓𓂻𓈖𓏤𓅱𓏏𓀀𓏤𓏏𓊪𓄿𓇋𓏤𓇳𓈖𓏏𓏤𓅓𓂝𓏤𓏏𓈖𓏤𓇯

34. THE INSTRUCTIONS OF AMENHEMET

The Instructions of Amenhemet is a short work of the sebayt *genre and is presented as the teachings that the ghost of the murdered Amenhemet I gives to his son Senusret I (Dynasty 12). It may have been composed at the request of Senusret I as a way to eulogize his father. Later Egyptian tradition ascribes authorship of the work to a scribe named Khety. The Millingen papyrus from the 18th dynasty, which contained the only complete copy of the text, no longer exists, but fortunately it was copied before it was lost.*

HERE BEGINS THE INSTRUCTION MADE BY THE MAJESTY OF THE KING OF UPPER AND LOWER EGYPT SEHTEPEBRE, SON OF THE SUN AMENEMHET, THE JUSTIFIED. HE SPEAKS THUS IN DISCOVERING WORDS OF TRUTH TO HIS SON, THE LORD OF THE WORLD:

1. Shine forth, he says, even as the God. Hearken to that which I say to you: that you may reign over the land, that you may govern the world, that you may excel in goodness.

2. Let one withdraw himself from his subordinates entirely. It happens that men give their hearts to one that causes them fear. Mix not among them alone; fill not your heart with a brother; know not a trusted friend; make for yourself no familiar dependents; in these things is no satisfaction.

3. When you lie down, have care for your very life, since friends exist not for a man in the day of misfortunes. I gave to the beggar, and caused the orphan to live; I made him that had not to attain, even as he that had.

4. But it was the eater of my food that made insurrection against me; to whom I gave my hands, he created disturbance thereby; they that arrayed them in my fine linen regarded me as a shadow; and it was they that anointed themselves with my spices that entered my harem.

5. My images are among the living; and my achievements are among men. But I have made an heroic story that has not been heard; a great feat of arms that has not been seen. Surely one fights for a lassoed ox that forgets yesterday; and good fortune is of no avail to one that cannot perceive it.

6. It was after the evening meal, and night was come. I took for myself an hour of ease. I lay down upon my bed, for I was weary. My heart began to wander. I slept, And lo! weapons were brandished, and there was conference concerning me. I acted as the serpent of the desert,

7. I awoke to fight; I was alone. I found one struck down, it was the captain of the guard. Had I received quickly the arms from his hand, I would have driven back the dastards by smiting around. But he was not a brave man on that night, nor could I fight alone; an occasion of prowess comes not to one surprised. Thus was I.

8. Behold, then! vile things came to pass, for I was without you; the courtiers knew not that I had passed on to you [my power], I sat not with you on the throne. Let me, then, make your plans. Because I awed them not I was not unmindful of them; but my heart brings not to remembrance the slackness of servants.

9. Have ever women gathered together assailants ? are assassins reared within my palace ? was the opening done by cutting through the ground? The underlings were deceived as to what they did. But misfortunes have not come in my train since my birth; nor has there existed the equal of me as a doer of valiance.

10. I forced my way up to Elephantine, I went down to the coast-lakes; I have stood upon the boundaries of the land, and I have seen its centre. I have set the limits of might by my might in my deeds.

11. I raised corn, I loved Nopi; the Nile begged of me every valley. In my reign none hungered; none thirsted therein. They were contented in that which I did, saying concerning me, 'Every commandment is proper.'

12. I overcame lions; I carried off crocodiles. I cast the Nubians under my feet; I carried off the Southern Nubians; I caused the Asiatics to flee, even as hounds.

13. I have made me an house, adorned with gold, its ceiling with lapis lazuli, its walls having deep foundations. Its doors are of copper, their bolts are of bronze. It is made for everlasting; eternity is in awe of it. I know every dimension thereof, O Lord of the World!

14. There are divers devices in buildings. I know the pronouncements of men when inquiring into its beauties; but they know not that it was without you, O my son, Senusret; life, safe and sound, be to you—by your feet do I walk; you are after my own heart; by your eyes do I see; born in an hour of delight, with spirits that rendered you praise.

15. Behold, that which I have done at the beginning, let me set it in order for you at the end; let me be the landing-place of that which is in your heart. All men together set the White Crown on the Offspring of the God, fixing it upon its due place. I shall begin your praises when in the Boat of Ra. Your kingdom has been from primaeval time; not by my doing, who have done valiant things. Raise

up monuments, make beautiful your tomb. I have fought against him whom you know; for I desire not that he should be beside your Majesty. Life, safe and sound, be to you."

IT IS FINISHED.

35. THE MAN WHO WAS TIRED OF LIFE

All but the beginning of this work of Wisdom Literature is preserved in the Berlin Papyrus 3024, the only surviving copy (Twelfth Dynasty). In it a depressed man is having a conversation with his own ba.

1. Then opened I my mouth unto my soul, that I might answer what it had said: This is too much for me at present, that my soul speaketh not with me – – – –. My soul goeth forth; it shall stand there for me – – – –. It fleeth on the day of misfortune. Behold, my soul thwarteth me, and I hearken not unto it, and drag me to death ere I be come to it, and cast me upon the fire in order to burn me – – – –. May it draw nigh to me on the day of misfortune and stand upon yon side, as a mourner doth - - - -. My soul, it is foolish, to hold back (?) one that is sorrowful on account of life; lead (?) me to death, ere I be come to it, and make the West pleasant for me. Is that then something grievous ? – – – – Tread thou upon wrongdoing. The unhappy one will endure: Thoth will judge me, he that contenteth the gods; Khons will defend me, he, the scribe of Right; Re will hearken unto my words, he that auideth (?) the sun's ship; Isdes will maintain my cause – My distress is heavy upon me and he beareth it for me . . The gods avert the secret of my body.

2. This is what my soul said unto me in answer: Thou art not a man (of high degree) – – – (and yet) thou carest for good hings like one that possesseth treasures.

3. I said: I go not away so long as that one remaineth on the earth – – – – I will carry thee away. Thy lot (?) is to die, while thy name liveth on, and yonder is the place where one alighteth – – – If my soul will hearken unto me – – and its heart agreeth (?) with me, it will be happy. I will cause it to reach the West, like the soul of one that is buried in his pyramid, and at whose burial there stood a survivor. The expedient, whereby the luckless one proposes to attain this, is unfortunately unintelligible to us; one can only see that he will do something which will safeguard his soul against the distresses feared. He assures it that it will despise another soul as a weary one, and it shall not freeze; it will despise another soul that is too hot, for he will drink water at the place of drawing, and it will also look down on another soul that hungereth. In this wise it is to lead him to death—otherwise hast thou no possibility of alighting in the West. Be so kind, my soul and my brother, and become mine heir (?), who shall make offering and stand upon my tomb on the day of burial, that he may prepare (?) the funeral bed.

4. Then my soul opened its mouth to me, to answer what I had said If thou callest burial to mind, it is sadness, it is the bringing of tears, it is making a man sorrowful, it is haling a man from

his house and casting him upon the hill. Never wilt thou go forth again to behold the sun. They that builded in granite and fashioned a hall (?) in the pyramid, that achieved what is goodly in this goodly work—when the builders are become gods, then their offering-tables are empty (and they are) even as the weary ones which die upon the dyke without a survivor; the flood hath taken its end (of them) and likewise the heat of the sun, and the fish of the river-bank hold converse with them. Hearken thou unto me, lo, it is good for a man when he hearkeneth. Follow the glad day and forget care.

5. Thus the advice of the soul now is that he had better give life a further trial, and then, probably in support of the theory that this is still to be endured by even the most unfortunate, he recounts to him two tales, of which we frankly understand but little:

6. A man of humble birth tilleth his field and loadeth his harvest on to a ship, that he may tow (it)..., when his festival approacheth. He seeth that the night of the flood (?) corneth on, keepeth watch in the ship until dusk, and goeth forth with his wife and his children; they perish upon the lake, endangered (?) in the night amid the crocodiles. Then he sitteth him down and when he hath a share in the voice (i.e. can speak again ?), he saith: I am not weeping for that maid, who cannot come forth from the West to another woman upon earth; I am troubled for her children that are broken in the egg, that behold the face of the crocodile before they are yet alive.

7. We understand still less of the second tale of the man of humble birth, who begs his supper of his wife.

8. Then opened I my mouth to my soul, that I might answer what it had said:

[FIRST POEM.]
Lo, my name is abhorred,
Lo, more than the odour of carrion
On days in summer, when the sky is hot.

Lo, my name is abhorred,
Lo, more than catching fish
On the day of the catch, when the sky is hot.

Lo, my name is abhorred,
Lo, more than the odour of birds,
More than the hill of willows with the geese.

Lo, my name is abhorred,
Lo, more than the odour of fishermen,
More than the shores of the swamps, when they have fished.

Lo, my name is abhorred,
Lo, more than the odour of crocodiles,
More than sitting on . . ., where are the crocodiles.

Lo, my name is abhorred,
Lo, more than that of a wife

When lies are told against her to the husband.

Lo, my name is abhorred,
Lo, more than that of a stalwart child
Against whom it is said, he ... to him that ha teth him,

Lo, my name is abhorred,
Lo, more than that of a ... city,
(Than) that of a rebel, whose back is seen.

[SECOND POEM.]
To whom do I speak to-day ?
Brothers are evil,
Friends of to-day, they are not lovable.

To whom do I speak to-day ?
Men are covetous,
Every one seizeth his neighbour's goods.

To whom do I speak to-day ?
Gentleness hath perished,
Insolence hath come to all men.

To whom do I speak to-day ?
He that hath a contented countenance is bad,
Good is disregarded in every place.

To whom do I speak to-day ?
He that maketh wrathful a (good) man by his evil deeds,
The same moveth all men to laughter, when his iniquity is grievous.

To whom do I speak to-day ?
Men rob,
Every man seizeth his neighbour's (goods).

To whom do I speak to-day ?
The sick man is the trusty friend,
The brother that is with him, hath become the enemy.

To whom do I speak to-day ?
None remembereth the past,
None at this moment doeth good to him that hath done it.

To whom do I speak to-day ?
Brothers are evil,
A man is treated as an enemy (?) in spite of (?) a right disposition.

To whom do I speak to-day ?
Faces are invisible,
Every man hath his face downcast against his brethren.'
To whom do I speak to-day ?
Hearts are covetous,
The man on whom men rely, hath no heart.

To whom do I speak to-day ?
There are none that are righteous.
The earth is given over to the workers of iniquity.

To whom do I speak to-day ?
A trusty friend is lacking,
A man is treated as one that is unknown, albeit (?) he have made (himself) known.

To whom do I speak to-day ?
There is none that is peaceable;
That one who went (?) with him, he is not existent (?).

To whom do I speak to-day ?
I am laden with misery,
And lack a trusty friend.

To whom do I speak to day ?
The sin that smiteth the land,
It hath no end.

[THIRD POEM.]
Death is before me to-day
As when a sick man becometh whole,
As when one walketh abroad after sickness.

Death is before me to-day
As the odour of myrrh,
As when one sitteth under the sail on a windy day.

Death is before me to-day
As the odour of lotus flowers,
As when one sitteth on the shore of drunkenness.

Death is before me to-day
As a well-trodden (?) path,
As when a man returneth from the war unto his house.
Death is before me to-day
As a clearing of the sky,
As a man … to that which he knew not.

Death is before me to-day
As when a man longeth to see his house again,
After he hath spent many years in captivity.

[FOURTH POEM.]
Why he that is yonder 1 will be
One that … as a living god,
And will inflict punishment for sin on him that doeth it.

Why he that is yonder will be
One that standeth in the sun's ship,
And will therein assign the choicest things unto the temples.

Why he that is yonder will be
A man of knowledge, and he is not hindered,
And he petitioneth Rê when he speaketh.

This is what my soul said unto me: Cast aside (?) lamentation, my comrade, my brother — — —
I will abide here, if thou rejectest the West. But when thou reachest the West, and thy body is united
with the earth, then I will alight after that thou restest. Let us have an abode together.

36. CONTRACT OF HEPZEFI

*Engraved on a wall in the cliff-tomb of the nomarch Hepzefi at Asyut (Dynasty 12) are ten contracts,
all intended to secure for Hepzefi certain ceremonies and offerings from the priesthood after his death.
This the eighth contract in the series, which is directed towards the priests of Anubis.*

Title

Contract which the count, the superior prophet, Hepzefi, triumphant, made, with the lay priests of the temple of Anubis; to-wit:

What Hepzefi Receives

There shall be given to him:

(a) A white loaf per each individual among them, for his statue, in the first month of the first season, on the seventeenth day, the night of the Wag-feast.

(b) And that they shall go forth, following his mortuary priest, and kindle for him (the count), the fire at his glorification, until they reach the lower steps of his tomb, just as they glorify their noble ones, on the day of kindling the fire.

(c) And that the priest belonging in each month shall give [...] of bread and a jar of beer for his statue, which is on the lower steps of his tomb, when he comes forth from offering in the temple every day.

What He Pays

He has given to them for it: grain from the first of the harvest of every field of the count's estate, as every citizen of Siut does from the first of his harvest. Now, behold, he begins with having his every peasant give it from the first of his field into the temple of Anubis.

Injunction to Future Nomarchs

Lo, the count, Hepzefi, said: "Behold, you know, that, as for every official and every citizen, who gives the first of his harvest into the temple, it is not agreeable to him that there should be lack therein. Therefore shall no future count diminish to future priests that which is secured by contract of another count."

Individual Payment and Remuneration

This grain shall belong to the lay priests, per each individual priest, who shall give to me this white bread. He shall not divide it to his colleagues, because they give this white bread, each by himself.

Conclusion

Lo, they were satisfied therewith.

37. AUTOBIOGRAPHY OF KHNUMHOTEP II

Khnumhotep II was a nomarch of the Oryx nome during the reigns of Amenhemet II and Senusret II. Like his uncle Ameni (reading #32), Khnumhotep's cliff-tomb is located at Beni Hasan. In the main chamber of the tomb appears this autobiography.

Introduction

The hereditary prince, count, king's-confidant, whom his god loves, governor of the eastern highlands, Nehri's son, Khnumhotep, triumphant; born of a count's daughter, the matron, Beket, triumphant.

The Tomb, its Paintings and Inscriptions

He made (it) as his monument; his first virtue was in adorning his city, that he might perpetuate his name forever, and that he might establish it for eternity in his tomb of the necropolis; that he might perpetuate the name of his official staff, establishing (them) according to their offices: the excellent ones, who were in his household, whom he raised over his peasant-slaves; every office that he sustained; all artificers according to their kind.

His Appointment as Count of Menet-Khufu

His mouth says: "The majesty of . . . . Amenemhet, who is given life, stability, satisfaction, like Re, forever, appointed me to be hereditary prince, count, governor of the eastern highlands, priest of Horus, and [priest] of Pakht; to the inheritance of my mother's father in Menet-Khufu. He established for me the southern landmark; he perpetuated the northern, like the heavens. He divided the great river along its middle, as was done for the father of my mother, by command which came forth from the mouth of the majesty of . . . . Amenemhet I, who is given life, stability, satisfaction, like Re, forever.

His Grandfather Appointed Count of Menet-Khzbfu

He appointed him to be hereditary prince, count, governor of the eastern highlands in Menet-Khufu. He established the southern landmark, perpetuating the northern, like the heavens; he divided the great river along its middle; its eastern side of the "Horizon of Horus," was as far as the eastern highland; at the coming of his majesty, when he cast out evil, shining like Atum himself, when he restored that which he found ruined; that which a city had taken from its neighbor; while he caused city to know its boundary with city, establishing their landmarks like the heavens, distinguishing their waters according to that which was in the writings, investigating according to that which was of old, because he so greatly loved justice.

His Grandfather Appointed Prince of Oryx Nome

Lo, he appointed him to be hereditary prince, count, [...], great lord of the Oryx nome. He established the landmarks: the southern on his boundary as far as the Hare nome; his northern as far as the Jackal nome. He divided the great river along its middle: its water, its fields, its trees, its sand as far as the western highlands.

Khnumhotep II's Uncle, Nakht, Made Count of Menet-Khufu

He (the king) appointed his (Khnumhotep I's) eldest son, Nakht (I) triumphant, revered, to the rule of his inheritance in Menet-Khufu as a great favor of the king, by the command which issued [from] the mouth of the majesty of king . . . . Sesostris (Senusret), who is given life, stability, satisfaction, like Re, forever.

Khnumhotep II's Birth

This my chief nobility is my birth, my mother having gone to be hereditary princess, and countess, as the daughter of the ruler of the Oryx nome, to Hat-Sehetepibre . . . . to be the wife of the hereditary prince, count, ruler of the "New Towns," the [...] of the king of Upper Egypt, the [...] of the king of Lower Egypt, [in] his rank of governor of the residence city, Nehri, triumphant, revered.

His Appointment as Count of Menet-Khufu

The King of Upper and Lower Egypt, Nubkure (Amenemhet II), who is given life, stability, satisfaction, like Re, forever, brought me, being the son of a count into the inheritance of the rule of my mother's father, because he so greatly loved justice. He is Atum himself, Nubkure (Amenemhet II), who is given life, stability, satisfaction, gladness of his heart, like Re, forever. He appointed me to be count in the year 19, in Menet-Khufu.

His Buildings and Piety

Then I adorned it, and its treasures grew in all things. I perpetuated the name of my father; I adorned the houses of the *kas* and the dwelling thereof; I followed my statues to the temple; I devoted for them their offerings: the bread, beer, water, wine, incense, and joints of beef credited to the mortuary priest. I endowed him with fields and peasants; I commanded the mortuary offering of bread, beer, oxen, and geese, at every feast of the necropolis: at the feast of the first of the year, of New Year's Day, of the great year, of the little year, of the last of the year, the great feast, at the great Rekeh, at the little Rekeh, at the feast of the 5 intercalary days, at [...], at the 12 monthly feasts, at the 12 mid-monthly feasts; every feast of the happy living, and of the dead. Now, as for the mortuary priest, or any person, who shall disturb them, he shall not survive, his son shall not survive in his place.

Khnumhotep II's Honors at Court

Greater was my praise at the court than (that of) any sole companion. He (the king) exalted me above his nobles, I was placed before those who had been before me. [...] the official body of the palace, giving praise according to my appointment, according to (my) favor which came to pass in the (royal) presence, the command of the king himself. Never happened the like to servants [...]. He knew the manner of my tongue, the [moderation] of my character. I was an honored one with the king; my praise was with his court, my popularity was before his "companions." The hereditary prince, count, Nehri's son, Khnumhotep, revered.

Appointment of K. II's Son, Nakht, as Prince of Jackal Nome

Another honor accorded me (was): my eldest son, Nakht, born of Kheti was appointed to the rule of the Jackal nome, to the inheritance of his mother's father; made sole companion; appointed to be forefront of Middle Egypt. There were given to him all ranks of nobility by the majesty of . . . . Sesostris, who is given life, stability, satisfaction, like Re, forever. He (the king) made his monuments in the Jackal nome, restoring that which he found obliterated, that which a city had taken from its neighbor; causing him to know his boundary according to the [record], investigating according to that which was of old, putting a landmark at his southern boundary, perpetuating the northern like the heavens, establishing on the fields of the low ground, a total amounting to 15 landmark; establishing upon its northern fields its boundary as far as Oxyrrhyncus. He divided the great river along its middle, its western side (going) to the Jackal nome as far as the western highlands; when the hereditary prince, count, Khnumhotep's son, Nakht, triumphant, revered, petitioned, saying: "My waters know not the great favor of the king's presence."

Honors of Khnumhotep II's Second Son, Khnumhotep

Another prince is counselor, sole companion, great [among] the sole companions, of numerous gifts to the palace, sole companion. There is not one possessed of his virtues; to whom the officers hearken, the unique mouth, closing (other) mouths, bringing advantage to its possessor, keeper of the door of the highlands, Khnumhotep, son of Khnumhotep, son of Nehri, who was born of the matron, Kheti.

His Restoration of Ancestors' Tombs

I kept alive the name of my fathers, which I found obliterated upon the doorways, (making them) legible in [form]; accurate in reading, not putting one in the place of another. Behold, it is an excellent son, who restores the name of the ancestors; Nehri's son, Khnumhotep, triumphant, revered.

His Father's Mortuary Buildings

My chief nobility was: I executed a cliff-tomb, (for) a man should imitate that which his father does. My father made for himself a house of the ka in the town of Mernofret, of good stone of Ayan, in order to perpetuate his name forever and establish it eternally; that his name might live in the mouth of the people and abide in the mouth of the living, upon his tomb of the necropolis, in his excellent house of eternity, his seat of everlastingness; according to the favor of the king's presence, his love in the court.

His Father's Excellent Administration

He ruled his city as a babe, before he was loosed from swaddling- clothes; he executed a royal commission, and his two plumes danced, as a child not yet circumcised; [for] the king knew the manner of his tongue, the [moderation] of his character, Sebekenekh's son, Nehri, triumphant, revered, whom he exalted before his nobles to be ruler of his city.

His Own Buildings

The achievements of the count, Khnumhotep: I made a monument in the midst of my city; I built a colonnaded hall which I found in [ruin]; I erected it with columns anew, inscribed with my own name. I perpetuated the name of my father upon them. I [recorded] my deeds upon every monument.

I made a door of 7 cubits, of cedar wood without [...] for the first doorway of the tomb; double doors for an opening of 5 cubits, 2 palms, for the shrine of the august chamber, which is in this tomb. A prayer for offerings, the mortuary oblations of bread, beer, oxen, geese, was upon every monument, which I made. I . . . . greater in monuments in this city than the fathers; a child of this city, more excellent in monuments of its burial place than the ancestors, [in the buildings] made before me.

Crafts Encouraged

I was munificent in monuments; I taught every craft which had been [neglected] in this city, in order that my name might be excellent upon every monument which I [made], ...

Conclusion

The hereditary prince, count, Nehri's son, Khnumhotep, born of Beket, triumphant, revered.

38. COFFIN TEXTS

The Coffin Texts are so named because they appear on coffins. They are based on the Pyramid Texts of the Old Kingdom and so contain funerary spells designed to help the deceased in the afterlife, but now that we see them on the coffins of common people, we know that spells of this sort are no longer reserved for royalty. A difference in content, however, is apparent, as they focus more on the subterranean realm of Osiris than on the celestial heavens. They first appear on coffins in the First Intermediate Period, but most of them come from the period of the Middle Kingdom.

CT 1130

Words spoken by Him-whose-names-are-hidden, the All-Lord, as he speaks before those who silence the storm, in the sailing of the court:

Hail in peace! I repeat to you the good deeds which my own heart did for me from within the serpent-coil,[1] in order to silence strife. I did four good deeds within the portal of lightland:

I made the four winds, that every man might breathe in his time. This is one of the deeds.

---

1   The serpent-dragon Apophis who symbolized the lurking dangers of the world.

I made the great inundation, that the humble might benefit by it like the great. This is one of the deeds.

I made every man like his fellow; and I did not command that they do wrong. It is their hearts that disobey what I have said. This is one of the deeds.

I made that their hearts are not disposed to forget the West, in order that sacred offerings be made to the gods of the nomes. This is one of the deeds.

I have created the gods from my sweat, and the people from the tears of my eye.[2]

CT 1031

I shall shine[3] and be seen every day as a dignitary of the All-Lord, having given satisfaction to the Weary-hearted.[4]

I shall sail rightly in my bark, I am lord of eternity in the crossing of the sky.

I am not afraid in my limbs, for Hu and Hike[5] overthrow for me that evil being.

I shall see lightland, I shall dwell in it. I shall judge the poor and the wealthy.

I shall do the same for the evil-doers; for mine is life, I am its lord, and the scepter will not be taken from me.

I have spent a million years with the Weary-hearted, the son of Geb, dwelling with him in one place; while hills became towns and towns hills, for dwelling destroys dwelling.

I am lord of the flame who lives on truth; lord of eternity maker of joy, against whom that worm shall not rebel.

I am he who is in his shrine, master of action who destroys the storm; who drives off the serpents of many names when he goes from his shrine.

Lord of the winds who announces the northwind, rich in names in the mouth of the Ennead.

Lord of lightland, maker of light, who lights the sky with his beauty.

I am he in his name! Make way for me, that I may see Nun and Amun! For I am that equipped spirit (*akh*) who passes by the guards. They do not speak for fear of Him-whose-name-is-hidden, who is in my body. I know him, I do not ignore him! I am equipped and effective in opening his portal!

As for any person who knows this spell, he will be like Re in the eastern sky, like Osiris in the netherworld. He will go down to the circle of fire, without the flame touching him ever!

---

2   A wordplay on *rmt*, "people," and *rmyt*, "tears," which occurs a number of times as an allusion to the creation of mankind.

3   This is a spell that is put in the mouth of the dead person.

4   Osiris.

5   The personifications of effective speech and of magic.

39. THE SECOND SEMNA STELA

At Semna in Nubia, two stelae carved from red granite and erected by Senusret III (Twelfth Dynasty) were discovered. He used them to mark his southern boundary after successfully campaigning against the Nubians. Here is the text of the second stela, which was put up in the temple in Senusret's Semna fortress in the sixteenth year of his reign.

Introduction

Live the King of Upper and Lower Egypt, Sesostris III, who is given life, stability, satisfaction forever.

Boundary Established

Year 16, third month of the second season, (occurred) his majesty's making the southern boundary as far as Heh. I have made my boundary beyond (that) of my fathers; I have increased that which was bequeathed to me. I am a king who speaks and executes; that which my heart conceives is that which comes to pass by my hand; (one who is) eager to possess, and [powerful] to [...]; not allowing a matter to sleep in his heart . . . . [attacking him who attacks], silent in a matter, or answering a matter according to that which is in it; since, if one is silent after attack, it strengthens the heart of the enemy. Valiance is eagerness, cowardice is to slink back; he is truly a craven who is repelled upon his border; since the Nubian hearkens [to] the [...] of the mouth; it is answering him which drives him back; when one is eager against him, he turns his back; when one slinks back, he begins to be eager. But they are not a people of might, they are poor and broken in heart. My majesty has seen them; it is not an untruth.

Plundering of Nubia

I captured their women, I carried off their subjects, went forth to their wells, smote their bulls; I reaped their grain, and set fire thereto. (I swear) as my father lives for me, I speak in truth, without a lie therein, corning out of my mouth.

Future Maintenance of Boundary

Now, as for every son of mine who shall maintain this boundary, which my majesty has made, he is my son, he is born to my majesty, the likeness of a son who is the champion of his father, who maintains the boundary of him that begat him, Now, as for him who shall relax it, and shall not fight for it; he is not my son, he is not born to me.

Royal Statue at Boundary

Now, behold, my majesty caused a statue of my majesty to be made upon this boundary, which my majesty made; in order that you might prosper because of it, and in order that you might fight for it.

40. HYMNS TO SENUSRET III

In a collection of Middle Kingdom papyri discovered at Kahun (el-Lahun) in the Faiyum region can be found four hymns dedicated to Senusret III (Dynasty 12). All four are provided here.

Horus, Neter-kheperu; lord of diadems, Neter-mesut, Horus that hath overcome Seth, Kheper, king of Upper and Lower Egypt, Khakaure, son of Re, Sesostris—he carried off the Two Lands in triumph.

[FIRST HYMN.]
Praise to thee, Khakaure! Our Horus, Neter-kheperu!
That protecteth the land and extendeth his boundaries,
That vanquisheth the foreign countries with his crown.
That encloseth the Two Lands in his arms,
And (strangleth?) the foreign lands with his grip;
That slayeth the People of the Bow, without stroke of the club,
Shooting of the arrow, or drawing of the string.
His might hath smitten the Troglodytes in their land,
And the fear of him hath slain the Nine Bows.
His slaughtering hath made thousands to die
Of the People of the Bow ..., that attacked his borders.
He that shooteth the arrow as doth Sekhmet,
When he overthroweth thousands of them that knew not his might.
It is the tongue of his majesty that confineth Nubia,
And it is his utterances that make the Bedouins to flee.
Sole youthful one that fighteth for his boundaries,
And suffereth not his people to wax faint;
That suffereth men to sleep unto daylight,
And his recruits to slumber, for his heart is their defender.
His decrees have made his boundaries,
And his word hath joined in one the Two River-banks.
[SECOND HYMN.]
How the gods rejoice: thou hast made their offerings to flourish.
How thy . . . rejoice: thou hast made their boundaries.
How thy (fathers) which were aforetime rejoice: thou hast increased their portions.
How the Egyptians rejoice in thy might: thou hast protected . . .
How the people rejoice in thy designs: thy might hath captured the . . .
How the Two River-banks rejoice in thy strength: thou hast enlarged that which they need.
How thy recruits rejoice in . . .: thou hast caused them to grow.
How thine honoured ones rejoice: thou hast renewed their youth.
How the Two Lands rejoice in thy strength thou hast protected their walls.

[THIRD HYMN.]

How great is the lord for his city: he alone is a million, little are other men.

How great is the lord for his city: he is like a dyke, that keepeth back the river in its water-floods.

How great is the lord for his city: he is like a cool lodge that letteth a man sleep unto daylight.

[*Two unintelligible verses: the second likens the king to a place of refuge.*]

How great is the lord for his city: he is like a bulwark that delivereth the fearful from his enemy.

How great is the lord for his city he is like the shade of the season of Overflowing for cooling in summer.

How great is the lord for his city: he is like a corner warm and dry in time of winter.

How great is the lord for his city: he is like a mountain, that keepeth back the storm-blast, at the time when the sky is in riot.

How great is the lord for his city: he is like Sekhmet unto foes that overstep his boundaries.

[FOURTH HYMN.]

He hath come unto us that he may carry away Upper Egypt; the double diadem hath rested on his head.

He hath come unto us and hath united the Two Lands; he hath mingled the reed(?) with the bee.

He hath come unto us and hath brought the Black Land under his sway; he hath apportioned to himself the Red Land.

He hath come unto us and hath taken the Two Lands under his protection; he hath given peace to the Two Riverbanks.

He hath come unto us and hath made Egypt to live; he hath banished its suffering.

He hath come unto us and hath made the people to live; he hath caused the throat of the subjects to breathe.

He hath come unto us and hath trodden down the foreign countries; he hath smitten the Troglodytes, that knew not the dread of him.

He hath come unto us and hath (done battle for) his boundaries; he hath delivered them that were robbed . . .

[*A destroyed verse.*]

He hath come unto us, that we may (nurture up?) our children and bury our aged ones . . .

41. INSCRIPTION OF IKHERNOFRET

Around the time of Senusret III's campaigns against Nubia, Senusret sent his chief treasurer Ikhernofret to Abydos to commission the building of monuments dedicated to Osiris. On a memorial tablet that he erected at Abydos, Ikhernofret narrates the story of the work he did there on behalf of the king.

Introduction

Live the King of Upper and Lower Egypt, Khekure (Senusret III), who is given life forever and ever.

Royal Commission

"Royal command to the hereditary prince, count, […], wearer of the royal seal, sole companion, lord of the double gold-house, lord of the double silver-house, chief treasurer, Ikhernofret, revered:

My majesty commands that you shall be sent up-river to Abydos, to make monuments for my father Osiris, First of the Westerners, to adorn his secret place with the gold, which he caused my majesty to bring from Upper Nubia in victory and in triumph. Lo, you shall do this in […] for offering, in satisfying my father Osiris, since my majesty sends you, my heart being certain of your doing everything according to the desire of my majesty; since you have been brought up in the teaching of my majesty; you have been in the training of my majesty, and the sole teaching of my palace. My majesty appointed you […], while you were a young man of 26 years. My majesty has done this, (because) I have seen you to be one excellent in character, ready of tongue on coming forth from the body, and sufficient in speech. My majesty [sends] you to do this, (since) my [majesty] has recognized that no one doing it possesses your good qualities. Quickly go, and do according to all that my majesty has commanded."

Execution of the Commission

I did according to all that his majesty commanded, by adorning all that my lord commanded for his father, Osiris, First of the Westerners, lord of Abydos, great, mighty one residing in Thinis. I acted as "Son, Whom He Loves," for Osiris, First of the Westerners, I adorned the great […] forever and ever. I made for him a portable shrine, the "Bearer-of-Beauty" of the "First-of-the-Westerners," of gold, silver, lazuli, fragrant woods, carob wood, and meru wood. (I) fashioned the gods belonging to his divine ennead, (I) made their shrines anew.

I caused the lay priests to [know how] to do their duties, (I) caused them to know the stipulation of every day, the feasts of the beginnings of the seasons. I superintended the work on the sacred barque, I fashioned (its) chapel. I decked the body of the lord of Abydos with lazuli and malachite, electrum, and every costly stone, among the ornaments of the limbs of a god. I dressed the god in his regalia by virtue of my office as master of secret things, and of my duty as (wtb-)priest. I was pure-handed in decking the god, a (sm-)priest of clean fingers.

I celebrated the (feast of) "Going Forth" of Upwawet, when he proceeded to champion his father. I repelled the foe from the sacred barque. I overthrew the enemies of Osiris. I celebrated the "Great-Going-Forth," following the god at his going. I sailed the divine boat of Thoth upon […]. I equipped the barque (called): "Shining-in-Truth" of the lord of Abydos, with a chapel. (I) put on his regalia when he went forth to […] Peker; I led the way of the god to his tomb before Peker; I championed Wennofer at "That Day of the Great Conflict;" I slew all the enemies upon the [flats] of Nedyt. I conveyed him into the barque (called): "The Great," when it bore his beauty; I gladdened the heart of the eastern highlands; I […]ed the rejoicing in the western highlands When they saw the beauty of the sacred barge, as it landed at Abydos, they brought [Osiris, First of the Westerners, lord] of Abydos to his palace, and I followed the god into his house, to attend to his […], when he [resumed] his seat. I loosed the knot in the midst of […] his [attendants], among his courtiers.

42. STELA OF SOBEKKHU

Sobekkhu was a military commander who served under Senusret III and Amenhemet III. On his mortuary stela that he had erected at Abydos, he recounts a campaign that he led into Retenu (Canaan) on behalf of Senusret III. It is the only record of a campaign this far north during the Middle Kingdom.

(1) His majesty went down the river to overthrow the Mentu of Setet. His majesty arrived at a region whose name is Sekmem. (2) His majesty made a prosperous beginning of returning to the Residence of Life, Prosperity and Health. Then Sekmem fell (upon him) together with the vile land of Retenu, (3) while I was acting as rear-guard. Then the soldiers of the army came to close quarters to fight with the Asiatics ('A'amu). (4) I smote an Asiatic, and caused his arms to be taken by two soldiers of the army, without ceasing from combat; my face pressed on, and I did not turn my back before an Asiatic. As Senusret lives, (5) I have spoken truly. Then he gave me a staff of electrum into my hand, and a bow and dagger worked with electrum and said:

(6) "The hereditary prince, firm of sandal, content of step, pressing close the path of him who makes him perfect, (7) to whom the Lord of the Two Lands has given his might, whose station his love advanced, the great *uartu*-official of the City, [Zaa], (8) says: I have made for myself this tomb, it being made glorious and its position established at the staircase of (9) the Great God, the Lord of Life, who is at the head of Abydos, in the region 'Mistress of Offerings' and in the region ' Mistress of Life.' I have smelt the incense (10) that comes forth and I am [equipped] with the divine aroma (?); the great *uartu* of the City, [Zaa], (11) He says; I was born in year 27 under the majesty of the King of Upper and Lower Egypt Nubkaura (Amenemhat II), justified. (12) When the majesty of the King of Upper and Lower Egypt Khakaura (Senusret III) arose in the double crown on the Horus-throne of the living, (13) his majesty caused me to adopt the profession of warrior of the guard by the side of his majesty among seven men of (14) the Residence. Behold, I was skilful at his side, and his majesty caused me to be made an 'Attendant of the Ruler,' and (15) there were given to me sixty men. When his majesty went upstream to overthrow the (16) Inu of Ta-sety, I captured a Nubian [.....]nkef, near my(!) city. (17) Then I came downstream in attendance among six men of the Residence. Then he made me inspector of the attendants, and there were given to me 100 men as a reward.

43. TALES OF KING KHUFU'S COURT

These five folk tales about priests and magicians come from the Westcar Papyrus, named for its discoverer, Henry Westcar, which survives in twelve rolls and dates to the Second Intermediate Period. All of the stories are set in the court of King Khufu of the Fourth Dynasty and are narrated by Khufu's sons, but they are fictional and were probably composed during the Twelfth Dynasty.

First Tale

[*Only the conclusion is preserved. It was set in the time of King Djoser, and after the tale is told, King Kheops (Khufu) commands that offerings be presented to that king and his magician in their tombs.*]

Second Tale

Then Prince Khephren (Khafre) stood up to speak and said: "I relate to thy majesty a wonder that came to pass in the time of thy father King Nebka, when he went to the temple of Ptah of Memphis. Now when his majesty went to Memphis, he also visited (?) the chief *kherheb* Ubaoner – – –

Ubaoner had a wife who was in love with a townsman, and who kept in touch with him through the medium of a handmaid; she had also sent him a box full of clothes as a present, and he came with the handmaid.

And after many days had passed—now there was a pleasurehouse in the lake of Ubaoner—the townsman said to the wife of Ubaoner: 'Why, there is a pleasure-house in the lake of Ubaoner. Behold, we will tarry therein.' And the wife of Ubaoner sent to the house-steward that had charge of the lake, saying: 'Let the pleasure-house which is in the lake be furnished.' Then went she thither and passed the day there drinking with the townsman, until the sun set. Now when it was evening, he came and went down into the lake, and the handmaid waited on him as bath attendant. And the housesteward observed it. Now when the earth became light and the next day was come, the house-steward went and reported this matter to his master – – – –. And Ubaoner said: 'Fetch me my ... of ebony and gold,' and with this gear he made a waxen crocodile that was seven spans long. And he recited a spell over it and said: 'Whoso cometh to bathe in my lake, him do thou seize.' And he gave it to the house-steward, and said unto him: 'When the townsman goeth down into the lake according to his daily wont, then do thou throw the crocodile into the water behind him.' So the house-steward went his way and took the waxen crocodile with him.

And the wife of Ubaoner sent unto the house-steward that was in charge of the lake, saying: 'Let the pleasure-house which is in the lake be furnished. Lo, I come to dwell therein.' And the pleasure-house was furnished with every good thing. Then they went and spent a mirthful day with the townsman.

Now when it was evening, the townsman came according to his daily wont. And the house-steward threw the waxen crocodile behind him into the water, and it became a crocodile of seven cubits, and it laid hold on the townsman — — —. But Ubaoner tarried for seven days with the majesty of King Nebka, and meantime the townsman was in the water without breathing. Now when the seven days were passed, King Nebka came ... and the chief *kherheb* Ubaoner presented himself before him. And Ubaoner said: '... May thy majesty come and view the wonder that hath come to pass in the time of thy majesty.' The king went with him, and Ubaoner called the crocodile and said: 'Bring thou hither the townsman.' Then the crocodile came forth and brought him — —. And the majesty of King Nebka said: 'Your pardon, but this crocodile is frightful(?).' Thereupon Ubaoner stooped down and took it, and it became a waxen crocodile in his hand.

Then the chief *kherheb* Ubaoner related unto the majesty of King Nebka this thing that the townsman had done in his house with his wife. And his majesty said unto the crocodile: 'Take that is thine.' Then the crocodile went down into the depths(?) of the lake, and none knew the place whither he went with him.

And the majesty of King Nebka caused the wife of Ubaoner to be taken to the field to the north of the Residence, and he set fire to her, and (her ashes) were thrown into the river.

Lo, this is a wonder that came to pass in the time of thy father Nebka, one of the deeds of the chief *kherheb* Ubaoner."

And the majesty of King Kheops said: "Let there be offered to King Nebka a thousand loaves of bread, a hundred jars of beer, one ox, and two measures of incense, and let there be given to the chief kherheb Ubaoner one cake, one jug of beer, a large piece of flesh, and one measure of incense, for I have seen an example of his learning." And it was done, according to all that his majesty commanded.

Third Tale

Then Prince Baufre stood up to speak, and said: "I relate to thy majesty a wonder that came to pass in the time of thy father Snefru, one of the deeds of the chief *kherheb* Zazamonkh. One day King Snefru was sad. So he assembled the officers of the palace in order to seek for him a diversion, but he found none. Then said he: 'Go, bring me the chief *kherheb*, the scribe of the book, Zazamonkh.' And he was brought unto him straightway. And his majesty said unto him: 'I had assembled the officers of the palace together in order to seek for me a diversion, but I could find none.' And Zazamonkh said unto him: 'If thy majesty would but betake thee to the lake of the Great House! Man thee a boat with all fair damsels from the inner apartments of thy palace. Then will the heart of thy majesty be diverted, when thou shalt see how they row to and fro. Then, as thou viewest the pleasant nesting-places of thy lake, and viewest its fields and its pleasant banks, thine heart will be diverted thereby.' His majesty said unto him: 'I will do this; get thee back to thine house(?), but I will go boating. Have brought to me twenty paddles of ebony inwrought with gold, the handles thereof being of *sekeb*-wood inwrought with fine gold. Have brought to me twenty women, of those with the fairest limbs, and with (beauteous) breasts and braided tresses, such as have not yet given birth, and moreover have brought to me twenty nets, and give these nets to these women instead of their clothes.' And it was done according to all that his majesty commanded. And they rowed to and fro, and the heart of his majesty was glad, when he beheld how they rowed.

Then a leader became entangled(?) with her braided tress, and a fish-pendant of new malachite fell into the water. And she became silent and ceased rowing, and her side became silent and ceased rowing. Then said his majesty: 'Is it that ye will not row then?' And they said: 'Our leader is silent and roweth not.' And his majesty said unto her: 'Wherefore rowest thou no ?' She said: 'It is the fishpendant of new malachite that hath fallen into the water.' He had another brought to her ?) and said: 'I give thee this instead.' And she said: 'I want my pot down to its bottom.'

Then said his majesty: 'Go to, and bring me the chief *kherheb* Zazamonkh.' And he was brought straightway. And his majesty said: 'Zazamonkh, my brother, I have done as thou saidst, and the heart of my majesty was diverted when I beheld how they rowed. But a fish-pendant of new malachite belonging to a leader fell into the water, and she was silent and rowed not, and so she spoilt her side. And I said unto her: Wherefore rowest thou not? And she said unto me: It is a fish-pendant of new malachite that hath fallen into the water. And I said unto her: Row, and lo, I will replace it. And she said unto me: I want my pot down to its bottom.'

Then the chief *kherheb* Zazamonkh said his say of magic, and he placed the one side of the water of the lake upon the other and found the fish-pendant lying on a potsherd. And he brought it and gave it to its mistress. — Now as for the water, it was twelve cubits deep in the middle, and it reached twenty-four cubits after it was turned back. Then he said his say of magic, and he brought the waters of the lake back to their place.

And his majesty spent the whole day in merriment with the entire palace, and he rewarded the chief *kherheb* Zazamonkh with all good things.

Lo, it is a wonder that came to pass in the time of thy father King Snefru, one of the deeds of the chief *kherheb*, the scribe of the book, Zazamonkh."

And the majesty of King Kheops said: "Let there be offered to the majesty of King Snefru a thousand loaves of bread, a hundred jars of beer, one ox, and two measures of incense, and let there be given to the chief *kherheb*, the scribe of the book, Zazamonkh, one cake, one jug of beer, and one measure of incense, for I have seen an example of his learning." And it was done according to all that his majesty commanded.

Fourth Tale

Then Prince Hardedef stood up to speak and said: "Hitherto hast thou heard only examples of what they knew that have gone before (us), and one knoweth not the truth from falsehood. But even in thine own time there is a magician." Then said his majesty: "Who is that, Har[dedef, my son?" And Prince Har]dedef said: "There is a townsman, Dedi by name, and he dwelleth in Ded-snefru. He is a townsman of no years, and he eateth five hundred loaves of bread, a haunch of beef in the way of meat, and drinketh one hundred jugs of beer, unto this very day. He knoweth how to put on again a head that hath been cut off, and he knoweth how to make a lion follow after him, with its leash trailing on the ground. He knoweth the number(?) of the locks(?) of the sanctuary of Thoth." — Now the majesty of King Kheops was always seeking for himself the locks(?) of the sanctuary of Thoth, to make for himself the like thereof for his Horizon.

Then said his majesty: "Thou thyself, Hardedef, my son, shalt bring him to me." And ships were made ready for Prince Hardedef, and he voyaged upstream to Ded-snefru. Now when the ships were moored to the bank, he went journeying by land, and sat in a carrying-chair of ebony, the poles of which were of sesenem-wood and overlaid with gold.

And when he was come to Dedi, the chair was set down. And he stood up to salute him, and found him lying on a mat on the threshold of his house, and a servant held his head and was stroking it for him, and another was rubbing his feet.

And Prince Hardedef said: "Thy condition is like life before growing old and before(?) old age, the place of decease, the place of enwrapping, the place of burial; (thou art still) one that sleepeth on into the daylight, free from sickness, and without becoming old in abhorrence. Greetings, revered one! I am come hither to summon thee with a message from my father Kheops, that thou mayest eat the dainties that the king giveth, the victuals of them that are in his service, that he may bring thee at a good time of life to thy fathers, who are in the realms of the dead." Said this Dedi: "In peace, in peace, Hardedef, thou king's son whom his father loveth! May thy father Kheops reward thee! May he advance thy station among the elders! May thy *ka* contend with thine adversary! May thy soul know the … way to the portal of Him-thathideth-Weakness! Greetings, king's son!"

And Prince Hardedef held out his hands to him and helped him up; and then he went with him to the riverside, giving him his hand the while. And Dedi said: "Let a ship be given me, that it may bring me the children together with my books." And two vessels with their crews were put at his service; but Dedi voyaged downstream in the ship in which was Prince Hardedef.

Now when he reached the Residence, Prince Hardedef entered in to make report to the majesty of King Kheops. And Prince Hardedef said: "O king, my lord, I have brought Dedi." Said his majesty: "Go, bring him to me." Then his majesty proceeded to the pillared hall of the palace, and Dedi was brought in unto him. And his majesty said: "How is it, Dedi, that I have never seen thee before ?" And Dedi said: "It is he who is summoned that cometh. The Sovereign summoned me, and lo, I am come." And his majesty said: "Is it true, what is said, that thou canst put on again a head that hath been cut off ?" And Dedi said: "Yea, that I can, O king, my lord." And his majesty said: "Have brought unto me a prisoner that is in the prison, that his punishment may be inflicted." And Dedi said: "But not on a man, O king, my lord! Lo, is not such a thing rather commanded to be done to the august cattle?"

And a goose was brought unto him, and its head was cut off; and the goose was placed on the western side of the hall, and its head on the eastern side of the hall. And Dedi said his say of magic, and thereupon the goose stood up and waddled, and its head likewise. Now when one part had reached the other, the goose stood up and cackled. And he had a duck brought unto him, and there was done unto it the like. And his majesty had an ox brought to him, and its head was made to tumble to the ground. And Dedi said his say of magic, and the ox stood up behind him, while its leash fell to the ground.

And King Kheops said: "It hath been said that thou knowest the number(?) of the locks(?) of the sanctuary of Thoth." And Dedi said: "So it please thee(?), I know not the number thereof, O king, my lord, but I know the place where they are." And his majesty said: "Where is that?" And Dedi said: "There is a chest of flint in the chamber named The Inventory in Heliopolis. (Lo, they are) in the chest." And Dedi said: "O king, my lord, lo, it is not I that bring it thee." And his majesty said: "Who then will bring it me?" And Dedi said: "It is the eldest of the three children who are in the belly of Red-dedet that will bring it thee." And his majesty said: "But I desire that(?) thou say who she is, this Reddedet." And Dedi said: "It is the wife of a priest of Re of Sakhebu, that hath conceived three children of Re, lord of Sakhebu. He hath told her that they will exercise this excellent office in this entire land, and that the eldest of them will be high priest in Heliopolis." Then his majesty's heart grew sad thereat. And Dedi said: "Pray, what is this mood, O king, my lord? Is it because of the three children? Then I say unto thee: thy son, his son, and then one of them." And his majesty said: "When will she give birth, pray, (this) Reddedet?" (And Dedi said): "She will give birth on the fifteenth day of the first winter month." And his majesty said: "She … the region(?) of the Canal of the Two Fishes; I myself would set foot(?) there; I will see the temple of Re, lord of Sakhebu." And Dedi said: "Then will I cause the water to stand four cubits deep over the region(?) of the Canal of the Two Fishes."

Then his majesty betook himself to his palace. And his majesty said: "Let the … be instructed (to consign) Dedi to the house of Prince Hardedef, that he may dwell with him. Fix his allowance at a thousand loaves of bread, an hundred jars of beer, one ox, and an hundred bunches of leeks." And it was done according to all that his majesty commanded.

Fifth Tale

Now on one of these days it came to pass that Red-dedet suffered the pangs of childbirth. Then said the majesty of Re of Sakhebu to Isis, Nephthys, Mesekhent, Heket, and Khnum: "Up, go ye and deliver Red-dedet of the three children that are in her womb, that will exercise this excellent office in this entire land. They will build your temples, they will furnish your altars with victuals, they will replenish your libationtables, and they will make great your offerings." Then these deities went, when they had taken on the forms of dancing-girls, and Khnum was with them and bore their carrying-chair(?).

And they came to the house of Rewoser and found him standing with loin-cloth hanging down. Then they presented to him their necklaces and rattles. And he said unto them: "My mistresses, behold there is a lady here who is in travail." And they said "Let us see her; lo, we understand midwifery." And he said unto them: "Come." Then they entered in before Red-dedet, and shut (the door of) the room upon them and her. And Isis placed herself in front of her, and Nephthys behind her, and Heket hastened the birth. And Isis said: "Be not lusty in her womb as truly as thou art named User-ref." This child slipped forth on to her hands, a child of one cubit with strong bones; the royal titulary of his limbs was of gold, and his head-cloth of true lapis lazuli. They washed him, cut his navel-string, and laid him on a sheet upon (?) a brick. And Mesekhent drew near unto him and she said: "A king that will exercise the kingship in the entire land." And Khnum gave health to his body.

[*The birth of the two other children is then related, both times in the same words and in the same detail. But the adjurations are of course different: "Draw not near in her womb, as truly as thou art named Sah-re," and "Be not dark in her womb, as truly as thou art named Keku."*]

And these divinities went forth, after that they had delivered Red-dedet of the three children. And they said: "Let thy heart be glad, Rewoser! Behold, three children are born unto thee." And he said unto them: "My mistresses, what can I do for you? I pray you give this one measure of barley to your chairman, and take it away for yourselves as payment into (your) vessels(?)." So Khnum loaded himself with the barley.

Now when they had gone their way to the place whence they had come, Isis said unto these deities: "What meaneth it, that we have come to her and yet have worked no wonder for these children, that we may make report to their father who sent us forth?" So they fashioned three royal crowns, and they placed them in the barley. And they caused storm and rain to come in the sky, and they went back to the house. And they said: "We pray you, let us lay the barley here in a lockedup chamber until we come again — — —." And they laid the barley in a locked-up chamber.

And Red-dedet purified herself with a fourteen days' purification. And she said unto her handmaid: "Hath the house been made ready?" And she said: "It hath been made ready with every good thing, save for pots, which cannot be brought." And Red-dedet said: "Wherefore, pray, cannot pots be brought?" And the handmaid said: "No good can be done here apart from the barley for the dancing girls, and that is in a chamber bearing their seal." And Red-dedet said: "Go down and fetch some of it, and Rewoser will recompense them therefore after he returneth."

So the handmaid went and opened the chamber. And she heard in the chamber the sound of singing, music, dancing, rejoicing(?), and all that is done in a king's honour. Then she went and told

Red-dedet all that she had heard. And she (Reddedet) went round the chamber, but could not find the place wherein it was being done. Then she laid her temple to the corn-bin, and she found that it was in this. And she put it in a chest, put this in another locker, corded it with hide, put it in a closet which contained her pots, and shut (the door) upon it.

And Rewoser came in from the field, and Red-dedet related unto him this matter. And he rejoiced greatly, and they sat them down and made merry.

Now after certain days had passed by, Red-dedet was enraged with her handmaid about a matter, and had her punished with a beating. And the handmaid said unto the people that were in the house: "Shalt thou do the ... ? She has born three kings. I will go and tell it unto the majesty of King Kheops." So she went and found her eldest brother by her mother binding yarn of flax on the threshing-floor. And he said unto her: "Whither art thou bound, little maiden?" Then she related unto him this matter. And her brother said unto her: "And so thou art come even unto me(?), and I am to take part in the betrayal(?)!" And he took a ... of flax to her, and dealt her a grievous blow. Then the handmaid went to fetch her a handful of water, and a crocodile seized her.

Then her brother went to tell it to Red-dedet, and he found Red-dedet sitting with her head upon her knee and her heart exceeding heavy. And he said unto her: "Wherefore art thou so troubled ?" And she said: "It is this girl, that hath grown up in the house. Lo, she is even now gone forth, saying: I will go to reveal it!" And he hung down(?) his head and said: "My mistress, she came and said unto me — — — — beside me, and I dealt her a grievous blow. And she went to draw her some water and a crocodile seized her."

[Here the manuscript breaks off.]

44. THE ELOQUENT PEASANT

Another fine work of fiction from the Twelfth Dynasty is this tale concerning a peasant named Khunanup, who impresses the pharaoh Nebkaure (Ninth Dynasty) with his rhetorical skills. No extant papyrus contains the whole story. The translation that follows is culled from Berlin Papyri 3023 and 3025, from the Middle Kingdom, and Ramesseum Papyrus A, from the New Kingdom.

Introductory Narrative

There was once a man whose name was Khunanup, a peasant of the Sekhet Ḥmuet and he had a wife whose name was [Ma]rye.

And this peasant said to her his wife: "Behold I am going down into Egypt to [bring] food thence for my children. Go now, measure out for me the corn which is in the barn, the remainder of [last harvest's (?)] corn." Then he measured out to her six (?)] gallons of corn.

And this peasant said to his wife:"Behold, [there are left over (?)] twenty gallons of corn to (be) food for thee and thy children; but make thou for me these six gallons of corn into bread and beer for every day in which [I shall be travelling (?)].

So this peasant went down into Egypt, after that he had loaded his asses with rushes, *rrmt*-plants, natron, salt, sticks of *tyw*, rods of Te-ehew, leopard skins, wolf furs, bamboo (?), pebbles (?), trim -plants, *hiprwr*-plants, *s3hwt*, *s3skwt*, *miswt*-plants, *snwt*-stones, *'ib[3]w*-stones, *ibs3*-plants, *inbi*-plants, doves, *n'rw*-birds, *wgs*-birds, *wbn*-plants, *tbsw*-plants, *gngnt*, earth-hair, *inst*,—full measure of all the goodly products of the Sekhet Hmuet. And this peasant departed southward toward Nenesu and arrived in the vicinity of Per-fiofi to the north of Medene; and he found a man standing on the river-bank named Dhutnakht, the son of a man whose name was Isry, a vassal of the high steward Rensi, the son of Meru.

And this Dhutnakht said, when he saw asses belonging to this peasant which were desirable in his heart: "Would that I had some potent idol that I might steal away the belongings of this peasant withal!" Now the house of this Dhutnakht was on the riverside path, which was narrow and not broad, equal to (?) the breadth of a loin-cloth; and the one side of it was under water, and the other under corn.

And this Dhutnakht said to his servant: "Go, bring me a cloth from my house!' And it was brought to him straightway. Then he stretched it over the riverside path, so that its fringe rested on the water and its hem on the corn. Then came this peasant along the public road.

And this Dhutnakht said: "Have a care, peasant; wouldst tread on my garments ?"

And this peasant said: "I will do thy pleasure; my course is a good one." So he went up higher.

And this Dhutnakht said: "Shalt thou have my corn for a path?"

And this peasant said: "My course is a good one. The bank is high and (our only) course is under corn; and still thou cumber est our way with thy garments. Wilt thou then not let us pass along the road?"

Thereupon one of the asses filled its mouth with a wisp of corn. And this Dhutnakht said: "Behold, I will take away thy ass, peasant, because it is eating my corn. Behold, it shall toil (?) because of its offence."

And this peasant said: "My course is a good one. Only one has been hurt I brought my donkey on account of its endurance (?), thou takest it away for the filling of its month with a wisp of corn. Nay, but I know the lord of this domain. It belongs to the high steward Rensi, the son of Meru. It is he who restrains every robber throughout the entire land; and shall I then be robbed in his (own) domain?"

And this Dhutnakht said: "Is this the proverb which people say: the poor mans name is (not) pronounced (save) for his master's sake? It is I who speak to thee, and it is the high steward whom thou callest to mind!"

Then he took up a rod of green tamarisk against him and belaboured all his limbs therewith; seized his asses and drove (them) into his domain.

Thereupon this peasant fell a-weeping very bitterly for the pain of that which was done to him. And this Dhutnakht said: "Lift not up thy voice, peasant. Behold, thou art bound for the abode of the Lord of Silence!"

And this peasant said:"Thou beatest me, thou stealest away my goods; and then takest thou the complaint from my mouth ! Thou Lord of Silence, give me back my chattels, so that I may cease to cry out to thy disturbance!"

And this peasant tarried for ten long spaces over ten days making petition to this Dhutnakht, but he paid no heed to it. So this peasant departed to Nenesu in order to make petition to the high steward Rensi, the son of Meru, and found him as he was coming forth from the door of his house to go down into his barge belonging to the judgment hall.

And this peasant said: "Would that I might be permitted to rejoice thy heart with this narration. Were it possible that a servant of thy choice might come to me, so that he might bear tidings from me to thee concerning it?"

So the high steward Rensi, the son of Meru, caused a servant of his choice to go in front of him in order that he might bring tidings from this peasant concerning this matter in its every aspect. Then the high steward Rensi, the son of Meru, laid an information against this Dhutnakht before the magistrates who were with him.

And they said to him: "Probably it is some peasant of his who has come to someone else beside him, Hehold, that is what they use to do to peasants of theirs who have come to others beside themselves. Is it a case for one s punishing this Dhutnakht on account of a trifle of natron and a trifle of salt? Let him be commanded to replace it, so that he may replace it."

But the high steward Rensi, the son of Meru, held his peace and answered not these magistrates, neither did he answer this peasant.

First Petition.

Then this peasant came to make petition to the high steward Rensi, the son of Meru, and said: "O high steward, my lord, greatest of the great, ruler of that which is not and of that which is! If thou go down to the sea of justice and sail thereon with a fair breeze, the sheet (?) shall not strip away thy sail, thy boat shall not lag, no trouble shall befall thy mast, thy yards (?) shall not break, thou shalt not founder (?) when thou touchest (?) on the land. The current shall not carry thee off, thou shalt not taste of the evils of the river, thou shalt not see a frighted face. The darting fish shall come to thee, and thou shalt attain of the fattest fowl. Forasmuch as thou art a father for the orphan, a husband for the widow, a brother for her that is put away, an apron for him that is motherless. Let me make thy name in this land in agreement with (?) every good ordinance—a ruler void of rapacity, a magnate void of baseness, a destroyer of falsehood, a fosterer of justice, one who comes at the voice of the caller. I speak; mayst thou hear. Do justice, thou praised one praised by them that are praised. Destroy (my) needs, behold I am heavy-laden. Prove me, behold I am in a loss."

Transition to the Second Petition.

Now this peasant made this speech in the time of king Nebkaure', the justified. And the high steward Rensi, the son of Meru, went before His Majesty and said: "My lord, I have found one of these peasants who is eloquent in very sooth, one whose goods have been stolen away; and behold, he is come to make petition to me concerning it."

Then said His Majesty: "As thou lovest to see me in health, cause him to linger here, without answering aught that he may say. For the sake of his continuing to speak, do thou keep silence. Then let it be brought to us in writing, that we may hear it. But provide for his wife and his children; behold, one of the peasants shall come to Egypt concerning the indigence of his house. Further, provide for this peasant himself Thou shalt cause him to be given food, without letting him know that it is thou who hast given it to him"So they gave him ten loaves and two jugs of beer every day. The high steward Rensi, the son of Mem, used to give it to a companion of his, and he used to give it to him. Then the high steward Rensi, the son of Meru, sent to the mayor of the Sekhet Ḥmuet concerning the making of food for the wife of this peasant, three gallons of wheat (?) every day.

Second Petition.

Then this peasant came to make petition to him a second time, and said: "O high steward, my lord, greatest of the great, richest of the rich, whose great ones have one greater, whose rich ones have one richer. Thou rudder of heaven, thou beam of earth, thou plumb-line that carries the weight. Rudder, diverge not; beam, tilt not; plumb-line, do not swing awry. A great lord takes (only) of that which has no lord, pillages (only) one. Thy sustenance is in thy house, a pint of beer and three loaves[1]. What canst thou expend in nourishing thy clients?

A mortal man dies along with his underlings; and shalt thou be a man of eternity?

"Is it not wrong, a balance which tilts, a plummet which deflects, a straightforward man who is become a shirker? Behold, justice escapes (?) from beneath thee, being expelled from its place; the magistrates make trouble; the norm of speech inclines to one side; the judges snatch at what he has taken(?). This means that a twister of speech from its exact sense makes travesty with it (?): the breath-giver languishes on the ground; he who takes his ease causes men to pant; the arbitrator is a spoiler; the destroyer of need commands its making; the town is its (own) flood; the redresser of wrong makes trouble—"

And the high steward Rensi, the son of Meru, said: "Is thy possession a greater matter in thy heart than that my servant should carry thee off?"

And this peasant said: "—the measurer of the corn-heaps converts to his own use; he who should render full account to another filches his belongings; he who should rule according to the laws commands to rob. Who then shall redress evil? He who should destroy poverty (?) acts perversely. One goes straight onward through crookedness, another gains repute through harm. Dost thou find (here aught) for thee (?) ?

"Redress is short, trouble is long. A good action comes back to its place of yesterday. Such is the precept, 'Do to the doer so as to cause him to do;' this is (like) thanking a man for what he does, the parrying of a thing before (its) casting, the order (given) to a craftsman. Would that an instant might destroy—make upheaval in thy vineyard (?), minish of thy birds, lay low among thy wild fowl. A seer is turned blind, a hearer deaf a ruler is become unruly.

"Thou......., hast thou ever......? What wouldst thou do......? Behold, thou art strong and power-ful. Thine arm is active, thy heart is rapacious. Mercy has passed thee by; how sorrowful is the poor man who is destroyed by thee. Thou art like a messenger from the Crocodile-god. Behold, thou surpassest the Lady of Pestilence. If thou possessest nought, then she possesseth nought; if nought is owing from her, then nought is owing from thee; if thou doest it not, then she does it not. He who has bread (?) should be (?) merciful, the criminal may be (?) hard. Thefts are natural to him who has no possessions, and the snatching at possessions by the criminal. An ill affair, but inevitable (?). One must not level reproach at him; it is but seeking for himself. But thou art sated with thy bread, and drunken with thy beer; thou art rich......all...... The face of the steersman is to the front; (yet?) the boat diverges as it pleases. The king is indoors, the rudder in thy hand; and trouble is spread in thy vicinity. The (task of the) petitioner is long, parting lags heavily. What signifies he who is yonder, men will be asking. Be a shelter, that thy coast may be clear; behold, thy habitation is infested (?). Let thy tongue be directed aright, do not stray away. The limb of a man may be his perdition (?).

"Speak no falsehood, take heed to the magistrates. It is a basket which......s judges; the speaking of lies is their herb, so that (?) it may be light in their hearts. Most instructed of all men, wilt thou know nothing of my circumstances? Destroyer of every waters need (?), behold I have a course without ship. Guider to port of all who are drowning, rescue one who is wrecked. Rescue me(?)......"

Third Petition.

Then this peasant came to make petition to him a third time, and said: "O high steward, my lord! Thou art Reʿ, the lord of heaven, in company with thy courtiers. The sustenance of all mankind is from thee, even like the flood. Thou art Ḥaʿpy who maketh green the meadows and furnisheth the wasted tracts. Restrain the robber; take counsel for the poor man; become not an inundation against the petitioner. Take heed to the approach of eternity. Will to live long, according to the saying: 'the doing of justice is the breath of the nose.' Deal punishment upon him who should be punished, and none shall resemble thy rectitude. Does the balance deflect? Does the stand-balance incline to one side? Does Thoth show leniency? (If so,) then mayst thou work trouble. Make thou thyself a seconder of these three; if the three show leniency, then do thou show leniency. Answer not good with evil; put not one thing in place of another. How doth speech grow more than a rank weed, more than suits the smeller! Answer it not, (then) trouble is watered so as to cause a coating (?) to grow (?). There have been (?) three times (?) to cause him to act (?). Guide thou the helm according to the sheet (?), stave off (?) the inundation according to (?) the doing of justice. Beware lest thou drive ashore (?) at the helm-rope (?). The true balancing of the land is the doing of justice. Speak not falsehood, being great. Be not light, being heavy. Speak not falsehood; thou art the, balance. Shrink not away; thou art rectitude. Behold, thou art on one level with the balance; if it tilt, then thou shalt tilt. Do not diverge but guide the helm.

Pull upon the helm-rope. Take not, but act against the taker. That great one is not great who is rapacious. Thy tongue is the plummet, thy heart the weight, thy two lips its arms. If thou veil thy face against the violent, who then shall redress evil?

"Behold, thou art a wretch of a washerman, one rapacious to damage a companion, forsaking (?) his partner (?) for the sake of his client; it is a brother of his who has come and fetched.

"Behold, thou art a ferryman who conveys across him who has a fare; a straight-dealer whose straight-dealing is dubious.

"Behold, thou art a head of the bakeries (?) who does not suffer one empty (?) to pass by in default(?).

"Behold, thou art a hawk to the common folk, living upon the meanest of the birds.

"Behold, thou art a purveyor whose joy is slaughter; the mutilation thereof is not (inflicted) on him.

"Behold, thou art a herdsman, not...... Thou hast not to pay. Accordingly thou shouldst(l) show less of the ravening crocodile, shelter being withdrawn (?) from the habitation of the entire land. Thou hearer, thou hear est not; wherefore dost thou not hear ? To-day have I quelled the savage one; the crocodile retires. What profits it thee that the secret of truth be found, and the back of falsehood be laid to the ground? (But) prepare not to-morrow ere it be come; none knows the trouble (that will be) in it."

Now this peasant spoke this speech to the high steward Rensi, the son of Meru, at the entrance of the judgment hall. Then he caused two apparitors to attend to him with whips, and they belaboured all his limbs therewith.

Then said this peasant: "The son of Meru goes on erring; his senses are blind to what he sees, deaf to what he hears, misguided as concerns what is related to him.

"Behold, thou art like a town not having a mayor, like a company not having a chief, like a ship in which is no commander, like a band of confederates not having a leader.

"Behold, thou art a sheriff who thieves, a mayor who will accept, a district inspector who should repress plundering, but is become a pattern for the criminal.

Fourth Petition.

Then this peasant came to make petition to him a fourth time, and found him coming forth from the door of the temple of Arsaphes, and said: "Thou praised one, may Arsaphes, from whose temple thou art come, praise thee. Perished is good, there is no cleaving to it; (yea, and) the flinging of falsehood's back to the ground. Is the ferry-boat brought to land? (Then) wherewith can one cross I The deed must be effected, however unwillingly(?). Grossing the river upon sandals, is (that) a good (way of) crossing? No! Who pray sleepeth (now) until dawn? Perished is walking by night, travel by day, and suffering a man to attend to his own right cause. Behold, it avails not him who says it to thee: 'mercy has passed thee by; how sorrowful is the poor man who is destroyed by thee.'

"Behold, thou art a hunter who slakes his ardour, one bent on doing his (own) pleasure, harpooning the hippopotami, piercing wild bulls, striking the fish, snaring the birds. There is none quick to speech who is free from overhaste, and none light of heart who can be heavy (in sinking his) caprice. Be patient that thou mayst discover justice; curb thy choice (?) so that one who is wont to enter silently (?) may be happy. There is none over-impetuous who practiseth excellence, none over-quick (whose) arm is sought. Let thine eyes behold; inform thou thy heart. Be not harsh in proportion to thy power, lest mischief befall thee. Pass over a case, and it will be twain. It is the eater who tastes; one addressed answers; the sleeper sees the vision; and as to the judge who ought to be punished, he is the pattern for the criminal. Fool, behold thou art hit. Dunce, behold thou art questioned. Baler out of water, behold thou art entered. Helmsman, let not drift thy boat. Life-giver, suffer one not to die. Destroyer, let one not be destroyed. Shade, act not as the sun-heat. Shelter, let not the crocodile seize. The fourth time of making petition to thee, shall I spend all day at it?"

Fifth Petition.

Then this peasant came to make petition to him a fifth time, and said: "O high steward, my lord! The fisher of ḥwdw-fishes makes ...... the.... yw slays the fish that chances (?), the piercer of fishes plays (?) the 'wbb-fishes, the ḏ3bḥw......, the netter of fish ravages the river. Behold, thou art in like case. Despoil not a humble man of his possessions, a feeble man with whom thou art acquainted. The poor mans possessions are breath to him, and one who takes them away stoppeth up his nose. Thou wast appointed to hear pleas, to decide between suitors, to repress the brigand; and behold, what thou dost is to support the thief. One puts faith in thee, and thou art become a transgressor. Thou wast set for a dam unto the poor man, take heed lest he drown; behold, thou art a swift current to him."

Sixth Petition.

Then this peasant came to make petition to him a sixth time, and said: "O high steward, my lord! (…) Every (true judgment (?)) lessens falsehood and fosters truth, fosters good and destroys ev[il]; even as satiety comes and ends hunger, clothing and ends nakedness; even as the sky becomes serene after a high storm, and warms all who are cold; even as a fire which cooks what is raw, and as water which quenches thirst See with thine (own) sight: the arbitrator is a spoiler; the peace-maker is a creator of sorrow; the smoother over (of differences) is a creator of soreness; the purloiner diminishes justice, (while) he who renders fidl and good account—then justice is neither filched from nor yet overflows in excess(?) (But) if thou takest, give to thy fellow, thou mouther (?) void of straight-forwardness.

"My sorrow leads to separation, my accusation bringeth departure; one knows not what is in the heart. Be not sluggish, but deal with the charge. If thou sever, who shall join? The boat-hook (?) is in thy hand like a free (?) pole, when deep water has been found (?). If the boat run aground (?) it is pushed off(?); but (?) its freight perishes and is lost(?) on every (sand-)bank (?).

"Thou art instructed, thou art clever, thou art fair, but not through despoiling. (And now ?) thou takest the likeness (?) of all mankind. Thy affairs are all awry; the perverter of the entire land goes straight onward. The cultivator of evil waters his plot with wrongdoing so as to make his plot grow with falsehood, so as to water trouble for eternity (?)."

Seventh Petition.

Then this peasant came to make petition to him a seventh time, and said: "O high steward, my lord! Thou art the rudder of the entire land; the land sails according to thy command. Thou art the peer of Thoth, judging without inclining to the one side. My lord, be patient, so that a man may invoke thee concerning his own right cause. Let not thine heart be restive; it beseems thee not. The far-sighted man is short tempered; brood not on that which is not yet come; rejoice not at that which has not yet happened. Forbearance prolongs companionship. Destroy a matter that is past. One knows not what is in the heart.

"The subverter of law, the infringer of the norm, there is no poor man can live whom he pillages, if (?) justice address him not. Verily, my belly was full, my heart was heavy-laden; there issued forth from my belly on account of the condition thereof It was a breach in the dam, and its water flowed; my mouth opened to speak. Then did I ply my sounding-pole (?); I baled out my water; I ventilated what was in my belly; I washed my soiled linen. (Now) my utterance is achieved; my misery is concluded in thy presence; what requirest thou yet?

"Thy sluggishness will lead thee astray. Thy rapacity will befool thee. Thy apathy (?) will beget thee enemies. But wilt thou ever find another peasant like me? A sluggard—will a petitioner stand at the door of his house? There is none silent whom thou hast caused to speak, none sleeping whom thou hast awakened, none downcast whom thou hast enlivened, none with shut mouth tuhom thou hast opened, none ignorant whom thou hast caused to know, none foolish whom thou hast taught; (albeit?) magistrates are the expellers of mischief and the lords of good, are artists to create whatever is and joiners together of the head that is cut off."

Eighth Petition.

Then this peasant came to make petition to him an eighth time, and said: "O high steivard, my lord! Men suffer a far fall through greed. The rapacious man lacks success, but he has a success in failure. Thou art rapacious and it beseems thee not; thou stealest and it benefits thee not; thou who shouldst (?) suffer a man to attend to his own right cause. It is because thy sustenance is in thy house; thy belly is full; the corn-measure flows over and, when it shakes (?), its superfluity is lost on the ground.

"O thou who shouldst (?) seize the robber, and who takest away the magistrates, (they) were made to redress trouble; they are shelters for the indignant; the magistrates, (they) were made to redress falsehood. No fear of thee causes me to make petition to thee. Thou perceivest not my heart; a silent one, who turns him ever back to make reproaches to thee. He does not fear him to whom he makes his claim; and his brother is not to be brought to thee from out of the street.

"Thou hast thy plot of ground in the country, and thy guerdon in the domain. Thy bread is in the bakery, and the magistrates give to thee. And (yet) thou takest! Art thou a robber? Are troops brought to thee to accompany thee for the divisions of the ground-plots?

"Do justice for the Lord of Justice, the justice of whose justice exists. Thou reed-pen, thou papyrus, thou palette, thou Thoth, keep aloof from the making of trouble. When what is well is well, then it is well. But justice shall be unto everlasting. It goes down into the necropolis with him who doeth it; he is buried and the earth envelops him; and his name is not obliterated upon earth, but he is remembered for goodness. Such is the norm in the word of god. Is he a balance? It does not tilt Is he a stand-balance? It does not incline to one side. Whether I shall come or another shall come, do thou address (him); answer not as one who addresses a silent man, or as one who attacks him who cannot attack. Thou dost not show mercy; thou dost not weaken (?); thou dost not annihilate (?); and thou givest me no reward for this goodly speech which comes forth from the mouth of Re[c] himself. Speak justice, and do justice; for it is mighty, it is great; it endureth long, its trustworthiness (?) is discovered, it bringeth unto revered old age. Does a balance tilt ? (If so), it is (through) its scales which carry the things. No inequality is possible to the norm. A mean act attaineth not to the city; the hinder-most (?) will reach land."

Ninth Petition.

Then this peasant came to make petition to him a ninth time, and said: "O high steward, my lord! The tongue of men is their stand-balance. The balance it is which searches out deficiencies. Deal punishment upon him who should be punished, and none shall resemble thy rectitude ...... falsehood, its business (?) is settled (?). Truth returneth confronting it (?). Truth is the wealth (?) of falsehood; it causes to flourish (?), it is not......ed. If falsehood walk (abroad), it strayeth, it doth not cross in the ferry-boat, it maketh no progress (?). As for him who grows rich through it, he hath no children, he hath no heirs upon earth. He who sails with it (for a cargo), reaches not land, his boat does not moor at its city.

"Be not heavy, who are not light; do not lag, who dost not haste. Be not partial; do not listen to (thy) heart. Veil not thy face from one whom thou knowest. Be not blind to one whom thou hast beheld. Rebuff not him who puts a claim upon thee. Forsake thou this sluggishness, in order that thy maxim 'Do (good) unto him who does (good) to thee' may be reported, yea in the hearing of all mankind, and in order that (?) a man may invoke (thee) concerning his own right cause. A sluggard has no yesterday; one deaf to justice has no companion; the rapacious man has no holiday. He against whom accusation is brought (?) becomes a poor man, and the poor man will be a petitioner; the enemy becomes a slayer (?). Behold, I make petition to thee, and thou hearest it not. I will go and make petition on thy behalf to Anubis."

Conclusion.

Then the high steward Rensi, the son of Meru, caused two apparitors to go and bring him back. And this peasant was afraid, thinking that it was being done in order to punish him for this speech which he had spoken.

And this peasant said: "The approach of a thirsty man to the waters, the reaching of a suckling's lips after milk, such is a death which has been desired to be seen in its coming, when his death comes tardily to him."

But the high steward Rensi, the son of Meru, said: "Fear not, peasant. Behold, thou shalt arrange to live(?) with me."

And this peasant said (?): "Am I to live saying 'Let me eat of thy bread and drink (of) thy (beer) to eternity?'"

The high steward Rensi, the son of Meru, said: "Well, tarry here, that thou mayst hear thy petitions." And he caused [them] to be read out from a new papyrus roll, every petition according to [its] content. And the high steward Rensi, the son of Meru, caused it to be sent in to the Majesty of the king Nebkaure', justified. And it was pleasant in the heart [of His Majesty] more than anything that is in this entire land. And [His Majesty] said: "Give judgment thou thyself, son of Meru."

And the [high stewardI] Rensi, the son of Meru, caused two apparitors to go and [fetch Dhutnakht]. And he was brought, awd arc- inventory was made of [all his property (?)], his......, six persons, besides [his]......, his Upper Egyptian corn, his barley, [his] asses......, his swine, [his] small cattle...... [And the house (?) of] this Dhutnakht [was given] to [this] peasant [together with] all his ...... And ......s[aid] to Dhutnakht......"

Colophon.

It is come [to an end in peace, even as it was found in writing].

45. THE SHIPWRECKED SAILOR

The following Middle Kingdom tale is preserved on only one papyrus copy, P. Leningrad 115. The story is told by the attendant of an official who has just returned from a long journey but apparently was unsuccessful in his mission.

A worthy henchman said: Be of good cheer, Prince, behold, we have reached the Residence. The mallet hath been taken, the mooring-post driven in, and the bow-rope run along the ground. There is praising and thanksgiving to God, and every one embraceth his fellow. Our crew hath come home safe and sound, and our soldiers have suffered no loss. We have reached the end of Wawat and have passed by Senmet. See, we have returned in peace and have reached our own land. Hearken to me, Prince; I am one that is free from exaggeration. Wash thyself and pour water on thy fingers. Answer when thou art greeted, speak to the king having thy wits about thee, and answer without faltering. It is a man's mouth that saveth him, and his speech maketh men forbearing towards him. Thou wilt do as thou willst; to speak to thee is irksome (to thee).

Yet I will relate to thee something like thereunto, that was experienced by me myself, when I had set out for the mines of the Sovereign and gone down to the sea in a ship of an hundred and twenty cubits in length and forty cubits in breadth; and therein were an hundred and twenty sailors of the pick of Egypt. They scanned the sky, they scanned the earth, and their hearts were more … than those of lions. They foretold a storm or ever it came, and a tempest when as yet it was not.

A storm burst while we were yet at sea, before we had reached land. We flew before the wind and it made a . . and a wave eight cubits high was within it. It was a piece of wood that … it to me.

Then the ship perished, and of them that were in it not one survived. And I was cast on to an island by a wave of the sea, and I spent three days alone with mine heart (only) as my companion. I slept under the shelter of a tree (?) and embraced the shade. Then I stretched forth my feet in order to find out what I could put into my mouth. I found figs and vines there, and all manner of fine leeks, kau-fruit together with nekut-fruit and cucumbers … There were fish there and fowl, and there was nothing that was not in it. Then I satisfied myself and still left over, for it was too much for my hands. When I had made me a fire-drill, I kindled a fire and made a burnt-offering for the gods.

Then I heard the sound of thunder and thought it was a wave of the sea; the trees brake, and the earth quaked. I uncovered my face and found that it was a serpent that drew nigh. He was thirty cubits long, and his beard it was longer than two cubits; his body was overlaid with gold, his eyebrows were of real lapis lazuli, and he coiled himself forward.

He opened his mouth at me, while I was on my belly in front of him, and he said unto me: "Who hath brought thee (hither), who hath brought thee (hither), little one? Who hath brought thee (hither)? If thou delayest in telling me who hath brought thee to this island, I will let thee know thyself to be but ashes, becoming as that which is not seen." (I answered:) "Thou speakest unto me, and yet I hear it not. I am in thy presence, but my wits have gone."

Then he took me in his mouth and brought me to his lair, and set me down without touching me, and I was whole and there was nothing torn from me. He opened his mouth at me, while I was on my belly in front of him. And he said unto me: "Who hath brought thee (hither), who hath brought thee (hither), little one? Who hath brought thee to this island of the sea, which is encompassed on both sides by the waters? "And I made answer to him, my arms being bent 1 in his presence, and said unto him: "I am one who went down to the mines on an errand of the Sovereign, with a ship of an hundred and twenty cubits in length and forty cubits in breadth, and therein were an hundred and twenty sailors of the pick of Egypt. They scanned the sky, they scanned the earth, and their hearts were more … than those of lions. They foretold the storm or ever it came, and the tempest when as yet it was not. Each one of them was … of heart and stronger of arm than his fellow, and there was no fool among them. A storm burst while we were yet at sea, before we had reached land. We flew before the wind and it made a … , and a wave eight cubits high was within it. It was a piece of wood that … it to me. Then the ship perished, and of them that were in it not one survived save me, and behold, here I am beside thee. And I was brought to this island by a wave of the sea."

Then he said unto me: "Fear not, fear not, little one; let not thy countenance . . ., now that thou art come to me. Lo, God hath preserved thee alive to bring thee to this Island of the Ka, in which there is nothing that is not in it, and it is full of all good things. Lo, thou shalt spend month after month in this island until thou completest four months. Then a ship will come from the Residence with sailors in it whom thou knowest, and thou shalt go with them to the Residence and die in thine own town.

"How glad is he that relateth what he hath experienced when the calamity hath passed! So I will relate to thee something like this which came to pass in this island. I was in it with my brethren, and children were in their midst, and we numbered in all seventy-five serpents, my children and my brethren, without my mentioning to thee the daughter of a humble woman that was brought to me by… . Then a star fell, and these went up (?) in fire because of it. Now it happened when I was not with the burned ones (?), and while I was not in their midst. And I (almost) died on their account when I found them as one heap of corpses.

"If thou art valiant, curb thine heart. Then thou wilt embrace thy children and kiss thy wife and see thine house— that is the best thing of all. Thou wilt arrive at the Residence, and dwell there in the midst of thy brethren."

Then I extended myself on my belly and touched the ground in (his) presence. And I said unto him: "I will discourse on thy nature to the Sovereign and acquaint him with thy greatness. I will cause *ibi*, *hekenu*, *iudeneb*, and *khesait* to be brought to thee, and incense of the temples, wherewith every god is made content. I will relate what befell me, and of what I have seen… . Thou shalt be thanked in the city in the presence of the officers of the entire land. I will slay for thee oxen for burnt-offering, and geese will I sacrifice for thee. I will send thee ships laden with all the precious things of Egypt, as should be done for a god, that loveth men, in a land far off which men know not."

Thereupon he laughed at me and at what I had said, as being but foolishness in his heart. And he said unto me: "Thou hast not myrrh in plenty, being (but) a possessor of frankincense. But I am the prince of Punt, and myrrh, that is my very own. As for that *hekenu* whereof thou didst say that it is to be brought (to me), why that is the chief product of this island. But it shall happen, when thou art parted from this place, that never shalt thou behold this island more, for it will become water."

And then that ship came, even as he had foretold. And I went and climbed a tall tree, and I descried them that were in it. And I went to report it, but found that he already knew it. And he said unto me: "Safely, safely home, little one, and see thy children, and give (me) a good name in thy city. Lo, that is all I require of thee."

Then I placed me on my belly, and my arms were bent in his presence. And he gave me a freight of myrrh, *hekenu*, *iudeneb*, *khesait*, *tishepes*, *shaas*, eye-cosmetic, giraffes' tails, a great mass (?) of incense, elephant-tusks, greyhounds, monkeys, apes, and all goodly treasures. And I stowed them on this ship.

Now when I had placed me on my belly to thank him, he said unto me: "Lo, thou shalt reach the Residence in two months, shalt hold thy children in thine embrace, grow young again at the Residence, and be buried."

And I went down to the shore where this ship lay. And I hailed the contingent that was in this ship, and gave praise upon the shore to the lord of this island, and they that were on board did likewise.

Then we voyaged northwards to the Residence of the Sovereign, and we reached the Residence in two months, according to all that he had said. And I entered in before the Sovereign and presented unto him all this treasure which I had brought from this island. And he thanked me in the sight of the officers of the entire land, and I was appointed to be a henchman and was presented with people of his (?).

Look at me after I reached land, after I saw what I had experienced. Hearken unto my speech. Lo, it is good for men to hearken!

And he said unto me: "Act not the superior person, my friend! Who giveth water at dawn to a bird that he will kill early in the morning?"

𓄿𓎡𓏏𓈖𓏤𓇋𓅓𓏏𓏭𓈖𓏏𓅓𓏏𓏭𓇋𓅓𓏏𓏭𓏛𓏏𓏤𓇋𓏤

46. THE INSTRUCTIONS OF DUA-KHETY

The Instructions of Dua-Khety, also known as The Satire of the Trades, is a work in the sebayt *genre, presented as an address to a boy named Pepy by his father Dua-Khety, a scribe from Sile. This may be the same Khety who is said to have written the Instructions of Amenhemet (reading #34), but by the later Middle Kingdom it seems Khety was already famous (see reading #47), and the present work may simply be pseudonymous. The text is preserved in its entirety in Papyrus Sallier II and partially in Papyrus Anastasi VII (both from Dynasty 19) but was composed during the Middle Kingdom.*

Instruction, which a ... man, named Duauf, the son of Khety, composed for his son, named Pepi, when he voyaged up to the Residence, in order to put him in the School of Books, among the children of the magistrates – – – –.

He said unto him: I have seen him that is beaten, him that is beaten: thou art to set thine heart on books. I have beheld him that is set free from forced labour: behold, nothing surpasseth books.

Read at the end of the Kemit; thou findest this sentence therein: "The scribe, his is every place at the Residence and lie is not poor in it. But he that acteth according to the understanding of another, he hath no success." The other professions also are as this sentence purporteth.

Would that I might make thee love books more than thy mother, would that I might bring their beauty before thy face. It is greater than any calling. – – – – If he hath begun to succeed, and is yet a child, men greet him. He is sent to carry out behests, and he cometh not home that he may don the apron.

Never have I seen a sculptor on an errand, nor a goldsmith as he was being sent forth. But I have seen the smith at his task at the mouth of his furnace. His fingers were like stuff from crocodiles, he stank more than the offal (?) of fishes.

Every artisan that wieldeth the chisel (?), he is wearier than he that delveth; his field is the wood and his hoe is the metal. In the night, when he is set free, he worketh beyond what his arms can do; in the night he burneth a light."

The stone-mason seeketh for work (?) in all manner of hard stone. When he hath finished it, his arms are destroyed and he is weary. When such an one sitteth down at dusk, his thighs and his back are broken.

The barber shaveth late into the evening – – – – he betaketh him from street to street, in order to seek (?) whom he may shave. He straineth his arms in order to fill his belly, even as a bee that feedeth at its work.

The ... sails down to the Delta in order to get the purchase money, and he worketh beyond that his arms can do. The gnats slay him – – – –.

The small bricklayer with the Nile mud (?), he spendeth his life among the cattle (?); he is somehow concerned with vines and swine, his clothes are stiff, – – – – he worketh (?) with his feet, he poundeth – – –.

Let me tell thee further of the builder of walls, that is ofttimes sick (?), his raiment is likewise vile; what he eateth is the bread of his fingers and he washeth himself once only. — He fares so ill that the sage has to devote a second paragraph to him, of which only a little is intelligible to us:

He is more miserable than one can rightly tell (?). He is like a block of stone (?) in a room, which measureth ten cubits by six cubits. – – – The bread, he giveth it unto his house; his children are beaten, beaten.

The gardener bringeth loads, and his arm and neck ache beneath them. At morn he watereth the leek, and at even the vines – — —. It also goeth more ill with him than any calling.

The field-worker, his reckoning endureth for ever; he bath a louder voice than the *abu*-bird – – –. He, too, is wearier than can be told (?), and he fareth as well as one fareth among lions; he is oft-times sick (?), – – – and when he cometh unto his house at eventide, the going hath cut him to pieces (?).

The weaver (?) in the workshop, he fareth more ill than any women. His thighs are upon his belly, and he breatheth no air. On a day, when no weaving is done, he must pluck (?) lotus flowers in the pond. He giveth bread to the doorkeeper, that he may suffer him to come into the daylight.

The fletcher, he fareth ill exceedingly, when he goeth up into the desert. Much giveth he for his ass, much giveth he for what is in the field. When he setteth out on the road (?) — — and cometh unto his house at eventime, the going hath cut him to pieces (?).

The ... goeth up into the desert, and (first) maketh over his goods to his children, for fear of the lions and the Asiatics — — — and cometh unto his house at eventide, the going hath cut him to pieces (?) — — — —.

The . . ., his fingers stink, and the odour thereof is abhorrent (?) — — —. He spendeth the day cutting reed, and clothes are his abhorrence.

The cobbler, he fareth ill exceedingly; he beggeth ever. He fareth as well as one fareth among ... What he biteth is leather ... ?

The fuller washeth upon the river bank, a near neighbour of the crocodile — — — —. This is no peaceful calling in thine eyes, that would be more tranquil than all callings — — —.

The fowler, he fareth ill exceedingly, when he looketh at the birds in the sky. When the passers-by are joined to the heaven, he saith: "Would that I had a net here." But God giveth him no success (?).

Let me tell thee further, how it fareth with the fisherman; it goeth more ill with him than any other calling. Is not his work upon the river, where he is mixed with the crocodiles ? — — —. One saith not: "There is a crocodile there"; fear hath blinded him — — — —. Behold, there is no calling that is without a director except (that of) the scribe, and he is the director.

If he knoweth the books, then true of him is: "They are good for thee"— — What I now do on the voyage up to the Residence, lo, I do it out of love for thee. A day at school is profitable to thee, and its work endureth even like the mountains — —.

[*Most of what is to be found in the following sections is unintelligible. As the introduction to them shows:*] Let me say to thee further yet other words in order to instruct thee ... [*They deal with a new theme; indeed, they may be a later addition. The one section teaches good behaviour in the presence of the great:*] If thou enterest, while the master of the house is in his house, and he hath to do with another first, while thou sittest with thine hand to thy mouth, ask not for anything. Further: Speak no hidden words and speak no insolent words — — — —. Then: If thou comest from school and midday is announced to thee, and thou goest shouting joyously in the streets, then — — — If a great man sendeth thee with a message, repeat it as he saith it; take nothing therefrom and add nothing thereto — — — —.

Be content with thy diet: If three loaves satisfy thee, and thou drinkest two pots of beer, and the belly is not yet contented, fight against it (?).

Behold, it is good if thou sendest away the multitude and hearkenest (alone) to the words of the great. — — — — Make a friend of a man of thy generation.

Behold, Renenet is upon the way of God; Renenet, the scribe hath her upon his arm on the day of his birth. He arriveth at the vestibule (?) of the officials, when he is grown up (?)

Behold, no scribe lacketh sustenance, the things of the king's house. Mesekhent hath vouchsafed success to the scribe; at the head of the officials is he set, and his father and his mother thank God for it — — —. Behold, this it is that I set before thee and thy children's children.

47. EULOGY OF WRITERS

This later Middle Kingdom work, praising the great scribes of old, is preserved in the Chester Beatty Papyrus IV, which dates to the New Kingdom.

[DO NOT FIND FAULT], BUT HAVE A CARE concerning words. Act (the part of) one who is silent as passenger [in the ferry-boat. Pay unto it the fare.] Reward the craftsman, that <he> may serve thee.

ACCORDING AS THE HEART INVITE THEE, thy name shall be .... thy deeds. Be not slothful, but make perfect all thy dealings. ...... Be not light in thy character, so that <thou> mayst be respected as a man. ...... [Better is ?] perseverance than sloth. He who is persevering after sloth (?).......

ACT THOU WITH RIGHTEOUS DEEDS. Be straight, be not crooked ...... thy excellent deeds. So shall thy superiors respect thee, and the commander [of] people ... hearken unto thee. ...... people. Persevere in thine office, and make perfect thy dealings, so that [all ?] things may hearken unto thee ......

[ATTACH ?] THYSELF TO A MAGISTRATE, that he may love thee on account of thy character, and may send thee (on missions), his heart confident .... excellent. Be (?) profitable to him even as the mistress of his house, and become to him like his son. Be not absent from him a moment. Beware ...... Fight against drawing nigh to a woman, lest thy name stink.

IF THOU ART WEALTHY, AND STRENGTH HATH COME to thee, thy god having built thee up, play not the ignorant with a man whom thou knowest. Greet everyone. Release another when thou hast found him bound. Be a protector to the miserable. He is called good who does not play the ignorant.

IF AN ORPHAN PETITION THEE, one who is weak and persecuted by another who would ruin him, fly to him and give him something. Constitute thyself his rescuer (?). It will be good in the heart of god, and men will (?) praise thee (?). A man whom his god hath built up should foster many.

NAY BUT IF THOU DOEST THESE THINGS, thou art versed in the writings. Those learned scribes from the time of the successors of the gods, (even) those who foretold the future, it hath befallen that their names endure for all eternity, (though) they be gone, having completed their lives, and (though) all their kindred be forgotten.

THEY MADE NOT UNTO THEMSELVES pyramids of brass, with tombstones of iron. They knew not how to leave heirs that were children [who should ?] pronounce their names, but they made heirs unto themselves of the writings and the books of instruction which they made.

THEY APPOINTED FOR THEMSELVES [the papyrus-roll] as a lector-priest, the writing-board as a loving-son. Books of instruction (became) their pyramids, and the reed-pen was their child. The stone-surface was (their) woman. (Persons) both great and small were made into their children, for the scribe, he is chief of them (all).

THERE WERE MADE FOR <THEM> DOORS AND HALLS, but these are fallen to pieces. Their *ka*-servants are [gone], their tombstones covered with dirt, their chambers forgotten. (But) their names are pronounced because of these books of theirs which they made, inasmuch as they were good, and the memory of him who made them (?) is for evermore.

BE A SCRIBE, PUT IT IN THY HEART, that thy name may fare similarly. More profitable is a book than a graven tombstone, than a chapel-wall (?) firmly established. This serves as chapels and pyramids to the end that a man's name may be pronounced. Assuredly profitable in the necropolis is a name on the lips of mankind!

A MAN HATH PERISHED and his corpse is become dirt. All his kindred have crumbled to dust. But writings cause him to be remembered in the mouth of the reciter. More profitable is a book than the house of the builder, than chapels in the West. Better is it than a stablished castle and than a memorial-stone in a temple.

IS (ANY) HERE LIKE Hardedef?[6] Is there another like Imhotep? There have been none among our kindred like Nofri[7] and Akhthoy,[8] that chief among them. I recall to thee the names of Ptahemdjedhuty and Kharkheperrarsonb. Is there another one like Ptahhotpe[9] or like Kairos?

THOSE SAGES WHO FORETOLD THE FUTURE, that which came forth from their mouths happened. It is found as a pronouncement, it was written in their books. The children of other folk

---

6   Son of King Khufu, featured in reading #43 and credited with writing *The Instruction of Hardedef*, only a fragment of which has survived (not included in this volume).
7   Possibly Neferty (see reading #30), though the 't' is missing here.
8   Vocalized more commonly today as Khety. This is perhaps the Khety of the previous reading.
9   Usually spelled Ptahhotep (the presumed composer of reading #19).

are given to them as heirs, as (though it had been) their own children. They concealed their magic from all the world, (but it is) read in a book of instruction. They are gone, their name is forgotten. (But) writings cause them to be remembered.

BE A SCRIBE. IT WILL SAVE THEE from taxation, and will protect thee from all labours. It will stop thee from bearing hoe and mattock, so that thou (need) not carry a basket. It sundereth thee from plying the oar, and stoppeth thee from hardships, that thou mayst not be under many lords and numerous masters. Of all that exercise a profession the scribe is the chief.

IT IS THE SCRIBE WHO ASSESSES both Upper and Lower Egypt. It is he who receives (the dues) from them. It is he who accounts for everything. All soldiers are dependent upon <him>. It is he who conducts officials into the Presence, and sets the pace for every man. It is he who commands the entire land. All business is under his control.

BE A SCRIBE, THAT THY LIMBS MAY BE SLEEK, and thy hands become soft, that thou mayst go forth in white attire, honour done to thee, and that the courtiers may salute thee. A man of value is sought and thou art found. One does not recognize a little one (?), but one finds (?) the man that is skilled, and he rises step by step until he has reached (the position of) magistrate, in praise corresponding to his good character.

NAY BUT THOU ART EXPERIENCED IN THE WRITINGS, thou hast penetrated into (moral) teachings. Sit not in the presence of one greater than thyself. Respect another, that thou (thyself) mayst be respected. Love men, that men may love thee. Speak no words in excess. Walk not upon the road (over-)ostentatiously when thy name has been recognized. Keep side by side (with others) (?) , relax not attention until thou hast attained a way for thy feet.

I SPREAD OUT instruction before thee, [I] testify [to thee] concerning the way of life. I set thee upon a path that is painless, a palisade protecting <against ?> the crocodile, a good and comfortable glow, shade without heat. Act accordingly, that thy name may be recognized, and that thou mayst attain the West.

BEWARE LEST THOU SAY: 'Every man is according to his (own) character; ignorant and learned are all alike; fate and upbringing are graven upon the character in the writing of God himself; every man passes his life within an hour.' Good is instruction without wearying of it, and that a son should make answer with the utterances of his father. I cause thee to know rectitude in thy heart. (But) do what is just in thy sight. (END.)

The breath of welcome, anointing with myrrh, and the north wind of hairdressers [be thine?] May they (?) exalt their moment of life when their names are pronounced. May they follow Sokaris in the Shetjit-shrine, and Osiris in Busiris! They all have blessed my name on reaching the conclusion.?

[REPETITION OF ?] LIFE, and the sight of the sun to the scribe Akhthoy, and invocation-offerings of bread and beer before Onnophris, libations and wine and linen to his *ka* and to his company— the excellent one, whose utterances are choice! I proclaim his name to eternity. It was he who made a book as the(?) Instruction of King Shetepebre, when he had gone to rest, joining heaven and entering among the lords of the necropolis, the ..., and causing to endure ...... beside Shetepebre ...... content ...... the generations which shall be. So let a man speak with instruction ... [Akh]thoy(?), the deceased.

48. THE BOOK OF THE HEAVENLY COW

The following text, sometimes called "The Legend of the Destruction of Mankind," was found in the tombs of the Egyptian New Kingdom pharaohs Seti I, Ramesses II, and Ramesses III, but it probably was composed earlier, as it is written in Middle Egyptian. It is a myth concerning the sun god Ra (Re) and how he came to be in heaven, having once resided on earth.

CHAPTER I.

[Here is the story of Ra,] the god who was self-begotten and self-created, after he had assumed the sovereignty over men and women, and gods, and things, the one god. Now men and women were speaking words of complaint, saying:—"Behold, his Majesty (life, strength, and health to him!) has grown old, and his bones have become like silver, and his members have turned into gold and his hair is like real lapis-lazuli." His Majesty heard the words of complaint which men and women were uttering, and his Majesty (life, strength, and health to him!) said to those who were in his train:—"Cry out, and bring to me my Eye, and Shu, and Tefnut, and Seb, and Nut, and the father-gods, and the mother-gods who were with me, even when I was in Nu side by side with my god Nu. Let there be brought along with my Eye his ministers, and let them be led to me here secretly, so that men and women may not perceive them [coming] here, and may not therefore take to flight with their hearts. Come with them to the Great House, and let them declare their plans (or, arrangements) fully, for I will go from Nu into the place wherein I brought about my own existence, and let those gods be brought to me there." Now the gods were drawn up on each side of Ra, and they bowed down before his Majesty until their heads touched the ground, and the maker of men and women, the king of those who have knowledge, spoke his words in the presence of the Father of the first-born gods. And the gods spoke in the presence of his Majesty, saying:—"Speak to us, for we are listening to them" (i.e., thy words). Then Ra spoke to Nu, saying:—"O first-born god from whom I came into being, O you gods of ancient time, my ancestors, take heed to what men and women [are doing]; for behold, those who were created by my Eye are uttering words of complaint against me. Tell me what you would do in the matter, and consider this thing for me, and seek out [a plan] for me, for I will not slay them until I have heard what you shall say to me concerning it."

Then the Majesty of Nu, to son Ra, spoke, saying:—"You are the god who is greater than he who made you, you are the sovereign of those who were created with you, your throne is set, and the fear of you is great; let your Eye go against those who have uttered blasphemies against you." And the Majesty of Ra, said:—"Behold, they have betaken themselves to flight into the mountain lands, for their hearts are afraid because of the words which they have uttered." Then the gods spoke in the presence of his Majesty, saying:—"Let your Eye go forth and let it destroy for you those who revile you with words of evil, for there is no eye whatsoever that can go before it and resist you and it when it journeys in the form of Hathor." Thereupon this goddess went forth and slew the men and the women who were on the mountain (or, desert land).

And the Majesty of this god said, "Come, come in peace, O Hathor, for the work is accomplished." Then this goddess said, "You have made me to live, for when I gained the mastery over men and women it was sweet to my heart;" and the Majesty of Ra said, "I myself will be master over them as [their] king, and I will destroy them." And it came to pass that Sekhet of the offerings waded about in the night season in their blood, beginning at Suten-henen. Then the Majesty of Ra, spoke [saying], "Cry out, and let there come to me swift and speedy messengers who shall be able to run like the wind ... .;" and straightway messengers of this kind were brought to him. And the Majesty of this god spoke [saying], "Let these messengers go to Abu, and bring to me mandrakes in great numbers;" and [when] these mandrakes were brought to him the Majesty of this god gave them to Sekhet, the goddess who dwells in Annu (Heliopolis) to crush. And behold, when the maidservants were bruising the grain for [making] beer, these mandrakes were placed in the vessels which were to hold the beer, and some of the blood of the men and women [who had been slain]. Now they made seven thousand vessels of beer. Now when the Majesty of Ra, the King of the South and North, had come with the gods to look at the vessels of beer, and behold, the daylight had appeared after the slaughter of men and women by the goddess in their season as she sailed up the river, the Majesty of Ra said, "It is good, it is good, nevertheless I must protect men and women against her." And Ra, said, "Let them take up the vases and carry them to the place where the men and women were slaughtered by her." Then the Majesty of the King of the South and North in the three-fold beauty of the night caused to be poured out these vases of beer which make [men] to lie down (or, sleep), and the meadows of the Four Heavens were filled with beer (or, water) by reason of the Souls of the Majesty of this god. And it came to pass that when this goddess arrived at the dawn of day, she found these [Heavens] flooded [with beer], and she was pleased thereat; and she drank [of the beer and blood], and her heart rejoiced, and she became drunk, and she gave no further attention to men and women. Then said the Majesty of Ra to this goddess, "Come in peace, come in peace, O Amit," and thereupon beautiful women came into being in the city of Amit (or, Amem). And the Majesty of Ra spoke [concerning] this goddess, [saying], "Let there be made for her vessels of the beer which produces sleep at every holy time and season of the year, and they shall be in number according to the number of my hand-maidens;" and from that early time until now men have been accustomed to make on the occasions of the festival of Hathor vessels of the beer which make them to sleep in number according to the number of the handmaidens of Ra.

And the Majesty of Ra spoke to this goddess, [saying], "I am smitten with the pain of the fire of sickness; from where comes to me [this] pain?" And the Majesty of Ra said, "I live, but my heart has become exceedingly weary with existence with them (i.e., with men); I have slain [some of] them, but there is a remnant of worthless ones, for the destruction which I wrought among them was not as great as my power." Then the gods who were in his following said to him, "Be not overcome by your inactivity, for your might is in proportion to your will." And the Majesty of this god said to the Majesty of Nu, "My members are weak for (or, as at) the first time; I will not permit this to come upon me a second time." And the Majesty of the god Nu said, "O son Shu, be you the Eye for your father ... and avenue (?) him, and you goddess Nut, place him . . . . And the goddess Nut said, "How can this be then, O my father Nu? Hail," said Nut . . . . . to the god Nu, and the goddess straightway became [a cow], and she set the Majesty of Ra upon [her] back . . . . . And when these things had been done, men and women saw the god Ra, upon the back [of the cow]. Then these men and women said, "Remain with us, and we will overthrow your enemies who speak words of blasphemy [against you] and [destroy them]." Then his Majesty [Ra] set out for the Great House, and [the gods who were in the train of Ra remained] with them (i.e., the men); during that time the earth was in darkness. And when the earth became light [again] and the morning had dawned, the men came forth with their bows and their [weapons], and they set their arms in motion to shoot the enemies [of Ra]. Then said the Majesty of this god, "Your transgressions of violence are placed behind you, for the slaughtering of the enemies is above the slaughter [of sacrifice];" thus came into being the slaughter [of sacrifice].

And the Majesty of this god said to Nut, "I have placed myself upon your back in order to stretch myself out." What then is the meaning of this? It means that he united (?) himself with Nut. [Thus came into being] . . . . . Then said the Majesty of this god, "I am departing from them (i.e., from men), and he must come after me who would see me;" thus came into being . . . . . Then the Majesty of this god looked forth from its interior, saying, "Gather together [men for me], and make ready for me an abode for multitudes;" thus came into being . . . . And his Majesty (life, health, and strength be to him!) said, "Let a great field (*sekhet*) be produced (*hetep*);" thereupon Sekhet-hetep came into being. [And the god said], "I will gather herbs (*aarat*) therein;" thereupon Sekhet-aaru came into being. [And the god said], "I will make it to contain as dwellers things (*khet*) like stars of all sorts;" thereupon the stars (*akhekha*) came into being. Then the goddess Nut trembled because of the height. And the Majesty of Ra said, "I decree that supports be to bear [the goddess up];" thereupon the props of heaven (*heh*) came into being. And the Majesty of Ra said, "O my son Shu, I pray you to set yourself under [my] daughter Nut, and guard you for me the supports (*heh*) of the millions (*heh*) which are there, and which live in darkness. Take you the goddess upon your head, and act as nurse for her;" thereupon came into being [the custom] of a son nursing a daughter, and [the custom] of a father carrying a son upon his head.

CHAPTER II.

[*describes a ritual done over the figure of a cow*]

CHAPTER III.

Then the majesty of this god spoke to Thoth, [saying] "Let a call go forth for me to the Majesty of the god Seb, saying, 'Come, with the utmost speed, at once.'" And when the Majesty of Seb had come, the Majesty of this god said to him, "Let war be made against your worms (or, serpents) which are in you; verily, they shall have fear of me as long as I have being; but you know their magical powers. Go to the place where my father Nu is, and say to him, 'Keep ward over the worms (or, serpents) which are in the earth and water.' And moreover, you shall make a writing for each of the nests of your serpents which are there, saying, 'Keep guard [lest you] cause injury to anything.' They shall know that I am removing myself [from them], but indeed I shall shine upon them. Since, however, they indeed wish for a father, you shall be a father to them in this land for ever. Moreover, let good heed be taken to the men who have my words of power, and to those whose mouths have knowledge of such things; verily my own words of power are there, verily it shall not happen that any shall participate with me in my protection, by reason of the majesty which has come into being before me. I will decree them to your son Osiris, and their children shall be watched over, the hearts of their princes shall be obedient (or, ready) by reason of the magical powers of those who act according to their desire in all the earth through their words of power which are in their bodies."

CHAPTER IV.

And the majesty of this god said, "Call to me the god Thoth," and one brought the god to him forthwith. And the Majesty of this god said to Thoth, "Let us depart to a distance from heaven, from my place, because I would make light and the god of light (Khu) in the Tuat and [in] the Land of Caves. You shall write down [the things which are] in it, and you shall punish those who are in it, that is to say, the workers who have worked iniquity (or, rebellion). Through you I will keep away from the servants whom this heart [of mine] loathes. You shall be in my place (*ast*) Asti, and you shall therefore be called, O Thoth, the 'Asti of Ra.' Moreover, I give you power to send (*hab*) forth . . . . .; thereupon shall come into being the Ibis (*habi*) bird of Thoth. I moreover give you [power] to lift up your hand before the two Companies of the gods who are greater than you, and what you do shall be fairer than [the work of] the god Khen; therefore shall the divine bird tekni of Thoth come into being. Moreover, I give you [Power] to embrace (*anh*) the two heavens with your beauties, and with your rays of light; therefore shall come into being the Moon-god (Aah) of Thoth. Moreover, I give you [power] to drive back (*anan*) the Ha-nebu; therefore shall come into being the dog-headed Ape (*anan*) of Thoth, and he shall act as governor for me. Moreover, you are now in my place in the sight of all those who see you and who present offerings to you, and every being shall ascribe praise to you, O you who are God."

CHAPTER V.

[*another ritual is described*] Then the Aged One himself (i.e., Ra) embraced (?) the god Nu, and spoke to the gods who came forth in the east of the sky, "Ascribe praise to the god, the Aged One, from whom I have come into being. I am he who made the heavens, and I set in order [the earth, and created the gods, and] I was with them for an exceedingly long period; then was born the year and . . . . . . but my soul is older than it (i.e., time). It is the Soul of Shu, it is the Soul of Khnemu (?), it is the Soul of Heh, it is the Soul of Kek and Kerh (i.e., Night and Darkness), it is the Soul of Nu and of Ra, it is the Soul of Osiris, the lord of Tettu, it is the Soul of the Sebak Crocodile-gods and of the Crocodiles, it is the Soul of every god [who dwells] in the divine Snakes, it is the Soul of Apep in Mount Bakhau (i.e., the Mount of Sunrise), and it is the Soul of Ra which pervades the whole world." [another ritual is described]

49. INSCRIPTION OF SEHETEPIBRE

Sehetepibre was a high official who served under Amenhemet III. In his tomb at Abydos was found a mortuary stela containing the following inscription. Not much of it is likely to be original, as we know sections of it were copied from the stela of an earlier official named Mentuhotep, who served under Senusret I. It is likely that the sebayt for his children was copied from elsewhere too.

Abydos Tomb

Now, I made this excellent tomb, and beautified its place. I gave contracts for the remuneration of the prophets of Abydos. I acted as "Son-Whom-He-Loves" in the conduct of the house of gold, in the secrets of the lord of Abydos. I conducted the work on the sacred barque, I fashioned its colors, I acted as Hakro of his Lord (at) every procession of Upwawet, making for him all the festal offerings, which the prophet read. I clothed the god at his processions by virtue of my office as master of secret things, and my duty as […]. I was one whose two hands were […] in adorning the god, a (sm-)priest with pure fingers. May I be a follower of the god, in order that I may be glorious and mighty at the stairway of the lord of Abydos.

The Instruction

The beginning of the teaching which he composed before his children. I speak great things, I cause you to hear, I cause you to know the eternal manner, the true manner of life—the passing of life in peace.

Adore the king, Nematre (Amenemhet III), living forever, in the midst of your bodies;
Enthrone his majesty in your hearts.
He is Esye in the hearts;
His two eyes, they search every body.
He is the Sun, seeing with his rays;
He illuminates the Two Lands more than the sun-disk.
He makes the Two Lands green more than a great Nile;
He hath filled the Two Lands with strength.
(He is) life, cooling the nostrils;
When he begins to rage, he is satisfied to […].
The treasures which he gives are food for those who are in his following;
He feeds those who tread his path.
The king is food,
His mouth is increase.
He is the one creating that which is;
He is the Khnum of all limbs;
The Begetter, who causes the people to be.
He is Bast protecting the Two Lands.
He who adores him shall [escape] his arm,
He is Sekhmet toward him who transgresses his command.
He is [gentle] toward him who has […].
Fight for his name,
Purify yourselves by his oath.
And ye shall be free from trouble.
The beloved of the king shall be blessed;
There is no tomb for one hostile to his majesty;
But his body shall be thrown to the waters.

Do ye this, and your limbs shall be sound;
Ye shall be glorious [...] forever.

50. LETTER OF KEMNY

This letter is an example of letters found written on papyri discovered at Kahun, where there lived a sizeable number of priests, officials and workers who were in charge of maintaining the funerary cult of Senusret II (Dynasty 12) after his death.

It is the servant of the estate Kemny who speaks:
[This is] a communication [to the lord, l.p.h.], to the effect that [all] business affairs [of the lord, l.p.h.], are prosperous and flourishing [wherever they are. In] the favor of Sobek the Crocodilopolite [and] his ennead, of Sobek, lord of Rosehwy, and his ennead, of the King of Upper and Lower Egypt Khakheperre (Senwosret II), the deceased, and of all the gods as I, your humble [servant], desire!

This is] a communication [to] the lord, l.p.h., about having attention paid to your royal slave Wadjhau in making him learn to write without being allowed to run away, in accordance with every good office that you, the lord, l.p.h., exercise, if you please, and about having attention paid to your household in accordance with every good office that you, the lord, exercise, if you please, because it is you, the lord, l.p.h., who can do whatever is necessary in turning(?) to me, your humble servant.

A communication to the effect that I, your humble servant, shall send the goods of the treasury with(?) Kheper[... (?)] when he comes southward since Soneb was already met as he was being sent coming southward after he had brought the nets in. It is a communication about this.

This is a communication to the lord, l.p.h. It is good if the lord, l.p.h. takes note.

Address: The lord, l.p.h., the steward Yey, l.p.h., from Kemny.

SECOND
INTERMEDIATE
PERIOD

51. THE NEFERHOTEP STELA

Neferhotep I was a king of the Thirteenth Dynasty. He was especially zealous in the care of the Osiris temple at Abydos, and there he erected a large sandstone stela, about six feet high and three feet wide, to testify to this. The text is in poor condition, but here are the parts of it we can read.

Year 2, under the majesty of King Neferhotep, born of the royal mother, Kemi, who is given life, stability, satisfaction, like Re, forever. His majesty appeared upon the throne of Horus in the palace, "[Structure]-of-Beauty." His majesty spake to the nobles, and companions, who were in his suite, the real scribes of the hieroglyphs, the masters of all secrets:

King's Speech

"My heart has desired to see the ancient writings of Atum; open for me for a great investigation; let the god know concerning his creation, and the gods concerning their fashioning, their offerings and [their] oblations . . . . (let) me know the god in his form, that I may fashion him as he was formerly, when they made the [statues] in their council, in order to establish their monuments upon earth." They have given to me the inheritance [of Re as far as] the circuit of the sun . . . . I will increase that which I shall have investigated, and they shall [increase] love for me to do according to that which they command."

Reply of Court

These companions said: "That which your *ka* has [commanded] is that which happens, O sovereign and lord. Let your majesty proceed to the libraries, and let your majesty see every hieroglyph."

Examination of Ancient Rolls

His majesty proceeded to the library. His majesty opened the rolls together with these companions. Lo, his majesty found the rolls of the House of Osiris, First of the Westerners, lord of Abydos.

King's Purpose

His majesty said to these companions: "My majesty hails my father Osiris, First of the Westerners, lord of Abydos. I will fashion [him, his limbs, his face, his fingers] according to that which my majesty has seen in the rolls [...] his [form] as King of Upper and Lower Egypt, at his coming forth from the body of Nut. . . . .

Messenger Sent to Abydos

His majesty had the king's-confidant, who was in his majesty's suite, called to him; his majesty said [to] him: "Betake yourself southward - - [together with] troops and marines. Sleep not night nor day until you arrive at Abydos; cause the First of the Westerners (Osiris) to proceed (forth). May I make his monuments according to the beginning."

Reply of Court

These companions said: "That which you command [is that which happens, O sovereign] and lord; you do all—in Abydos for your father, First of the Westerners."

Messenger Departs

This official betook himself southward [to do] that which his majesty commanded him. He arrived at [Abydos] - - -. The majesty of this god came to the sacred barge of the lord of eternity - - the banks of the river were flooded [with his fragrance and with] the odors of Punt. [The majesty of this god] arrived in the midst - - - -. One came to inform his majesty, saying: "This god has proceeded in peace."

King Goes to Abydos

His majesty proceeded [in] the sacred ship . . . . together with this god, causing that sacred offerings be presented to his father, the First of the Westerners: myrrh—and sacred things for Osiris, First of the Westerners, in all his names . . . . those hostile to the sacred barge were overthrown. Lo, the majesty of this god appeared in procession, his ennead united [with him]. Upwawet was before him, he opened the ways . . . .

King Executes Temple Works

Lo, [his majesty caused that this god should proceed] to [...] that he should rest [on] his throne in the house of gold; in order to fashion the beauty of his majesty and his ennead, his oblation-tables of every splendid, costly stone of God's-Land. Behold, [the king] himself led the work on them—gold, (for) his majesty was pure with the purity of a god. . . . .

King's Concluding Speech

. . . . Be vigilant for the temple, look to the monuments which I have made. I put the eternal plan before me, I sought that which was useful for the future by putting this example in your hearts, which is about to occur in this place, which the god made, because of my desire to establish my monuments in his temple, to perpetuate my contracts in his house. His majesty loves that which I have done for him, he rejoices over that which I have decreed to do, (for) triumph [has been given] to him. I am his son, his protector, he gives to me the inheritance of the earth." [I] am the king, great in strength, excellent in commandment. He shall not live who is hostile to me; he shall not breathe the air who revolts against me; his name shall not be among the living; his *ka* shall be seized before the officials; he shall be cast out for this god, [together with] him who shall disregard the command of my majesty and those who shall not do according to this command of my majesty, who shall not exalt me to this august god, who shall not honor that which I have done concerning his offerings [who shall not] give to me praise at every feast of this temple, of the entire [lay priesthood] of the sanctuary of this temple, and every office of Abydos. Behold, my majesty has made these monuments, for my father, Osiris, First of the Westerners, Lord of Abydos, because I so much loved him, more than all gods; that he might give to me a reward for this [which I have done], - - - consisting of millions of years . . . .

52. THE ADMONITIONS OF IPUWER

The date of this lament is disputed. The only surviving copy is on Papyrus Leiden I 344, which comes from the New Kingdom. Earlier scholars believed the work described conditions in the First Intermediate Period, but recently the view that it reflects the conditions of the Second Intermediate Period has become more common. The speaker is Ipuwer, clearly an Egyptian nobleman, who appears to be addressing the god Atum.

The collection of words, the gathering together of sayings, the quest of utterances with ingenious mind, made by the priest of Heliopolis, the .... Khekheperre-sonbu, called Onkhu.

He said: — Would that I had words that are unknown, utterances that are strange, (expressed) in new language that has never occurred (before), void of repetitions; not the utterance of past speech, spoken by the ancestors. I squeeze out my body for that which is in it, in the loosing of all that I say. For what has been said is repeated, when what has been said has been said; there is no ...... the speech of men of former times, when those of later times find it.

Not speaks one who has (already) spoken; there speaks one that is about to speak, and of whom another finds what he speaks. Not a tale of telling afterwards: 'they had made (it) before.' Not a tale which shall say: 'it is searching after what had perished; it is lies; there is none who shall recall his name to others'; I have said this in accordance with what I have seen, beginning with the first generation down to those who shall come afterwards; they are like what is past. Would that I knew that of which others are ignorant, even things that have never been related: in order that I might say them, and my heart might answer me; that I might explain to it concerning my sufferings, and thrust aside for it the load that is upon my back, (that I might speak) words about that which oppresses me, that I might express to it what I suffer through it, that I might say .... about my mood.

I am meditating on what has happened, the things that have come to pass throughout the land. Changes take place; it is not like last year. One year is more burdensome than the other. The land is in confusion and has become waste; it is made into ...... Right is cast outside. Wrong is inside the council-chamber. The plans of the gods are violated; their ordinances are neglected. The land is in distress. Mourning is everywhere. Towns and provinces are in sorrow. Everybody alike is subjected to wrongs. Reverence, an end is put to it. The lords of quiet are disturbed. Morning occurs every day, and the face shrinks at what has happened. I speak concerning it. My limbs are heavy-laden. I am distressed because of my heart. It is painful to hold my peace concerning it. Another heart would bend (under such a burden). A brave heart in evil case is the companion of its lord. Would that I had a heart able to suffer! Then I would rest upon it. I would load it with words of ...... I would ward off from it my malady.

He said to his heart: Come, my heart, that I may speak to you, and that you may answer for me my words, and may explain to me what is in the land ...... I am meditating on what has happened. Afflictions have entered in today; in the morning, . . . have not passed away. All people are silent concerning it. The entire land is in a great stir. There is nobody free from wrong; all people alike do it. Hearts are sad. He who gives commands is as one who receives commands; both of them are content. People rise in the morning to (find) it (so) daily, and (yet) hearts thrust it not aside. The state of yesterday therein is like today, and resembles it because of much. Men's fares are stolid; there is no one wise (enough) to know, there is no one angry (enough) to speak out. People rise to suffer every day. Long and heavy is my malady. The poor man has no strength to protect himself from him who is stronger than himself. It is pain to keep silence about things heard. It is misery to answer one who is ignorant. To find fault with a speech breeds hostility. The heart does not accept the truth. The reply to a speech is not tolerated. All that a man loves is his (own) utterance. Everyone puts his trust in ...... Rectitude has abandoned speech.

I speak to you, my heart; answer me. A heart that is approached does not keep silence. Behold the affairs of the slave are like (those of) the master. Manifold is that which weighs upon you.

53. MEDICAL PRESCRIPTIONS

The oldest known Egyptian surgical treatise on trauma is contained in the Edwin Smith Medical Papyrus, which comes from the Sixteenth or Seventeenth Dynasty. It is a composite text compiled by a single scribe, parts of which may come from the Old Kingdom, as it contains many archaic forms of expression. Here are some examples of the medical advice found within it.

CASE NINE: WOUND IN THE FOREHEAD PRODUCING A COMPOUND COMMINUTED FRACTURE OF THE SKULL (IV 19-V 5)

TITLE

Instructions concerning a wound in his forehead, smashing the shell of his skull.

EXAMINATION

If thou examinest a man having a wound in his forehead, smashing the shell of his head, (*conclusion in treatment*)

TREATMENT

Thou shouldst prepare for him the egg of an ostrich, triturated with grease (and) placed in the mouth of his wound. Now afterward thou shouldst prepare for him the egg of an ostrich, triturated and made into poultices for drying up that wound. Thou shouldst apply to it for him a covering for physician's use; thou shouldst uncover it the third day, (and) find it knitting together the shell, the color being like the egg of an ostrich.

That which is to be said as a charm over this recipe:
Repelled is the enemy that is in the wound!
Cast out is the evil that is in the blood,
The adversary of Horns, on everyl side of the mouth of Isis.
This temple does not fall down;
There is no enemy of the vessel therein.
I am under the protection of Isis;
My rescue is the son of Osiris.
Now afterward thou shouldst cool [it] for him [with] a compress of figs, grease, and honey, cooked, cooled, and applied to it.

Gloss A

As for: "A covering for physician's use," it is a bandage which is in the hand of the embalmer, and which he (the physician) applies to this remedy which is on this wound which is in his forehead. O Sekhmet; I am thy unique one, O Buto. I die not by thee; I die not by thee. I am the rejoicing one, I am the jubilating one. O son of Bastet, descend not upon me; O Dweller in the Sepsepu, approach me not, draw not near me. I am the king in the midst of his [shelter].

RECIPE FOR FEMALE TROUBLES (XX 13—XXI 3)

EXAMINATION

If thou examinest a woman suffering in her abdomen, so that the menstrual discharge cannot come away for her; and thou findest trouble in the upper part of her vulva, (conclusion follows in diagnosis).

DIAGNOSIS

Thou shouldst say concerning her: "It is obstruction of the blood in her vulva."

FIRST TREATMENT, INTERNAL AND EXTERNAL

Thou shouldst prepare for her:

Wam,	16
Grease,	18
Sweet beer,	8

Cooked and drunk for four days.

Besides preparing for her (the prescription called) "Discharge of the blood" (as follows): Oil, *tepnenet*, eye-paint, sweet frankincense. Mix, (and) anoint the organ therewith very frequently.

ALTERNATIVE EXTERNAL TREATMENT

Thou shouldst put *hezret*-ears into ointment. If afterward she has an evil odor, wipe her off and anoint her two labia therewith very frequently. Thou shouldst apply frankincense and incense between her two loins, (and) cause the smoke thereof to enter her flesh.

TWO RECIPES FOR THE COMPLEXION (XXI 3-8)

RECIPE FOR TRANSFORMING THE SKIN

A recipe for transforming the skin:

Honey,	1
Red natron,	1
Northern salt,	1

Triturate together (and) anoint therewith.

RECIPE FOR BEAUTIFYING THE FACE

Another (recipe) for beautifying the face:

Alabaster [kernels],	1
Natron [kernels],	1
Northern salt,	1
Honey,	1

Mix together, (and) anoint therewith.

RECIPE FOR TRANSFORMING AN OLD MAN INTO A YOUTH (XXI 9-XXII 10)

TITLE

Beginning of the Book of Transforming an Old Man into a Youth.

DIRECTIONS FOR MAKING THE RECIPE

Let there be brought a large quantity of *hemayet*-fruit, about two khar. It should be bruised and placed in the sun. Then when it is entirely dry let it be husked as grain is husked, and it should be winnowed until (only) the fruit thereof remains. Everything that comes therefrom shall be measured, (and) let it be sifted after the manner of the rthreshing floor with the sieve. Measure likewise everything that comes from these fruits and make them into two portions: one consisting of these fruits and the other even so. Treat one like the other.

(First Process)

Let it be set aside, mixed with water. Make into a soft mass and let it be placed in a new jar over the fire (and) cooked very thoroughly, making sure that they boil, evaporating the juice thereof and drying them, until it is like dry, without moisture therein. Let it be dug out (of the jar). Now when it is cool, let it be put into (another) jar in order to wash it in the river. Let it be washed thoroughly, making sure that they are washed by tasting the taste of this water that is in the jar (until) there is no bitterness at all therein. It should be placed in the sun, spread out on launderer's linen. Now when it is dry, it should be ground upon a grinding mill-stone.

(Second Process)

Let it be set aside in water. Make like a soft mass and let it be placed in a jar over the fire and cooked thoroughly, making sure that it boils, that the fluids of the mass may go forth therefrom. A man shall dip out the mass that has come of it with a dipper. Put into a *hin*-jar after it is (of the consistency) of clay. Rub and make thick its consistency. Dip out this mass and put upon a linen cover on the top of this *hin*-jar. Now afterward it should be put into a vase of costly stone.

DIRECTIONS FOR USE

Anoint a man therewith. It is a remover of wrinkles from the head. When the flesh is smeared therewith, it becomes a beautifier of the skin, a remover of blemishes, of all disfigurements, of all signs of age, of all weaknesses which are in the flesh. Found effective myriads of times.

RECIPE FOR SOME AILMENT OF THE ANUS AND VICINITY (XXII 11-14)

EXAMINATION XXII

If thou inspectest a man ailing in his anus, (and) whether standing or sitting, suffering very greatly with seizures in both his legs, (conclusion in treatment).

TREATMENT XXII

Thou shouldst give to him a recipe, an ointment of great protection (as follows): Acacia leaves, ground, triturated and cooked together. Smear a strip of fine linen therewith and place in the anus, that he may recover immediately.

54. THE COPTOS DECREE

This legal ruling from the reign of Nubkheperre Intef (Dynasty 17) was found on the wall of the temple of Min in Qift (Coptos) in Upper Egypt. It concerns the degradation of an official named Teti for treason.

Date

Year 3, third month of the second season, day 25, under the majesty of the King of Upper and Lower Egypt, Nubkheprure, Son of Re, Intef, who is given life, like Re, forever.

Title of Decree

Royal decree to:
The wearer of the royal seal, the count of Coptos, Minemhet; The king's-son, commandant of Coptos, Kinen;
The wearer of the royal seal, the priest of Min, scribe of the temple, Neferhotepur;
The whole army of Coptos,
And the entire lay priesthood of the temple.

Discovery of Culprit

Behold, there is brought to you this decree, to let you know: that my majesty, L. P. H., has sent the scribe of the sacred treasury of Amon, Siamon, and the [...] Amenusere, to make an inspection in the temple of Min; and that the lay priesthood of the temple of my father, Min, applied to my majesty, L. P. H., saying: "An evil thing is about to happen in this temple. Foes have been [stirred up] by, a curse to his name! Teti, son of Minhotep.

Punishment of Culprit

Cause him to be deposed from the temple of my father, Min; cause [him to be] cast out of his temple office, from son to son, and heir to heir; [...] upon the earth; take away his bread, his [food], and his joints of meat. His name shall not be remembered in this temple, according as it is done toward one like him, who is hostile toward the enemies of his god. His entries shall be cast out from the temple of Min, from the treasury, and on every book likewise.

No King or Dynast to Show Him Mercy

As for any king or any ruler, who shall be merciful to him, he shall not receive the white crown, he shall not wear the red crown, he shall not sit upon the Horus-throne of the living, the two patron goddesses shall not be gracious to him gas their beloved. As for any commandant or any official who shall apply to the king, L. P. H., to be merciful to him (the traitor), his (the applicant's) people, his goods, his fields shall be given to the sacred property of my father, Min, lord of Coptos.

Culprit's Office Given to Minemhet

No one of his connections, or of the family of his father or of his mother shall be inducted into this office, but this office shall be given to the wearer of the royal seal, the overseer of royal property, Minernhet. Its bread, its [food] and its joints of meat shall be given to him, established for him in writing, in the temple of my father Min, lord of Coptos, from son to son and heir to heir.

55. KAMOSE TABLET

Two texts prepared at Thebes for the pharaoh Kamose of the Seventeenth Dynasty have been uncovered, both of which recount the king's military campaigns against the Hyksos to the north. The later of the two is on a stone stela discovered at Karnak. The first was found on a hieratic writing-board (Carnarvon Tablet No. 1) at Deir el-Bahri and no doubt was intended to be placed on a stone stela later. It is incomplete, but the text is translated below.

Year III, Horus "Manifest-on-his-Throne," Two Goddesses "Repeating-Monuments," Horus of Gold "Making-Content-the-Two-Lands," King of Upper and Lower Egypt [Wazkhe]per[re^c, Son of Re^c] Kamose, given life like Re^c for ever and ever; beloved of Amenre^c, Lord of Karnak.

The powerful King within Thebes, Kamose, given life for ever, was beneficent King, and Re^c [caused] him to be a veritable King, and handed over to him the power in very truth. And His Majesty spoke in his palace to the council of grandees who were in his suite: "To what end am I cognizant of it, this power of mine, when a chieftain is in Avaris, and another in Kush, and I sit in league with an 'A'am and a Nubian, every man holding his slice of this Egypt? He who shares the land with me, I do not pass him as far as Memphis, the water of Egypt. See, he holds *Shmnn*, and no man rests, being toasted through servitude of the Setyu. I will grapple with him and rip open his belly; my desire is to deliver Egypt and to smite the Asiatics."

And the grandees of his Council said: "Behold, the Asiatics have [advanced] as far as Cusae, they have pulled out their tongues all together. We are at ease holding our (part of) Egypt. Elephantine is strong, and the midland is with us as far as Cusae. Men till for us the finest of their land; our cattle are in the papyrus marshes. Spelt is trodden out for our swine. Our cattle are not taken away......on account of it. He holds the land of the 'A'amu, we hold Egypt. But [whoever] comes to land and to oppose us, then would we oppose him."

And they were displeasing to the heart of his Majesty: "As to this counsel of yours ...... these 'A'amu who ...... [Behold I will fight] with the 'A'amu. Success will come. If ...... with weeping, the entire land [shall acclaim me the powerful ruler] within Thebes, Kamose the protector of Egypt."

I sailed down as a champion to overthrow the 'A'amu by the command of Amun, just of counsels, my army being valiant in front of me like a blast of fire, troops of Mazoi being in advance of our strongholds in order to spy out the Setyu in order to destroy their positions, East and West bringing their fat, and my army abounding in supplies everywhere. I sent forth a powerful troop of Mezay while I spent the day......to coop up......Teti the son of Piopi within Nefrusi. I was not going to allow him to escape. I turned back the 'A'amu who had encroached upon Egypt and he acted like one who......the might of the 'A'amu. I spent the night in my boat, my heart being happy.

When day dawned I was on him as it were a hawk. When the time of perfuming the mouth came I overthrew him, I destroyed his wall, I slew his folk, I caused his wife to go down to the river-bank. My army were like lions with their spoil, with slaves, herds, fat and honey, dividing up their possessions, their hearts being glad. The district of Nefr[usi] was falling; it was no great thing for us to confine its soil. The......Per-shak was lacking when I reached it; their horses were fled within. The garrison......

NEW KINGDOM

56. AUTOBIOGRAPHY OF AHMOSE OF NEKHEB

Ahmose of Nekheb, not to be confused with the pharaoh Ahmose, was a naval officer who served under the latter at the time of the founding of the New Kingdom (Dynasty 18). His career continued under Amenhotep I and Thutmose I. Ahmose was a native of Nekheb (El-Kab) and was buried there in a rock-cut tomb after his death. On two of its walls can be found his autobiography, which reads as follows:

Introduction

The naval captain Ahmose, son of the justified Abana, he says:

I speak to you, all men, I cause you to know the favours which have accrued to me: how I have been rewarded with gold seven times in the sight of the entire land, and with men slaves and women slaves in like manner, and how I have been vested with very many lands. For the name of a valiant man (resides) in that which he has done; it will not be obscured in this land forever.

Thus he spoke:

Service under Ahmose I

I had my upbringing in the town of Nekhab, my father being a soldier of the King of Upper and Lower Egypt, the justified Seknenre͗, whose name was Baba, son of Re͗dnet. I took service as soldier in his stead, in the ship of "The Wild Bull" in the time of the Lord of Both Lands, the justified Nebpehtire͗ (Ahmose I), when I was a youth, and had not taken a wife, but spent my nights in a hammock of net.

Now when I had established a household, I was taken upon the ship "Northern" because I was valiant; and I used to accompany the Sovereign upon foot in the course of his goings abroad in his chariot. And when they sat down before the town of Avaris, I displayed valour on foot in His Majesty's presence. Hereupon I was promoted to the "Manifestation in Memphis."

And when they proceeded to fight on the water in (the canal) Pzedku of Avaris, I made a capture and brought away a hand, and it was reported to the King's Informant, and the gold of valour was given to me.

Fighting was repeated in this place, and I proceeded to make a second capture there and brought away a hand. And the gold of valour was given to me over again.

And when they fought in the (part of) Egypt south of this town (i.e. Avaris), I brought away a male living prisoner. I went down into the water—(for he was taken prisoner on the city side)—and carried him over the water with me. It was reported to the King's Informant, and thereupon, behold, I was rewarded with gold afresh.

Then they proceeded to spoil Avaris; and I brought away spoil from there: one man; three women; a total of four heads. And His Majesty gave them to me for slaves.

And they sat down before Sharuhen for three years. And when His Majesty spoiled it I brought away spoil from there: two women, and a hand. And I was given the gold of valour. And lo, my spoil was given to me for slaves.

Now when His Majesty had slain the Mentyu of Asia, he fared southwards to Khenthennufer to destroy the Nubian Beduins. And His Majesty proceeded to make a great slaughter among them. Then I brought away spoil from there: two living men and three hands. And I was rewarded with gold afresh. Lo, two female slaves were given to me. And His Majesty fared northwards, his heart being glad, in valour and victory, having taken possession of the Southerners and Northerners.

Then there came 'A'ata of the South, whose doom his fate drew on, the gods of Upper Egypt taking hold on him. He was found by His Majesty in Tentta'a. And His Majesty brought him a living prisoner, and all his people as easy spoil. Then I brought two skirmishers as captives from the ship of 'A'ata. And five heads were given to me, and a portion of land, five arurae, in my city; and it was done likewise for the whole navy.

Then that wretch came, whose name was Teti'an. He had collected the rebels to himself. And His Majesty slew him, his crew being made non-existent. Then three heads and five arurae of land were given to me in my city.

Service under Amenhotep I

And I conveyed by water the King of Upper and Lower Egypt, the justified Zeserkere^c (Amenhotep I), when he was going southward to Kush to enlarge the frontiers of Egypt. And His Majesty smote down that Nubian Beduin in the midst of his army, he being brought away in a stranglehold, nor was any missing, he who sought flight being laid low like those who had never been. Now I was in front of our army; I fought in very deed, and His Majesty saw my valour. I brought away two hands, which were offered to His Majesty. And when they proceeded to search for his folk and his cattle, I brought away a living prisoner, who was offered to His Majesty. I brought His Majesty in two days to Egypt from the well Hraw. Then was I rewarded with gold. Then I brought away two female slaves as spoil, apart from those which I had offered to His Majesty. And they made me a Warrior of the Ruler.

Service under Thutmose I

And I conveyed by water the King of Upper and Lower Egypt, the justified ^cAkheperkere^c (Thutmose I), when he was going southward to Khenthennufer to abolish sedition throughout the lands, and to drive forth the influx of the desert region. And I displayed valour in his presence on the bad waters, in forcing the ships over the cataract. And I was thereupon made a Naval Captain.

And His Majesty [heard that]; and His Majesty became enraged thereat like a leopard; His Majesty shot, and his first arrow fastened in the neck of that wretch. And these [rebels] were...... and confounded at his royal Uraeus. And there was made there an hour of execution; their people were brought away as living prisoners. His Majesty fared northwards, with all foreign lands in his grasp, and that wretched Beduin of Nubia head downwards in front of His Majesty's falcon ship. And they landed at Karnak.

After that (His Majesty) made an expedition to Retenu,[1] that his ardour might be slaked throughout the foreign lands. His Majesty arrived at Naharayin;[2] His Majesty found that wretch while he was marshalling his forces. And His Majesty made a great slaughter among them. There was no counting of the living prisoners which His Majesty brought away from his victories. Now I was in front of our army, and His Majesty saw how valiant I was. I brought away a chariot and its horse, (with him) who was in it as a living prisoner. These were offered to His Majesty, and I was rewarded with gold afresh.

Conclusion

I am grown infirm, I have reached old age, and the favours shown me are like the first ......, ... I [rest] in the upland tomb which I myself made.

57. PRAYERS OF PAHERI

In another rock-cut tomb at El-Kab was found a lengthy mortuary text. The tomb belonged to Paheri, grandson of Ahmose (reading #56) and mayor of Nekheb (El-Kab) and Iunyt (Esna) during the reign of Thutmose I (Dynasty 18). The inscription contains many of the usual features of texts of this kind: the virtues of the deceased, prayers for a happy future, and the desire for visitors to make offerings on behalf of the deceased.

O excellent satisfier of the heart of his master! may you go in and out, your heart enlarged, in the favours of the lord of gods; a good burial after a long life of honourable service: when old age comes and you arrive at your place in the coffin and join the earth in the necropolis of the West, becoming a living soul. O may it enjoy bread, water, and breath, may it make its transformations into a heron, swallow, hawk, or egret, as you desire may you cross (the river) in the barge and not be driven back; and sail upon the waves of the stream; may your life come to you a second time; may your soul not depart from your body; may your soul be strong with the glorious spirits, may the noble souls speak with you, your image associated therewith receiving what is given upon earth; that you may drink water, smell the breezes and enjoy your heart's desire; may your eyes be given you to see, your ears to hear speech: your mouth speaking, your feet walking, may your hands and arms return to you; may your flesh be firm, your muscles pleasant, may you rejoice in all your limbs: may you reckon your limbs entirely healthful, no ills in you at all: your stomach with you in very truth, your heart of former days: may you go out to heaven and pi[erce the earth]: may a summons be given to you daily to the altar of Unnefer: may you receive cakes that have appeared in the Presence, offerings of the Lord of Ta-Zeser.

---

1   Canaan.
2   Mitanni.

(all the above) for the *ka* of the prince of Nekheb (El Kab), the prince of Anyt (Esneh): accountant of corn from Ant (Bender) to Nekheb, overseer watchful and free of weariness, the scribe Paheri, justified.

May you eat the *shens*-cake with the god at the great staircase of the lord of the divine cycle: may you return from it to the place where he is amongst the chief divine officials: may you walk with them and associate with the followers of Horns may you depart and come without being turned back or stopped at the gate of Tuat: may the doors of the horizon be opened to you, and the bolts unlock themselves for you; and may you arrive at the Hall of the two Truths, and the god who is in it salute you, and may you sit within the Amhet, and walk abroad in the City of the Nile, and your heart be enlarged with your ploughing in your portion of the Field of Aaru; may you have possessions of your own getting, and may the harvest of fruits come to you; may the rudder line be guided for you in the barge, and may you voyage according to the bent of your desire; may you go forth every morning and betake yourself home every evening; may a lamp be lighted for you at nighttime until the light (of the sun) rises upon your breast: may one say to you: "Come, come into this your house of the living!" may you see Ra on the horizon of heaven and view Amen at his rising: may your waking be good each day, destroying utterly for you all evil: may you draw out eternity in pleasure of heart, by the favour of the god who is in you: your heart (stomach) with you not torturing you, and your food remaining in its place.

(all the above) to the *ka* of the scribe Paheri, justified: he says,

"I am a departed soul that was good to his lord, wise of countenance, without failure of heart: I walked upon the road that I had planned, I knew that which results from life: I reckoned the boundaries in writing, the dykes with all the care of royal affairs: all matters of the royal house, L. P. H., were like the Nile flowing to the Great Green (sea). My mouth was firm in improvement for my master: I feared for the matter of the balance (of account): I did not forget (or turn away my face), there were no exchanges, I did not receive bribes from the results; my own [heart] guided me to the road of those who are praised of the king: my pen made me very learned: [it] justified [my words before the] auditors: it caused me to be distinguished. I informed the nobles in the Presence: my good quality advanced me. When I was placed upon the scales [I turned out true], when I was counted, I had the full number.

"I prospered when I went out and when I returned, my heart was likewise: I did not speak to deceive another: I knew the god who is in men, I recognized him: I knew this from that: I performed matters according to the commands, I did not alter a message in delivering it, I did not speak words above the station of serfs: I did not repeat to those who had no constant character. I brought enjoyment to the patient man—I who am praised and born of the body of the praised," the prince of Nekheb, Paheri, justified, begotten of the nurse (tutor) of the king's son, the scribe Atefrura justified, and born of the mistress of the house Kam, justified—he says,

"Hear, you who are to come into existence, I speak to you and there is no deceit in what I say.

"O you living and existing nobles and people upon earth, servants of gods, and priests and those connected with them, every scribe who takes the palette, skilful in divine words, and every excellent man of his inferiors, opening his mouth in boasting of his occupation—May Ra, lord of Eternity, favour you, and Nekhebt the white goddess of Nekhen: and all you who are established in your offices, may you bequeath them to your children.

"If you say 'May the king propitiate in accordance with that which is in the writings,' comings forth in answer to words in the formula of the ancients like the utterance of a god, and whosoever bends his hand in prayer may he act in the correct manner, and perform his devotion according to the rules, testifying from the reading of the command here written: 'may you have loaves by the thousand, beer by the thousand, and by the hundred thousand all things good and sanctified by offering and pure'—to the ghost of Osiris, the prince of Nekheb and Anyt, who satisfied the heart of the superintendent of seal-bearers in the southward voyage (of inspection), the excellent scribe of accounts, Paheri, justified.

"I say to you and cause you to know, that is by reading (this memorial): it has no boasts, there is no injury or protest in it, it is not a quarrel with another, nor a contradiction of a man who was miserable in his time: they are pleasant words of cheerfulness, which the heart wearies not to hear: it is the breath of the mouth which is not eaten, which hastens not and delays not: it will be well for you to do the like: [you would have] found [it true] if you had come here when I was in this land of the living, not a shame to my god. I have become a [soul] well furnished, I have established my place in Kher-neter; my possessions of all kinds are with me, that I may not refrain from answering ...... my father('s mummy) was an object of reverent care to him whom he created, he lacked not (the son) whom he had begotten.

"May your hearing of this be pleasant."

58. LETTER OF THE SCRIBE AHMOSE

Yet another Ahmose (not to be confused with either the pharaoh of that name or the officer) speaks to us from this period. He was a scribe who worked for a man named Peniati, director of public works at Armant (Hermonthis). Peniati, we know, lived during the reigns of Amenhotep I, Thutmose I, Thutmose II, Hatshepsut, and Thutmose III (Dynasty 18). In the following letter (from Papyrus Louvre 3230), Ahmose addresses Peniati's supervisor, the treasurer Tai, regarding a female slave.

(1) What Aahmose of Peniati says to his master, the treasurer Tai. (2) Why has the female slave who was with me been taken away and given to another? Am (3) I not thy servant, hearkening to thy commands by night as well as by day? (4) Let her value be taken along with mine, for truly she is a child, she cannot (5) work. Or let my lord command that I should be made to deliver her tasks (6) like those of any female slave of my lord: for her mother has written to me (7) saying, "It is thou who hast allowed my daughter to be taken away when she was here with thee, and I have refrained (8) from complaining to my lord since she was in thy charge in the capacity of a child." Thus said she to me by way of complaint.

59. THE CORONATION OF HATSHEPSUT

At Queen Hatshepsut's great mortuary temple at Deir el-Bahri, there are reliefs and inscriptions on the walls that tell her story. The section concerning her coronation is of special interest as a piece of propaganda. There is a scene with Hatshepsut's father, Thutmose I, sitting on his throne with his daughter Hatshepsut before him. Three rows of courtiers stand next to them. According to the accompanying inscription, Thutmose I had crowned Hatshepsut as his successor, rather than Hatshepsut's brother (and husband) Thutmose II. It reads as follows:

Thutmose I Summons His Daughter to be Crowned

There saw herb the majesty of her father, this Horus; how divine is her great fashioner! Her heart is glad, (for) great is her crown; she advocates her cause [in] truth, [exalter] of her royal dignity, and of that which her *ka* does. The living were set before her in his palace of [...]. Said his majesty to her: "Come, glorious one; I have placed (you) before me; that you may see your administration in the palace, and the excellent deeds of your *kas* that you may assume your royal dignity, glorious in your magic, mighty in your strength. You shall be powerful in the Two Lands; you shall seize the rebellious; you shall appear in the palace, your forehead shall be adorned with the double diadem, resting upon the head of the heiress of Horus, whom I begat, daughter of the white crown, beloved of Buto. The diadems are given to you by him who presides over the thrones of the gods.

Thutmose I Summons the Court

"My majesty caused that there be brought to him the dignitaries of the king, the nobles, the companions, the officers of the court, and the chief of the people, that they may do homage, to set the majesty of the daughter of this Horus before him in his palace of [...]." There was a sitting of the king himself, in the audience-hall of the right of the [court], while these people prostrated themselves in the court.

Thutmose I's Address to the Court

Said his majesty before them: "This my daughter, Khnemet-Amon, Hatshepsut, who lives, I have appointed [her] - -; she is my successor upon my throne, she it assuredly is who shall sit upon my wonderful seat. She shall command the people in every place of the palace; she it is who shall lead you; you shall proclaim her word, you shall be united at her command. He who shall do her homage shall live, he who shall speak evil in is blasphemy of her majesty shall die. Whosoever proclaims with unanimity the name of her majesty shall enter immediately into the royal chamber, just as it was done by the name of this Horus (viz., by my name). For you are divine, O daughter of a god, for whom even the gods fight; behind whom they exert their protection every day according to the command of her father, the lord of the gods."

The Court and People Acknowledge the New Queen

The dignitaries of the king, the nobles and the chief of the people hear this command for the advancement of the dignity of his daughter, the king of Upper and Lower Egypt, Makere (Hatshepsut) living forever. They kissed the earth at his feet, when the royal word fell among them; they praised all the gods for the King of Upper and Lower Egypt, Okheperkere (Thutmose I), living forever. They went forth, their mouths rejoiced, they published his proclamation [to] them. All the people of all the dwellings of the court heard; they came, their mouths rejoicing, they proclaimed (it) beyond everything, dwelling on dwelling therein was announcing (it) in his name; soldiers on soldiers [...], they leaped and they danced for the double joy of their hearts. They [proclaimed], they [proclaimed] the name of her majesty as king; while her majesty was a youth, while the great god was [turning] their hearts to his daughter, Makere (Hatshepsut), living forever, when they recognized that it was the fa[ther] of the divine daughter, and thus they were excellent in her great soul beyond everything. As for any man who shall love her in his heart, and shall do her homage every day, he shall shine, and he shall flourish exceedingly; [but] as for any man who shall speak against the name of her majesty, the god shall determine his death immediately, even by the gods who exercise protection behind her every day. The majesty of this her father has published this, all the people have united upon so the name of this his daughter for king. While her majesty was a youth, the heart of his majesty inclined to [her] exceedingly.

Proclamation of the Queen's Names

His majesty commanded that the ritual priests be brought to [proclaim] her great names that belonged to the assumption of the dignities of her royal crown and for insertion in (every) work and every seal of the Favorite of the Two Goddesses, who makes the circuit north of the wall, who clothes all the gods of the Favorite of the Two Goddesses. He has recognized the auspiciousness of the coronation on New Year's Day as the beginning of the peaceful years and of the spending of myriads (of years) of very many jubilees. They proclaimed her royal names, for the god caused that it should be in their hearts to make her names according to the form with which he had made them before:

Her great name, Horus: [Wosretkew], forever;
Her great name, Favorite of the Two Goddesses: "Fresh in years," good goddess, mistress of offering;
Her great name, Golden Horus: "Divine of diadems;"
Her great name of King of Upper and Lower Egypt: "Makere, who liveth forever."
It is her real name which the god made beforehand.

60. ANNALS OF THUTMOSE III

Thutmose III had his annals inscribed on walls he had constructed around the great temple of Amun at Karnak. They form the most complete account of the military campaigns of any Egyptian king that we have. The following excerpt from these annals recounts the famed Battle of Megiddo, in which the pharaoh defeated a powerful coalition of Canaanite kings.

Departure from Gum

[Year 23] first month of the third season (ninth month), on the fifth day; departure from this place in might, - - in power, and in triumph, to overthrow that wretched foe, to extend the boundaries of Egypt, according as his father, Amon-Re, [had commanded - -] that he seize.

Arrival at Yehem

Year 23, first month of the third season (ninth month), on the sixteenth day, (he arrived) at the city of Yehem.

Council of War

[His majesty] ordered a consultation with his valiant troops, saying as follows: "That [wretched] enemy, [the chief] of Kadesh, has come and entered into Megiddo; he [is there] at this moment. He has gathered to himself the chiefs of [all] the countries [which are] on the water of Egypt, and as far as Naharin, consisting of [the countries] of the Kharu, the Kode, their horses, their troops, thus he speaks, 'I have arisen to [fight against his majesty] in Megiddo.' Tell me."

Advice of the Officers

They spoke in the presence of his majesty, "How is it, that [we] should go upon this road, which threatens to be narrow? While they [come] and say that the enemy is there waiting, [hold]ing the way against a multitude. Will not horse come behind [horse and man behind] man likewise? Shall our [advance-guard] be fighting while our [rear-guard] is yet standing yonder in Aruna not having fought? There are yet two (other) roads: one road, behold, it [will] - - us, for it comes forth at Taanach, the other, [behol]d, it will [bring us upon] the way north of Zefti, so that we shall come out to the north of Megiddo. Let our victorious lord proceed upon [the road] he desires; (but) cause us not to go by a difficult road."

Decision of the King

Then - - [messengers] concerning [this] design which they had uttered, in view of what had been said [by] the majesty of the Court, L. P. H.: "I [swear], as Re loves me, as my father Amon, favors me, as my [nostrils] are rejuvenated with satisfying life, my majesty will proceed upon this road of Aruna. Let him who will among you, go upon those roads you have mentioned, and let him who will among you, come in the following of my majesty. Shall they think among those enemies whom Re detests: 'Does his majesty proceed upon another road? He begins to be fearful of us,' so will they think."

Submission of the Officers

They spoke before his majesty: "May your father Amon, lord of Thebes, presider over Karnak, [grant you life] Behold, we are the following of your majesty in every place to where [your majesty] proceeds, as the servant is behind [his] master."

Departure from Yehem

[Then his majesty] commanded the entire army [to march] - - [upon] that road which threatened to be [narrow. His majesty] swore, saying: "None shall go forth [in the way] before my majesty." He went forth at the head of his army himself, [showing the way] by his (own) footsteps; horse behind [horse], [his majesty] being at the head of his army.

Arrival at Arum

Year 23, first month of the third season (ninth month), on the nineteenth day; the watch in [safety] in the royal tent was at the city of Aruna. "My majesty proceeded northward under (the protection of my) father, Amon-Re, lord of Thebes, [who went] before me, while Harakhte [strengthened my arms] (my) father, Amon-Re, lord of Thebes, victorious of the sword over my majesty."

Battle in the Mountains

[The enemy] went forth in numerous battle array. The southern wing was in Taa[nach], the northern wing was on the ground south of Megiddo. His majesty cried out to them before they fell; behold, that wretched foe of [the city of] Aruna.

Danger of the Rear

Now, the rear of the victorious army of his majesty was at the city of Aruna, the front was going forth to the valley of ... ; they filled the opening of this valley. Then [they] said in the presence of his majesty, L. P. H.: "Behold, his majesty goes forth with his victorious army, and it has filled the hollow of the valley; let our victorious lord hearken to us this time and let our lord protect for us the rear of his army and his people. Let the rear of this army come forth to us behind; then shall they (also) fight against these barbarians; then we shall not (need to) take thought for the rear of our army." His majesty halted outside and waited there, protecting the rear of his victorious army.

Exit from the Mountains

Behold, when the front had reached the exit upon this road, the shadow had turned, and when his majesty arrived at the south of Megiddo on the bank of the brook of Kina, the seventh hour was turning, (measured) by the sun.

Camp in Plain of Megiddo

Then was set up the camp of his majesty, and command was given to the whole army, saying: "Equip yourselves! Prepare your weapons! for we shall advance to fight with that wretched foe in the morning." [Therefore] the king rested in the royal tent, the [affairs] of the chiefs were arranged, and the provisions of the attendants. The watch of the army went about, saying, "Steady of heart! Steady of heart! Watchful! Watchful! Watch for life at the tent of the king." One came to say to his majesty, "The land is well, and the infantry of the South and North likewise."

Battle of Megiddo

Year 23, first (month) of the third season (ninth month), on the twenty-first day, the day of the feast of the new moon, [corresponding to] the royal coronation, early in the morning, behold, command was given to the entire army to move - - . His majesty went forth in a chariot of electrum, arrayed in his weapons of war, like Horus, the Smiter, lord of power; like Montu of Thebes, while his father, Amon, strengthened his arms. The southern wing of this army of his majesty was on a hill south of the [brook of]a Kina, the northern wing was at the northwest of Megiddo, while his majesty was in their center, with Amon as the protection of his members, [...] the valor - - of his limbs. Then his majesty prevailed against them at the head of his army, and when they saw his majesty prevailing against them they fled headlong to Megiddo in fear, abandoning their horses and their chariots of gold and silver. The people hauled them (up), pulling (them) by their clothing, into this city; the people of this city having closed (it) against them [and lowered] clothing to pull them up into this city. Now, if only the army of his majesty had not given their heart to plundering the things of the enemy, they would have [captured] Megiddo at this moment, when the wretched foe of Kadesh and the wretched foe of this city were hauled up in haste to bring them into this city. The fear of his majesty had entered [their hearts], their arms were powerless, his serpent diadem was [victorious] among them.

The Spoil

Then were captured their horses, their chariots of gold and silver were made spoil; their champions lay stretched out like fishes on the ground. The victorious army of his majesty went around counting their portions. Behold, there was captured the tent of that wretched foe [in] which was [his] son - - . The whole army made jubilee, giving praise to Amon for the victory which he had granted to his son on [this day, giving praise] to his majesty, exalting his victories. They brought up the booty which they had taken, consisting of hands, of living prisoners, of horses, chariots of gold and silver, of - - .

The Rebuke

Then his majesty spoke [on hearing] the words of his army, saying: "Had you captured [this city] afterward, behold, I would have given Re this day; because every chief of every country that has revolted is within it; and because it is the capture of a thousand cities, this capture of Megiddo. Capture [mightily, mightily] - - ."

Siege of Megiddo

[His majesty commanded] the [officers] of the troops to go - - , [assigning to] each his place. They measured this city, [surrounding it] with an enclosure, walled about with green timber of all their pleasant trees. His majesty himself was upon the fortification east of this city, [inspecting] - - .

It was [wa]lled about with a thick wall - - - with its thick wall. Its name was made: "Menkheperre (Thutmose III)-is-the-Surrounder-of-the-Asiatics." People were stationed to watch over the tent of his majesty; to whom it was said: "Steady of heart! Watch." His majesty [commanded, saying: "Let not one among them [come forth] outside, beyond this wall, except to come out in order to [knock] at the door of their fortification."

Now, all that his majesty did to this city, to that wretched foe and his wretched army, was recorded on (each) day by its (the day's) name, under the title of: "- - - -". Then it was recorded upon a roll of leather in the temple of Amon this day.

Surrender of Megiddo

Behold, the chiefs of this country came to render their portions, to do obeisance to the fame of his majesty, to crave breath for their nostrils, because of the greatness of his power, because of the might of the fame of his majesty - - the country came to his fame, bearing their gifts, consisting of silver, gold, lapis lazuli, malachite; bringing clean grain, wine, large cattle, and small cattle - - for the army of his majesty. [Each of the Kode] among them bore the tribute southward. Behold, his majesty appointed the chiefs anew for - -.

Spoil of Megiddo

- - living prisoners; 83 hands; 2,041 mares; 191 foals; 6 stallions; - - young - - ; a chariot, wrought with gold, (its) [pole] of gold, belonging to that foe; a beautiful chariot, wrought with gold, belonging to the chief of [Megiddo]; 892 chariot[s] of his wretched army; total, 924 (chariots); a beautiful [suit] of bronze armor, belonging to that foe; a beautiful [suit] of bronze armor, belonging to the chief of Megiddo; - - , 200 suits of armor, belonging to his wretched army; 502 bows; 7 poles of (mry) wood, wrought with silver, belonging to the tent of that foe. Behold, the army of [his majesty] took , 297 - - , 1,929 large cattle, 2,000 small cattle, 20,500 white small cattle.

61. INSCRIPTION OF REKHMIRE

Near Thebes lies the rock-cut tomb of Rekhmire, vizier of Thutmose III during the latter part of his reign, the highest official of the country next to the pharaoh. One of the inscriptions in the tomb depicts the appointment of Rekhmire to this high office and instructions he was given by the pharaoh at that time. We believe these instructions were standard. Unfortunately, they are not in the best condition and are hard to read.

Regulation laid upon the vizier, Rekhmire. The officials were brought to the audience-hall, [his majesty] commanded that the vizier, Rekhmire, be presented [for] appointment for the first time.

His majesty spoke before him: "[Take heed] to yourself for the hall of the vizier; be watchful over all that is done therein. Behold, it is a support of the whole land; behold, as for the vizier, behold, he is not sweet, behold, bitter is he, when he addresses - - of copper is he, a wall of gold for the house of his - - . Behold, he is not one setting his face toward the officials and councilors, neither one making [brethren] of all the people. Behold, - - - a man is in the dwelling of his lord, he [does] good for him; behold [he] does not - - for another.

Behold, the petitioner of the South, [the North] and the whole land, shall come, supplied - - - - - - . May you see to it for yourself, to do everything after that which is in accordance with law; to do everything according to the right thereof. Do not - - - that he may be just. Behold, as for an official, when he has reported water and wind of all his doings, behold, his deeds shall not be unknown - -. - - - - - -, he is not brought in because of the speech of the responsible officer, [but] it is known by the speech of his messenger as the one stating it; he is by the side of the responsible officer as the speaker; he is not one lifting up the voice, a messenger petitioning or an official. Then one shall not be ignorant of his deeds; lo, it is the safety of an official to do things according to the regulation, by doing that which is spoken by the petitioner . . . .

It is an abomination of the god to show partiality. This is the teaching: you shall do the like, shall regard him who is known to you like him who is unknown to you, and him who is near to [you] like him who is far; an official who does like this, then shall he flourish greatly in the place. Do not [avoid] a petitioner, nor nod your head when he speaks. As for him who draws near, who will approach you, do not - - - - the things which he says in speaking. You shall punish him when you have let him hear that on account of which you punish him. Lo, they will say, the petitioner loves him who nods the head - - - - - - .

Be not enraged toward a man unjustly, but be enraged concerning that about which one should be enraged; show forth the fear of you; let one be afraid of you, (for) a prince is a prince of whom one is afraid. Lo, the true dread of a prince is to do justice. Behold, if a man shows forth the fear of him a myriad of times, there is something of violence in him. Be not known to the people; and they shall not say: "He is (only) a man."

He who speaks a lie shall go forth according to his docket, Lo, [...] you shall do your office, as you do justice. Lo, one shall desire to do justice . . . . Lo, one shall say of the chief scribe of the vizier: "A scribe of justice," shall one say of him. Now, as for the hall, wherein you hold hearings there shall be a broad-hall therein . [He who dispenses] justice before all the people, he is the vizier. Behold, a man shall be in his office, (as long as) he shall do things according to that which is given to him. Lo, a man is [...] when he shall act according to that which has been told him. Do not - - your - - in - - that you know the law thereof. Lo, let one [- -] to the proud-hearted; the king loves the fearful more than the proud-hearted. Do according to [that which is given] to you; lo, ...

𓀀𓁐𓃀𓅓𓆓𓇳𓈖𓉐𓊖𓋹𓌂𓍑𓎛𓏏𓀀𓁐𓃀𓅓𓆓𓇳𓈖𓉐𓊖𓋹𓌂𓍑𓎛𓏏

62. SPHINX STELA OF THUTMOSE IV

A large red granite tablet sitting between the paws of the Great Sphinx at Giza commemorates the maintenance of the Sphinx by Thutmose IV (Dynasty 18), who his reign cleared away the sands covering the great monument in the first year of his reign. It is sometimes called the "Dream Stela," because it describes Thutmose as having received his commission to rescue the Sphinx by the god in a dream.

Introduction

Year 1, third month of the first season, day 19, under the majesty of Horus: Mighty-Bull-Begetting-Radiance; Favorite of the Two Goddesses: Enduring-in-Kingship-like-Atum; Golden Horus: Mighty-of-Sword, Repelling-the-Nine-Rows; King of Upper and Lower Egypt; Menkheprure, Son of Re: [Thutmose, Shining] in Diadems; beloved of - - , given life, stability, satisfaction, like Re, forever. Live the Good God, son of Atum, Protector of Harakhte, living image of the All-Lord; sovereign, begotten of Re; excellent heir of Khepri; beautiful of face like his father; who came forth [...] equipped with the form of Horus upon him; a king who - - the gods; who - - favor with the ennead of gods; who purifies Heliopolis, who satisfies Re; who beautifies Memphis; who presents truth to Atum, who offers it to Him-Who-is-South-of-His-Wall (Ptah); who makes a monument by daily offering to Horus; who does all things, seeking benefits for the gods of South and North; who builds their houses of limestone; who endows all their offerings; son of Atum, of his body, Thutmose, Shining in Diadems, like Re; heir of Horus upon his throne, Menkheprure, given life.

Youth of Thutmose

When his majesty was a stripling like Horus, the youth in Khemmis, his beauty was like the protector of his father, he seemed like the god himself. The army rejoiced because of love for him, the king's-children and all the nobles. Then his strength overflowed him, and he repeated the circuit of his might like the son of Nut.

Hunting Expedition

Behold, he did a thing that gave him pleasure upqn the highlands of the Memphite nome, upon its southern and northern road shooting at a target with copper bolts, hunting lions and wild goats, coursing in his chariot, his horses being swifter than the wind; together with two of his followers, while not a soul knew it.

Midday Rest

Now, when his hour came on for giving rest to his followers, (it was always) at the [shoulder] of Harmakhis, beside Sokar in Rosta, Renutet in [...] in heaven, Mut - - of the northern - the mistress of the Wall of the South, Sekhmet presider over Khas [...] the splendid place of the beginning of time, over against the lords of Khereha, the sacred road of the gods to the necropolis west of On (Heliopolis). Now, the very great statue of Khepri, rests in this place; the great in prowess, the splendid in strength; upon which the shadow of Re tarries. The quarters of Memphis and all the cities which are by him come to him, (raising) their hands for him in praise to his face, bearing great oblations for his *ka*.

The Vision

One of those days it came to pass that the king's-son, Thutmose, came, coursing at the time of midday, and he rested in the shadow of this great god. A [vision] of sleep seized him at the hour (when) the sun was in the zenith, sand he found the majesty of this revered god speaking with his own mouth, as a father speaks with his son, saying: "Behold me! See me! my son Thutmose. I am your father, Harmakhis-Khepri-Re-Atum, who will give to you my kingdom on earth at the head of the living. You shall wear the white crown and the red crown upon the throne of Keb, the hereditary prince. The land shall be yours in its length and breadth, that which the eye of the All-Lord shines upon. The food of the Two Lands shall be yours, the great tribute of all countries, the duration of a long period of years. My face is yours, my desire is toward you. You shall be to me a protector (for) my manner is as I were ailing in all my limbs [...]. The sand of this desert upon which I am, has reached me; turn to me, to have that done which I have desired, knowing that you are my son, my protector; [come here], behold, I am with you, I am your leader." When he had finished this speech, this king's-son [awoke] hearing this - - ; he understood the words of this god, and he kept silent in his heart. He said: "Come, let us hasten to our house in the city; they shall protect the oblations for this god which we bring for him: oxen [...] and all young vegetables; and we shall give praise [to] Wennofer, --- Khaff[re], the statue made for Atum-Harmakhis ---.

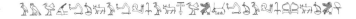

63. THE INSTRUCTION OF ANY

The Instruction of Any, presented as advice from the scribe Any to his son, differs from earlier works of the sebayt *genre in that it is directed toward members of the common class, rather than to the nobility. Papyrus Boulaq 4, from Dynasty 21 or 22, contains the most complete version, but fragments of the work appear in several extant papyri and ostraca. The work was likely composed during the Eighteenth Dynasty.*

Follow My Words

(I tell thee) that which is excellent, that which thou shalt observe (?) in thine heart. Do it, and so thou wilt be good, and all evil is far from thee. — — — — It will be said of thee: a good character, and not: he is ruined, he is idle. Accept my words, and so will all evil be far from thee.

Be Prudent in Speech (?)

[*Unintelligible.*]

Be Reticent

Guard thyself against ought that injureth (?) great people, by talking of secret affairs. If (anyone) speaketh (of them) in thine house, make (thyself?) deaf — — — —.

Boast Not of Thy Strength (?)

[*Unintelligible.*]

Found a Family

Take to thyself a wife when thou art a youth, that she may give thee a son. Thou shouldest beget him for thee whilst thou art yet young, and shouldest live to see him become a man (?). Happy is the man who hath much people, and he is respected because of his children (?).

Be Pious

Celebrate the feast of thy god — — — — —. God is wroth with him that disregardeth it. Let witnesses stand by thine offering; it is best (?) for him that hath done it (?) — — — Singing, dancing, and frankincense appertain to his maintenance (?), and the receiving of reverence appertaineth to his possessions.' Bestow them on the god in order to magnify his name — — — —.

Be Discreet on Visits

Enter not the (house ?) of another, – – – –. Gaze not on that which is not right in (his ?) house; thine eye may see it, but thou keepest silent. Speak not of it to another outside, that it may not become for thee a great crime worthy of death, when it is heard (?).

Beware of the Harlot

Beware of a strange woman, one that is not known in her city. Wink (?) not at her – – – – have no carnal knowledge of her (?). (She is) a deep water whose twisting men know not. A woman that is far from her husband, "I am fair," she saith to thee every day, when she hath no witnesses – – – –. It is a great crime worthy of death, when one heareth of it, and although it is not related outside – – – –.

Be Reserved in Thy Conduct

Go not in and out in the court of justice, that thy name may not stink – – – –. Speak not much, be silent, that thou mayest be happy. Be not a gossip.

The True Piety

The dwelling of God, it abhorreth clamour. Pray with a loving heart, all the words whereof are hidden. Then he will do what thou needest; he will hear what thou sayest and accept thine offering.

Piety Towards Parents

Offer water to thy father and thy mother, who rest in the desert-valley – – – –. Omit not to do it, that thy son may do the like for thee.

Be Not A Drunkard

Take not upon thyself (?) to drink a jug of beer. Thou speakest, and an unintelligible utterance issueth from thy mouth. If thou fallest down and thy limbs break, there is none to hold out a hand to thee. Thy companions in drink stand up and say: "Away with this sot !" If there (then) cometh one to seek thee in order to question thee, thou art found lying on the ground, and thou art like a little child.

Lead an Honest Life

Go not forth from thine house to one that thou knowest not (?) – – – – let every place that thou favourest be known.

Be Mindful of Death

Make for thyself a fair abode in the desert-valley, the deep which will hide thy corpse. Have it before thine eyes in thine occupations – – – – even as (?) the great elders, who rest in their sepulchre (?). He who maketh it (for himself) meeteth with no reproof; good is it if thou too art furnished in like manner. Thy messenger 1 cometh to thee – – – – he placeth himself in front of thee (?). Say not "I am too young for thee to carry off," for thou knowest not thy death. Death cometh and leadeth away the babe that is still in the bosom of its mother, even as the man when he hath become old.

[*Here begins a fresh section of some length, in which, firstly, caution in social intercourse is enjoined—most of it frankly unintelligible.*]

Behold, I tell thee yet other excellent things, which thou shalt heed (?) in thine heart. Do them, and thou wilt be happy, and all evil will be far from thee – – – –.

Caution in Social Intercourse

Keep thyself far from an hostile man, and take him not to thee for a companion. Make to thyself a friend (rather) of one that is upright and righteous, when thou seest what he hath done (?) – – – –.

Make not a friend of the slave of another, whose name stinketh – – – If one pursueth him in order to seize him, and to take away him that is in his house, thou art wretched and sayest: "What am I to do ?"– –

Possessions Do Not Make for Happiness

A man constructeth a house for himself. A piece of ground (?) is laid out for thee, thou hast fenced in (?) a garden of herbs in front of thine arable land; thou hast planted sycamores inside – – – – and thou fillest thine hand with all flowers that thine eye perceiveth. (But) with them all one is wretched — — — —.

Put not thy trust in the possessions of another; guard thyself from doing that (?). Rely not on the things of another — — say not: "The father of my mother hath an house — —. For when it cometh to the division with thy brethren, thy share (is only) a storehouse. If thy god grants that a child be born to thee — — — —.

Be Respectful

Sit not when another standeth, one that is older than thou, or that hath occupied himself in his calling longer than thou — — —.

[*The subject with which the passages immediately following are concerned, cannot even be conjectured, so are here omitted.*]

Usefulness of Knowledge

Men do all that thou sayest, if thou art skilled in the writings. Devote thyself to the writings, and put them in thine heart, and then all that thou sayest is excellent. To whatsoever office the scribe is appointed, he consulteth the writings. There is no son for the superintendent of the treasury, no heir for the superintendent of the fortress — — — — the offices, which have no children — — —.

Be Cautious in Speech

Speak not out thine heart to the … man — — —. A wrong word that hath come forth from thy mouth, if (he ?) repeateth it, thou makest enemies (for thyself). A man falleth in ruin because of his tongue — — — —. A man's belly is broader than a granary, and is full of all manner of answers. Choose thou out the good and speak them, while the bad remain imprisoned in thy belly. — — — —

Of a truth thou will ever be with me and answer him that injureth me with falsehood, in spite of God who judgeth the righteous. His fate cometh to carry him off.

Relations with Thy God

Make offering to thy god and keep thyself from trespassing against him. Inquire not concerning his form; walk not with swaggering gait, when he goeth forth in procession; press not forward to carry him. — — — — Let thine eye mark how he is wroth, and have respect for his name. It is he that giveth power (?) to millions of forms, and (only) he is made great whom he maketh great. The god of this land is the sun which is in the horizon, (but) his images are on earth; to them let incense be offered daily.

Be Grateful to Thy Mother

Double the bread that thou givest to thy mother, and carry her as she carried (thee). She had a heavy load in thee, and never left it to me. When thou wast born after thy months, she carried thee yet again about her neck, and for three years her breast was in thy mouth. She was not disgusted at thy dung, she was not disgusted and said not: "What do I?"

She put thee to school, when thou hadst been taught to write, and daily she stood there …with bread and beer from her house.

When thou art a young man and takest to thee a wife and art settled in thine house, keep before thee how thy mother gave birth to thee, and how she brought thee up further in all manner of ways. May she not do thee harm nor lift up her hands to God, and may he not hear her cry.

On Wealth and its Instability

Eat not bread, if another is suffering want, and thou dost not stretch out the hand to him with bread. — — — —. One is rich and another is poor — — — —. He that was rich in past years, is this year a groom. Be not greedy about filling thy belly — — — —. The course of the water of last year, it is this year in another place. Great seas have become dry places, and banks have become abysses. — — — —

On Paying Visits

Go not freely to a man in (his) house, but enter in (only) when thou art bidden. When he hath said to thee "Praise to thee" with his mouth, — — — —. [*Then after an unintelligible passage:*] give him to God and give him daily again to God. The morrow is as to-day. Thou wilt see what God will do, if he besmircheth (?) him that hath besmirched (?) thee.

Keep Thyself Far from Tumults

Enter not into a crowd, if thou findest that it standeth ready for beating — — — — that thou mayest not be blamed in the Court before the magistrates after the tendering of evidence. Keep thee far from hostile people — — — —.

Treat Thy Wife Well

Act not the official over thy wife in her house, if thou knowest that she is excellent. Say not unto her: "Where is it? Bring it us," if (?) she hath put (it) in the right place. Let thine eye observe and be silent, that so (?) thou mayest know her good deeds. (She is) happy when thine hand is with her — — — —. Thereby the man ceaseth to stir up strife in his house — — —.

Be Careful of Women

Go not after a woman, in order that she may not steal thine heart away.

Behaviour Towards Superiors

Answer not a superior who is enraged, get out of his way. Say what is sweet, when he saith what is bitter to any one, and make calm his heart. Contentious answers carry rods, and thy strength collapseth. Rage directeth itself (?) against thy business, therefore vex (?) not thine own self. He turneth about and praiseth thee quickly, after his terrible hour. If thy words are soothing for the heart, the heart inclineth to receive them. Seek out silence for thyself, and submit to what he doeth.

Stand Well with the Police

Make a friend of the herald of thy quarter, and let him not become enraged with thee. Give him dainties when there are any in thine house, and pass him not by at his prayers. Say to him: "Praise to thee"— — —.

[An unintelligible passage is followed by a dialogue, with which the book concludes.]

Conclusion

The scribe Khenshotep answered his father, the scribe Anii: "Ah, would that I were as thou (?) — — — — so would (?) I act in accordance with thy teaching, that (?) the son should be promoted to his father's place — — — —. Thou art a man with lofty desires, all of whose words are choice. A son that imagineth (?) evil within himself, he saith — — — — in books. Thy words are soothing for mine heart, and mine heart inclineth to receive them. Mine heart rejoiceth. (But) let not thine excellence be too abundant, — — — — a boy doth not yet do according to the teaching that instructs, albeit (?) the books are on his tongue."

The scribe Anii answered his son, the scribe Khenshotep: "Trust not in these hazardous things (?). Avoid further complaining, mine heart heedeth it not. Even the fighting bull, that hath slain the stall, cannot leave the ring, and receiveth his instructions from the drover. The fierce lion abateth his rage and doefully passeth by the ass. The horse submitteth to his yoke. The dog, he hearkeneth to words and followeth his master. The *kaeri*-animal carrieth the … vessel, which his mother carried not. The goose alighteth on the cool pool, when it is chased, and then fretteth itself in the net. Nubians are taught to speak Egyptian, and Syrians, and all strangers likewise. I too have discoursed on all the callings that thou mayest hear, and know what is to be done."

[What the son replies to this is unintelligible; he probably alludes to the fact that most men are worthless.] There is a multitude of all that is evil (?), and none knoweth his teaching. If there be one that is prudent, the bulk is foolish. *[He then probably would vow obedience to his father:]* All thy words are excellent — — — I give thee oaths, place them upon thy way.

The scribe Anii answered his son, the scribe Khenshotep: "Turn thy back on these many words, which are far from being heard. The bent (?) stick that lieth in the field, exposed to (?) sun and shade, the craftsman fetcheth it and maketh it straight, and maketh it into the whip of a notable. But the straight piece of wood, that maketh he into a board (?). O heart that cannot deliberate, is it thy will to give oaths, or dost thou miscarry?"

[Anii then probably expresses the hope that his son, who already knows the strength in his hand, may be as sensible as the child in its mother's arms.] When it cometh to years of discretion and no longer wishes to suck, it findeth its mouth in order to say: "Give me bread."

𓎛𓏤𓆑𓄿𓈖𓏏𓈖𓂋𓏤𓈖𓇋𓏏𓀁𓊪𓈖𓏏𓂝𓈖𓏤𓇋𓏏𓏤

64. GREAT HYMN TO OSIRIS

This hymn, containing the longest version of the Osiris myth written in Egyptian, comes from a limestone stela erected by an official named Amenmose and his wife Nefertari, who lived during the Eighteenth Dynasty.

1. Homage to thee, Osiris, Lord of eternity, King of the gods, whose names are manifold, whose transformations are sublime, whose form is hidden in the temples whose *ka* is holy, the Governor of Tetut, the mighty one of possessions (?) in the shrine, the Lord of praises in the nome of Anetch, President of the *tchef* food in Anu, Lord who art commemorated in [the town of] Maati, the mysterious (or, hidden) Soul, the Lord of Qerret, the sublime one in White Wall, the Soul of Ra [and] his very body, who hast thy dwelling in Henensu, the beneficent one, who art praised in Nart, who makest to rise up thy Soul, Lord of the Great House in the city of the Eight Gods, [who inspirest] great terror in Shas-hetep, Lord of eternity, Governor of Abtu (Abydos).

Thy seat (or, domain) reacheth far into Ta-tchesert, and thy name is firmly stablished in the mouth[s] of men. Thou art the two-fold substance of the Two Lands everywhere (?), and the divine food (*tchef*) of the Kau, the Governor of the Companies of the Gods, and the beneficent (or, perfect) Spirit-soul among Spirit-souls. The god Nu draweth his waters from thee, and thou bringest forth the north wind at eventide, and wind from thy nostrils to the satisfaction of thy heart. Thy heart flourisheth, and thou bringest forth the splendour of *tchef* food.

The height of heaven and the stars [thereof] are obedient unto thee, and thou makest to be opened the great gates [of the sky]. Thou art the lord to whom praises are sung in the southern heaven, thou art he to whom thanks are given in the northern heaven. The stars which never diminish are under the place of thy face, and thy seats are the stars which never rest. Offerings appear before thee by the command of Keb. The Companies of the Gods ascribe praise unto thee, the Star-gods of the Tuat smell the earth before thee, the domains [make] bowings [before thee], and the ends of the earth make supplication to thee [when] they see thee.

Those who are among the holy ones are in terror of him, and the Two Lands, all of them, make acclamations to him when they meet His Majesty. Thou art a shining Noble at the head of the nobles, permanent in [thy] high rank, stablished in [thy] sovereignty, the beneficent Power of the Company of the Gods. Well-pleasing [is thy] face, and thou art beloved by him that seeth thee. Thou settest the fear of thee in all lands, and because of their love for thee [men] hold thy name to be pre-eminent. Every man maketh offerings unto thee, and thou art the Lord who is commemorated in heaven and upon earth. Manifold are the cries of acclamation to thee in the Uak festival, and the Two Lands shout joyously to thee with one accord. Thou art the eldest, the first of thy brethren, the Prince of the Company of the Gods, and the stablisher of Truth throughout the Two Lands. Thou settest [thy] son upon the great throne of his father Keb. Thou art the beloved one of thy mother Nut, whose valour is most mighty [when] thou overthrowest the Seba Fiend. Thou hast slaughtered thy enemy, and hast put the fear of thee into thy Adversary.

Thou art the bringer in of the remotest boundaries, and art stable of heart, and thy two feet are lifted up (?); thou art the heir of Keb and of the sovereignty of the Two Lands, and he (i.e., Keb) hath seen thy splendid qualities, and hath commanded thee to guide the lands (i.e., the world) by thy hand so long as times [and seasons] endure.

Thou hast made this earth with thy hand, the waters thereof, the winds thereof, the trees and herbs thereof, the cattle thereof of every kind, the birds thereof of every kind, the fish thereof of every kind, the creeping things thereof, and the four-footed beasts thereof. The land of the desert belongeth by right to the son of Nut, and the Two Lands have contentment in making him to rise upon the throne of his father like Ra.

Thou rollest up into the horizon, thou settest the light above the darkness, thou illuminest [the Two Lands] with the light from thy two plumes, thou floodest the Two Lands like the Disk at the beginning of the dawn. Thy White Crown pierceth the height of heaven saluting the stars, thou art the guide of every god. Thou art perfect in command and word. Thou art the favoured one of the Great Company of the Gods, and thou art the beloved one of the Little Company of the Gods.

Thy sister [Isis] acted as a protectress to thee. She drove [thy] enemies away, she averted seasons [of calamity from thee], she recited the word (or, formula) with the magical power of her mouth, [being] skilled of tongue and never halting for a word, being perfect in command and word. Isis the magician avenged her brother. She went about seeking for him untiringly. She flew round and round over this earth uttering wailing cries of grief, and she did not alight on the ground until she had found him. She made light [to come forth] from her feathers, she made air to come into being by means of her two wings, and she cried out the death cries for her brother. She made to rise up the helpless members of him whose heart was at rest, she drew from him his essence, and she made therefrom an heir. She suckled the child in solitariness and none knew where his place was, and he grew in strength. His hand is mighty (or, victorious) within the house of Keb, and the Company of the Gods rejoice greatly at the coming of Horus, the son of Osiris, whose heart is firmly stablished, the triumphant one, the son of Isis, the flesh and bone of Osiris. The Tchatcha of Truth, and the Company of the Gods, and Neb-er-tcher himself, and the Lords of Truth, gather together to him, and assemble therein. Verily those who defeat iniquity rejoice in the House of Keb to bestow the divine rank and dignity upon him to whom it belongeth, and the sovereignty upon him whose it is by right.

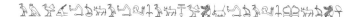

65. CORRESPONDENCE BETWEEN TARHUNTA-RADU OF ARZAWA AND AMENHOTEP III

The Amarna Letters are a collection of diplomatic letters written in cuneiform on clay tablets from the reigns of Amenhotep III and Amenhotep IV (Akhenaten) that were found at the site of Akhetaten (el-Amarna), the latter pharaoh's capital city. Included are several letters from Arzawa, a kingdom in Western Anatolia that was a neighbour to the Hittite empire. The following is an exchange between Tarhunta-radu, the king of Arzawa and Amenhotep III.

Tarhunta-radu to Amenhotep

(1-3) Kalbaya (your messenger) has just now said this to me. He quoted (you as saying) this: "We ought to establish a relationship by marriage." (4-6) But I do not trust Kalbaya (in this matter). He conveyed it orally, but it was not written on the tablet. (7-9) If you are really seeking my daughter (in marriage), will I really not give (her) to you? I will give (her) to you! (10-13) So send Kalbaya back to me quickly together with my messenger, and write back to me on a tablet concerning this matter.

Amenhotep to Tarhunta-radu

(1-6) Thus speaks Nimuwareya, Great King, king of Egypt:
Say to Tarhunta-radu, the king of Arzawa: With me it is well. With my houses, my wives, my children, my great men, my troops, my chariot-fighters, my property?—everything in my lands   all is well. (7-10) With you too may all be well. With your houses, your wives, your children, your great men, your troops, your chariot-fighters, your property?—everything in your lands-may all be well.

(11-16) I have herewith sent to you Irsappa, my messenger (with the instructions): "Let us see the daughter whom they will conduct to My Majesty for marriage. And pour oil on her head." I have herewith sent to you one set of good-quality leather sacks of gold. (17-21) But as for the ceremonial garments about which you wrote me (saying): "Send it/them here to me!," I will send them to you, but later.

Send back quickly your messenger together with my messenger, and let them come. (22-26) Then they—my messenger and the messenger from you who came and … -ed—will proceed to bring to you the bride-price for (your) daughter. And send me people of the Kagka land. I have heard that everything is finished, (27-38) and that the land of Hattuša is paralyzed …

I have herewith sent you a gift as a token of good will, in the charge of my messenger Irgappa: a leather sack (?) of gold weighing twenty minas, three sheer linen garments, three sheer linen tunics, three linen ḫuzzi, eight linen *kušitti*, one hundred *walga*-linen, one hundred linen ḫappa-..., one hundred linen *putalliyašša*, four large stone jars of perfumed oil, six small stone jars of perfumed oil, three beautiful ebony cross-legged chairs overlaid with gold, ten chairs of ebony inlaid with ivory, one hundred (beams of) ebony as a token of good will.

66. LETTER FROM TUSHRATTA OF MITANNI TO AMENHOTEP III

Here is another letter from the Amarna archive. It is one of several written by Tushratta, the king of Mitanni, a large empire in Syria and northern Mesopotamia. In it Tushratta requests a large quantity gold from the pharaoh Amenhotep III as a sign of friendship between the two countries.

[To] Nimmuriya the great king, the king of Egypt, [my] brother, my son-in-law, who loves me, and whom I love it is said as follows: Tušratta, the great king, your father in law who loves you, the king of Mitanni, your brother.

Onto myself (is) peace; onto you may there be peace, to your house, to my sister, and to the rest of your wives, to your sons, to your chariots, to your horses, to your noble(s), to your country and to your property may there be abundant peace!

Until the time of your fathers, they with my fathers were in closest alliance; since then you have perfected (it), and with my father were in exceedingly close alliance. Now you, since (you) and I love one another, have established (it) ten times more than in my father's time. May the gods direct them, and this our alliance may Rimmon my lord and Amanum for ever as now confirm.

And when my brother sent Mane his ambassador, saying: 'O my brother, let your daughter be my wife and mistress of the land of Egypt,' I did not vex the heart of my brother and spoke publicly according to (his) wish, and her whom my brother asked for I showed to Mane, and he saw her. When he had seen her he much approved of her; and in peace in the country of my brother may I know her: may Ištar and Amanum according to the heart of my brother advise her!

Giliya my messenger reported to me the words of my brother. When I heard (them) it was very good, I rejoiced very exceedingly saying: 'Truly to me has this favour happened, and whereas in consequence of the alliance that (was) between us we loved (each other), now in consequence of these words we shall love (each other) for ever.'

When I had sent to my brother and had said this: 'As for me, very exceedingly do we love (each other) and in alliance we have been friendly,' then to my brother I said this: 'My brother has honoured me ten times above my father!'

And I asked much gold of my brother saying: 'Above my father may my brother set me and may my brother send (it) to me.' And to my father did you send much gold; an oblation-dish of solid gold and a cup of solid gold did you send to him; a brick of gold like molten bronze did you send to me.

I sent Giliya on an embassy to my brother and [much] gold I asked for saying: 'As for me may my brother above my father honour me, and much gold which cannot be counted may he send me, may my brother send me more than to my father.' And then I said this to my brother: 'Your standard, which my grandfather made saying: As for me, that it may last I have painted the work red, I have constructed (it) again for you'; and thereupon I further said: 'The gold which my brother will send let him send for the dowry.'

Again my brother sends gold (and) I say this: 'The amount is much, for the supply of the amount is much; and to the (fitting) quantity it reaches, for thus it reaches exactly to the (fitting) quantity; and on this account I have rejoiced greatly, and for all that my brother has sent for this I have rejoiced exceedingly.'

Now again I send to my brother, and may my brother grant me friendship above what (he granted) to my father. Now have I asked gold of my brother, and the gold which of my brother I have asked, has twice been asked for, once because of your standard and a second time for the dowry.

And, O my brother, gold in good earnest which cannot be counted may my brother send to me, and may my brother send more gold than (he sent) my father, since in the midst of the country of my brother gold is as plentiful as dust. May the gods reveal it, and as at present in the country of my brother gold is plentiful, so ten times more than at present may he extract gold; and may the gold, which I have asked for, in the heart of my brother not cause vexation, and O my loved one, my heart let not my brother vex, but let my brother the gold which cannot be counted in good earnest send to me!

And whatsoever my brother desires let him send for to the house where it is, and let (the messenger) go and I will give the present which my brother has asked for. This country (is) my brother's country, and this house (is) my brother's house.

Now I send my ambassador Giliya to my brother, and let my brother not detain him. Let him dismiss him with a costly present, and let him go. May I rejoice very exceedingly when I hear of my brother's present; may I hear for ever of my brother's present. And as for this letter which we have sent may Rimmon my lord and Amanum direct them, and to their destination may they attain, and as (things are) at present so may they continue with them. As at present we love (one another), so, as at present, for ever may we love (one another)!

Now for a present to my brother, one goblet of gold set with crystals (around) its cup; one heavy necklace of 20 crystal beads, and 19 (beads) of gold, in its centre a crystal (amulet) encased in gold; one heavy necklace of 42 *khulalu* stones (and) 40 gold beads, the metal of which (is) ... of Ištar, (in) its centre an (amulet) of *khtdalu* stone cased in gold; 10 pairs of horses; 10 chariots of wood, together with their furniture; and 30 eunuchs I have sent for a present to my brother.

67. LETTER FROM ŠUPPILULIUMA TO AKHENATEN

Suppiluliuma was one of the most powerful kings of the Hittite empire. In this letter from the Amarna archive, Suppiluliuma requests a marriage alliance with Akhenaten.

(1-3) [Thus speaks His Majesty], Šuppiluliuma, G[reat] King, [king of Ḫat]ti: Say to Ḫuriya, [king] of Egypt, my brother:

(4-6) [With me all is] well. With you may all be well (too). [With] your [wives], your sons, your household, your troops, your chariots, [and] in your country, may all be very well.

(7-13) Neither my messengers, whom I sent to your father, nor the request that your father made, saying, "Let us establish only the most friendly relations between us," did I indeed refuse. Whatsoever your father said to me, I indeed did absolutely everything. (12) And my own request, indeed, that I made to your father, he never refused; he gave me absolutely everything. (14-15) Why, my brother, have you held back the shipments (of gifts) that your father was sending to me, when he was alive?

(16-22) Now, my brother, [yo]u have ascended the throne of your father, and just as your father and I were desirous of (exchanging) greeting gifts between us, so now too should you and I enjoy good relations with one another. The request (that) I expressed to your father [I shall express] to my brother, too. Let us establish a [mar]riage bond between us.

(23-28) [You], my [brother], should not hold back [anything] that [I asked] of your father. [As to the two st]atues of gold, one [should be standing], one should be seated. And [let] my brother [send me] two [silver] statues of women, and a large (amount of) lapis lazuli for their large stand [...].

(29-38) ...... (31) If my brother [wants to give], let my brother give them. [But] if my brother does not want to give them, when my chariots are readied for ... linen ḫuzzi, I will return them to my brother. Whatever you want, my brother, write to me so I can send it to you.

(39-43) I herewith send you as your greeting gift: one silver vessel in the shape of a stag, five minas its weight; one silver vessel in the shape of a young ram, three minas its weight; two silver disks, ten minas their weight, (and) two large medicinal shrubs.

68. GREAT HYMN TO THE ATEN

This hymn dedicated to the sun god Aten, reproduced here in full, is a product of the reign of Akhenaten (Dynasty 18), the religious reformer who supplanted traditional polytheism with a new monotheistic cult. The hymn has been found on the walls of several tombs of Akhenaten's capital city, Akhetaten, and is the longest of several Aten hymns that were written at the time. It may have been written by Akhenaten himself.

A Hymn of praise of Horakhty, the living one exalted in the Eastern Horizon in his name of Shu who is in the Aten, who lives for ever and ever, the living and great Aten, he who is in the Sed-Festival, the lord of the Circle, the Lord of the Disk, the Lord of heaven, the Lord of earth, the lord of the House of the Aten in Akhetaten, [of] the King of the South and the North, who lives in Truth, lord of the Two Lands (i.e., Egypt), Nefer-kheperu-Ra Wa-en-Ra, the son of Ra, who lives in Truth, Lord of Crowns, Akhenaten, great in the period of his life, [and of] the great royal woman whom he loves, Lady of the Two Lands, Nefer-nefru-Aten Nefertiti, who lives in health and youth for ever and ever.

He says: Your rising [is] beautiful in the horizon of heaven, O Aten, ordainer of life. You shoot up in the horizon of the East, you fill every land with your beneficence. You are beautiful and great and sparkling, and exalted above every land. Your arrows (i.e., rays) envelop (i.e., penetrate) everywhere all the lands which you have made.

You are as Ra. You bring [them] according to their number, you subdue them for your beloved son. You yourself are afar off, but your beams are upon the earth; you are in their faces, they [admire] your goings. You set in the horizon of the west, the earth is in darkness, in the form of death. Men lie down in a booth wrapped up in cloths, one eye cannot see its fellow. If all their possessions, which are under their heads, be carried away they perceive it not.

Every lion emerges from his lair, all the creeping things bite, darkness [is] a warm retreat. The land is in silence. He who made them has set in his horizon. The earth becomes light, you shoot up in the horizon, shining in the Aten in the day, you scatter the darkness. You send out your arrows (i.e., rays), the Two Lands make festival, [men] wake up, stand upon their feet, it is you who raises them up. [They] wash their members, they take [their apparel] and array themselves therein, their hands are [stretched out] in praise at your rising, throughout the land they do their works. Beasts and cattle of all kinds settle down upon the pastures, shrubs and vegetables flourish, the feathered fowl fly about over their marshes, their feathers praising your Ka (person). All the cattle rise up on their legs, creatures that fly and insects of all kinds spring into life, when you rise up on them. The boats drop down and sail up the river, likewise every road opens (or shows itself) at your rising, the fish in the river swim towards your face, your beams are in the depths of the Great Green (i.e., the Mediterranean and Red Seas). You make offspring to take form in women, creating seed in men. You make the son to live in the womb of his mother, making him to be quiet that he cries not; you are a nurse in the womb, giving breath to vivify that which he has made. [When] he drops from the womb ... on the day of his birth [he] opens his mouth in the [ordinary] manner, you provide his sustenance. The young bird in the egg speaks in the shell, you give breath to him inside it to make him to live. You make for him his mature form so that he can crack the shell [being] inside the egg. He comes forth from the egg, he chirps with all his might, when he has come forth from it (the egg), he walks on his two feet. O how many are the things which you have made! They are hidden from the face, O One God, like whom there is no other. You did create the earth by your heart (or will), you alone existing, men and women, cattle, beasts of every kind that are upon the earth, and that move upon feet (or legs), all the creatures that are in the sky and that fly with their wings, [and] the deserts of Syria and Kush (Nubia), and the Land of Egypt. You set every person in his place. You provide their daily food, every man having the portion allotted to him, [you] compute the duration of his life. Their tongues are different in speech, their characteristics (or forms), and likewise their skins [in colour], giving distinguishing marks to the dwellers in foreign lands. You make Hapi (the Nile) in the Tuat (Underworld), you bring it when you wish to make mortals to live, inasmuch as you have made them for yourself, their Lord who supports them to the uttermost, O Lord of every land, you shine upon them, O Aten of the day, great one of majesty. You make the life of all remote lands. You set a Nile in heaven, which comes down to them.

It makes a flood on the mountains like the Great Green Sea, it makes to be watered their fields in their villages. How beneficent are your plans, O Lord of Eternity! A Nile in heaven art you for the dwellers in the foreign lands (or deserts), and for all the beasts of the desert that go upon feet (or legs). Hapi (the Nile) comes from the Tuat for the land of Egypt. Your beams nourish every field; you rise up [and] they live, they germinate for you. You make the Seasons to develop everything that you have made:

The season of Pert (i.e., Nov. 16-March 16) so that they may refresh themselves, and the season Heh (i.e., March 16-Nov. 16) in order to taste you. You have made the heaven which is remote that you may shine therein and look upon everything that you have made. Your being is one, you shine (or, shoot up) among your creatures as the Living Aten, rising, shining, departing afar off, returning. You have made millions of creations (or, evolutions) from your one self (viz.) towns and cities, villages, fields, roads and river. Every eye (i.e., all men) beholds you confronting it. You are the Aten of the day at its zenith.

At your departure your eye ... you created their faces so that you might not see. ... one you made ... You are in my heart. There is no other who knows you except your son Nefer-kheperu-Ra

Wa-en-Ra (Akhenaten). You have made him wise to understand your plans [and] your power. The earth came into being by your hand, even as you have created them (i.e., men). You rise, they live; you set, they die. As for you, there is duration of life in your members, life is in you. [All] eyes [gaze upon] your beauties until you set, [when] all labours are relinquished. You set in the West, you rise, making to flourish ... for the King. Every man who [stands on his] foot, since you laid the foundation of the earth, you have raised up for your son who came forth from your body, the King of the South and the North, Living in Truth, Lord of Crowns, Akhenaten, great in the duration of his life [and for] the Royal Wife, great of majesty, Lady of the Two Lands, Nefer-nefru-Aten Nefertiti, living [and] young for ever and ever.

69. LETTER FROM ABIMELECH OF TYRE TO AKHENATEN

Abimelech (technically Abimilku), king of Tyre, was a vassal of Egypt. There are ten letters from him in the Amarna archive. In the one presented here, Abimelech offers praise to Akhenaten and then informs him of the king of Sidon's duplicitous activity.

To the King my Lord, my God, my Sun thus (says) Abimelec your servant: seven and seven (times) at the feet of the King my Lord I bow. I (am) the dust beneath the eyes of the King my Lord my master—the Sun God who declares in presence of the lands that are meted out for all, and just it is as the decree of the Sun God his gracious father: who fulfils the breadth of its circuit, and gives light' to what is obscure: who conquers all lands, enjoying good (fortune) from the abject ones he smites; who gives this his compassion from heaven, like the God Adonis, and causes all lands to rest through his mercy.

This is the message of a servant to his Lord. Lo! I hear the gracious message of the King which reaches his servant, and the breadth of the circuit which is laid down on the side of the King my Lord for his servant; and the extent it makes clear, since the arrival of the messenger of the King my Lord. Does not he make it clear?—the extent is clear. The lands of my fathers behold he has left. Lo! the extent is laid down, O King, to enlarge me, and you make great my boundary, and the region that they have taken away from the people—the race of this people. For my boundary increases. Well pleased behold I hear the gracious messenger from my Lord, and all my land has been afraid as to my Lord's countenance. Lo! I hear the extent of the circuit; and the gracious messenger who reaches me, behold he says, O King my Lord, that the region (is) to be established by the presence of many soldiers; and the servant says for his Lord that my plain is my land over against my gardens, over against the plain of my cities. He has followed the order of the King my Lord listening to the King his Lord, and has followed the power of his (orders), and the Sun God he has proclaimed before him; and he makes clear the breadth of the circuit from the side of his Lord, and does he not listen to the order of his Lord? The portion of his town he has divided. His word none shall overthrow in all the lands for ever, after the deed which his Lord now hears. His city will rest, will rest from overthrowing his utterance for all time. You are the Sun God whom he has proclaimed before him; and the decision which shall set at rest is lasting for one. And because she judges that the King my Lord is just, our land obeys —the land that I am given. This Abimelec says to the Sun God. My Lord I am given what appears before the King my Lord. And now to be taken by the city of Tyre (Tsuru) the city Zarbitu I behold, because of the King my Lord.

70. LETTERS FROM LABAYA AND ADDURBILU TO AKHENATEN

These two letters from the Amarna archive are from vassals of Akhenaten in Canaan. They illustrate the tension between vassals of Egypt at this time and their expectation of the pharaoh to redress their grievances.

Letter from Labaya

To the King my Lord and my Sun thus Labaya your servant, and the dust of your feet. At the feet of the King my Lord and my Sun seven times seven times I bow. I have heard the message which the King sent to me; and who am I? and the King will afflict his country before me. (I swear) I am myself a faithful servant, and I have not sinned, and I have not murmured at my tribute, and I have not murmured at the wishes of my friends (or subjects). Lo! this province my destroyers eat up, and I have had no food. The King my Lord (says) it is my fault. Once more he makes it my fault. Lo! I strive with the city Gezer and I complain of the young men. The King one hears will march. I restrained the band of Milcilu and my band desirous to fight The quarrel of Milcilu against me is relinquished; as to Ben Zachariah the King has sent not to attack. Lo! Ben Zachariah with men of blood was known to us to march, and I marched, and we are conquering him. He gives up Abukasu. Once more he has made peace. The King has sent to my band (saying), "I order peace." I am desirous of peace, since the King has sent to me. Stay your sword, ponder in your heart, and is the peace hollow? Nay!

Letter from Addurbilu

To the King my Lord by letter thus (says) Addurbilu your servant, at the feet of the King my Lord seven times and seven times I bow. The King my Lord will know the hate which is desired by the son of the sinful chief who hated me—the second son of Labaya. His face is estranged, I foresee estrangement of the land of the King my Lord. He has plotted as plotted (against me) the chief who was his father; and the King my Lord shall know it. Lo! he has built a fort … against me. The second son of Labaya (says), "Why has a vain papyrus taken from us the lowlands of the Gittites? … your Lord, O city of those who besieged the chief our father." As I am saying speaks to us the second son of Labaya. He has made war for me with the chiefs of the Land of Gina which I hold—a gift to us. And when (there was) a battle he has not been confounded, and the fight was great, but he has made it his dwelling, bereaving me in the sight of the King my Lord, for he has made war in … of Gina (with) the servants of the King my Lord. And truly a master of great men exceeding strong (is) Bimyapiza. (And you shall hear) what is said as to him. [*The text becomes broken, but still refers to the doings of the second son of Labaya, and continues with an important passage on the back of the tablet:*]

And as I say speaks to us the second son of Labaya who is making war: "As to our possessions from the King your Lord, lo! this is the boundary; over against the city of Sunasu and over against the city Burku and over against the city Kharabu. And behold the boundary of the dwelling of my race. Ask them how (it is) of my Lords, and it includes the city of Giti Rimuna (Gath Rimmon). And the King your Lord is (breaking the bond of our …)." And I strive with him …… he deprives me of it in sight of the King my Lord. Because of his making wars with the King my Lord—my King my Lord—I and my brethren have gone down. The field is my portion. And did not the messenger of Milcilu proclaim the decree before the face of the second son of Labaya? It was made complete. I foresee estrangement of the land of the King my Lord. They disturb a peaceful region, and in vain I repeat the letter about me. The guard of my Lord …. to go down, and the King my Lord shall hear what the message says.

71. LETTER FROM ADONIZEDEK OF JERUSALEM TO AKHENATEN

In another letter from the Amarna archive, the king of Jerusalem, a vassal of Akhenaten, complains of attacks upon his territory by a people called the 'Apiru or 'Abiru, who some have speculated could be the ancestors of the Israelites.

To the King my Lord is mourning thus this Adonizedek your servant. At the feet of my Lord, of the King, seven times and seven times I bow. What shall I ask of the King my Lord? They have prevailed, they have (taken the fortress of Jericho) they who have gathered against the King of Kings, which Adonizedek has explained to the King his Lord. Behold, as to me, my father is not and my army is not. The tribe that has ground me in this place is very rebellious to the King, the same is gathering near me for the house of my father. Why has the tribe sinned against the King my Lord? Behold O King my Lord arise! I say to the Paka (resident) of the King my Lord: "Why is the land in slavery to the chief of the 'Abiru and the rulers fear the end? So now they must send from the presence of the King my Lord." Behold I say that the land of the King my Lord is ruined. So now they must send to the King my Lord, and let the King my Lord know this; behold the King my Lord has placed a garrison to stop the way ...... (Yankhamu?) ...... of kings .... chiefs of the garrison ...... the king as master to his land , ... as to his land she has rebelled, the (lands) of the King my Lord—the whole of it. Ilimelec cuts off all the King's land. And let one warn the King as to his land. I myself speak pleading with the King my Lord and (for once) let the King my Lord behold the entreaties. And the wars are mighty against me, and am not I forced to ask—to ask a letter from the King my Lord? And let an order return from the King (my Lord). Whether will he not order chiefs for garrison? And let him be kind, and let the King my Lord regard the entreaties. This tribe behold, O King my Lord, has risen up. Lo the Paka they have expelled. I say the lands of the King my Lord are ruined. Do not you hear this same of me? They have destroyed all the rulers. There is no ruler now O King my Lord. Let the King give his countenance to the chiefs; and whether shall the chiefs of the Egyptian soldiers remain at rest? They have lingered, O King my Lord. The lands are failing to the King my Lord. The 'Abiru chiefs plunder all the King's lands. Since the chiefs of the Egyptian soldiers have gone away quitting the lands this year, O King my Lord, and since there is no chief of the Egyptian soldiers there is ruin to the lands of the King my Lord. They have ... O King my Lord, and Adonizedek (is) dust . . .messages (are asked) of the King my Lord, there is destruction by the foe of the lands of the King my Lord.

72. EDICT OF HOREMHEB

From a stela erected at Karnak by Horemheb, last pharaoh of the Eighteenth Dynasty, comes legislation containing a series of enactments designed to protect the common people from abuses of power by fiscal officers in the collection of taxes.

I. Introduction (ll. 1-9)

....

II. The King's Zeal for the Relief of the People (ll. 10-14)

His majesty took counsel with his heart [how he might] ... [exp]el evil and suppress lying. The plans of his majesty were an excellent refuge, repelling violence behind ... [and delivering the Egyptians from the oppressions] which were among them. Behold, his majesty spent the whole time seeking the welfare of Egypt and searching out instances [of oppression in the land]. ... [came the scribe] of his majesty. Then he seized palette and roll; he put it into writing according to all that his majesty, the king himself said. He spoke as follows: "[My majesty] commands [concerning all] instances of oppression in the land.

III. Enactment Against Robbing the Poor of Dues for the Royal Breweries and Kitchens (ll. 14-17)

If the poor man made for himself a craft with its sail, in order to be able to serve the Pharaoh, L. P. H., [loading it with the dues for the breweries and kitchens of the Pharaoh, and he was robbed of the craft and] the dues, the poor man stood reft of his goods and stripped of his many [labors]. [This is wrong, and the Pharaoh will suppress it by] his excellent measures. If there be a [poor man] who pays the dues of the breweries and kitchens of the Pharaoh, L. P. H., [to the two] deputies, [and he be robbed of his goods and his craft, my majesty commands: that every officer who seizes the dues] and takes the craft of any citizen of the army or of any person who is in the whole land, the law shall be executed against him, in that his nose shall be cut off, and he shall be sent to Tha[ru].

IV. Against Robbing the Poor of Wood Due the Pharaoh (ll. 17, 18)

[Furthermore, concerning the impost of wood, my majesty commands that if any officer finds] a poor man without a craft, then let him bring to him a craft for his impost from another, and let him send him to bring for him the wood; thus he shall serve [the Pharaoh].

V. Against Exacting Dues from a Poor Man Thus Robbed (ll. 18-20)

[Furthermore, my majesty commands that if any poor man is oppressed by] [robbe]ry, his cargo is emptied by theft of them, and the poor man stands reft of hi[s good]s, [no further exactions for dues shall be made from him] when he has nothing. For it is not good, this report of very great injustice. My majesty commands that restitution be made to him; behold, ...

VI. Against Robbing the Poor of Dues for the Harem or the Gods by the Soldiers (ll. 20-22)

[Furthermore, as for those who] ... and those who bring to the harem, likewise for the offerings of all gods, paying dues to the [two] deputies of the army and ... [my majesty commands that if any officer is guilty of extortions or thefts], the law [shall be executed] against him, in that his nose shall be cut off, and (he) shall be sent to Tharu likewise.

VII. Against Unlawful Appropriation of Slave Service (ll. 22-24)

When the officers of the Pharaoh's house of offerings have gone about tax-collecting in the towns, to take [katha-plant], [they have seized the slaves of the people, and kept them at work] for 6 days or 7 days, without one's being able to depart from them [afar], so that it was an excessive detention indeed. It shall be done likewise [against them]. If there be any place [where the stewards shall be tax-collecting, and any one] shall hear, saying: "They are tax-collecting, to take katha-plant [for themselves,]" and another shall come to report, saying: "My man slave (or) my female slave has been taken away [and detained many days at work by the stewards;" it shall be done likewise against them].

VIII. Against Stealing of Hides by the Soldiers (ll. 25-28)

The two divisions of troops which are in the field, one in the southern region, the other in the northern region, stole hides in the whole land, not passing a year, without applying the [brand] of [the royal house to cattle which were not due to them, thereby increasing] their number, and stealing that which was stamped from them. They went out from house to house, beating and [plundering] without leaving a hide for [the people .... Then the officer] of Pharaoh went about [to each one,] [to collect the hides charged against him, and came to the people demanding] [them], but the hides were not found with them (although) the [amount charged] against them could be established. They satisfied them, saying: "They have been stolen from us." A wretched case is this; [therefore] it shall be [done] likewise.

When the overseer of the cattle of Pharaoh, L. P. H., goes about to attend to the loan-herds in the whole land, and there be not brought to him the hides of the ..., which are on the [lists], [he shall not hold the people responsible for the hides if they have them not, but they shall be released by command of his majesty,] according to his just purposes. As for any citizen of the army, (concerning) whom one shall hear, saying: "He goes about stealing hides," beginning with this day, the law shall be executed against him, by beating him a hundred blows, opening five wounds, and taking from him by force the hides which he took.

IX. Against Connivance of Dishonest Inspectors with Thievish Tax-Collectors, for a Share of the Booty (ll. 28-32)

Now, as for this other instance of evil which the [official staff were accustomed to commit, when they held inspection] in the land, of that which happened [against the law], [the table-scribe of] the queen and the table-scribe of the harem went about after the official staff, punishing them and investigating the [affair] ... of the one who sailed down- or up-river. One investigated it among the officials in the time of the King Menkheperre (Thutmose III). Now, when the one who sailed down- or up-river whom they took; and when [the superior officials of] [the king], Menkheperre, went about [after these officials] [each year,] [that they might make an] expedition to the [city,] and that these superior officials might come to these officials, saying: "Give [to us] the consideration for the careless expedition;" then, behold, the Pharaoh, L. P. H., made the expedition at the feast of Opet each year without carelessness. One prepared the way before the Pharaoh [and questioned the local magistrate, wherever he] landed, [concerning the corrupt official] causing him to ... what he (the corrupt official) was like. As for the one who goes about again, afterward, to seek the consideration ..., then these officials shall go about with the expedition concerning the affairs of these poor people. My majesty commands to prevent that one shall do thus, beginning with this day the landing; he is the one against whom one shall prosecute it.

X. Against Stealing Vegetables under the Pretense of Collecting Taxes (ll. 32-35)

Likewise the [collection] of vegetables for the breweries [and kitchens of the Pharaoh and] .... [Extortion was practiced, and the officials plundered] the poor, taking the best of their vegetables, saying: "They are for the impost [of the Pharaoh]." [Thus they] robbed the poor of their [labors,] so that a double [impost was levied. Now, my majesty commands that as for any officials who come to] collect vegetables [for] the impost of Pharaoh, L. P. H., in the arbors, and the ... houses of the estates of Pharaoh, L. P. H., and the ... of Pharaoh which contain vegetables, (concerning whom) one shall hear, saying: "They ... for any ... of any citizen of the army, or [any] people, [beginning with this day, the law shall be executed against them] ...... transgressing commands.

XI. Enactments Too Fragmentary for Analysis (ll. 35-39, and right side, ll. 1, 2)

[*The fragmentary condition of ll. 35-39 makes any coherent rendering impossible. They contain, however, a new enactment of the greatest interest regarding taxation of grain, in which there is an apparent contrast between the property owners, or citizens of the city, and the poor.*]

XII. Narratives of the King's Reforms, Containing Also an Enactment Against Corrupt Judges (ll. 3-7)

Appointment of Two Judges

I have improved this entire land ... I have sailed it, as far as south of the wall, I have given ..., I have learned its whole interior, I have traveled it entirely in its midst, I have searched in ... [and I have sought two officials] perfect in speech, excellent in good qualities, knowing how to judge the innermost heart, hearing the words of the palace, the laws of the judgment-hall. I have appointed them to judge the Two Lands, to satisfy those who are in .... [I have given to each one] his seat; I have set them in the two great cities of the South and the North; every land among them comes to him without exception; I have put before them regulations in the daily register [of the palace].... I have directed [them] to the way of life, I lead them to the truth, I teach them, saying: "Do not associate with others of the people; do not receive the reward of another, not hearing .... How, then, shall those like you judge others, while there is one among you committing a crime against justice?

Now, as to the obligation of silver and gold ... [my] majesty remits it, in order that there not be collected an obligation of anything from the official staff of the South and North.

Punishment of Bribery

Now, as for any official or any priest (concerning whom) it shall be heard, saying: "He sits, to execute judgment among the official staff appointed for judgment, and he commits a crime against justice therein;" it shall be against him a capital crime. Behold, my majesty has done this, to improve the laws of Egypt, in order to cause that another should not be ....

Appointment of Local Courts

[Behold, my majesty appointed] the official staff of the divine fathers, the prophets of the temples, the officials of the court of this land and the priests of the gods who comprise the official staff out of desire that they shall judge the citizens of every city. My majesty is legislating for Egypt, to prosper the life of its inhabitants; when he appeared upon the throne of Re. Behold, the official staffs have been appointed in the whole land ... all ... to comprise the official staffs in the cities according to their rank.

XIII. The King's Audiences and Largesses (ll. 7-10)

They went around ... times a month, [which] he made for them like a feast; every man sat down at a portion of every good thing, of good bread, and meat of the storehouses, of royal provision their voices reached heaven, praising all benefits the heart of all the soldiers of the army. [The king appeared to the people] ... throwing (gifts) to them from the balcony while every man was called by his name by the king himself. They came forth from the presence rejoicing, laden with the provision of the royal house; yes, they took [grain-heaps] in the granary, every one of them [bore] barley and spelt, there was not found one who had nothing their cities. [If] they did not complete the circuit therein within three days, ... their *khetkhet*-officers hastened after them to the place where they were immediately. They were found there ....

XIV. Laudation of the King, and Conclusion

[*Little can be made out of these nine lines. In line 9, the conclusion of the whole edict can be discerned*:] Hear these commands which my majesty has made for the first time governing the whole land, when my majesty remembered these cases of oppression which occur before this land.

73. KANAIS TEMPLE INSCRIPTION OF SETI I

On a desolate road about 35 miles east of Edfu at the Wadi Kanais lies a small temple built during the reign of Seti I (Dynasty 19). The temple was cut into a cliff face and was a place of shelter for those travelling to the gold mines further east. On the door jamb of the entrance to the main hall appear three inscriptions. This is the first, which was composed in the ninth year of Seti's reign.

The ninth year, the third month of summer, the twentieth day of the month, under the Majesty of Horus, Victorious Bull, Manifest in Thebes, Nourishing the Two Lands; Two Goddesses, Renewing Birth, Mighty of Scimetar, Repressing the Nine Bows; Horus of Gold, Renewing Manifestations, Mighty of Bows in all lands; King of Upper and Lower Egypt, Menmare^c; Son of Re^c, Setoy-Maneptah, given life for ever and ever.

This day:—

Now His Majesty was surveying the desert lands towards the hills, for his heart desired to see the cuttings from where the fine gold is brought. And as His Majesty was mounting up with the knowledge of many streams, he made a halt upon the way to exchange counsel with his heart. And he said: How wretched is a way that has no water! What indeed is done by travellers to stop the parching of their throats? Who quenches their thirst, the homeland being far away, and the desert wide? Woe to him, a man that is athirst in the wilderness! Come now, let me take thought for their welfare. I will make for them the means of preserving them alive, that they may bless my name in the future years that are to come, that generations yet to be may come to glory in me for my energy. For I am indeed compassionate and regardful of wayfarers.

Now when His Majesty had said these his words to his own heart, he went round about over the desert seeking a place to make a watering-station.—Now God was guiding him, so as to grant the request which he desired. —And workers in stone were appointed to dig a well on the hills, in order that he (the king) might uplift the weary one, and refresh the heart that is burnt up in summer. Then this place was finished off, bearing the great name Menmareᶜ. And the waters flooded it very greatly, like the cavern of the two Nile-sources of Elephantine.

And His Majesty said: See, God has given effect to my prayers; he causes water to spring forth for me on the hills; a way which since (the time of) the gods had been wretched was made pleasant during my reign. Pasture-lands profit the herdsman; the breadth of the land is fortunate, when the King is active. Every deed that was unknown is made [known] in my time.

Another good deed is come into my heart, by God's command, the founding of a town in which shall be an Abode—the place which possesses a temple is noble. I will build an Abode in this place, bearing the great name of [my] fathers [the gods]; then shall they cause my deeds to endure, and my name to flourish, bruited abroad over the foreign lands.

Thereupon His Majesty commanded that directions be given to the foreman of the King's work-men, who were with him as stonecutters. And there was made an excavation in this hill, a temple of these [gods]: Amun was in it, Reᶜ was inside it, Ptah and Osiris were in its Main Hall, Horus, Isis and Menmareᶜ, the company of gods which is in this temple.

And after the monument was completed, and adorned, and its pictures and inscriptions made, came His Majesty to adore his fathers, all the gods, and said:

Hail to you, great gods who founded heaven and earth at your good pleasure! You shall show me favour to all eternity, you shall perpetuate my name for ever, inasmuch as I am serviceable, am of good to you, am watchful over the matters that you wish.

Therefore you shall tell those who shall come, kings, officials and people, to confirm for me my deeds under the supervision of my House at Abydos. He who acts upon the word of God is happy, because his plans fail not. Speak yourselves, and your word shall be acted on, for it is you who are the lords. I have spent my life being staunch to you to seek my betterment with you. Cause my monuments to endure for me, my name being perpetuated upon them.

74. LETTER OF MAISETI

Several letters on papyrus have been discovered that were written by a Lower Egyptian standard bearer named Maiseti, who served under Seti I. This is a translation of one of them, which is addressed to some garrison commanders under his authority.

It is the standard-bearer Maiseti who addresses the garrison captains who are in the Northern Region:

I have learned that you have been interfering with the god's personnel in Tell el-Balamun who are under the authority of the royal scribe Iuny. What's the meaning of your acting this way? By Amon and by the Ruler, [l.p.h.], if I learn that you have further interfered with the god's personnel who are in your vicinity, see, I shall severely reprimand you, if that's what you want, for the officials of Pharaoh, l.p.h., are severely reprimanding me personally.

Please carry out your assignment properly. Don't be remiss concerning the orders which I entrusted to you. As regards all this that is in the orders, don't ignore it but procure for us men who have been dismissed from this and no longer constitute a squad. And don't create a commotion in the place which is sublime, but come that you may return.

When this letter reaches you, you shall prevent service for the god there from remaining inactive, or you will go to jail. Please take note of this.

Address: It is the standard-bearer Maiseti who addresses the squad leaders who are in the Northern Region.

75. LETTER TO A DEPARTED WIFE

From the Leiden Papyrus 371 comes a letter written hastily in hieratic by a man to his deceased wife 'Ankhere.

(1) To the excellent Spirit 'Ankhere! What evil thing have I done to thee, (2) that I should have come into this wretched state in which I am? What have I done to thee? What (3) thou hast done, is that thou hast laid hands on me, although I had done nothing evil to thee. Since I lived with thee (4) as husband down to this day, what have I done to thee that I must hide (it)? (5) What (have I done) to thee? What thou(?) hast done is that I must bring this accusation against thee. What have I done to thee? (6) I will lay a plaint against thee in the presence with words of my mouth, in the presence of the Divine Ennead of the West, (7) and it shall be decided betwixt thee and me <by means of> this writing, (even) this which (?) disputes with <thee concerning> what is written (8) about (?). What have I done to thee? I made thee a (married) woman when I was a youth. I was with thee when I was performing (9) all (manner of) offices. I was with thee, and did not put thee away. I did not cause thy heart (10) to grieve. And I did it when I was a youth and when I was performing all (manner of) important offices (11) for Pharaoh, without putting thee away but saying, "She has (always) been (??) with (me)—so said I! And everyone who (12) came to me before thee, I did not receive them on thy account, saying "I will act (13) according to thy desire." And now, behold, thou dost not suffer my heart to take comfort. I will be judged (14) with thee, and one shall discern wrong from right.

Now behold, when I was training (15) officers for the soldiery and the cavalry of Pharaoh, (16) I <caused> them to come and lie on their bellies before thee, bringing all (manner of) good (17) things to lay before thee, and I hid nothing from thee in thy (18) day of life.

I did not cause [thee to (?)] suffer pain (in) aught that I did (19) with thee, after the fashion of a lord. Nor didst thou find me (?) (20) disregarding (?) thee after the fashion of a peasant in entering into a strange house. I caused no (21) man to chide me (in) aught that I did with thee. And when they placed me in the position in which I am, (22) I became unable to go abroad in my (wonted) fashion, and I came (23) to do that which one like me does, when he is at home (?), (concerning) thy unguent, (24) likewise thy provisions, and likewise thy clothes, and they were brought to thee, and I did not (25) put them in a strange place, saying, 'The woman is [there (?)]. So said I, and did not (26) disregard (?) thee. But behold, thou dost not know the good that I have done with thee. (27) I am sending to let thee know that which thou art doing. And when thou (28) didst sicken of the sickness which thou didst have, I <caused to be brought> a master-physician, and he treated (29) thee, and he did everything whereof thou didst say 'Do it.' And when I followed after Pharaoh (30) journeying to the south, and this condition had come to pass with thee, I spent this sum (?) of eight months without eating or drinking like a man. And when I arrived in Memphis, I asked (leave) of Pharaoh, arad I (came) to the (place) (33) where thou wast, and I wept exceedingly together with my people in front of my (34) street-quarter. I gave linen clothes to wrap thee, and I caused many clothes to be (35) made, and I left no good thing that it should not be done for thee. And now, behold, I have passed (36) three years dwelling (alone) without entering into a house, though it be not right that one like me should be caused (37) to do it. And behold, I have done it on thy account. But behold, thou dost not know good from bad. (38) It shall be decided betwixt thee and me. And behold, the sisters in the house, I have not entered in to one of them.

𓀀𓀁𓀂𓀃𓀄𓀅𓀆𓀇𓀈𓀉𓀊𓀋𓀌𓀍𓀎𓀏𓀐𓀑𓀒𓀓𓀔𓀕𓀖𓀗𓀘𓀙𓀚

76. THE GREAT ABYDOS INSCRIPTION

This is a selection from the longest inscription we have from the reign of Ramesses II (Dynasty 19), cut into a wall in the temple of Seti I at Abydos. It comes from the early part of Ramesses' reign.

Ramesses Addresses His Father, Narrating His Good Deeds to Him

Then spoke the King of Upper and Lower Egypt, Ramses II, given life, sending up that which he had done for his father, the Osiris, King Menmare (Seti I), triumphant; saying: "Awake, (lift) your face to heaven, that you may see Re, O my father, Merneptah (Seti I), who are a god. Behold, I am making your name to live, I have protected you, I give attention to your temple, your offerings are established. You rest in the Nether World, like Osiris, while I shine as Re for the people, being upon the great throne of Atum, like Horus, son of Isis, who protected his father. How [happy] for you, who begat me ... since you come as one living again. I have fashioned you, I have built the house you love, wherein is your statue in the cemetery of Abydos, region of eternity. I have founded offerings [for] your s[tatues], the daily offerings come to you. [I] am he that does that which is lacking to you; I do it for you, every desire of your heart, the excellent thing in your name. I assess for you the [officials] ... works for your *ka*, in order to offer for you upon the ground, with bread and drink. I have come myself, myself, in order to see your temple beside Wennofer, sovereign of eternity. I have [finished] the work in it, I have laid out the [ground], I ... that which you desire, making your every house wherein I have established your name forever. [I] am he that does according to truth, that it (truth) may flourish."

"I have given to you the Southerners, offering gifts to your temple, and the Northerners, (bringing) their tribute before your beautiful face. I have collected all them that owe you dues, united in one body, under the administration of the prophet of your temple, in order to make your property a permanent whole, to be brought [to] your temple ... forever."

"I made splendid your treasury, filled with possessions, the heart's desire, which I have given to you, together with your dues. I have given to you a ship, bearing cargoes upon the sea, conveying to you the great [marvels] of God's-Land, and the merchants doing merchandising, bearing their wares and their impost therefrom in gold, silver, and copper."

"I have made for you calculations of the fields, which had been only verbal on high [land], calculated in fields. I equipped them with inspectors, together with husbandmen, to produce clean grain for your divine offerings. I have given to you barges with crews, and artisans hewing without ceasing to sail to your temple."

"I have formed for you herds of all small cattle, faithfully to supply your offerings. I levied for you wild fowl from the [enclosed] marsh; others ... live geese for maintaining those that were hatched. I put fishermen on the waters, on every pool, in order to furnish for you imposts by the shipload."

"I equipped your temple with every office ... of my majesty. Your lay priesthood of the temple has its full complement of heads. The peasant-slaves are assessed for woven stuff, for your wardrobe, and (as for) your serfs of the fields of every district, every man brings their (sic!) impost, to fill your house."

"Lo, you have entered into heaven, you follow Re, you mingle with stars and moon. You rest in the nether world, like those who are therein, beside Wennofer, lord of eternity; your two [arms] draw Atum in heaven and in earth, like the unresting stars and the imperishable stars, while you are on the prow of the barque of myriads of years. When Re rises in heaven, your two eyes are upon his beauty; when Atum [enters] into the earth, you are among his followers. You have entered into the hidden chamber before its lord; your going is afar in the midst of the Nether World; you have associated yourself with the mortuary gods. Lo, [I] pray for the breath of your august nostrils. I mention your name many times daily, I ... my father ...... I tell of your valor, when I am in a foreign country. I lay down for you gifts, my hand bears offerings for your name, for your ... in your every place."

Ramesses Prays His Father to Intercede in His Behalf

"May you speak to Re ...... life to his son, Wennofer, with a loving heart. Grant lifetime upon lifetime, united in jubilees for Usermare-Setepnere (Ramesses II), given life. It will be well for you, that I should be king forever, (for) you will be ... by a good son, who remembers his father; (for) I will take counsel for your temple, every day, and for the affairs of your *ka*, in every matter. If I hear of any damage about to happen, I will command to remove it instantly in every matter. You shall be as if you lived, while I reign. I shall look to your house every day. ... I have ..., my heart shall incline after you, I shall champion you and your name, while you are in the nether world. Excellent indeed shall it be for you, while I am; while Ramses, given life, like Re, forever, [the son] of Re, lives."

The Deceased Seti I Replies to His Son's Prayer

Then was King Menmare (Seti I), triumphant, an excellent soul (*ba*), like Osiris, rejoicing over all that which his son, the doer of excellent things, King Ramses (II), had done, and praising all his beauty, to Re-Harakhte, and to the gods who are in the nether world, while he spoke in ... as a father on earth speaks with his son, saying:

"Let your heart be very glad, O my beloved son, Usermare-Setepnere, given life, in ... giving to you [myriads] of years, eternity upon the Horus-throne of the living. Osiris has besought for you the duration of heaven, wherein you rise like Re at early morning. Life and prosperity shall be with you, ... truth, might, and joy of heart, for him who is rich in years. Yours shall be might and victory, O you great in victory; health shall be for your limbs like (those of) Re in heaven. Joy and rejoicing shall be in your every abode, O king, defending Egypt, binding the barbarians, spending the eternity of your lifetime as King of Upper Egypt, and as King of Lower Egypt, as Atum flourishes at rising and setting. Behold, I say to Re with a loving heart: 'Grant to him eternity upon earth like Khepri.' I have repeated to Osiris when I entered before him: 'Double for him the duration of your son, Horus.' Behold, Re said in the horizon of heaven: 'Grant eternity, everlastingness, myriads of years of royal jubilees for the son of his body, the beloved Meriamon-Ramses, given life, doer of excellent things.' Atum has decreed to you his duration as king. Might and victory shall be united behind you. Thoth writes them at the side of the All-Lord, and the Great Ennead say: 'Re, in his barque, lord of the morning-barque, collects them for him; his eye sees that which you have so excellently done. When he sails the heavens with the wind every day, great joy is behind him, because he remembers your beauty; until Atum sets in the land of the West, your love is in his body every day.' Behold, Wennofer is lord of triumph through that which your majesty has done in the place of truth. I [Horus] awake him at the reminder of your goodness; my heart has joy indeed, because of the eternity which he has decreed for you. Behold, I have received the things which you have given to me: my bread and my water with gladness of heart, breath [reaches my, nostrils, because of the deeds of a son, whose heart chooses to protect, free from negligence, knowing that which is seemly. You have repeated monument on monument for Osiris under my authority in the presence ... [in] the midst of Abydos. I am magnified because of all that which you have done for me; I am placed at the head of the abode of the dead, I am transformed, I have become a god more beautiful than before, since your heart has inclined to me, while I am in the nether world. I am your true father, who am a god; I have mingled with the gods, following Aton; I [know] him who dwells in the barque ... like one in ... who is in .... He [remem]bers your beauty .... Behold, you have a long life, Re has decreed to you ..., forever, like .... You are the living ... of Atum, your every word comes to pass like (that of) the All-Lord. You are the favorite egg of Khepri, the water of a god [which came forth] from him. What you beget is that which Re himself has made; he said to you: '... [as the maker of] ... a guardian, you come as living

Re to the people; the Southland and Northland [are beneath] your feet, beseeching myriads of royal jubilees for Usermare-Setepnere, the duration of the All-Lord, when [he] rises.'"

𓀭𓏤𓈖𓆓𓀀𓅓𓏏𓊪𓆑𓈖𓏤𓊪𓅓𓏏𓊪𓆑𓈖𓏤𓊪𓅓𓏏𓊪𓆑𓈖𓏤𓊪

77. QADESH BATTLE INSCRIPTIONS OF RAMESSES II

Ramesses was so proud of his performance at the Battle of Qadesh that he had images and inscriptions concerning it put in temples all over Egypt. Here are presented some of the inscriptions, copies of which were found in Thebes, in the Ramesseum (his mortuary temple across the Nile from Thebes), and at Abu Simbel. The first section is a narrative describing Ramesses' march toward Qadesh. The second section consists of inscriptions that accompany wall reliefs and which recount the battle itself.

Record of the March to Qadesh

Date

Year 5, third month of the third season, day 9; under the majesty of Horus: Mighty Bull, Beloved of Truth; King of Upper and Lower Egypt: Usermare-Setepnere; Son of Re; Ramses-Meriamon, given life forever.

Camp South of Qadesh

Lo, his majesty was in Zahi on his second victorious campaign. The goodly watch in life, prosperity and health, in the tent of his majesty, was on the highland south of Kadesh.

False Message of the Shasu near Shabtuna

When his majesty appeared like the rising of Re, he assumed the adornments of his father, Montu. When the king proceeded northward, and his majesty had arrived at the locality south of the town of Shabtuna, there came two Shasu,[3] to speak to his majesty as follows: "Our brethren, who belong to the greatest of the families with the vanquished chief of Kheta,[4] have made us come to his majesty, to say: "We will be subjects of Pharaoh, L. P. H., and we will flee from the vanquished chief of Kheta; for the vanquished chief of Kheta sits in the land of Aleppo, on the north of Tunip. He fears because of Pharaoh, L. P. H., to come southward." Now, these Shasu spoke these words, which they spoke

---

3   Bedouins.
4   Hatti.

to his majesty, falsely, (for) the vanquished chief of Kheta made them come to spy where his majesty was, in order to cause the army of his majesty not to draw up for fighting him, to battle with the vanquished chief of Kheta.

Positions of the Two Armies

Lo, the vanquished chief of Kheta came with every chief of every country, their infantry and their chariotry, which he had brought with him by force, and stood, equipped, drawn up in line of battle behind Kadesh the Deceitful, while his majesty knew it not. Then his majesty proceeded northward and arrived on the northwest of Kadesh; and the army of his majesty [made camp] there.

Examination of Hittite Scouts

Then, as his majesty sat upon a throne of gold, there arrived a scout who was in the following of his majesty, and he brought two scouts of the vanquished chief of Kheta. They were conducted into the presence, and his majesty said to them: "What are you?" They said: "As for us, the vanquished chief of the Kheta has caused that we should come to spy out where his majesty is." Said his majesty to them: "He! Where is he, the vanquished chief of Kheta? Behold, I have heard, saying: 'He is in the land of Aleppo.'" Said they: "See, the vanquished chief of Kheta is stationed, together with many countries, which he has brought with him by force, being every country which is in the districts of the land of Kheta, the land of Naharin, and all Kode. They are equipped with infantry and chariotry, bearing their weapons; more numerous are they than the sand of the shore. See, they are standing, drawn up for battle, behind Kadesh the Deceitful."

The Council of War

Then his majesty had the princes called into the presence, and had them hear every word which the two scouts of the vanquished chief of Kheta, who were in the presence, had spoken. Said his majesty to them: "See the manner wherewith the chiefs of the peasantry and the officials under whom is the land of Pharaoh, L. P. H., have stood, daily, saying to the Pharaoh: 'The vanquished chief of Kheta is in the land of Aleppo; he has fled before his majesty, since hearing that, behold, he came.' This they spoke to his majesty daily. But see, I have held a hearing in this very hour, with the two scouts of the vanquished chief of Kheta, to the effect that the vanquished chief of Kheta is coming, together with the numerous countries [that are with] him, being people and horses, like the multitudes of the sand. They are stationed behind Kadesh the Deceitful. But the governors of the countries and the officials under whose authority is the land of Pharaoh, L. P. H., were not able to tell it to us."

Said the princes who were in the presence of his majesty: "It is a great fault, which the governors of the countries and the officials of Pharaoh, L. P. H., have committed in not informing that the vanquished chief of Kheta was near the king; and (in) that they told his report to his majesty daily."

The Divisions in the South Are Ordered Up

Then the vizier was ordered to hasten the army of his majesty, while they were marching on the south of Shabtuna, in order to bring them to the place where his majesty was.

The Attack of the Asiatics

Lo, while his majesty sat talking with the princes, the vanquished chief of Kheta came, and the numerous countries, which were with him. They crossed over the channel on the south of Kadesh, and charged into the army of his majesty while they were marching, and not expecting it. Then the infantry and chariotry of his majesty retreated before them, northward to the place where his majesty was. Lo, the foes of the vanquished chief of Kheta surrounded the bodyguard of his majesty, who were by his side.

Ramesses' Personal Attack

When his majesty saw them, he was enraged against them, like his father, Montu, lord of Thebes. He seized the adornments of battle, and arrayed himself in his coat of mail. He was like Baal in his hour. Then he betook himself to his horses, and led quickly on, being alone by himself. He charged into the foes of the vanquished chief of Kheta, and the numerous countries which were with him. His majesty was like Sutekh, the great in strength, smiting and slaying among them; his majesty hurled them headlong, one upon another into the water of the Orontes.

Ramesses' Own Statement

"I charged all countries, while I was alone, my infantry and my chariotry having forsaken me. Not one among them stood to turn about. I swear, as Re loves me, as my father, Atum, favors me, that, as for every matter which his majesty has stated, I did it in truth, in the presence of my infantry and my chariotry."

Relief Inscriptions

Over King's Horses and Chariot

The Good God, mighty in valor, great in victory, crushing all countries, King of Upper and Lower Egypt: Usermare-Setepnere; Son of Re; Ramses-Meriamon. The stand which his majesty made while he was camping on the north west of Kadesh. He charged into the midst of the foe belonging to the vanquished chief of Kheta, while he was alone by himself, and no other with him. He found surrounding him 82,500 horse in four bodies on his every side. He slaughtered them, making (them) heaps beneath his horses. He slew all the chiefs of all the countries, the allies of the vanquished chief of Kheta, together with his own great chiefs, his infantry and his chariotry. He overthrew them prostrate upon their faces, and hurled them down, one upon another into the waters of the Orontes. His majesty was behind them like a fierce-eyed lion in their place. Lo, the vanquished chief of Kheta stood extending backward his arms in praise of the Good God.

Among the Fleeing Enemy

Tergen.
Tergenenes, charioteer of the vanquished chief of Kheta.

The great horse of his majesty: "Victory-in-Thebes;" of the great stable: "Usermare-Setepnere,-Beloved-of-Amon."

Kemeth, chief of the Warriors.

_____es, charioteer of the vanquished chief of Kheta.

Tergetetethes, chief of the archers of the Thebes.

Kherpesar, scribe of the vanquished chief of Kheta.

Egem, chief of the archers of the vanquished chief of Kheta.

Teyeder, chief of the bodyguard of the vanquished chief of Kheta.

Pcycs, charioteer of the vanquished chief of Kheta.

Gerbetes, chariot-warrior of the vanquished chief of Kheta.

Semretes.

Peyes, charioteer of the vanquished chief of Kheta.

Teder, chief of the warriors (Tw-hy-r).

Methrem.

Rebesnen, chief of the archers of Enenes.

Septher, brother of the vanquished chief of Kheta.

Thewethes, chief of the country of Tenes.

Rebeyer.

The wretched chief of Aleppo turned upside down by his soldiers, after his majesty hurled him into the water.

Warriors, who are in front of the [commander], 8,000.

Town of Kadesh.

By the King of Kheta

The vanquished, wretched chief of Kheta, standing before his infantry and chariotry with his face turned round, and his heart afraid. He went not forth to battle, for fear of his majesty, after he saw his majesty prevailing [against the vanquished chief] of Kheta and all the chiefs of all the countries [who] were with him. His majesty ... he overthrew them .... [The vanquished chief of Kheta] said: "He is like Sutekh, great in might; Baal is in his limbs."

In Front of Troops

The arrival of the recruits of Pharaoh, L. P. H., from the land of Amurru. They found that the force of the vanquished chief of Kheta had surrounded the camp of his majesty on its western side. His majesty had been camping alone, no army with him, [waiting the] arrival of his [officers] and his army and the division with which Pharaoh, L. P. H., was, had not finished setting up the camp.

Now the division of Re and the division of Ptah were on the march; they had not (yet) arrived, and their officers were in the [forest] of Bewey. Then the recruits cut off the foe belonging to the vanquished chief of Kheta, while they (the foe) were entering into the camp, and Pharaoh's officers slew them; they left not a single survivor among them. Their hearts were filled with the mighty valor of Pharaoh, their good lord; he was behind them like a steward of ..., like a wall of iron, forever and ever.

78. TREATY BETWEEN RAMESSES II AND HATTUSHILI

Two versions of the treaty made between Ramesses II of Egypt and Hattushili of Hatti exist, and translations of both are reproduced here side by side for comparison. The one on the left comes from the Hittite archives discovered at Boğhazkale in Turkey and is written in Akkadian. The one on the right was found at Karnak and at the Ramesseum and is written, of course, in Egyptian.

Explanatory Introduction (in Egyptian only)

Year 21, first month of winter, day 21, under the Majesty of the King of Upper and Lower Egypt Usima᷂re᷂-setpenre᷂, son of Re᷂, Ra᷂messe-mi-Amun, granted life eternally and forever, beloved of Amen-Re᷂, Harakhte, Ptah South-of-His-Wall, lord of ᷂Onkhtowe, Mut lady of Ishru and Khons-Neferhotpe, being arisen upon the Horus-throne of the Living like his father Harakhte eternally and for evermore.

On this day, when His Majesty was at the town of Pi-Ra᷂messe-mi-Amun doing the pleasure of his father Amen-Re᷂, Harakhte, Atum lord-of-the-two-lands-of-Heliopolis, Amun of Ra᷂messe-mi-Amwn, Ptah of Ra᷂messe-mi-Amun and Setekh great-of-valour, son of Nut, according as they give to him an infinity of Sed-festivals and an eternity of peaceful years, all lands and all hill-countries being prostrate under his sandals eternally; (3) there came the king's messenger, the deputy-commander .... the king's messenger ...... [Usima᷂re᷂]-setpen[re᷂], ... -tesub and the messenger of Hatti ......, carrying [the tablet of silver which (?)] (4) the great chief of Hatti, Hattušili, [caused] to be brought to Pharaoh in order to beg pe[ace from the Majesty of Usima᷂re᷂-setpenre᷂, son of Re᷂, Ra᷂messe-mi-Amun, granted life eternally and forever like his father Re᷂ every day.

Heading to the Egyptian Translation of the Treaty

Copy of the tablet of silver which the great chief of Hatti, Hattušili, caused to be brought to Pharaoh by the hand of his messenger (5) Tartesub and his messenger Ra᷂mose, in order to beg peace from the Majesty [of Usima᷂re᷂-setpenre᷂], son of Re᷂, Ra᷂messe-mi-Amun, bull of rulers, who makes his boundary where he will in every land.

§1. Preamble of the actual Treaty

Hittite-Babylonian Text.

(1) [And so be it. Riamasesa-mai-]Amana, the great king, king [of Egypt, the strong], (2) [with Hattušili, the great king], king of the land Hatti, his brother, in order to give good peace, (3) [good brotherhood and to obtain] a mighty [king]dom between them as long as we [live] (and) [forever] (4) [a treaty] has made.

Egyptian Text.

The treaty which the great prince of Hatti, Hattušili, the strong, the son of Mursili, (6) the great chief of Hatti, the strong, the son of the son of Šubbi[luliuma, the great chief of Hatti, the str]ong, made upon a tablet of silver for Usima^{c}re^c-setpenre^c, the great ruler of Egypt, the strong, the son of Menma^{c}re^c, the great ruler of Egypt, the strong, the son of the son of Menpehtire^c, (7) the great ruler of Egypt, the strong: the good treaty of peace and brotherhood, giving peace [and brotherhood]....... between us by means of a treaty of Hatti with Egypt] forever.

Riamasesa-mai-Amana, the great king, king of Egypt, the strong in all lands, son [of] (5) Minmuaria, the great king, king of Egypt, the strong, son of the son of Minpahiritaria, the great king, (6) [king of Egy]pt, the strong, unto Hattušili, the great king, king of the land Hatti, the strong, the son of Mursili, the great king, (7) king of the land Hatti, the strong, son of the son of Šubbiluliuma, the great king, king of the land Hatti, the strong, behold now I give (8) [good] brotherhood, good peace between us forever, in order to give good peace, good brotherhood (9) by means of [a treaty] of Egypt with Hatti forever. So it is.

§ 2. The Treaty is the resumption of old peaceful relations

Hittite-Babylonian Text.

Behold, the policy of the great king, of Egypt, (10) [and of the great king], king of Hatti since eternity—god did not permit the making of hostility between them, (11) [by means of a treaty] forever.

Egyptian Text.

Now aforetime, since eternity, as regards the policy of the great ruler of Egypt and the great chief of Hatti—the god did not permit hostility to be made between them, by means of a treaty.

But in the (8) time of Muwattalli, the great chief of Hatti, my brother, he fought with [Ra^{c}messe-mi-Amun], the great ruler of Egypt.

Behold, Riamasesa-mai-Amana, the great king, king of Egypt, in order to make the policy (12) [which Samas and] Tesub made for Egypt with the land Hatti because of his policy which is from eternity, (13) wickedly [will not become host]ile to make hostility between them unto everlasting and unto all (time).

But hereafter, beginning from this day, behold Hattušili, the great chief of Hatti, is [in] a treaty for making permanent the policy which Preᶜ made and Setekh made for the land of Egypt (9) with the land of Hatti, so as not to permit hostilities to be made between them forever.

§ 3. Declaration of the new treaty.

Hittite-Babylonian Text.

(14) Riamasesa-mai-Amana, the great king, king of Egypt, has made himself in a treaty upon a silver tablet (15) with Hattušili, the great king, king of the land Hatti, to brother, from this day to give good peace and good brotherhood (16) between us forever; and he is a brother to me and at peace with me, and I am a brother to him and at peace with him (17) forever.

Egyptian Text.

Behold, Hattušili, the great chief of Hatti, has made himself in a treaty with Usimaᶜreᶜ-serpenreᶜ, the great ruler of Egypt, beginning with this day, to cause to be made good peace and good brotherhood between us forever; (10) and he is in brotherhood with me and at peace with me, and I am in brotherhood with him and at peace with him forever.

And since Muwattalli, the great chief of Hatti, my brother, hastened after his fate, and Hattušili took his seat as (11) great chief of Hatti on the throne of his father; behold I have become with Raᶜmesse-mi- Amun, the great ruler of Egypt, we being [together in] our peace and our brotherhood;

And we have made brotherhood, peace and goodwill more than the brotherhood and peace of former times, (18) which was between [Egypt and] Hatti.

and it is better than the peace and the brotherhood of formerly, which was in the land.

Behold, Riamasesa-mai-Amana, the great king, king of Egypt, is in good peace and good brotherhood (19) with Hattušili, the great king, king of the land Hatti.

Behold, I, being the great chief of Hatti, am with (12) [Raᶜmesse-mi-Amun], the great ruler of Egypt, in good peace and good brotherhood.

Behold, the sons of Riamasesa-mai- Amana, the king of Egypt, (20) are at peace (and) are bro[thers with] the sons of Hattušili, the great king, king of the land Hatti, forever; and they are according to our policy (21) of [our] brotherhood [and] our peace.

And the children of the children [of] the great chief of Hatti shall be in brotherhood and at peace with the children of the children of Raᶜmesse-mi- Amun, the great ruler of Egypt; they being in our policy of brotherhood and our policy (13) [of peace].

And Egypt with the land Hatti—they are at peace, they are brothers like us forever.

[And the land of Egypt] with the land Hatti [shall be] at peace and in brotherhood like us forever; and hostilities shall not be made between them forever.

§ 4. Mutual Assurances with regard to Invasion

Hittite-Babylonian Text.

(22) And Riamasesa-mai-Amana, the great king, king of Egypt, shall not trespass into the land Hatti to take aught (23) from therein [forever]; and Hattušili, the great king, king of the land Hatti, shall not trespass into Egypt (24) to take aught from therein [forever].

Egyptian Text.

And the great chief of Hatti shall not trespass into the land of Egypt forever to take aught from it; and Usinmareᶜ-setpenreᶜ the great ruler of Egypt, shall not trespass into the land (14) [of Hatti to take] (aught) from it forever.

§ 5. Formal Renewal of the former Treaty

Hittite-Babylonian Text.

Behold, the decree of eternity which Samas and Tesub have made (25) for Egypt and the land Hatti [to make peace] and brotherhood in order not to give hostility between them. (26) And behold, Riamasesa-mai-A[mana, the great king], king of Egypt, takes hold of it to make peace from this day.

(27) Behold, Egypt and Hatti [are at peace, and] they are brothers forever.

Egyptian Text.

As to the regular treaty which there was in the time of Subbiluliuma, the great chief of Hatti, and likewise the regular treaty which was in the time of Muwattalli (sic!), the great chief of Hatti, my father, I take hold of it. Behold, Raᶜmesse-mi-Amun, the great ruler of Egypt, takes hold (15) [of the peace which it] makes together with us from this day;

and we will act according to this regular policy.

§ 6. Undertaking of a Defensive Alliance (cf. § 8)

Hittite-Babylonian Text.

And if another enemy (28) come [against] the land Hatti, and Hattušili, [the great king of the land Hat]ti, send to me saying, 'Come unto me (29) for [my] help against him'; then Ri[amasesa-mai-Ama]na, the great king, king of Egypt (30) shall send his troops (and) his chariots and shall slay [his enemy and] he shall restore [con]fidence to the land Hatti.

Egyptian Text.

And if another enemy come to the lands of Usimaᶜreᶜ-setpenreᶜ, the great ruler of Egypt, and he send to the great chief of Hatti saying, 'Come with me as help against him; the great chief of Hatti shall (16) [come to him], the great chief of Hatti [shall] slay his enemy.

But if it be not the desire of the great chief of Hatti to come, he shall send his troops and his chariotry and shall slay his enemy.

§ 7. Common Action to be taken against Rebellious Subjects (cf. § 9)

Hittite-Babylonian Text.

(31) And if Hattušili, the great king, king of the land Hatti, [become incensed] against servants of his [and they] sin against him, (32) and thou send to Riamasesa, the great king, king of [Egypt] concerning it;

straightaway] Riamasesa-mai-Amana (33) his troops (and) his chariots shall send, and they shall destroy all [of them] against whom [thou art become incensed].

Egyptian Text.

Or if Ra^cmesse-mi-Amun, (17) [the great ruler of Egypt], become incensed against servants of his, and they do another offence against him, and he go to slay his enemy;

the great chief of Hatti shall act with him [to destroy] everyone [against whom] they shall be incensed.

§ 8. Reciprocal Clause (corresponding to § 6)

Hittite-Babylonian Text.

[And if] another enemy come (34) against Egypt, and Riamasesa-mai-Amana, the king of Egypt, thy brother, [send] to Hattušili, (35) king of the land Hatti, his brother, saying, [Co]me for my help against him'; straightway then shall Ha[ttušili], king of the land Hatti, (36) send his troops (and) his [chariots]; he [shall slay] my enemy.

Egyptian Text.

But [if] another enemy [come] against the great chief [of Hatti];

[then shall Usi]ma^c[re^c]-setpenre^c (18) [the great ruler of Egypt] come to him as help to slay his enemy.

(But) if it be (not) the desire of Ra^cmesse-mi-Amun, the great ruler of Egypt, to come, he—.......Hatti, [and he shall send his troops and his] (19) chariotry, besides returning answer to the land of Hatti.

§ 9. Reciprocal Clause (corresponding to § 6)

Hittite-Babylonian Text.

And if Riamasesa, [the great king, king] of Egypt, (37) become incensed against servants of his, and they commit sin against [him, and I send] (38) to Hattušili, king of the land Hatti, my brother, concerning [it];

then Hattušili, the great king, king of Egypt, (39) shall send his troops (and) his chariots and they shall destroy all [of them]; and I will.......

Egyptian Text.

But if servants of the great chief of Hatti trespass against him,

and Ra^cmes[se]-mi-Amun, [the great ruler of Egypt,].................

§ 10. A Clause relating to Succession (?)

Hittite-Babylonian Text.

(40) And behold the son of Hattušili, king of the land Hatti, [the treaty which] we have made..........(41) in the place of Hattušili, his father, after years..........(42).......of the land Hatti have committed sin........(43)..............chariots where shall I return...,(44)....in the land Hatti

[*The text breaks off here.*]

Egyptian Text.

............the [land] of Hatti (and) the land (?) [of Egypt]......(20)..the life. Supposing I shall go after [my] fate, then Raᶜmesse-mi-Amun, the great ruler of Egypt, living forever, shall act ...coming [to] the [land of Hat]ti to cause to make (21) them to make him for themselves to lord, so as to cause Usimaᶜreᶜ-setpen[reᶜ], the great ruler of Egypt, to be silent with his mouth forever. And after......the land of Hatti and he return to place the great chief of Hatti and similarly the....

§ 11. Extradition of Important Fugitives

Egyptian Text.

[If any great man flee from the land of Egypt and he come to the lands of] the great chief of Hatti; or a town (22) (or a district) [belonging to the lands of Raᶜmesse-mi-Amun, the great ruler of Egypt, and they come to the great chief of Hatti: the great chief of Hatti shall not receive them. The great chief of Hatti shall cause them to be brought to Usimaᶜreᶜ-setpenreᶜ, the great ruler of Egypt, their lord, [on accou]nt of it.

§ 1-2. Extradition of Fugitives of Humble Birth

Egyptian Text.

Or if one man or two men who are unknown flee (23), and they come to the land of Hatti to be servants of another, they shall not be left in the land of Hatti, they shall be brought to Raᶜmesse-mi-Amun, the great ruler of Egypt.

§ 13. Reciprocal Clause (corresponding to § 11)

Egyptian Text.

Or if a great man flee from the land of Hatti, and [he come to the lands of(?) Usi]maᶜ[reᶜ]-setpenreᶜ, the [great] ruler of Egypt; or a town or a district or (24)......belonging to the land of Hatti, and they come to Raᶜmesse-mi-Amun, the great ruler of Egypt: Usimaᶜreᶜ-setpenreᶜ, the great ruler of Egypt, shall not receive them. Raᶜmesse-mi-Amun, the great ruler of Egypt, shall cause them to be brought to the chief...... they shall not be left.

§ 14. Reciprocal Clause (corresponding to § 12)

Egyptian Text.

Likewise, if one man or two men (25) who are [not] known flee to the land of Egypt to be subjects of others, Usimaᶜreᶜ-setpenreᶜ, the great ruler of Egypt, shall not leave them; he shall cause them to be brought to the great chief of Hatti.

§ 15. The Gods of Hatti and Egypt are Witnesses to the Treaty

Egyptian Text.

As for these worlds of the treaty [made by] the great chief of Hatti with Ra‑mes[se- mi-Amun], the great ruler (26) [of Egypt, in] writing upon this tablet of silver; as for these words, a thousand gods, male gods and female gods of those of the land of Hatti, together with a thousand gods, male gods and female gods of those of the land of Egypt—they are with me as witnesses [hearing] these words: Prethe lord of the sky; Pre‑ of the town of Arinna; (27) Setekh, the lord of the sky; Setekh of Hatti; Setekh of the town of Arinna; Setekh of the town of Zippalanda; Setekh of the town of Betiarik; Setekh of the town of Hissashapa; Setekh of the town of Sarissa; Setekh of the town of Halab; Setekh of the town of Lihzin; Setekh (28) of the town of...r(?)...; Setekh [of the town of......; Setekh of the town] of [S ?]-*m*(?)-*s*; Setekh of the town of *S-h-p-n*; Astarte of the land of Hatti; the god of Zitharias; the god of Karzis (?); the god of Hapanta[ri]as; (29) the goddess of the town Karahna; the goddess of Tyre; the goddess of *?-w-k*(?); the goddess of *D-n-* ?; the god of *P*(?)-*n-t*; the god of *?-r*; the god of *H-?-b-t*; the queen of the sky; the gods lords of swearing; this goddess, the mistress of the earth; the mistress of swearing Ishara; the mistress of (...); (30) (the) mountains and the rivers of the land of Hatti; the gods of the land of Kizuwadna; Amun; Pre‑; Setekh; the male gods and the female gods; the mountains and the rivers of the land of Egypt; the sky; the earth; the great sea; the winds; the clouds.

§ 16. Curses or Blessings on those who Violate or Keep the Treaty

Egyptian Text.

As to these words (31) which are upon this tablet of silver of the land of Hatti and of the land of Egypt, as to him who shall not keep them, a thousand gods of the land of Hatti and a thousand gods of the land of Egypt shall destroy his house, his land and his servants. But he who shall keep these words which are on this tablet of silver, be they Hatti, or be they (32) Egyptians, and who do not neglect them, a thousand gods of the land of Hatti and a thousand gods of the land of Egypt will cause him to be healthy and to live, together with his houses and his (land) and his servants.

§ 17. Amnesty for Extradited Persons

Egyptian Text.

If one man flee from the land of Egypt, or two, or three, and (33) they come to the great chief of Hatti, the great chief of Hatti shall seize them and shall cause them to be brought back to Usima‑re‑-setpenre‑, the great ruler of Egypt. But as for the man who shall be brought to Ra‑messe-mi-Amun, the great ruler of Egypt, let not his crime be charged against him, let not (34) his house, his wives or his children be destroyed, [let him not] be [killed], let no injury be done to his eyes, to his ears, to his mouth or to his legs, let not-any [crime be charged] against him.

§ 18. Reciprocal Clause (corresponding to § 17)

Egyptian Text.

Likewise if a man flee from the land of Hatti, be he one, be he two, or be he three, and they come to Usima‑re‑-setpenre‑ (35) the great ruler of Egypt, let Ra‑ messe-mi-Amun, the [great] ruler [of Egypt, cause] them to be brought to the great chief of Hatti, and the great chief of Hatti shall not charge their crime against them, and they shall not destroy his house, his wives or his children, and they shall not kill him, and they shall not do injury to his ears, (36) to his eyes, to his mouth or to his legs, and they shall not charge any crime against him.

§ 19. Description of the Silver Tablet

Egyptian Text.

What is in the middle of the tablet of silver. On its front side: a reliefs) consisting of an image of Setekh embracing an image of the great prince of Hatti, surrounded by a legend, saying: the seal of Setekh, the ruler of the sky, the seal of the treaty made by Hattušili, the great chief (37) of Hatti, the strong, the son of Mursili, the great chief of Hatti, the strong. What is within the surrounding (frame) of the relief: the seal [of Setekh, the ruler of the sky]. [What is on] its other side: a relief consisting of a female image of [the] goddess of Hatti embracing a female image of the chieftainess of Hatti, surrounded by a legend saying: the seal of (28) Pre^c of the town of Arinna, the lord of the land, the seal of Puduhepa, the chieftainess of the land of Hatti, the daughter of the land of Kizuwadna, the [priestess] of [the town of] Arinna, the lady of the land, the servant of the goddess. What is within the surrounding (frame) of the relief: the seal of Pre^c of Arinna, the lord of every land.

79. THE MERNEPTAH STELA

This inscription comes from a stela erected by pharaoh Merneptah (Dynasty 19) in his mortuary temple at Thebes. He wrote it on the back of a stela that had belonged to Amenhotep III (Dynasty 18) and that had originally been standing in Amenhotep's mortuary temple. The inscription, which commemorates Merneptah's military victories in Libya and Palestine, has gained wide attention because it contains the earliest reference to Israel in ancient literature.

Date and Introduction

Year 5, third month of the third season (eleventh month), third day, under the majesty of Horus: Mighty Bull, Rejoicing in Truth; King of Upper and Lower Egypt: Binre-Meriamon, Son of Re: Merneptah-Hotephirma, magnifying might, exalting the victorious sword of Horus, mighty Bull, smiter of the Nine Bows, whose name is given forever and ever.

The Great Deliverance

His victories are published in all lands, to cause that every land together may see, to cause the glory of his conquests to appear; King Merneptah, the Bull, lord of strength, who slays his foes, beautiful upon the field of victory, when his onset occurs; the Sun, driving away the storm which was over Egypt, allowing Egypt to see the rays of the sun, removing the mountain of copper from the neck of the people so that he might give breath to the people who were smothered. He gratified the heart of Memphis on their foes, making Tatenen rejoice over his enemies. He opened the gates of the walled city which were stopped up, and caused his temples to receive their food (even), King Merneptah, the unique one, who establishes the hearts of hundreds of thousands of myriads, so that breath enters into their nostrils at the sight of him. He has penetrated the land of Temeh in his lifetime, and put eternal fear sin the heart of the Meshwesh. He has turned back Libya, who invaded Egypt, and great fear of Egypt is in their hearts

The Rout of the Libyans

Their advanced columns they left behind them, their feet made no stand, but fled. Their archers threw down their bows, and the heart of their fleet ones was weary with marching. They loosed their water skins and threw them to the ground, their ... were taken and thrown out.

The Fall of the Libyan Chief

The wretched, fallen chief of Libya, fled by favor of night alone, with no plume upon his head, his two feet [failed]. His women were taken before his face, the grain of his supplies was plundered, and he had no water in the skin to keep him alive. The face of his brothers was hostile to slay him, one fought another among his leaders. Their camp was burned and made a roast, all his possessions were food for the troops. When he arrived in his country, he was the complaint of every one in his land. [Ashamed], he bowed himself down, an evil fate removed (his) plume. They all spoke against him, among the inhabitants of his city: "He is in the power of the gods, the lords of Memphis; the lord of Egypt has cursed his name, Meryey, the abomination of Memphis, from son to son of his family, forever. Binre-Meriamon is in pursuit of his children; Merneptah-Hotephirma is appointed to be his fate."

Merneptah's Fame in Libya

He has become a proverb for Libya; the youth say to youth, concerning his victories: "It has not been done to us [before] since the time of Re," say they. Every old man says to his son: "Alas for Libya!" They have ceased to live in the pleasant fashion of walking in the field; their going about is stopped in a single day. The Tehenu are consumed in a single year. Sutekh has turned his back upon their chief; their settlements are desolated with his [consent]. There is no work of carrying ... in these days. Concealment is good; there is safety in the cavern. The great lord of Egypt, possessor of might and victory! Who will fight, knowing his stride? The fool, the witless is he who receives him; he shall not know the morrow, who transgresses his boundary.

Divine Protection of Egypt

Since the time of the gods, say they, Egypt has been the only daughter of Re; his son is he who sits upon the throne of Shu. No one can make a design to invade her people, for the eye of every god is behind him who would violate her; it (the eye) captures the rear of her foes. ... A great wonder has happened for Egypt, the power of which has made her invader a living prisoner. The divine king [exults] over his enemies, in the presence of Re. Meryey, the evil-doer, whom the god, the lord who is in Memphis, has overthrown, he has been judged with him in Heliopolis, and the divine ennead declared him guilty of his crimes.

Merneptah Divinely Appointed

The All-Lord has said: "Give the sword to my son, the upright of heart, the good and kindly Merneptah, the [champion] on behalf of Memphis, the advocate of Heliopolis, who opens the towns that were closed up. Let him set free multitudes who are bound in every district, let him give offerings to the temples, let him send in incense before the god, let him cause the princes to [recover] their possessions, let him cause the poor to [re-enter] their cities."

Heliopolis Praises Merneptah

They say among the lords of Heliopolis regarding their son, Merneptah: "Give to him duration like Re, let him be advocate of him who is oppressed in every country. Egypt has been assigned to him as the portion of [him who has gained it] for himself forever. His strength is its people. Lo, when one dwells in the time of this hero, the breath of life comes immediately. . . . . so they say.

The Gods Delivered Meryey to Merneptah

Meryey, the wretched, vanquished chief of Libya, came to invade the "Walls-of-the-Sovereign" (Memphis), [who is its lord,] whose son shines on his throne, the King Merneptah. Ptah said concerning the vanquished (chief) of Libya: "All his crimes shall be gathered and returned upon his (own) head. Deliver him into the hand of Merneptah, that he may make him disgorge what he has swallowed, like a crocodile. Behold, the swift is the captor of the swift; and the king shall snare him, (though) his strength be known; for Amon shall bind him in his hand and shall deliver him to his *ka* in Hermonthis, (to him) the King Merneptah."

Rejoicing of the Egyptians

Great joy has come in Egypt, rejoicing comes forth from the towns of Tomeri. They converse of the victories which Merneptah has achieved among the Tehenu: "How amiable is he, the victorious ruler! How magnified is the king among the gods! How fortunate is he, the commanding lord! Sit happily down and talk, or walk far out upon the way, (for) there is no fear in the heart of the people. The strongholds are left to themselves, the wells are opened (again). The messengers [skirt] the battlements of the walls, shaded from the sun, until their watchmen wake. The soldiers lie sleeping, and the border scouts are in the field at their (own) desire. The herds of the field are left as cattle sent forth, without herdmen, crossing (at will) the fulness of the stream. There is no uplifting of a shout in the night: 'Stop! Behold, one comes, one comes with the speech of strangers!' One comes and goes with singing, and there is no lamentation of mourning people. The towns are settled again anew; as for the one that plows his harvest, he shall eat it. Re has turned himself to Egypt; he was born, destined to be her protector, the King Merneptah."

Concluding Strophe

The kings are overthrown, saying: "Salam!"[5]
Not one holds up his head among the Nine Bows.
Wasted is Tehenu,
Kheta is pacified,
Plundered is Canaan, with every evil,
Carried off is Askalon,
Seized upon is Gezer,
Yenoam is made as a thing not existing.
Israel is desolated, his seed is not;
Palestine has become a widow for Egypt.
All lands are united, they are pacified;
Everyone that is turbulent is bound by King Merneptah, given life like Re, every day.

80. LETTER OF BAKENAMON

This papyrus letter found at Thebes and dating to the reign of Merneptah or Seti II (Dynasty 19) from Bakenamon, "the scribe of the offering table," to his father in Memphis sheds some light on agricultural labor on temple lands during this period.

The scribe of the offering table Bakenamon to the prophet of the Temple of Thoth Ramose.

The scribe of the offering table Bakenamon greets his father, the prophet Ramose of the Temple of Thoth, Content-of-Heart, in Memphis: In life, prosperity and health and in the favor of Amon-Re, King of the Gods! I am calling upon Pre-Harakhti in his rising and in his setting, upon Amon, Pre and Ptah of Ramesses (II), l.p.h., and upon all the gods of Pi-Ramessumiamon, l.p.h., the great Ka of Pre-Harakhti, to give you health, to give you life, to give you prosperity, and to let me see you in health and fill my embrace with you.

A further matter: I have taken note of the message you wrote inquiring after my welfare. It is Pre and Ptah who will inquire after your welfare. I didn't know that my boy would reach you since it was to the town of Sekhempehty that I had sent him. Otherwise I would have sent you a letter by his hand. Moreover, don't cease writing to me regularly that I may learn about your condition.

Further, I investigated the matter of the Syrian of the Temple of Thoth about whom you had written me, and I discovered that he was assigned to be a cultivator of the Temple of Thoth under your authority in Year 3, second month of the third season, day 10, from among the slaves of the ships' cargoes that the superintendent of fortresses had brought back. To inform you of his identity:

---

5 "Peace!"

the Syrian Nekedy, son of Serertja whose mother is Kedy, of the land of Aradus, a slave of the ship's cargo belonging to this temple in the ship captain Kel's boat, whose certificate reads, "It is the captain of heralds of the soldiers of the garrison of Pharaoh, l.p.h., Khaemope who received him in charge in order to have him conscripted." I went to the captain of heralds of the soldiers of the garrison of Pharaoh, l.p.h., Khaemope. He disclaimed responsibility for him with me; he told me in short, "It is the vizier Merysakhmet who received him in charge in order to have him conscripted." I went to the vizier Merysakhmet, and he and his scribes disclaimed responsibility, saying, "We never even saw him." I am after the captain of assault officers daily, saying, "Produce the Syrian cultivator of the Temple of Thoth whom you received in charge that he may be taken to his prophet." I am now contending with him in the great court.

Moreover, I have taken note of the matter of the sacred standard of Thoth, about which you wrote me. It has not been brought to me straightaway, even though I had arranged for it to proceed in procession. But don't worry about it, although it is better if you send it to me so that I may have it proceed in procession.

Moreover, don't worry about the seed-order. I examined it, and I found that three men and one boy, totaling four persons, produce 700 *khar*-measures (of grain). I spoke with the chief record keepers of the granary and told them, "Take the three cultivators of the god to serve this year." And they answered me, "We will do so, look, we will do so. We shall heed your request"; so they said to me. I am staying in their presence until they have caused the registration documents to go out to the fields and you find out about everything which I shall have done for you, because it is only one man, producing 200 *khar*-measures (of grain) that they have determined for me to carry it out, leaving at your disposal two men and one boy, producing 500 *khar*-measures (of grain).

Now regarding this Syrian cultivator who was assigned to you, he was assigned to you during the summer months. As long as he survives, his summer shall be charged against you.

81. LETTER OF KENHIKHOPESHEF

Many letters have been found at Deir el-Medina, the site of a New Kingdom village on the west side of Thebes, the inhabitants of which prepared tombs in the Valley of Kings and the Valley of Queens for the government. The literacy rate of the village was quite high (5%). This letter from the latter half of Dynasty 19 comes from an otherwise unknown Kenhikhopeshef.

Kenhikhopeshef addresses the woman Inerwau:

What means your failing to go to the woman diviner on account of the two infants who died while in your charge? Inquire of the woman diviner about the death of the two infants, whether it was their fate or their destiny. And you shall inquire about them for me and get a view of my own life and their mother's life. As for whatever god shall be [mentioned] to you afterwards(?), you shall write me concerning his identity. You [will be rendering ser]vice for one who knows her occupation(?).

82. THE TALE OF TWO BROTHERS

Dating approximately to the reign of Seti II (Dynasty 19), the Papyrus D'Orbiney contains an interesting folk tale concerning two brothers, Anubis (Anpu in this translation) and Bata, their falling out and later reconciliation. The scribe who wrote down the story identifies himself as Ennana. Although this does not necessarily indicate that he is the author, his handwriting is exquisite.

There were two brothers, (children) of one mother and of one father. Anpu was the name of the elder, Bata that of the younger.

Anpu had a house and a wife, and his younger brother was like a son to him. He it was who .... clothes for him. He followed after his cattle ...... he who did the ploughing .... did all the labours of the fields.

Behold, his younger brother was so good a labourer that there was not his equal in the whole land. But when the days had multiplied after this the younger brother was with his cattle according to his daily custom; he took them to his house every evening; he was laden with all the herbs of the field

(The elder brother) sat with his wife and ate and drank (while the younger was in) the stable with his cattle. But when the day dawned.......he rose before his elder brother, took bread to the field and called the (labourers) to eat in the field.

He followed after his cattle and they told him where the best grasses were. He understood all that they said and he took them to the place where the best herbage was which they wanted.

And the cattle which was before him became exceedingly beautiful, and they multiplied exceedingly. And when the time for ploughing came his elder brother said to him, "Let us take our teams for ploughing, because the land has made its appearance. The time is excellent for ploughing it. So do come with seed for we shall accomplish the ploughing." So said he.

And the younger brother proceeded to do whatever his elder told him......But when the day dawned they went to the field with their......and worked at their tillage and they enjoyed themselves exceedingly at their work.

But when the days had multiplied after this they were in the field.....(the elder brother) sent his junior, saying, "Go and fetch seed for us from the village."

And the younger brother found the wife of the elder sitting at her dressing table. And he said to her, "Arise and give me seed that I may go back to the field because my elder brother wishes me to return without delay."

And she said to him, "Go, open the bin, and take yourself whatever you will; my hair would fall by the way."

The youth entered his stable, he took a large vessel for he wished to take a great deal of seed and he loaded himself with grain and went out with it.

And she said to him, "How much have you on......" And he said to her, "Two measures of barley and three of wheat; in all five, which are on my arm."

And she spoke to him saying, "What strength there is in you; indeed, I observe your vigour every day." Her heart knew him...... She seized upon him and said to him, "Come let us lie down for an instant. Better for you … beautiful clothes."

The youth became like a panther with fury on account of the shameful discourse which she had addressed to him. And she was alarmed exceedingly.

He spoke to her, saying, "Truly, I have looked upon you in the light of a mother and your husband in that of a father to me. (For he is older than I, as much as if he had begotten me.) What a great abomination is this which you have mentioned to me. Do not repeat it again to me, and I will not speak of it to any one. Truly, I will not let any thing of it come forth from my mouth to any man."

He took up his load and went forth to the field. He came to his elder brother and they accomplished the task of their labour. But when the time of evening had come the eider brother returned to his house. His younger brother behind his cattle .... loaded with all things of the field. He led his cattle before him to lie down in their stable....

Behold, the wife of his elder brother was alarmed at the discourse which she had held. She .... She made herself like one who has suffered violence from a man for she wished to say to her husband, "It is your younger brother who has done me violence."

Her husband returned home at evening according to his daily custom. He came to his house and he found his wife lying as if murdered by a ruffian.

She did not pour water upon his hand according to her custom. She did not light the lamp before him; his house was in darkness. She was lying uncovered.

Her husband said to her, "Who has been conversing with you?" She said, "No one has conversed with me except your younger brother; when he came to fetch seed for you, he found me sitting alone, and he said to me, 'Come and let us lie down for an instant,' that is what he said to me.

"But I did not listen to him. 'Behold, am I not your mother and your elder brother is he not like a father to you,' that is what I said to him, and he got alarmed and did me violence that I might not make a report to you, but if you let him live I shall kill myself. Behold he was come....

And the elder brother became like a panther .... he made his dagger sharp, and took it in his hand. And the elder brother put himself behind the door of his stable to kill his younger brother on his return at evening to bring his cattle to the stable.

But when the sun set he loaded himself with all the herbs of the field, according to his daily custom. And he came, and the first cow entered into the stable and it said to its keeper, "Truly, your elder brother is standing before you with his dagger to slay you. Betake yourself from before him."

He heard the speech of the first ox; the next one entered and it spoke in the same way. He looked under the door of the stable, and he saw the two feet of his elder brother, who was standing behind the door with a dagger in his hand.

He laid down his load upon the ground and betook himself to flight, his elder brother following him with his dagger.

The younger brother invoked the Sun-god Horus of the two horizons, saying, "My good Lord, it is you who distinguish wrong from right!" The Sun-god stopped to listen to all his wailings. And the Sun-god made a large stream, which was full of crocodiles between him and his elder; one of them was on one bank and one upon the other.

And the elder brother struck his hand twice (with rage) at not killing him: he did.

And the younger brother called to him from the bank, saying, "Stop till daybreak, and when the sun's disc comes forth I shall have an explanation with you in its presence to give the......of the truth, for I have never done wrong to you but I will never live in the places wherein you are. I am going to the mountain of the Cedar."

But when the day dawned the Sun-god, Horus of both horizons, came forth and each of them saw the other.

The young man spoke to his elder brother, saying, "What is this, your coming to kill me wrongfully? Hear you not what my mouth speaks? Truly, I am your younger brother, in very deed, and you were to me as a father, and your wife as a mother.

"Behold, is it not because you did send me to fetch seed for us, your wife said to me, 'Come let us lie down for an instant,' but see, she has turned it to you the wrong way."

And he made him understand what had happened with reference to himself with his wife. He swore by the Sun-god, Horus of both horizons saying, "Your intent is to slay me wrongfully; you are with your dagger ... and he took a sharp knife, cut off his phallus and threw it into the water and the fish swallowed it.

But he became faint and swooned away. And his elder brother felt compassion exceedingly. And he stood weeping and crying, not being able to pass over to the place where his younger brother was, on account of the crocodiles.

But the younger brother called to him saying, "Behold you did imagine a crime: you did not imagine that it was a virtuous action or a thing which I had done for you.

"Now return to your house, and do you look after your cattle, yourself; for I will no longer remain in a place where you are. I go to the mountain of the Cedar.

"But as to what you shall do for me, and your coming to look after me, you shall learn, namely: things will happen to me.

"I shall take my heart and place it in the top of the flower of the Cedar, and when the Cedar is cut down, it will fall to the ground.

"You shall come to seek it. If you are seven years in the search of it let not your heart be depressed, and when you have found it you shall place it in a cup of cold water; oh then I shall live (once more) and fling back a reply to an attack.

"And this you shall learn, namely, that the things have happened to me. When you shall take a jug of beer into your hand and it turns into froth, then delay not; for to you of a certainty is the-issue coming to pass."

Then he departed to the mountain of the Cedar and the elder brother returned to his house. He put his hand upon his head and smeared it with dust; and when he came to his house he slew his wife and flung her to the dogs. But he continued mourning for his younger brother.

But when the days had multiplied after this, the younger brother was at the mountain of the Cedar. There was no one with him and his time was spent in hunting the animals of the country. He returned at evening to lie down under the Cedar on the top of whose flowers his heart lay.

But when the days had multiplied after this he built with his hands a dwelling on the mountain of the Cedar, which was filled with all the good things which the possessor of a house desires.

And having gone out of his dwelling he met the company of the gods who were going forth to do their will in their land of Egypt.

The divine company spoke by one of them who said to him "Ho! BATA, Bull of the divine company! do you remain alone and abandon your country on account of the wife of ANPU, your elder brother? Behold, his wife is slain, because you have flung back replies to all the attacks made upon you."

Their hearts pitied him exceedingly. And the Sun-god, HORUS of both horizons said to CHNUM, "O, make a wife for BATA, that he may not remain alone."

And CHNUM made him a companion who as she sat was more beautiful in her limbs than any woman in the whole earth; the whole godhead was in her.

The seven Hathors came to see her, and they said with one mouth that she would die a violent death. And he loved her exceedingly and she remained in his house while he spent his time in hunting the animals of the country and bringing the game to her.

And he said to her, "Do not go out, lest the Sea carry you off, and I may not know how to rescue you from him, because I am a woman even as you are, for my heart is on the top of the flower of the Cedar and if any one finds it I shall be overcome by him." And he revealed to her his heart in all its height.

And when the days had multiplied after this, BATU went out to hunt the animals after his daily custom, and the young woman went out to take a turn under the Cedar which was near her house.

And the Sea beheld her and dashed its waters in pursuit of her and she betook herself to flight before it and entered into her house.

And the Sea cried to the Cedar saying, "O that I could seize upon her!" And the Cedar earned off one of her fragrant locks, and the Sea carried it to Egypt, and deposited it in the place where the washers of the King were.

And the odour of the lock grew into the clothes of the King. And a quarrel arose fimong the royal washers on account of the overpowering odour in the clothes of the King. The quarrel continued among them day after day, so that they no longer knew what they were doing.

And the Chief of the washers of the King went out to the water-side and his heart was exceedingly oppressed on account of the quarrels in which he was every day involved.

And he stopped and stood at the spot in the midst of which lay the fragrant lock in the water. And he stooped down and picked it up and he found the odour of it delicious, exceedingly, and he took it to the King.

And it was carried to the doctors, the magicians of the King. They said to the King, "The lock belongs to a daughter of the Sun-god, HORUS of both horizons, the essence of the whole godhead is in her.

"But the whole earth is in obeisance before you, send therefore envoys to every place to seek her; but as for the envoy who is for the mountain of the Cedar, send out with him troops in great numbers to bring her."

His Majesty replied, "Good exceedingly is that which ye have said to us!" And the envoys were sent.

But when the days had multiplied after this the troops that went to every place returned to give their reports to His Majesty, but those returned not who had gone to the mountain of the Cedar; BATA had slain them.

One of them returned to tell the tale to His Majesty. And His Majesty once more sent out troops, many bow-men and also cavalry to fetch her, and there was a woman with them, into whose hand one had given all the most beautiful trinkets for a woman.

And the woman came with her into Egypt, and rejoicing was made for her throughout the whole land. And His Majesty loved her exceedingly and she was raised to the dignity of a Princess.

And it was said to her that she should reveal the ways of her husband and she said to His Majesty, "Cause the Cedar to be cut down and he will be destroyed."

And troops were sent out with their swords to cut down the Cedar. They came to the Cedar and cut down the flower upon which lay the heart of BATA. He fell dead in an instant.

But when the dawn of the next day appeared the Cedar was cut down, and ANPU the elder brother of BATA entered his house. He sat down and washed his hand and there was given to him a jug of beer, but this turned into froth. Another jug was then given him of wine, but this at once became troubled.

Thereupon he took his staff and his sandals, likewise his clothes and his instruments of labour; and he betook himself to a journey towards the mountain of the Cedar.

He came to the dwelling of his younger brother and found him lying dead upon the floor. He wept when he saw his younger brother lying in the state of death, and he went out to seek for his brother's heart under the Cedar where he used to lie in the evening.

Three years he sought without finding. But when the fourth year was come his heart longed to return to Egypt and he said, "I will go tomorrow." Such was his intention.

But when the dawn of the next day appeared, he continued to walk under the Cedar, occupied with his search and he returned in the evening.

He looked after his search once more and found a pod. He examined under it; and, behold, there was the heart of his younger brother. He brought a vessel of cold water, dropped the heart into it, and sat down according to his daily custom.

But when the night was come the heart absorbed the water. BATA trembled in all his limbs and continued looking at his elder brother, but his heart was faint.

Then ANPU took the vessel of cold water which his brother's heart was in. And when the latter had drunk it up his heart rose in its place and he became as he had been before. Each embraced the other and each one of them held conversation with his companion.

And BATA said to his elder brother, "Behold I am about to become a great Bull with all the sacred marks, but with an unknown history.

"Do you sit upon my back and when the Sun-god rises we shall be in the place where my wife is. (Answer whether you will take me there ?) For there will be given to you all good things, yes, you shall be loaded with silver and gold for bringing me to the King, for I shall become a great marvel and there will be rejoicing for me in the whole land. Then do return to your village."

But when the dawn of the next day appeared BATA had assumed the form which he had mentioned to his elder brother. And ANPU, his elder brother, sat upon his back at dawn of day.

And he arrived at the place which had been spoken of and information was given to His Majesty, who inspected him and rejoiced exceedingly and celebrated a festival above all description, a mighty marvel and rejoicings for it were made throughout the whole land.

And there was brought silver and gold for the elder brother who staid in his village. But to (the Bull) there were given many attendants and many offerings and the King loved him exceedingly above all men in the whole land.

But when the days had multiplied after this he entered the sanctuary and stood in the very place where the Princess was. And he spoke to her, saying: "Look upon me, I am alive indeed."

And she said to him, "And who then are you?" And he said to her, "I am BATA, you gave information for the cutting down of the Cedar to the King as to where I was that I might no longer live. But look upon me for I am really alive. I am a Bull."

And the Princess was frightened exceedingly at the speech which her husband addressed to her. And he went out of the sanctuary.

But when the King sat down to make a holiday with her, and as she was at the table of His Majesty and he was exceedingly gracious to her she said to him, "Come swear to me by God that you will grant whatever I ask."

And he granted all that she asked, saying, "Let me eat the liver of the Bull for you have no need of him,"

This she spoke to him, and it grieved him exceedingly that she spoke it, and the heart of His Majesty was exceedingly troubled.

But when the dawn of the next day appeared there was celebrated a great festival with offerings to the Bull.

But one of the Chief Royal Officers of His Majesty was made to go and slay the Bull. And as they were killing him and he was in the hands of the attendants, he shook his neck and two drops of blood fell upon the two doorposts of His Majesty; one was on the one side of the great staircase of His Majesty, the other upon the other side; and they grew up into two mighty Persea trees, each of which stood alone.

And they went and told His Majesty saying: "Two mighty Persea trees have sprung up as a great omen of good fortune to His Majesty during the night, near the great staircase of His Majesty and there is rejoicing for them through the whole land and offerings are made to them."

And when the days had multiplied after this His Majesty was wearing the collar of lapis lazuli with a wreath of all kinds of flowers upon his neck. He was in his bronze chariot, and he went forth from the royal palace to see the Persea tree.

And the Princess went out on a two-horsed car behind the King. And His Majesty sat under one of the Perseas and (the Tree) said to his wife, "Ho! you false one! I am BATA, I am living still, I have transformed myself. You gave information to the King of where I was that I might be slain. I then became a Bull and you did cause me to be slain."

And when the days had multiplied after this the Princess was in the good graces of His Majesty, and he showed her favour. And she said to him, "Come swear to me by God, saying, 'Whatever the Princess shall ask me I will consent to it.'"

And he consented to all that she said. And she said, "Cause the two Persea trees to be cut down and let them be made into beautiful planks." And he consented to all that she said.

And when the days had multiplied after this, His Majesty made cunning workmen come to cut down the two Persea trees of the King, and there stood by looking on the royal spouse, the Princess. And there flew a splinter and it entered into the mouth of the Princess and she perceived that she had conceived......all that she desired.

And when the days had multiplied after this she brought forth a male child, and they went to the King and said to him, "There is born to you a male child."

And the child was brought and there were given to it a nurse and waiting woman, and rejoicings were made through the whole land. They sat down to make a holiday (and they gave him his name) and His Majesty at once loved him exceedingly and raised him to the dignity of Prince of Ethiopia.

But when the days had multiplied after this, His Majesty made him hereditary Prince of the whole land.

And when the days had multiplied after this, and he had completed many years as hereditary Prince......His Majesty flew up to heaven and (the Prince) said, "Let the Princes and Nobles of His Majesty be summoned and I shall inform them of all the events which have happened to me......" His wife was brought to him and he had a reckoning with her in presence of them, and they spoke their speech.

And his elder brother was brought to him, and he made him hereditary Prince of the whole land. And he reigned for thirty years as King of Egypt.

And when he had completed (those) thirty years of life, his elder brother arose in his place, on the day of his death.

(Finished) happily as an offering from the Scribe of the double white house, KAKABU, of the double white house of His Majesty. The Scribe HORA, and the Scribe MERIEMAP. Made by the Scribe ANNA, the Master of the Rolls. Whatsoever he says in the Rolls may THOTH guard from contradiction!

The Standard Bearer at the King's left hand, the Commander in Chief of the bowmen, the Royal Prince SETI, beloved of PTAH.

This is the name and title of the owner of the papyrus. It is here written in large characters, and it is repeated on the back of the book.

83. TRUTH AND FALSEHOOD

This late New Kingdom morality tale, which comes from the Chester Beatty Papyrus II, also concerns two brothers—in this case, Truth and Falsehood personified.

[*The lost beginning may be summarized as follows: Truth and Falsehood are brothers. Falsehood, the younger brother, has denounced Truth to the Ennead. He claims that he had lent to Truth a wondrous dagger of extraordinary size, and Truth had failed to return it to him. He proceeds to describe the dagger:*]

[All the copper of Mount Yal had gone into the making of its blade. The timber of the grove of Coptus was its haft]. The god's tomb was its sheath. The cattle of Kal formed its belt. Then Falsehood said to the Ennead: "Let Truth [be brought], let him be blinded in both eyes, and let him be given to me as door-keeper of my house." And [the] Ennead did all that he had asked.

Now many days after this, Falsehood raised his eyes to see, and he observed the virtue of Truth, his elder brother. Then Falsehood said to two servants of Truth: "Take your master and [cast] him to a savage lion with many lionesses....... [So they] took him. Now as they went up with him, Truth [said to his servants]: "Do not take [me]....... Find me a little bread. Go and tell Falsehood: 'When [we] had left [him] [a lion] came out of......."

Now many days after this, the Lady[6] went out [of her] house, [accompanied by her servants. They] saw him (Truth) [lying beneath a thicket, and he was a handsome man; there was none] like [him in the] whole land. They went [to where] the Lady was and [said]: "Come [with] us and see [the blind man] lying beneath the thicket. He should be brought back and made door-keeper of our house." The Lady said: "Hasten to him, I want to see him." They went and brought him back. [And when the Lady] saw him she desired him very much, for she saw that he was [handsome] in all his [body]. He slept with her that night and knew her with the knowledge of a man. And she conceived a son that night.

Now many days after this, she gave birth to a boy whose like did not exist in the [whole] land. [He was] tall; he was like the child of a god. He was sent to school and learned to write very well. He practiced all the arts of war, and he surpassed his older companions who were at school with him. Then his companions said to him: "Whose son are you? You don't have a father!" And they reviled him and mocked him: "Hey, you don't have a father!"

Then the youth said to his mother: "What is the name of my father? I want to tell it to my companions, for they quarrel with me. 'Where is your father?' So they say; and they mock me." His mother said to him: "You see the blind man who sits by the door; he is your father." So she said to him. Then he said to her: "You deserve that your family be gathered and a crocodile be summoned." The youth brought his father inside; made him sit on an armchair; placed a footrest under his feet; and put food before him. He gave him to eat, he gave him to drink. Then the youth said to his father: "Who blinded you? I will avenge you!" He said to him: "My young brother blinded me." And he told him all that had happened to him.

He went off to avenge his father. He took ten loaves of bread, a staff, a pair of sandals, a waterskin, and a sword. He fetched an ox of very beautiful color. And he went to where the herdsman of Falsehood was. He said to him: "Take for yourself these ten loaves, the staff, the waterskin, the sword and the sandals, and guard my ox for me until I return from town."

Now many days after this, when his ox had spent many months with Falsehood's herdsman, Falsehood came to the fields to view his cattle. Then he saw the ox of the youth which was exceedingly beautiful in color. He said to his herdsman: "Give me this ox, I want to eat it. The herdsman said to him: "It is not mine; I cannot give it to you." Then Falsehood said to him: "Look, all my cattle are in your charge; give one of them to its owner."

Then the youth heard that Falsehood had taken his ox. He came to where the herdsman of Falsehood was and said to him: "Where is my ox? I do not see it among your cattle." The herdsman

<hr>

6 Who "the Lady" is supposed to be is not known, but it has been surmised that she is Desire personified.

said to him: "All my cattle are yours; take one you like. The youth said to him: "Is there another ox as big as my ox? If it stood on Amun's Island, the tip of its tail would lie on the papyrus marshes, while one of its horns would be on the western mountain and the other on the eastern mountain. The Great River is its resting place, and sixty calves are born to it daily." The herdsman said to him: "Does there exist an ox as big as you say?" Then the youth seized him and took him to where Falsehood was. And he took Falsehood to court before the Ennead.

Then (they) said to the youth: "[What you have said] is false. We have never seen an ox as big as you say." The youth [said to the Ennead]: "Is there a dagger as big as you said? One that has Mount Yal in it for copper, in whose haft is [the grove] of Coptus, whose sheath consists of the tomb of the god, and its belt of the herds of Kal?" And he said to the Ennead: "Judge between Truth and Falsehood! I am his son; I have come to avenge him!"

Then Falsehood took an oath by the lord, saying: "As Amun lives, as the Ruler lives, if Truth is found alive, I shall be blinded in both eyes and shall be made door-keeper of the house of Truth!" Then the youth [led the Ennead to where his father was] and he was found to be alive. Then they [inflicted punishment upon Falsehood. He was smitten] with five open wounds, blinded in [both his eyes, and made door-keeper of] the house of Truth....... [thus they settled the dispute] between Truth and Falsehood.......

Colophon: [It has been finished successfully under the scribe of] the temple, the pure of hands, Amen, ... [the scribe of] the palace.......

84. THE INSTRUCTION OF AMENEMOPE

The Instruction of Amenemope is a good example of New Kingdom values. While still clearly in the sebayt genre, the values we see are not, as they have been in the past, focused on achieving material and political success through practical action, but rather on inner qualities that can bring one a happy life. Portions of the text are preserved on a handful several papyrus scraps and writing tablets, the earliest of which is from the late New Kingdom, but the most complete version is on the British Museum Papyrus 10474, which comes from the late Third Intermediate Period. There are many similarities between this text and the biblical book of Proverbs.

Preface.

Beginning of teaching how to live, guidance for welfare; every direction for intercourse with elders, rules for (intercourse with ?) courtiers; knowledge how to answer a statement to its pronouncer, and return a report to one that has sent him; to direct him to the path of life, and make him prosper upon earth; to let his heart enter its shrine, and steer it (?) clear of evil; to save him from the mouth of others, praised in the mouth of men.

Made by a superintendent of the soil, experienced in his office, the fruit of a scribe of Egypt. Superintendent of cereals, regulating the waze-measure, who ordained the corn-yield (?) for his lord. Who inscribed islands and new lands in the great name of His Majesty,. and set a land-mark boundary of the sown; who safeguarded the king by his markings and made the terrier of the Black Land. Scribe establishing divine endowments of all the gods, giver of leases to other people. Superintendent of cereals, provider (?) of food, transporting (?) magazine(s) (?) of(?) cereals. Tranquil indeed in Thinite Tew-wer,[7] justified in A-pe;[8] possessing a pyramid-tomb on the west of Sen-ut,[9] possessing a sepulchre in Abydos. Amenemopi son of Kanakht, justified in Tew-wer.

(For) his son, the youngest of his children, little compared to his relations; over the mysteries of Min Kamephis (i.e., Bull of his Mother), water-pourer of Wennofri; who installs Horus upon the throne of his father; his (?) guardian (?) in his noble shrine; fuller (?) [of the garments of Isis ?] the Great, watcher (?) of the Mother of God; inspector of the black kine of the terrace of Min, protecting Min in his shrine; Harmaᶜkher his true name, child of a nobleman of A-pe: son of the sistrum-player of Shu and Tefnut, chief cymbalist of Horus, Tewosri.

He saith:

Chapter I. Charge to the Pupil.

Give thine ears, hear (the words) that are said, give thy mind to interpret them; to put them in thy heart is good, (but there is) woe to him who neglecteth them; let them rest in the casket of thy belly, that they may be the threshold(?) in thy heart; verily (?) when there cometh a gale of speech, they will be a mooring-post in (?) thy tongue. If thou spend thy life-time with these things in thy heart, thou wilt find it a success; thou wilt find my words a storehouse of life, and thy body will prosper upon earth.

Chapter II. Humanity, and Various Advice.

Beware of robbing a poor wretch, of being valorous against the man of broken arm.

Put not forth thine hand to touch an old man, nor snatch (?) at the word of the aged.

Let not thyself be sent on a wicked mission, nor desire (the company of) him that hath performed it.

Clamour not against him whom thou hast injured, nor return him an answer to justify (?) thyself.

Him who hath done ill, the quay slips away(?) from him, his wetted land it (?) carries him away; the north wind cometh down to end his hour, it uniteth with the tempest; the thunder is loud, the crocodiles are vicious. Thou passionate man, what is thy condition? He cries out, his voice (reacheth) to heaven. Thou Moon, bring forward his crime!

Steer that we may carry the bad man over for we will not do as he (hath done). Lift him up, give him thy hand, commit him to the arms of God; fill his belly with bread of thine, that he may be satisfied and understand (?).

Another thing good in the heart of God is to pause before speaking.

---

7 The sacred quarter of Abydos, perhaps to be read as Nef-wer.
8 Panoplis.
9 A name of Panoplis (Ekhmin) or of a temple there.

Chapter III. Prudence in Argument.

Do not join wrangling with the hot-mouthed, nor goad him with words.

Pause before an intruder, and give way unto him that attacketh.

Sleep a night before speaking; the storm, it bursts forth like flame in straw.

The passionate man in his hour—withdraw thyself before him; leave him to his own devices; God will know how to reply to him.

If thou spend thy life-time with these things in thy heart, thy children shall see them.

Chapter IV. The Passionate Man and the Tranquil Man.

As to the passionate man in the temple, he is like a tree grown in the forest (?); in a moment comes its loss of foliage; its end is reached in the dock-yard (?); or (?) it is floated far from its place, the flame is its winding-sheet.

The truly tranquil man, he setteth himself aside, he is like a tree grown in a plot (?); it grows green, it doubles its yield, it (stands) in front of its lord, its fruit is sweet, its shade is pleasant, and its end is reached in the garden.

Chapter V. Honesty and Tranquillity in the Temple.

Misuse (?) not the shares of the temple, be not greedy, (thus) wilt thou find excess (beyond your expectation), remove not a servant of a god, in order to do a benefit to another.

Say not "to-day is as to-morrow"; how will these things end? The morrow is come, to-day is gone, the deep hath become the edge of the waves, the crocodiles are uncovered, the hippopotami on dry land, the fishes gasping (?); the jackals are sated, the wild-fowl in festival, the nets are empty (?).

As to all the tranquil in the temple, they say "Great is the good pleasure of Re^c." Hold fast to the tranquil man, (thus) wilt thou find life, (and) thy body shall prosper upon earth.

Chapter VI. Encroachment on the Land of Others.

Remove not the landmark on the boundaries of the sown, nor shift the position of the measuring-cord;. covet not a cubit of land, nor throw down the boundaries of the widow. The rut of trampling (?), the wear of time, he who wrongfully seizes it in the field, if(?) he snare by false oaths, is lassoed by the Power of the Moon.

Mark well him who hath done this on earth, for he is an oppressor of the weak, he is an enemy working destruction within thee, deprival of life is in his eye, his house is an enemy to the town; (but) his barns are destroyed, his goods are taken out of the hand of his children, and his property is given to another.

Beware of throwing down the boundaries of the sown, lest a terror carry thee away; a man propitiates God by the Power of the Lord, when he defines the boundaries of the sown.

Desire then to make thine own self prosperous; beware of the Universal Lord; trample not the furrow of another, it is good for thee to be sound in regard to them.

Cultivate the fields, that thou mayest find what thou needest; and receive the bread of thine own threshing-floor; better is a bushel that God giveth thee than five thousand (obtained) by force; they stay not a day in store and barn, they make no food in the beer-jar; a moment is their duration in the granary, when morning cometh they have gone below.

Better is poverty at the hand of God than riches in the storehouse; better is bread with happy heart than riches with vexation.

Chapter VII. The Search for Wealth.

Cast not thy heart after riches; there is no ignoring of Shay and Renent.[10]

Place not for thyself thy thoughts (on things) outside; every man is (destined) for his hour.

Labour not to seek increase, (then ?) thy needs shall be secure for thee; if riches be brought to thee by robbery, they shall not stay the night with thee; day dawneth and they are not in thy house, their places shall be seen, but they are not (there); (perchance) the earth hath opened its mouth, "It adjusts it and swallows it" and has sunk them in Tei, (or) they have made for themselves a great breach of their measure, and they have sunk themselves in the corn-store, (or) they have made themselves wings like geese, they have flown to heaven.

Rejoice not thyself (because of) riches by robbery, nor groan over poverty; when an archer in front pushes forward (?) his troop leaves him (in difficulty); the boat of the covetous is left (in) the mud, while the bark of the tranquil sails (with the breeze).

Thou shalt pray to the Aten when he rises, saying, "Grant me prosperity and health," and he will give thee thy needs in life, and thou wilt be safe from fear.

Chapter VIII. Speak no Evil.

Set thy goodness in the bowels of men that everyone salute thee; (for) one acclaims the Uraeus, and spits on the Apophis-serpent.

Keep sound thy tongue from words of detraction; (thus) wilt thou be the favourite of the others, thou wilt find thy place within the temple, and thy provisions in the bread-offerings of thy lord; thou wilt be revered in old age and be hidden (in) thy coffin, and be safe from the Power of God.

Cry not "crime" at a man; hide the manner of (a fugitive's) flight. If thou hearest (to judge ?) a thing that may be either good or bad, do this outside, (where) it is not heard; put a good report upon thy tongue, while the ill is hidden in thy belly.

Chapter IX. Avoid the Passionate Man and his Ways.

Do not associate to thyself the passionate man, nor approach him for conversation.

Keep sound thy tongue from answering thy chief, and guard thyself from reviling him. Cause him not to cast his speech to lasso thee, and give not free rein to thine answer; thou shalt discuss the answer with (?) a man of thine own measure, and beware of headlong utterance of it. Swift is speech when the heart is hurt, more than wind before water (?). He is ruined and he is built up by his tongue, yet he speaks an ugly (?) speech; he makes an answer worthy of a beating, (for) its freight (?) is of ill; he makes a voyage like all the world, but he is laden with false words; he acts the ferryman (?) of weaving (?) speech, he goes and comes with wrangling; when he eats, when he drinks within, his answer is (heard) without; verily the day of charging his crime is a misery for his children. Would that Khnum might bring in indeed, indeed (?), the potter s wheel for the fiery-mouthed, to mould and burn hearts (like vessels)(and reform his ways !). (He is like a ...), he is like a wolf's whelp in the

10   Deities of fortune.

farmyard, he turns one eye contrary to the other, he sets brethren to wrangling; he goes before every breeze like clouds, he diminishes the colour of the sun, he bends (?) his tail like a young crocodile, he gathers himself together, crouched (?), his lips are sweet, his tongue cold (?), (but) flame burns in his belly.

Leap not to cleave to that (fellow), lest a terror carry thee away.

Chapter X. Sincerity.

Do not salute thy passionate (opponent), forcing thyself, nor grieve thine own heart (thereby); say not to him "Hail to thee" in falsehood, when there is terror in thy belly.

Speak not to a man in falsehood, the abomination of God; sever not thy heart from thy tongue, that all thy ways may be successful.

Be thou resolute before other people, for one is safe at the hand of God; hated of God is the falsifier of words, his great abomination is the dissembler (?).

Chapter XI. The Dependent.

Covet not the property of a dependent, nor hunger for his bread. Verily the property of a dependent, it is a chokingly for the throat, it is a vomiting(?) for the gullet.

When he has obtained it by false oaths, his desire is perverted(?) by his belly. It is through (?) the treacherous that success (?) is missed (?), (both) bad and good fail.

When thou failest before thy chief and art feeble (?) in thy speeches, thy entreaties are replied to by curses, thine obeisances by beating. The (too) great mouthful of bread, thou swallowest it and vomitest it, thou art emptied of thy good.

Mark well the examination (?) of a dependent, when staves reach him, and all his people are fast in fetters, and where (?) is the executioner?

(Even) when thou art released before thy chief, then thou art disgraced (?) unto thy subordinates.

Thou shalt steer away from the dependent on the road, thou shalt see him and keep clear of his goods.

Chapter XII. The Honest Factor.

Be not greedy of the things of a noble, do not give (away) a great feed of bread in extravagance; if he setteth thee to manage his affairs, refrain from what is his, that what is thine may prosper.

Do not take (a share) with the passionate man, nor associate to thyself a treacherous (?) person.

If thou art sent to transport straw, refrain from its corn-measure.

The detection(?) of a man in a poor business prevents a repetition of his employment another time also.

Chapter XIII. The Kindly Scribe of Accounts.

Do not pervert a pen-man (?) in regard to a papyrus, the abomination of God.

Bear not witness by a false statement, nor displace another man by thy tongue.

Do not make assessment (?) (of) one who hath nought, nor falsify thy pen.

If thou find a large debt against a poor man, make it into three parts; forgive two, let one remain; thou wilt find it a path of life; thou wilt lie down at night and sleep soundly. On the morrow thou wilt find it like good news.

Better is the praise and (?) love of men than riches in the storehouse;. better is bread with happy heart than riches with vexation.

Chapter XIV. Dignity.

Do not have consideration (?) of a person, nor labour to seek his hand; if he say to thee "Receive a present" it is no indigent man who accepts (?) it, be not shy (?) to him nor bend down upon thyself, nor be cast down in thy gaze; salute him with thy mouth; say to him "Hail to thee"; (when) he ceases thy attainment will come. (Yet) do not repel him at his first (approach); another occasion will take him away.

Chapter XV. Thoth and the Scribe.

Do well that thou mayest reach what I(?) am; do not ink a pen to do an injury. The beak of the Ibis is the finger of the scribe; beware of disturbing it. The Ape dwelleth in the House of Khmun, (but) his eye travels round the Two Lands; if he sees him that perverts with his finger, he takes away his provisions in the deep waters. As for a scribe who perverts with his finger, his son shall not be registered.

If thou spend thy life-time with these things in thy heart, thy children shall see them.

Chapter XVI. False Weights and Sham.

Tamper not with the scales, nor falsify the *kite*-weights, nor diminish the fractions of the corn-measure. Desire not the corn-measure of the fields, and then neglect those of the Treasury.

The Ape sitteth by the balance, his heart being the plummet. Where is a god so great as Thoth, he that discovered these things, to make them?

Fashion not for thyself deficient kite-weights; they abound in armies (?) by the Power of God. If thou seest another perverting, thou shalt pass by him at a distance.

Covet not copper, avoid beautiful linen; what is the good of it, a cloak of *mek*? when it is a perversion before God if gold-bases (?) be overlaid (?) to (appear as) pure gold (?), at dawn it is of lead.

Chapter XVII. The Corn-measurer.

Beware of covering up(?) the waze-measure, to falsify its fractional parts; do not the injustice of(?) Wbn-nakht(?); cause it not to be empty in its belly; let it measure according to its size precisely (?), thy hand clearing exactly.

Make not for thyself a bushel-measure of two capacities, (for then) thou wilt make (only) for the deep waters; the bushel is the Eye of Re^c, its abomination is he who abstracts. A corn-measurer who multiplies cheating, his eye seals (the accusation) upon him.

Do not receive harvest-dues from a farmer and then (?) tie up (?) a document against him, that he may be injured; conspire not with the corn-measurer, nor play the game of "Arranging the Interior." The floor for threshing barley is greater in Power than an oath by the Great Throne.

Chapter XVIII. Over-anxiety.

Lay thee not down at night fearing the morrow; when day appears, what is the morrow like? Man knoweth not how the morrow will be (The events of the morrow are in the hand of God);

God is (ever) in his success, Man is (ever) in his failure. The words which men say are one thing, The things which God doeth are another.

Say not "I have no crime" nor labour to seek strife. Crime belongeth to God, it is sealed with his finger.

There is no success with God, nor is there failure before him; if he turn him to seek success, in a moment the man (?) mars it.

Be resolute in thy heart, make firm thy mind; steer not with(?) thy tongue; the tongue of a man is the rudder of a boat, (but) the Universal Lord is its pilot.

Chapter XIX. Speech in the Law-court.

Enter not the law-court before a noble, and then falsify thy words; go not up and down with thy reply when thy witnesses are set up. Do not labour (with) oaths by thy lord, (with) speech of the place of inquisition.

Tell the truth before the noble, lest he get power over thy body; (then) if next day thou come before him, he will consent to all thou sayest; he will tell thy statement within before the Council of Thirty; it will be kindly (?) another time also.

Chapter XX. Professional Honesty.

Do not pervert(?) a man in the law-court, nor disturb the just man(?). Give not (all) thy attention to one that is clothed (?) in shining white and accept him in rags;

Receive not the gift of a strong man, nor repress the weak for him. Justice is a great gift of God, he will give it to him whom he will; verily the strength of him who is like unto him, it saves the poor wretch from his beating.

Make not for thyself false documents; they are a gross treason (?) (worthy) of death, they are great oaths of *szf-tr*, they are for enquiry by the informer.

Do not falsify the bread(?) upon the record, and so mar the design of God; do not find for thine own self the Power of God; without (the decree of) Shay and Renent.

Hand over property to its owners, and seek life for thyself. Let not thy heart build in their house, (for thus) thy bone(s) are for the execution-block.

Chapter XXI. Reticence.

Say not "Find me a strong chief for a man in thy city hath injured me"; say not "Find me a redeemer, for a man who hateth me hath injured me."

Verily thou knowest not the designs of God, thou canst not realise (?) the morrow. Sit thee down at the hands of God; thy tranquillity will overthrow them.

Verily a crocodile which is void of proclaiming, inveterate is the dread of it.

Empty not thine inmost soul to everybody, nor spoil (thereby) thine influence; spread not thy sayings about to others, nor associate to thyself one who lays bare his heart.

Better is a man that (hides) his report within himself than he who tells a thing to disadvantage. One does not run to reach perfection; one does not throw (?) to injure himself (?).

Chapter XXII. Debate.

Plot (?) not against thine opponent in debate, nor (make) him tell his talk of hearts; leap not to go in and meet him when thou hast not seen what he doeth. Thou shalt perceive first from his reply, and be still, (then) will thine attainment come. Leave it to him that he may empty his inmost soul; know how to sleep, and he will be comprehended. Seize his feet, do not slight (?) him; fear him, do not neglect him.

Verily thou knowest not the designs of God, thou canst not realise (?) the morrow. Sit thee down at the hands of God; thy tranquillity will overthrow them.

Chapter XXIII. Spare the Official's Hospitality.

Eat not bread in presence of a noble, nor apply thy mouth at the beginning. If thou art satisfied (with) false munchings, they are a diversion in thy saliva. Look at the cup that is before thee, and let it do thy need. Even as a noble is great in his office, he is like as a well aboundeth (in) drawings (of water).

Chapter XXIV. The Secretary.

Hear not the replies of a noble in a house, and then report him to another without; let not thy speech be carried abroad, lest thine heart be bitter (?).

The heart of man is the nose of God; beware lest thou neglect it.

A man who stands by the side of a noble, verily his name should not be known.

Chapter XXV. Respect for Infirmity.

Laugh not at a blind man, nor tease a dwarf, nor mar the design of a lame (?) man; tease not a man who is in the hand of God, nor be fierce of countenance against him when he has transgressed.

Verily man is clay and straw, God is his fashioner; he pulls down and builds up each day; he makes a thousand dependents at his will, (or) he makes a thousand men into overseers (?) when he is in his hour of life.

How happy is he who hath reached the West when he is safe in the hand of God.

Chapter XXVI. Conduct towards Seniors in Society.

Sit not in the beer-house, and then join(?) one senior to thyself, whether he be young (but) great in his office, or old by birth; associate with thyself a man of thine own rank; Re^c is helpful from afar.

(But) if thou see one greater than thyself outside and attendants following him, do (him ?) reverence; give a hand to an old man when he is sated with beer,. reverence (?) (him) as (?) his children (would).

The strong arm is not softened (?) by being uncovered; the back is not broken by bending it; poverty will not be made for a man when he says the pleasant thing, any more than riches when his speech is straw (?).

A pilot who sees from afar, he will not make his boat a wreck.

Chapter XXVII. Submission to the Old.

Curse not one older than thou, for he hath seen Re^c before thee; cause him not to accuse thee to the Aten at its rising, saying "Another, a youth, hath cursed an old man"; very painful before Re^c is a youth who curses an old man.

Let him beat thee, with thy hand in thy bosom; let him curse thee, while thou keepest silence. If next day thou come before him, he will give thee bread without stint. The food of a hound is (the affair) of his master, and he barks unto him that gives it

Chapter XXVIII. Benevolence.

Identify (?) not a widow when thou hast caught her in the fields, nor fail to be long-suffering (?) to her reply. Pass not over the stranger (with) thine oil-jar, that it may be doubled before thy brethren .

God loveth the happiness of the humble more than that the noble be honoured.

Chapter XXIX. The Ferry.

Hinder (?) not people from crossing a river, when thou hast room in the ferry-boat; if a steering-paddle be brought to thee in the midst of the deep waters, thou wilt bend back(?) thy hands to take it. There is no abomination (for thee to suffer) from God if a sailor doth not welcome (thee).

Make not for thyself a ferry-boat upon the river and then labour to seek its fare; take the fare from the person of wealth, and welcome him who hath nothing.

Chapter XXX. Epilogue.

See for thyself these thirty chapters, they please, they educate; they are the foremost of all books; they instruct the ignorant. If they be read before the ignorant, he will be cured (?) by reason of them. Fill thyself with them; put them in thy heart, and be an interpreter of them, explaining as a teacher.

As to a scribe who is experienced in his office, he will find himself worthy (?) to be a courtier.

Colophon.

That is its end. Written by Senu son of the divine father Pemu.

85. THE QUARREL OF APOPHIS AND SEKNENRE

A young scribe named Pentewere, who lived in the Ramessid period, is responsible for our only extant copy of this tale, on the Sallier I Papyrus. This work of historical fiction is set near the end of the Second Intermediate Period, when the rulers of Dynasty 17 were waging war with the

Hyksos rukers of Dynasty 15. The protagonist is Theban king Seqnenre Tao and the villain Apepi (Apophis). Unfortunately, the ending is missing.

Now it befell that the land of Egypt was in dire affliction and that there was no Sovereign (as) King of the time. And it happened that, behold, King Seknenre^c was Ruler of the Southern City. But dire affliction was in the 'A'amu town, the Prince Apophis being in Avaris, and the entire land was tributary to him with their produce in full, as well as with all good things of Timuris.[11] Then King Apophis took Setekh[12] to himself as lord, and did not serve any god which was in the entire land except Setekh. And he built a temple of fair and everlasting work by the side of [the palace of] Apophis, and he arose [every] day to make the daily sacrifice of [cattle] to Setekh, and the officials of [His Majesty] bore garlands of flowers (?), exactly as it is done (in) the temple of Phra^c-Harakhte. Now as to King Apophis, his desire was to bring up a matter of offence (against) King Seknenre^c, [the] Prince of the Southern City.

Now when many days were passed after this, King [Apophis] caused to be summoned [his] ...., his chief..............

[*At this point the text is interrupted by a lacuna which extends, save for a few isolated words, to the end of the first page of the papyrus. The loss amounts to rather more than half of the passage already translated, and would have obscured the purport of the tale very seriously but for the fact that a consultation between King Apophis and his councillors was clearly here narrated, the contents of which are repeated almost verbatim later on.*]

[..............and said to them, "The desire of My Majesty is] to send [a messenger to the Southern City in order to bring] an accusation [against King Seknenre^c." And his...... and his.......... .knew not how to answer him. Then he caused to be summoned his] scribes and wise men [concerning it. And they made answer to him and said, "O] Sovereign, [our Lord...... There is] a hippopotamus pool [in the Southern City ....the] river [.........] and they (the hippopotami) do not allow [sleep to come to us either by day or by] night, [but] noise[is in our ear. Let therefore y]our [Majesty send] to the Prince of [the Southern City........... King Seknenre^c and let the messenger say to him: 'King] Apophis[...] commands [you to cause to be abandoned the hippopotamus pool.'.........So shall your Majesty see who is] [*The second page begins here.*] with him as helper, (for) he does not incline to any god which is in [the entire land] except Amen-re^c, King of the Gods."

[And] when many days were passed after this, King Apophis sent to the Prince of the Southern City concerning the accusation which his scribes and wise men had said to him. And the messenger of King Apophis reached the Prince of the Southern City; and they took him into the presence of the Prince of the Southern City. And that one said to the messenger of King Apophis: "What is your message to the Southern City; how did you come to make this journey?" And the messenger said to him, "King Apophis sends to you to say: 'Let cause to be abandoned the hippopotamus pool which is in the flowing spring of the City, for they do not allow sleep to come to me either by day or by night'; but noise is [in] his ear." And the Prince of the Southern City remained silent and wept a long time, and he did not know how to return answer to the messenger of King Apophis. And the Prince of the Southern City said to him: "How did your lord hear of [the pool which is in the] flowing spring of the Southern City?" And [the messenger said to him: "...........the] matter concerning which he

11   A name for Egypt.
12   Seth. Perhaps a reference to the Canaanite god Hadad, who was considered an equivalent to Seth.

sent to you." [And the Prince of the Southern City caused] the [messenger of King Apophis] to be tended [with] all good [things], meat, cakes............ [And the Prince of the Southern City said to him: "Return to King Apophis your master. .... and] whatever you say to him, I will do it, [when you comes]" .... [And the messenger of King] Apophis betook him to journey to the place where his lord was.

Then the Prince of the Southern City caused to be summnoned his great officers, and likewise all the chief soldiers that he had, and he repeated to them the accusation concerning which King Apophis had sent to him. They were silent with one accord for a long time, and knew not anything to answer him whether good or bad. And King Apophis sent to........

[*Here the tale breaks off, the scribe not having bothered to finish copying it. This story seems to have been simply the local variant of a theme popular throughout the entire Near East. The kings of those times were accustomed to send one another problems to be solved on all sorts of matters, the condition being that they should pay one another a kind of tribute or fine according as they should answer well or ill the questions put to them.*]

𓀀𓁐𓃾𓆑𓏏𓍯𓊃𓎡𓂋𓈖𓏤𓀁𓅓𓏤𓂝𓏏𓈖𓇋𓊪𓏏𓆑𓏛𓄿𓅓𓏏𓊪𓃀𓏏𓆑

86. THE DOOMED PRINCE

On the back side of the Papyrus Harris 500 (Ramessid Period) are two Egyptian folk tales, and this is the second. It concerns a prince whose death is predicted in advance by the seven Hathors and his father's attempts to save him. The ending, sadly, is missing.

(4:1) It is said that there was once a king to whom no male child had been born. [He] begged for himself a son from the gods of his time (2) and they decreed that one should be born to him. Now on that night he slept with his wife and [his wife] conceived. And when she had fulfilled the months (3) of childbirth a son was born. The Hathors came to decree for him a destiny. They said, (4) he shall die either by the crocodile or the snake or the dog. And the people who were about the child heard it and told it (5) to his majesty. Then his majesty became exceeding sore at heart. And his majesty caused to be built [for him a house] of stone (6) on the desert, equipped with servants and with every good thing pertaining to a royal house, and the child was not to go outside it. Now when the child (7) grew up he went up on to his roof and saw a greyhound following a man who was (8) walking on the road. He said to his attendant who was beside him, What is that which is following the man who is coming along the road? And he (9) said to him, It is a dog. Then the child said to him, Let there be brought to me one like it. And the attendant went and told (10) it to his majesty. His majesty said, Let a little puppy be taken to him lest (?) his heart be grieved. So they took (11) him the dog.

Now when many days had gone by the child grew in body and in mind. And he sent to his father saying, What boots it that I sit here. Behold I am delivered over to Fate. Let me be released (?) (13) that I may do after my own desire; the god will surely do what is in his heart. They hearkened to him. They ordered (?) that there should be given to him a chariot furnished with (5:1) every kind of martial equipment, and his [servant] followed him by way of esquire. They ferried him over to the east bank (2) and they said to him, Go where thou wilt. Now his dog was with him. And he fared northward following his heart's desire, upon the desert, living upon the choicest of every kind of (3) game of the desert. And so he reached the chief of Naharin. Now there had been born to the chief of (4) Naharin no child save a daughter. And (he) (?) had built for her a house whose window was at a height of (5) fifty-six (?) cubits from the ground. He had summoned all the sons of all the chiefs of the land of Syria and said to them, (6) He who shall reach the window of my daughter shall have her to wife.

Now when many days had gone by, (7) as they were at their daily occupation the youth came by them. And (8) they took the youth to their house and washed him and gave fodder to his (9) horses. They did every service for the youth: they anointed him and swathed his feet and they (10) gave food to his attendant. And they said to him by way of converse, Whence comest thou, beauteous (11) youth? He said to them, I am the son of an officer of the land of Egypt. My mother died and my (12) father took to him another wife, a stepmother. But she began to hate me and I came away in flight before her. Then they (13) embraced him and kissed him repeatedly.

Now when many days had gone by he said to the (14) youths, What is this which ye do........... [And they said to him, We have been] here for months past, (6:1) spending our time in flying, and he who shall reach the window of the daughter of the chief of Naharin, he will (2) give her to him to wife. And he said to them, Would that she might be mine. Could I but enchant my legs, I would go to fly (3) with you. Now they went to fly after their daily custom, but the youth (4) stood afar off watching. And the glance of the daughter of the chief of Naharin was upon him.

Now when many days had gone by (5) the boy came to fly with the children of the chiefs. And he flew (6) and he reached the window of the daughter of the chief of Naharin. She kissed him and embraced him (7) repeatedly. Now they went to inform her father and they said to him, A man has reached the window (8) of thy daughter. The chief asked him saying, The son of which of the chiefs And they said to him, (9) An officers son, who has come as an exile from the land of Egypt before the face of his stepmother. But (10) the chief of Naharin grew exceeding wroth and said, Shall I give my daughter to the exile (11) of Egypt? Let him take himself off again. They came to tell him saying, Get thee back to the place from which thou didst come. (12) But the daughter seized him and made an oath saying, As Reᶜ-Horus-of-the-Horizon lives, if they take him away (13) from me I will neither eat nor drink, and I will die straightway. Then the messenger (14) went and told her father all that she had said. And the chief sent men to slay him (15) on the spot. But the girl said, As Reᶜ lives, if they slay him, when the sun sets I shall be dead: (16) I will not outlive him by an hour. They [went] to tell it to her father. And the (7:1) ....daughter. Then....., and awe of him (2) .... entered into the chief. He embraced and he kissed him repeatedly. He said to him, Tell me thy condition. Behold (3) thou art to me as a son. He said to him; I am a son of an officer of the land of Egypt. My mother died and my father took (4) to himself another wife; And she began to hate me and I came away in flight before her face. Then he gave him his daughter to wife, and he (5) gave him a house with land likewise and all manner of goodly cattle.

Now when many days had gone by the youth said to (6) his wife, I am ordained to three fates, the crocodile, the snake or the dog. She said to him, Let the dog (7) which follows thee be killed. But he said to her,...........I will not have my dog killed whom I reared (8) when he was a puppy.

So she began to watch over her husband very closely, not allowing him to go out alone. (9) Now behold the............the.............the land of Egypt to retreat (?). Lo, (10) the crocodile of the lake...... It came over against him in the town in which the (11) youth was...................lake. Now there was a water-spirit in it and the water-spirit would not suffer (12) the crocodile to go out. But when the crocodile slept (?) the water-spirit went forth to take a walk. But when the sun shone (13) they stood fighting (?) the two of them daily for a space of two whole months.

Now (14) when many days had gone by the youth sat down to enjoy himself in his house. And when night (15) came the youth slept on his bed and sleep took possession of his body. But (8:1) his wife filled a [bowl with]........and another bowl with beer. There came forth [a snake from his] hole (2) to sting the youth. But lo his wife was sitting beside him wide awake. The .... (3) .... the snake. It drank, it became drunk and went to sleep on its back. Then his wife caused it to meet (4) destruction by means of her axe. She woke her husband .... (5) him. She said to him, Behold thy god hath delivered one of thy fates into thy hand, he will [also deliver the others in like wise]. He (6) made offering to Re^c, praising him and glorifying his might daily.

Now when many days had gone by (7) the youth went out to take a walk on the banks (?) in his domain (?) without going outside .... (8) Now his dog was following him, and his dog received power of speech .... and he (9) ran away from it. He reached the Lake and went down into the [lake to escape from his ?] (10) dog. The crocodile seized (?) him and carried him off to the place in which the water-spirit lived. ....Then the (11) crocodile said to the youth, I am thy fate who has been pursuing thee, and .... (12) [for many days] past. I am about to fight with the water-spirit and behold I will release thee. But if. .... (13) to fight .... and thou shalt applaud (?) me when the water-spirit is killed (?). And if thou see .... (14) see the .... Now when day dawned and the second day came, ... came ....

87. LOVE POEMS

This collection of love poems are taken from the Chester Beatty Papyrus I and the Papyrus Harris 500, both from the Ramessid Period. These poems probably were not spontaneous expressions by young lovers, but carefully crafted works of literature. Nevertheless it is interesting to hear the voices of both males and females here. Keep in mind that the expressions "brother" and "sister" are terms of endearment and not to be taken literally in most cases.

I. Stanza the First

BEGINNING OF THE WORDS OF THE GREAT DISPENSER OF ENTERTAINMENT,   VERSO, C1
One alone, a sister without her peer,
Comelier than all mankind.

Behold she is like the Star-goddess arising   2
At the beginning of a happy year;
Of sheen surpassing, of radiant skin,
Lovely of eyes wherewith to gaze,   3
Sweet are her lips wherewith to speak,
She hath not a word too much;
Long of neck and radiant of nipple,   4
Of true sapphire is her hair;
Her arm surpasseth gold,
Her fingers are like lotus-lilies,
Drooping of buttocks, firm-girt in her midst;   5
Her legs show forth her beauty.
Fair of gait she treadeth upon the earth,
She hath captured my heart in her embrace,   6
She maketh the necks of all men
To be turned away dazzled at the sight of her.
Joyous is whoso embraceth her,   7
He is like the chiefest of lusty youths.
One regardeth her going forth abroad
Even as hers yonder, the only One.   8

Stanza the Second

The brother[13] troubleth my heart with his voice,
He maketh sickness to lay hold on me;
He is a neighbour of my mother's house,   9
Yet am I not able to go unto him.
Good is my mother in charging him (?) thus,   Verso, C 2 1
Forgo seeing her,
For behold, my heart is vexed when he is remembered,
Love of him hath captured me.
Behold, he is foolish,   2
But I—I am like unto him.
He knoweth not my desire to embrace him,
Or he would send to my mother.   3
Brother—O, I am decreed unto thee
By the Golden among women.[14]
Come unto me, that I may see thy beauty.
My father and mother will be glad,   4
All men will rejoice at thee with one accord,
They will rejoice at thee, O brother.

---

13 "Brother" and "sister" are terms of endearment and not to be taken literally in most cases.
14 Hathor, the goddess associated with love.

Stanza the Third

My heart purposed to see its beauty,   5
Sitting within it.
I found Mehy a-riding on the road,
Together with his lusty youths.   6
I knew not how to remove myself from before him.
Should I pass by him boldly?
Lo, the river is the road,   7
I know not a place for my feet.
Witless art thou, O my heart, exceedingly,
Why wilt thou brave Mehy?
Behold, if I pass before him,   8
I shall tell him of my turnings;
Behold, I am thine, I shall say unto him,
And he will boast of my name,
Allotting me to the first-come hareem   9
Of some one among his followers.

Stanza the Fourth

It fleeth away, my heart, quickly,
When I recall my love of thee,   10
Nor suffereth me to walk in human wise,
But is affrighted (from) its place.
It suffereth me not to don a tunic,   Verso, C 3 1
Nor to attire myself with my fan.
I put not paint upon mine eyes,
Nor anoint myself at all.
Bide not, but get thee home,   2
Saith it to me as often as I recall him.
Act not the fool, O my heart;
Wherefore playest thou the madman?   3
Sit calm, until the brother come to thee,
Mine eye ...(?)
Let not the folk say concerning me,
A woman distraught with love.   4
Stand fast as often as thou recallest him,
O my heart, and do not flee.

Stanza the Fifth

I adore the Golden one, I extol Her Majesty,   5
I exalt the Lady of Heaven,
I give praise unto Hathor,

And thanksgiving unto my Mistress.   6
I appealed unto her, and she heard my petition,
She decreed unto me my mistress,
And she came of her own accord I to see me.   7
How great is that which hath happened unto me.
I rejoice, I exult, I am puffed up,
Ever since it was said, Hey, here is she!
Behold, she came, and the lusty youths did obeisance   8
For the greatness of their love of her.
I make prayer unto I my goddess,   9
That she may give me the sister as a gift.
Three days it is to yesterday since first I made my petition
In her name, but she hath gone from me for five days.

Stanza the Sixth   10

I passed in the neighbourhood of his house,
And I found his door open,
And the brother standing beside his mother,
All his brothers and sisters with him;   Verso, C 4 1
Love of him captureth the heart of all who tread upon the road,
An excellent stripling, without his like,
A brother outstanding in virtues.
He looked at me when I passed by,   2
And I was alone to rejoice.
How exulted my heart with jubilation,
O brother, I because of the seeing of me.   3
If only (thy) mother had known my heart;
Then had she gone indoors betimes.
Golden one, put it into her heart;   4
Then will I haste unto the brother,
And will kiss him before his companions;
would not weep at any one,
But would rejoice at their perceiving   5
That thou knowest me.
I will make a festival for my goddess.
My heart is a-flutter to go forth,
To make the brother look upon me in the night.   6
How happy is it in the passing.

Stanza the Seventh

Seven days it is from yesterday that I have not seen the sister,
And sickness hath crept upon me,   7

And I am become all heavy in my limbs,
And am forgetful of mine own body.
If the master-physicians come unto me,   8
My heart hath no comfort (of) their remedies;
The magicians, no resource is in them;
My sickness is not discerned.
That which I have said, behold it is what reviveth me,   9
Her name is that which can raise me up.
The coming and going of her messengers,
Is that which reviveth my heart.   10
More beneficial unto me is the sister than any remedies,
More important is she unto me than the entire compendium of medicine,
My salvation is her coming in from without,   1 Verso, C 5
When I see her, then am I well;
Openeth she her eye, then my limbs become young again;
Speaketh she, then I am strong,   2
And when I embrace her, she banisheth evil from me,
But she hath gone from me for seven days.

II.

O that thou mayst come to the sister quickly,   Verso, G 1 1
Like a royal envoy whose lord is impatient for his message,   2
And his heart is set upon hearing it;
An envoy for whom all the stables have been requisitioned,
And he hath horses at the resting-places,   3
And the chariot stands harnessed in its place,
Nor is there any breathing-space for him upon the road.   4
He hath reached the house of the sister,
And his heart jubilates.

O that thou mayst come (to the sister quickly),   5
Like a horse belonging to the king,
Picked from a thousand steeds of every kind,   6
Chief of the stables.
It is distinguished above others in its provender,
And its lord knoweth its paces.
If it hear the sound of the whip,   7
It knoweth no restraining,
Nor is there any chief among the charioteers,   8
Who can draw level with it.
How well knoweth the heart of the sister,
That he is not far from the sister.   G 2 1

O that thou mayst come to the sister quickly,
Like a gazelle bounding over the desert,
Its feet reel (?), and its limbs are faint, 2
And panic hath entered into its limbs;
For a huntsman is after it,
And hounds are with him, 3
But they see not its dust,
For it hath seen a resting-place like a . . .,
It hath taken the river as a road (?) 4
Thou shalt attain to her grotto
In the kissing of thy hand four times,
Being in pursuit of the sister's love. 5
The Golden one hath decreed her unto thee,
O my friend.

III.

BEGINNING OF THE SWEET SAYINGS FOUND WHILE USING A PAPYRUS (?)—
COMPOSED BY THE SCRIBE OF THE NECROPOLIS NAKHTSOBK. 9 RECTO, 16
Thou shalt bring it into the house of the sister,
When thou stormest (?) into her grotto;
It is made (?) like her . . ., 10
A place of slaughter (?), it is (in) her bower (?).
Furnish her with songs of the throat (?);
Wine and strong ale are her protection,
That thou mayst confound her senses (?), 11
And mayst restore them (?) in her night.
She will say unto thee, Take me in thy embrace,
Day dawneth, and we (?) will be after this sort.

Thou shalt bring it (into) the hall of the sister,
Alone and without another,
That thou mayst work thy pleasure with her ...(?); 12
The porticoes will be a-blowing (?),
And the heaven descends in wind,
Yet shall this not remove it,
That she may bring unto thee her fragrance,
Perfume I spread abroad (so that) those present are intoxicated. RECTO, 17 1
The Golden one hath decreed her unto thee as reward (?)
To cause her (?) to restore thy life.

How clever is she, the sister, in casting a noose (?), 2

She ... eth not the inspection,
She casteth a noose (?) upon me with her hair,
She will catch me with her eye,   3
She will subjugate me with her ruddle (?),
That she may brand me with her seal.

When thou speakest with thy heart,   4
Prithee after her, that I may embrace her;
By Amun, it is I who come to thee,
My tunic upon my arm.
I found the brother in the rill (?),   5
His foot placed upon the river.
He was making a day-time altar (?),
And (?) waiting for (?) the beer.
He taketh the skin of my side (?),   6
It is longer than it is broad.

The wrong that she hath done unto me, the sister,
Shall I conceal it from her?
That she let me stand at the door of her house,
When she went within,   7
Nor granted she me a fair relief,
Sharing in my night.

I passed by her house in the darkness,   8
I knocked, and it was not opened unto me.
It is a good night for our door-keeper.
O bolt, I will open;
O door, thou art my fate.   9
Art thou mine own good spirit?
One slaughtereth our ox within,
O door, exert not thy power,
That an ox may be slaughtered to the bolt,   10
A short-horn to the threshold,
A stout goose to the jambs,
Tender meat (?) to the . . .;
But all the choicest portions of our ox   11
Are for the carpenter lad
Who shall make for us a bolt of papyrus
And a door of straw (?),   12
That the brother may come at any time,
And may find her house open,
And may find a bed laid with fine linen,   13

And a fair maiden together with it (?),
And the maiden shall say to me (?),
This (?) house belongeth to the son of (?) the city-prefect.

88. THE GREAT INSCRIPTION OF THE SECOND PYLON AT MEDINET HABU

On the second pylon of the mortuary temple of Ramesses III (Dynasty 20) at Medinet Habu on the west bank of the Nile near Thebes appears this lengthy inscription. It recounts Ramesses III's defeat of the Sea Peoples.

Introduction: Praise of Ramesses

Year 8, under the majesty of Horus: mighty Bull, valiant Lion, strong-armed, lord of might, capturing the Asiatics; Favorite of the Two Goddesses: Mighty in Strength, like his father, Montu, destroying the Nine Bows, driving (them) from their land; Hawk, divine at his birth, excellent and favorite egg of Harakhte, sovereign, excellent heir of the gods, fashioning their images on earth, doubling their offerings; King of Upper and Lower Egypt, Lord of the Two Lands: Usermare-Meriamon; Son of Re, Ramses, Ruler of Heliopolis; king lord of valor, extending (his) two arms, and taking away the breath from the countries by the heat of his limbs, great in the power of Montu, ... the fray like Re, [daily] ...... valiant upon (his) horse, fighting hand to hand upon his feet, warrior like the shooting-stars in heaven, King Ramses; charging into the thick of the fray like turning hack the Asiatics, fighting in the territory of rebels who know not Egypt, who tell how they have heard of his might, who come with praise, trembling in all their limbs ...... of the Asiatics. His form and his limbs are [straight], the equal of Baal, mighty in the multitude, without his like. He smites millions, alone by himself; all lands are despised and contemptible before him, appearing ...... They come ... [to] look upon Egypt, prostrate, bowing down before him. They say every day: "Montu is in his great form, which is in Egypt among you, bearing his mighty sword. Let us all come, that we may make for him ...... him [in] his grasp, the King Ramses (III)." Beautiful is the appearance of the king, like the son of Isis the defender, firstborn son of Re-Atum, ... wearing the white crown, wearing the red crown, beautiful of face, wearing the double plume like Tatenen. His loveliness ...... in the early morning, beautiful, sitting upon the throne like Atum, when he has assumed the regalia of Horus and Set; Nekhbet and Buto, the serpent-crown of the South and the serpentcrown of the North, they take their place upon his head. His two hands grasp the crook-staff and hold the scourge, ... conscious of strength ... [among] the Nine Bows .... Plentiful are fowl and provision in his reign, like his father, the Beautiful-Faced (Ptah), Nun, great in love as king, like Shu, son of Re. When he appears, there is rejoicing over him, like Aton; strong and valiant, mustering the lands at his] desire, ... like [Montu], creating them like Ptah; ready and skilled in law, there is none like him; like Re when he took the land as a kingdom, King Ramses, ... numerous in monuments, great in wonderful works, making festive the temples, ... the son of Re, ... who came forth from his limbs, ... firstborn [of] the gods. He was appointed as a youth to be king of the Two Lands, to be ruler of every circuit of Aton, a shield protecting Egypt in his time. They sit under the shadow of his might, the strong one victorious hand laid upon their head; King Ramses, the king himself, he saith:

Ramesses' Speech; His Accession

"Hearken to me all the land, gathered in [one place], the court, the king's-children, the butlers, ... living, the ..., the youth, all the young men who are in this land. Give your attention to my utterance, that ye may know my plans for sustaining you alive, that ye may learn of the might of my august father, Amon-Kamephis, creator of my beauty. His great might ..., victorious against every fallen foe, beneath my feet. He decrees to me victory, and his hand is with me, so that every invader of my boundary is slain in my grasp; his chosen one whom he found among hundreds of thousands, who was established upon his throne for safety ... [when there was not a single man among them to rescue (them)] from the Nine Rows. I surrounded her, I established her by my valiant might. When I arose like the sun as king over Egypt, I protected her, I expelled for her the Nine Bows."

Northern Invasion of Syria

"The countries ......, the [Northerners] in their isles were disturbed, taken away in the [fray] ... at one time. Not one stood before their hands, from Kheta,[15] Kode, Carchemish, Arvad, Alasa,[16] they were wasted. [The]y [set up] a camp in one place in Amor.[17] They desolated his people and his land like that which is not. They came with fire prepared before them, forward to Egypt. Their main support was Peleset,[18] Tjekker, Shekelesh, Denyen, and Weshesh. (These) lands were united, and they laid their hands upon the land as far as the Circle of the Earth. Their hearts were confident, full of their plans."

Ramesses' Preparations

"Now, it happened through this god, the lord of gods, that I was prepared and armed to [trap] them like wild fowl. He furnished my strength and caused my plans to prosper. I went forth, directing these marvelous things. I equipped my frontier in Zahi, prepared before them. The chiefs, the captains of infantry, the nobles, I caused to equip the harbor-mouths, like a strong wall, with warships, galleys, and barges, ... They were manned [completely] from bow to stern with valiant warriors bearing their arms, soldiers of all the choicest of Egypt, being like lions roaring upon the mountain-tops. The charioteers were warriors ..., and all good officers, ready of hand. Their horses were quivering in their every limb, ready to crush the countries under their feet. I was the valiant

---

15 Hatti.
16 Cyprus.
17 Amurru.
18 Philistines.

Montu, stationed before them, that they might behold the hand-to-hand fighting of my arms. I, King Ramses, was made a far-striding hero, conscious of his might, valiant to lead his army in the day of battle."

Defeat of the Enemy

"Those who reached my boundary, their seed is not; their heart and their soul are finished forever and ever. As for those who had assembled before them on the sea, the full flame was in their front, before the harbor-mouths, and a wall of metal upon the shore surrounded them. They were dragged, overturned, and laid low upon the beach; slain and made heaps from stern to bow of their galleys, while all their things were cast upon the water. (Thus) I turned back the waters to remember Egypt; when they mention my name in their land, may it consume them, while I sit upon the throne of Harakhte, and the serpent-diadem is fixed upon my head, like Re. I permit not the countries to see the boundaries of Egypt to ... [among] them. As for the Nine Bows, I have taken away their land and their boundaries; they are added to mine. Their chiefs and their people (come) to me with praise. I carried out the plans of the All-Lord, the august, divine father, lord of the gods."

Ramesses' Song of Triumph

"Rejoice, O Egypt, to the height of heaven, for I am ruler of the South and North upon the throne of Atum. The gods have appointed me to be king over Egypt, to be victor, to expel them for her from the countries; they decreed to me the kingdom while I was a child, and my reign is full of plenty ...... Strength has been given to me, because of my benefactions to the gods and goddesses, from a heart of love. I have expelled your mourning, which was in your heart, and I have made you to dwell in peace. Those whom I have overthrown shall not return, the tribute ...... their land, their detestation is the daily mention of my name, King Ramses. I have covered Egypt, I have protected her by my valiant might, since I assumed the rule of the kingdom ...... the might of my two arms, bringing terror among the Nine Rows. Not a land stays at hearing my name, (but) they leave their cities, starting in their places, forsaking ...... before them. I am a goring Bull, confident in his two horns. My hand is equal to my courage following my valor, when my heart says to me: 'Make ...' ... my office ...... in the bow of the morning-barque, I bring to you jubilation. Mourning is in the countries, trembling is in every land which I wrought. My heart is filled as a god ...... valiant, lord of the sword. I know that his might is greater than (that of) the gods. The [lifetime] which the gods who are in ... decree ...... There is not a moment in your presence, which brings not plunder by the plans of the counsel which is in my heart, for the support of Egypt. Desolated is ...... the chief of their cities, wasted at one time. Their groves, and all their people are consumed by fire. They lament in their hearts: 'We will ...... their ... to Egypt.'

"I am the strong and valiant one; my designs come to pass without fail. I have shown my excellence, since I [know] this god, the father of the gods ...... I have not ignored his temple, (but) my heart has been steadfast to double the feasts and food-offerings above what was before. My heart is filled with truth every day, my abhorrence is lying ...... the gods are satisfied with truth. Their hands are for me the shield of my body, to ward off evil and misfortune from my limbs; the king, ruler of the Nine Bows, Lord of the Two Lands, Ramses, given life, stability, satisfaction, like Re, forever and ever."

89. RECORDS OF THE HAREM CONSPIRACY

The Harem Conspiracy Papyrus (also known as the Judicial Papyrus of Turin), the Papyrus Lee, and Papyrus Rollin all contain a record of trials that were held after an assassination attempt against Ramesses III. Apparently involved in the conspiracy was Tiye, wife of Ramesses III, who was attempting to place her son Pentewere on the throne. The following translation is taken from these three papyri.

I. Appointment of the Court

Introduction

...... Ruler of Heliopolis .... t[he] wh[ole] land .... the whole land .... their cattle .... to bring them .... all ... before them .... for them; the ... are .... people saying .... they are the abhorred of the land.

Commission of the Court

I commission:
The overseer of the White House, Mentemtowe;
The overseer of the White House, Pefroi;
The standard-bearer, Kara;
The butler, Pebes;
The butler, Kedendenna;
The butler, Maharbaal;
The butler, Payernu;
The butler, Thutrekhnefer;
The king's-herald, Penrenut;
The scribe, Mai;
The scribe of the archives, Peremhab;
The standard-bearer of the infantry, Hori; saying:

Instructions to the Court

As for the words which the people have spoken, I know them not. Go and examine them. When they go out, and they examine them, they shall cause to die by their own hand, those who should die, without [my] knowing it. They shall execute the punishment [upon] the others, likewise without my knowing it. When [you] go, [see to it] that you give heed, and have a care lest you execute punishment upon ...... unjustly ...... Now, I say to you in very truth, as for all that has been done, and those who have done it, let all that they have done fall upon their (own) heads; while I am protected and defended forever, while I am [among] the just kings, who are before Amon-Re, king of gods, and before Osiris, ruler of eternity.

II. The Condemned of the First Prosecution

First Prosecution

Persons brought in because of the great crimes which they had committed, and placed in the court of examination before the great nobles of the court of examination, that they might be examined by:

Composition of the Court

The overseer of the White House, Mentemtowe;
The overseer of the White House, Pefroi;
The standard-bearer, Kara;
The butler, Pebes;
The scribe of the archives, Mai;
The standard-bearer, Hori.

They examined them; they found them guilty; they brought their punishment upon them; their crimes seized them.

The Condemned and Their Crimes

The great criminal, Pebekkamen, formerly chief of the chamber. He was brought in because of his collusion with Tiy and the women of the harem. He made common cause with them, and began bringing out their words to their mothers and their brothers who were there, saying: "Stir up the people! Incite enemies to hostility against their lord." He was placed before the great nobles of the court of examination; they examined his crimes; they found that he had committed them. His crimes seized him; the nobles who examined him brought his punishment upon him.

The great criminal, Mesedsure, formerly butler. He was brought in because of his collusion [with] Pebekkamen, formerly chief of the chamber, and with the women, to stir up enemies to hostility against their lord. He was placed before the great nobles of the court of examination; they examined his crimes; they found him guilty; they brought his punishment upon him.

The great criminal, Peynok, formerly overseer of the king's ... of the harem, [in the suite]. He was brought in because of his making common cause with Pebekkamen and Mesedsure, to commit hostility against their lord. He was placed before the great nobles of the court of examination; they examined his crimes; they found him guilty; they brought his punishment upon him.

The great criminal, Pendua, formerly scribe of the king's ... of the harem, [in the suite]. He was brought in because of his making common cause with Pebekkamen and Mesedsure, the other criminal, formerly overseer of the king's ..., and the women of the harem, to make a conspiracy with them, to commit hostility against their lord. He was placed before the nobles of the court of examination; they examined his crimes; they found him guilty; they brought his punishment upon him.

The great criminal, Petewnteamon, formerly inspector of the harem, [in the suite]. He was brought in because of his hearing the words which the people discussed with the women of the harem, without reporting them. He was placed before the great nobles of the court of examination; they examined his crimes; they found him guilty; they brought his punishment upon him.

The great criminal, Kerpes, formerly inspector of the harem, [in the suite]. He was brought in because of the words which he had heard and had concealed. He was placed before the nobles of the court of examination. They found him guilty; they brought his punishment upon him.

The great criminal, Khamopet, formerly inspector of the harem, [in the suite]. He was brought in because of the words which he had heard and had concealed. He was placed before the nobles of the court of examination. They found him guilty; they brought his punishment upon him.

The great criminal, Khammale, formerly inspector of the harem, [in the suite]. He was brought in because of the words which he had heard and had concealed. He was placed before the nobles of the court of examination; they found him guilty; they brought his punishment upon him.

The great criminal, Setimperthoth, formerly inspector of the harem, [in the suite]. He was brought in because of the words which he had heard and had concealed. He was placed before the nobles of the court of examination; they found him guilty; they brought his punishment upon him.

The great criminal, Setimperamon, formerly inspector of the harem, [in the suite]. He was brought in because of the words which he had heard and had concealed. He was placed before the nobles of the court of examination; they found him guilty; they brought his punishment upon him.

The great criminal, Weren, who was butler. He was brought in because of his hearing the words from the chief of the chamber, and when he had [withdrawn from] him, he concealed them and did not report them. He was placed before the nobles of the court of examination; they found him guilty; they brought his punishment upon him.

The great criminal, Eshehebsed, formerly assistant of Pebekkamen. He was brought in because of his hearing the words from Pebekkamen; and when he had left him, he did not report them. He was placed before the nobles of the court of examination; they found him guilty; they brought his punishment upon him.

The great criminal, Peluka, formerly butler and scribe of the White House. He was brought in because of his collusion with Pebekkamen, having heard the words from him, without reporting them. He was placed before the nobles of the court of examination; they found him guilty; they brought his punishment upon him.

The great criminal, the Libyan, Yenini, formerly butler. He was brought in because of his collusion with Pebekkamen, having heard the words from him, without reporting them. He was placed before the nobles of the court of examination; they found him guilty; they brought his punishment upon him.

Wives of the people of the harem-gate, who united with the men, when the things were discussed; who were placed before the nobles of the court of examination; they found them guilty; they brought their punishment upon them: six women.

The great criminal, Pere, son of Ruma, formerly overseer of the White House. He was brought in because of his collusion with the great criminal, Penhuibin, making common cause with him to stir up enemies to hostility against their lord. He was placed before the nobles of the court of examination; they found him guilty; they brought his punishment upon him.

The great criminal, Binemwese, formerly captain of archers in Nubia. He was brought in because of the letter, which his sister, who was in the harem, [in the suite], had written to him, saying: "Incite the people to hostility! And come to begin hostility against your lord." He was placed before

Kedendenna, Maharbaal, Pirsun, and Thutrekhnefer; they examined him; they found him guilty; they brought his punishment upon him.

III. The Condemned of the Second Prosecution

Persons brought in because of their crimes and because of their collusion with Pebekkamen, Peyes and Pentewere. They were placed before the nobles of the court of examination in order to examine them; they found them guilty; they left them in their own hands in the court of examination; they took their own lives; and no punishment was executed upon them.

The great criminal, Peyes, formerly commander of the army. The great criminal, Messui, formerly scribe of the house of sacred writings.

The great criminal, Perekamenef, formerly chief. The great criminal, Iroi, formerly overseer of the ... of Sekhmet.

The great criminal, Nebzefai, formerly butler.

The great criminal, Shedrneszer, formerly scribe of the house of sacred writings.

Total, 6.

IV. The Condemned of the Third Prosecution

Persons who were brought in, because of their crimes, to the court of examination, before Kedendenna, Maharbaal, Pirsun, Thutrekhnefer, and Mertusamon. They examined them concerning their crimes; they found them guilty; they left them in their place; they took their own lives.

Pentewere, who bore that other name. He was brought in because of his collusion [with] Tiy, his mother, when she discussed the words with the women of the harem, being hostile against his lord. He was placed before the butlers, in order to examine him; they found him guilty; they left him in his place; he took his own life.

The great criminal, Henutenamon, formerly butler. He was brought in because of the crimes of the women of the harem; having been among them and having heard (them), without reporting them. He was placed before the butlers, in order to examine him; they found him guilty; they left him in his place; he took his own life.

The great criminal, Amenkha, formerly deputy of the harem, [in the suite]. He was brought in because of the crimes of the women of the harem; having been among them, and having heard (them), without reporting them. He was placed before the butlers, in order to examine him; they found him guilty; they left him in his place; he took his own life.

The great criminal, Pere, formerly scribe of the king's ... of the harem, [in the suite]. He was brought in because of the crimes of the women of the harem; having been among them, and having heard (them), without reporting them. He was placed before the butlers, in order to examine him; they found him guilty; they left him in his place; he took his own life.

V. The Condemned of the Fourth Prosecution

Persons upon whom punishment was executed by cutting off their noses and their ears, because of their forsaking the good testimony delivered to them. The women had gone; had arrived at their place of abode, and had there caroused with them and with Peyes. Their crime seized them.

This great criminal, Pebes, formerly butler. This punishment was executed upon him; he was left (alone); he took his own life.

The great criminal, Mai, formerly scribe of the archives.

The great criminal, Teynakhte, formerly officer of infantry.

The great criminal, Oneney, formerly captain of police.

VI. The Acquitted

Person who had been connected with them; they had contended with him, with evil and violent words; he was dismissed; punishment was not executed upon him:

The great criminal, Hori, who was standard-bearer of the infantry.

VII. The Practicers of Magic

First Case of Magic

He began to make magic rolls for [hindering] and terrifying, and to make some gods of wax, and some people, for enfeebling the limbs of people; and gave them into the hand of Pebekkamen, whom Re made not to be chief of the chamber, and the other great criminals, saying: "Take them in;" and they took them in. Now, when he set himself to do the evil (deeds) which he did, in which Re did not permit that he should succeed, he was examined. Truth was found in every crime and in every evil (deed), which his heart had devised to do. There was truth therein, he had done them all, together with all the other great criminals. They were great crimes of death, the great abominations of the land, the things which he had done. Now, when he learned of the great crimes of death which he had committed, he took his own life.

Second Case of Magic

...... the king, L. P. H., for provisioning ...... "...... any ... of my place of abode, to any person in the world." Now, when Penhuibin, formerly overseer of herds, said to him: "Give to me a roll for enduing me with strength and might," he gave to him a magic roll of Usermare-Meriamon (Ramesses III), L. P. H., the Great God, his lord, L. P. H., and he began to [employ the magic powers of a god] upon people. He arrived at the side of the harem, this other large, deep place. He began to make people of wax, inscribed, in order that they might be taken in by the inspector, Errem, [hindering] one troop and bewitching the others, that a few words might be taken in, and others brought out. Now, when he was examined concerning them, truth was found in every crime and in every evil (deed), which his heart had devised to do. There was truth therein, he had done them all, together with the other great criminals, the abomination of every god and every goddess all together. The great punishments of death were executed upon him, of which the gods have said: "Execute them upon him."

Third Case of Magic

...... in the ... upon the measure. He went away his hand enfeebled .... Now, when [he was examined concerning] them, truth was found in every crime and in [every] evil (deed), which his heart had devised to do. There was truth [therein, he had done them all, together with the othe]r great criminals, the abomination of every god and every goddess all together. They were great crimes of death, the great abominations of [the land, the things which he had done. Now, when he learned of the] great [crim]es of death, which he had committed, he took his own life. Now, when the nobles, who examined him, learned that he had taken his own life ...... Re, altogether, of which the sacred writings say: "Execute it upon him."

𓈖𓏤𓆑𓎛𓏤𓅱𓂋𓏤𓇋𓏤𓈖𓏤𓂋𓆑𓏤𓄿𓏤𓈖𓏤𓅱𓏤𓂋𓏤𓇋𓏤𓈖𓏤𓄿𓏤𓅱𓏤𓂋𓏤𓇋𓏤𓈖

90. THE GREAT HARRIS PAPYRUS

One of the longest papyri still in existence from ancient Egypt is the Great Harris Papyrus, found in a hole in the floor of a cliff-tomb at Deir el-Medina near Thebes. Written at the beginning of the reign of Ramesses IV (Dynasty 20), it is a tribute to the reign of his father, Ramesses III, listing offerings and gifts that his father gave to the temples and giving a historical account of much of his father's reign. Here is the latter.

Introduction

Said King Usermare-Meriamon (Ramses III), L. P. H., the Great God, to the princes, and leaders of the land, the infantry and chariotry, the Sherden, the numerous archers, and all the citizens of the land of Egypt:

Former Anarchy

"Hear, that I may inform you of my benefactions which I did while I was king of the people. The land of Egypt was [overthrown] from without, and every man was (thrown out) of his right; they had no chief mouth for many years formerly until other times. The land of Egypt was in the hands of chiefs and of rulers of towns; one slew his neighbor, great and small. Other times having come after it, with empty years, Yarsu, a certain Syrian was with them as chief. He set the whole land tributary before him together; he united his companions and plundered their possessions. They made the gods like men, and no offerings were presented in the temples.

Rule of Setnakht

"But when the gods inclined themselves to peace, to set the land (in) its right according to its accustomed manner, they established their son, who came forth from their limbs, to be Ruler, L. P. H., of every land, upon their great throne, (even) Userkhare-Setepnere-Meriamon, L. P. H., Son of Re, Setnakht-Mererre-Meriamon, L. P. H. He was Khepri-Set, when he is enraged; he set in order the entire land, which had been rebellious; he slew the rebels who were in the land of Egypt; he cleansed the great throne of Egypt; he was Ruler, L. P. H., of the Two Lands, on the throne of Atum. He gave [ready faces, which had been turned away]. Every man knew his brother who had been walled in. He established the temples in possession of divine offerings, to offer to the gods according to their customary stipulations.

Rise of Ramesses III and Death of Setnakht

"He appointed me to be hereditary prince in the place of Keb, I was the great chief mouth of the lands of Egypt, and commander of the whole land united in one. He went to rest in his horizon, like the gods; there was done for him that which was done for Osiris; he was rowed in his king's-barge upon the river, and rested in his eternal house west of Thebes.

Accession of Ramesses III

"Then my father, Amon-Re, lord of gods, Re-Atum, and Ptah, beautiful of face, crowned me as Lord of the Two Lands on the throne of him who begat me; I received the office of my father with joy; the land rested and rejoiced in possession of peace, being joyful at seeing me as ruler, L. P. H., of the Two Lands, like Horus when he was called to rule the Two Lands on the throne of Osiris. I was crowned with the *etef*-crown bearing the uraeus; I assumed the double-plumed diadem, like Tatenen. I sat upon the throne of Harakhte. I was clad in the regalia, like Atum.

Internal Organization

"I made Egypt into many classes, consisting of: butlers of the palace, great princes, numerous infantry, and chariotry, by the hundred-thousand; Sherden and Kehek without number; attendants by the ten-thousand; and serf-laborers of Egypt.

War with Northern Asiatics

"I extended all the boundaries of Egypt; I overthrew those who invaded them from their lands. I slew the Denyen in their isles, the Tjekker and the Peleset were made ashes. The Sherden and the Weshesh of the sea, they were made as those that exist not, taken captive at one time, brought as captives to Egypt, like the sand of the shore. I settled them in strongholds, bound in my name. Numerous were their classes like hundred-thousands. I taxed them all, in clothing and grain from the storehouses and granaries each year.

Edomite War

"I destroyed the people of Seir, of the tribes of the Shasu; I plundered their tents of their people, their possessions, their cattle likewise, without number. They were pinioned and brought as captive, as tribute of Egypt. I gave them to the gods, as slaves into their house[s].

Libyan Wars

"Behold, I will inform you of other things, done in Egypt since my reign. The Libyans and the Meshwesh were dwelling in Egypt, having plundered the cities of the western shore, from Memphis to Kerben. They had reached the great river on both its banks. They it was who plundered the cities of Egwowe during very many years, while they were in Egypt. Behold, I destroyed them, slain at one time. I laid low the Meshwesh, the Libyans, the Esbet, the Keykesh, the Shai, the Hes and the Beken; they were overthrown in their blood and made heaps. I turned them back from trampling the border of Egypt. I carried away those whom my sword spared, as numerous captives, pinioned like birds before my horses, their wives and their children by the ten-thousand, their cattle in number like hundred-thousands. I settled their leaders in strongholds in my name. I gave to them captains of archers, and chief men of the tribes, branded and made into slaves, impressed with my name; their wives and their children were made likewise. I led their cattle into the house of Amon; they were made for him into herds forever.

Well in Ayan

"I made a very great well in the country of Ayan. It was surrounded by a wall like a mountain of gritstone, with 20 [courses] in the ground foundation, and a height of 30 cubits, having battlements. Its doorposts and doors were hewn of cedar, their bolts were of copper, with mountings.

Punt Expedition

"I hewed great galleys with barges before them, manned with numerous crews, and attendants in great number; their captains of marines were with them, with inspectors and petty officers, to command them. They were laden with the products of Egypt without number, being in every number like ten-thousands. They were sent forth into the great sea of the inverted water, they arrived at the countries of Punt, no mishap overtook them, safe and bearing terror. The galleys and the barges were laden with the products of Land, consisting of all the strange marvels of their country: plentiful myrrh of Punt, laden by ten-thousands, without number. Their chief's children of God's-Land went before their tribute advancing to Egypt. They arrived in safety at the highland of Coptos; they landed in safety, bearing the things which they brought. They were loaded, on the land-journey, upon asses and upon men; and loaded into vessels upon the Nile, (at) the haven of Coptos. They were sent forward down-stream and arrived amid festivity, and brought (some) of the tribute into the (royal) presence like marvels. Their chief's children mere in adoration before me, kissing the earth, prostrate before me. I gave them to all the gods of this land, to satisfy the two serpent-goddesses every morning.

Expedition to Atika

"I sent forth my messengers to the country of the Atika, to the great copper mines which are in this place. Their galleys carried them; others on the land-journey were upon their asses. It has not been heard before, since kings reign. Their mines were found abounding in copper; it was loaded by ten-thousands into their galleys. They were sent forward to Egypt, and arrived safely. It was carried and made into a heap under the balcony, in many bars of copper, like hundred-thousands, being of the color of gold of three times. I allowed all the people to see them, like wonders.

Sinai Expedition

"I sent forth butlers and officials to the malachite-country, to my mother, Hathor, mistress of the malachite. There were brought for her silver, gold, royal linen, mek-linen, and many things into her presence, like the sand. There were brought for me wonders of real malachite in numerous sacks, brought forward into my presence. They had not been seen before, since kings reign.

Ramesses III's Good Works at Home

"I planted the whole land with trees and verdure, and I made the people dwell in their shade. I made the woman of Egypt to go ... to the place she desired, (for) no stranger nor any one upon the road molested her. I made the infantry and chariotry to dwell (at home) in my time; the Sherden and Kehek were in their towns, lying the [length] of their backs; they had no fear, (for) there was no enemy from Kush, (nor) foe from Syria. Their bows and their weapons reposed in their magazines, while they were satisfied and drunk with joy. Their wives were with them, their children at their side; they looked not behind them, (but) their hearts were confident, (for) I was with them as the defense and protection of their limbs. I sustained alive the whole land, whether foreigners, ([common]) folk, citizens, or people, male or female. I took a man out of his misfortune and I gave to him breath; I rescued him from the oppressor, who was of more account than he. I set each man in his security, in their towns; I sustained alive others in the hall of petition. I equipped the land in the place where it was laid waste. The land was well satisfied in my reign. I did good to the gods, as well as the men, sand I had nothing at all belonging to any ([other]) people. I exercised my sovereignty over the land as ruler of the Two Lands, while you were my servants under my feet, without .... You were well pleasing to my heart, for you did excellently, and you were zealous for my commands and my commissions.

Ramesses III's Death

"Behold, I have gone to rest in the Nether World, like (my) father Re, I have mingled with the great gods in heaven, earth and, the Nether World. Amon-Re has established my son on my throne; he has taken my once in peace, as ruler of the Two Lands, sitting on the throne of Horus as lord of the two shores. He has assumed the *etef*-crown, like Tatenen, as: Usermare-Setepnamon, L. P. H., firstborn son of Re, the self-begetter: Ramses (IV)-Hekma-Meriamon; the child, son of Amon, who came forth from his limbs, shining as Lord of the Two Lands; he is like a true son, praised for his father's sake.

Faithfulness to Ramesses IV Urged

"Be attached to his sandals, kiss the earth in his presence, bow down to him, follow him at all times, adore him, praise him, magnify his beauty as you do to Re every morning. Present to him your tribute (in) his august palace, bring to him the gifts of the lands and countries. Be zealous for his commissions, the commands which are spoken among, you. [Obey] his behests, that you may prosper under him. Labor for him as one man in every work; drag for him monuments, dig for him canals, do for him the work of your hands, that you may enjoy his favor, in possession of his provision every day. Amon has decreed to him his reign upon earth; he has doubled to him his lifetime more than (to) any king; (even) the King of Upper and Lower Egypt, Lord of the Two Lands; Usermare-Setepnamon, L. P. H.; Son of Re, Lord of Diadems: Ramses (IV)-Hekma-Meriamon, L. P. H., given life forever:

91. LETTER OF NAKHTSOBEK

Another letter from the group found at Deir el-Medina (see reading #81) is this one from the scribe Nakhtsobek, who writes to an old friend who has recently been causing him trouble. It comes from the time of Ramesses V (Dynasty 20).

[The scribe] Nakhtsobek to the workman Amennakht:

In life, prosperity and health and in the favor of Amon-Re, King of the Gods! Every day I am calling upon Amon, Mut, Khonsu, and all gods of Thebes and every god and goddess who resides [in] the West of Ne (Thebes) to give you life, to give you health, and to give you a long [lifetime] and a ripe old age, while you continue in the favor of Amenophis, the lord of the Village, your good lord who looks after you.

And further: What's up? What have I done against you? Am I not your old table companion? Has the time come when you must turn your [back(?)]? What shall I do? Please write me of the wrong that I've done against you through the policeman Bes. And if you refuse to write me either good or bad, this day is really bad! I won't request anything else of you. A person is delighted when he is together with his old table companion. While certain new [things] are good to have, an old companion is better.

As soon as my letter reaches you, [you] shall send word about your condition through the policeman Bes. Inform me of the situation today. Don't make me be told not to enter your house and not to make [my] way within the walls and to flee [from] the Village. And don't [turn a deaf ear(?)] to me. I am going to enter the house and leave therefrom. I must have access [to this] abode of mine.

May Amon be before you! If [he] lives, I shall (also) live. When I die, may Amon still be before you (text: him)! Farewell!

ᛀᛊᛊ ᛊᛊᛊ (hieroglyphic text)

92. THE CONTENDINGS OF HORUS AND SETH

This tale from the Chester Beatty Papyrus I concerns a fight between Horus and Seth over the throne of their father Osiris. One can see that the myth of the two gods has developed significantly by the later Twentieth Dynasty, when this narrative was composed (cf. reading #10).

I

The tale of how a decision was reached in the case of Horus versus Seth, those two mysterious entities, those enormous beings, great and ancient deities from the time of the Beginning:

Now a young god was seated before Ra the lord of all, demanding the royal title of his father Osiris —Osiris, beautiful as the dawn, the son of Ptah, Osiris whose visage illuminates the underworld. As this young god, Horus, was making his claim, Thoth brought to Ra, great and ancient chief of Heliopolis, the Wedjat. This magic object, which looks like a human eye and also like that of a falcon, is the spiritual essence of the sun, of the kingship and of all well-being. Whoever holds it rules Egypt.

Shu said to his father Ra: "Right should rule over might: make it so, order that the kingship be given to Horus."

Thoth said: "That's a million times right!"

Isis gave a great shriek, for she was very, very delighted; she came before Ra and said: "O North wind, travel West, beyond the sunset to the land of the dead! There cheer the heart of good King Osiris with this news."

Shu said: "The passing on of the Wedjat to Horus seems right to the gods."

Ra, lord of all things, said: "What's that supposed to mean? Are the lot of you going to make my decision for me?"

The minor war god Onuris said: "Let the royal ring be put on Horus' finger and the White Crown of Upper Egypt on his head!"

Ra remained silent for a long moment, furious with the gods.

II

Seth the son of Nut said: "Have him dragged outside with me so I can show you my power, let me wrestle with him in front of the gods. Since it doesn't look like this will be settled by words, my hands will take what your tongues won't give."

Then Thoth said to Seth: "Don't you think we can recognize the lie here? Are we giving the crown of Osiris to you even though Osiris' son Horus stands here waiting for it?"

Then Ra became really furious — his intention was to give the kingship to Seth, Nut's powerful son.

Meanwhile Onuris bellowed at the whole pantheon: "What are we going to do?"

The great lord of Heliopolis, Ra, said: "Have someone fetch Ba-Neb-Djedy, the ram-headed god of Mendes, that great and vigorous deity: let him decide between the young fellows who'll be king."

III

Then Ba-Neb-Djedy was brought from Setchet, where they call him K'num. There, in his temple at the first cataract, he controls the level of the flooding Nile. Ba-Neb-Djedy came accompanied by Ptah-Ta-Tenen, lord of the Nile's rich silt and clay. These two were told:

"Judge the two young fellows so they can stop their constant squabbling."

Ba-Neb-Djedy replied: "We shouldn't make a recommendation without knowing all the facts. Let a letter be sent to great Neith, the divine mother, goddess of war and creation! Whatever she says, we'll do."

The gods replied: "Why do you hesitate to pronounce on the case? It was already decided in the courtroom called "Thus-The-World-Is-Ordered," back in primordial times."

But honoring the suggestion of Ba-Neb-Djedy, the gods turned to Thoth there in front of Ra and said: "God of scribes and knowledge, write a letter to Neith, the divine great mother, in the name of Ra, lord of all, the great bull of Heliopolis."

Thoth said: "I will , I will, oh yes indeed, to be sure!" He sat down on his mat and took up his brush and ink-pot to write.

IV

The letter went: "From Ra, the King of Egypt, whom Thoth loves, Lord of the Two Lands, who resides in his temple at Heliopolis, the solar orb who illumines the country with his glance, who fills it with fertility like the Nile, "— in full acknowledgement of the majesty of Neith, the divine and primordial great mother, who shone upon the first created face that ever saw this world — may you live, be well, and remain forever young —

"I, Ra, active manifestation of the universal Deity and lord of all, the Bull of Heliopolis, Egypt's good king, I say that I, your unworthy servant, spend my nights worrying about this matter of who shall inherit from Osiris, and all my days taking counsel with Egypt on his behalf. I've been at it for more years than a crocodile lives.

"What should we do for these two persons, Horus and Seth, who have been wrangling in court for eighty years now? Write to us with your instructions!"

V

Neith's reply was: "Give Osiris' office to his son Horus. Cease to multiply these great, lying, inappropriate wrongs, or I will become angry and the sky will crash down to earth! Let this be told to Mr. Ra as well: Double Seth's inheritance! Give him your daughters Anat and Astarte, goddesses of Canaan. But place Horus on the throne of his father Osiris."

VI

Neith's letter was brought to the gods as they sat in the hall named "Long-Horned-Horus Prevails." It was given to Thoth. He read it before Ra and the gods, who said with one voice "This goddess is right!"

The lord of all things, Ra, became angry at Horus as a result of this, and said to him: "You're a puny weakling, the job of kingship's too big for you. You're just a little boy with sour milk-breath from sucking your mother's tit."

Then Onuris began to rage, and the whole divine senate with him. A minor demon named Baba pulled himself up to his full height and said to Ra: "Oh, who cares what you think, you're nothing but an implausible old superstition."

Ra was terribly hurt by this. He lay down on his back, with his heart just aching.

The gods left, shouting at Baba: "Leave us, what you have done is a terrible, awful crime" Then they retired to their tents.

VII

The supreme god passed a day lying on his back in his pavilion, all alone, his feelings brutally wounded. Now after a long while the tree-goddess Hathor came along, stood before the lord god her father, lifted her skirt, bent over and wiggled her ass and cunt at him.

This made the great god laugh. He got up, went back to his seat among the pantheon and said to Horus and Seth: "Let's hear what you two have to say for yourselves."

VIII

Powerful Seth, the son of Nut, said: "Me, I'm Seth, strongest god in the pantheon, I'm the one who re-slays Apophis, Ra's eternal enemy, each day. To do this, I stand at my post in the prow of the solar barque, and no other god can. I will inherit the title from Osiris."

The gods said: "Seth, the son of Nut, is right!"

Onuris and Thoth shouted: "Are we really going to award the royal title to the uncle while the son and heir stands before us?"

Then Ba-Neb-Djedy said: "Are we really going to award the royal title to this child? I've heard it said that Seth standing before us is actually Horus' older brother, and thus the legitimate heir."

At this the assembled gods shrieked in front of Ra and answered Ba-Neb-Djedy: "What kind of worthless nonsense is this you're saying? If we gave weight to every obscure variant tradition in Egyptian mythology none of us would know who we were."

Horus said to Ba-Neb-Djedy: "It's not nice to attack me like this in front of the gods, calling me 'this child!' Do you all mean to rob me of my own father's title."

Here Isis became angry with the gods on her son's behalf, and she swore this solemn oath before them: "By the life of my mother, the All-Mother Neith, goddess of the primordial waters, and by the life of Ptah-Ta-Tenen, god of the first land mass to emerge from Neith's world-birthing flood — yes, by Ptah-Ta-Tenen who wears the two tall plumes, before whom all gods bow, these matters shall be laid before Ra lord of Heliopolis, and before Kepri in the Solar Barque. The supreme gods will decide, not this debating club."

The whole pantheon said to her: "Don't get mad! Whoever the true heir is will be given his rights, and all you have said shall be done."

IX

Then Seth became very angry on account of their yielding to Isis the great divine mother. He said: "I am going to take my forty-five hundred pound scepter and kill one of you gods each day."

Then swearing an oath in the name of Ra, Seth continued: "And I will not try my case before this tribunal as long as Isis sits on it."

Thereupon Ra said to them all: "Cross over to the island in the midst of the river, let their claims be settled there without interference, and tell Nemty the ferryman not to bring over any woman who even looks like Isis."

The pantheon went to the isle in mid-river, and there they sat down to eat bread.

X

Meanwhile Isis came over to Nemty, who sat beside his boat: she transformed herself into an old human woman who walked all bent over. She wore a small gold signet ring on her hand, and said to him:

"I'm here to have you ferry me across to that isle in mid-river; I've brought a bowl of porridge for the little boy there. He's been looking after his father's herds there for five days now and he must be very hungry."

Nemty said: "They told me not to ferry any woman across."

"Oh, they only meant Isis when they said that to you — if you don't take Isis, that more than suffices!" said Isis with a grin.

For Nemty a rhyme was as good as a reason, so he said: "What will you give me to take you over?"

"I'll give you this cake . . ."

"What do I care about your cake? They told me not to ferry any woman at all — am I going to ignore my orders for a cake?"

"I'll give you the gold ring on my hand, this signet ring here."

"Give me the ring."

So she gave him the ring and he ferried her to the isle in mid river.

XI

Once there she proceeded on foot till she found herself under the trees. Looking around she saw the gods: they were eating their bread with Ra in his tent.

Then Seth looked up and saw her approaching in the distance. Isis spoke magic words and transformed herself into a young girl with a beautiful body — more beautiful in fact than any woman in the country. Seth fell greatly, terribly, painfully in love with her. As he sat there with the gods eating bread under the sun god's tent, his kilt made a second little tent right there in his lap. He got up and went to intercept her before anyone else saw her.

Seth stood behind a sycamore tree and called out to her: "I'm over here, close by, you beautiful girl!"

She said to him: "Great lord! consider this:

"I was the wife of a cattle herder, and I bore him one child, a boy. When my man died, the boy began to look after his father's cattle, his inheritance. Then a stranger showed up, sat down by my cattle-pen, and here's how he spoke to my child: I'm going to beat you, then I'll take your cattle, your inheritance from your father, and then I'm throwing you out.

"That's how he spoke to my boy! Now I'm asking you, will you defend him?"

Seth said: "How can the rightful possession of the cattle be given to a stranger while the man's son is right there?"

Then Isis transformed herself into a kite and flew off; she perched at the top of an acacia tree and called to Seth: "Now it's your turn to cry! You said it with your own mouth! You're so smart you knew how to pronounce your own verdict! What more do want?"

XII

Seth stood up weeping, and went in tears to where Ra was.

But Ra also said: "What more do you want?"

Seth said: "That awful person, that Isis, came to me again so she could cheat me like she always does. She changed herself into a beautiful girl to catch my eye, and said:

"As for me, I was the wife of a cattle herder who died, and I bore him one child, a boy, who now tends the little herd that used to be his father's. One day a stranger followed my son back to my cattle-pen, where my son was, and I gave him food, but after he had been with us many days this drifter said to my son:

"I'm going to beat you, then I'll take your father's cattle — they'll be mine!

"That's just what he said to my defenseless little boy!

"And that," said, Seth, "was Isis' story to me."

Ra asked: "And what did you say?"

Seth said: "My words were: We can't let the cattle go to a stranger when the man's son is right there — my very words — we've got to get a stick and give that stranger a crack on the head, then throw him out and put the boy in possession of his father's estate — my very words — "

Ra said: "Now look here, you've pronounced your own sentence —what do you want from me?"

Seth said: "Have the ferryman Nemty brought! let a heavy punishment be inflicted on him, ask him why he ferried Isis across, let's see what he has to say about that!"

The ferryman Nemty was brought before the gods, and they deprived him of his toes.

Nemty stood before the deities and foreswore all contact with gold from that day to this: "Gold is taboo to me and to all who dwell in my city."

XIII

The gods then shipped across to the Nile's western shore and sat themselves down on the hills at river-valley's edge. When evening came, Ra and Atum sent a message to the gods saying: "What do you hope to accomplish by sitting there? Look at these boys: do you mean to make them spend their whole lives in court? When this letter reaches you place Egypt's white crown on the head of Horus the son of Isis, name him rightful successor to the office of his father Osiris."

Then Seth became most greatly and terribly angry. The gods said to him: "What are you raging about? Surely you don't think we should disobey the orders of the supreme god Ra?"

The white crown was placed on Horus' head, and Seth let out a mighty cry against the gods and said in his indignation: "Shall a younger kinsman be given the title while I, the elder, first in line for the succession, am passed over? Will you discount my just claim even though I'm standing right here in front of you?"

Then Seth swore this oath: "The white crown must be withdrawn from Horus' head and thrown into the Nile so I can wrestle Horus for it beneath the waves."

Ra decreed that it should be so.

Seth said to Horus: "Come, let's turn ourselves into a pair of Hippopotami and dive under flood in deepest Nile: whoever surfaces before three months are up forfeits the kingship."

They dove in together.

Isis sat weeping, saying: "Seth will hurt my little Horus!" Then she got a ball of cord, made a slip knot on one end; she took a few ounces of copper and cast it into a hook, secured this to the end of her cord and threw it into the water at the spot where Horus and Seth had plunged under.

First the copper hook tasted the royal flesh of Horus, a tiny fish-hook caught on the great tough hide of a hippo! He bellowed as if a mighty spear-head had bit into his vitals: "O mommy, O Isis, help! Tell your hook to let me go! I'm your son Horus!"

Isis shouted to the copper: "Let him go! He's my little boy, my Horus." The copper hook let Horus go.

Then Isis threw it into the water once again, and this time the tiny fish-hook was caught in the armored calluses of the second hippo: Seth bellowed: "What did I do to you, Isis my sister? Call to your copper hook, have it release me! I'm your brother, Nut was my mother too!"

This made Isis feel terribly sorry for Seth, but not that terribly sorry. Then Seth called to her again: "Do you love this one, who came late into your life, more than you love your Seth, who grew up with you, the son of your own mother?"

Isis called out to the copper hook: "Let go of him. That's the son of Isis' mother you're biting into!" The copper released him.

XIV

Horus was angry with his mother Isis: when he came out of the water his face was fierce as that of a south Egyptian panther; with his three pound knife in his hand he removed Isis' head, and went up the hills at the Nile valley's edge, hugging it to him.

Isis changed herself into a statue made of flint which had no head. Then Ra said to Thoth: "What's this thing that's come here without a head?"

Thoth replied: "This, my good lord, is Isis the great, the divine mother; her little boy Horus has taken away her head."

Ra cried to the gods: "Let's go right now and give him a tremendous punishment."

So the pantheon set out for the mountains to search for Horus. As for Horus, he was now lying under a certain fruit-bearing tree in an oasis.

Seth found him, seized him, threw him back-first against the mountainside, tore his two eyes from their sockets, and buried them there. Towards dawn, the pupils of the pair of eyes emerged from underground as a pair of buds: they were lotuses, and opened their blossoms.

Seth came and lied to Ra: "I didn't find Horus," he said, though found him he surely had.

Then Hathor went and found Horus lying, crying in the desert; she took a gazelle, milked it, and said to him: "Open your eyes so I can put this milk in."

He opened his eyes, she applied the milk, both to the right eye and the left, and said: "Open your eyes." He opened his eyes; she examined him and found him to be quite restored.

She left to tell Ra: "I found Horus, Seth had injured his eyes, but I set him right again. He's on his way here now."

XV

The gods said: "Let Horus and Seth be called, and let them be judged."

They were brought before the gods, and Ra, lord of all, said to Horus and Seth in the presence of that great divine assembly: "Now listen up and listen well to what I'm telling you: eat and drink and try to relax and stop the ongoing endless squabbling right now!"

Seth said to Horus: "Let's have a party at my house."

Horus said: "Oh boy oh boy, a party! I'm ready for that!"

That evening when a bed was made up for them, they lay down on it together it to sleep. But Seth got his cock hard and put in between Horus' thighs from behind. Feeling something there, Horus stuck his hand back between his thighs and got a palm-full of Seth's cum. He ran to tell his mother: "Mommy, come see what Seth did to me — "

He opened his hand and let her see the cum in it; she screamed, took her axe, cut off his hand and threw it into the Nile. She got a replacement hand for him. Then she took some high-grade cooking fat and put it on Horus' cock. She got him hard, placed his member over the mouth of a jar and he squirted his cum into it.

XVI

When morning came, she took that cum to Seth's garden and asked his gardener: "Which of these plants here does Seth usually eat?"

"The only plant," said the gardener, "that Seth is accustomed to eat is lettuce."

So Isis poured the cum of Horus on that. Then Seth came along, as was his daily custom, and ate some lettuce — just like he always did. He became pregnant from Horus' cum.

Seth went to Horus and said: "Come on, let's get moving, I'm going to challenge you in court."

Horus replied: "I'll do that, yesiree!"

They arrived together at the tribunal, stood before the awesome council of the gods, who told them: "If you have anything to say on your own behalf, say it now."

Seth said: "Let the kingship, that sublime office, with all its high prerogatives, be given to me, because this Horus here has served me as a woman."

The gods gave a cry of horror.

They spit in Horus' face!

Horus laughed at them!

Horus swore a great oath by the life of all the gods, saying: "Everything Seth has said is a lie. Let the cum of Seth be called before the court as a witness — we'll just see where it answers from. Then let mine be called — let's see where that answers from."

Thoth, master of hieroglyphics, honest scribe of the gods, put his hand on Horus' shoulder and said: "Come forth, O jism of Seth!" It answered from the water that was irrigating a cucumber patch.

Then Thoth put his hand on Seth's shoulder and said: "Come forth, O jism of Horus!"

It answered from Seth's tum: "Where should I come out?"

Thoth said: "Come out through his ear."

It answered: "Shall I then emerge from his ear like common wax, I who am slime divine?"

Thoth said: "Come out then through the top of his head."

So it emerged as a golden sun-disk atop Seth's head. Seth got really, really, terribly angry, and stretched out his hand to sieze the sun-disk.

Thoth snatched it away from him and place it as a glorious crown on his own head.

The gods said: "Horus is vindicated, Seth is a crook."

XVII

When they said that, Seth got really, really, terribly, extremely angry, raising a frightful great howl.

Seth took a great oath, swearing by the name of Ra: "Horus shall not be given the kingship before you send him off with me to build a couple of ships out of stone and have a race! Winner take the kingdom!"

(This was of course a thing impossible, and Seth hoped thus to defer decision forever. However...)

Horus built himself a boat from cedar, whitewashed it with plaster, and pushed it off into the water at night when no one in the whole country could see. The next morning when Seth saw the boat of Horus, he thought it was really made of stone. He went to the nearest mountain, cut off a big outjutting cliff, and carved it into a stone boat 240 feet long.

Then the two rivals went down to their boats, in the presence of the pantheon.

Seth's boat sank. So Seth transformed himself into a hippo and battered Horus' ship.

Horus grabbed a weapon and struck Seth's royal form with it.

All the gods said to him: "Don't whack him with that!"

XVIII

Horus withdrew his fishing spear, placed it in his boat and sailed downstream to Sais in the western delta, the home of great Neith, primordial divine mother — a goddess of terrible power.

He said to her: "Come, judge between Seth and me, for we've been in court over this for eighty years now. No one has been able to finally decide our case, even though a verdict was never given in his favor and I've been found right every day a thousand times now—he just disregards what the pantheon says. I've rebutted his claims in all the courtrooms—I was vindicated in every hall of justice: "Way of Truth," "Horus Triumphant," "Elysian Fields," "Pool of Paradise." From the names of the courtrooms where I've won my case against him you'd think I'd gone through all of eschatology, you'd think one of these would have been the Last Judgement!

"—and all the gods told Shu, Ra's firstborn, himself a former king and now protector of the Wedjat (the orb the king holds, which represents monarchical power and justice), they told Shu himself: "Every one of Horus' claims is valid."

XIX

Thoth said to Ra the lord of all: "Have a letter sent to Osiris asking him to judge between these two."

Shu said: "Thoth's words to us all are right a million times over."

Ra said to Thoth: "Sit and write a letter to Osiris, let's find out what he'll say."

Thoth sat down, took up his pen to write. This is how the message went.

It began with full formality, listing the great names a pharaoh assumes on his accession:

"Osiris, you who are:
The Embodiment of Horus' power:
King *May-Behes-En-Ef* ("Lion-Who-Kills-What-He-Wants-To;")
He Who Is Fostered by the Two Goddesses of Upper and Lower
Egypt: *Mekey-Netcherew-Waf-Tawey* ("Protector-of-the-Gods, Subduer-of-All-Egypt;")
The Victorious God:
Gemey-Remetch-Em-Sep-Tepey ("Who-in-Primordial-Time-Invented Humankind;")

The Uniter of Egypt: *Ka-Em-Jewnew* ("Bull-of-Heliopolis,")
— long may you live!

Osiris, heir of Ptah, the benefactor of the two lands, you who manifest yourself in glory as the creator of all the other gods, son of the creator of the universe Ptah, "Holy-Monarch-Who-Dines-Upon-Plates-of-Faience-and-Drinks-from-Cups-of-Gold," lord of the burial grounds, long may you live in health and wealth! May you write to us informing us what to do regarding Horus and Seth, so that we may not make a decision in ignorance."

It took a great while, but the letter finally arrived in Hell and was received by Osiris, the Embodiment of Horus' power, who in his character of lord of the underworld bears the titles: King *A'a-Tchetef-Neb-Djefa* ("Great Lord of Superabundant Sustenance") etc. etc. When the letter was read before Osiris he gave a great cry. He sent his reply with the utmost haste to Ra and the rest of the pantheon, saying:

"Why is my son Horus being injured—deprived of his rights? And this despite the fact that I created grain for the gods to live on, the barley and the emmer which would later sustain the rest of creation as well, when no other god or goddess could even imagine it!"

XX

The letter made its way to where Ra sat with the nine gods in the fields of Xoïs which gleamed white with grain (for now it was the time of the harvest). Then after it was read before them all, Ra said:

"Send me a reply to Osiris fast, tell him, with reference to his epistle: If you'd never existed, if you'd never been born, there'd still be wheat and barley all the same."

This letter of Ra's made its way to Osiris, it was read before him and he sent a reply to Ra, lord of all, to this effect:

"Good, fair and excessively excellent is what you have done on the advice of the gods — Truth has been driven from the earth and sunk in the depths of Hell! Now take a good look at this policy of yours, and what will come of it. This place where I am, it's full of raging creatures I can send to do my bidding — they fear neither goddess nor god. I'll dispatch them to bring me the hearts of all evildoers, and then the wicked will find themselves here beside me!

"That's what I'm here for, to judge and punish the wicked. Didn't you ever wonder why I rest here in the uttermost depths of the West while all the rest of you stay far from me, out there in the world? Who among you is more powerful than I? And what you *were* strong enough to do is wrong.

"When Ptah made the sky — great Ptah whose temple dominates Memphis, lord of life for all Egypt — when Ptah created the heavens, did he not then say to the stars: At the end of each night you will rest in the West, the realm of King Osiris, and in time all of the gods, all mankind, noble and humble, they too will come to rest with Osiris.

"That's what Ptah said: in the end, all come to me."

XXI

After a time this letter from Osiris reached Ra and the gods: Thoth took it and read it out before them all.

They replied: "He's right, he's right in everything he said, the king of generosity, lord god of food, great Osiris, long may he reign!"

Then Seth said: "Take us back to the isle in mid-river so I can settle this with Horus."

He went to the island, but the gods simply declared for Horus without further contest.

Then Ra, lord of the two lands, whose great temple stands in On, sent a message to Isis: "Bring Seth, bound, his neck and wrists in a wooden yoke."

Isis brought Seth bound like a common criminal.

Ra said to him: "Why did you go off to that island, refusing to accept the authority of this court, continuing to claim on your own account the rights that belong to Horus?"

Seth said: "Quite to the contrary, my good lord. Let Horus the son of Isis be called, and let the rank and office of his father Osiris be given him."

Horus was brought, the white crown of Southern Egypt was placed on his head, they sat him on his father's throne and said to him: "You are Egypt's good king, the excellent master of the world henceforth and forever, long may you live!"

Then Isis shouted: "You are the good king of this land beloved of the gods! My heart is glad! Your radiant face will shine out over the country!"

Great Ptah, templed in Memphis, who makes all Egypt live, said: "What shall be done for Seth, now that Horus has been given his father's throne?"

Ra said: "Let Seth the son of Nut be given to me, to dwell with me as my son, his voice shall be the thunder in the heavens and all men shall fear him."

When the coronation of Horus was officially announced throughout the land, Ra was exceedingly pleased and said to the gods: "Let the country rejoice for Horus the son of Isis!"

"Horus has taken the throne, long live the king!

"All the gods are glad, the skies brighten for you, put wreaths upon your heads in honor of my son arisen to the kingship of Egypt, long may he live! All the gods rejoice, the entire land is gleeful now that they've seen Horus, the son of Isis, successor to the throne of Osiris, Lord of Busiris."

And so it all turned out well, and Horus was crowned king in Egypt's capital, Thebes, the city of justice.

93. LETTER OF WENENAMON

This late Twentieth-Dynasty letter from a builder at Thebes to a merchant concerns the unfair seizure of a slave woman and her son.

The builder Wenenamon of the Temple of Amon-Re, King of the Gods, greets the merchant Amenkhau of the Temple of Amon-Re, King of the Gods:

In life, prosperity and health and in the favor of Amon-Re, King of the Gods! Every day I am calling upon Amon, Mut, and Khonsu to keep you alive, to keep you healthy, and to invigorate you.

And further: Before you left here from Ne, I had entrusted to you the slave-woman Tentuendjede and the slave Gemiamon, her son, and you had given them to the fisherman Pamershenuty and the retainer Hori, who told you while I was present, "It was by stealth that this woman was gotten" So they said to you, but you replied, "That's wrong! It was from the master of serfs Ikhterpay that I bought this woman" so you told them, "and I gave full payment for her." And they told you, "We shall corroborate this with the man who sold [her] to you," so they said to you. And I went with you before the commander of foreign Tuhir-troops Iuhepy, your superior, who told me, "Leave the maidservant be! She has been entrusted to the merchant Amenkhau" so he said. I had confidence in you and entrusted you with this maidservant up until today.

Now look, you sent the scribe Efnamon to me with the message, "It is just like those many others who were carried off that your maidservant has been carried off.' So you said in writing to me, although you know that it was while I was inside the walled enclosure of (the Temple of) Mut that some came and took my maidservant away, [persuading(?)] people saying, "She is our sister," so they were saying regarding her. So you deal with her affair while you are there.

As soon as my letter reaches you, you shall deal with the affair of this maidservant [and go to(?)] those people who removed her, and if they prevail over you, you will realize that she is a conscriptable servant, it being the master of serfs who conscripted her. You will make him give you (as replacement) a satisfactory maidservant who has a son at her bosom just like the two of them, and you will bring them south when you return. See, I've written in order to provide you with authorization.

Now you know the many good things that I've done for you. Don't forget them and disobey me, or your misdemeanors will get the better of you.

Address: The builder Wenenamon of the Temple of Amon to the merchant Amenkhau of the Temple of Amon.

94. RECORDS OF ROYAL TOMB ROBBERIES

The weaknesses of the government of the late New Kingdom can be seen in the following documents, which recount efforts by the authorities to prevent the plundering of royal tombs and to arrest and prosecute the thieves involved. The first document (Papyrus Abbott), from the reign of Ramesses IX (Dynasty 20), is a report of an inspection made by the pharaoh's vizier Khamwese of the cemeteries near Thebes, which were under the jurisdiction of the mayor of the west side of the city, Pewero. The survey was initiated after the mayor of the east side of the city, Peser, complained that Pewero was not guarding the tombs effectively. The second set of documents (Mayer Papyri), from the reign of Ramesses X, contain a record of the trial of the men who had recently robbed the tombs of Sobekemsaf II and his wife Nubkhaes.

Papyrus Abbott

Date

[Year 16, third month of the first season, day 18], under the majesty of the King of Upper and Lower Egypt, the Lord of the Two Lands: Neferkere-Setepnere, L. P. H., Son of Re, Lord of Diadems: [Ramses (IX)-] Meriamon, L. P. H., beloved of [Amon]-Re, king of gods, and of Harakhte; given life forever and ever.

First Commission of Inspection

[There were sent] the inspectors of the great and august necropolis, the scribe of the vizier and the scribe of the overseer of the White House of Pharaoh, L. P. H., [in order to inspect the] sepulchers of former kings, the tombs and resting-places of the nobles, [located on] the west of the city; by: (1) the governor of the city and vizier, Khamwese; (2) the king's-butler, Nesuamon, the scribe of [Pharaoh]; (3) the major-domo of the house of the Divine Votress, L. P. H., of Amon-Re, king of gods, king's-butler, Neferkereem-Per-Amon, the herald of Pharaoh, L. P. H., [because of the] thieves [on] the west of the city, concerning whom the mayor, the chief of police of the great and august necropolis [of] Pharaoh [on] the west of Thebes, Pewero, had reported to the vizier, the nobles and butlers of Pharaoh, L. P. H.

List of Members of the Commission

[People] sent on this day:
The mayor and chief of police of the necropolis, Pewero;
[Chief of polic]e of this house, Beknurel.
...................of the necropolis].
...................of this house.
...................of this house.
...................-amon.
Chief of police of this house, Menthirkhepeshef.
The scribe of the vizier, Penebik.
Chief scribe of the magazine of the overseer of the White House, Paynofer.
Prophet of the House of (King) Amenhotep, L. P. H., Pe'enkhew.
Prophet of the wine-cellar of the house of Amon, Uramon.
The police of the cemetery, who were with them.

List of Tombs Inspected

The pyramids, sepulchers, and tombs, investigated on this day, by the inspectors:

Tomb of Amenhotep I

The eternal horizon of King Zeserkere, L. P. H., son of Re, Amenhotep (I), L. P. H., which is 120 cubits deep (measured) from its superstructure, which is called: "The-High-[Ascent]," north of the "House-of-Amenhotep,-L.-P.-H.,-of-the-Garden," concerning which the mayor of the city, Peser, had reported to the governor of the city and vizier, Khamwese; the king's-butler, Nesuamon, the scribe of Pharaoh, major-domo of the house of the Divine Votress, L. P. H., of Amon-Re, king of gods; the king's-butler, Neferkere-em-Per-Amon, the herald of Pharaoh, L. P. H., and the great nobles, saying: "The thieves have broken into it." Inspected on this day; it was found uninjured by the inspectors.

Pyramid of King Intef I

The pyramid of the king, the son of Re, Intefo, L. P. H., which is on the north of the "House-of-Amenhotep,-L.-P.-H.,-of-the-Court," upon which the pyramid is destroyed, before which its stela (still) stands; the figure of the king stands upon this stela, his hound being between his feet, named Behka. It was inspected on this day; it was found uninjured.

Pyramid of King Nubkheprure-Intef

The pyramid of King Nubkheprere, L. P. H., Son of Re, Intef, L. P. H., it was found in course of being tunneled into by the thieves; they had tunneled 2 cubits into its [masonry], cubit (distant) from the outer chamber of the tomb of the chief of the oblation-bearers of the House of Amon, Yuroi, which is in ruins. It was uninjured; the thieves had not been able to enter it.

Pyramid of King Sekhemre-Intef

The pyramid of King Sekhemre-Upmat, L. P. H.; Son of Re, Intefo, L. P. H. It was found in course of being tunneled into by the thieves, at the place where its stela of its pyramid was set up. Inspected on this day; it was found uninjured; the thieves had been unable to enter it.

Pyramid of King Sebekemsaf

The pyramid of King Sekhemre-Shedtowe, L. P. H., Son of Re, Sebekemsaf. It was found, that the thieves had broken into it by mining work through the base of its pyramid, from the outer chamber of the tomb of the overseer of the granary of King Menkheperre (Thutmose III), L. P. H., Nebamon. The burial-place of the king was found void of its lord, L. P. H., as well as the burial-place of the great king's-wife, Nubkhas, L. P. H., his royal wife; the thieves having laid their hand upon them. The vizier, the nobles, and the inspectors made an examination of it, and the manner in which the thieves had laid their hands upon this king and his royal wife, was ascertained.

Pyramid of King Sekenenre-Tao I

The pyramid of King Sekenenre , L. P. H., Son of Re, Tao, L. P. H. Inspected on this day by the inspectors; it was found uninjured.

Pyramid of King Sekenenre-Tao II

The pyramid of King Sekenenre, L. P. H., Son of Re, Taoo, L. P. H., the second King Tao, L. P. H. Inspected on this day by the inspectors; it was found uninjured.

Pyramid of King Kamose

The pyramid of King Uzkheperre, L. P.H., Son of Re, Kemose, L.P. H. Inspected on this day; it was uninjured.

Pyramid of King Ahmose-Sepir

The pyramid of King Ahmose-Sepir, L. P.H. Inspected; found uninjured.

Pyramid of Mentuhotep II

The pyramid of King Nibhepetre, L. P. H., Son of Re, Mentuhotep (II), L. P. H., which is in Zeseret; it was uninjured.

Summary

Total of pyramids of the former kings, inspected on this day by the inspectors:

Found uninjured	9 pyramids
Found broken into	1
Total	10

Tombs of Queens and Noble Families

The tombs of the singing-women of the house of the Divine Votress, L. P. H., of Amon-Re, king of gods:

Found uninjured	2
Found broken into by the thieves	2
Total	4

These are the tombs and sepulchers in which the nobles, the ..., the Theban women, and the people of the land rest, on the west of the city; it was found that the thieves had broken into them all, that they had pulled out their occupants from their coverings and coffins, they (the occupants) being thrown upon the ground; and that they had stolen their articles of house-furniture, which had been given them, together with the gold, the silver, and the ornaments which were in their coverings.

Report of the Commission

The mayor and chief of police of the great and august necropolis, Pewero, together with the chiefs of police, and the inspectors of the necropolis, the scribe of the vizier, and the scribe of the overseer of the White House, who were with them, made a report upon them (the tombs) to:

The governor of the city and vizier, Khamwese;
The king's-butler, Nesuamon;
The scribe of Pharaoh, L. P. H., the major-domo of the house of the Divine Votress, L. P. H., of Amon-Re, king of gods, king's-butler, Neferkere-em-Per-Amon, the herald of Pharaoh, L. P. H.;

And the great nobles. The mayor of the West, chief of police of the necropolis, Pewero, handed in the names of the thieves in writing before the vizier, the nobles and butlers. They were seized and imprisoned; they were examined, and confessed the facts.

Vizier's Inspection

Year 16, third month of the first season, day 19; day on which there went to inspect the great seats of the king's-children, the king's-wives, and the king's-mothers, which are in "The-Place-of-Beauty:"

The governor of the city and vizier, Khamwese; and the king's-butler, Nesuamon, the scribe of Pharaoh, L. P. H., after the copper-smith, Pekharu, of the west of the city, son of Kharu, his mother, being Mitshere, a serf of "The-House-of-Usermare-Meriamon (Ramses III),-L.-P.-H.,-in-the-House-of-Amon," under charge of the High Priest of Amon-Re, king of gods, Amenhotep, (being) the man who was found there and arrested, while he was with the three people of the (said) temple, beside the tombs, whom the vizier, Nibmare-nakht, had examined in the year 14, had told, saying: "I was in the tomb of the king's-wife, Isis, L. P. H., of King Usermare-Meriamon (Ramses III), L. P. H.; I carried off a few things from it; I took possession of them."

Examination of the Coppersmith

Then the vizier and the butler had the coppersmith taken before them to the tomb, while he was blindfolded as a man .... He was permitted to see (again), when he had reached them. The officials said to him: "Go before us to the tomb, from which you said: 'I carried away the things.'" The coppersmith went before the nobles to one of the ... tombs of the king's-children of King Usermare-Setepnere (Ramses II), L. P. H., the Great God, in which no one was buried, which was left open, and (to) the hut of the workman of the necropolis, Amenemyenet, son of Huy, which was in this place, saying: "Behold, the tombs in which I was." The nobles examined the coppersmith with a [severe] examination in the great valley, (but) he was not found to know any place there, except the two places upon which he had laid his hand. He took an oath of the king, L. P. H., that he should be mutilated (by cutting off) his nose and his ears and placed upon the rack (if he lied), saying: "I know not any place here among these tombs, except this tomb which is open, together with the hut upon which I have laid your hands."

Conclusion of Inspection

The officials examined the tombs of the great seats which are in "The-Place-of-Beauty," in which the king's-children, king's-wives, king's-mothers, the goodly fathers and mothers of Pharaoh, L. P. H., rest. They were found uninjured. The great officials caused the inspectors, the administrators, the workmen of the necropolis, the chiefs of police, the police, and all the serf-laborers of the necropolis of the west of the city to go around as a great deputation to the city.

The Indiscretion of the Mayor of the City (East Side)

Year 16, third month of the first season, day 19; on this day, at the time of evening, beside the House of Ptah, lord of Thebes there came along the king's-butler, Nesuarnont, he scribe of Pharaoh, L. P. H.; and the mayor of the city, Peser; and they came upon the chief workman, Userkhepesh;

the scribe, Amennakht; and the workman of the necropolis, Amenhotep. The mayor of the city spoke to the people of the necropolis in the presence of the (said) butler of Pharaoh, saying: "As for this deputation which ye have made this day, it is no deputation at all. It is (only) your jubilation, which you have made?" This he spoke to them. He took an oath of the king, L. P. H., in the presence of the (said) butler of Pharaoh, L. P. H., saying: "The scribe of the necropolis, Horishere, son of Amennakht, and the scribe of the necropolis, Pebes, have told me five very serious accusations worthy of death against you. Yes, I am writing concerning them to Pharaoh, L. P. H., my lord, L. P. H., that a man of Pharaoh, L. P. H., may be sent to take you all in charge." This he spoke.

Pewero's Letter of Complaint

Year 16, third month of the first season, day 20. Copy of the letter which the mayor of the west of the city, the chief of police of the necropolis, Pewero, sent to the vizier, concerning the words, which the mayor of the city, Peser, spoke to the people of the necropolis, in the presence of the butler of Pharaoh, L. P. H., and of the scribe of the overseer of the treasury, Paynozem.

That which the mayor of the west of the city, Pewero, said, to wit:

The king's-butler, Nesuamon, the scribe of Pharaoh, L. P. H., happened by, when the mayor of the city, Peser, was with him, while he (the mayor) stood quarreling with the people of the necropolis, beside the House of Ptah, lord of Thebes. The mayor of the city spoke to the people of the necropolis, saying: 'You exult over me at the door of my house! Oh, indeed! Although I am the mayor who makes report to the ruler, L. P. H., and you therefore exult over him. You were there; it was inspected; you found it uninjured! Broken into were (the tomb of) Sekhemre-Shedtowe, L. P. H., Son of Re, Sebekemsaf, L. P. H., and (that of) Nubkhas, L. P. H., his royal wife; one great ruler, L. P. H., while he makes ten reports. (I invoke) the [severity] of Amon-Re, king of gods, this great god, on behalf of his monuments, standing in his hall this day.' Then spoke the workman, Userkhepesh, who is under the hand of the chief workman of the necropolis, Nakhtemhet, saying: 'But all the kings, together with their king's-wives, king's-mothers, and king's-children, who rest in the necropolis, together with those who rest in "The-Place-of-Beauty," they are uninjured, they are protected and defended forever. It is the goodly designs of Pharaoh, L. P. H., their son, which protect them and examine them [closely].' The mayor of the city spoke to him, saying: 'Are your deeds as great as your speech?' For this is indeed no little word which this mayor of the city spoke.

"This mayor of the city spoke to him again, a second word, saying: 'The scribe of the necropolis, Horishere, son of Amennakht, came to the chief side of the city, to my place of abode, and he told me three very serious accusations. My scribe and the scribe of the two districts of the city put them in writing. Moreover, the scribe of the necropolis, Pebes, told me two other matters; in all five. They were put in writing likewise. He that has them cannot keep silence. Forbid, for they are great and capital crimes, worthy of bringing to the block, and of executing every penalty because of them. Now, I shall write concerning them to Pharaoh, my lord, L. P. H., that a man of Pharaoh, L. P. H., may be sent to take you all in charge.' So spoke he to them, this mayor of the city. He made ten oaths of the king, L. P. H., saying: 'So will I do.'

"I heard these words which the mayor of the city spoke to the people of the great and august necropolis of millions of years, of Pharaoh, L. P. H., on the west of Thebes; and I report them to my lord, for it were a crime for one like me to hear (such) words and conceal them. But I was not able to apprehend the very serious words which the mayor of the city spoke; the scribes of the necropolis who stood among the people told me them, (but) my feet were not present with them. I report them to my lord, that my lord may bring in one who apprehended the words, which the mayor of the city spoke, and the scribes of the necropolis told me. 'I am writing of them to Pharaoh, L. P. H.,' said he. This is a crime of these two scribes of the necropolis, that they should have applied to this mayor of the city, to report to him; for their fathers did not report to him, but they reported to the vizier when he was in the South. When he was in the North, however, the necropolis-police of the suite of his majesty, L. P. H., went North to the place where the vizier was, bearing their writings. [I have] made (this) deposition in the year 16, third month of the first season, day 20, of the words which I have heard from the mayor of the city. I put them in writing before my lord, that those who apprehended them may be summoned for tomorrow."

Hearing of Peser's Accusations

Year 16, third month of the first season, day 21;on this day in the great courtd of the city, beside the two stela of ... the forecourt of Amon in the gate (called): "Praise."

Composition of the Court

People and nobles who sat in the great court of the city on this day:

1. Governor of the city and vizier, Khamwese.
2. The High Priest of Amon-Re, king of gods, Amenhotep.
3. The prophet of Amon-Re, king of gods, [scribe] of "The-House-of-Millions-of -Years-of -King-Neferkere-Setepnere,-L.-P.-H.," Nesuamon.
4. The king's-butler, Nesuamon, the scribe of Pharaoh, L. P. H.
5. The major-domo of the house of the Divine Votress, L. P. H., of Amon-Re, king of gods, king's-butler, Neferkere-em-Per-Amon, the herald of Pharaoh, L. P. H.
6. The deputy of ..., Hori.
7. The standard-bearer of the marines, Hori.
8. The mayor of the city, Peser.

The governor of the city and vizier, Khamwese, had brought in the coppersmith, Pekharu, son of Kharu; the coppersmith, Tharoy, son of Khamopet; and the coppersmith, Pekamen, son of Tharoy, of "The-House-of-Usermare-Meriamon (Ramses III),-L.-P.-H.," under charge of the High Priest of Amon.

Said the vizier to the great nobles of the great court of the city: "This mayor of the city said a few words to the inspectors and workmen of the necropolis, in the year 16, third month of the first season, day 19, in the presence of the king's-butler, Nesuamon, the scribe of Pharaoh, L. P. H., delivering himself of slanders concerning the great seats, which are in 'The- Place-of - Beauty.' Now, I, the vizier of the land, have been there, with the king's-butler, Nesuamon, the scribe of Pharaoh, L.P.H. We inspected the tombs, where the mayor of the city said that the coppersmiths of 'The-House-of-Usermare-Meriamon (Ramses III),-L.-P.-H.,-in-the-House-of-Amon,' had been. We found them uninjured; and all that he said was found to be untrue. Now, behold, the coppersmiths stand before you; let them tell all that has occurred." They were examined. It was found that the people did not know any place in the seat of Pharaoh, L. P. H., of which the mayor had spoken the words. He was found wrong therein.

The great nobles granted life to the coppersmiths of "The-House-of -Usermare- Meriamon,- L.-P.-H.,-[in- the-House- of] -Amon." They were reassigned to the High Priest of Amon-Re [king of gods], Amenhotep, on this day.

The documents thereof are: one roll; it is deposited in the office of the vizier's archives.

Later Dockets

Year 1, first month of the first season, day 2, corresponding to the year 19. Copy of the records of the necropolis-thieves, the thieves of the tombs, which was placed before Pharaoh, L. P. H., by the mayor of the west of the city, Pewero:

Here follow the names of sixteen people, forming the list of thieves, of which the above is the title.

Year 1, second month of the first season, day 25, corresponding to the year 19. Copy of the records of the necropolis-thieves, which was laid before the vizier, Nibmare-nakht, by the mayor of the west of the city, Pewero:

Here follow the names of twenty-nine people, forming the list of which the above is the title.

Mayer Papyri

Trial of Robbers of Ramesses II ard Seti I's Tombs

Year 1, of Uhem-mesut, fourth month of the third season, day 15. On this day occurred the examination of the thieves of the tomb of King Usermare-Setepnere (Ramses II), L. P. H., the great god; and the tomb of King Menmare, L. P. H., Seti (I), L. P. H., which are [recorded] in the treasury of "The-House-of-King-Usermare-Meriamon (Ramses III),-L.-P.-H.," concerning whom the chief of police, Nesuamon, had reported, in this roll of names; for he was there, standing with the thieves, when they laid their hands upon the tombs; who were tortured at the examination on their feet and their hands, to make them tell the way they had done exactly.

Composition of the Court

By the governor of the city and vizier, Nibmarenakht; Overseer of the White House and overseer of the granary, Menmarenakht;

Steward and king's-butler, [In], the [herald] of Pharaoh, L. P. H.;

Steward of the court, king's-butler, Pemeriamon, the scribe of Pharaoh.

Testimony of the Prisoner, Paykamen

Examination. The X,[19] Paykamen, under charge of the overseer of the cattle of Amon, was brought in; the oath of the king, L. P. H., was administered to him, not to tell a lie. He was asked: "What was the manner of thy going with the people who were with you, when you robbed the tombs of the kings which are [recorded] in the treasury of 'The-House-of-King-Usermare-Meriamon,-L.-P.-H.?" He said: "I went with the priest Teshere, son of the divine father, Zedi, of 'The House;' Beki, son of Nesuamon, of this house; the X, Nesumontu of the house of Montu, lord of Erment; the X, Paynehsi of the vizier, formerly prophet of Sebek of Peronekh; Teti … who belonged to Paynehsi, of the vizier, formerly prophet of Sebek of Peronekh; in all six."

Testimony of the Chief of Police

The chief of police, Nesuamon, was brought in. He was asked: "How did you find these men?" He said: "I heard that these men had gone to rob this tomb. I went and found these six men. That which the thief, Paykamen, has said is correct. I took testimony from them on that day …….. The examination of the watchman of the house of Amon, the thief, Paykamen, under charge of the overseer of the cattle of Amon, was held by beating with a rod, the bastinade was applied to his feet. An oath was administered to him that he might be executed if he told a lie; he said: 'That which I did is exactly what I have said.' He confirmed it with his mouth, saying: 'As for me, that which I did is what [they] did; I was w[ith the]se six men, I stole a piece of copper therefrom, and I took possession of it.'"

Testimony of the Prisoner, Nesumontu

The X, the thief, Nesumontu, was brought in; the examination was held by beating with a rod; the bastinade was applied on (his) feet and his hand(s); the oath of the king, L. P. H., was administered to him, that he might be executed if he told a lie. He was asked: "What was the manner of your going to rob in the tomb with thy companions?" He said: "I went and found these people; I was the sixth. I stole a piece of copper therefrom, I took possession of it."

Testimony of Karu

The watchman of the house of Amon, the X, Karu, was brought in; he was examined with the rod, the bastinade was applied to his feet and his hands; the oath of the king, L. P. H., was administered to him, that he might be executed if he told a lie. He was asked: "What was the manner of your going with the (sic!) companions when you robbed in the tomb?" He said: "The thief, the X, Pehenui, he made me take some grain. I seized a sack of grain, and when I began to go down, I heard the voice of the men who were in this storehouse. I put my eye to the passage, and I saw Paybek and Teshere, who were within. I called to him, saying, 'Come!' and he came out to me, having two pieces of copper in his hand. He gave them to me, and I gave to him I measures of spelt to pay for them. I took one of them, and I gave the other to the X, Enefsu.

---

19   A title common among people in the necropolis, but it's meaning is unknown, so it is here indicated simply by an X.

Testimony of Nesuamon

The priest, Nesuamon, son of Paybek, was brought in, because of his father. He was examined by beating with the rod. They said to him: "Tell the manner of thy father's going with the men who were with him." He said:"My father was truly there. I was (only) a little child, and I know not how he did it." On being (further) examined, he said: "I saw the workman, Ehatinofer, while he was in the place where the tomb is, with the watchman, Nofer, son of [Merwer], and the artisan; ..., in all three (men). They are the ones I saw distinctly. Indeed, gold was taken, and they are the ones whom I know." On being (further) examined with a rod, he said: "These three men are the ones I saw distinctly."

Testimony of Wenpehti

The weaver of "The House," Wenpehti, son of ..., was brought in. He was examined by beating with a rod, the bastinade was applied to his feet and his hands. The oath of the king, L. P. H., was administered, not to tell a lie. They said to him: "Tell what was the manner of thy father's going, when he committed theft in the tomb with his companions." He said: "My father was killed when I was a child. My mother told me: 'The chief of police, Nesuamon, gave some chisels of copper to your father; then the captains of the archers and the X slew your father.' They [held] the examination, and Nesuamon took the copper and gave it to [me]. It remains [in the possession of] my mother."

Testimony of Enroy

A Theban woman, Enroy, the mistress of the priest, Teshere, son of Zedi, was brought in. She was examined by beating with a rod; the bastinade was applied to her feet and her hands. The oath of the king, L. P. H., not to tell a lie, was administered to her; she was asked: "What was the manner of your husband's going when he broke into the tomb and carried away the copper from it?" She said: "He carried away some copper belonging to this tomb; we sold it and devoured it."

95. THE BOOK OF THE DEAD

The Book of the Dead, or more properly, "The Book of the Coming Forth by Day," represents the next stage in the development of Egyptian funerary texts that began with the Pyramid Texts in the Old Kingdom and the Coffin Texts in the Middle Kingdom. Instead of the texts being written on objects, as in earlier times, these were written on papyri, either in hieroglyphics or hieratic, often with illustrations, and placed in tombs. Not all versions are exactly the same, but they contain much in common and were used from the New Kingdom to the Ptolemaic period. Here are some selections.

Chapter (VI) whereby the funereal Statuettes may be made to do work for a person in the Netherworld.

O Statuette there! Should I be called and appointed to do any of the labours that are done in the Netherworld by a person according to his abilities, lo! all obstacles have been beaten down for thee; be thou counted for me at every moment, for planting the fields, for watering the soil, for conveying the sands of east and west.

Here am I, whithersoever thou callest me.

Chapter (XIV) for removing displeasure from the heart of the god against the deceased person.

Hail to thee, oh god who sendest forth the Moment, who presidest over all the Secret things, and protectest the utterance of my words.

Here is a god displeased against me; let wrong be overwhelmed and let it fall upon the hands of the Lord of Law. Remove the impediments which are in me and the evil and the darkness, oh Lord of Law, and let that god be reconciled to me, removing that which detaineth me from thee.

Oh, lord of offerings in Kenu, let me offer to thee the propitiary offering by which thou livest, and let me live by it and be reconciled.

Let all the displeasure which is in thy heart against me be removed.

Chapter (XXI) whereby the mouth of a person is given to him in the Netherworld.

Hail to thee, Lord of Eight, who art Prince of the House which is encircled by Darkness and Obscurity. I am come to thee glorified and purified.

My hands are behind thee; thy portion is that of those who have gone before thee.

Give me my mouth that I may speak with it; and guide my heart at its hour of Darkness and Night.

Another Chapter (XXII) whereby the Mouth of a person is given to him in the Netherworld.

I shine forth out of the Egg which is in the unseen world. Let there be given my mouth that I may speak with it in presence of the great god, Lord of the Tuat. Let not my hand be repulsed by the Divine Circle of the great god.

I am Osiris, the Lord of Restau, the same who is at the head of the Staircase.

I am come to do the will of my heart, out of the Tank of Flame, which I extinguish when I come forth.

Chapter (XXIII) whereby the Mouth of a person is opened for him in the Netherworld.

He saith: Let my mouth be opened by Ptah, and let ti e muzzles which are upon my mouth be loosed by the god of my domain,

Then let Thoth come, full and equipped with Words of Power, ar.d let him loose the muzzles of Sutu which are upon my mouth, and let Tmu lend a hand to fling them at the assailants.

Let my mouth be given to me. Let my mouth be opened by I'tah with that instrument of steel wherewith he openeth the mouths of the gods.

I am Sechit Uat'it who sitteth on the right side of Heaven: I am Sahit encircled by the Spirits of Heliopolis.

And all the Words of Power, and all the accusations which are uttered against me—the gods stand firm against them: the cycles of the gods unitedly.

Chapter (XXIV) whereby the Words of Power are brought to a Person in the Netherworld.

I am Chepera, the self-produced, on his Mother's thigh.

The speed of bloodhounds is given to those who are in Heaven, and the mettle of hyaenas to those who belong to the Divine Circle.

Lo, I bring this my Word of Power, and I collect this Word of Power from every quarter in which it is, more persistently than hounds of chase and more swiftly than the Light.

O thou who guidest the Bark of Ra, sound is thy rigging and free from disaster as thou passest on to the Tank of Flame.

Lo, I collect this my Word of Power from every quarter in which it is, in behalf of every person whom it concerneth more persistently than hounds of chase and more swiftly than Light; the same who create the gods out of Silence, or reduce them to inactivity: the same who impart warmth to the gods.

Lo, I collect this my Word of Power from every quarter in which it is, in behalf of every person whom it concerneth, more persistently than hounds of chase and more swiftly than the Light.

Chapter (XXV) whereby a person remembereth his name in the Netherworld.

Let my name be given to me in the Great House, Let me remember my name in the House of Flame on the Night wherein the Years are counted and the Months are reckoned, one by one.

I am He who dwelleth in Heaven, and who sitteth on the Eastern side of Heaven: and if there be any god who cometh not in my train, I utter his name at once.

Chapter (XXVI) whereby the Heart is given to a person in the Netherworld.

He saith: Heart mine to me, in the place of Hearts! Whole Heart mine to me, in the place of Whole Hearts!

Let me have my Heart that it may rest within me; but I shall feed upon the food of Osiris, on the eastern side of the mead of amaranthine flowers.

Be mine a bark for descending the stream and another for ascending.

I go down into the bark wherein thou art.

Be there given to me my mouth wherewith to speak, and my feet for walking; and let me have my arms wherewith to overthrow my adversaries.

Let two hands from the Earth open my mouth: Let Seb, the Erpa of the gods, part my two jaws; let him open my two eyes which are closed, and give motion to my two hands which are powerless: and let Anubis give vigour to my legs, that I may raise myself up upon them.

And may Sechit the divine one lift me up, so that I may arise in Heaven and issue my behest in Memphis.

I am in possession of my Heart, I am possession of my Whole Heart, I am possession of my arms and I have possession of my legs.

[I do whatsoever my Genius willeth, and my Soul is not bound to my body at the gates of Amenta.]

Chapter (XXVII) whereby the Heart of a person is not taken from him in the Netherworld.

O ye gods who seize upon Hearts, and who pluck out the Whole Heart; and whose hands fashion anew the Heart of a person according to what he hath done; lo now, let that be forgiven to him by you.

Hail to you, O ye Lords of Everlasting Time and Eternity!

Let not my Heart be torn from me by your fingers.

Let not my Heart be fashioned anew according to all the evil things said against me,

For this Heart of mine is the Heart of the god of mighty names, of the great god whose words are in his members, and who giveth free course to his Heart which is within him.

And most keen of insight is his Heart among the gods. Ho to me! Heart of mine; I am in possession of thee, I am thy master, and thou art by me; fall not away from me; I am the dictator to whom thou shalt obey in the Netherworld.

Chapter (LXXIX) whereby the Soul is united to the dead Body.

Oh thou who Bringest; Oh thou Runner, who dwellest in thy Keep, thou great god; grant that my Soul may come to me from whatsoever place wherein it abideth.

But if there be a delay in the bringing of my soul to me, thou shalt find the Eye of Horus standing firm against thee, like those undrowsy Watchers who lie in Annu, the land wherein are thousands of reunions.

Let my Soul be caught, and the Chu which is with it, wheresoever it abideth.

Track out among the things in heaven and upon earth that soul of mine, wherever it abideth.

But if there be a delay in thy causing me to see my Soul and my Shade, thou shalt find the Eye of Horus standing firm against thee.

Oh ye gods who draw along the Bark of the Eternal one: ye who lift up above the Tuat, and who raise up the Sky: ye who enable the Souls to enter into the mummied forms; ye whose hands grasp the cordage, hold firm with your ropes and stop the adversaries that the Bark may rejoice and the god proceed in peace.

And now grant that my Soul may come forth in your train from the Eastern horizon of Heaven for ever and ever.

Chapter (XC) whereby Memory is restored to a person.

Oh thou who choppest off heads and cuttest throats, but restorest memory in the mouth of the dead through the Words of Power which they possess: thou seest me not with thine eyes, thou perceivest not with thy feet; thou turnest back thy face, thou seest not the executioners of Shu, who are coming behind thee to chop off thine own head and to cut thy throat. Let not my mouth be closed, through the Words of Power which I possess; even as thou hast done to the dead, through the Words of Power which they possess.

Away with the two sentences uttered by Isis when thou earnest to fling remembrance at the mouth of Osiris and the heart of Sutu, his enemy, saying:—

Chapter (XCI) whereby the Soul is secured from imprisonment in the Netherworld.

Oh thou who art exalted and worshipped, all powerful, almighty one, who grantest thy terrors to the gods, who displayest thyself upon thy throne of grandeur, let the way be made for my Soul, my Chu and my Shade. Let me be thoroughly equipped.

I am a powerful Soul; let the way be made for me to the place where Ra is and Hathor.

If this Chapter is known, he taketh the form of a fully equipped Chu in the Netherworld, and does not suffer imprisonment at any door in the Amenta, either in coming in or going out.

Chapter (XCII) whereby the Tomb is opened to the Soul and to the Shade of the person, that he may come forth by day and may have mastery of his feet.

That standeth open which thou openest, and that is closed which thou closest, oh thou who art at rest; thou openest and thou closest to my Soul, at the bidding of the Eye of Horus: who delivereth me, who established the glory upon the brow of Ra: [the god] of stretched out steps and rapid paces, who maketh for me a wide path and vigorous limbs.

I am Horus, the avenger of his father, who lifteth up his father and who lifteth up his mother with his staff.

Let the path be opened to him who hath mastery of his feet, that he may look upon the great god within the Bark of Ra on the day of the Soul's Reckoning; and my Soul is then at the front during the Reckoning of the Years.

May the Eye of Horus deliver for me my Soul, and establish my splendour upon the brow of Ra, and may my radiance be upon your faces who are attached to the person of Osiris: imprison not rny Soul, put not in custody my Shade.

Let the path be open to my Soul and to my Shade that it may see the great god within his sanctuary, on the day of the Soul's Reckoning, and may repeat the words of Osiris whose place is unseen, and of those who are attached to the person of Osiris and have the custody of Souls and Spirits, and who shut up the Shades of the Dead who would do an injury to me.

Let the path be thrown open to thy Genius and to thy Soul, Glorified one, who art provided with those who conduct thee; sit thou at the head of the Great ones in thy place; thou shalt not be imprisoned by those who are attached to the person of Osiris and who have the custody of Souls and Spirits and who shut up the Shades of the Dead. It is Heaven that shall hold thee.

Chapter (CV) whereby one propitiateth the Ka.

Hail to thee, my Ka, my coeval!

May I come to thee and be glorified and made manifest and ensouled, let me have strength and soundness.

Let me bring to thee grains of incense wherewith I may purify myself and may also purify thine own overflow.

The wrong assertions that I have uttered, and the wrong resistance which I have offered: let them not be imputed to me.

For I am the green gem, fresh at the throat of Ra, given by those who are at the Horizon: their freshness is my freshness [said twice] the freshness of my Ka is like theirs, and the dainties of my Ka are like theirs.

Thou who liftest the hand at the Balance, and raisest Law to the nose of Ra in this day [of my Ka]: do not thou put my head away from me. For I am the Eye which seeth and the Ear which heareth; and am I not the Bull of the sacrificial herd, are not the mortuary gifts upon me and the supernal powers [otherwise said: the powers above Nut].

Grant that I may pass by thee, and may purify myself and cause the triumph of Osiris over his adversaries.

Chapter CXXV.

Part I.

Said on arriving at the Hall of Righteousness, that Ar may be loosed from all the sins which he hath committed and that he may look upon the divine countenances.

He said: Hail to thee, mighty god, lord of Righteousness !

I am come to thee, oh my Lord: I have brought myself that I may look upon thy glory, I know thee, and I know the name of the Forty-two gods who make their appearance with thee in the Hall of Righteousness; devouring those who harbour mischief, and swallowing their blood, upon the Day of the searching examination in presence of Unneferu.

Verily, 'Thou of the Pair of Eyes, Lord of Righteousness' is thy name.

Here am I; I am come to thee; I bring to thee Right and have put a stop to Wrong.

I am not a doer of wrong to men.

I am not one who slayeth his kindred.

I am not one who telleth lies instead of truth.

I am not conscious of treason, am not a doer of mischief.

I do not exact as the first fruits of each day more work than should be done for me.

My name cometh not to the Bark of the god who is at the Helm,

I am not a transgressor against the god. am not a tale-bearer,

I am not a detractor.

I am not a doer of that which the gods abhor,

I hurt no servant with his master,

I cause no famine,

I cause not weeping,

I am not a murderer,
I give not orders for murder,
I cause not suffering to men.
I reduce not the offerings in the temples,
I lessen not the cakes of the gods,
I rob not the dead of their funereal food,
I am not an adulterer.
I am undefiled in the Sanctuary of the god of my domain,
I neither increase nor diminish the measures of grain,
I am not one who shorteneth the palm's length.
I am not one who cutteth short the field's measure.
I put not pressure upon the beam of the balance,
I tamper not with the tungue of the balance,
I snatch not the milk from the mouth of infants,
I drive not the cattle from their pastures,
I net not the birds of the manors of the gods.
I catch not the fish of their ponds,
I stop not the water at its appointed time,
I divide not an arm of the water in its course,
I extinguish not the lamp during its appointed time,
I do not defraud the Divine Circle of their sacrificial joints.
I drive not away the cattle of the sacred estate.
I stop not a god when he cometh forth.
I am pure, I am pure, I am pure, I am pure.

My purity is that of the Great Bennu in Sutenhunen, for I am the Nose of the Lord of Air, who giveth life to all mortals; on the day when the Eye is full in Annu, on the last day of Mechir; in presence of the Lord of this land.

And I am one who see the fulness of the Eye in Annu, let no harm come to me in this land, in the Hall of Righteousness; because I know the names of those gods who make their appearance in it.

Part II.

1. Oh thou of long strides, who makest thine appearance in Annu; 1 am not a doer of wrong.
2. Oh thou who boldest the fire, and makest thine appearance in Cher-aba; I am not a man of violence.
3. Oh thou of the Nose, who makest thine appearance at Chemunnu; I am not evil minded.
4. Oh Eater of the Shadow, who makest thine appearance at Elephantine; I am not rapacious.
5. Oh thou Facing-backward god, who makest thine appearance at Re-Stau; I am not a slayer of men.
6. Oh thou of Lion form, who makest thine appearance in Heaven; I am not fraudulent in measures of grain.
7. Oh thou whose eyes [pierce] like swords, who makest thine appearance in Sechem;[X]I commit no fraud.

8. Oh thou of fiery face, whose motion is backwards; I am not a robber of sacred property.
9. Oh Breaker of bones, who makest thine appearance in Sutenhunen; I am not a teller of lies.
10. Oh thou who orderest the flame, who makest thine appearance in Memphis;' I am not a robber of food.
11. Oh thou of the Two Caverns, who makest thine appearance in Amenta; I am not sluggish.
12. Oh thou of the Bright Teeth, who makest thine appearance in the Unseen Land; I am not a transgressor.
13. Oh Eater of Blood, who makest thine appearance at the Block; I have not slaughtered the sacred animals.
14. Oh Eater of Livers, who makest thine appearance at Mabit; I deal not fraudulently.
15. Oh Lord of Righteousness, who makest thine appearance in the place of Righteousness; I am not a land-grabber.
16. Oh thou who turnest backwards, who makest thine appearance in Bubastis; I am not an eaves-dropper.
17. Oh Aati, who makest thine appearance at Annu; I am not one of prating tongue.
18. Oh Tutu, who makest thine appearance in Ati; I trouble myself only with my own affairs.
19. Oh Uammetu, who makest thine appearance at the Block; I commit not adultery with another's wife.
20. Oh Maa-antu-f, who makest thine appearance in Pa-Amsu, I am not unchaste with any one.
21. Oh thou who art above Princes, and who makest thine appearance in Amu; (19) I do not cause terrors.
22. Oh Chemiu, who makest thine appearance in Kauu; I am not a transgressor.
23. Oh thou who raisest thy voice, and makest thine appearance in Urit; I am not hot of speech.
24. Oh divine Babe, who makest thy appearance in Annu; I lend not a deaf ear to the words of Righteousness.
25. Oh high-voiced one, who makest thy appearance in Unsit; I am not boisterous in behaviour.
26. Oh Basit, who makest thine appearance at the Shetait; I am not the cause of weeping to any.
27. Oh thou whose face is behind thee, and who makest thine appearance at thy cavern; I am not given to unnatural lust.
28. Oh thou, hot of foot, who makest thy appearance at even; I indulge not in anger.
29. Oh Kenemtu, who makest thine appearance in Kenemit; I am not given to cursing.
30. Oh thou who carriest thine own offering, and makest thine appearance in Syut; I am not of aggressive hand.
31. Oh thou who hast different faces, and makest thine appearance in Net'efit; I am not one of inconstant mind.
32. Oh Busy one, who makest thine appearance at Utenit; I do not steal the skins of the sacred animals.
33. Oh thou Horned one, who makest thine appearance at Sais I am not noisy in my speech.
34. Oh Nefertmu, who makest thine appearance in Memphis; I am neither a liar nor a doer of mischief.
35. Oh Tem-sepu, who makest thine appearance in Tattu; I am not one who curseth the king.
36. Oh thou who doest according to thine own will, and makest thine appearance in Tebuu; I put no check upon the water in its flow.

37. Oh Striker, who makest thine appearance in Heaven; I am not one of loud voice.
38. Oh thou who makest mortals to flourish, and who makest thine appearance at Sals; I curse not a god.
39. Oh thou of beautiful shoulder, who makest thine appearance at ... ; I am not swollen with pride.
40. Oh Neheb-kau, who makest thy appearance at thy cavern; I have no unjust preferences.
41. Oh thou of raised head, who makest thine appearance at thy cavern; I have no strong desire except for my own property.
42. Oh thou who liftest an arm, and who makest thine appearance in the Netherworld, 1 do not that which offendeth the god of my domain.

Part III.

[Said upon approaching to the gods who are in the Tuat.]

Hail ye gods, I know you and I know your names; let me not be stricken down by your blows: report not the evil which is in me to the god whom ye follow. Let not reverse of mine come to pass through you.

Let not evil things be said against me in presence of the Inviolate One; because I have done the light in Tamerit.

I revile not the god: let not reverse of mine come to pass through the King who resideth within His own Day.

Hail ye gods who are in the Hall of Righteousness, who have nothing wrong about you; who subsist upon Righteousness in Annu, and who sate themselves with cares, in presence of the god who resideth within his own Orb: deliver me from Babai who feedeth upon the livers of princes on the Day of the Great Reckoning.

Behold me: I am come to you, void of wrong, without fraud, a harmless one: let me not be declared guilty; let not the issue be against me.

I subsist upon Righteousness: I sate myself with uprightness of heart: I have done that which man prescribeth and that which pleaseth the gods.

I have propitiated the god with that which he loveth. I have given bread to the hungry, water to the thirsty, clothes to the naked, a boat to the shipwrecked. I have made oblations to the gods and funeral offerings to the departed: deliver me therefore: protect me therefore: and report not against me in presence of the great god,

I am one whose mouth is pure, and whose hands are pure, to whom there is said "Come, come in peace, by those who look upon him.

For I have listened to the words which were spoken by the Ass and the Cat in the house of Hept-ro.

And I have undergone the inspection of the god Whose face is behind him, who awardeth my verdict, so that I may behold what the Fersea tree covereth in Restau.

I am one who glorifieth the gods and who knoweth the things which concern them.

I am come and am awaiting that inquisition be made of Rightfulness and that the Balance be set upon its stand within the bower of amaranth.

Thou who art exalted upon thy pedestal and who callest thy name, Lord of Air: deliver me from those messengers of thine who inflict disasters and bring about mishaps. No covering have they upon their faces.

For I have done the Righteousness of a Lord of Righteousness.

I have made myself pure: my front parts are washed, my back parts are pure, and my inwards steeped in the Tank of Righteousness. There is not a limb in me which is void of Righteousness.

I purify me in the Southern Tank, and I rest me at the northern lake, in the Garden of Grasshoppers.

The Boatmen of Ra purify them there at this hour of the night or day and the hearts of the gods are appeased when I pass through it by night or by day.

Let him come: that is what they say to me.

Who, pray, art thou ? that is what they say to me.

What, pray, is thy name? that is what they say to me.

"He who groweth under the Grass and who dwelleth in the Olive tree" is my name.

Pass on, then: that is what they say to me.

I pass on to a place north of the Olive.

What, prithee, didst thou see there

A thigh and a leg.

And what, prithee, said they to thee ?

That I shall see the greetings in the lands there of the Fenchu:

What, prithee, did they give to thee?

A flame of fire and a pillar of crystal.

And what, prithee, didst thou to them?

I buried them on the bank of the Lake of Maait as Provision of the Evening.

What, prithee, didst thou find there on the bank of the Lake of Maait?

A sceptre of flint: 'Giver of Breath' is its name.

And what didst thou to the flame of fire and to the pillar of crystal after thou hadst buried them?

I cried out after them and drew them forth: and I extinguished the fire, and I broke the pillar, and I made a Tank.

Thou mayest now enter through the door of the hall of Righteousness, for thou knowest us.

I allow thee not to pass by me, saith the Leaf of the Door, unless thou tell my name:

"The Pointer of Truth" is thy name.

I allow thee not to pass by me, saith the right side post of the Door, unless thou tell my name.

"The Scale-pan of one who lifteth up Right" is thy name.

I allow thee not to pass by me, saith the left side post of the Door, unless thou tell my name:

"The Scale-pan of Wine" is thy name.

I allow thee not to pass over me, saith the Threshold of the Door, unless thou tell my name:

"Ox of Seb" is thy name.

I open not to thee, saith the Lock of the Door, unless thou tell my name:

"Bone of An-maut-ef" is thy name.

I open not to thee, saiih the Latch, unless thou tell my name.

"The Eye of Sebak, Lord of Bachau," is thy name.

I open not to thee, and I allow thee not to pass by me, saith the Keeper of the Door, unless thou tell my name:

"The Knee of Shu, which he hath lent for the support of Osiris," is thy name.

We allow thee not to pass by us, say the Lintels of the Door, unless thou tell our names:

"The dragon brood of Renenut" is your name.

Thou knowest us; pass therefore by us.

I allow thee not to pass over me, saith the Floor of the Hall, for the reason that I am noiseless and clean, and because we know not the names of thy two feet, wherewith thou wouldst walk upon us. Tell me, then, their names,

"He who goeth before Amsu" is the name of my right foot: and "The Truncheon of Hathor" is the name of my left foot.

Thou mayest walk over us: for thou knowest us.

I do not announce thee, saith the Doorkeeper, unless thou tell my name:

"He who knowelh the heart and exploreth the person" is thy name.

Then I will announce thee.

But who is that god who abideth in his own hour? Name him.

He who provideth for the Two Worlds.

Who, pray, is it? It is Thoth.

Come hither, saith Thoth, wherefore hast thou come?

I am come, and wait to be announced.

And what manner of man, prithee, art thou?

I have cleansed myself from all the sins and faults of those who abide in their own day; for I am no longer among them.

Then I shall announce thee.

But who is he whose roof is of fire, and whose walls are living Uraei, and the floor of whose house is of running water? Who is it?

It is Osiris,

Proceed then: for behold, thou art announced.

Thy bread is from the Eye, thy beer is from the Eye, and the funeral meals offered upon earth will come forth to thee from the Eye. So is it decreed for me.

This chapter is said by the person, when purified and clad in raiment; shod with white sandals; anointed from vases of anta; and presenting oblations of beeves, birds, incense, bread, beer and vegetables.

And thou shall make a picture, drawn upon a clean brick of clay, extracted from a field in which no swine hath trod.

And if this chapter be written upon it—the man will prosper and his children will prosper: he will rise in the affection of the king and his court: there will be given to him the shesit cake, the measure of drink, the person cake and the meat offering upon the altar table of the great god; and he shall not be cut off at any gate of Amenta, but he shall be conveyed aton° with the Kings of North and South, and make his appearance as a follower of Osiris: undeviatingly and for times infinite.

The Chapter (CLII) of building a house on earth.

O rejoice. Seb, [Name] has been set in motion with his vital power ..... he has given to men and gods their creative strength.

There is cheering, when it is seen that Seshait has come towards Seb; when Anubis has commanded to [Name]: build a house on earth, the foundations of which be like On, and the circuit like Cher-aba; let the god of the sanctuary be in the sanctuary. I also decree that it should contain the sacrificial victim, brought by slaves, and held up by ministrants.

Said by Osiris to the gods in his following: come hastily, and see the house which has been built for the glorified, the well equipt, who cometh every day. Look at him, hold him in awe, and give him praise, which is well pleasing to him.

You see what I have done myself, I the great god who cometh every day. Look ye, Osiris brings me cattle, the south wind brings me grain, the north wind brings me barley as far as the end of the earth.

I have been exalted by the mouth of Osiris, applause surrounds him on his left and on his right.

Look ye men, gods, and Chus, they applaud him, they applaud him, and I am well pleased.

The Chapter (CLIV) of not letting the body decay in the Netherworld.

Hail to thee, my father Osiris. I have come to embalm thee. Ho thou embalm this flesh of mine, for I am perfect like my father Chepera, who is my image, he who does not know corruption.

Come, take hold of my breath of life, lord of the breath, lofty above his equals; vivify me, build me up, thou lord of the funeral chest.

Grant me to go down into the land of eternity, as thou doest when thou art with thy father Tmu, he whose body never decays, he who does not know destruction.

I have not done what thou hatest, the command (which I obey) is that which thy ka loveth, I have not transgressed it.

I have been delivered, being thy follower, O Tmu, from the rottenness which thou allowest to come over every god, every goddess, every animal, every creeping thing which is corruptible.

After his soul has departed he dies, and when it has gone down he decays: he is all corruption; all his bones are rottenness, putrefaction seizes his limbs and makes his bones break down, his flesh becomes a fetid liquid, his breath is stink, he becomes a multitude of worms.

(As for me) there are no worms. He is impotent whoever has lost the eye of Shu among all gods and goddesses, all birds and fishes, all snakes and worms, all animals altogether, for I cause them to crawl before me, they recognise me and the fear of me prevails over them, and behold every being is alike dead among all animals, all birds, all fishes, all snakes, all worms, their life is like death.

Let there be no food for the worms all of them. Let them not come to me when they are born, I shall not be handed over to the destroyer in his cover, who destroys the limbs, the hidden one who causes corruption, who cuts to pieces many dead bodies, who lives from destroying.

He lives who performs his commands, but i have not been delivered into his fingers, he has not prevailed upon me, for I am under thy command, lord of the gods.

Hail to thee, my father Osiris! thy limbs are lasting, thou dost not know corruption; there are no worms with thee, thou art not repugnant, thou dost not slink, thou dost not putrefy, thou wilt not become worms.

I am Chepera, my limbs are lasting for ever. I do not know corruption. I do not rot, I do not putrefy, I do not become worms. I do not lose the eye of Shu.

I am, I am, I live, I live, I grow, I grow, and when I shall awake in peace, I shall not be in corruption, I shall not be destroyed in my bandages. I shall be free of pestilence, my eye will not be corrupted, my skin will not disappear. My ear will not be deaf, my head will not be taken away from my neck, my tongue will not be torn away, my hair will not be cut off. my eyebrows shall not be shaven off. No grievous harm shall come upon me, my body is firm, it shall not be destroyed. It shall not perish in this earth for ever.

96. THE STORY OF WENAMON

A hieratic text (Papyrus Pushkin 120) dating to the Twenty-second Dynasty was found at el-Hiba, the site of ancient Tayu-djayet (Coptic: Teudjoi). It is dated to the fifth year of Ramesses XI's Era of Renaissance (Dynasty 20) and claims to be a report by a priest of Amon at Karnak named Wenamon concerning a journey he made to Byblos to buy timber to build a ship to transport an important cult image of Amon. In the past scholars generally agreed it to be an authentic autobiography of Wenamon, but in recent years a case has been made that the story is a work of literature, though it may be based on an original report by Wenamon. The ending of the tale is missing.

Departure from Thebes

Year five, third month of the third season (eleventh month), day 16, day of the departure of the "eldest of the hall," of the house of Amon, [the lord of the] lands, Wenamon, to bring the timber for the great and august barge of Amon-Re, king of gods, which is on [the river] ...... (called): "Userhet" of Amon.

Arrival at Tanis

On the day of my arrival at Tanis, at the place of abode of Nesubenebded and Tentamon,[20] I gave to them the writings of Amon-Re, king of gods, which they caused to be read in their presence; and they said: "I will do (it), I will do (it) according to that which Amon-Re, king of gods, our lord, saith." I abode until the fourth month of the third season: being in Tanis.

Voyage to Dor

Nesubenebded and Tentamon sent me with the ship-captain, Mengebet, and I descended into the great Syrian sea,[21] in the fourth month of the third season, on the first day. I arrived at Dor, a

---

20 Or Nesbanedbjed (i.e., Smendes) and his wife, who were ruling Lower Egypt.
21 The Mediterranean Sea.

city of Tjekker, and Bedel, its king, caused to be brought for me much bread, a jar of wine, and a joint of beef.

The Robbery at Dor

Then a man of my ship fled, having stolen:

[vessels] of gold, [amounting to]	5 deben
4 vessels of silver, amounting to	20 deben
A sack of silver	II deben
[Total of what] he [stole]	5 deben of gold
	31 deben of silver

In the morning then I rose and went to the abode of the prince, and I said to him: "I have been robbed in your harbor. Since you are the king of this land, you are therefore its investigator, who should search for my money. For the money belongs to Amon-Re, king of gods, the lord of the lands; it belongs to Nesubenebded, and it belongs to Hrihor, my lord, and the other magnates of Egypt; it belongs also to Weret, and to Mekmel, and to Zakar-Baal, the prince of Byblos," He said to me: "To your honor and your excellence! but, behold, I know nothing of this complaint which you have lodged with me. If the thief belonged to my land, he who went on board your ship, that he might steal your treasure, I would repay it to you from my treasury till they find your thief by name; but the thief who robbed you belongs to your ship. Wait a few days here with me, and I will seek him." When I had spent nine days, moored in his harbor, I went to him, and said to him: "Behold, you have not found my money; [therefore let me depart] with [the] ship-captain, and with those who go ......" ...... the sea. He said to me, "Be silent. ...."

Departure from Tyre for Byblos

...... the harbor .... [I arrived at] Tyre. I went forth from Tyre at early dawn .... Zakar-Baal, the prince of Byblos......

Seizure of Security from Tjekker Travelers

...... the ...... I found 30 deben of silver therein. I seized [it, saying to them: "I will take] your money, and it shall remain with me until ye find [my money. Was it not a man of Tjekker who stole it, and no thief [of ours]? I will take it ." They went away, while I ....

Arrival at Byblos

[I] arrived ...... the harbor of Byblos. [I made a place of concealment, I hid] "Amon-of-the-Way," and I placed his things in it. The prince of Byblos sent to me, saying: "Be[take yourself] (from) my harbor." I sent to him, saying: "...... ...... if they sail, let them take [me] to Egypt." ...... I spent nineteen days in his [harbor], and he continually sent to me daily, saying: "Take yourself away from my harbor."

A Prophet of Byblos

Now, when he sacrificed to his gods ..., the god seized one of his noble youths, making him frenzied, so that he said: "Bring [the god] here! Bring the messenger of Amon who has him. Send him, and let him go."

Wenamon's Departure Prevented

Now, while the frenzied (youth) continued in frenzy during this night, I found a ship bound for Egypt, and I loaded in all my belongings into it. I waited for the darkness, saying: "When it descends I will embark the god also, in order that no other eye may see him."

Wenamon is Summoned

The harbor-master came to me, saying: "Remain until morning by the prince." I said to him: "Are not you he who continually came to me daily, saying: 'Take yourself away from my harbor'? Do you not say, 'Remain in the [land]', in order to let depart the ship that I have found? that you may come and say again, 'Away!'? He went and told it to the prince, and the prince sent to the captain of the ship, saying: "Remain until morning by the king."

Wenamon Visits Zakar-Baal

When morning came he sent and had me brought up, when the divine offering occurred in the fortress wherein he was, on the shore of the sea. I found him sitting in his upper chamber, leaning his back against a window, while the waves of the great Syrian sea beat against the ... behind him. I said to him: "[Kindness] of Amon!" He said to me: "How long is it until this day since you came (away) from the abode of Amon?" I said: "Five months and one day until now."

He said to me: "Behold, if you are true, where is the writing of Amon, which is in your hand? Where is the letter of the High Priest of Amon, which is in your hand?" I said to him: "I gave them to Nesubenebded and Tentamon." Then he was very angry, and he said to me: "Now, behold, the writing and the letter are not in your hand! Where is the ship of cedar, which Nesubenebded gave to you? Where is its Syrian crew? He would not deliver your business to this ship-captain ...... to have you killed, that they might cast you into the sea. From whom would they have sought the god then? And you, from whom would they have sought you then?" This he spoke to me. I said to him: "There are indeed Egyptian ships and Egyptian crews who sail under Nesubenebded, (but) he has no Syrian crews." He said to me: "There are surely twenty ships here in my harbor, which are in connection with Nesubenebded; and at this Sidon, to where you also [would go] there are indeed 10,000 ships also which are in connection with Berket-el and sail to his house."

Then I was silent in this great hour. He answered and said to me: "On what business have you come here?" I said to him: "I have come after the timber for the great and august barge of Amon-Re, king of gods. Your father did it, your grandfather did it, and you will also do it." This I spoke to him.

He said to me: "They did it, truly. If you give me (something) for doing it, I will do it.. Indeed, my agents transacted the business; he Pharaoh, L. P. H., sent six ships, laden with the products of Egypt, and they were unloaded into their storehouses. And you also shall bring something for me." He had the journal of his fathers brought in, and he had them read it before me. They found 1,000 deben of every (kind of) silver, which was in his book.

He said to me: "If the ruler of Egypt were the owner of my property, and I were also his servant, he would not send silver and gold, saying: 'Do the command of Amon.' It was not the payment of [tribute] which they exacted of my father. As for me, I am myself neither your servant nor am I the servant of him that sent you. If I cry out to the Lebanon, the heavens open, and the logs lie here on the shore of the sea. Give me the sails which you have brought to propel your ships which bear your logs to [Egypt]. Give me the cordage [which you have brought to bind] the trees which I fell, in order to make them [fast] for you I make them for you [into] the sails of your ships, and the tops are (too) heavy and they break, and you die in the midst of the sea when Amon thunders in heaven, and puts Sutekh in his time. For Amon equips all lands; he equips them, having first equipped the land of Egypt, from where you come. For artisanship came forth from it, to reach my place of abode; and teaching came forth from it, to reach my place of abode. What (then) are these miserable journeys which they have had you make?"

I said to him: "O guilty one! They are no miserable journeys on which I am. There is no ship upon the river, which Amon does not own. For his is the sea, and his is Lebanon of which you say, 'It is mine.' It grows for 'Userhet' (the barge) of Amon, the lord of every ship. Yes, so spoke Amon-Re, king of gods, saying to Hrihor, my lord: 'Send me,' and he made me go, bearing this great god. But, behold, you have let this great god wait twenty-nine days, when he had landed [in] your harbor, although you did certainly know he was here. He is indeed (still) what he (once) was, while you stand and bargain for the Lebanon with Amon, its lord. As for what you say, that the former kings sent silver and gold, if they had given life and health, they would not have sent the valuables; (but) they sent the valuables [to] your fathers instead of life and health. Now, as for Amon-Re, king of gods, he is the lord of life and health, and he was the lord of your fathers, who spent their lifetime offering to Amon. And you also, you are the servant of Amon. If you say to Amon, 'I will do (it), I will do (it),' and you execute his command, you shall live, and you shall be prosperous, and you shall be healthy, and you shall be pleasant to your whole land and your people. Wish not for yourself a thing belonging to Amon-Re, [king of] gods. Yes, the lion loves his own. Let my scribe be brought to me, that I may send him to Nesubenebded and Tentamon, the rulers whom Amon has given to the North of his land, and they will send all that of which I shall write to them, saying: 'Let it be brought;' until I return to the South and send you all, all your trifles again." This I spoke to him.

Timber is Shipped; Messenger Brings Payment

He gave my letter into the hand of his messenger. He loaded in the [keel], the head of the bow and the head of the stern, with four other hewn timbers, together seven; and he had them taken to Egypt. His messenger went to Egypt, and returned to me, to Syria in the first month of the second season. Nesubenebded and Tentamon sent:

Gold: 4 *Tb*-vessels, 1 *K'k-mn*-vessel;
Silver: 5 *Tb*-vessels;
Royal linen: 10 garments, 10 *ḥm-ḥrd*;
Papyrus: 500 rolls;
Ox-hides: 500;
Rope: 500 (coils);

Lentils: 20 measures;

Fish: 30 measures;

She sent me:

Linen: 5 ..., 5 [ḥm-ḥrd];

Lentils: 1 measure;

Fish: 5 measures.

More Timber Felled

The prince rejoiced, and detailed 300 men and 300 oxen, placing overseers over them, to have the trees felled. They spent the second season therewith .... In the third month of the second season (seventh month) they dragged them [to] the shore of the sea. The prince came forth and stood by them.

Timber Delivered to Wenamon

He sent to me, saying: "Come." Now, when I had presented myself before him, the shadow of his sunshade fell upon me. Penamon, a butler, he stepped between me, saying: "The shadow of Pharaoh, L. P. H., your lord, falls upon you." He was angry with him, saying: "Let him alone!" I presented myself before him, and he answered and said to me: "Behold, the command which my fathers formerly executed, I have executed, although you for your part have not done for me that which your fathers did for me. Behold, there has arrived the last of your timber, and there it lies. Do according to my desire and come to load it, for they will indeed give it to you. Come not to contemplate the terror of the sea, (but) if you do contemplate the terror of the sea, you shall (also) contemplate my own. Indeed, I have not done to you that which they did to the messengers of Khamwese, when they spent seventeen years in this land. They died in their place." He said to his butler: "Take him, and let him see their tomb, wherein they sleep."

I said to him: "Let me not see it! As for Khamwese, (mere) people were the messengers whom he sent to you; but people ... there was no [god among] his messengers. And yet you say, 'Go and see your companions.' Lo, are you not glad? and do you not have made for you a tablet, whereon you say: 'Amon-Re, king of gods, sent to me "Amon-of-the-Way," his [divine] messenger, and Wenamon, his human messenger, after the timber for the great and august barge of Amon-Re, king of gods? I felled it, I loaded it, I supplied him (with) my ships and my crews, I brought them to Egypt, to beseech for me 10,000 years of life from Amon, more than my ordained (life), and it came to pass.' Then in future days when a messenger comes from the land of Egypt, who is able to write, and reads your name upon the stela, you shall receive water in the West, like the gods who are there."

He said to me: "It is a great testimony which you tell me."

I said to him: "As for the many things which you have said to me, when I reach the place of abode of the High Priest of Amon, and he shall see your command in your command, [he] will have something delivered to you."

Tjekker Ships Lie in Wait

I went to the shore of the sea, to the place where the timbers lay; I spied eleven ships coming from the sea, belonging to the Tjekker, saying: "Arrest him! Let not a ship of his (pass) to Egypt!" I sat down and began to weep. The letter-scribe of the prince came out to me, and said to me: "What is the matter with you?" I said to him: "Surely you see these birds which twice descend upon Egypt. Behold them! They come to the pool, and how long shall I be here, forsaken? For you see surely those who come to arrest me again."

Zakar-Baal Reassures Wenamon

He went and told it to the prince. The prince began to weep at the evil words which they spoke to him. He sent out his letter-scribe to me, he brought me two jars of wine and a ram. He sent to me Tentno, an Egyptian singer (feminine), who was with him, saying: "Sing for him; let not his heart feel apprehension." He sent to me, saying: "Eat, drink, and let not your heart feel apprehension. You shall hear all that I have to say in the morning."

Interview with the Tjekker

Morning came, he had (the Tjekker) called into his ..., he stood in their midst and said to the Tjekker: "Why have you come?" They said to him: "We have come after the stove-up ships which you send to Egypt with our ... comrades." He said to them: "I cannot arrest the messenger of Amon in my land. Let me send him away, and you shall pursue him, to arrest him."

Escape to Alasa

He loaded me on board, he sent me away ... to the harbor of the sea. The wind drove me to the land of Alasa;[22] those of the city came forth to me to slay me. I was brought among them to the abode of Heteb, the queen of the city. I found her as she was going forth from one of her houses and entering into her other. I saluted her, I asked the people who stood about her: "There is surely one among you who understands Egyptian?" One among them said: "I understand (it)." I said to him: "Say to my mistress: 'I have heard as far as Thebes, the abode of Amon, that in every city injustice is done, but that justice is done in the land of Alasa; (but), lo, injustice is done every day here." She said: "Indeed! What is this that you say?" I said to her: "If the sea raged and the wind drove me to the land where I am, you will not let them take [advantage of] me to slay me; I being a messenger of Amon. I am one for whom they will seek unceasingly. As for the crew of the prince of Byblos whom they sought to kill, their lord will surely find ten crews of yours, and he will slay them, on his part." She had the people called and stationed (before her); she said to me: "Pass the night ." ...... [*ending missing*]

---

22 Cyprus.

97. LETTER OF DHUTMOSE

During the reign of Ramesses XI, the community of tomb builders at Deir el-Medina moved inside the temple compound at Medinet Habu, where it was safer. A group of papyrus letters from there have been discovered, quite a few having been written by the necropolis scribe Dhutmose (nicknamed Tjaroy). This one comes from the sixth year of Ramesses XI's Era of Renaissance, when Dhutmose was on a journey north of Thebes.

The scribe of the great and noble necropolis Dhutmose to the scribe Butehamon and the chantress of Amon Shedemdua:

In life, prosperity and health and in the favor of Amon-Re, King of the Gods! Every single day I am calling upon Amon-Re-Harakhti, Arsaphes, the great god, Thoth, lord of Hermopolis, and every god and every goddess by whom I pass to give you life, prosperity and health, a long lifetime, and a good ripe old age.

And [further]: I've taken note of all matters you wrote me about through the retainer Nesamon, namely, what you stated regarding the matter of the vessels of smaragdus and two flagons which you said you are having finished up, as well as the matter of the donkeys which you said you gave to the wab-priest Tjaumehi[em]hab in order to carry in the grain, as you said. It's all right, this which you have done. If he has finished carrying in the grain, you shall receive it enregistered in full and enter it into its granary. And you shall turn them (the donkeys) over to the police captain Sermontu in order to carry in his grain which is in the fields, excluding any of that which is stowed in the settlements, for it is only that which is scattered about in the fields that you should have brought in, while that which is in the magazines should be retained where it is.

As soon as this floodwater rises, you shall receive in charge this transport boat which I sent to you and give it to the fishermen and the policemen. And they shall bring in the balance of it (the grain); and you shall receive it fully enregistered, the scribe Pentahunakht, son of Sobeknakht, being with you, for he shall supervise for you, and you shall enter it. And you shall receive this transport boat, its oars, its mast, and the fittings(?) and take care of it, for you will find it useful to carry out your assignments with it, along with the wood and the charcoal to have them transported. And you shall enter [them] into their proper place, along with the wood which [the] men [will] cut; and you shall take [it] to my house. Indeed you have a full day ahead of you!

And you are to look after the little children and take care of them properly in the same way as this daughter of Hemesheri, her mother and her nurse. And you shall look after their need.

And you shall attend to the soldiers and watch over them closely.

And you shall give your personal attention to the men who are in the country and make them perform their field labors properly.

And you shall not let the young boys who are in school cease studying.

And you shall look after the people who are in my house and give them clothing. Don't let them go naked! And you shall claim back the three garments which Pakhor has in his possession.

And you shall look after these three riparian plots of ours and have the trees which are on their mounds pruned in the same way as the holding which Nesmontu used to cultivate. And you shall prune its trees beginning from the district of Pre as far as the well of the district.

And you shall see this daughter of Khonsmose and have her write a letter and send it to me.

And you shall not let Hemesheri and Shedemdua nor their little children be lacking in anything.

And you shall tell Tapeses that I met Paturaa at the Northern Promontory (El-Hiba).

And you shall write to me the house in which you found the covering(?), and you shall write me whether you have handed Hori's grain over to him.

And you shall have this courtyard finished up, protected with stone patchwork.

And you shall look after the yoke of oxen which are in the charge of the herdsman Nesamon, son of Djahy, and hand them over to Paydegesh.

And you shall take water to Amon of the Thrones of the Two Lands and tell him to keep [me] safe.

And you shall not neglect [...] Paykamen, my brother. Don't neglect them [...] on the day I return.

And you shall tell Amon to remove this illness which is in me.

98. A DAUGHTER TO HER MOTHER'S LOVER

The background to this letter is a bit difficult to determine, but it appears that the writer is confronting a man named Nesamenemope, who has had an illicit affair with her mother Neferti. Like the previous letter, this one also comes from Medinet Habu and likely is from the reign of Ramesses XI.

To wit: Your people, including the eldest of them and the youngest of them, both male and female, have moved off by dark of night. They were coming saying, "We are going to beat her and her people up." [It was] the steward who said to them, "What means your going [to the house(?)] of my scribe in order to beat up my(?) people, while she isn't there?" And he held them at bay and said to them, "Was it your man who was encountered there as an emissary? Tell me the one whom you found fit to go and beat up. Please tell him to me" so he said to them. And they answered saying to him, "It is eight whole months till now that he has been having sex with this woman while he is not a married man. [Now] if he were a married man, would he not then swear off your woman?" so they said to him.

And the steward sent word to my mother in the presence of Audjar, this workman from whom you took counsel as well, saying, "As for Nesamenemope, why did you accept him as your sexual partner [and so] gain for yourself adversaries? If only [they had not gone] by dark of night to deliver the things of a nice fledgling-child saying, 'We are going to [...] also,' so they said. If this man yearns for you, let [him] enter the court together with his wife and let him swear off [her (his wife)] and come to your house. But if not, he will be one who has to find the way for you to put your lips in touch with his lips. Even if I held them at bay on this occasion, I won't hold them at bay again" so he said.

When my letter reaches you, you shall refuse to go to the woman Neferti in this m[anner].

THIRD INTERMEDIATE PERIOD

99. STELA OF THE BANISHMENT

Menkheperre was High Priest of Amon at Thebes and pharaoh of Upper Egypt while his brother Psusennes I of Dynasty 21 ruled in the north. This stela inscription, erected during Menkheperre's reign, recounts a successful campaign of Menkheperre against some rebels while he was yet commander of the armies under his father Pinedjem I. Then it relates Menkeheperre's later decision to recall all those who had been banished to the Southern Oasis and to forbid any further banishments from taking place. Who the banished were is unclear, but they may have been captured rebels from his earlier campaign.

Date and Introduction

Year 25, third month of the third season, day 29, corresponding to the feast of Amon-Re, king of gods, at his [beautiful] feast......

......Nesuhor in their increase thereof. The majesty of this august god was Thebes. Then he took (his) way to the scribes, inspectors, people......

Departure for Thebes

Year 25, first month of the ... [season, day] .... [Then spoke his majesty] to the people: "Amon-[Re], lord of Thebes ...... their heart is firm ...... their multitude ... the High Priest of Amon-Re, king of gods, commander in chief of the army, Menkheperre, triumphant, son of King Pinedjem-Meriamon ...... his ...... companion of his footsteps, while their hearts rejoiced because he had desired to come to the South in might and victory, in order to make satisfied the heart of the land, and to expel his enemies, that he might give ...... [as] they were in the time of Re.

Arrival at Thebes

He arrived at the city (Thebes) with a glad heart; the youth of Thebes received him, making jubilee, with an embassy before him. The majesty of this august god, lord of gods, Amon-Re, [lord of] Thebes, appeared (in procession) ...... that he might ... him very greatly, very greatly, and establish him upon the throne of his father, as High Priest of Amon-Re, king of gods, commander in chief of the armies of the South and North. He (the god) decreed to him many gracious wonders, (such as) had never been seen since the time of Re.

New Year's Feast

[Now, after] the fourth month of the third season, on the fifth day of the (feast), "Birth of Isis," corresponding to the feast of Amon at the New Year, the majesty of this august god, lord of gods, Amon-Re, king of gods, appeared (in procession), came to the great halls of the house of Amon, and rested before the [inclosure wall] of Amon. The High Priest of Amon-Re, king of gods, commander in chief of the army, Menkheperre, triumphant, went to him and praised him exceedingly, exceedingly, many times, and he founded [for him] his offering, even [every] good thing.

Recall of the Banished

Then the High Priest of Amon, Menkheperre, triumphant, recounted to him, saying: "O my good lord, (when) there is a matter, shall one recount it ... ?" Then the great god nodded exceedingly, exceedingly. Then he went again to the great god, saying: "O my good lord, (it is) the matter of these servants, against whom you are angry, who are in the oasis, to where they are banished." Then the great god nodded exceedingly, while this commander of the army, with his hands uplifted was praising his lord, as a father talks with his own son: "Hail to you, [maker] of all [that is], creator of all that exists, father of the gods, fashioner of goddesses; who equips them in the cities and districts; begetter of men, and fashioner of women, maker of the life of all men. He is Khnum, building excellently, [giving] the breath of life; the north wind .... Men live from his provision, who supplies the necessities of gods and men; the sun by day, the moon by night, sailing the heavens without ceasing. Great in fame, he is mightier than Sekhmet, like fire ...... for him that prays to him; he is healthy to heal the sick, when the people look [to him] .... You shall hearken to my voice on this day, and you shall [relent] toward the servants, whom you have banished to the oasis, and they shall be brought (back) to Egypt." The great god nodded exceedingly.

Abolishment of Banishment

Then he (the High Priest) spoke again, saying: "[O my good lord], as for any writing which any ... makes, in order to bring it, let it be said ...." Then the great god nodded exceedingly. Then he went again to the great god, saying: "O my good lord, you shall make a great decree in your name, that no people of the land shall be [banished] to the distant region of the oasis, nor ...... from this day on." Then the great god nodded exceedingly. He spoke again, saying: "You shall say that it shall be made into a decree upon a stela ...... in your ..., abiding and fixed forever."

Thanksgiving to Amon

Then the High Priest of Amon, Menkheperre, triumphant, spoke again, saying: "O my good lord, then my ... is for myriads of times, and the command is for father and mother in every family. My every word shall please the heart in [your] presence, I am your faithful servant, profitable to your ka. I was a youth in your city, I produced your provision and your ..., while I was in the womb, when you did form (me) in the egg, when you did bring me forth [to the great joy] of your people. Grant that I may spend a happy life as a follower of your *ka*. There is purity and health wherever you linger. Set my feet in your way, and direct me on your path. Incline my heart ... to do .... Grant that I may pass a happy [old age] in peace, while I am established, living in your august house, like every favorite ...."

Slaying of Murderers

Then the High Priest of Amon, Menkheperre, triumphant, went to the great god, saying: "As for any person, of whom they shall report before you, saying, 'A slayer of living people ... (is he);' you shall destroy him, you shall slay him." Then the great god nodded exceedingly, exceedingly.

100. ABYDOS STELA OF PASIBAKHANU II

With this inscription, found on a red granite stela at Abydos, we learn something of Shoshenq I, founder of the Twenty-second Dynasty before he became pharaoh, this man was an important chief of the Meshwesh ("Ma") in Lower Egypt during the reign of Pasibakhanu (Psusennes) II (Dynasty 21). This inscription of Pasibakhanu recounts his handling of Shoshenq's complaint that his father Nimlot's tomb at Abydos has not been treated with respect by the officials in charge of it.

Speech to Amon

"... great chief of chiefs, Sheshonk, triumphant, his son, in the glorious place by his father, Osiris, [that he might] lay his beauty [to rest] in the city of Abydos over against .... You will let him survive to attain old age, while his [heart] .... You will let him join the feasts of his majesty, receiving full victory." This great god saluted exceedingly.

Amon Condemns the Thieves

Then his majesty spoke again before this great god: "O my good lord, you shall slay the ..., the administrator, the scribe, the inspector, every one who was sent on any commission to the field, of those who stole of his [things] from the offering-table of the Osiris, the great chief of Ma, Namlot, triumphant, son of Mehetnusekhet, who is in Abydos; all the people who plundered from his divine offerings, his people, his cattle, his garden, his every oblation and all his excellent things. You will do according to your great spirit throughout; fill them up and fill up (the number of) the women and their children." The great god saluted exceedingly.

Final Prayer to Amon

His majesty smelled the earth before him; his majesty said; "Make to triumph, Sheshonk, triumphant, the great chief of Ma, chief of chiefs, the great ..., and all who are before you, all the troops...." [Said to] him, Amon-Re, king of gods: "... I will do ... for you, you shall attain old age, abiding on earth; your heir shall be upon your throne forever."

Statue of Nimlot Sent to Abydos

His majesty sent the statue of Osiris, the great chief of Ma, great chief of chiefs, Namlot, triumphant, northward to Abydos. There were ...... a great army, in order to protect it, having [numerous] ships, ... without number, and the messengers of the great chief of Ma, in order to deposit it in the august palace, the sanctuary of the right eye of the sun, in order to make his offerings belonging in Abydos, according to the stipulations for making his offerings, incense ... in the hall of petition.

Records of Endowment

His contract was recorded in the hall of writings, according to that which the lord of gods (Amon) had said. A stela was erected for him of granite of Elephantine, bearing the decree ... in his name, in order to deposit it in the divine sanctuary to the end of eternity, (even) forever. Then was established the offering-table of Osiris, the great chief of Ma, Namlot, triumphant, son of Mehetnusekhet, who is in Abydos.

People of Endowment

There were brought the [people] of the ... of the great chief of Me, who came with the statue: a Syrian servant (named) Ikhamon ..., a Syrian (named) Ekptah; [the price of the first] was 14 deben of silver; his majesty gave for the second] 20 deben of silver; total, 35 deben of silver, the tale thereof.

𓊪𓄿𓎛𓆄𓇋𓏤𓏭𓊪𓄿𓎛𓆄𓇋𓏤𓏭𓊪𓄿𓎛𓆄𓇋𓏤𓏭

101. THE GREAT KARNAK RELIEF OF SHOSHENQ I

This is an excerpt from a large relief on the south wall of the temple at Karnak put there by Shoshenq I, founder of the Twenty-second Dynasty. It pertains to his military campaign against the sister kingdoms of Judah and Israel soon after they split in two (compare reading #106).

Before the King

Sheshonk I, king, great in fame, smiting the countries that assail him, achieving with his sword, that the Two Lands may know that he has smitten the chiefs of all countries.

With Amon

"Welcome! my beloved son, Sheshonk, ... mighty in strength. You have smitten the lands and the countries, you have crushed the Nubian Troglodytes, [your] sword was mighty among the Asiatics; they were made fragments every moment. Your victorious fame ... all lands. You went forth in victory, and you have returned in might; [you have united] ... ; I have ... for you the countries that knew not Egypt, that had begun to invade [your] boundaries, in order to cut off their heads. Victory is given into your hands, all lands and all countries are united ..., the fear of you is as far as the four pillars [of heaven], the terror of your majesty is among the Nine Bows: you have ... the hearts of the countries. You are Horus over the Two Lands, you are ... against your enemies, when you have smitten the foe. Take my victorious sword, you whose war-mace has smitten the chiefs of the countries."

Utterance of Amon-Re .... "My heart is very glad, when I see your victories, my son, Meriamon-Sheshonk, my beloved, who came forth from me, in order to be my champion. I have seen the excellence of your plans; which you have executed, the ... of my temple, which you have established [for] me, in Thebes, the great seat to which my heart [inclines]. You have begun to make monuments in Southern Heliopolis, Northern Heliopolis, and every city ... thereof for the [sole] god of its district. You have made my temple of millions of years, ... of electrum, wherein I .... Your heart is satisfied over .... You have - more than any king of them all. You have smitten every land, my mighty sword was the source of the victories which I have given ...... all the Asiatics. Your fire raged as a flame behind them, it fought against every land, which you did gather together, which your majesty gave to it, (being) Montu the mighty overwhelming his enemies. Your war-mace, it struck down your foes, the Asiatics of distant countries; your serpentcrest was mighty among them.

"I made your boundaries as far as you desired; I made the Southerners come in obeisance to you, and the Northerners to the greatness of your fame. You have made a great slaughter among them without number, falling in their valleys, being multitudes, annihilated and perishing afterward, like those who have never been born. All the countries that came ......; your majesty has destroyed them in the space of a moment. I have trampled for you them that rebelled against you, overthrowing [for] you the Asiatics of the army of Mitanni; I have humbled them ... beneath your feet. I am your father, the lord of gods, Amon-Re, lord of Thebes, sole leader, whose remnant escapes not, that I may cause your valor to be [remembered] in the future through all eternity."

102. THE PIANKHI STELA

Found in the remains of the temple at Gebel Barkal near Napata in Kush, the Piye Stela narrates the successful military campaign of Piye (Piankhi) of Kush against the Egyptian forces of Tefnakhte I (Dynasty 24) and other rival kings of the Delta area.

Date and Introduction

Year 21, first month of the first season, under the majesty of the King of Upper and Lower Egypt, Meriamon-Piankhi, living forever.

Command which my majesty speaks: "Hear of what I did, more than the ancestors. I am a king, divine emanation, living image of Atum, who came forth from the womb, adorned as a ruler, of whom those greater than he were afraid; whose father knew, and whose mother recognized that he would rule in the egg, the Good God, beloved of the gods, achieving with his hands, Meriamon-Piankhi."

Tefnakhte's Advance

One came to say to his majesty: "A chief of the west, the great prince in Neter, Tefnakhte is in the nome of ..., in the nome of Xois, in Hapi, in ..., in Ayan, in Pernub, and in Memphis. He has seized the whole west from the back-lands to Ithtowe, coming southward with a numerous army, while the Two Lands are united behind him, and the princes and rulers of walled towns are as dogs at his heels. No stronghold has closed [its doors in] the nomes of the South: Mer-Atum (Medum), Per-Sekhemkheperre, the temple of Sebek, Permezed, Theknesh; and every city of the west; they have opened the doors for fear of him. He turned to the east, they opened to him likewise: Hatbenu, Tozi, Hatseteni, Pernebtepih. Behold, [he] besieges Heracleopolis, he has completely invested it, not letting the comers-out come out, and not letting the goers-in go in, fighting every day. He measured it off in its whole circuit, every prince knows his wall; he stations every man of the princes and rulers of walled towns over his (respective) portion."

Then [his majesty] heard [the message] with courageous heart, laughing, and joyous of heart.

These princes and commanders of the army who were in their cities sent to his majesty daily, saying: "Will you be silent, even to forgetting the Southland, the nomes of the [court], while Tefnakhte advances his conquest and finds none to repel his arm? Namlot ..., prince of Hatweret, he has overthrown the wall of Nefrus, he has demolished his own city, for fear of him who might take it from him, in order to besiege another city. Behold, he goes to follow at his (Tefnakhte's) heels, having cast off allegiance to his majesty (Piankhi). He tarries with him (Tefnakhte) like one of [his vassals in] the nome of Oxyrhyncus, and gives to him (Tefnakhte) gifts, as much as he desires, of everything that he has found."

Piankhi Commands the Capture of Hermopolis

Then his majesty sent to the princes and commanders of the army who were in Egypt: the commander, Purem; and the commander, Lemersekeny; and every commander of his majesty who was in Egypt (saying): "Hasten into battle line, engage in battle, surround [Hermopolis], capture its people, its cattle, its ships upon the river. Let not the peasants go forth to the field, let not the plowmen plow, beset the frontier of the Hare nome, fight against it daily." Then they did so.

Piankhi Sends His Army to Engage Tefnakhte

Then his majesty sent an army to Egypt, charging them earnestly: "[Delay] not day nor night, as at a game of draughts; (but) fight on sight. Force battle upon him from afar. If he says to the infantry and chariotry of another city, 'Hasten;' (then) you shall abide until his army comes, that you may fight as he says. But if his allies be in another city, (then) let one hasten to them; these princes, whom he has brought for his support: Libyans and favorite soldiers, force battle upon them [first]. Say, 'We know not what he cries in mustering troops. Yoke the war horses, the best of your stable; draw up the line of battle! You know that Amon is the god who has sent us.'

"When you arrive at Thebes, before Karnak, you shall enter into the water, you shall bathe in the river, you shall dress in [fine linen]; unstring the bow, loosen the arrow. Let not the chief boast as a mighty man; there is no strength to the mighty without him (Amon). He makes the weak-armed into the strong-armed, so that multitudes flee from the feeble, and one alone takes a thousand men. Sprinkle yourselves with the water of his altars, sniff the ground before him. Say to him, 'Give to us the way, that we may fight in the shadow of your sword. (As for) the generation whom you have sent out, when its attack occurs, multitudes flee before it.'"

Then they threw themselves upon their bellies before his majesty (saying): "It is your name which endues us with might, and your counsel is the mooring-post of your army; your bread is in our bellies on every march, your beer quenches our thirst. It is your valor that gives us might, and there is strength at the remembrance of your name; (for) no army prevails whose commander is a coward. Who is your equal therein? You are a victorious king, achieving with his hands, chief of the work of war."

They sailed down-stream, they arrived at Thebes, they did according to all that his majesty had said.

Battle on the River

They sailed down-stream upon the river; they found many ships coming up-stream bearing soldiers, sailors, and commanders; every valiant man of the Northland, equipped with weapons of war, to fight against the army of his majesty. Then there was made a great slaughter among them, (whose) number was unknown. Their troops and their ships were captured, and brought as living captives to the place where his majesty was.

Battle of Heracleopolis

They went to the [frontier] of Heracleopolis, demanding battle.

List of the princes and kings of the Northland: namely:
1. King Namlot and
2. King Yewepet.
3. Chief of Ma, Sheshonk, of Per-Osiris (Busiris), lord of Ded.
4. Great chief of Ma, Zeamonefonekh, of Per-Benebded (Mendes), together with
5. His eldest son, who was commander of the army of Per-Thutuprehui.
6. The army of the hereditary prince, Beknenef, together with
7. His eldest son, chief of Ma, Nesnekedi in the nome of Hesebka.
8. Every chief wearing a feather who was in the Northland; together with
9. King Osorkon, who was in Per-Bast (Bubastis) and the district of Ranofer.
10. Every prince, the rulers of the walled towns in the West, in the East, (and) the islands in the midst, were united of one mind as followers of the great chief of the West, ruler of the walled towns of the Northland, prophet of Neit, mistress of Sais, *sem*-priest of Ptah, Tefnakhte.

They went forth against them; then they made a great slaughter among them, greater than anything. Their ships were captured upon the river. The remnant crossed over and landed on the west side before Per-Peg.

When the land brightened early in the morning, the army of his majesty crossed over against them. Army mingled with army; they slew a multitude of people among them; horses of unknown number; a rout ensued among the remnant. They fled to the Northland, from the blow, great and evil beyond everything.

List of the slaughter made among them:
People: ... men.

Namlot Flees into Hermopolis

King Namlot fled up-stream southward, when it was told him: "Hermopolis is in the midst of the foe from the army of his majesty, who capture its people and its cattle." Then he entered into Hermopolis, while the army of his majesty was upon the river, in the harbor of the Hare nome. Then they heard of it, and they surrounded the Hare nome on its four sides, not letting the comers-out come out, and not letting the goers-in go in.

Piankhi Determines to go to Egypt Himself

They sent to report to the majesty of the King of Upper and Lower Egypt, Meriamon-Piankhi, given life, on every conflict which they had fought, and on every victory of his majesty. Then his majesty was enraged thereat like a panther (saying): "Have they allowed a remnant of the army of the Northland to remain? allowing him that went forth of them to go forth, to tell of his campaign? not causing their death, in order to destroy the last of them? I swear: as Re loves me! As my father Amon favors me! I will myself go northward, that I may destroy that which he has done, that I may make him turn back from fighting, forever.

"Now, afterward when the ceremonies of the New Year are celebrated, I will offer to my father, Amon, at his beautiful feast, when he makes his beautiful appearance of the New Year, that he may send me forth in peace, to behold Amon at the beautiful Feast of Opet; that I may bring his image forth in procession to Luxor at his beautiful feast (called): "Night of the Feast of Opet," and at the feast (called): "Abiding in Thebes," which Re made for him in the beginning; and that I may bring him in procession to his house, resting upon his throne, on the "Day of Bringing in the God," in the third month of the first season, second day; that I may make the Northland taste the taste of my fingers."

Capture of Oxyrhyncus

Then the army, which was there in Egypt, heard of the wrath which his majesty felt toward them. Then they fought against Per-Mezed of the Oxyrhynchite nome, they took it like a flood of water, and they sent to his majesty; (but) his heart was not satisfied therewith.

Capture of Tetehen

Then they fought against Tetehen, great in might. They found it filled with soldiers, with every valiant man of the Northland. Then the battering-ram was employed against it, its wall was overthrown, and a great slaughter was made among them, of unknown number; also the son of the chief of Ma, Tefnakhte. Then they sent to his majesty concerning it, (but) his heart was not satisfied therewith.

Capture of Hatbenu

Then they fought against Hatbenu, its interior was breached, the army of his majesty entered into it. Then they sent to his majesty, (but) his heart was not satisfied therewith.

Surrender of Hermopolis

First month of the first season, ninth day; his majesty went northward to Thebes, and completed the Feast of Amon at the Feast of Opet. His majesty sailed northward to the city of the Hare nome (Hermopolis); his majesty came forth from the cabin of the ship, the horses were yoked up, the chariot was mounted, the terror of his majesty reached to the end of the Asiatics, every heart was heavy with the fear of him.

Then his majesty went forth ... to hate his soldiers, enraged at them like a panther (saying): "Is the steadfastness of your fighting this slackness in my affairs? Has the year reached its end, when the fear of me has been inspired in the Northland? A great and evil blow shall be smitten them."

He set up for himself the camp on the southwest of Hermopolis and besieged it daily. An embankment was made, to enclose the wall; a tower was raised to elevate the archers while shooting, and the slingers while slinging stones, and slaying people among them daily.

Days passed, and Hermopolis was foul to the nose, without her (usual) fragrance. Then Hermopolis threw herself upon her belly, and plead before the king. Messengers came forth and descended bearing everything beautiful to behold: gold, every splendid costly stone, clothing in a chest, and the diadem which was upon his head, the uraeus which inspired the fear of him; without ceasing during many days, pleading with his diadem.

Then they sent his wife, the kings'-wife, and king's-daughter, Nestent, to plead with the king's-wives, king's-concubines, king's-daughters, and king's-sisters, to throw herself upon her belly in the harem, before the king's-wives (saying): "We come to you, O king's-wives, king's-daughters, and king's-sisters, that you may appease Horus, lord of the palace, whose fame is great and his triumph mighty. Grant that he ...... me; lo, he him. Lo, ... [Speak] to him, that he may incline to the one that praises him ...."

[*Piankhi addresses Namlot*] "Lo, who has led you? who has led you? Who, then, has led you? Who has led you? ...... you did [forsake] the way of life. Did heaven rain with arrows? I am [content] when the Southerners do obeisance and the Northerners (say): 'Put us in your shadow.' Lo, it is evil ...... bearing his food. The heart is a steering-oar; it capsizes its owner through that which is from the god. It seeth flame as coolness [in] the heart .... There is no old man, ... Your nomes are full of youths."

He [Namlot] threw himself upon his belly before his majesty (saying): "[Be appeased], Horus, lord of the palace, it is your might which has done it. I am one of the king's slaves, paying impost into the treasury ...... their impost. I have brought for you more than they."

Then he presented much silver, gold, lapis lazuli, malachite, bronze, and all costly stones. Then he filled the treasury with this tribute; he brought a horse in the right hand and a sistrum in the left hand, of gold and lapis lazuli.

Piankhi's Triumphant Entry into Hermopolis

Then his [majesty] appeared in splendor in his palace, proceeded to the house of Thoth, lord of Hermopolis, and he slew bulls, calves, and fowl for his father, lord of Hermopolis, and the eight gods in the house of the eight gods. The army of the Hare nome acclaimed and rejoiced, saying: "How beautiful is Horus, resting in his city, the Son of Re, Piankhi! Celebrate for us a jubilee, even as you have protected the Hare nome."

His majesty proceeded to the house of King Namlot, he entered every chamber of the king's-house, his treasury and his magazines. He caused that there be brought to him; the king's-wives and king's-daughters; they saluted his majesty in the fashion of women, (but) his majesty turned not his face to them.

His majesty proceeded to the stable of the horses and the quarters of the foals. When he saw that they had suffered hunger, he said: "I swear, as Re loves me, and as my nostrils are rejuvenated with life, it is more grievous in my heart that my horses have suffered hunger, than any evil deed that you have done, in the prosecution of your desire. It has borne witness of you to me, the fear of your associates for you. Did you not know that the god's shadow is over me? and that my fortune never perishes because of him? Would that another had done it to me! I could not but [condemn] him on account of it. When I was being fashioned in the womb, and created in the divine egg the seed of the god was in me. By his *ka*, I do nothing without him; he it is who commands me to do it."

Then his [Namlot's] possessions were assigned to the treasury, and his granary to the divine offerings of Amon in Karnak.

Loyalty of Heracleopolis

The ruler of Heracleopolis Pefnefdibast came, bearing tribute to the palace: gold, silver, every costly stone, and horses of the choicest of the stable. He threw himself upon his belly before his majesty; he said: "Hail to you, Horus, mighty king, Bull subduer of Bulls! The Nether World had seized me, and I was submerged in darkness, upon which the light has (now) shone. I found not a friend in the evil day, who was steadfast in the day of battle; but you, O mighty king, you have expelled the darkness from me. I will labor together with (your) subjects, and Heracleopolis shall pay taxes into your treasury, you likeness of Harakhte, chief of the imperishable stars. As he was, so are you king; as he perishes not so you shall not perish, O King of Upper and Lower Egypt, Piankhi, living forever.

Surrender of Per-Sekhemkheperre

His majesty sailed north to the opening of the canal beside Illahun; he found Per-Sekhemkhperre with its wall raised, and its stronghold (htm) closed, filled with every valiant man of the Northland. Then his majesty sent to them, saying: "You living in death! You living in death! You insignificant ... and miserable ones! You living in death! If an hour passes without opening to me, behold, you are of the number of the fallen; and that is [painful] to the king. Close not the gates of your life, to be brought to the block this day. Love not death, nor hate life .... before the whole land."

Then they sent to his majesty, saying: "Lo, the shadow of the god is over you; the son of Nut, he gives to you his two arms; the thought of your heart comes to pass immediately, like that which comes forth from the mouth of a god. Lo, you are fashioned as the face of a god; we see by the decree of your hands. Lo, your city, his stronghold; [do] your [pleasure] therewith. Let the goers-in go in there, and the comers-out come out. Let his majesty do what he will." Then they came out, with the son of the chief of Ma, Tefnakhte. The army of his majesty entered into it, without slaying one of all the people. He found ...... and treasurers to seal his possessions. His treasuries were assigned to the Treasury, and his granaries to the divine offerings of his father, Amon-Re, lord of Thebes.

Surrender of Medum

His majesty sailed northward; he found that Mer-Atum (Medum), the house of Sokar, lord of Sehez, had been closed, and was inaccessible. It had set fighting in its heart, taking .... Fear [seized] them; terror sealed their mouth. Then his majesty sent to them, saying: "Behold, two ways are before you; choose as you will: open, and you shall live; close, and you shall die. My majesty will not pass by a closed city." Then they opened immediately; his majesty entered into this city, and offered ... [to] Menhy of Sehez. His treasury was assigned [to the Treasury], his granaries to the divine offerings of Amon of Karnak.

Surrender of Ithtowe

His majesty sailed north to Ithtowe; he found the rampart closed, and the walls filled with the valiant troops of the Northland. Then they opened the stronghold, and threw themselves upon [their] bellies [before] his majesty (saying): "Your father has assigned to you his inheritance. Yours are the Two Lands, yours is what is therein, yours is all that is on earth." His majesty entered to cause a great oblation to be offered to the gods residing in this city, consisting of bulls, calves, fowl, and everything good and pure. Then his treasury was assigned to the Treasury, and his granaries to the divine offerings [of Amon].

Piankhi Approaches Memphis

[His majesty sailed north to] Memphis; then he sent to them, saying: "Shut not up, fight not, you abode of Shu in the beginning. As for him that would go in, let him go in; as for him that would come out, let him come out; and let not them that would leave be hindered. I would offer an oblation to Ptah and to the gods dwelling in Memphis, I would sacrifice to Sokar in the mysterious place, I would behold 'Him-Who-is-South-of-His-Wall,' that I may sail north in peace. [The people] of Memphis [shall be] safe and sound; not (even) a child shall weep. Look to the nomes of the South; not a single one has been slain therein, except the enemies who blasphemed against the god, who were dispatched as rebels."

Then they closed their stronghold; they sent forth an army against some of the soldiers of his majesty, being artisans, chief builders and sailors ...... the harbor of Memphis.

Tefnakhte Arrives at Memphis and Then Leaves to Get Reinforcements

Lo, that chief of Sais (Tefnakhte) arrived at Memphis in the night, charging his infantry and his sailors, all the best of his army, a total of 8,000 men, charging them very earnestly: "Behold, Memphis is filled with troops of all the best of the Northland; (with) barley and spelt and all kinds of grain, the granaries are running over; (with) all weapons of [war. It is fortified with] a wall; a great battlement has been built, executed with skillful workmanship. The river flows around the east side, and no (opportunity of) attack is found there. Cattle yards are there, filled with oxen; the treasury is supplied with everything: silver, gold, copper, clothing, incense, honey, oil. I will go, and I will give something to the chiefs of the North, and I will open to them their nome. I will be ...... [There will be but a few] days until I return."

He mounted upon a horse, he asked not for his chariot, he went north in fear of his majesty.

Capture of Memphis

When day broke, at early morning, his majesty reached Memphis. When he had landed on the north of it, he found that the water had approached to the walls, the ships mooring at [the walls of] Memphis. Then his majesty saw that it was strong, and that the wall was raised by a new rampart, and battlements manned with mighty men. There was found no way of attacking it. Every man told his opinion among the army of his majesty, according to every rule of war. Every man said: "Let us besiege [it] ...; lo, its troops are numerous." Others said: "Let a causeway be made against it; let us elevate the ground to its walls. Let us bind together a tower; let us erect masts and make the spars into a bridge to it. We will divide it on this (plan) on every side of it, on the high ground and ... on the north of it, in order to elevate the ground at its walls, that we may find a way for our feet."

Then his majesty was enraged against it like a panther; he said: "I swear, as Re loves me, as my father, Amon [who fashioned me], favors me, this shall befall it, according to the command of Amon. This is what men say: [The Northland] and the nomes of the South, they opened to him from afar, they did not set Amon in their heart, they knew not what he commanded. He (Amon) made him (Piankhi) to show forth his fame, to cause his might to be seen.' I will take it like a flood of water. I have commanded ...."

Then he sent forth his fleet and his army to assault the harbor of Memphis; they brought to him every ferry-boat, every [cargo]-boat, every [transport], and the ships, as many as there were, which had moored in the harbor of Memphis, with the bow-rope fastened among its houses. [There was not] a citizen who wept, among all the soldiers of his majesty.

His majesty himself came to line up the ships, as many as there were. His majesty commanded his army (saying): "Forward against it! Mount the walls! Penetrate the houses over the river. If one of you gets through upon the wall, let him not halt before it, [so that] the (hostile) troops may not repulse you. It were vile that we should close up the South, should land [in] the North and lay siege in 'Balances of the Two lands.'"

Then Memphis was taken as (by) a flood of water, a multitude of people were slain therein, and brought as living captives to the place where his majesty was.

Piankhi Honors the Temples of Memphis

Now, afterward, when it dawned, and the second day came, his majesty sent people into it, protecting the temples of the god. He ... the holy of holies of the gods, offered to the community of gods of Hatkeptah (Memphis), cleansed Memphis with natron and incense, installed the priests in their places.

His majesty proceeded to the house of [Ptah], his purification was performed in the Dewat-chamber, and every custom that is practiced upon a king was fulfilled upon him. He entered into the temple, and a great oblation was made for his father, "Ptah-South-of-His-Wall", consisting of bulls, calves, fowl, and everything good. His majesty proceeded to his house.

Submission of the Memphis Nomes

Then all the nomes which were in the district of Memphis, heard (of it): Herypeclemy, Penineywe, the Tower of Beyew, the Oasis of Bit; they opened the strongholds, and fled away; none knew the place where they had gone.

Submission of Delta Dynasts

King Yewepet came, and the chief of Ma, Akenesh, and the hereditary prince, Pediese, together with all the princes of the Northland, bearing their tribute, to behold the beauty of his majesty.

Wealth of Memphis Assigned

Then the treasuries and granaries of Memphis were assigned to the divine offerings of Amon, of Ptah, and of the gods dwelling in Hatkeptah (Memphis).

Piankhi Visits Heliopolis

When the land brightened, very early in the morning, his majesty proceeded eastward, and an offering was made for Atum in Khereha, the divine ennead in the house of the ennead, the cavern and the gods dwelling in it; consisting of bulls, calves, and fowl; that they might give life, prosperity, and health to the King of Upper and Lower Egypt, Piankhi, living forever.

His majesty proceeded to Heliopolis, upon that mount of Khereha, on the highway of (the god) Sep to Khereha. His majesty proceeded to the camp, which was on the west of Eti. His purification was performed, and he was cleansed in the pool of Kebeh, and he bathed his face in the river of Nun, in which Re bathes his face.

Proceeding to the Sand-hill in Heliopolis, a great oblation was made upon the Sand-hill in Heliopolis, in the presence of Re, at his rising, consisting of white oxen, milk, myrrh, incense, and every sweet-smelling wood.

He came, proceeding to the house of Re, and entered into the temple with great praise. The chief ritual priest praised the god, that rebels might be repelled from the king. The Dewat-chamber was visited, that the *sedeb*-garment might be fastened on; he was purified with incense and libations; garlands for the pyramidion-house were presented to him, and flowers were brought to him. He ascended the steps to the great window, to behold Re in the pyramidion-house. The king himself stood alone, he broke through the bolts, opened the double doors, and beheld his father, Re, in the glorious pyramidion-house, the Morning-Barque of Re, and the Evening-Barque of Atum. He closed the double doors, applied the clay, and sealed (them) with the king's own seal. He charged the priests: "I have proved the seal; no other shall enter therein, of all the kings who shall arise." They threw themselves upon their bellies before his majesty, saying: "To abide, to endure, without perishing, O Horus, beloved of Heliopolis."

He came and entered into the house of Atum, following the image of his father, Atum Khepri the Great, of Heliopolis.

King Osorkon came to see the beauty of his majesty.

Piankhi Visits Athribis

When the land brightened, very early in the morning, his majesty proceeded to the harbor, and the [best] of his ships crossed over to the harbor of the nome of Athribis. The camp of his majesty was set up on the south of Keheni, on the east of the nome of Athribis.

Then came those kings and princes of the Northland, all the chiefs who wore the feather, every vizier, all chiefs, and every king's-confidant, from the west, from the east, and from the islands in the midst, to see the beauty of his majesty.

The hereditary prince, Pediese, threw himself upon his belly before his majesty, and said: "Come to Athribis, that you may see Khentikhet, that you may worship Khuyet, that you may offer an oblation to Horus in his house, consisting of: bulls, calves, and fowl; and that you may enter my house. My treasury is open to you, to ... yourself with my paternal possessions. I will give to you gold, as much as you desire; malachite shall be heaped up before you; many horses of the best of the stable, and the first of the stall."

His majesty proceeded to the house of Harkhentikhet, and there were offered bulls, calves, and fowl to his father, Harkhentikhet, lord of Kemwer. His majesty went to the house of the hereditary prince, Pediese; he (Pediese) presented to him silver, gold, lapis lazuli, and malachite, a great heap of everything; clothing of royal linen of every number; couches laid with fine linen; myrrh and ointment in jars; horses, both stallions and mares, of all the best of his stable.

He (Pediese) purified himself by a divine oath, before these kings and great chiefs of the Northland (saying): "Every one of them, if he conceals his horses and hides his obligation shall die the death of his father. So be it to me, till you bear witness of the servant there, in all that you know of me; say (whether) I have concealed (anything) from his majesty, of all the possessions of my father's house: [of] gold, silver; of costly stone; of all kinds of vessels, ...; of golden bracelets, of necklaces, and collars wrought with costly stones; amulets for every limb, chaplets for the head rings for the ears: all the adornments of a king; all the vessels of the king's purification, in gold and - all costly stones. All these I have presented in the (royal) presence: garments of royal linen by thousands of all the best of my house, where-with I knew you would be pleased. Go to the stable that you may choose as you desire, of all the horses that you will." Then his majesty did so.

Said these kings and princes to his majesty: "Dismiss us to our cities, that we may open our treasuries, that we may choose as much as your heart desires, that we may bring to you the best of our stables, the first of our horses." Then his majesty did so.

List of names belonging thereto:

1. King Osorkon in Bubastis, the district of Ranofer.
2. King Yewepet in Tentremu and Tayan.
3. The prince Zeamonefonekh in "The Granary of Re," of Per-Benebded (Mendes).
4. His eldest son, commander of the army, in Per-Thutuprehui, Enekhhor.
5. The prince Akenesh in Sebennytos, in Per-heby, and in Samhudet.
6. The prince, chief of Ma, Pethenef, in Per-Soped and in "Granary of Memphis."
7. The prince, chief of Ma, Pemou, in Per-Osiris (Busiris), lord of Ded.
8. The prince, chief of Ma, Nesnekedy in the nome of Hesebka.
9. The prince, chief of Ma, Nekhtharneshenu in Per-Gerer.

10. The chief of Ma, Pentewere.

11. The chief of Ma, Pentibekhenet.

12. The prophet of Horus, lord of Letopolis, Pediharsomtous.

13. The prince Hurabes in the house of Sekhmet, mistress of Sais, and the house of Sekhmet, mistress of Rehesu.

14. The prince Zedkhiyu in Khentnofer.

15. The prince Pebes in Khereha in Per -Hapi.

Bearing all their good tribute: gold, silver, ..., couches laid with fine linen, myrrh in jars, ..., as goodly dues; horses of ......

Revolt of Mesed

[Many days after] this, came one to say to his majesty: "The ... army ...... his wall [for fear] of you; he has set fire to [his] treasury [and to the ships] upon the river. He has garrisoned Mesed with soldiers and .... Then his majesty caused his warriors to go and see what had happened there, among the forced of the hereditary prince, Pediese. One came to report to his majesty, saying: "We have slain every man whom we found there." His majesty gave it as a reward to the hereditary prince, Pediese.

Tefnakhte Submits

Then the chief of Ma, Tefnakhte, heard of it and caused a messenger to come to the place where his majesty was, with flattery, saying: "Be appeased! I have not beheld your face for shame; I cannot stand before your flame, I tremble at your might. Lo, you are Nubti, presiding over the Southland, Montu, the Bull of mighty arm. To whatsoever city you have turned your face, you have not found the servant there, until I reached the islands of the sea, trembling before your might, and saying, 'His flame is hostile to me.' Is not the heart of your majesty appeased, with these things that you have done to me? For I am truly a wretched man. You should not smite me according to the measure of the crime; weighing with the balances, knowing with the *kidet*-weights. You increase it to me threefold; leave the seed that you may [spare] it in [time]; do not hew down the grove to its [root]. By your *ka*, the terror of you is in my body, and the fear of you in my bones. I have not sat in the beer-hall, nor has the harp been played for me; but I have eaten bread in hunger, and I have drunk water in thirsts, since that day when you heard my name. [Disease] is in my bones, my head is bare, my clothing is rags, till Neit is appeased toward me. Long is the course which you have brought to me; [your face is against me - the year has undone me]. Cleanse (your) servant of his fault, let my possessions be received into the Treasury, of gold and every costly stone, and the best of the horses, (even) [payment for] everything. Send to me a messenger quickly, that he may expel fear from my heart. Let me go forth before him to the temple, that I may cleanse myself with a divine oath."

His majesty dispatched the chief ritual priest, Pediamenesttowe, and the commander of the army, Purme. He [Tefnakhte] presented him with silver and gold, clothing and every splendid, costly stone. He went forth to the temple, he worshiped the god, he cleansed himself with a divine oath, saying: "I will not transgress the command of the king, I will not overstep that which the king says. I will not do a hostile act against a prince without your knowledge; I will do according to that which the king says, and I will not transgress that which he has commanded." Then his majesty was satisfied therewith.

Submission of the Fayum, Atfih, and the Last Kings of the Delta

One came to say to his majesty: "The temple of Sebek, they have opened its stronghold, Metenu throws itself upon its belly, there is not a nome closed against his majesty of the nomes of the South and North; the west, the east, and the islands in the midst are upon their bellies in fear of him, causing that their possessions be presented at the place where his majesty is, like subjects of the palace." When the land brightened, very early in the morning these two rulers of the South and two rulers of the North, with serpent-crests (uraei), came to sniff the ground before the fame of his majesty, while, as for these kings and princes of the Northland who came to behold the beauty of his majesty, their legs were as the legs of women. They entered not into the king's-house, because they were unclean and eaters of fish; which is an abomination for the palace. Lo, King Namlot, he entered into the king's-house, because he was pure, and he ate not fish. There stood three upon their feet, (but only) one entered the king's-house.

Piankhi's Return to the South

Then the ships were laden with silver, gold, copper, clothing, and everything of the Northland, every product of Syria, and all sweet woods of God's-Land. His majesty sailed up-stream, with glad heart, the shores on his either side were jubilating. West and east, they seized the ..., jubilating in the presence of his majesty; singing and jubilating as they said: "O mighty, mighty Ruler, Piankhi, O mighty Ruler; you come, having gained the dominion of the Northland. You make bulls into women. Happy the heart of the mother who bore you, and the man who begat you. Those who are in the valley give to her praise, the cow that has borne a bull. You are to eternity, your might endures, O Ruler, beloved of Thebes."

103. THE SHABAKA STONE

The inscription on this piece of black granite was produced during the reign of King Shabaka of Kush (Dynasty 25), who reunified Egypt under his authority. It is purported that Shabaka found an ancient papyrus scroll in the temple of Ptah and, in order to preserve the text, had it inscribed upon the stone, which he then displayed in the temple of Ptah in Memphis. At one time scholars believed the creation myth on the stone (dubbed The Memphite Theology) came from the Old Kingdom, it is now believed to have been roughly contemporary with the time of Shabaka and deliberately made to look archaic in language to give it an air of authority. Because someone later bored a hole in the stone and used it as a millstone, the condition of the text is rather poor. The myth portion of the text is provided here.

(3) This Ptah is he, who is proclaimed under this great name. (4) The Southland and the Northland are this Uniter, who appears as King of Lower Egypt. [(5) *left blank*]. (6) He that begat him is Atum, who formed the Nine Gods, (7) to whom the gods offered when he had judged Horus and Set. (8) He defended their litigation, in that he set up Set as King of Upper Egypt in the Southland, from the place where he was born, Sesu; whereas Keb, he set Horus as King of Lower Egypt in the Northland, from the place where his father was drowned; (9) at the division of the Two Lands. It is Horus and Set who stood on the ground; they joined the Two Lands at Enu; it is the boundary of the Two Lands.

(10a) Keb (to) Set, speech; "Hasten from the place, wherein you were born."

(11a) Keb (to) Horus, speech: "Hasten from the place wherein your father was drowned."

(12a) Keb (to) Horus and Set, speech: "I will judge you."

(13a-17a) Keb (to) the gods: "I have assigned the inheritance to that heir, to the son of the first-born son."

(10b) (To) Set the Southland! It is evil to the heart of Keb, that the portion of Horus should be (only) equal to the portion of Set.

(11b) (to) Horus the Northland! It is Keb, who gives his inheritance to Horus, he being the son (12b) of his first-born son.

(13c) Horus stands on the earth, he is the uniter of this land, proclaimed under the great name, "Totenen south of his wall," lord of eternity. (14c) The double crown flourishes on his head; he is Horus, appearing as King of Upper and Lower Egypt, Uniter of the Two Lands at the stronghold, at the place where the Two Lands are united. (15c) Now when the ... and the column were at the front of the house of Ptah, Horus and Set were united, joined, they became brothers, they no longer strove together. (16c) .... united in the House of Ptah, in the place .... wherein the Southland and the Northland join; it is this land.

[*Broken references to the Osiris-myth follow, and then comes the great central lacuna.*]

(48) Ptah is the Being of the gods (??)

(49a) Ptah upon the Great Throne is

(49b) fashioner of the gods.

(50a) Ptah-Nun is the father of Atum.

(50b) fashioner of the gods.

(51a) Ptah-Nekhabet is the mother who bore Atum.

(51b) ....

(52a) Ptah the Great is the heart and the tongue of the gods.

(52b) at the nose of Re every day.

(53) He that became heart, and he that became tongue are an emanation of Atum.. . .their Ka's being this heart and this tongue.

(54) Horus came into existence through him, Thoth came into existence through him, through Ptah, from whom proceeded the power of the heart and the tongue. ... He is the one who makes to [*lost causative verb*] that which comes forth from every body (thought), and from every mouth (speech), of all gods, of all people, of all cattle, of all reptiles, which live, thinking and commanding everything that he wills.

(55) His Ennead is before him, being the teeth and the lips, the phallus and the hands of Atum....
(For) the Ennead of Atum came into existence from his phallus and his fingers; the Ennead indeed being the teeth and the lips in this mouth, which proclaims the name of everything; and from which Shu and Tefnut came forth.

(56) The gods fashioned the sight of the eyes, the hearing of the ears, and the smelling of the nose, that they might furnish the desire of the heart. It (the heart) is the one that brings forth every successful issue. It is the tongue which repeats the thought of the heart; it (the heart) is the fashioner of all gods, at the time when every divine word even, came into existence by the thought (57) of the heart, and command of the tongue. It (the heart) is the maker of *ka*s.... the maker of every food-offering and every oblation, by this word, the maker of that which is loved and that which is hated; it is the giver of life to him who bears peace (the innocent), the giver of death to him who bears guilt. It (the heart) is the maker of all handiwork, and of every handicraft, the doing of the hands, the going of the feet; the movement of every member is according to its command (viz.,) the expression of the heart's thought that comes forth from the tongue and does the totality of everything Ptah-Totenen, he being the fashioner of the gods; everything has come forth from him, whether offering or food or (59) divine oblation, or any good thing.

He is Thoth, the Wise; greater is his strength than (that of the gods. He united with Ptah after he had made all things, every divine word; when he formed the gods, made the towns, equipped the nomes, placed the gods in their adyta, (60) made their offerings flourish, equipped their adyta, made likenesses of their bodies to the satisfaction of their hearts; then the gods entered into their bodies, of every wood, of every costly stone, of every metal, and everything, that grows upon his. .... (61) from which they come. It is he to whom all the gods sacrifice, their *ka*s being united, associated with the Lord of the Two Lands. The divine storehouse of Totenen is the Great Seat attached to the heart of the gods who are in the house of Ptah, lord of life, lord.... wherein the life of the Two Lands is made.

(62) .... Osiris, he was drowned in his water; Isis and Nephthys saw; when they beheld him, they were of service to him. Horus gave command to Isis and Nephthys in Dedu, that they should save Osiris, and that they should prevent that he drown. (63) They went around...., they brought him to the land, he entered his secret structure in.... of the lords of eternity, at the footsteps of him who rises in the horizon upon the highways of Re in the Great Seat. (64) He associates with the court, he becomes a brother to the gods.

Totenen-Ptah, lord of years, he has become Osiris in the land, in.... on the north side of this land. His son Horus comes to him, appearing as King of Upper Egypt, appearing as King of Lower Egypt, in the presence of his father, Osiris and the gods, his ancestors, who are behind him.

104. DREAM STELA OF TANWETAMANI

The following inscription comes from a granite stela found at Napata in Kush and is from the reign of the Kushite king Tanwetamani (Dynasty 25), who in his first year briefly ruled all of Egypt. This was during the period of Assyrian domination, when Nekau I was running the country on behalf of the Assyrians. Here Tanwetamani narrates his defeat of Nekau's forces and the brief return of his dynasty to power in Egypt.

Introduction

"Good God" on the day when he was born; Atum is he for the people, lord of two horns, ruler of the living, prince, seizing every land, victorious in might on the day of battle, facing the front on the day [of conflict], lord of valor, like Montu, great in strength, like a fierce-eyed lion, wise-hearted, like Thoth; crossing the sea in pursuit of his opponent, carrying off the ends of .... He has [taken] this land; none fighting and none standing before him, (even) the King of Upper and Lower Egypt, Bekere, Son of Re, Tanutamon (Tanwetamani), beloved of Amon of Napata.

The Dream

In the year 1 of his coronation as king ... his majesty saw a dream by night: two serpents, one upon his right, the other upon his left. Then his majesty awoke, and he found them not. His majesty said: "Wherefore [has] this [come] to me ?" Then they answered him, saying: "Yours is the Southland; take for yourself (also) the Northland. The 'Two Goddesses' shine upon your brow, the land is given to you, in its length and its breadth. [No] other divides it with you."

Journey to Napata

When his majesty was crowned upon the throne of Horus in this first year, his majesty went forth from the place where he had been, as Horus went forth from Khemmis. He went forth from ..., while there [came] to him millions and hundreds of thousands coming after him. Said his majesty: "Lo, the dream is true! It is profitable for him who sets it in his heart, (but) evil for him who understands [it] not." His majesty went to Napata, while none stood before him.

His majesty arrived at the temple of Amon of Napata, residing in the Pure Mountain. As for his majesty, his heart was glad when he saw his father, Amon-Re, lord of Thebes, residing in the Pure Mountain. Garlands for this god were brought to him; then his majesty brought forth in splendor Amon of Napata; and he made for him a great festival offering, founding for him a [feast]: 39 oxen, 40 jars of beer, and 100 *šw*.

Ceremonies at Elephantine

His majesty sailed down-stream toward the Northland, that he might behold Amon, whose name is hidden from the gods. His majesty arrived at Elephantine; then his majesty sailed across to Elephantine, he arrived at the temple of Khnum-Re, lord of the cataract, and he caused this god to be brought forth in splendor. He made a great festival offering, and he gave bread and beer for the gods of the two caverns. He appeased [Nun] in his cavern.

Ceremonies at Thebes

Then his majesty sailed down-stream to the city Thebes of Amon. His majesty sailed to the frontier of Thebes, and he entered the temple of Amon-Re, lord of Thebes. There came to his majesty the servant of the great ..., and the lay priests of the temple of Amon-Re, lord of Thebes, and they brought to him garlands for Amon, whose name is hidden. As for his majesty, his heart rejoiced when he saw this temple. He brought forth Amon-Re, lord of Thebes, in splendor, and there was celebrated a great feast in the whole land.

Departure for the Delta

His majesty sailed down-stream to the Northland, while the west and the east made great jubilee, saying: "Welcome is your coming, and welcome your *ka*! To sustain alive the Two Lands; to erect the temples which have begun to fall to ruin; to set up their statues in their shrines; to give divine offerings to the gods and goddesses, and mortuary offerings to the glorified (dead); to put the priest in his place; to furnish all things of the sacred property." As for those who had fighting in their hearts, they became rejoicers.

Capture of Memphis

When his majesty arrived at Memphis, there came forth the children of rebellion, to fight with his majesty. His majesty made a great slaughter among them; their number being unknown. His majesty took Memphis, and he entered into the temple of Ptah, "South-of-His-Wall;" he made a great festival oblation for Ptah-Sokar; he appeased Sekhmet, the great, who loves him.

New Buildings in Napata

As for his majesty, his heart was glad in giving ... to his father, Amon, of Napata. His majesty issued a command concerning it, to Nubia, to build for him a hall anew; it was not found built in the time of the ancestors. His majesty caused it to be built of stone, mounted with gold; its panel was of cedar incensed with myrrh of Punt. The double doors thereof were of electrum, the two bolts of [tin]. He built for him another hall at the rear exit, for furnishing his milk of his numerous herds, in tens of thousands, thousands, hundreds, and tens; the number of the young calves with their mothers was unknown.

Submission of the Delta Dynasts

Now, after these things, his majesty sailed north, to fight with the chiefs of the North. Then they entered their strongholds [as beasts crawl into] their holes. Then his majesty spent many days before them, (but) there came not forth one of them to fight with his majesty. Then his majesty sailed southward to Memphis.

He sat in his palace deliberating and counseling with his heart how to cause his army to reach and to ... them. Then his army said that one had come to report to him, saying: "These chiefs come to the place where his majesty is, [O king], our lord." Said his majesty: "Come they to fight? Come they to submit, they shall live from this hour." They said [to] his majesty: "They come to submit to the king, our lord." Said his majesty: "As for my lord, this august god, Amon-Re, lord of Thebes, residing in the Pure Mountain, great and [excellent] god, whose name is [known], vigilant ... for his beloved, and giving valor to him who serves him; he who possesses his plans does not go astray; nor does he whom he leads err. Behold, he told (it) me by night, and I behold (it) by day." Said his majesty: "Where are they in this hour?" Said they before his majesty: "They are here, waiting at the hall."

Then his majesty went forth from his [palace] to ..., as Re shines in his bright dwelling. He found them prostrate upon their bellies, kissing the ground to his majesty. Said his majesty: "Lo, it is true that which he uttered, the word [of his design. Lo, he knows what] shall happen. It is the decree of the god; (hence) it comes to pass. I swear as Re loves me, as Amon favors me in his house, [behold, I saw] this august god, Amon, of Napata, residing in the Pure Mountain, while he was standing by me, he said to me: 'I am your leader in every way. You may not say: "Would that I had ...." Then they answered him, saying: "Lo, this god, he has [revealed] to you the beginning; he has completed for you the [end] in prosperity. Lo, you do not ... that comes out of his mouth, O king, our lord." Then the hereditary prince of Per-Soped, Pekrur, arose to speak, saying: "You slay whom you will; and let live whom you will ...." They answered him with one accord, saying: "Give to us breath, O lord of life, without whom there is no life. Let us serve you like the serfs who are subject to you, as you said at the first on the day when you were crowned as king." The heart of his majesty rejoiced when he heard this word, and he gave to them bread, beer, and every good thing.

Brief Reign at Memphis

Now, when some days had passed, after these events, and [everything had been given in plenty] ..., they said: "Wherefore are we (still) here, O king, our lord?" Said his majesty: "Wherefore!" Said they to his majesty: "Let us go to our cities, that we may command our peasant-serfs that we may bring our impost to the court." His majesty (let) them go to their cities, and they became [subjects].

The Southerners went north, and the Northerners went south to the place where his majesty was, bearing every good thing of the Southland, and all provision of the Northland, to satisfy the heart of his majesty, (when) the King of Upper and Lower Egypt, Bekere, Son of Re, Tanutamon, L. P. H., appeared upon the throne of Horus, forever.

LATE KINGDOM

105. ADOPTION STELA OF NITOCRIS

This inscription from a stela found at Karnak records the adoption of Nitocris, the daughter of Psamtik I (Dynasty 26) by Shepenupet II, the Divine Adoratrice, to be her successor. The top of the stela is broken off and missing, and so the translation begins in the middle of a speech by Psamtik.

Psamtik's Declaration of Adoption

"I am his son, first in the favor of the father of the gods, offering to the gods; whom he begat for himself, to satisfy his heart. I have given to him my daughter, to be Divine Consort, that she [may invoke protection for the king] more than those who were before her; that he may indeed be satisfied with her prayers, and that he may protect the land of him who gave her to him.

"Lo, I have now heard saying, a king's-daughter of Taharka, triumphant, is there whom he gave to his sister to be her 'Great Daughter,' who is there as 'Divine Votress.' I am not one to expel an heir from his place, for I am a king who loves truth; my particular abomination is lying; (I am) a son protecting his father, taking the inheritance of Keb, uniting the two portions as a youth. Hence I give her to her, to be her 'Great Daughter' as her father (once) conveyed her to (his) sister."

Then they bowed to the ground, they gave thanks to the King of Upper and Lower Egypt, Wahibre (Psamtik I), living forever; and they said: "Abiding and enduring through eternity! Your every command shall abide and endure. How beautiful is this which the god does for you! How excellent is that which your father does for you! .... He loves to remember your *ka*, and he rejoices at the mention of your name, O Horus, ' Great-of-Heart,' King of Upper and Lower Egypt, Psamtik, living forever. He has done this as his monument for his father, Amon, lord of heaven, ruler of gods. He has given his beloved eldest daughter, Nitocris, whose 'beautiful name' is Shepnupet, to be Divine Consort, to play the sistrum before his (Amon's) beautiful face."

Installation of Nitocris

In the year 9, first month of the first season (first month), day 28, went forth his eldest daughter from the king's family apartments, clad in fine linen, and newly adorned with malachite. The attendants conducting her were legion in number, and marshals cleared the path, for beginning the goodly way to the harbor, to turn up-stream for Thebes. The vessels bearing her were very numerous, the crews were mighty men; and they were deeply laden [to the decks] with every good thing of the king's-palace. The commander thereof was the sole companion, nomarch of Heracleopolis, commander in chief of the army, chief of the harbor, Somtous-Tefnakhte. Messengers sailed to the South, to make splendid provision before her. Sail was set .... The great men took their weapons, and every noble [had] his provision, supplied with every good thing: bread, beer, oxen, geese, ..., dates, herbs, and every good thing. One transferred (her) to his neighbor, until she reached Thebes.

In the year 9, second month of the first season (second month), day 14, they arrived at the city of the gods, Thebes. As she advanced, she found (all) Thebes, men and women alike, standing, rejoicing at her approach, surrounding her with great offerings, a multitude in number. Then they said: "The daughter of the King of Upper Egypt, Nitocris, comes to the house of Amon, that he may receive her and be satisfied with her. The daughter of the King of Lower Egypt, Shepnupet, comes to Karnak, that the gods therein may honor her. Every monument of the King of Upper and Lower Egypt, Psamtik, abides and endures forever and ever. Amon, lord of heaven, king of gods, has received what his son, Horus, 'Great-of-Heart,' living forever and ever, made for him. Amon, ruler of gods, has praised that which his son, Favorite of the Two Goddesses, Nebe, living forever and ever, made for him .... The reward therefore is with Amon, and with Montu, even a million years of life, a million years of stability, a million years of satisfaction. All health and joy of heart are with them for their beloved son, the King of Upper and Lower Egypt, Lord of the Two Lands, Wahibre, Son of Re, Psamtik, living forever and ever ...."

Conveyance of the Fortune from Shepnupet to Nitocris

Now, afterward when she came to the Divine Votress, Shepnupet, she saw her, was satisfied with her, and loved her beyond everything. She conveyed to her the fortune which her father and her mother had conveyed to her and to her 'Great Daughter,' Amenardis, king's-daughter of King ..., triumphant. It was put into writing concerning them, saying: "We have given to you all our property in field and in town. You abide upon our throne, abiding and enduring forever and ever." The witnesses concerning them were the prophets, the priests and all the adherents of the temple.

List of all the property given to her [by them] in the towns and nomes of the South and North, that which his majesty gave to her in seven nomes of the Southland:

1. In the district of Heracleopolis, the nome called Yuna, which is in the district thereof lands, 300 stat.

2. In the district of Oxyrhyncus, the estate of Putowe, which is in the district thereof lands, 300 stat.

3. In the district of Sep, the estate of Kewkew, which is in the district thereof lands, [300] stat.

4. In the district of the Hare nome, (Hermopolis), the estates of Nesumin, which are in the district thereof, 600 stat.

5. In the district of Aphroditopolis, (the town of) Kay, which is in the district thereof, 300 stat.

6. In the district of ..., the estateof Harsiese, which is in the district thereof, 200 stat.

All this added together lands, 1,800 stat together with all the income thereof from field and town; with their arid lands, and their canals.

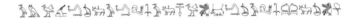

106. THE DEUTERONOMIC HISTORY (FIRST EDITION)

From the kingdom of Judah comes this narrative, which is an excerpt from a lengthy history that was composed under the auspices of King Josiah of Judah (640-609 BCE) during the reign of

Psamtik I of Egypt. This passage, which is now to be found in the Second Book of Kings in the Hebrew Bible, concerns the invasion of Judah by Shoshenq I (see reading #101) two centuries previously.

^{11:14}Now Yahweh[1] raised up an adversary against Solomon:[2] Hadad the Edomite—he was of the king's seed in Edom.

^{11:15}It had happened that when David[3] had been in Edom, when Joab the captain of the army had gone up to bury the slain and had struck down every male in Edom ^{11:16}(for Joab and all Israel had remained there six months until he had cut off every male in Edom), ^{11:17}that Hadad fled—he and Edomite men from among his father's servants with him—to go into Egypt. Hadad was a child (at the time). ^{11:18}They arose from Midian and entered Paran, and taking men with them from Paran, they came to Egypt, to Pharaoh the king of Egypt, who gave him a house, commanded he be provided food rations, and gave him land.

^{11:19}And Hadad found great favor in the eyes of Pharaoh the king of Egypt, so he gave him a woman, the sister of his wife, the sister of Tahpenes[4] the queen of Egypt. ^{11:20}And the sister of Tahpenes bore him Genubath his son, whom Tahpenes weaned in Pharaoh's palace; and Genubath was in Pharaoh's palace among the sons of Pharaoh.

^{11:21}When Hadad, in Egypt, heard that David slept with his fathers[5] and that Joab the captain of the army was dead, Hadad said to Pharaoh, "Let me depart, so that I may go to my country." ^{11:22}And Pharaoh said to him, "But with me what have you lacked that you now look to go to your country?" And he said to him, "Nothing, but let me depart anyway." ...

^{11:26}And a servant of Solomon, Jeroboam ben-Nebat, an Ephraimite from the Zeredah, whose mother's name was Zeruah, a widowed woman—he also lifted up his hand against the king. ^{11:27}And this was the reason that he lifted his hand against the king: Solomon had built the Millo—he had repaired the breach of the city of David, his father.... ^{11:40}And Solomon sought to put Jeroboam to death, so Jeroboam rose and fled to Egypt, to Shishaq the king of Egypt. And he was in Egypt until the death of Solomon.... ^{11:43}And Solomon slept with his fathers, being buried in the city of David his father, and Rehoboam his son reigned in his place....

^{12:1}And Rehoboam went to Shechem, because to Shechem all Israel had come to make him king. ^{12:2}And it came to be that Jeroboam ben-Nebat heard of it (for he was still in Egypt, where he had fled from the presence of king Solomon, and Jeroboam lived in Egypt), ^{12:3}and they sent and called for him. So they came—Jeroboam and the whole assembly of Israel—and they spoke to Rehoboam, saying: ^{12:4}"Your father made our yoke grievous; now therefore make lighter your father's grievous service and heavy yoke that he put upon us, and we will serve you."...^{12:16} And when all Israel saw that the king would not listen to them, the people returned word to the king, saying: "What portion in David do we have? We have no inheritance in the son of Jesse. To your tents, O Israel! Now see to your (own) house, O David." So Israel left for their tents.... ^{12:19}And Israel has been in rebellion against the house of David to this day.

---

1 Judah's national God.
2 The king of Judah.
3 The previous king of Judah, Solomon's father.
4 Perhaps a corruption of the name Tentsepeh, a common female name in the Libyan royal family.
5 That is, in the grave, not literally.

¹²:²⁰So it happened that, when all Israel heard that Jeroboam was returned, they sent for and called him to the assembly, and they made him king over all Israel; there was none that followed the house of David, except the tribe of Judah alone....

¹⁴:²⁵Now in the fifth year of King Rehoboam, it came to be that Shishaq the king of Egypt came up against Jerusalem, ¹⁴:²⁶and he took away the treasures of the temple of Yahweh, and the treasures of the king's palace, and everything else. He (even) took away the shields of gold that Solomon had made. ¹⁴:²⁷So King Rehoboam made shields of bronze instead, and he committed them to the hands of the captains of the guards, who watched the door of the king's palace. ¹⁴:²⁸And it would happen that every time the king would enter the temple of Yahweh, the guards would carry them and bring them back into the guard-chamber.

𓈖𓆓𓂝𓏏𓇋𓀀𓊖𓅱𓏏𓈖𓅓𓏏𓇋𓂋𓏏𓊖𓀀𓏏𓇯𓈖𓅱𓏏𓏏𓇋𓂋

107. PROPHECIES OF JEREMIAH

These two prophecies, taken from the book of Jeremiah in the Hebrew Bible (Chapter 46), date to the reign of Nekau II. In the first prophecy, Jeremiah celebrates the defeat of Egypt's forces at by Nebuchadnezzar the king of Babylon at Carchemish. The defeat is portrayed as a divine punishment upon Nekau for his treatment of Judah (see reading #108). He warns the Egyptians to prepare for worse. In the second, Jeremiah forecasts a successful invasion of Egypt itself by Nebuchadnezzar. It turned out, however, that Nebuchadnezzar was never able to conquer Egypt.

For Egypt: concerning the army of Pharaoh Neko, the king of Egypt, which was near the Euphrates River at Carchemish, (and) which Nebuchadrezzar, the king of Babylon, struck down in the fourth year of Jehoiakim, the son of Josiah, the king of Judah.[6]

Ready buckler and shield, and advance to battle!

Harness the horses and mount, O horsemen!

And stand ready with helmets, and furbish the spears, and put on the scale armor!

Why then have I seen them terrified, turning back?

Their warriors are beaten, and they are fleeing a flight.

They do not look back, terror on every side.—the oracle of Yahweh.

The swift one cannot flee, and the mighty man cannot escape.

In the north by the Euphrates River, they have stumbled, and they have fallen.

Who is this that rises like the Nile, like the great river whose waters surge?

Egypt rises like the Nile and like the great river, the waters surge,

For he said, "I shall rise, I shall cover the land, I will destroy city and inhabitants thereof."

Go up, O horses! And rush like mad, O chariots! May the mighty men go forth,

---

6   605 BCE.

Kush and Put[7] handling the buckler and Ludim[8] handling and bending the bow!
And that day is for the Lord Yahweh Sebaot,
A day of vengeance, to avenge himself on his foes,
And the sword has consumed, and it has been sated,
And it has become drunk from their blood.
For a sacrificial feast for the Lord Yahweh Sebaot
Was in the northland by the Euphrates River.
Go up into Gilead and get balm, O virgin daughter Egypt!
In vain do you search for remedies; there is no healing for you.
Nations have heard of your disgrace; your cry has filled the land,
For mighty man with a mighty man—they have stumbled; together they both have fallen.

The message that Yahweh spoke to Jeremiah the prophet about the coming of Nebuchadrezzar, the king of Babylon, to strike down the land of Egypt:
Declare in Egypt and announce in Migdol[9] and announce in Nop[10] and say in Tahpanhes:[11]
Standy ready and prepare yourself, for the sword has consumed those around you!
So why is your mighty bull lying flat? It does not stand, because Yahweh thrust him down.
He kept making stumble even one man upon another,
And they said, "Get up and let us return to our people,
And to the land of our birth, before the oppressing sword."
Call the name of Pharaoh, the king of Egypt: "Noise Who Has Let the Appointed Time Pass."
"As I live"—the oracle of the King, Yahweh Sebaot his name—
"Assuredly as Tabor is among the mountains and Carmel is by the sea, so shall he[12] come."
Luggage for captivity prepare for yourself, O inhabitant daughter Egypt,
For Nop will become a desolation and burned without an inhabitant.
A beautiful, beautiful heifer was Egypt, but a gladfly from the north has come, has come.
Even the mercenaries in her midst were like staff heifers,
But even they—they turned back, they fled together, they did not stand,
For the day of their disaster came upon them, their time of reckoning.
Her sound is like that of a moving snake, for with strength they come,
And with axes they come against her, like those cutting down trees.
They cut down her forest—oracle of Yahweh—it has not even been searched out,
For they are more numerous than locusts, and there is not even a number for them.
Daughter Egypt has been put to shame; she has been given into the hand of people of the north.
Yahweh Sebaot, the God of Israel, has said: "Lo! I will bring a reckoning upon Amon of No,[13] and upon Pharaoh, and upon Egypt, and upon her gods, and upon her kings, and upon Pharaoh, and

---

7   Probably Libya.
8   Lydians.
9   A city somewhere in the eastern Delta.
10 Memphis.
11 Tjafanet.
12 Nebuchdrezzar.
13 Thebes.

upon those trusting in him. And I will give them into the hand of those who seek their life, and into the hand of Nebuchadrezzar, the king of Babylon, and into the hand of his servants.

"But afterward, she will dwell as in the days of old."—the oracle of Yahweh.

108. THE DEUTERONOMIC HISTORY (SECOND EDITION)

In this excerpt from the revised Deuteronomic History (see reading #107), which was produced probably by the Jewish community in exile in Babylon at the time that Ahmose (Amasis) II ruled Egypt, the narrator recounts the activities of Pharaoh Nekau (Necho) II against the kingdom of Judah that occurred some decades earlier. 23:29

In [Josiah's] days, Pharaoh Nekoh[14] king of Egypt went up to the king of Assyria to the Euphrates River, and King Josiah went to engage him; but Pharaoh Nekoh slew him at Megiddo when he saw him.[23:30] And his servants conveyed him in a chariot, dead, from Megiddo, and brought him into Jerusalem, and interred him in his tomb. Then the people of the land took Jehoahaz the son of Josiah and anointed him, and they made him king in his father's place. [23:31]

Twenty-three years old was Jehoahaz at his accession, and he reigned three months in Jerusalem. His mother's name was Hamutal the daughter of Jeremiah of Libnah.[23:32] And he did what was bad in the eyes of Yahweh, the same as all his fathers had done.[23:33] And Pharaoh Nekoh put him in bonds at Riblah in the land of Hamath, so that he might not reign in Jerusalem, and he laid upon the land a tribute of a hundred talents of silver and (one) talent of gold.[23:34] Then Pharaoh Nekoh made Eliakim the son of Josiah king in the place of Josiah his father, and he changed his name to Jehoiakim. Jehoahaz he took away; and he came to Egypt and died there.[23:35]

Now the silver and the gold Jehoiakim delivered to Pharaoh. However, he taxed the land to give the silver according to Pharaoh's command. Each according to his assessment he exacted the silver and the gold of the people of the land to give it to Pharaoh Nekoh.

---

14 Nekau II.

PERSIAN PERIOD

109. STATUE INSCRIPTION OF UDJAHORRESNET

Udjahorresnet was high priest of Neith and chief physician of the Persian emperor Cambyses II in Egypt. He had previously served as a naval officer under the last two kings of the Late Kingdom, Ahmose II and Psamtik III. This biographical inscription, dating to the time of Darius I, appears on a green basalt statue of Udjahorresnet who is holding an image of Osiris. It was found in his shaft tomb at Abusir near Memphis.

I.

When the great King of all lands, Cambyses, came to Egypt, the people of all (foreign) lands were with him. He exercised sovereignty in the land in its entire extent; they settled down in it, he being the great King of Egypt, the mighty Sovereign of this country. His Majesty conferred upon me the dignity of Chief San,[1] and granted that I should be by him as Smer and Provost of the temple. He assumed the official title in his name of Mestu-Ra. I made known to His Majesty the grandeur of Sais, as being the abode of Neith, the Great Mother, who gave birth to the Sun-god Ra, the First-born, when as yet no birth had been; together with the doctrine of the grandeur of the house of Neith, as being a Heaven in its whole plan; together with the doctrine of the grandeur of the (other) temples of Neith, and of all the gods and goddesses who dwell in them, also of the grandeur of the Hat-nat, as being the abode of the Sovereign and Lord of Heaven, together with the doctrine of the grandeur of the South Chapel, and of the North Chapel, of the house of Ra, and of the house of Tmu, as being the mysterious abodes of all the gods.

II.

I made supplication to the King Cambyses against the people who had taken up their abode in this temple of Neith, that they should be dislodged from it in order that the temple of Neith should be restored to all its splendours as formerly. His Majesty ordered that all the people should be dislodged who had taken up their abode in the temple of Neith, that all their houses should be destroyed, and that all their belongings which were in the temple they should themselves carry out of the precincts of this temple. His Majesty gave order that the temple of Neith should be purified, that all its own people should be restored to it ...... people, Hours[2] of the temple. His Majesty gave order that the sacred revenue should be restored to Neith, the Great Mother, and the great gods of Sais, as formerly. His Majesty gave orders to (restore) all their panegyries, and all their possessions as formerly. His Majesty did this because I had instructed him as to the grandeur of Sais, as being the city of all the gods who dwell upon their thrones within it for evermore.

---

1 Physician.
2 This is a title given to certain persons in temple service.

III.

When King Cambyses arrived at Sais, His Majesty came himself to the temple of Neith and made presents to the almighty goddess of all good things; to Neith, the mighty one, the Divine Mother, and to the gods who are in Sais, as all pious Kings have done. His Majesty did this because I had instructed him as to the grandeur of the goddess, as being the Mother of the Sun-god himself.

IV.

His Majesty performed all the rites at the temple of Neith. He established the offering of a libation to the Lord of Eternity within the temple of Neith, as all Kings had done of old. His Majesty did this because I had instructed him as to all the rites at this temple performed by all the Kings on account of the grandeur of this temple, as being the dwelling of all the gods who abide for evermore.

V.

I established the property of Neith, the mighty one, the Divine Mother, as His Majesty had ordered, for an everlasting duration, I provided the monuments of Neith, the Mistress of Sais, with all good things, as doth every dutiful servant for his lord. I was a good man before his face. I saved the population in the dire calamity which took place throughout the whole land, such a one as had never happened in this land. I shielded the weak against the strong, I protected him who honoured me, and was to him his best portion. I did all good things for them when the time came to do them.

VI.

I was pious towards my father and did the will of my mother; kind-hearted towards my brethren. I established for them what His Majesty had ordered, giving to them splendid lands for an everlasting duration, as His Majesty had pleased. I made a good sarcophagus for one who had no coffin. I made all their children to live, I made firm all their houses, I did for them all good things as a father does for his son when the calamity came to pass in this nome, yes when the dire calamity befell the entire land.

VII.

His Majesty, the King Darius, everliving, gave orders that I should come to Egypt while His Majesty was in Arma[3] (for he was Sovereign of all provinces and great King of Egypt), to re-establish the school of the Hierogrammatists and (restore) what had fallen in ruin. And strangers conveyed me from province to province, bringing me in safety to Egypt according to the command of the Lord of the Two Lands. I did what His Majesty had commanded. I chose them from their schools out of the children of the inhabitants to the great sorrow of the childless. I gave them to a skilful teacher who should instruct them in every kind of work. I provided all those who distinguished themselves with all that was necessary for the scribe's profession according to their progress. His Majesty did this in consequence of his knowing that this work was the best means of restoring what had fallen into ruin, of rendering firm the names of the gods, their temples, their revenues, and the celebration of their festivals for evermore.

---

3   Aram (Syria).

VIII.

I was devoted to all the masters that I had, and they bestowed upon me decorations of gold and gave me all glory.

IX.

O all you gods who are in Sais! declare all the glorious things which the Chief San, Udjahorresnet, has done; O grant to him all glory, establish for him a good name in this land for evermore.

X.

Osiris, Lord of Eternity! the Chief San, Udjahorresnet, puts his arms behind you to guard your image. Be there done to him all glorious things as he has done who protects your shrine for evermore.

XI.

A royal table of offerings grant Osiris Hemaka, abundance of bread, beer, beeves, geese, and all good and pure things to the image of the Chief San, Udjahorresnet, pious towards the gods of Sais.

XII.

A royal table of offerings grant Osiris abiding in Hat-nat, funeral offerings, bread, beer, beeves, geese, mummy bands, incense, and all good things to the image of the great San, Udjahorresnet, pious towards all the gods.

110. THE PETITION OF PETEÊSI

Nine demotic papyri from the site of ancient Teudjoi (modern el-Hiba) were disovered, which belonged to a priestly family that worked at the temple of Amon there. The latest of these, dating to the ninth year of the Persian emperor Darius I (512 BCE), is one of the most interesting of the lot. It is a petition by the priest Peteêsi to the Persian satrap to be able to return to his house in safety after being attacked by the other local priests. In it he provides much information concerning the history of his family.

(**5/13**) Oh, may Amun prolong his existence!
To inform the Governor of the events (14) what happened to my father.

In the 4th year[4] of Perᶜo[5] Psammetk the elder,[6] Ptores[7] was in the charge of Peteesi son of 'Ankhsheshonk, (15) the Master of the Shipping, from the southern guard-house of Menfi[8] to Suan.[9]

(Now) Peteesi son of 'Ankhsheshonk, the Master of the Shipping, (16) was son of a priest of Amenra'senter . He had been brought to Perᶜo's house before he became priest of Amun; he became (17) priest of Harshafe, and he became priest of Sobk. And he had a colleague, son of his father's younger brother, named Peteesi son of Ieturou, who (18) was a second to Peteesi, the Master of the Shipping: he it was that inspected from the southern guard-house to Suan.

(Now) in (19) the 4th year of Perᶜo Psammetk, Peteesi son of 'Ankhsheshonk, the Master of the Shipping, went before Perᶜo, and said: 'My great lord, (20) Oh, may he make the duration of Preᶜ! I am grown old: may this good thing be done to me before Perᶜo. I have a colleague named Peteesi son of (6/1) Ieturoti; he it is that administers Ptorés, and fosters its silver and its *boti*-corn: and it has come to pass that Ptores is very prosperous: (2) its silver and its boti have made one into one-and-a-half. Let him be brought before Perᶜo, let a good thing be said to him before Perᶜo, let it be said to him, (3)"Ptores is committed to you," it being committed to me also—he being able to make levy thereby.'

Peteesi son of Ieturou was brought before Perᶜo, and Perᶜo said to him: (4) 'The Master of the Shipping has told me what a marvel of a man you are.' And Perᶜo said, Let a ship be given him, let a chariot be given him. (5) And Perᶜo said to him, You go inspecting to Ptores: I will cause it to be reckoned with you. Said Peteesi, ' My great lord, it has been committed (6) to Peteesi, the Master of the Shipping.' (But) Perᶜo said to him, 'It is committed to him also together with you: except that they shall tell its account with you.' And they gave him gold and byssus (7) before Perᶜo.

Peteesi son of Ieturou came southward, inspecting, from the southern guard-house to Suan; (8) (but) Peteesi son of ᶜAnkhsheshonk, the Master of the Shipping, settled in Hnes, and report was rendered to him of everything that happened in Ptores.

(9) Peteesi soii of Ieturou reached Teuzoi:[10] he went to the temple and inspected every place that was in the temple of (10) Teuzoi. And behold he found the temple of Teuzoi to be in the style of a very large House, but that it was short (11) of men: he found not a man in the temple except one aged priest and a (shrine)-opener. And Peteesi son of Ieturou caused (12) the priest to be brought, and said to him, 'Behold, since you are not deficient in age, tell me, please, the manner in which this town has been destroyed.'

(13) And the priest said to him, 'The thing has happened (in this way): No man was priest here except the priests of Amenra'senter; (14) but your ancestors were priests here, and they made this shrine glorious with all things: endowment-estates in abundance (15) were appropriated to Amun of Teuzoi, and this House was spoken of as the first seat of Amenra'senter. (16) When that evil time came the great shrines of Kemi were made to pay taxes, and this town was burdened with (17) heavy taxes: the people could not pay the taxes with which they were burdened, and they departed away.

---

4   660 BCE.
5   Pharaoh.
6   Psamtik I.
7   Per-Hathor.
8   Memphis.
9   A town at the southernmost border of Egypt.
10   Tayu-djayet.

And behold, though discharge has been made (18) to the great shrines of Kemi, they come to us, saying, "Produce (your) taxes" until now.'

(19) Peteesi son of Ieturou went down to Hnes, he stood before Peteesi, the Master of the Shipping, and told him the whole condition which he had found (20) to have befallen Teuzoi, and he told him all the events that the old priest whom he found in Teuzoi had told him, and he said to him, 'This priest said to me, "No (21) man was priest here except the priests of Amenraesenter."'

And Peteesi, the Master of the Shipping, said to him, 'As Amenraᶜsenter lives, this has all happened (indeed): (7/1) everything that you tell me I used to hear from the mouth of our notables/ He caused the scribes of the nome and the agents to be fetched, (2) he caused the men to be fetched whom he could question, and they were all questioned before the Master of the Shipping, saying, 'Teuzoi, were taxes customarily to be paid (3) from it before that evil time took place?' And they all agreed, saying, 'Nothing on earth used to be paid therefrom: it is one of the great Houses (4) of this nome.' And the Master of the Shipping caused them to receive a severe beating on account of it, saying, 'You did never tell me, saying, (5)"We are causing it to be paid."' And the Master of the Shipping said to Peteesi son of Ieturou, 'Go, let a writing be taken for the things that have been paid from Teuzoi since discharge was made to the (6) great fanes of Ptores; let the (amount) be given to the priests of Amun of Teuzoi.'

Peteesi son of Ieturou came to Teuzoi, (7) he caused the men to be brought who did handicraft, and gave them 200 pieces of refined silver and 20 pieces of gold, he caused them to make them into cups of silver and gold for Amun, he caused them to make (8) the shrine of Amun upon-the-great-place. He caused the priests, the shrine-openers, and the other classes of men who (are qualified to) enter the temple to be brought to Teuzoi; (9) (even) if there was a man among them who had gone as far as Ne he caused all to be brought. He caused the endowment-estates which he found to have been appropriated to Amun to be given, (10) and he caused 1,000 aruras[11] to be added to the endowment-estates of Amun. He caused offerings and linen to be laid before Amun and before Usiri[12] of Ieruoz. He made (11) Teuzoi glorious like one of the great shrines of Ptores. He made his children priests[8] of Amun of Teuzoi, and he caused (12) a house to be built measuring 40 divine cubits by 40 divine cubits, with a rope of land about it for (its) courtyard; and he caused (13) his temple-place to be built.

He went to Ptores, inspecting, and reached Ieb,[13] he caused (14) a tablet of stone of Ieb to be quarried and the blocks for two statues of *temgy*-stone, and caused (15) them to be brought to Teuzoi, He came north and reached Teuzoi, he caused the granite-workers, the (16) engravers, the scribes of the House of Life, and the draughtsmen to be brought. He caused the good deeds that he had done in Teuzoi to be put upon (17) the tablet, and he caused his two statues of *temgy*-stone to be made, kneeling on their feet, a figure (18) of Amun being in the lap of the one and a figure of Usiri in the lap of the other statue; he caused one to be placed (19) at the entrance of the shrine of Amun, he caused the other to be placed at the entrance of the shrine of Usiri.

Peteesi son of (20) Ieturou went down to Hnes and stood before the Master of the Shipping, and made report to him of everything that he had done in Teuzoi. (8/1) And Peteesi, the Master of the

---

11   About 2 sq. miles.
12   Osiris.
13   Or Abu.

Shipping, said to him, 'Harshafe, king of the Two Lands, praise you! Amun shall give you its requital in benefit! You know the fact that the share of the prophet of Amun of Teuzoi (2) and his Ennead of deities belongs to me, and since you have chosen it as a dwelling I will write a title for you to the share of the prophet of Amun of Teuzoi and his Ennead of deities.' And the Master (3) of the Shipping caused a school-scribe to be fetched, and wrote a title for him to the share of the prophet of Amun of Teuzoi and his Ennead of deities.

Peteesi son of Ieturou came south, (4) he reached the nome of Pemze, inspecting. And he found a priest of Amenra⁣ᶜ⁣senter who had been sent by the priests of Amun for the pasturing (5) of cattle and geese which are furnished by the nome: his name was Haruoz son of Peftu⁣ᶜ⁣ubasti. And it happened that 'steward of the treasury of Amun' was the title given to the priest who was sent for the pasturing, (6) during the time he was sent for the pasturing. Peteesi son of Ieturou brought Haruoz son of Peftu⁣ᶜ⁣ubasti, the steward of the treasury of Amun, with him to Teuzoi, (7) he caused him to purify himself with him in his house which he had caused to be built in Teuzoi: he caused his wife and her female children to be brought (8) up, and they drank beer before them.

And Haruoz son of Peftu⁣ᶜ⁣ubasti saw a girl belonging to Peteesi named Nitemhe. And Haruoz (9) son of Peftu⁣ᶜ⁣ubasti said to Peteesi, 'Let his Honour cause me to find my employment. Behold his Honour is a priest of Amenra⁣ᶜ⁣senter; (10) my father used to be priest here in Teuzoi, and I will show to his Honour that he used to be priest here, I will bring the patents of my father (11) before his Honour. Let his Honour cause the girl Nitemhe to be given to me to wife.' And Peteesi said to him, 'Her time has not yet come. But act as priest of (12) Amenra⁣ᶜ⁣senter, and I will give her to you, and on every occasion on which the pasturing in Pemze is committed to you you shall stay at Teuzoi: (13) behold it is a wonder of a House, a House for a priest. There are not two classes of men in it beside priests and men who enter the temple.' And (14) Haruoz blessed (him) and said, 'It is well.'

In year 15[14] of Per⁣ᶜ⁣o-Psammetk, Ptores was exceedingly prosperous. Peteesi son of Ieturou was taken to the House of (15) Record, and its silver and its boti made one into two. Peteesi son of Ieturou was taken before Per⁣ᶜ⁣o: he was anointed with lotus-(oil), and Per⁣ᶜ⁣o said to him, 'Is there a good thing (16) of which you say, "Let it be done to me"?' And Peteesi said before Per⁣ᶜ⁣o, 'My father was priest of Amenra⁣ᶜ⁣senter, he was priest in the temples of the province of Ne,[15] (17) he was priest of Harshafe, he was priest of Sobk.' And Per⁣ᶜ⁣o called to the scribe in charge of letters, saying, 'Write a letter to the temples of which Peteesi son of Ieturou shall say (18)"My father was priest in them," saying, "Let Peteesi be priest in them if it were fitting."' And letters were written to the temples of which Peteesi said (19) 'My father was priest in them.' And Peteesi son of Ieturou was dismissed from before Per⁣ᶜ⁣o, and came south: he became priest of Harshafe, priest of Sobk of Sheti, priest of Amenra⁣ᶜ⁣senter, priest of Usiri, lord of Ebot, priest of Anhuri of Tin, and priest of Min.

And Peteesi son of Ieturou came north, inspecting, (9/1) and reached Pemze, and found Haruoz son of Peftu⁣ᶜ⁣ubasti, the priest of Amun who was sent for the pasturing; he came (2) to Teuzoi with Peteesi son of Ieturou, and Haruoz son of Peftu⁣ᶜ⁣ubasti brought the patents of his father to Peteesi, (3) and showed him the fact that Peftu⁣ᶜ⁣ubasti his father used to be priest of Anhuri of Teuzoi. And Peteesi caused (4) Haruoz son of Peftu⁣ᶜ⁣ubasti to be made priest of Amun of Teuzoi and gave him Nitemhe his daughter to wife.

---

14   649 BCE.
15   The nome of which Waset (Thebes) was the capital.

And Peteesi son of Ieturou went down (5) to Hnes; he caused his women and children to be brought on board (ship), and caused them to be brought to Ne. He reached Teuzoi, (6) and found Haruoz son of Peftuᶜubasti in Teuzoi. Peteesi went up to his house which is in Teuzoi, and said to Haruoz, 'It is (7) fitting to let us spend today in drinking beer before Amun in Teuzoi, before we go to Ne.' (8) Peteesi spent the day in drinking beer with his women and children and with Haruoz son of Peftuᶜubasti.

And Haruoz son of Peftuᶜubasti said to him, (9) 'Behold, his Honour goes to Ne: what are the things which his Honour bids me do?' And Peteesi said to him, (10) 'Settle here in Teuzoi. I will go and cause the priests of Amun to make your account, and I will give them the amount (11) that shall remain against you: and (any) balance (due to you) beyond the amount that reaches you when the pasturing is committed to you I will cause to reach you while you are settled (12) here in Teuzoi, without your suffering fatigue, Behold, mine is the share of the prophet of Amun of Teuzoi, together with other sixteen shares. (13) But you are he that shall perform service to Amun and his Ennead of deities, and the fifth part of the endowment revenues of Amun shall be given to you. But you shall pay to me the amount that (14) shall remain against you.'

And Nitemhe daughter of Peteesi wept, saying, 'Take me to Ne with you.' And Peteesi said to her, (15) 'Why would you go to Ne? I will leave you with your life good beyond all the girls. (16) Take to you this house which is here in Teuzoi, and name a prophet's share for which you desire me to write you a title.' And Haruoz son of Peftuᶜubasti, (17) her husband, said, 'Let his Honour write her a title to the share of the prophet of Khons.' And Peteesi wrote her a title to the share of the prophet of Khons.

Peteesi (18) sailed to Ne with his women and his children, and Haruoz son of Peftuᶜubasti settled in Teuzoi with Nitemhe (19) daughter of Peteesi, doing service to Amun and his cycle of deities, while the fifth part of the endowment revenues were given to him. And Peteesi son of Ieturou reached Ne, (20) he caused his women and his children to go up to Ne, and placed them in the house of his father which was in Ne.

In year 8[16] of Perᶜo (10/1) Psammetk Peteesi son of ᶜAnkhsheshonk, the Master of the Shipping, went to his fathers. And Perᶜo caused Peteesi son of Ieturou to be brought, and said to him, Ptores (2) is committed to you; it is you that shall be able to administer it.' And Peteesi said before Perᶜo, 'As your face lives, I shall be able to administer it if there be also a noble (3) to whom it is committed together with me.' And Perᶜo said to him, 'Tell me, pray, the noble of whom you say, "Let it be entrusted to him."' And Peteesi said, ' My great lord, (4) Peteesi son of ᶜAnkhsheshonk, the Master of the Shipping, has his son; he is a man of the household of Perᶜo, and a marvel of a man exceedingly; his name is Semtutefnakhti: (5) Perᶜo will find that he is a marvel of a man. Let Perᶜo cause the office of his father to be committed to him.' And Perᶜo questioned the nobles concerning it, and they agreed, saying before Perᶜo, 'Let it be done, he is a marvel of a man.'

And Perᶜo made Semtutefnakhti Master of the Shipping, and Ptores was committed to him again even as it had been to his father. And Semtutefnakhti the Master of the Shipping was dismissed from before Perᶜo, and came to Hnes. (8) And he said to Peteesi son of Ieturou, 'Depart south, inspect in the province, and let nothing spoil: I will stay here in Hnes (9) until the Master of the Shipping be buried.'

---

16   646 BCE.

And Peteesi son of Ieturou came south inspecting again according to his (former) manner. And Peteesi the Master of the Shipping remained (10) seventy days lying in state, and was buried in his tomb in Pusirer. ... Now Peteesi son of Ieturou was administering Ptores, (11) its account was made with him yearly, and it did not deteriorate, for what he did was to add silver and spelt to it each year.

In year 19[17] of Per‛o (12) Psammetk the account of the land was made with Peteesi, and its account was good. And Per‛o said to him, 'Is there a thing of which you say "Let it be done"?' And Peteesi said (13) before Per‛o, 'Let this good thing be done to me before Per‛o. I am aged in years, let me be dismissed from before Per‛o, (for) I shall not be able to endure (14) fatigue.' And Per‛o said to him, 'Have you a son who knows how to administer?' And he said before Per‛o, 'Many are the servants of Per‛o who shall be able to administer; (15) they will administer under the hand of the Master of the Shipping, and will not allow a thing to spoil.' And Per‛o said to him, 'Is there property that you desire?' And Peteesi said, 'May (16) Per‛o be enriched! There is no good thing that Per‛o has not caused to be done to me.' And Per‛o said to Semtutefnakhti the Master of the Shipping, 'Consider this that Peteesi (17) says, saying, "I am old in years, let me be dismissed." If I shall have sent him away will you be able to administer Ptores?' And Semtutefnakhti said to him, (18) 'Let him be dismissed, my great lord—he is our father—spending the balance of his life resting: but he shall yet be our guardian.'

(19) Peteesi son of Ieturou was dismissed from before Per‛o, and came south and reached Teuzoi. He went up and prayed before Amun, and caused burnt sacrifice (20) and drink-offering to be made before Amun, and was conveyed to his house which was in Teuzoi. He purified himself therein with Haruoz son of Peftu‛ubasti, and detailed the affair (21) to Haruoz, saying, 'I have caused myself to be dismissed from before Per‛o.' And Haruoz said, 'Let [not] these priests who are here know it, they are rascals.' And Peteesi said to him, 'Behold (**11**/1) I will take you to Semtutefnakhti the Master of the Shipping, and the thing that is unseemly to you, you shall go and tell it to him.' And Peteesi sent for the elder brethren of (2) the priests, and caused them to purify themselves before him; he spent days purified in Teuzoi, and sailed to Ne.

In the 31st year,[18] Pamenhotp,[19] the *boti* (3) that had resulted to the endowment-estate of Amun of Teuzoi was brought up and turned out in front of the temple. The priests assembled at the temple. They said, 'Tell (us) please, as Pre‛ lives! (4) Shall he still take the fifth of the divine endowment? this outcast of a southerner is in our power.' They charged some youths, rascally fellows, saying, 'Come with (5) your staves in the evening, lie down on the face of this *boti*, and bury your staves in it till the morning. Now it happened that there were two boys of (6) Haruoz son of Peftu‛ubasti who were grown up: and in the morning the priests came to the temple to divide the corn to the orders, and the two boys of Haruoz son of Peftu‛ubasti (7) came to the temple, saying, 'Let the fifth part be measured'; then the young priests drew out their staves from the corn and surrounded the two sons of Haruoz, and gave (8) them a beating. They fled up to the holy place before them, (but) they (also) ran up after them: and lo they caught them at the entrance of the shrine of Amun, and slew (9) them with beating and cast them into a store-chamber in the interior of the stone platform.

---

17   645 BCE.
18   633 BCE.
19   The harvest month (Phamenoth).

Now it happened that Haruoz son of Peftuᶜubasti was not in Teuzoi; (10) he was on the west in the villages of Tkohi. But Nitemhe daughter of Peteesi, the mother of the two boys, made fast her house upon her. And when (11) Haruoz son of Peftuᶜubasti heard that his two children had been slain he made his raiment into mourning, and went to the Chief of Police of Tkohi and informed him of it. The Chief (12) of Police collected the soldiers of Tkohi and took them to Teuzoi, armed with their shields and spears, and he set a watch about (13) the house in which Nitemhe was.

And Haruoz hastened to Ne in his mourning-raiment. And when Haruoz came to Peteesi, Peteesi embarked on his ship (14) with his children and his people, and came down (the river). And when he reached Teuzoi he found no man on earth in Teuzoi except the men of the Chief of Police who were on guard (15) around the house in which Nitemhe was. And Peteesi went to the temple, (but) found not a man in the temple except two (16) aged priests and one shrine-opener. They fled to the holy place from Peteesi; and Peteesi put men to guard them, and sent to Hnes to Semtutefnakhti the (17) Master of the Shipping concerning all the events that had happened while Peteesi was in Teuzoi.

And the Master of the Shipping caused a Captain of the host to come, saying, 'Go, seize every man of whom Peteesi shall (18) say to you, "Let them be seized."' The Captain came to Teuzoi, and Peteesi caused the two priests to be seized, and he went down the river with them to the house of Perᶜo. (19) And Peteesi told before Perᶜo everything that had been done. And Perᶜo caused punishment to be inflicted on the two priests.

Peteesi was dismissed from before Perᶜo, and reached Hnes, (20) and stood with the Master of the Shipping. And Semtutefnakhti the Master of the Shipping said to him, 'I have heard the things that have been done to you by these outcasts of evil men, scum of men of Teuzoi, whom you did make (21) rich.'/ And Peteesi said to him, 'Has not the detector of crime heard that he who nurtures the wolf shall die by it? As Preᶜ lives, this is what has befallen me with the priests of Amun (12/1) of Teuzoi.'

Now it happened that Haruoz son of Peftuᶜubasti was in Hnes with Peteesi, and Peteesi took the hand of Haruoz and brought him (2) before the Master of the Shipping, saying, 'Behold, my brother who is in Teuzoi; let the Master of the Shipping charge the Chief of Police of Tkohi (3) and the commissary of Tkohi to cause him to be protected.' And Semtutefnakhti said to him, 'I will charge every man belonging to me, saying, 'The man of Teuzoi (4) that you shall find, let him be brought to me that I may cause him to die in the prison in Hnes.'

But Peteesi said to him, 'Let not the Master of the Shipping do so: (5) as Amun lives, and the breath of the Master of the Shipping prospers! I will not go to Ne without having furnished Teuzoi and brought its (6) people again into it.' And the Master of the Shipping said, 'I have caused Harshafe, king of the two lands, to be named when it is said "Your love that you had to Teuzoi (7) it has not yet ceased."' And Peteesi said to him, 'You have imagined to yourself. As your breath prospers! exceeding great gods are they that are in it, it is a house to which comes (8) Amenraᶜsenter the great god: many are the divine things that I have known in it.'

The Master of the Shipping dismissed Peteesi. He came southward, and reached (9) Teuzoi, and spent (some) days in Teuzoi. And it befell that the Chief of Police came to Teuzoi with fifty fighting men: and he came (10) before Peteesi and did obeisance. And the Chief of Police said to Peteesi, 'What grievous thing is this, that his Honour, the detector of crime, has caused the Master of the Shipping to send to me, saying, (11)"Let a guard be kept over the people of Peteesi who shall happen to be in Teuzoi." Is not his Honour he that has nurtured us? From the time that I heard that (12) these priests had done injury did I not come instantly and have a watch set about this house, because they were (13) molesting this great lady? If his Honour say to me, "Come even to Ne," can I refuse to come ?'

And Peteesi said to him, 'Amun shall make you live! (14) I caused the Master of the Shipping to send to you to prevent another task being laid upon you. Do this business for me: depart, go round in the nome (15) of Pemze and the nome of Hartai seeking for the men of Teuzoi whom you shall find: gather them to the place (16) to which they shall desire me to come in order to make oath to them not to cause anything to be done to them; and tell them, saying, "The injury that you have done, I have caused (17) its requital to be done to you." Is it right to cause Amun to slay the rest of these youths and let his town be destroyed?'

And Peteesi took the hand of the Chief of Police (18) and took him into the dromos of Amun. He bound himself by oath before him, saying, 'All men that you shall bring me, if they come to Teuzoi, I will not allow a mischief to be done to them (19) I will bind myself by oath to them not to cause a mischief to be done to them. I have bound myself by oath before you, because they would have said, "The chief of police has sought for (20) us to cause a mischief to be done to us."

The Chief of Police prostrated himself upon the ground and did obeisance. And the Chief of Police went out to the places of the nome of (21) Pemze, the nome of Khmun, the nome of Hartai: he gathered the men of Teuzoi to Hartai. The Chief of Police came to (13/1) Teuzoi and reported to Peteesi son of Ieturou, saying, 'I reached as far as Khmun, and I left not a man of Teuzoi, as far as Khmun, until I brought him to Hartai, the place to which they agreed (2) in saying, "Let an oath be sworn to us in it. Let Essemteu son of Peteesi come and bind himself by oath to us, or, if not (him, then) one of the youths that is with his Honour."' And Peteesi said, 'As Amun lives! it is I (3) myself that will come.' Peteesi sailed to Hartai, and swore an oath to the priests and the shrine-openers and every man that had come to Teuzoi, saying, 'I will not cause a thing to be done to you on account of a thing (4) that is past.'

Peteesi came to Teuzoi with the men of Teuzoi whom he had found, and all their women and children came. Peteesi caused the priests to be assembled (5) at the temple, and said to them, 'Oh, may they live! Have I done to you a thing beyond a thing that you desired? Behold, when I was sent (officially) did I do a thing in the manner of one in authority? (6) You said to me, "Four stipends is that which is given to the prophet of Hor, lord of Hnes, and the prophet of Anup, lord of Hartai," and I said to you, "That is what you shall give to me." You said (7) "One stipend is given as the share of a prophet," and I said to you, "That is what you give." I have stipend of four in the name of the share of the prophet of Amun, and I have besides sixteen stipends in the name (8) of the gods to whom I have been prophet, making in all twenty stipends. Twenty is the number of priests which you make up for one order: and one order of priests makes the fifth part of the divine endowment.'

The priests placed their clothes (9) to their necks, they prostrated themselves on the ground before Peteesi, and said, 'Know we not that his Honour is he that has made us to live, when his Honour established our (10) city, and you did cause it to be equal to the great Houses of Kemi. These youths who left the path, let his Honour cause them to be brought, let (11) them be cast into a furnace. The good things that his Honour has done to Amun remain to eternity.'

And Peteesi said, 'The good deeds that I have done before Amun, I know the fact: it is not that I (12) did them to your fathers: I did them to Amun. These priests who slew my boys, shall I not be able to cause them to be brought? Except that I have caused (13) punishment to be inflicted upon their fathers, and have let them go, (I) together with the god. Behold, since I am overcome by you (even) while my strength exists and while I live, (14) a time may come when the son of mine who shall be here shall be weaker than you, so that you shall be able to exclude him and take his shares which are in this city. (15) Does any know the event? This tablet which I caused to be made and taken to the holy place, I had it made before I became priest, before (16) a title had been written for me to those shares of prophets which are in this city; and you will be able to say, 'You were not priest upon it.'

And the priests said to him, 'What is the thing of which his Honour (17) says "Do it"? And Peteesi son of Ieturou said to them, 'I will cause a tablet to be made upon the stone platform on the way by which Amun goes to the cleansing-place, (18) I will set the good deeds which I did to Amun upon it, and I will set my priestly offices upon it.' And the priests said, 'All things that are (19) favourable to the affairs of his Honour let them be done. We shall know the fact that we are alive by means of his Honour, if his Honour cause it to be done.'

And Peteesi caused the scribes of the House of Life (20) and the draughtsmen to be brought, he caused the tablet to be written upon the stone platform, saying, 'In case the priests and the notables who shall come to inspect in the temple shall see (14/1) it.'

Peteesi son of Ieturou rode to the shore, saying, 'I will sail to go to Ne.' (2) But Nitemhe his daughter wept before him, saying, 'The boys who were slain they are in the temple, they have not been brought out.' (3) And Peteesi went to the temple and caused them to seek for the two boys; they found them in a store-chamber in the holy place, and he had them (4) brought down, linen was put upon them, and a great lamentation took place in the city, and the boys were buried.

And Peteesi (5) was about to go on board ship: but Nitemhe wept before him, saying, 'Take me to Ne with you; otherwise (6) these priests will cause me to be slain.' And Peteesi said to her, 'They cannot. As Amun lives, never again shall they cease to fear you.' (7) And Nitemhe said, 'If it be that you will cause us to be here, let Essemteu son of Peteesi stay here with me, doing service (8) to Amun.' And Peteesi caused Essemteu son of Peteesi to stay in Teuzoi, and said to him, 'Take to yourself the share of the prophet of Amun of Teuzoi and his Ennead of gods.' (9) And Peteesi caused a papyrus to be brought, and wrote (a title) for Essemteu son of Peteesi to the offices of prophet of Amun in Teuzoi and his Ennead of gods. (10) And Essemteu stayed in Teuzoi with Nitemhe his sister and Haruoz her husband.

And Essemteu son of Peteesi dwelt in Teuzoi (11) doing service to Amun and his Ennead of gods, and the fifth part of the divine endowment of Amun was given to him. And Essemteu son of Peteesi went and stood before (12) Semtutefnakhti, the Master of the Shipping, and said to him, 'I am he whom Peteesi set in Teuzoi to do service to Amun and his Ennead of gods. He wrote me (a title) to (13) the share of the prophet of Amun and his Ennead of gods.' And the Master of the Shipping caused a seal-ring of gold .... to be given to Essemteu, and said to him, 'I have not caused (14) byssus to be given you because the succession to the linen of Amun belongs to you. Do not fail to tell me your business on [every] occasion.' Essemteu son of Peteesi spent the (15) days that he spent in life doing service to Amun and his Ennead of gods, and they gave him the fifth part of the divine endowment of Amun.

And Essemteu went to his fathers, (16) and Peteesi son of Essemteu, his son, succeeded him. He performed service to Amun and his Ennead of gods, and the fifth part of the divine endowment of Amun was given to him likewise.

And in the 4th year[20] of (17) Per‘o Psammetk Nefrebre‘,[21] messages were sent to the great temples of Upper and Lower Egypt, saying, 'Per‘o goes to the land of Khor:[22] let (18) the priests come with the bouquets of the gods of Kemi to take them to the land of Khor with Per‘o.' And a message was sent to Teuzoi, (19) saying, 'Let a priest come with the bouquet of Amun to go to the land of Khor with Per‘o.' And the priests assembled and agreed in (20) saying to Peteesi son of Essemteu, 'You are he that are meet to go to the land of Khor with Per‘o: there is no man [here] in this city who (21) can go to the land of Khor except you. Behold, you are a scribe of the House of Life: there is not a thing that they shall ask you to which there is not a suitable answer. (22) For you are the prophet of Amun, and the prophets of the great gods of Kemi are they who are going to the land of Khor with Per‘o.' They (15/1) persuaded Peteesi to go to the land of Khor with Per‘o, and he equipped himself (for the journey).

Peteesi son of Essemteu went to the land of Khor, no man (2) accompanying him except his servant and one guard named Usirmose. And when the priests knew that Peteesi had gone to the land of Khor with Per‘o (3) they went to Haruoz son of Harkhebi, a priest of Sobk, who was ruler of Hnes, and said to him, 'Does his Honour know the fact that the share of the prophet of Amun of Teuzoi is Per‘o's share, and it belongs to (4) his Honour? Now, Peteesi son of Ieturou, a priest of Amun, took it when he was Ruler in Hnes, and behold it is held by his sons son until now.' And Haruoz son of Harkhebi said to them, 'Where is he, his son?' (5) and the priests said to him, 'We have caused him to go to the land of Khor with Per‘o. Let Ptahnufi son of Haruoz come to Teuzoi, that we may write him a title to the share of the prophet of Amun.' And Haruoz made (6) Ptahntifi son of Haruoz, his son, come to Teuzoi, and they wrote him a title to the share of the prophet of Amun of Teuzoi. They divided the other sixteen shares to the four orders, four shares to each order. And they went to fetch (7) Ptahnufi son of Haruoz, and brought him and caused him to anoint the hands and to perform service to Amun.

Peteesi son of Essemteu came down from the land of Khor (8) and reached Teuzoi, and everything that the priests had done was told to him. Peteesi hastened northward to the gate of the House of Per‘o, but he was treated contemptuously, and they said to him, 'Destruction! Per‘o is (9) sick, Per‘o does not come out.' And Peteesi made plea to the judges. They brought Ptahnfifi son of Haruoz, and their declarations were written in the House of Judgement, (10) saying, 'This share which Ptahnfifi has taken, his father being Master in Hnes, is Per‘o's share.' Peteesi son of Essemteu spent many days in the House of Judgement (11) (striving) with Ptahnufi son of Haruoz.

And Peteesi was worsted in the House of Judgement, and came south; and he went away to Ne, saying, 'I go to let my brethren (12) who are in Ne know it,' and found the sons of Peteesi son of Ieturou who were priests of Amun in Ne; and he told them every event that happened to him with the priests of Amun of (13) Teuzoi. And they took Peteesi and made him stand before the priests of Amun, and the priests of Amun said to him, 'What is it of which you say, "Do it"? It has befallen that report has been sent (14) to the priests of Amun, saying, "Per‘o Psammetk Nefrebre‘ has deceased." Behold, when they said "Per‘o has deceased" we were about to send to the House of Per‘o concerning everything (15) that these priests of Amun have done to you: you should make plea to these (judges)

20   590 BCE.
21   Psamtik II.
22   Western Asia.

who have given their declarations in writing in the House of Judgement against this priest of Sobk who takes of your share, (16) for they will not be able to have leisure to finish an affair of yours in this length of time.'

The priests caused 5 pieces of silver to be given to Peteesi, and his brethren gave him five more, in all 10 pieces of silver, and they said to him, 'Go to the House (17) of Judgement against this man who takes of your share; when you spend this silver, come that we may give you other silver.'

Peteesi son of Essemteu came north (18) and reached Teuzoi, and the men with whom he stood said to him, 'There is no profit in going to the House of Judgement; your adversary in speech is richer than you. If (19) there be a hundred pieces of silver in your hand he will defeat you.' And they persuaded Peteesi not to go to the House of Judgement. The priests did not give stipend (20) for the sixteen shares which the priests had divided to the orders, but the priests who happened to enter did service in their name, and stipend of four was given to Ptahnufi (**16**/1) in the name of the share of the prophet of Amun, from the first year[23] of Per⁽ᶜ⁾o Uehabre⁽ᶜ⁾[24] to the fifteenth year[25] of Per⁽ᶜ⁾o Ahmosi.[26]

In the 15th year of Ahmosi, the Superintendent of farm-land came (2) to Hnes, and caused the scribes of the nome of Hnes to be brought, and said to them, 'Is there a *ꞗanakh* belonging to Harmakher son of Ptahertais (3) in this nome? for the Superintendent of farm-land is ardent against Harmakher.' And Peftu⁽ᶜ⁾ubasti son of Khepekhrat, a scribe of the nome, who was not a priest of Amun of (4) Teuzoi, said to him, 'There is no *ꞗanakh* belonging to Harmakher son of Ptahertais in this nome. But if the Superintendent of farmland desires to cause mischief to be done (5) to Harmakher, I can cause a thing to be done to him for which he will be more ardent than for his *ꞗanakh*.' The Superintendent of farmland said to him, 'Tell it,' and Peftu⁽ᶜ⁾ubasti said to him, 'There is not a man (6) on earth belonging to Harmakher except these priests of Amun of Teuzoi: for he made his brethren into priests of (7) Amun of Teuzoi. There is an island held by the priests of Amun of Teuzoi in which 484 aruras are appropriated to them, (but) it will complete 1000 aruras. (When) the statue of Per⁽ᶜ⁾o Ahmosi was brought to Teuzoi (8) he (Harmakher) caused Ptahertais son of Meibptah to act for him as prophet of the statue, and he caused 120 aruras to be appropriated to the statue of Per⁽ᶜ⁾o, while not a single arura was given (9) to the statue of Per⁽ᶜ⁾o which was brought to Hnes.'

The Superintendent of farm-land sailed southward and reached the island of Teuzoi. He moored at (10) its extremity, and caused two land-measurers to go up (on shore) and go round the island. They included the sands and the trees in the island, and (11) made it 929 aruras. He took away the island from Teuzoi. The 120 aruras belonging to the statue were in the Field of Shekeke, a place (so-called), and he took them away (12) also.

The Superintendent of farm-land called to the captain of the host Mananuehabre⁽ᶜ⁾, saying, 'Let the priests of Amun of Teuzoi give 4,000 measures of corn...........of the harvest (13) of this island which was held by them.' The captain of the host came to Teuzoi, and took possession of the granary, and caused all the corn that he found in the granary and in the houses to be carried (14) to the entrance of the temple. It was put under seal at the entrance of the temple.

---

23 589 BCE.
24 Haiibre⁽ᶜ⁾.
25 556 BCE.
26 Ahmose II.

The priests hastened northward to the entry of the House of Perᶜo, and (15) the shrine-opener of Ptah, in whose house they purified themselves, said to them, 'There is no man belonging to Perᶜo who can defend you except Khelkhons son of Hor, a man who petitions (16) Perᶜo (even) in the closet. They do not say "there is a man within the House of Perᶜo who is hearkened to in a thing as he is."' They made (17) the shrine-opener of Ptah go to fetch Harkhebi the eunuch of Khelkhons, and they stood with him and said to him, 'If Khelkhons defend us in our affairs and (18) cause this island which is appropriated to Amun to be given to us, we will give him 300 artabas of boti, 200 hins of *tekem* oil, 50 hins of honey, and 30 geese .... as his (19) stipend yearly.'

Harkhebi went and told it to Khelkhons, (but) Khelkhons said, 'These southerners, the gape of their mouths is great. Let them give them (20) to me this year; (otherwise) when they know that I have saved them they will not pay me. Tell them that I act as priest of Hor of Puto,[27] and I have my brother a priest (21) of Hor-in-Pe. Write him a title to an office of prophet of your House, and write for him to give (him) these things as its levy each year, (17/1) that I may protect you in your affairs.'

Now it befell that Nekumosi son of Ptahntifi, the priest of Sobk, who was prophet of Amun of Teuzoi, was in Menfi. (2) The priests went to him, and said to him, 'Nekumosi, the endowment-state of Amun of Teuzoi has been taken back by the Superintendent of farm-land to the *u*-land. (3) Are you able to protect us? If not, behold, when we went to a (certain) magnate he said to us, "Write me a title to the share of the prophet of Amun (4) that I may protect you in every affair of yours." For you know the fact that we were they who wrote your father Ptahnfifi son of Haruoz a title (5) to the share of the prophet of Amun, when his father Haruoz son of Harkhebi was ruler of Hnes, though it is not a share that belonged to him. We (6) gave it to him, saying, "He will protect us."' And Nekumosi son of Ptahnufi said to them, 'Go, write a title for any man that will protect you to the share of (7) the prophet of Amun. Sobk is with you! bring me the document that you shall make that I may subscribe to it.'

And the priests went to Harkhebi (8) the son of Ienharou, the man of Khelkhons, and they wrote a title to the share of the prophet of Amun to Psammetkmenempe son of Hor, the brother of Khelkhons, (9) and they took the writing to Khelkhons. (Then) Khelkhons son of Hor pleaded before Perᶜo, saying, 'My father used to act as (10) prophet of Amun of Teuzoi, a notable House in the nome of Hnes. The Superintendent of farm-land went to it and took away (11) its endowment-state, and caused everything that was in the city to be seized, saying, "I will make them give the harvest of the land," which he had taken away.'

(12) The Superintendent of farm-land was brought before Perᶜo, and said, 'My great lord, I found a river-island at the centre of Teuzoi, and (13) the nome-scribes said to me, "It will make 1,000 aruras.' I had it measured, and it made 929 aruras. As the face of Perᶜo lives, (14) it is not fitting that it be given as endowment-estate to god or goddess, it will be proper for Perᶜo. It will come to 20 measures of boti (15).............to one arura. I asked the scribes, saying, "Is it appropriated to Amun of Teuzoi?" and they said to me, "484½ aruras (16) are appropriated to Amun in it." I said to the priests of Amun, "Come, that I may cause them to be given you adjoining your endowment-estate (17) which is in the Field on the mainland of Teuzoi." But they did not listen to me. As to Amun of Teuzoi, it was the endowment of (18) a very great House that I found in his occupation. I found 33

---

27   Buto.

measures of boti...........appropriated to Amun of Teuzoi daily. I will (19) obtain them in full from him (?).'

Much disputing took place between Khelkhons and the Superintendent of farm-land before Per⁽o: the (20) end was that the Superintendent of farm-land could not be dispossessed of the island of Teuzoi. But Khelkhons caused him to make a letter (**18**/1) of divine inspiration to cause the 484½ aruras to be given as the equivalent of the 484½ aruras which had been found (2) appropriated to the endowment-estate of Amun on the island of Teuzoi, adjoining the endowment-estate of Amun which was (in) the Field of the mainland of Teuzoi, (3) and to cause remission to be made of the corn that had been brought out of Teuzoi, they saying that it would be taken from the harvest (4) of the island of Teuzoi, which had been confiscated.

Psammetkmenempe son of Hor, the brother of Khelkhons, came to Teuzoi, he anointed (5) *khemen*, he performed service to Amun, and the things were given him of which they had said to Khelkhons, 'We will give them to you.' And Psammetkmenempe said to them, (6) 'This papyrus which you made me for the share of the prophet of Amun, I took it to the House of Judgement, and a judge said to me, "It is invalidated, (7) because of the fact that these priests will say to you, 'Had this share no owner?' Its owner can come to you (8) another time and say, 'It is mine' and he will be justified against you." Behold, I have heard saying, "This priest of Sobk in whose possession it was, the priests (9) wrote him a title for it likewise, when his father was Master in Hnes." Had it not an owner before him?' Then (10) Zeubestef⁽onkh son of Aho the *le-shoni* said to him, 'I will bring you its owner and make him write you a title to it.'

Now it befell that Peteesi son of (11) Essemteu had gone to his fathers in year 13²⁸ of Per⁽o Uehabre⁽, and Essemteu his son was (living). A man came to Essemteu, (12) saying, 'They are coming to you to make you write a title to the share of the prophet of Amun for Psammetkmenempe son of Hor by force.' And Essemteu went away (13) with his wife and children to a boat by night, and went to Khmun.

And when the next day came the (14) priests and the *le-shoni* heard it; they went to his house and took everything that belonged to him, and pulled down his house and his temple-place: they caused (15) a stonemason to be brought, and made him deface the tablet which Peteesi son of Ieturou had caused to be made upon the stone platform.

They went (16) to the other tablet, of stone of Ieb, which was in the holy place, saying, 'We will have it defaced,' (but) the stonemason said, 'I cannot (17) deface it: it is a granite- worker (only) that can deface (it): my tools will slip.' And a priest said, 'Let it alone: behold, no (18) man sees it; moreover, he caused it to be made before he had acted as priest, before Peteesi the Master of the Shipping had written him a title (19) to the share of the prophet of Amun. We can repel him by means of it, saying, "Your father did not act as prophet of Amun."' (So) they left the tablet of (20) stone of Ieb and did not deface it.

They went to his two statues of *temgi*-stone, one at the entrance of the chapel (21) of Amun, its figure of Amun being in its lap, and cast it into the river; and they went to the other, which was in the House of Usiri at the entrance of the chapel of Usiri, (22) its figure of Usiri being in its lap, and cast it into the river.

---

28   577 BCE.

And Essemteu son of Peteesi heard everything that the priests had done to him in (**19**/1) Teuzoi. Now it befell that there was a scribe of accounts belonging to the Superintendent of the treasury named Imhotp son of Pshenesi, whom the Superintendent of the treasury had sent (2) to make account of the affairs of Khmun. Essemteu son of Peteesi said to his son Peteesi, 'Behold, since you are a scribe, go and write with Imhotp son of Pshenesi (3) this scribe of accounts belonging to the Superintendent of the treasury. When he knows your necessity he will be able to make plea to the Superintendent of the treasury for you, and cause us to be protected.'

(4) Peteesi went and wrote with Imhotp son of Pshenesi, and he finished the affairs which he had been sent to Khmun to record in writing. I came to Menfi (5) with Imhotp, and he caused the scribes of the Superintendent of the treasury to write the affairs of Khmun, and he made report of them to the Superintendent of the treasury. And the Superintendent of the treasury spoke a good word to him, (6) and Imhotp made plea to the Superintendent of the treasury, saying, 'I have a brother, a priest of Amun of Teuzoi. Zeubestefonkh son of Aho, the *le-shoni* of Amun of (7) Teuzoi, went with his brethren to his house and his temple-place, and took everything that belonged to him, and pulled down his house and his temple-place.'

(8) The Superintendent of the treasury caused a letter to be written to Harbes son of Hanef-eu, the (Sheikh) of Hnes, saying, 'The scribe Imhotp (9) son of Pshenesi, who is under me, has made plea to me, saying, "I have a brother a priest of Amun of Teuzoi, whose name is Peteesi son of Essemteu. Zeubestefonkh son of Aho, (10) the *le-shoni* of Amun of Teuzoi, went with his brethren to his house and temple-place, and took everything that was in them, and pulled down his house and his (11) temple-place." The moment that this letter reaches you go to Teuzoi, and let every man be seized of whom Peteesi son of (12) Essemteu this priest shall say to you, "Let them be seized"; let them be brought bound to the place in which I am.' He caused its like to be written (13) to Psammetkᶜaneit the Captain of the host that was in the nome of Hnes, and a young man was made to carry the letters. He came to (14) Hnes with me, and we reached the prince of Hnes and the Captain of the host, and stood before them in the House of Record, and the letters (15) of the Superintendent of the treasury were read.

And Herbes the (Sheikh) of Hnes said, 'As Usiri lives, Zeubestefonkh the *le-shoni* of Amun of Teuzoi is not in this nome. (16) I have heard that he went to Puto to mourn for Hor the father of Khelkhons, who has gone to his fathers.' He called (17) to Pete-harshafe his attendant, saying, 'Go to Teuzoi, take 50 men with you, let them seize every man of whom Peteesi the priest shall (18) say, "Let them be seized," and bring them to me bound.

And the Captain of the host called to his attendant, saying, 'Go to Teuzoi, take much men (19) with you, let them bring the men of whom Peteesi son of Essemteu shall say, "Let them be seized": let them be seized, and bring them (20) bound to me.'

We came to Teuzoi in two ships, we did not find Zeubestefonkh the *le-shoni* in Teuzoi, (21) but his brethren whom we found were seized and brought to Hnes before the Sheikh of Hnes and the Captain of the host. They prayed before (**20**/1) the (Sheikh) of Hnes and the Captain of the host, saying, 'As Perᶜo lives, we have not taken property belonging to Peteesi, we did not pull down a house belonging to him: (2) Psammetkmenempe son of Hor, the prophet of Amun, was he who pulled down his house and temple-place.'

The (Sheikh) of Hnes said, 'Peteesi: behold, (3) since they found not Zeubestefonkh the *le-shoni*, what is your profit in having these priests taken to the Superintendent of the treasury? They will go and say before the Superintendent of the treasury (4)"We have not taken property of yours, we have not caused a house of yours to be pulled down."' I said to the (Sheikh) of Hnes, 'Did Imhotp the (5) scribe of the Superintendent of the treasury set me before the Superintendent of the treasury and cause one to be sent to the (Sheikh) of Hnes and the Captain of the host before me saying, "His Honour will cause (6) my affair to be despised here in the nome"?'

And the (Sheikh) of Hnes seized my hand and took me apart, and said to me, 'As Usiri lives, I love you more than these priests. (7) It has happened that Khelkhons was gone to speak with the Superintendent of the treasury on behalf of these priests, and cause them to be let go, and your affair to (8) fail. Behold the mild letter which Imhotp caused to be brought to me about you, that through which I am ardent for your rights, says, (9)"He is my brother: let him be taken care of, and let the affair for which he has come to you be made much of." These priests, I will cause them to give you 10 teben of silver coin, (10) and I will cause them to make oath to you besides before Harshafe and before Usiri of Naref, saying, "We took no property of yours, we did not pull down a house of yours," and I will cause them besides to pay the expense of this man of the Superintendent of the treasury who is before you.'

Harbes the (Sheikh) of Hnes (12) persuaded me to make remission to the priests: and the (Sheikh) of Hnes said to the priests, 'Behold, Peteesi, I have persuaded him to make remission (13) to you: you shall give him 20 teben of silver.' But they cried aloud, saying, 'We cannot give him five pieces of silver.' I said to the (Sheikh) of Hnes, 'As the breath (14) of his Honour prospers, they took (the worth of) ten pieces of silver in beams and binding from these houses that they pulled down, and spoiled another twenty pieces besides in stonework (15) in them.' And the (Sheikh) of Hnes said to them, 'As Usiri lives, I have heard everything that you have done to him: if you be taken to the Superintendent of the treasury, 50 pieces of silver shall not bring you (16) out. Let 10 pieces be given to him, and I will make him forgive you the other 10 pieces, and you shall make oath to him, saying, "We took not property of yours, (17) we caused (it) not to be taken, we caused not your house and your temple-place to be pulled down."'

In the end it was arranged so that the hand (18) of the priests was taken for the 10 pieces of silver, they made the oath to me before Harshafe and before Usiri of Naref, they gave one piece of silver to the man of (the) Superintendent of the treasury that was (19) before me, remission was made to the priests, and the (Sheikh) of Hnes said to me, 'Converse not with your heart. As Usiri lives, if Zeubestef·onkh (20) the *le-shoni* come southward I will make him give you the balance (due to you) of the property that these priests gave you, and I will do to you my own benefit also. As Pre[c] lives (**21/1**) I have heard the wrongs they have done to you. I did not cause these priests to be taken to the Superintendent of the treasury, (for I) said, "Lest Khelkhons (2) cause your word to be denied and your affair fail."'

The (Sheikh) of Hnes and the Captain of the host sent me away. I went to Khmun, (3) and brought my father Essemteu, with my mother and my brethren and all my people, to Teuzoi: we caused bricks to be moulded, (4) and our house to be built. They finished its street-front, and we dwelt in it. (But) its temple-place (is) (5) lying in ruins until now.

After a few days Khelkhons son of Hor went to (his) fathers; (6) Psammetkmenempe son of Hor did not come to Teuzoi until now, but what he did was to send men to fetch his property, (7) until year 44 of Ahmosi.[29]

In year 3[30] of Kam'oze[31] Hor son of Psammetkmenempe, the prophet of Amun, came to (8) Teuzoi, and stood with the priests: but they spoke not with him as to any man on earth, and they did not let rations be taken to him. They went to (9) Pshenah son of Ienharou, the brother of Harkhebuesikem, and wrote him the title to the share of the prophet of Amun of Teuzoi in year 4 [32]of Kam'oze.

𓀀 𓏤 𓎡 𓈖 𓂋 𓏏 𓅱 𓆓 𓊮 𓅃 𓈖 𓏏 𓏤 𓂧 𓏏 𓆑 𓈖 𓊃 𓏏 𓅃 𓈖 𓏏 𓂋 𓏭 𓏏 𓅱 𓆓 𓊮 𓅃 𓈖 𓏏 𓏤 𓂧 𓏏

111. HERODOTUS' *ENQUIRIES*

Herodotus of Halicarnassus wrote his famous history during the reign of Artaxerxes I of Persia. Although the work chiefly concerns relations between the Greeks and Persians, he devotes almost the entirety of his second volume to Egypt, which he visited while doing research. Here are some excerpts.

2. Now the Egyptians, before the reign of their king Psammetichus, believed themselves to be the most ancient of mankind. Since Psammetichus, however, made an attempt to discover who were actually the primitive race, they have been of opinion that while they surpass all other nations, the Phrygians surpass them in antiquity. This king, finding it impossible to make out by dint of inquiry what men were the most ancient, contrived the following method of discovery:— He took two children of the common sort, and gave them over to a herdsman to bring up at his folds, strictly charging him to let no one utter a word in their presence, but to keep them in a sequestered cottage, and from time to time introduce goats to their apartment, see that they got their fill of milk, and in all other respects look after them. His object herein was to know, after the indistinct babblings of infancy were over, what word they would first articulate. It happened as he had anticipated. The herdsman obeyed his orders for two years, and at the end of that time, on his one day opening the door of their room and going in, the children both ran up to him with outstretched arms, and distinctly said "Becos." When this first happened the herdsman took no notice; but afterwards when he observed, on coming often to see after them, that the word was constantly in their mouths, he informed his lord, and by his command brought the children into his presence. Psammetichus then himself heard them say the word, upon which he proceeded to make inquiry what people there was who called anything "becos," and hereupon he learnt that "becos" was the Phrygian name for bread.

---

29 527 BCE.
30 523 BCE.
31 Cambyses.
32 522 BCE.

In consideration of this circumstance the Egyptians yielded their claims, and admitted the greater antiquity of the Phrygians.

3. That these were the real facts I learnt at Memphis from the priests of Hephaestus.[33] The Greeks, among other foolish tales, relate that Psammetichus had the children brought up by women whose tongues he had previously cut out; but the priests said their bringing up was such as I have stated above. I got much other information also from conversation with these priests while I was at Memphis, and I even went to Heliopolis and to Thebes, expressly to try whether the priests of those places would agree in their accounts with the priests at Memphis. The Heliopolitans have the reputation of being the best skilled in history of all the Egyptians. What they told me concerning their religion it is not my intention to repeat, except the names of their deities, which I believe all men know equally. If I relate anything else concerning these matters, it will only be when compelled to do so by the course of my narrative.

4. Now with regard to mere human matters, the accounts which they gave, and in which all agreed, were the following. The Egyptians, they said, were the first to discover the solar year, and to portion out its course into twelve parts. They obtained this knowledge from the stars. (To my mind they contrive their year much more cleverly than the Greeks, for these last every other year intercalate a whole month, but the Egyptians, dividing the year into twelve months of thirty days each, add every year a space of five days besides, whereby the circuit of the seasons is made to return with uniformity.) The Egyptians, they went on to affirm, first brought into use the names of the twelve gods, which the Greeks adopted from them ; and first erected altars, images, and temples to the gods; and also first engraved upon stone the figures of animals. In most of these cases they proved to me that what they said was true. And they told me that the first man who ruled over Egypt was Men, and that in his time all Egypt, except the Thebaic canton, was a marsh, none of the land below lake Moeris then showing itself above the surface of the water. This is a distance of seven days' sail from the sea up the river.

5. What they said of their country seemed to me very reasonable. For any one who sees Egypt, without having heard a word about it before, must perceive, if he has only common powers of observation, that the Egypt to which the Greeks go in their ships is an acquired country, the gift of the river. The same is true of the land above the lake, to the distance of three days' voyage, concerning which the Egyptians say nothing, but which is exactly the same kind of country.

35. Concerning Egypt itself I shall extend my remarks to a great length, because there is no country that possesses so many wonders, nor any that has such a number of works which defy description. Not only is the climate different from that of the rest of the world, and the rivers unlike any other rivers, but the people also, in most of their manners and customs, exactly reverse the common practice of mankind. The women attend the markets and trade, while the men sit at home at the loom; and here, while the rest of the world works the woof up the warp, the Egyptians work it down; the women likewise carry burthens upon their shoulders, while the men carry them upon their heads. They eat their food out of doors in the streets, but retire for private purposes to their houses, giving as a reason that what is unseemly, but necessary, ought to be done in secret, but what has nothing unseemly about it, should be done openly. A woman cannot serve the priestly office,

---

33   Ptah.

either for god or goddess, but men are priests to both; sons need not support their parents unless they choose, but daughters must, whether they choose or no.

36. In other countries the priests have long hair, in Egypt their heads are shaven; elsewhere it is customary, in mourning, for near relations to cut their hair close; the Egyptians, who wear no hair at any other time, when they lose a relative, let their beards and the hair of their heads grow long. All other men pass their lives separate from animals, the Egyptians have animals always living with them; others make barley and wheat their food, it is a disgrace to do so in Egypt, where the grain they live on is spelt, which some call zea. Dough they knead with their feet, but they mix mud, and even take up dirt, with their hands. They are the only people in the world—they at least, and such aa have learnt the practice from them[1]—who use circumcision. Their men wear two garments apiece, their women but one. They put on the rings and fasten the ropes to sails inside, others put them outside. When they write or calculate, instead of going, like the Greeks, from left to right, they move their hand from right to left; and they insist, notwithstanding, that it is they who go to the right, and the Greeks who go to the left. They have two quite different kinds of writing, one of which is called sacred, the other common.

37. They are religious to excess, far beyond any other race of men, and use the following ceremonies:— They drink out of brazen cups, which they scour every day: there is no exception to this practice. They wear linen garments, which they are specially careful to have always fresh washed. They practise circumcision for the sake of cleanliness, considering it better to be cleanly than comely. The priests shave their , whole body every other day, that no lice or other impure thing may adhere to them when they are engaged in the service of the gods. Their dress in entirely of linen, and their shoes of the papyrus plant: it is not lawful for them to wear either dress or shoes of any other material. They bathe twice every day in cold water, and twice each night. Besides which they observe, so to speak, thousands of ceremonies. They enjoy, however, not a few advantages. They consume none of their own property, and are at no expense for anything; but every day bread is baked for them of the sacred corn, and a plentiful supply of beef and of goose's flesh is assigned to each, and also a portion of wine made from the grape. Fish they are not allowed to eat; and beans,—which none of the Egyptians ever sow, or eat, if they come up of their own accord, either raw or boiled—the priests will not even endure to look on, since they consider it an unclean kind of pulse. Instead of a single priest, each god has the attendance of a college, at the head of which is a chief priest; when one of these dies, his son is appointed in his room.

84. Medicine is practised among them on a plan of separation; each physician treats a single disorder, and no more; thus the country swarms with medical practitioners, some undertaking to cure diseases of the eye, others of the head, others again of the teeth, others of the intestines, and some those which are not local.

85. The following is the way in which they conduct their mournings and their funerals :—On the death in any house of a man of consequence, forthwith the women of the family beplaster their heads, and sometimes even their faces, with mud; and then, leaving the body indoors, sally forth and wander through the city, with their dress fastened by a band, and their bosoms bare, beating themselves as they walk. All the female relations join them and do the same. The men too, similarly begirt, beat their breasts separately. When I do not think it religious to name in connexion with such a matter; the second sort is inferior to. the first, and less costly; the third is the cheapest of all. All this the embalmers explain, and then ask in which way it is wished that the corpse should

be prepared. The bearers tell them, and having concluded their bargain, take their departure, while the embalmers, left to themselves, proceed to their task. The mode of embalming, according to the most perfect process, is the following:— They take first a crooked piece of iron, and with it draw out the brain through the nostrils, thus getting rid of a portion, while the skull is cleared of the rest by rinsing with drugs; next they make a cut along the flank with a sharp Ethiopian stone, and take out the whole contents of the abdomen, which they then cleanse, washing it thoroughly with palm wine, and again frequently with an infusion of pounded aromatics. After this they fill the cavity with the purest bruised myrrh, with cassia, and every other sort of spicery except frankincense, and sew up the opening. Then the body is placed in natrura for seventy days, and covered entirely over. After the expiration of that space of time, which must not be exceeded, the body is washed, and wrapped round, from head to foot, with bandages of fine linen cloth, smeared over with gum, which is used generally by the Egyptians in the place of glue, and in this state it is given back to the relations, who enclose it in a wooden case which they have had made for the purpose, shaped into the figure of a man. Then fastening the case, they place it in a sepulchral chamber, up-right against the wall. Such is the most costly way of embalming the dead.

87. If persons wish to avoid expense, and choose the second process, the following is the method pursued:— Syringes are filled with oil made from the cedar-tree, which is then, without any incision or disembowelling, injected into the abdomen. The passage by which it might be likely to return is stopped, and the body laid in natrum the prescribed number of days. At the end of the time the cedar-oil is allowed to make its escape; and such is its power that it brings with it the whole stomach and intestines in a liquid state. The natrum meanwhile has dissolved the flesh, and so nothing is left of the dead body but the skin and the bones. It is returned in this condition to the relatives, without any further trouble being bestowed upon it.

The third method of embalming, which is practised in the case of the poorer classes, is to clear out the intestines with a clyster, and let the body lie in natrum the seventy days, after which it is at once given to those who come to fetch it away.

The wives of men of rank are not given to be embalmed immediately after death, nor indeed are any of the more beautiful and valued women. It is not till they have been dead three or four days that they are carried to the embalmers. This is done to prevent indignities from being offered them. It is said that once a case of this kind occurred: the man was detected by the information of his fellow-workman.

Whensoever any one, Egyptian or foreigner, has lost his life by falling a prey to a crocodile, or by drowning in the river, the law compels the inhabitants of the city near which the body is cast up to have it embalmed, and to bury it in one of the sacred repositories with all possible magnificence. No one may touch the corpse, not even any of the friends or relatives, but only the priests of the Nile, who prepare it for burial with their own hands—regarding it as something more than the mere body of a man—and themselves lay it in the tomb.

99. Thus far I have spoken of Egypt from my own observation, relating what I myself saw, the ideas that I formed, and the results of my own researches. What follows rests on the accounts given me by the Egyptians, which I shall now repeat, adding thereto some particulars which fell under my own notice.

The priests said that Men was the first king of Egypt, and that it was he who raised the dyke which protects Memphis from the inundations of the Nile. Before his time the river flowed entirely along the sandy range of hills which skirts Egypt on the side of Libya. He, however, by banking up the river at the bend which it forms about a hundred furlongs south of Memphis, laid the ancient channel dry, while he dug a new course for the stream half-way between the two lines of hills. To this day, the elbow which the Nile forms at the point where it is forced aside into the new channel is guarded with the greatest care by the Persians, and strengthened every year; for if the river were to burst out at this place, and pour over the mound, there would be danger of Memphis being completely overwhelmed by the flood. Men, the first king, having thus, by turning the river, made the tract where it used to run, dry land, proceeded in the first place to build the city now called Memphis, which lies in the narrow part of Egypt; after which he further excavated a lake outside the town, to the north and west, communicating with the river, which was itself the eastern boundary. Besides these works he also, the priests said, built the temple of Hephaestus which stands within the city, a vast edifice, very worthy of mention.

100. Next, they read me from a papyrus, the names of three hundred and thirty monarchs, who (they said) were his successors upon the throne. In this number of generations there were eighteen Ethiopian kings, and one queen who was a native: all the rest were kings and Egyptians. The queen bore the same name as the Babylonian princess, namely, Nitocris. They said that she succeeded her brother; he had been king of Egypt, and was put to death by his subjects, who then placed her upon the throne. Bent on avenging his death, she devised a cunning scheme by which she destroyed a vast number of Egyptians. She constructed a spacious underground chamber, and, on pretence of inaugurating it, contrived the following:— Inviting to a banquet those of the Egyptians whom she knew to have had the chief share in the murder of her brother, she suddenly, as they were feasting, let the river in upon them, by means of a secret duct of large size. This, and this only, did they tell me of her, except that, when she had done as I have said, she threw herself into an apartment full of ashes, that she might escape the vengeance whereto she would otherwise have been exposed.

101. The other kings, they said, were personages of no note or distinction, and left no monuments of any account, with the exception of the last, who was named Moeris, He left several memorials of his reign—the northern gateway of the temple of Hephaestus, the lake excavated by his orders, whose dimensions I shall give presently, and the pyramids built by him in the lake, the size of which will be stated when I describe the lake itself wherein they stand. Such were his works: the other kings left absolutely nothing.

102. Passing over these monarchs, therefore, I shall speak of the king who reigned next, whose name was Sesostris.[34] He, the priests said, first of all proceeded in a fleet of ships of war from the Arabian gulf along the shores of the Erythraean sea, subduing the nations as he went, until he finally reached a sea which could not be navigated by reason of the shoals. Hence he returned to Egypt, where, they told me, he collected a vast armament, and made a progress by land across the continent, conquering every people which fell in his way. In the countries where the natives withstood his attack, and fought gallantly for their liberties, he erected pillars, on which he inscribed his own name and country, and how that he had here reduced the inhabitants to subjection by the might of his arms: where, on the contrary, they submitted readily and without a struggle, he inscribed on the

---

34 Senusret. The tradition seems to combine the accomplishments of both Senusret I and III into one person and adds a bit of Ramesses II in there as well.

pillars, in addition to these particulars, an emblem to mark that they were a nation of women, that is, unwarlike and effeminate.

103. In this way he traversed the whole continent of Asia, whence. he passed on into Europe, and made himself master of Scythia and of Thrace, beyond which countries I do not think that his army extended its march. For thus far the pillars which he erected are still visible, but in the remoter regions they are no longer found. Returning to Egypt from Thrace, he came, on his way, to the banks of the river Phasis. Here I cannot say with any certainty what took place. Either he of his own accord detached a body of troops from his main army and left them to colonise the country, or else a certain number of his soldiers, wearied with their long wanderings, deserted, and established themselves on the banks of this stream[2]

104. There can be no doubt that the Colchians are an Egyptian race. Before I heard any mention of the fact from others, I had remarked it myself. After the thought had struck me, I made inquiries on the subject both in Colchis and in Egypt, and I found that the Colchians had a more distinct recollection of the Egyptians, than the Egyptians had of them. Still the Egyptians said that they believed the Colchians to be descended from the army of Sesostris. My own conjectures were founded, first, on the fact that they are black skinned and have woolly hair; which certainly amounts to but little, since several other nations are so too; but further and more especially, on the circumstance that the Colchians, the Egyptians, and the Ethiopians, are the only nations who have practised circumcision from the earliest times. The Phoenicians and the Syrians of Palestine themselves confess that they learnt the custom of the Egyptians; and the Syrians who dwell about the rivers Thermodon and Parthenius, as well as their neighbours the Macronians, say that they have recently adopted it from the Colchians. Now these are the only nations who use circumcision, and it is plain that they all imitate herein the Egyptians. With respect to the Ethiopians, indeed, I cannot decide whether they learnt the practice of the Egyptians, or the Egyptians of them—it is undoubtedly of very ancient date in Ethiopia—but that the others derived their knowledge of it from Egypt is clear to me, from the'fact that the Phoenicians, when they come to have commerce with the Greeks, cease to follow the Egyptians in this custom, and allow their children to remain uncircumcised.

105. I will add a further proof of the identity of the Egyptians and the Colchians. These two nations weave their linen in exactly the same way, and this is a way entirely unknown to the rest of the world; they also in their whole mode of life and in their language resemble one another. The Colchian linen is called by the Greeks Sardinian, while that which comes from Egypt is known as Egyptian.

106. The pillars which Sesostris erected in the conquered countries, have for the most part disappeared, but in the part of Syria called Palestine, I myself saw them still standing, with the writing above-mentioned, and the emblem distinctly visible. In Ionia also, there are two representations of this prince engraved upon rocks, one on the road from Ephesus to Phocaea, the other between Sardis and Smyrna. In each case the figure is that of a man, four cubits and a span high, with a spear in his right hand and a bow in his left, the rest of his costume being likewise half Egyptian, half Ethiopian, There is an inscription across the breast from shoulder to shoulder, in the sacred character of Egypt, which says, "With my own shoulders I conquered this land." The conqueror does not tell who he is, or whence he comes, though elsewhere Sesostris records these facts. Hence it has been imagined by some of those who have seen these forms, that they are figures of Memnon; but such as think so err very widely from the truth.

107. This Sesostris, the priests went on to say, upon his return home accompanied by vast multitudes of the people whose countries he had subdued, was received by his brother, whom he had made viceroy of Egypt on his departure, at Daphnae near Pelusium, and invited by him to a banquet, which he attended, together with his sons. Then his brother piled a quantity of wood all round the building, and having so done set it alight. Sesostris, discovering what had happened, took counsel instantly with his wife, who had accompanied him to the feast, and was advised by her to lay two of their six sons upon the fire, and so make a bridge across the flames, whereby the rest might effect their escape. Sesostris did as she recommended, and thus while two of his sons were burnt to death, he himself and his other children were saved.

108. The king then returned to his own land and took vengeance upon his brother, after which he proceeded to make use of the multitudes whom he had brought with him from the conquered countries, partly to drag the huge masses of stone which were moved in the course of his reign to the temple of Hephaestus—partly, to dig the numerous canals with which the whole of Egypt is intersected. By these forced labours the entire face of the country was changed; for whereas Egypt had formerly been a region suited both for horses and carriages, henceforth it became entirely unfit for either. Though a flat country throughout its whole extent, it is now unfit for either horse or carriage, being cut up by the canals, which are extremely numerous and run in all directions. The king's object was to supply Nile water to the inhabitants of the towns situated in the mid-country, and not lying upon the river; for previously they had been obliged, after the subsidence of the floods, to drink a brackish water which they obtained from wells.

109. Sesostris also, they declared, made a division of the soil of Egypt among the inhabitants, assigning square plots of ground of equal size to all, and obtaining his chief revenue from the rent which the holders were required to pay him every year. If the river carried away any portion of a man's lot, he appeared before the king, and related what had happened; upon which the king sent persons to examine, and determine by measurement the exact extent of the loss; and thenceforth only such a rent was demanded of him as was proportionate to the reduced size of his land. From this practice, I think, geometry first came to be known in Egypt, whence it passed into Greece. The sun-dial, however, and the gnomon, with the division of the day into twelve parts, were received by the Greeks from the Babylonians.

110. Sesostris was king not only of Egypt, but also of Ethiopia. He was the only Egyptian monarch who ever ruled over the latter country. He left, as memorials of his reign, the stone Statues which stand in front of the temple of Hephaestus, two of which, representing himself and his wife, are thirty cubits in height, while the remaining four, which represent his sons, are twenty cubits. These are the statues, in front of which the priest of Hephaestus, very many years afterwards, would not allow Darius the Persian to place a statue of himself; "because," he said, "Darius had not equalled the achievements of Sesostris the Egyptian: for while Sesostris had subdued to the full as many nations as ever Darius had brought under, he had likewise conquered the Scythians, whom Darius had failed to master. It was not fair, therefore, that he should erect his statue in front of the offerings of a king, whose deeds he had been unable to surpass." Darius, they say, pardoned the freedom of this speech.

111. On the death of Sesostris, his son Pheron,[35] the priests said, mounted the throne. He undertook no warlike expeditions; being struck with blindness, owing to the following circumstance. The

---

35   This is basically just the word Pharaoh; the story is a folk tale.

river had swollen to the unusual height of eighteen cubits, and had overflowed all the fields, when, a sudden wind arising, the water rose in great waves. Then the king, in a spirit of impious violence, seized his spear, and hurled it into the strong eddies of the stream. Instantly he was smitten with disease of the eyes, from which after a little while he became blind, continuing without the power of vision for ten years. At last, in the eleventh year, an oracular announcement reached him from the city of Buto, to the effect, that "the time of his punishment had run out, and he should recover his sight by washing his eyes with urine. He must find a woman who had been faithful to her husband, and had never preferred to him another man." The king, therefore, first of all made trial of his wife, but to no purpose— he continued as blind as before. So he made the experiment with other women, until at length he succeeded, and in this way recovered his sight. Hereupon he assembled all the women, except the last, and bringing them to the city which now bears the name of Erythrabfilus (Red-soil), he there burnt them all, together with the place itself. The woman to whom he owed his cure, he married, and after his recovery was complete, he presented offerings to all the temples of any note, among which the best worthy of mention are the two stone obelisks which he gave to the temple of the Sun. These are magnificent works; each is made of a single stone, eight cubits broad, and a hundred cubits in height.

112. Pheron, they said, was succeeded by a man of Memphis, whose name, in the language of the Greeks, was Proteus. There is a sacred precinct of this king in Memphis, which is very beautiful, and richly adorned, situated south of the great temple of Hephaestus. Phoenicians from the city of Tyre dwell all round this precinct, and the whole place is known by the name of the camp of the Tyrians. Within the enclosure stands a temple, which is called that of Aphrodite the Stranger.

121. (1.) When Proteus died, Rhampsinitus, the priests informed me, succeeded to the throne. His monuments were, the western gateway of the temple of Hephaestus, and the two statues which stand in front of this gateway, called by the Egyptians, the one Summer, the other Winter, each twenty-five cubits in height. The statue of Summer, which is the northernmost of the two, is worshipped by the natives, and has offerings made to it; that of Winter, which stands towards the south, is treated in exactly the contrary way. King Rhampsinitus was possessed, they said, of great riches in silver,— indeed to such an amount, that none of the princes, his successors, surpassed or even equalled his wealth. For the better custody of this money, he proposed to build a vast chamber of hewn stone, one side of which was to form a part of the outer wall of his palace. The builder, therefore, having designs upon the treasures, contrived, as he was making the building, to insert in this wall a stone,[3] which could easily be removed from its place by two men, or even by one. So the chamber was finished, and the king's money stored away in it. Time passed, and the builder fell sick, when finding his end approaching, he called for his two sons, and related to them the contrivance he had made in the king's treasure-chamber, telling them it was for their sakes he had done it, that so they might always live in affluence. Then he gave them clear directions concerning the mode of removing the stone, and communicated the measurements, bidding them carefully keep the secret, whereby they would be Comptrollers of the Royal Exchequer so long as they lived. Then the father died, and the sons were not slow in setting to work; they went by night to the palace, found the stone in the wall of the building, and having removed it with ease, plundered the treasury of a round sum.

(2.) When the king next paid a visit to the apartment, he was astonished to see that the money was sunk in some of the vessels wherein it was stored away. Whom to accuse, however, he knew not, as the seals were all perfect, and the fastenings of the room secure. Still each time that he repeated his visits, he found that more money was gone. The thieves in truth never stopped, but plundered the treasury ever more and more. At last the king determined to have some traps[3] made, and set near the vessels which contained his wealth. This was done, and when the thieves came, as usual, to the treasure-chamber, and one of them entering through the aperture, made straight for the jars, suddenly he found himself caught in one of the traps. Perceiving that he was lost, he instantly called his brother, and telling him what had happened, entreated him to enter as quickly as possible and cut off his head, that when his body should be discovered it might not be recognised, which would have the effect of bringing ruin upon both. The other thief thought the advice good, and was persuaded to follow it;—then, fitting the stone into its place, he went home, taking with him his brother's head.

(3.) When day dawned, the king came into the room, and marvelled greatly to see the body of the thief in the trap without a head, while the building was still whole, and neither entrance nor exit was to be seen anywhere. In this perplexity he commanded the body of the dead man to be hung up outside the palace wall, and set a guard to watch it, with orders that if any persons were seen weeping or lamenting near the place, they should be seized and brought before him. When the mother heard of this exposure of the corpse of her son, she took it sorely to heart, and spoke to her surviving child, bidding him devise some plan or other to get back the body, and threatening, that if he did not exert himself, she would go herself to the king, and denounce him as the robber.

(4.) The son said all he could to persuade her to let the matter rest, but in vain: she still continued to trouble him, until at last he yielded to her importunity, and contrived as follows:—Filling some skins with wine, he loaded them on donkeys, which he drove before him till he came to the place where the guards were watching the dead body, when pulling two or three of the skins towards him, he untied some of the necks which dangled by the asses' sides. The wine poured freely out, whereupon he began to beat his head, and shout with all his might, seeming not to know which of the donkeys he should turn to first. When the guards saw the wine running, delighted to profit by the occasion, they rushed one and all into the road, each with some vessel or other, and caught the liquor as it was spilling. The driver pretended anger, and loaded them with abuse; whereon they did their best to pacify him, until at last he appeared to soften, and recover his good humour, drove his asses aside out of the road, and set to work to re-arrange their burthens; meanwhile, as he talked and chatted with the guards, one of them began to rally him, and make him laugh, whereupon he gave them one of the skins as a gift. They now made up their minds to sit down and have a drinking-bout where they were, so they begged him to remain and drink with them. Then the man let himself be persuaded, and stayed. As the drinking went on, they grew very friendly together, so presently he gave them another skin, upon which they drank so copiously that they were all overcome with the liquor, and growing drowsy lay down, and fell asleep on the spot. The thief waited till it was the dead of the night, and then took down the body of his brother; after which, in mockery, he shaved off the right side of all the soldiers' beards, and so left them. Laying his brother's body upon the asses, he carried it home to his mother, having thus accomplished the thing that she had required of him.

(5.) When it came to the king's ears that the thief's body was stolen away, he was sorely vexed. Wishing therefore, whatever it might cost, to catch the man who had contrived the trick, he had recourse (the priests said) to an expedient, which I can scarcely credit. He sent his own daughter[6] to the common stews, with orders to admit all comers, but to require every man to tell her what was the cleverest and wickedest thing he had done in the whole course of his life. If any one in reply told her the story of the thief, she was to lay hold of him and not allow him to get away. The daughter did as her father willed, whereon the thief, who was well aware of the king's motive, felt a desire to outdo him in craft and cunning. Accordingly he contrived the following plan:—He procured the corpse of a man lately dead, and cutting off one of the arms at the shoulder, put it under his dress, and so went to the king's daughter. When she put the question to him as she had done to all the rest, he replied, that the wickedest thing he had ever done was cutting off the head of his brother when he was caught in a trap in the king's treasury, and the cleverest was making the guards drunk and carrying off the body. As he spoke, the princess caught at him, but the thief took advantage of the darkness to hold out to her the hand of the corpse. Imagining it to be his own hand, she seized and held it fast; while the thief, leaving it in her grasp, made his escape by the door.

(6.) The king, when word was brought him of this fresh success, amazed at the sagacity and boldness of the man, sent messengers to all the towns in his dominions to proclaim a free pardon for the thief, and to promise him a rich reward, if he came and made himself known. The thief took the king at his word, and came boldly into his presence; whereupon Rhampsinitus, greatly admiring him, and looking on him as the most knowing of men, gave him his daughter in marriage. "The Egyptians," he said, "excelled all the rest of the world in wisdom, and this man excelled all other Egyptians."

122. The same king, I was also informed by the priests, afterwards descended alive into the region which the Greeks call Hades, and there played at dice with Demeter, sometimes winning and sometimes suffering defeat. After a while he returned to earth, and brought with him a golden napkin, a gift which he had received from the goddess. From this descent of Rhampsinitus into Hades, and return to earth again, the Egyptians, I was told, instituted a festival, which they certainly celebrated in my day. On what occasion it was that they instituted it, whether upon this or upon any other, I cannot determine. The following are the ceremonies:— On a certain day in the year the priests weave a mantle, and binding the eyes of one of their number with a fillet, they put the mantle upon him, and take him with them into the roadway conducting to the temple of Demeter, when they depart and leave him to himself. Then the priest, thus blindfolded, is led (they say) by two wolves to the temple of Demeter, distant twenty furlongs from the city, where he stays awhile, after which he is brought back from the temple by the wolves, and left upon the spot where they first joined him.

123. Such as think the tales told by the Egyptians credible are free to accept them for history. For my own part, I propose to myself throughout my whole work faithfully to record the traditions of the several nations. The Egyptians maintain that Demeter and Dionysus preside in the realms below. They were also the first to broach the opinion, that the soul of man is immortal, and that, when the body dies, it enters into the form of an animal which is born at the moment, thence passing on from one animal into another, until it has circled through the forms of all the creatures which tenant the earth, the water, and the air, after which it enters again into a human frame, and is born anew. The whole period of the transmigration is (they say) three thousand years. There are Greek writers, some of an earlier, some of a later date, who have borrowed this doctrine from the Egyptians, and put it forward as their own. I could mention their names, but I abstain from doing so.

124. Till the death of Rhampsinitus, the priests said, Egypt was excellently governed, and flourished greatly; but after him Cheops succeeded to the throne, and plunged into all manner of wickedness. He closed the temples, and forbade the Egyptians to offer sacrifice, compelling them instead to labour, one and all, in his service. Some were required to drag blocks of stone down to the Nile from the quarries in the Arabian range of hills; others received the blocks after they had been conveyed in boats across the river, and drew them to the range of hills called the Libyan. A

hundred thousand men laboured constantly, and were relieved every three months by a fresh lot. It took ten years' oppression of the people to make the causeway for the conveyance of the stones, a work not much inferior, in my judgment, to the pyramid itself. This causeway is five furlongs in length, ten fathoms wide, and in height, at the highest part, eight fathoms. It is built of polished stone, and is covered with carvings of animals. To make it took ten years, as I said—or rather to make the causeway, the works on the mound where the pyramid stands, and the underground chambers, which Cheops intended as vaults for his own use: these last were built on a sort of island, surrounded by water introduced from the Nile by a canal. The pyramid itself was twenty years in building. It is a square, eight hundred feet each way,1 and the height the same, built entirely of polished stone, fitted together with the utmost care. The stones of which it is composed are none of them less than thirty feet in length.

The wickedness of Cheops reached to such a pitch that, when he had spent all his treasures and wanted more, he sent his daughter to the stews, with orders to procure him a certain sum—how much I cannot say, for I was not told; she procured it, however, and at the same time, bent on leaving a monument which should perpetuate her own memory, she required each man to make her a present of a stone towards the works which she contemplated. With these stones she built the pyramid which stands midmost of the three that are in front of the great pyramid, measuring along each side a hundred and fifty feet.

Cheops reigned, the Egyptians said, fifty years, and was succeeded at his demise by Chephren, his brother.

Chephren imitated the conduct of his predecessor, and, like him, built a pyramid, which did not, however, equal the dimensions of his brothers. Of this I am certain, for I measured them both myself. It has no subterraneous apartments, nor any canal from the Nile to supply it with water as the other pyramid has. In that, the Nile water, introduced through an artificial duct, surrounds an island, where the body of Cheops is said to lie. Chephren built his pyramid close to the great pyramid of Cheops, and of the same dimensions, except that he lowered the height forty feet. For the basement he employed the many-coloured stone of Ethiopia. These two pyramids stand both on the same hill, an elevation not far short of a hundred feet in height. The reign of Chephren lasted fifty-six years.

Thus the affliction of Egypt endured for the space of one hundred and six years, during the whole of which time the temples were shut up and never opened. The Egyptians so detest the memory of these kings that they do not much like even to mention their names. Hence they commonly call the pyramids after Philition, a shepherd who at that time fed his flocks about the place.

After Chephren, Mycerinus (they said) son of Cheops, ascended the throne. This prince disapproved the conduct of his father, re-opened the temples, and allowed the people, who were ground down to the lowest point of misery, to return to their occupations, and to resume the practice of sacrifice. His justice in the decision of causes was beyond that of all the former kings. The Egyptians praise him in this respect more highly than any of their other monarchs, declaring that he not only gave his judgments with fairness, but also, when any one was dissatisfied with his sentence, made compensation to him out of his own purse, and thus pacified his anger. Mycerinus had established his character for mildness, and was acting as I have described, when the stroke of calamity fell on him. First of all his daughter died, the only child that he possessed. Experiencing a bitter grief at this visitation, in his sorrow he conceived the wish to entomb his child in some unusual way. He therefore caused a cow to be made of wood, and after the interior had been hollowed out, he had the whole surface coated with gold; and in this novel tomb laid the dead body of his daughter.

The cow was not placed underground, but continued visible to my times: it was at Sa'is, in the royal palace, where it occupied a chamber richly adorned. Every day there are burnt before it aromatics of every kind; and all night long a lamp is kept burning in the apartment. In an adjoining chamber are statues which the priests at Sais declared to represent the various concubines of Mycerinus. They are colossal figures in wood, of the number of about twenty, and are represented naked. Whose images they really are, I cannot say—I can only repeat the account which was given to me.

Concerning these colossal figures and the sacred cow, there is also another tale narrated, which runs thus: "Mycerinus was enamoured of his daughter, and offered her violence—the damsel for grief hanged herself, and Mycerinus entombed her in the cow. Then her mother cut off the hands of all her tiring-maids, because they had sided with the father, and betrayed the child; and so the statues of the maids have no hands." All this is mere fable in my judgment, especially what is said about the hands of the colossal statues. I could plainly see that the figures had only lost their hands through the effect of time. They had dropped off, and were still lying on the ground about the feet of the statues.

As for the cow, the greater portion of it is hidden by a scarlet coverture; the head and neck, however, which are visible, are coated very thickly with gold, and between the horns there is a representation in gold of the orb of the sun. The figure is not erect, but lying down, with the limbs under the body; the dimensions being fully those of a large animal of the kind. Every year it is taken from the apartment where it is kept, and exposed to the light of day—this is done at the season when the Egyptians beat themselves in honour of one of their gods, whose name I am unwilling to mention in connexion with such a matter. They say that the daughter of Mycerinus requested her father in her dying moments to allow her once a year to see the sun.

After the death of his daughter, Mycerinus was visited with a second calamity, of which I shall now proceed to give an account. An oracle reached him from the town of Buto, which said, "Six years only shalt thou live upon the earth, and in the seventh thou shalt end your days." Mycerinus, indignant, sent an angry message to the oracle, reproaching the god with his injustice—"My father and uncle," he said, "though they shut up the temples, took no thought of the gods, and destroyed multitudes of men, nevertheless enjoyed a long life; I, who am pious, am to die so soon!" There came in reply a second message from the oracle—"For this very reason is your life brought so quickly to a close—thou hast not done as it behooved you. Egypt was fated to suffer affliction one hundred and fifty years—the two kings who preceded you upon the throne understood this —thou hast not understood it." Mycerinus, when this answer reached him, perceiving that his doom was fixed, had lamps prepared, which he lighted every day at eventime, and feasted and enjoyed himself unceasingly both day and night, moving about in the marsh-country and the woods, and visiting all the places that he heard were agreeable sojourns. His wish was to prove the oracle false, by turning the nights into days, and so living twelve years in the space of six.

134. He too left a pyramid, but much inferior in size to his father's.

136. After Mycerinus, the priests said, Asychis[36] ascended the throne. He built the eastern gateway of the temple of Hephaestus, which in size and beauty far surpasses the other three. All the four gateways have figures graven on them, and a vast amount of architectural ornament, but the gateway

---

36 Probably referring to Shoshenq I.

of Asychis is by far the most richly adorned. In the reign of this king, money being scarce and commercial dealings straitened, a law was passed that the borrower might pledge his fathers body to raise the sum whereof he had need. A proviso was appended to this law, giving the lender authority over the entire sepulchre of the borrower, so that a man who took up money under this pledge, if he died without paying the debt, could not obtain burial either in his own ancestral tomb, or" in any other, nor could he during his lifetime bury in his own tomb any member of his family. The same king, desirous of eclipsing all his predecessors upon the throne, left as a monument of his reign a pyramid of brick. It bears an inscription, cut in stone, which runs thus:— "Despise me not in comparison with the stone pyramids; for I surpass them all, as much as Zeus surpasses the other gods. A pole was plunged into a lake, and the mud which clave thereto was gathered; and bricks were made of the mud, and so I was formed." Such were the chief actions of this prince.

137. He was succeeded on the throne, they said, by a blind man, a native of Anysis, whose own name also was Anysis. Under him Egypt was invaded by a vast army of Ethiopians, led by Sabacos, their king. The blind Anysis fled away to the marsh-country, and the Ethiopian was lord of the land for fifty years, during which his mode of rule was the following:—When an Egyptian was guilty of an offence, his plan was not to punish him with death: instead of so doing, he sentenced him, according to the nature of his crime, to raise the ground to a greater or a less extent in the neighbourhood of the city to which he belonged. Thus the cities came to be even more elevated than they were before. As early as the time of Sesostris, they had been raised by those who dug the canals in his reign; this second elevation of the soil under the Ethiopian king gave them a very lofty position. Among the many cities which thus attained to a great elevation, none (I think) was raised so much as the town called Bubastis, where there is a temple of the goddess Bubastis, which well deserves to be described. Other temples may be grander, and may have cost more in the building, but there is none so pleasant to the eye as this of Bubastis. The Bubastis of the Egyptians is the same as the Artemis of the Greeks.

138. The following is a description of this edifice:— Excepting the entrance, the whole forms an island. Two artificial channels from the Nile, one on either side of the temple, encompass the building, leaving only a narrow passage by which it is approached. These channels are each a hundred feet wide, and are thickly shaded with trees. The gateway is sixty feet in height, and is ornamented with figures cut upon the stone, six cubits high and well worthy of notice. The temple stands in the middle of the city, and is visible on all sides as one walks round it; for as the city has been raised up by embankment, while the temple has been left untouched in its original condition, you look down upon it wheresoever you are. A low wall runs round the enclosure, having figures engraved upon it, and inside there is a grove of beautiful tall trees growing round the shrine, which contains the image of the goddess. The enclosure is a furlong in length, and the same in breadth. The entrance to it is by a road paved with stone for a distance of about three furlongs, which passes straight through the market-place with an easterly direction, and is four hundred feet in width. Trees of an extraordinary height grow on each side the road, which conducts from the temple of Bubastis to that of Mercury.

The Ethiopian finally quitted Egypt, the priests said, by a hasty flight under the following circumstances. He saw in his sleep a vision:—a man stood by his side, and counselled him to gather together all the priests of Egypt and cut every one of them asunder. On this, according to the account which he himself gave, it came into his mind that the gods intended hereby to lead him to commit an act of sacrilege, which would be sure to draw down upon him some punishment either at the hands of gods or men. So he resolved not to do the deed suggested to him, but rather to retire from Egypt, as the time during which it was fated that he should hold the country had now (he thought) expired. For before he left Ethiopia he had been told by the oracles which are venerated there, that he was to reign fifty years over Egypt. The years were now fled, and the dream had come to trouble him; he therefore of his own accord withdrew from the land.

As soon as Sabacos was gone, the blind king left the marshes, and resumed the government. He had lived in the marsh-region the whole time, having formed for himself an island there by a mixture of earth ashes. While he remained, the natives had orders ring him food unbeknown to the Ethiopian, and latterly, at his request, each man had brought him, with the food, a certain quantity of ashes. Before Amyrtaeus, no one was able to discover the site of this island, which continued unknown to the kings of Egypt who preceded him on the throne for the space of seven hundred years and more. The name which it bears is Elbo. It is about ten furlongs across in each direction.

141. The next king, I was told, was a priest of Hephaestus, called Sethos. This monarch despised and neglected the warrior class of the Egyptians, as though he did not need their services. Among other indignities which he offered them, he took from them the lands which they had possessed under all the previous kings, consisting of twelve acres of choice land for each warrior. Afterwards, therefore, when Sanacharib, king of the Arabians and Assyrians, marched his vast army into Egypt, the warriors one and all refused to come to his aid. On this the monarch, greatly distressed, entered into the inner sanctuary, and before the image of the god, bewailed the fate which impended over him. As he wept he fell asleep, and dreamt that the god came and stood at his side, bidding him be of good cheer, and go boldly forth to meet the Arabian host, which would do him no hurt, as he himself would send those who should help him. Sethos, then, relying on the dream, collected such of the Egyptians as were willing to follow him, who were none of them warriors, but traders, artisans, and market people; and with these marched to Pelusium, which commands the entrance into Egypt, and there pitched his camp. As the two armies lay here opposite one another, there came in the night a multitude of field-mice, which devoured all the quivers and bowstrings of the enemy, and ate the thongs by which they managed their shields. Next morning they commenced their flight, and great multitudes fell, as they had no arms with which to defend themselves. There stands to this day in the temple of Hephaestus, a stone statue of Sethos, with a mouse in his hand, and an inscription to this effect—"Look on me, and learn to reverence the gods."

142. Thus far I have spoken on the authority of the Egyptians and their priests. They declare that from their first king to this last-mentioned monarch, the priest of Hephaestus, was a period of three hundred and forty-one generations; such, at least, they say, was the number both of their kings, and of their high priests, during this interval. Now three hundred generations of men make ten thousand years, three generations filling up the century; and the remaining forty-one generations make thirteen hundred and forty years. Thus the whole number of years is eleven thousand, three hundred and forty; in which entire space, they said, no god had ever appeared in a human form; nothing of this kind had happened either under the former or under the later Egyptian kings. The sun, however, had within this period of time, on four several occasions, moved from his wonted course, twice rising where he now sets, and twice setting where he now rises. Egypt was in degree affected by these changes; the productions of the land, and of the river, remained the same; nor was there anything unusual either in the diseases or the deaths.

147. In what follows I have the authority, not of the Egyptians only, but of others also who agree with them. I shall speak likewise in part from my own observation. When the Egyptians regained

their liberty after the reign of the priest of Hephaestus, unable to continue any while without a king, they divided Egypt into twelve districts, and set twelve kings over them. These twelve kings, united together by intermarriages, ruled Egypt in peace, having entered into engagements with one another not to depose any of their number, nor to aim at any aggrandisement of one above the rest, but to dwell together in perfect amity. Now the reason why they made these stipulations, and guarded with care against their infraction, was, because at the very first establishment of the twelve kingdoms, an oracle had declared—"That he among them who should pour in Hephaestus's temple a libation from a cup of bronze, would become monarch of the whole land of Egypt." Now the twelve held their meetings at all the temples.

151. The twelve kings for some time dealt honourably by one another, but at length it happened that on a certain occasion, when they had met to worship in the temple of Hephaestus, the high-priest on the last day of the festival, in bringing forth the golden goblets from which they were wont to pour the libations, mistook the number, and brought eleven goblets only for the twelve princes. Psammetichus was standing last, and being left without a cup, he took his helmet, which was of bronze, from off his head, stretched it out to receive the liquor, and so made his libation. All the kings were accustomed to wear helmets, and all indeed wore them at this very time. Nor was there any crafty design in the action of Psammetichus. The eleven, however, when they came to consider what had been done, and bethought them of the oracle which had declared "that he who, of the twelve, should pour a libation from a cup of bronze, the same would be king of the whole land of Egypt," doubted at first if they should not put Psammetichus to death. Finding, however, upon examination, that he had acted in the matter without any guilty intent, they did not think it would be just to kill him; but determined, instead, to strip him of the chief part of his power and to banish him to the marshes, forbidding him to leave them or to hold any communication with the rest of Egypt.

152. This was the second time that Psammetichus had been driven into banishment. On a former occasion he had fled from Sabacos the Ethiopian, who had put his father Necos to death; and had taken refuge in Syria, from whence, after the retirement of the Ethiop in consequence of his dream, he was brought back by the Egyptians of the Sa'itic canton. Now it was his ill-fortune to be banished a second time by the eleven kings, on account of the libation which he had poured from his helmet; on this occasion he fled to the marshes. Feeling that he was an injured man, and designing to avenge himself upon his persecutors, Psammetichus sent to the city of Buto, where there is an oracle of Latona, the most veracious of all the oracles of the Egyptians, and having inquired concerning, means of vengeance, received for answer, that "Vengeance would come from the sea, when brazen men should appear." Great was his incredulity when this answer arrived, for never, he thought, would brazen men arrive to be his helpers. However, not long afterwards certain Carians and Ionians, who had left their country on a voyage of plunder, were carried by stress of weather to Egypt, where they disembarked, all equipped in their brazen armour, and were seen by the natives, one of whom carried the tidings to Psammetichus, and, as he had never before seen men clad in brass, he reported that brazen men had come from the sea and were plundering the plain. Psammetichus, perceiving at once that the oracle was accomplished, made friendly advances to the strangers, and engaged them, by splendid promises, to enter into his service. He then, with their aid and that of the Egyptians who espoused his cause, attacked the eleven and vanquished them.

153, When Psammetichus had thus become sole monarch of Egypt, he built the southern gateway of the temple of Hephaestus in Memphis, and also a court for Apis, in which Apis is kept whenever he makes his appearance in Egypt. This court is opposite the gateway of Psammetichus, and is surrounded with a colonnade and adorned with a multitude of figures. Instead of pillars, the colonnade rests upon colossal statues, twelve cubits in height. The Greek name for Apis is Epaphus.

154. To the Ionians and Carians who had lent him their assistance Psammetichus assigned as abodes two places opposite to each other, one on either side of the Nile, which received the name of "the Camps." He also made good all the splendid promises by which he had gained their support; and further, he intrusted to their care certain Egyptian children, whom they were to teach the language of the Greeks. These children, thus instructed, became the parents of the entire class of interpreters in Egypt. The Ionians and Carians occupied for many years the places assigned them by Psammetichus, which lay near the sea, a little below the city of Bubastis, on the Pelusiac mouth of the Nile. King Amasis, long afterwards, removed the Greeks hence, and settled them at Memphis to guard him against the native Egyptians. From the date of the original settlement of these persons in Egypt, we Greeks, through our intercourse with them, have acquired an accurate knowledge of the several events in Egyptian history, from the reign of Psammetichus downwards; but before his time no foreigners had ever taken up their residence in that land. The docks where their vessels were laid up, and the ruins of their habitations, were still to be seen in my day at the place where they dwelt originally, before they were removed by Amasis. Such was the mode by which Psammetichus became master of Egypt.

157. Psammetichus ruled Egypt for fifty-four years, during twenty-nine of which he pressed the siege of Azotus1 without intermission, till finally he took the place. Azotus is a great town in Syria. Of all the cities that we know, none ever stood so long a siege.

158. Psammetichus left a son called Necos, who succeeded him upon the throne. This prince was the first to attempt the construction of the canal to the Red Sea,—a work completed afterwards by Darius the Persian—the length of which is four days' journey, and the width such as to admit of two triremes being rowed along it abreast. The water is derived from the Nile, which the canal leaves a little above the city of Bubastis, near Patumus, the Arabian town, being continued thence until it joins the Red Sea. At first it is carried along the Arabian side of the Egyptian plain, as far as the chain of hills opposite Memphis, whereby the plain is bounded, and in which lie the great stone quarries; here it skirts the base of the hills running in a direction from west to east; after which it turns, and enters a narrow pass, trending southwards from this point, until it enters the Arabian Gulf. From the northern sea to that which is called the southern or Erythraean, the shortest and quickest passage, which is from Mount Casius, the boundary between Egypt and Syria, to the Gulf of Arabia, is a distance of exactly one thousand furlongs. But the way by the canal is very much longer, on account of the crookedness of its course. A hundred and twenty thousand of the Egyptians, employed upon the work in the reign of Necos, lost their lives in making the excavation. He at length desisted from his undertaking, in consequence of an oracle which warned him "that he was labouring for the barbarian." The Egyptians call by the name of barbarians all such as speak a language different from their own.

159. Necos, when he gave up the construction of the canal, turned all his thoughts to war, and set to work to build a fleet of triremes, some intended for service in the northern sea, and some for the navigation of the Erythraean. These last were built in the Arabian Gulf, where the dry docks in which they lay are still visible. These fleets he employed wherever he had occasion; while he also made war by land upon the Syrians, and defeated them in a pitched battle at Magdolus, after which he made

himself master of Cadytis, a large city of Syria. The dress which he wore on these occasions he sent to Branchidae in Milesia, as an offering to Apollo. After having reigned in all sixteen years, Necos died, and at his death bequeathed the throne to his son Psammis.

160. In the reign of Psammis, ambassadors from Elis arrived in Egypt, boasting that their arrangements for the conduct of the Olympic games were the best and fairest that could be devised, and fancying that not even the Egyptians, who surpassed all other nations in wisdom, could add anything to their perfection. When these persons reached Egypt, and explained the reason of their visit, the king summoned an assembly of all the wisest of the Egyptians. They met, and the Eleans having given them a full account of all their rules and regulations with respect to the contests, said that they had come to Egypt for the express purpose of learning whether the Egyptians could improve the fairness of their regulations in any particular. The Egyptians considered awhile, and then made inquiry, "If they allowed their own citizens to enter the lists?" The Eleans answered, "That the lists were open to all Greeks, whether they belonged to Elis or to any other state." Hereupon the Egyptians observed, "That if this were so, they departed from justice very widely, since it was impossible but that they would favour their own countrymen, and deal unfairly by foreigners. If therefore they really wished to manage the games with fairness, and if this was the object of their coming to Egypt, they advised them to confine the contests to strangers, and allow no native of Elis to be a candidate." Such was the advice which the Egyptians gave to the Eleans.

161. Psammis reigned only six years. He attacked Ethiopia and died almost directly afterwards. Apries, his son, succeeded him upon the throne, who, excepting Psammetichus, his great-grandfather, was the most prosperous of all the kings that ever ruled over Egypt. The length of his reign was twenty-five years, and in the course of it he marched an army to attack Sidon, and fought a battle with the king of Tyre by sea. When at length the time came that was fated to bring him woe, an occasion arose which I shall describe more fully in my Libyan history, only touching it very briefly here. An army despatched by Apries to attack Cyrene having met with a terrible reverse, the Egyptians laid the blame on him, imagining that he had, of malice prepense, sent the troops into the jaws of destruction. They believed he had wished a vast number of them to be slain, in order that he himself might reign with more security over the rest of the Egyptians. Indignant therefore at this usage, the soldiers who returned and the friends of the slain broke instantly into revolt.

162. Apries, on learning these circumstances, sent Amasis to the rebels, to appease the tumult by persuasion. Upon his arrival, as he was seeking to restrain the malcontents by his exhortations, one of them, coming behind him, put a helmet on his head, saying, as he put it on, that he thereby crowned him king. Amasis was not altogether displeased at the action, as his conduct soon made manifest: for no sooner had the insurgents agreed to make him actually their king, than he prepared to march with them against Apries. That monarch, on tidings of these events reaching him, sent Patarbemis, one of his courtiers, a man of high rank, to Amasis, with orders to bring him alive into his presence. Patarbemis, on arriving at the place where Amasis was, called on him to come back with him to the king, whereupon Amasis broke a coarse jest, and said, "Please take that back to your master." When the envoy, notwithstanding this reply, persisted in his request, exhorting Amasis to obey the summons of the king, he made answer, "that this was exactly what he had long been intending to do; Apries would have no reason to complain of him on the score of delay; he would shortly come himself to the king, and bring others with him." Patarbemis, upon this, comprehending the intention of Amasis, partly from his replies, and partly from the preparations which he saw in

progress, departed hastily, wishing to inform the king with all speed of what was going on. Apries, however, when he saw him approaching without Amasis, fell into a paroxysm of rage; and not giving himself time for reflection, commanded the nose and ears of Patarbemis to be cut off. Then the rest of the Egyptians, who had hitherto espoused the cause of Apries, when they saw a man of such note among them so shamefully outraged, without a moment's hesitation went over to the rebels, and put themselves at the disposal of Amasis.

163. Apries, informed of this new calamity, armed his mercenaries, and led them against the Egyptians: this was a body of Carians and Ionians, numbering thirty thousand men, which was now with him at Sais, where his palace stood—a vast building, well worthy of notice. The army of Apries marched out to attack the host of the Egyptians, while that of Amasis went forth to fight the strangers; and now both armies drew near the city of Momemphis, and prepared for the coming fight.

112. THE BENTRESH STELA

This inscription, found at Karnak on a black sandstone stela (sometimes called the Bakhtan Stela), is an example of a priestly propagandistic work. It was deliberately made to appear as if it had been composed in the time of Ramesses II in order to glorify the cult of the Theban god Khons.

Horus: Mighty Bull, Likeness of Diadems, Abiding in Kingship, like Atum; Golden Horus: Mighty of Strength, Expelling the Nine Bows; King of Upper and Lower Egypt, Lord of the Two Lands: Usermare-Setepnere; Son of Re, of his Body: Ramses-Meriamon, beloved of Amon-Re, lord of Thebes, and all the gods of Thebes ....

Lo, his majesty was in Naharin according to his yearly custom, while the chiefs of every country came bowing down in peace, because of the fame of his majesty. From the marshes was their tribute; silver, gold, lapis lazuli, malachite and every sweet wood of God's-Land were upon their backs, each one leading his neighbor.

Then the chief of Bekhten caused his tribute to be brought, and he placed his eldest daughter in front thereof, praising his majesty, and craving life from him. Now, she was exceedingly beautiful to the heart of his majesty, beyond everything. Then they affixed her titulary as: "Great King's-Wife, Nefrure." When his majesty arrived in Egypt, she fulfilled all the functions of king's-wife.

When the year 23, the tenth month, the twenty-second day, came, while his majesty was in Thebes, the victorious, the mistress of cities, performing the pleasing ceremonies of his father, Amon-Re, lord of Thebes, at his beautiful feast of Southern Opet (Thebes), his favorite seat, of the beginning (of the world), came one to say to his majesty: "A messenger of the chief of Bekhten has come, bearing many gifts for the King's-Wife." Then he was brought before his majesty together with his gifts. He said, praising his majesty: "Praise to thee, Sun of the Nine Bows! Give us life from you." So he spoke, smelling the earth before his majesty. He spoke again before his majesty: "I come to you,

O king, my lord, on account of Bentresh, your great sister of the King's-Wife, Nefrure. Sickness has penetrated into her limbs. May your majesty send a wise man to see her."

Then said his majesty: "Bring to me the sacred scribes and the officials of the court." They were led to him immediately. Said his majesty: "Let one read to you, till you hear this thing. Then bring to me one experienced in his heart, who can write with his fingers, from your midst." The king's-scribe, Thutemhab, came before his majesty, and his majesty commanded that he go to Bekhten together with this messenger.

The wise man arrived in Bekhten; he found Bentresh in the condition of one possessed of a spirit. He found her [unable] to contend with him.

The chief of Bekhten repeated in the presence of his majesty, saying: "O king, my lord, let his majesty command to have this god brought." [Then the wise man whom his majesty had sent, returned] to his majesty in the year 26, the ninth month, at the feast of Amon, while his majesty was in Thebes.

Then his majesty repeated (it) before Khonsu-in-Thebes-Beautiful-Rest, saying: "O my good lord, I repeat before you concerning the daughter of the chief of Bekhten." Then they led Khonsu-in-Thebes-Beautiful-Rest to Khonsu-the-Plan-Maker, the great god, smiting the evil spirits. Then said his majesty before Khonsu-in-Thebes-Beautiful-Rest: "O good lord, if you incline your face to Khonsu-the-Plan-Maker, the great god, smiting the evil spirits, he shall be conveyed to Bekhten." There was violent nodding. Then said his majesty: "Send your protection with him, that I may cause his majesty to go to Bekhten, to save the daughter of the chief of Bekhten." Khonsu-in-Thebes-Beautiful-Rest nodded the head violently. Then he wrought the protection of Khonsu-the-Plan-Maker-in-Thebes four times.

His majesty commanded to cause Khonsu-the-Plan-Maker-in-Thebes to proceed to a great ship, five transports, numerous chariots and horses of the west and the east.

This god arrived in Bekhten in a full year and five months. Then the chief of Bekhten came, with his soldiers and his nobles, before Khonsu-the-Plan-Maker. He threw himself upon his belly, saying: "You come to us, you are welcome with us, by command of the King Usermare-Setepnere (Ramses II)."

Then this god went to the place where Bentresh was. Then he wrought the protection of the daughter of the chief of Bekhten. She became well immediately.

Then said this spirit which was in her before Khonsu-the-Plan-Maker-in-Thebes: "You come in peace, great god, smiting the barbarians. Your city is Bekhten, your servants are its people, I am your servant. I will go to the place whence I came, to satisfy your heart concerning that, on account of which you come. (But) let your majesty command to celebrate a feast-day with me and with the chief of Bekhten." Then this god nodded to his priest, saying: "Let the chief of Bekhten make a great offering before this spirit." While these things were happening, which Khonsu-the-Plan-Maker-in-Thebes wrought with the spirit, the chief of Bekhten stood with his soldiers, and feared very greatly. Then he made a great offering before Khonsu-the-Plan-Maker-in-Thebes and the spirit; and the chief of Bekhten celebrated a feast-day [with] them. Then the spirit departed in peace to the place he desired, by command of Khonsu-the-Plan-Maker-in-Thebes, and the chief of Bekhten rejoiced very greatly, together with every man who was in Bekhten.

Then he took counsel with his heart, saying: "I will cause this god to remain with me in Bekhten; I will not permit that he return to Egypt." Then this god waited three years and nine months in Bekhten.

Then the chief of Bekhten slept upon his bed, and he saw this god coming to him, to forsake his shrine; he was a hawk of gold, and he flew upward toward Egypt. He (the chief) awoke in fright.

Then he said to the priest of Khonsu-the-Plan-Maker-in-Thebes: "This god, he is still with us; let him depart to Egypt; let his chariot depart to Egypt." Then the chief of Bekhten caused this god to proceed to Egypt, and gave to him very many gifts of every good thing, very many soldiers and horses.

They arrived in peace at Thebes. Then came the city of Thebes, and-the-Plan-Maker-in-Thebes to the house of Khonsu-in-Thebes-Beautiful-Rest. He set the gifts which the chief of Bekhten had given to him, of good things, before Khonsu-in-Thebes-Beautiful-Rest, (but) he gave not every thing thereof into his house. Khonsu-the-Plan-Maker-in-Thebes arrived [at] his [plac]e in peace in the year 33, the second month, the ninth day, of King Usermare-Setepnere; that he might be given life like Re, forever.

𓎛𓄿 𓋴𓂝𓈖𓏏𓃀𓏛𓈖𓂋𓏏𓊪𓅱𓈖𓐍𓏏𓊪𓅆𓈖𓏏𓊪𓐍𓏏𓊪𓏛

113. THE METTERNICH STELA

The Metternich Stela, or "Magical Stela", which was erected at Heliopolis during the reign of Nekhtnebef (Nectanebo) II of the Thirtieth Dynasty, was designed to heal people, particularly those who had been bitten by venomous snakes or other poisonous creatures. Water would be poured over the stela, collected, and then drunk by the person suffering the ailment. Magical spells and incantations, which are written on the stela, would be also be recited. Stories, also, appear on the object, including this one, the tale of Isis and the Seven Scorpions.

"I am Isis, [and] I have come forth from the dwelling (or, prison) wherein my brother Set placed me. Behold the god Thoth, the great god, the Chief of Maat [both] in heaven and on the earth, said to me, "Come now, O Isis, goddess, moreover it is a good thing to hearken, [for there is] life to one who shall be guided [by the advice] of another. Hide yourself with [your] son the child, and there shall come to him these things. His members shall grow, and two-fold strength of every kind shall spring up [in him]. [And he] shall be made to take his seat upon the throne of his father, [whom] he shall avenge, [and he shall take possession of] the exalted position of Heq of the Two Lands."

I came forth [from the dwelling] at the time of evening, and there came forth the Seven Scorpions which were to accompany me and to strike for me with [their] stings. Two scorpions, Tefen and Befen, were behind me, two scorpions, Mestet and Mestetef, were by my side, and three scorpions, Petet, Thetet, and Maatet (or, Martet), were for preparing the road for me. I charged them very strictly (or, in a loud voice), and my words penetrated into their ears: "Have no knowledge of [any], make no cry to the Tesheru beings, and pay no attention to the 'son of a man' (i.e., anyone) who belongs to a man of no account," [and I said,] "Let your faces be turned towards the ground [that you may show me] the way." So the guardian of the company brought me to the boundaries of the city of Pa-Sui, the city of the goddesses of the Divine Sandals, [which was situated] in front of the Papyrus Swamps.

When I had arrived at the place where the people lived, I came to the houses wherein dwelt the wives [and] husbands. And a certain woman of quality spied me as I was journeying along the road, and she shut her doors on me. Now she was sick at heart by reason of those [scorpions] which were with me. Then [the Seven Scorpions] took counsel concerning her, and they all at one time shot out their venom on the tail of the scorpion Tefen; as for me, the woman Taha opened her door, and I entered into the house of the miserable lady.

Then the scorpion Tefen entered in under the leaves of the door and smote (i.e., stung) the son of Usert, and a fire broke out in the house of Usert, and there was no water there to extinguish it; [but] the sky rained upon the house of Usert, though it was not the season for rain.

Behold, the heart of her who had not opened her door to me was grievously sad, for she knew not whether he (i.e., her son) would live [or not], and although she went round about through her town uttering cries [for help], there was none who came at [the sound of] her voice. Now my own heart was grievously sad for the sake of the child, and [I wished] to make to live [again] him that was free from fault. [Thereupon] I cried out to the noble lady, "Come to me. Come to me. Truly my mouth possesses life. I am a daughter [well] known in her town, [and I] can destroy the demon of death by the spell (or, utterance) which my father taught me to know. I am his daughter, the beloved [offspring] of his body."

Then Isis placed her two hands on the child in order to make to live him whose throat was stopped, [and she said],

"O poison of the scorpion Tefent, come forth and appear on the ground! You shall neither enter nor penetrate [further into the body of the child]. O poison of the scorpion Befent, come forth and appear on the ground! I am Isis, the goddess, the lady (or, mistress) of words of power, and I am the maker of words of power (i.e., spells), and I know how to utter words with magical effect. Hearken you to me, O every reptile which possesses the power to bite (i.e., to sting), and fall headlong to the ground! O poison of the scorpion Mestet, make no advance [into his body]. O poison of the scorpion Mestetef, rise not up [in his body]. O poison of the scorpions Petet and Thetet, penetrate not [into his body]. [O poison of] the scorpion Maatet (or, Martet), fall down on the ground."

[Here follows the] "Chapter of the stinging [of scorpions]."

And Isis, the goddess, the great mistress of spells (or, words of power), she who is at the head of the gods, to whom the god Keb gave his own magical spells for the driving away of poison at noonday, and for making poison to go back, and retreat, and withdraw, and go backward, spoke, saying, "Ascend not into heaven, through the command of the beloved one of Ra, the egg of the Smen goose which comes forth from the sycamore. Truly my words are made to command the uttermost limit of the night. I speak to you, [O scorpions] I am alone and in sorrow because our names will suffer disgrace throughout the nomes. Do not make love, do not cry out to the Tesheru fiends, and cast no glances upon the noble ladies in their houses. Turn your faces towards the earth and [find out] the road, so that we may arrive at the hidden places in the town of Khebt. Oh the child shall live and the poison die! Ra lives and the poison dies! Truly Horus shall be in good case (or, healthy) for his mother Isis. Truly he who is stricken shall be in good case likewise."

And the fire [which was in the house of Usert] was extinguished, and heaven was satisfied with the utterance of Isis, the goddess.

Then the lady Usert came, and she brought to me her possessions, and she filled the house of the woman Tah, for the Ka of Tah, because [she] had opened to me her door. Now the lady Usert suffered pain and anguish the whole night, and her mouth tasted (i.e., felt) the sting [which] her son [had suffered]. And she brought her possessions as the penalty for not having opened the door to me. Oh the child shall live and the poison die! Truly Horus shall be in good case for his mother Isis. Truly everyone who is stricken shall be in good case likewise.

Lo, a bread-cake [made] of barley meal shall drive out (or, destroy) the poison, and natron shall make it to withdraw, and the fire [made] of hetchet-plant shall drive out (or, destroy) fever-heat from the limbs.

"O Isis, O Isis, come to your Horus, O woman of the wise mouth! Come to your son"—thus cried the gods who dwelt in her quarter of the town—"for he is as one whom a scorpion has stung, and like one whom the scorpion Uhat, which the animal Antesh drove away, has wounded."

[Then] Isis ran out like one who had a knife [stuck] in her body, and she opened her arms wide, [saying] "Behold me, behold me, my son Horus, have no fear, have no fear, O son my glory! No evil thing of any kind whatsoever shall happen to you, [for] there is in you the essence (or, fluid) which made the things which exist. You are the son from the country of Mesqet, [you have] come forth from the celestial waters Nu, and you shall not die by the heat of the poison. You were the Great Bennu, who are born (or, produced) or; the top of the balsam-trees which are in the House of the Aged One in Anu (Heliopolis). You are the brother of the Abtu Fish, who orders what is to be, and are the nursling of the Cat who dwells in the House of Neith. The goddess Reret, the goddess H̱at, and the god Bes protect your members. Your head shall not fall to the Tchat fiend that attacks you. Your members shall not receive the fire of that which is your poison. You shall not go backwards on the land, and you shall not be brought low on the water. No reptile which bites (or, stings) shall gain the mastery over you, and no lion shall subdue you or have dominion over you. You are the son of the sublime god who proceeded from Keb. You are Horus, and the poison shall not gain the mastery over your members. You are the son of the sublime god who proceeded from Keb, and thus likewise shall it be with those who are under the knife. And the four august goddesses shall protect your members."
[Here are placed some hymns, and then the narrative resumes:]

"I am Isis, who conceived a child by her husband, and she became heavy with Horus, the divine [child]. I gave birth to Horus, the son of Osiris, in a nest of papyrus plants. I rejoiced exceedingly over this, because I saw [in him one] who would make answer for his father. I hid him, and I concealed him through fear of that [fiend]. I went away to the city of Am, [where] the people gave thanks [for me] through [their] fear of my making trouble [for them]. I passed the day in seeking to provide food for the child, [and] on returning to take Horus into my arms I found him, Horus, the beautiful one of gold, the boy, the child, without [life]. He had bedewed the ground with the water of his eye, and with foam from his lips. His body was motionless, his heart was powerless to move, and the sinews (or, muscles) of his members were [helpless]. I sent forth a cry, [saying]:

'I, even I, lack a son to make answer [for me]. [My] two breasts are full to overflowing, [but] my body is empty. [My] mouth wished for that which concerned him. A cistern of water and a stream of the inundation was I. The child was the desire of my heart, and I longed to protect him. I carried him in my womb, I gave birth to him, I endured the agony of the birth pangs, I was all alone, and the great ones were afraid of disaster and to come out at the sound of my voice. My father is in the Tuat, my mother is in Aqert, and my elder brother is in the sarcophagus. Think of the enemy and of how prolonged was the wrath of his heart against me, [when] I, the great lady, was in his house.'

I cried then, [saying,] 'Who among the people will indeed let their hearts come round to me?' I cried then to those who dwelt in the papyrus swamps (or, Ateh), and they inclined to me straightway. And the people came forth to me from their houses, and they thronged about me at [the sound of] my voice, and they loudly bewailed with me the greatness of my affliction. There was no man there who set restraint on his mouth, every person among them lamented with great lamentation. There was none there who knew how to make [my child] to live.

And there came forth to me a woman who was [well] known in her city, a lady who was mistress of her [own] estate. She came forth to me. Her mouth possessed life, and her heart was filled with the matter which was therein, [and she said,] 'Fear not, fear not, O son Horus! Be not cast down, be not cast down, O mother of the god. The child of the Olive-tree is by the mountain of his brother, the bush is hidden, and no enemy shall enter therein. The word of power of Tem, the Father of the gods, who is in heaven, makes to live. Set shall not enter into this region, he shall not go round about it. The marsh of Horus of the Olive-tree is by the mountain of his brother; those who are in his following shall not at any time . . . . . . it. This shall happen to him: Horus shall live for his mother, and shall salute [her] with his mouth. A scorpion has smitten (i.e., stung) him, and the reptile Aun-ab has wounded him.'"

Then Isis placed her nose in his mouth so that she might know whether he who was in his coffin breathed, and she examined the wound of the heir of the god, and she found that there was poison in it. She threw her arms round him, and then quickly she leaped about with him like fish when they are laid upon the hot coals, [saying]:

"Horus is bitten, O Ra. Your son is bitten, [O Osiris]. Horus is bitten, the flesh and blood of the Heir, the Lord of the diadems of the kingdoms of Shu. Horus is bitten, the Boy of the marsh city of Ateh, the Child in the House of the Prince. The beautiful Child of gold is bitten, the Babe has suffered pain and is not. Horus is bitten, he the son of Un-Nefer, who was born of Auh-mu. Horus is bitten, he in whom there was nothing abominable, the son, the youth among the gods. Horus is bitten, he for whose wants I prepared in abundance, for I saw that he would make answer for his father. Horus is bitten, he for whom [I] had care [when he was] in the hidden woman [and for whom I was afraid when he was] in the womb of his mother. Horus is bitten, he whom I guarded to look upon. I have wished for the life of his heart. Calamity has befallen the child on the water, and the child has perished."

Then came Nephthys shedding tears and uttering cries of lamentation, and going round about through the papyrus swamps. And Serq [came also and they said]: "Behold, behold, what has happened to Horus, son of Isis, and who [has done it]? Pray then to heaven, and let the mariners of Ra cease their labours for a space, for the Boat of Ra cannot travel onwards [while] son Horus [lies dead] on his place."

And Isis sent forth her voice into heaven, and made supplication to the Boat of Millions of Years, and the Disk stopped in its journeying, and moved not from the place whereon it rested. Then came forth Thoth, who is equipped with his spells (or, words of power), and possesses the great word of command of *maa-kheru*, [and said:] "What [ails you], what [ails you], O Isis, goddess who has magical spells, whose mouth has understanding? Assuredly no evil thing has befallen [your] son Horus, [for] the Boat of Ra has him under its protection. I have come this day in the Divine Boat of the Disk from the place where it was yesterday, —now darkness came and the light was destroyed—in order to heal Horus for his mother Isis and every person who is under the knife likewise."

And Isis, the goddess, said: "O Thoth, great things [are in] your heart, [but] delay belongs to your plan. Have you come equipped with your spells and incantations, and having the great formula of *maa-kheru*, and one [spell] after the other, the numbers whereof are not known? Truly Horus is in the cradle of the poison. Evil, evil is his case, death, [and] misery to the fullest [extent]. The cry of his mouth is towards his mother. I cannot [bear] to see these things in his train. My heart [has not] rested because of them since the beginning [when] I made haste to make answer [for] Horus-Ra, placing [myself] on the earth, [and] since the day [when] I was taken possession of by him. I desired Neheb-ka . . . . "

[And Thoth said:] "Fear not, fear not, O goddess Isis, fear not, fear not, O Nephthys, and let not anxiety [be to you]. I have come from heaven having life to heal the child for his mother, Horus is . . . Let your heart be firm; he shall not sink under the flame. Horus is protected as the Dweller in his Disk, who lights up the Two Lands by the splendour of his two Eyes; and he who is under the knife is likewise protected. Horus is protected as the First-born son in heaven, who is ordained to be the guide of the things which exist and of the things which are not yet created; and he who under the knife is protected likewise. Horus is protected as that great Dwarf (Nemu) who goes round about the Two Lands in the darkness; and he who is under the knife is protected likewise. Horus is protected as the Lord in the night, who revolves at the head of the Land of the Sunset (Manu); and he who is under the knife is protected likewise. Horus is protected as the Mighty Ram who is hidden, and who goes round about in front of his Eyes; and he who is under the knife is protected likewise. Horus is protected as the Great Hawk which flies through heaven, earth, and the Other World (Tuat); and he who is under the knife is protected likewise. Horus is protected as the Holy Beetle, the mighty wings of which are at the head of the sky; and he who is under the knife is protected likewise. Horus is protected as the Hidden Body, and as he whose mummy is in his sarcophagus; and he who is under the knife is protected likewise. Horus is protected [as the Dweller] in the Other World [and in the] Two Lands, who goes round about 'Those who are over Hidden Things'; and he who is under the knife is protected likewise. Horus is protected as the Divine Bennu who alights in front of his two Eyes; and he who is under the knife is protected likewise. Horus is protected in his own body, and the spells which his mother Isis has woven protect him. Horus is protected by the names of his father [Osiris] in his forms in the nomes; and he who is under the knife is protected likewise. Horus is protected by the weeping of his mother, and by the cries of grief of his brethren; and he who is under the knife is protected likewise. Horus is protected by his own name and heart, and the gods go round about him to make his funeral bed; and he who is under the knife is protected likewise."

[And Thoth said:]

"Wake up, Horus! Your protection is established. Make happy the heart of your mother Isis. The words of Horus shall bind up hearts, he shall cause to be at peace him who is in affliction. Let your hearts be happy, O you who dwell in the heavens (Nut). Horus, he who has avenged (or, protected) his father shall cause the poison to retreat. Truly that which is in the mouth of Ra shall go round about (i.e., circulate), and the tongue of the Great God shall repulse [opposition]. The Boat [of Ra] stands still, and travels not onwards. The Disk is in the [same] place where it was yesterday to heal Horus for his mother Isis, and to heal him that is under the knife of his mother likewise. Come to the earth, draw near, O Boat of Ra, make the boat to travel, O mariners of heaven, transport provisions of . . . . . . Sekhem to heal Horus for his mother Isis, and to heal him that is under the knife of his mother likewise. Hasten away, O pain which is in the region round about, and let it (i.e., the

Boat) descend upon the place where it was yesterday to heal Horus for his mother Isis, and to heal him that is under the knife of his mother likewise. Get you round and round, O bald fiend, without horns at the seasons, not seeing the forms through the shadow of the two Eyes, to heal Horus for his mother Isis, and to heal him that is under the knife likewise. Be filled, O two halves of heaven, be empty, O papyrus roll, return, O life, into the living to heal Horus for his it mother Isis, and to heal him that is under the knife likewise. Come to earth, O poison. Let hearts be glad, and let radiance (or, light) go round about.

"I am Thoth, the firstborn son, the son of Ra, and Tem and the Company of the gods have commanded me to heal Horus for his mother Isis, and to heal him that is under the knife likewise. O Horus, O Horus, your Ka protects you, and your Image works protection for you. The poison is as the daughter of its [own] flame; [it is] destroyed [because] it smote the strong son. Your temples are in good condition for you, [for] Horus lives for his mother, and he who is under the knife likewise."

And the goddess Isis said:

"Set his face towards those who dwell in the North Land (Ateh), the nurses who dwell in the city Pe-Tept (Buto), for they have offered very large offerings in order to cause the child to be made strong for his mother, and to make strong him that is under the knife likewise. Do not allow them to recognize the divine Ka in the Swamp Land, in the city of Nemhettu [and] in her city."

Then spoke Thoth to the great gods who dwell in the Swamp-Land [saying]: "O you nurses who dwell in the city of Pe, who smite [fiends] with your hands, and overthrow [them] with your arms on behalf of that Great One who appears in front of you [in] the Sektet Boat, let the Matet (Mantchet) Boat travel on. Horus is to you, he is counted up for life, and he is declared for the life of his father [Osiris]. I have given gladness to those who are in the Sektet Boat, and the mariners [of Ra] make it to journey on. Horus lives for his mother Isis. and he who is under the knife lives for his mother likewise. As for the poison, the strength thereof has been made powerless. Truly I am a favoured one, and I will join myself to his hour to hurl back the report of evil to him that sent it forth. The heart of Ra-Heru-Khuti rejoices. Your son Horus is counted up for life [which is] on this child to make him to smite, and to retreat from those who are above, and to turn back the paths of the Sebiu fiends from him, so that he may take possession of the throne of the Two Lands. Ra is in heaven to make answer on behalf of him and his father. The words of power of his mother have lifted up his face, and they protect him and enable him to go round about wheresoever he pleases, and to set the terror of him in celestial beings. I have made haste ......"

PTOLEMAIC PERIOD

114. DECREE OF PTOLEMY LAGIDES

After Alexander the Great's death, his empire was divided into satrapies with Ptolemy Lagides (the later Ptolemy I Soter) becoming satrap of Egypt. Alexander's brother, Philip Arrhidaeus, was given the empire, but since Arrhidaeus was mentally incompetent, a regent would rule on his behalf. After the assassination of Arrhideaus in 317 BCE, Alexander Aegus (also known as Alexander IV), the son of Alexander the Great, was made king, but being only a boy, he also would have a regent rule for him. This decree, found on a black basalt slab near Cairo, was made by Ptolemy and is dated to the seventh year of Alexander Aegus (311 BCE), which also happens to be the year the boy was murdered.

In the year seven, beginning of inundation, and the Holiness of Horus, the youthful, rich in strength, Lord of the diadems, loving the gods (who) gave him his father's dignity, the golden Horus, the ruler in the whole world, King of Upper and Lower Egypt, Lord of both lands, delight of Amen's heart, chosen by the sun, Son of the Sun, of Alexander the immortal, of the gods of the city Pe (and) Tep the friend. He being as King in the stranger's world, as was His Holiness in Inner Asia, so there was a great Viceroy in Egypt, Ptolemaeus was he called. A person of youthful energy was he, strong in both arms, prudent of mind, powerful amidst men, of firm courage, steady foot, repelling the raging, not turning his back, striking the face of his foes amidst their combat. When he had seized the bow not a shot is from the opponent' a flourish of his sword in the fight no one could stand his ground, of mighty hand, nor was his hand repulsed, nor repented he of what his mouth utters, none is like him in the stranger's world. He had restored the sculptures of the gods, found in Asia, and all the furniture and books of the temples of Northern and Southern Egypt, he had restored them to their place. He had made as his residence the fortress of the King, "Loving the name of Amen the sun-chosen the Son of the Sun, Alexander," as it is called on the shore of the great sea of the Ionians. Rakotis was its former name. He had gathered Ionians many and their cavalry (and) their numerous ships, with their crew. When he marched with his men to the Syrians' land, who were at war with him, he penetrated its interior, his courage was as mighty as the eagle amongst the young birds. He took them at one stroke, he led their princes, their cavalry, their ships, their works of art, all to Egypt. After this, when he set out for the region of Mermerti, he took it in one time, he brought home their folk, men, women, with their horses, as revenge for what they did to Egypt. When he arrived in Egypt, his heart was rejoicing on what he had done, he solemnized a holiday, (and) this great Viceroy seeking the best for the gods of Upper Egypt (and) Lower Egypt.

Spoke to him his Sidesman, and the Elders of Lower Egypt, the maritime land called land of Buto, whereto the King had an Image of Tanen chosen by PTAH, Son of the Sun, Knabash, ever-living, to the gods of Pe (and) Tep after His Holiness had gone to Pe-Tep to investigate the littoral, all in their domain, to go into the inner marshes, to see each arm of the Nile, that goes into the great sea, to keep back Asia's fleet from Egypt, spoke His Holiness to his Sidesman, "This littoral country I wish to learn about." They spoke before His Holiness, "The sea-land, the land of Buto is its name, was from old the property of the gods of Pe-Tep, it was overthrown by foe Xerxes, who never gave anything to the gods of Pe-Tep." Then spoke His Holiness to bring to him the Priests (and) Archons of Pe-Tep. They hastily brought (them) to him. His Holiness said, "I wish to know the souls of the gods of Pe-Tep about this? What they did to the impious for the bad action he had done?" They replied, "The impious Xerxes had acted wrongfully to Pe-Tep, he took away his possession." They spoke to His Holiness the King, "Lord and Horus, Son of Isis, Son of Osiris, Ruler of Rulers, King of Kings of Upper Egypt, King of Kings of Lower Egypt, avenger of his father, Lord of Pe, origin of the gods, there being afterwards no King like him, threw away the impious Xerxes from his palace with his eldest son, making themselves known in the city Sais of Neith on this day at the side of the Holy Mother." Thus spoke His Holiness, "This mighty god amongst the gods, there is no King after him, may he be bestowed on the way of holiness! I swear it." Then spoke the Priests (and) Archons of Pe-Tep, "May Your Holiness decree, to give the littoral, the land of Buto it is called, to the gods of Pe-Tep, with bread, drinks, oxen, birds, all good things, that it may be renewed in your name for its donation to the gods of Pe-Tep a second time, as remunerating the distinguishing action of yours." Then answered this great Viceroy: "Let a decree be made in writing at the seat of the King's scribe of the audit to this effect:

"Ptolemaeus, Satrap of land of Buto, I give it to Horus the avenger of his father, Lord of Pe, (and) to Buto, the Lady of Pe-Tep, from this day and for ever, with its villages all, its cities all, all its inhabitants, all its meads, all its waters, all its oxen, all its birds, all its cattle herds, (and) all things produced therein, what was (formerly) and its additions (and) with the donation given by King, Lord of both lands, Khabash, everliving. Its South limit is domain of the city Buto and Hermopolis, on the North against the mouths of the Nile on the North, the downs on the shore of the great sea, on the West the mouths of the oarsmen............. against the downs in the East of the nome of Sebennys, so that its calves may be for the Great Hawk, its oxen for the face of Nebtauit, its cattle for the Living Hawk, its milk to the Glorious Child, its birds to him in Sa, who ... life his.................. is, all the fruits of its ground on the table of Horus himself, Lord of Pe, and of Buto (lady) to the crown of Ra-Harmachis for ever. All which is given to the utmost by the King, Lord of both lands, Image of Tanen, chosen by Ptah, Son of the Sun, Khabash, ever-living, (and the gift) is renewed by this great ruling Viceroy of Egypt, Ptolamaeus, the donations to the gods of Pe-Tep for ever. In reward of this for what he has done, may he receive victory and strength to his heart's content, so that he may always be dreaded as now by strange people. The land of Buto, whoever tries to plan its removal of any part thereof, let him be excommunicated by those in Pe, let him be cursed by those in Tep, that he may be in the burning breath of the goddess Aptaui on the day of her dread, with neither a son nor a daughter to give him water."

𓂝𓏤𓏏𓏥𓈖𓂋𓏏𓏥𓈖𓏏𓏏𓏥𓏏𓈖𓂋𓏏𓏥𓏏𓏏𓏥𓈖

115. MARRIAGE CONTRACT OF HERACLIDES AND DEMETRIA

This marriage contract comes from a papyrus found at Elephantine and is written in Greek. The bride and groom are of Greek background, which can be told by their names and the somewhat stringent provisions of the contract. The contract is dated to the seventh year of Alexander Aegus (311 BCE), the same year as the previous document.

In the seventh year of the reign of Alexander the son of Alexander, the fourteenth year of the satrapy of Ptolemaeus, the month Dios. Contract of marriage between Heraclides and Demetria.

Heraclides takes Demetria of Cos as his lawful wife from her father Leptines of Cos and her mother Philotis, both parties being freeborn, and the bride bringing clothing and adornment of the value of 1000 drachmas, and let Heraclides provide for Demetria all things that are fitting for a freeborn woman, and that we should live together wherever shall seem best to Leptines and Heraclides in consultation together. And if Demetria shall be detected doing anything wrong to the shame of her husband Heraclides, let her be deprived of all that she has brought, and let Hcraclides prove his charge against Demetria in the presence of three men, whom both shall approve. And let it not be allowed to Heraclides to bring in another woman to the insult of Demetria, nor to beget children by another woman, nor shall Heraclides do any wrong to Demetria on any pretext. And if Heraclides shall be detected doing any of these things, and Demetria shall prove it in the presence of three men, whom both shall approve, let Heraclides repay to Demetria the dowry which she brought to the value of 1000 drachmas, and let him pay in addition 1000 drachmas of Alexander's coinage. And let the right of execution be as if a formal decree of the court had been obtained to Demetria and to those acting with Demetria or Heraclides himself and all Heraclides' property both on land and sea. And let this contract be valid under all circumstances, as if the agreement had been come to in that place wheresoever Heraclides brings the charge against Demetria, or Demetria and those acting with Demetria bring the charge against Heraclides. And let Heraclides and Demetria enjoy equal legal lights both in preserving their own contracts, and in bringing charges against one another. Witnessed by Cleon of Gela, Anticrates of Temnos, Lysis of Temnos, Dionysius of Temnos, Aristomachus of Cyrene, and Aristodicus of Cos.

116. MANETHO'S *AEGYPTICA*

Manetho was an Egyptian priest from Sebennytos in Lower Egypt who lived during the reigns of Ptolemy I, II and III. His Aegyptica *was a full history of Egypt, written in Greek, perhaps completed during the reign of Ptolemy II. No copy of the work exists anymore; however several ancient writers quote extracts from it, including this passage quoted by Flavius Josephus in his book* Against Apion *(late first century CE). It deals with the Hyksos invasion of Egypt during the Second Intermediate Period.*

There was a king of ours whose name was Timaus (Dedumose I). Under him it came to pass, I know not how, that God was averse to us, and there came, after a surprising manner, men of ignoble birth out of the eastern parts, and had boldness enough to make an expedition into our country, and with ease subdued it by force, yet without our hazarding a battle with them. So when they had gotten those that governed us under their power, they afterwards burnt down our cities, and demolished the temples of the gods, and used all the inhabitants after a most barbarous manner; nay, some they slew, and led their children and their wives into slavery. At length they made one of themselves king, whose name was Salatis (Sheshi); he also lived at Memphis, and made both the upper and lower regions pay tribute, and left garrisons in places that were the most proper for them. He chiefly aimed to secure the eastern parts, as foreseeing that the Assyrians, who had then the greatest power, would be desirous of that kingdom, and invade them; and as be found in the Saite Nomos, a city very proper for his purpose, and which lay upon the Bubastic channel, but with regard to a certain theologic notion was called Avaris: this he rebuilt, and made very strong by the walls he built about it, and by a most numerous garrison of two hundred and forty thousand armed men which be put into it to keep it. There Salatis came in summer time, partly to gather his corn and pay his soldiers their wages, and partly to exercise bis armed men, and thereby to terrify foreigners. When this man had reigned thirteen years, after him reigned another, whose name was Beon, for forty-four years; after him reigned another, called Apachtias thirty-six years and seven months; after him Apophis reigned sixty-one years, and then Janias fifty years and one month; after all these reigned Assis forty-nine years and two months. And these six were the first rulers among them, who were all along making war with the Egyptians, and were very desirous gradually to destroy them to the very roots. This whole nation was styled Hycsos, that is, shepherd-kings; for the first syllable Hyc, according to the sacred dialect, denotes, a king, as is sos a shepherd; but this according to the ordinary dialect; and of these is compounded Hycsos: but some say; that these people were Arabians.

These people, whom we have before named kings and called shepherds also, and their descendants, kept possession of Egypt five hundred and eleven years. After these, the kings of Thebais and of the other parts of Egypt made an insurrection against the shepherds, and that there a terrible aud long war was made between them.... Under a king, whose name was Alisphragmuthosis, the shepherds were subdued by him, and were, indeed, driven out of other parts of Egypt, but were shut up in a place that contained ten thousand acres: This place was named Avaris.... The shepherds built a wall round all this place, which was a large and a strong wall, and this in order to keep all their possessions and their prey within a place of strength, but Thummosis, the son of Alisphragmuthosis, made an attempt to take them by force and by siege, with four hundred and eighty thousand men to lie round about them; but upon his despair of taking the place by that siege, they came to a composition with them, that they should leave Egypt, and go, without any harm to be done to them, wherever they would; and after this composition was made, they went away with their whole families and effects, not fewer in number than two hundred and forty thousand, and took their journey from Egypt through the wilderness for Syria; but that, as they were in fear of the Assyrians, who had then the dominion over Asia, they built a city in that country which is now called Judea, and large enough to contain this great number of men, and called it Jerusalem....

When this people or shepherds were gone out of Egypt to Jerusalem, Tethmosis the king of Egypt who drove them out reigned afterward twenty-five years and four months, and then died; after him his son Chebron took the kingdom for thirteen years; after whom came Amenophis, for twenty years and seven months; then came his sister Amesses, for twenty-one years and nine months; after her came Mephres, for twelve years and nine months; after him was Mephramuthosis, for twenty-five years and ten months; after him was Thmosis, for nine years and eight months; after him came

Amenophis, for thirty years and ten months; after him came Orus, for thirty-six years and five months; then came his daughter Acenchres, for twelve years and one month; then was her brother Rathotis, for nine years; then was Acencheres, for twelve years and five months; then came another Acencheres, for twelve years and three months; after him Armais, for four years and one mouth; after him was Harnesses, for one year and four months; after him came Armesses Miammonn, for sixty years and two months; after him Amenophh, for nineteen years and six months; after him came Sethosis and Harnesses, who had an army of horse, and a naval force. This king appointed his brother Armais to be his deputy over Egypt. He also gave him all the other authority of a king, but with these only injunctions, that he should not wear the diadem, nor be injurious to the queen, the mother of his children; and that he should not meddle with the other concubines of the king, while he made an expedition against Cyprus and Phoenicia, and besides against the Assyrians and the Medes. He then subdued them all, some by his arms, some without fighting, and some by the terror of his great army; and, being puffed up by the great successes hie had had, he went still on the mans boldly, and overthrew the cities and countries that lay in the eastern parts. But after some considerable time, Armais, who was left in Egypt, did all those very things, by way of opposition, which his brother had forbid him to do, without fear; for he used violence to the queen, and continued to make use of the rest of the concubines, without sparing any of them: nay, at the persuasion of his friends, he put on the diadem, and set up to oppose his brother. But then be who was set over the priests of Egypt wrote letters to Sethosis, and informed him of all that had happened, and how his brother had set up to oppose him: be, therefore, returned back to Pelusium immediately, and recovered his kingdom again. The country also was called from his name Egypt; for Sethosis was himself called Egyptus, as was his brother Armais, called Danaus.

117. THE CANOPUS DECREE

This is the earliest bilingual inscription we have from Egypt, a decree honoring Ptolemy III, his wife Berenice, and their daughter Berenice from the year 238 BCE, which was found at Canopus in the Nile delta. It is written on a stone stela in three scripts: hieroglyphics, demotic, and Greek. Here is a translation of the hieroglyphs.

On the seventh day of the month Apellaios, which [corresponds] to the seventeenth day of the first month of the season Pert, of the inhabitants of the Land of the Inundation, [in] the ninth year of the reign of [His] Majesty, the King of the South Ptolemy, the everliving, the beloved of Ptah, the son of Ptolemy, and Arsinoe, the two Brother-Gods; [when] Apollonides, the son of Moschion, was libationer of Alexander, whose word is law, and of the two Brother-Gods, and of the two Good-doing Gods; and when Menekrateia, the daughter of Philammon, was the bearer of the basket before Arsinoe Philadelphos: [on] this day [was passed the following] Decree: The chiefs of the temples, and the servants of the gods, and those who are over the secret things of the gods, and the priests [who]array the gods in their ornamental apparel, and the scribes of the divine hooks, and the learned men, and the divine fathers, and the libationers, according to their various classes and grades, who were accustomed to come from both groups of sanctuaries of the South and the North on the fifth day of the month Dios, whereon is celebrated the new year (i.e., the birthday) of His Majesty, and also on the twenty-fifth day of the same month, whereon His Majesty received his exalted rank from his father, gathered themselves together in the temple of the two Good-doing Gods which is in Canopus, and they spoke thus:— Inasmuch as Ptolemy, the everlivirig, the beloved of Ptah, the King of the South and North, the son of Ptolemy and Arsinoe, the two Brother Gods, and the Queen Berenice, his sister and wife, the two Good-doing Gods, are performing many great and benevolent deeds for the temples of the Land of the Inundation, and are on every occasion sanctifying the words of the renown of the gods exceedingly; and behold, at all seasons they provide for the temporal wants of Hapi, and Merur (i.e., Apis and Mnevis), and for all the other animals who live in holy houses and are venerated in Egypt, and they supply the things [they need] in large quantities, and provisions in overflowing abundance in order to ensure their performance of the proper service; and in the matter of the divine images which the vile men of Persia carried off to [a country] outside Egypt, His Majesty set out on an expedition to the lands of Asia, and he recaptured the images and brought them back to the Land of the Inundation and set them upon their thrones in the temples wherein they had stood originally; and he has made Egypt safe and secure exceedingly by fighting outside it, in the valley, and on the plain, and in many foreign desert and mountain lands, and [he has vanquished] the debased chiefs who were their overlords; and they (i.e., the King and Queen) have made safe and secure all living people of the Land of the Inundatiou, and the inhabitants of all the lands which are subject to their Majesties; and behold, when during their reign there came a year with a very low Nile, and the hearts of all men and women in Egypt were smitten with grief, because there came into their minds the memory of the misery and want which had come upon the inhabitants of the Land of the Inundation during their own time when a low Nile came in the reign of former kings, His Majesty himself and his sister were exceedingly careful in their minds for every one of those who dwelt in the houses of the gods, and for the [ordinary] inhabitants of Egypt, and they took great and exceeding forethought on their behalf, and turned their backs upon much revenue [due to them] in their desire to keep men and women alive, and they caused corn to be brought to Egypt from Eastern Syria, and from the Land of Keftet (Phoenicia), and from the Island of Inthanai (Cyprus) which is in the middle of the Great Green Sea (i.e., the Mediterranean), and from vast foreign lands, and they expended much gold in purchasing the grain at a high price, being anxious only to keep safe the men and women who were living in the Divine Land: [hereby] making to know their beneficence, which is everlasting, and their virtues (or, good qualities), [which are] many, both those who live at the present time, and those who shall come after them, and in return for these [deeds] the gods have given stability to their exalted dignity of the sovereignty of the lands of the South and North, and they shall reward them with good things of each and every kind for ever and ever. Strength and health!

And the priests of the Land of the Inundation have set it in their hearts to multiply in many respects the honour [which is paid to] the King of the South and North, Ptolemy, the everliving, the beloved of Ptah, and to Queen Berenice, the two Good-doing Gods, in the temples, and that which is paid to the two Brother-Gods who begot them, and that which is paid to the two Saviour-Gods who begot them; and the priests who are in all the temples of Egypt of each and every kind shall be magnified, and, in addition to the honourable priestly titles which they now bear, they shall be called "Priests of the two Good-doing Gods"; and their title of priests of the two Good-doing Gods shall be inscribed upon all documents, and cut upon the rings which they wear upon their hands; and there shall be formed another tribe among the priests who are now living in each and every temple, in addition to the four tribes of priests which exist at the present day, and it shall be called the "Fifth tribe of the two Good-doing Gods," since there happened the most auspicious event, with strength and health, that the King of the South and North, Ptolemy, the everliving, the beloved of Ptah, the son of the two Brother-Gods, was born on the fifth day of the month Dios, and this day was, in consequence, the beginning of great prosperity and happiness of all living men and women; and the priests whom the King made to enter into the temples in the first year of His Majesty's reign, and also those who have entered [them] until the fourth month of the season Shemu (i.e., Mesore), and also their children, shall be in this tribe for ever; and the priests who existed before these up to the first year [of His Majesty's reign] shall remain in the tribes wherein they were formerly, and their children likewise, from this day forward and for ever, shall be written down in the tribes wherein are their fathers; and instead of the twenty Priests Councillors who are elected at a certain period each year from the four tribes, five from each tribe, the Priests Councillors shall be twenty-five [in number], and the five additional priests shall be brought from the fifth tribe of the two Good-doing Gods, and the priests of the fifth tribe of the two Good-doing Gods shall be permitted to have a share in all the appointed ceremonies, and they shall go into the temple to assist in the services of libations and in all the other duties which they [i.e., the priests of the four tribes] have to perform in them; and a prophet in the fifth tribe shall be Chief of the tribe (Phylarch) as in the other four tribes.

And moreover, because a festival is celebrated in honour of the Good-doing Gods in all the temples in the course of every month, on the fifth day, and on the ninth day, and on the twenty-fifth day, according to the decree which has been set down in writing in times past, and because the festival which is made in honour of the great gods is observed universally as a very great festival throughout the Land of the Inundation at the proper season of the year, in like manner there shall be celebrated a great festival at the proper season of the year in honour of the King of the South and North, Ptolemy, the everliving, the beloved of Ptah and Queen Berenice, the two Good-doing Gods, in the sanctuaries of the South and North, and throughout all Egypt, on the day when the divine star Sothis makes its [first] appearance, which is called in the Books of the House of Life "the opening of the year" (i.e., New Year), which corresponds to the first day of the second month of the season Shemu (Payni) in the ninth year, on which shall be celebrated the festival of the New Year, and the festival of Bast, and the great festival of Bast in this month, because it is the season of the ingathering of fruits of all kinds, and the increase of the Nile.

Now behold, when it happens that the festival of the divine star Sothis changes to another day every four years, the day on which the festival of Ptolemy shall be celebrated shall not change also because of it, but the festival shall be celebrated on the first day of the second month of the season Shemu (Payni) even as it was celebrated on that day in the ninth year; and this festival shall be kept for five days, and [the people] shall wear garlands of flowers upon their heads and ornaments, and they shall lay offerings upon the altars, and they shall make drink offerings, and shall perform all things whatsoever it is right and proper to do. And thus it shall happen that they shall do whatsoever it is their duty to do, and their seasons of the year shall at all times be in accordance with ordinances (or, plans) whereon the heavens are founded to this very day; and it shall never once happen that the general festivals which are celebrated throughout Egypt in the season Pert (i.e., the Winter), shall be observed in the season Shemu (i.e., the Summer) because of the change of the festival of the divine star Sothis one day every four years; for, behold, the other festivals which at the present time it is customary to celebrate in the season Shemu (i.e., the Summer) would be observed in the season Pert (i.e., the Winter) in the times to come, even as it has already happened in the times of our ancestors, and it would happen again if the year consisted [only] of 360 days and the five days which it is customary to add to them at the end [of them].

And moreover, from this day onward, one day, a festival of the Good-doing Gods, shall be added every four years, in addition to the five additional days, at the beginning of the New Year, so that it may be known to all men that the arrangement of the seasons of the year was somewhat defective (or, short a little), and that the year [itself], and the rules which exist as to the laws of the science of the ways of heaven have now been set right, and [what was lacking] has been supplied by the two Good-doing Gods.

And in respect of the daughter who was born to the King of the South and North, Ptolemy, everliving, of Ptah beloved and the lady of the two lands Berenice, the two Good-doing Gods, whose name was called Berenice and who was straightway appointed Queen, since it has happened that this goddess, being a virgin, entered heaven suddenly while the priests who came from Egypt every year to the King of the South and North were in the house with His Majesty, they made a great lamentation immediately because of that which had happened. And they made supplication before the King and Queen, and put it in their hearts to allow this goddess to rest with the god Osiris in the temple of Canopus, because it is among the temples of the first rank, and because it is held in very great honour, both by the King and by all the men and women who live in the Land of the Inundation—behold, now the god Osiris makes his entry into this temple in the Sektet Boat at the stated time each year from the temple of Akerbemret (i.e., Herakleion), on the twenty-ninth day of the fourth month of the season Shat (i.e., Choiakh), when all those who are in the temples of the first class make offerings by fire upon the altars of the temples of the first rank on the right and left hand sides of the courtyard of this temple—and after these things they performed everything which it was right and proper to do in respect of making her a deity, and in concluding the mourning [which was made] for her, and they did it with the same readiness of heart and warmth which it is customary to show to Apis and Mnevis. And moreover, they passed a resolution to make the word[s] of everlasting renown of Queen Berenice, the daughter of the two Good-doing Gods, to be [known] in all the temples of the Land of the Inundation. And since it came to pass that she entered among the gods in the first month of the season Per (i.e., Tybi), which is the month wherein the daughter of Ea entered into heaven, and he called her name the "Eye of Ra," and the "Mehen Crown on his brow," because he loved her, and [since] festivals of procession in the great temples of the first class in this month wherein her majesty was made a goddess originally are celebrated in her [honour], there shall likewise be celebrated a festival and a procession for Queen Berenice, daughter of the two Good-doing Gods, in each and all the temples of the South and North, in the first month of the season Per (i,e., Tybi), and this festival and procession shall begin on the seventeenth day of the month, wherein her procession and the purification (or, conclusion) of the mourning for her were made originally, and shall last for four days; and moreover, a divine image of this goddess, made of gold and inlaid with precious stones of all kinds shall be set up in each and every temple of the first and second class, and the statue shall be placed upon its pedestal in the temple, and a servant of the god (prophet), or one of the libationers who has been chosen to make the great libation and to array the gods in their festal apparel, shall carry it in his arms on the day of the great, general festival, on each and every one of the festivals of the god, so that all people may see that it is adored according to its sanctity, and the statue shall be called "Berenice mistress of virgins." And behold, the crown which shall be on the head of the divine image shall not be [like to those] which are on the images of her mother, the goddess Berenice; for there shall be made [for it] two ears of corn, between which shall be an uraeus, and behind this uraeus there shall be placed, in an upright position, a sceptre of papyrus plants, similar to that which is in the hands of the goddesses, and the tail of the uraeus shall be twined round this sceptre, so that the construction (or, fashion) of this crown shall proclaim the name of Berenice according to its symbols in the writing (or, letters) of the House of Life (i.e., the hieroglyphics).

And moreover, at the festival [which takes place] in the days of Kaaubekh, in the fourth month of the season Shat (i.e., Khoiak), preceding the procession of Osiris, the virgin daughters and wives of the priests shall give (i.e., provide) another statue of Berenice, the "mistress of virgins," and burnt offerings shall be made to it, and there shall be performed for it every other thing which it is right and proper to do on the days of this festival, and the other virgins shall be at liberty to perform for this goddess in this respect whatsoever is right (or, customary) according to their desire. And behold, hymns of praise shall be sung to this goddess by the *qemat* priestesses [and by those who are] chosen to minister to the gods and [to place] the crowns of the gods [on their heads], and who are therefore their priestesses; and behold, when there are firstfruits of the crops ears of corn shall be carried by the *qemat* priestesses into the sanctuary, and presented to the divine image of this goddess, and the companies of the singing women [of the temple], and men and women [in general] shall sing to her image at the festivals, and [during] the processions of the gods, the hymns of praise which shall be composed by the learned men of the House of Life, and shall be given to the choirs of singing men, and copies [of the said hymns] shall be inscribed in the books of the House of Life; and when they (i.e., the priests) are made to enter into the temple by the King when the divine offerings of the priests are made in the temples, provision (or, food) shall be given to the female children of the priests, from the holy offerings which are made to the gods from the day whereon they are born, and the amount of the same shall be determined by the priests who are the Councillors in the temples, each and all of them, in proportion to the [amount of] the holy offerings. And the bread which shall be given to the wives of the priests shall be distinguished by being made in the form of the *qefen* loaf, and shall be called by name the "Bread of Berenice."

And the Councillors in the temples, and the governors of the temples, and the temple-scribes shall set this Decree in writing, and it shall be cut upon a stele of stone or bronze in the writing of the House of Life, and in the writing of the books, and in the writing of the Greeks, and it shall be set up in the hall of the congregation in the temples of the first, and second, and third orders, to inform every person of the honour which has been done by the priests of the temples of Egypt to the two Good-doing Gods, and to their children, according to what is right and proper to do to them.

118. THE TALE OF SETNE KHAEMWESET AND NANEFERKAPTAH

Khaemweset was a famous son of Ramesses II (Dynasty 19), who was known for his work on the restoration of temples and other monuments. By the time of the Ptolemaic dynasty he had taken on legendary status and was known by the nickname "Setne." There were several fictional tales written about him, including this one, sometimes called by the short-hand name "Setne 1." It concerns Setne's discovery of a magic book in the tomb of Prince Naneferkaptah. The text is written in demotic on Cairo Museum Papyrus 30646, but the first two pages of the six-page work are missing. Another papyrus (Cairo Museum 30692) contains a portion of the missing section, but it is not included in this translation.

(The missing part of this may perhaps be restored somewhat as follows:)—[And she said, 'It happened in the time of Pharaoh Mernebptah that the king grew old and he had no child but myself, whose name is Ahure, and Neneferkaptah, my elder brother, who is beside me. And the king desired that there should be a child to his children, and he commanded that a feast should be made before Pharaoh after three days, and that the sons of the generals and the daughters of the generals should be bidden. But my elder brother Neneferkaptah and I loved each other exceedingly, and I feared that the king would take me and give me in marriage to the son of a general and would marry Neneferkaptah to the daughter of another general in order that the family might be enlarged, and that so we should be separated. Now the king had a steward, an aged man, who loved Neneferkaptah and me exceedingly, and when he saw that we loved each other he spoke to me on the second day and said, "Do you not love your brother Neneferkaptah?" and I said, "Speak to the king that he may marry me with Neneferkaptah, and that he do not separate us." And he said, "I will go and speak to the king, for it is right that the son of the king should marry the daughter of the king": and my heart was glad exceedingly. And he went to the king and returned. And he said, "I went to the king and spoke with him, saying, 'My great lord the king, may he accomplish the duration of Ra. Is it not appropriate that the king should follow the law of Egypt and that he should marry Neneferkaptah with Ahure that a son may be born in the family of the king?' And the king was silent, and his heart was troubled exceedingly. And I said to him, 'What is it that troubles the king?'] *(Here the papyrus begins with the third page of the original manuscript.)*

III. '"[And he said to me] 'You are he that wrongs me. If it be that I have not a child beside two children, does custom make one marry with the other of them? I will make Neneferkaptah marry with the daughter of a general, [I will make Ahure marry] with the son of another general. May it be for the abounding of our family!'"

'The hour came, the banquet was set before Pharaoh; I was sent for and taken to the banquet [named, and it came to pass that] my [heart was] sad exceedingly, my demeanour not being as the day before.

'Said Pharaoh to me, "Ahure, did you send to me in these anxious affairs, saying, 'Marry me with [Neneferkaptah, my] elder [brother]?'" I said to him, "Let me marry with the son of a general, let him marry with the daughter of another general: may it be for the abounding of our family!" I laughed, Pharaoh laughed.

'......Pharaoh [said], "O steward of the king's house! let Ahure be taken to the house of Neneferkaptah tonight, and let all beautiful things be taken with her." So I was taken as wife to the house of Neneferkaptah.

'[There came the morning of the next day, and Pharaoh caused] to be brought to me a present of silver and of gold, and all the household of Pharaoh caused themselves to be brought to me; and Neneferkaptah made a good day with me, and he entertained all the household of Pharaoh. And in that same night he slept with me, and lo! he found me [pleasing. And it came to pass that he did not ......] with me, ever, ever; and lo! each of us loved his fellow.

'And when there came my time of making purification, I made not purification again: report of it was made to Pharaoh; his heart was glad exceedingly, and he caused much stuff to be taken [immediately to me]; he caused to be carried to me a present of silver and gold and royal linen, beautiful exceedingly. And when my time of bearing came, I bore this child that is before you, who is named Merab; and they caused it (or him) to be recorded in the House of Life.

'[It came to pass that my brother Neneferkaptah had no pursuit on earth but to walk on the necropolis hill of Memphis reading the writings that were in the tombs of the Pharaohs and on the tablets of the scribes of the House of Life, and the writings that were on [the temples, and his zeal] concerning writings was great.

'After these things it befell that there was a procession in honour of Ptah, and Neneferkaptah went to the temple to worship; and it chanced that he was walking behind the procession reading the writings that were upon the shrines of the gods. [But a certain priest perceived him, greater in age] than he, and laughed. And Neneferkaptah said to him, "Why do you laugh at me?"

'And he said, "I laugh not at you, but you laugh and read that of which no [man upon earth] has [the like. If it be that] you seek to pronounce a spell, come to me that I may cause you to be taken to the place wherein is the book which Thoth wrote with his own hand when he went down following the gods. (There are) two formulae in writing that are upon it, and when you [read the first formula you will] enchant the heaven, the earth, the underworld, the mountains, the seas; you will discover all that the birds of heaven and the creeping things shall say; you will see the fish of the deep, there being [power of God resting in water] over [them]. If you read the second formula, though you be in Amenti, you shall take again your form upon earth; you will see Ra shining forth in heaven with all the gods of his company, and the moon rising [in] its wise......"

'[And Neneferkaptah said to him], "O king, live for ever! let there be told to me some good thing that you seek, and I will cause it to be done to you, that you may direct me to the place in which this book is."

'And the priest said to Neneferkaptah, "If it be that [you] seek to be directed to [the place where this book is], you shall give to me a hundred *teben* of silver for my burial, and you shall cause to be given to me two priestly offices without fee."

'Neneferkaptah called a youth, and caused to be given to the priest the hundred *teben* of silver; he caused..........two...............to be made, he caused them to be given [to him without fee.

'And the priest said to] Neneferkaptah, "The book named, it is in the midst of the Sea of Coptos, in a box of iron, the box of iron being [in] a box [of bronze, the box of bronze] in a box of *kete*-wood, the box [of] *kete*-wood in a box of ivory and ebony, the box of ivory and ebony in a [box of silver, and the box] of silver in a box of gold, wherein is the book: there [being a schoenus] of every kind of serpent, scorpion, and reptile around the box wherein is the book, there being [an endless snake about] the box named."

'Now when the priest told these things [to] Neneferkaptah, Neneferkaptah knew not in what place on earth he was. He came forth from the temple, he told [to me all] that had befallen him, all. He [said] to me, "I will go to Coptos, I will bring this box and return without delay to the north."

'It came to pass that I reproached the priest, saying, "May Amen curse you in that you have related to him these [ill-omened things! You have prepared for me the] battle, you have brought to me the quarrel. (As for) the Thebaid, I have found it [cruel."

'I did all] in my power with Neneferkaptah that he should not go to Coptos, but he hearkened [not] to me. He went into the presence of [Pharaoh, and told before] Pharaoh of everything that the priest had told him, all; and Pharaoh said to him, "What is it that [you desire]?" He said to him, "Let the pleasure-boat of Pharaoh be given to me with its equipment, and I will take Ahure [with Merab, her ch]ild, with me to the south and bring the book straightway."

'There was given to him the pleasure-boat of Pharaoh with its equipment; we went up on board thereof, we made sail, we reached [Coptos. Report] of it [was made] to the priests of Isis of Coptos and the chief priest of Isis: they came down to meet us; they came forthwith to meet Neneferkaptah; and their women also came down to meet me. [We went up from the shore, we went into] the temple of Isis and Harpochrates. And Neneferkaptah caused to be brought ox, goose, wine, and made offering and libation before Isis of Coptos and Harpochrates. They took us to a house beautiful exceedingly......and Neneferkaptah spent four days making holiday with the priests of Isis of Coptos, the women also of the priests of Isis making holiday with me.

'And when the morning of our next day came, Neneferkaptah caused [to be brought] to him [much wax] and pure, and (thereof) he made a boat manned with its rowers and its navigators. He read a spell to them and made them to live; he gave them breath and launched them upon the sea. And having filled the pleasure-boat of Pharaoh with sand, [and made it fast to the magic vessel], he went on board. As for me, I sat over against the Sea of Coptos, saying, "I will find what shall become of him."

'And he said, "Row on, O rowers! with me to the place where[in] is this book." [And they rowed on with him, at night] as at midday. And lo! on the third day he reached it. He cast sand before him, and the waters were divided. And lo! he found a schoenus of every kind of serpent, scorpion, and reptile around [the place] wherein [the book was]; and lo! he found an endless snake around the box named. He pronounced a spell against the schoenus of every kind of snake, scorpion, and reptile that was around the box; he suffered them not to rise up. [He came to the place] in which was the endless [snake]. He fought with it, he slew it; it lived, it made its form again. He fought with it again a second time; he slew it, it lived again. He [fought with it again] a third [time]; he cut it in twain and put sand between the one piece and its fellow; [it] died, it became not itself again, ever.

'Neneferkaptah came to the place wherein the box was, [and found that it was a box of] iron. He opened it and found a box of bronze. He opened it and found a box of *kete*-wood. He opened it and found a box of ivory and ebony. [He opened it and found a box of] silver. He opened it and found a box of gold. He opened it and found the book in it. He took up the book out of the box of gold; he read from it a formula of writing; [he enchanted heaven, earth, the underworld, the] mountains and the seas; he became aware of all that the birds of the heaven, the fishes [of] the deep, and the beasts of the mountains spoke of. He read another formula of writing; he saw [Ra shining forth in heaven with all his divine cycle, and the moon rising and the stars in their forms]; he saw the fishes of the deep, there being divine power resting in water over them.

'And Neneferkaptah read a spell to the [water; he caused it to become as it had been. He went on] board; he said to the rowers, "Row on with me to the place which.........." And they rowed on with him at night as at midday. And lo! he arrived at the place wherein I was; [he found me sitting] over against the Sea of Coptos, not having eaten nor drunk, nor had I done anything on earth, but I was as one who has reached the Good House.

'I said to Neneferkaptah ....." let me see this book for which we have thus.......toiled." **IV.** He put the book in my hand. I read in it a written formula; I enchanted the heaven, the earth, the underworld, the mountains, and the seas; I discovered the things that the birds of the heaven, the fishes of the deep, and the animals say, all. And when I read another formula of writing, I saw Ra shining in heaven with all his divine cycle; I saw the moon rising with all the stars in heaven, and their procedure; I saw the fishes in the deep, there being power of God resting in water over them.

'But I was no scribe—I mean as compared to my elder brother Neneferkaptah, who was a good scribe and a learned man exceedingly. He caused to be brought to him a piece of new papyrus; he wrote (thereon) every word that was before him on the roll, all. Having caused it to be soaked with beer, he dissolved it in water, he made certain that it was dissolved, he drank it, he knew according to that in which it was.

'We returned to Coptos that same day. We made a good day before Isis of Coptos and Harpochrates. We embarked, we travelled down stream, we reached (a place) one schoenus to the north of Coptos.

'But behold! Thoth had learned all that had become of Neneferkaptah concerning the book. Thoth delayed not; he pleaded before Ra, saying, "Know my right and my cause with Neneferkaptah the son of Pharaoh Mernebptah!

He went to my chamber and plundered it, he took my box containing my book, he slew my guard that kept it." It was said to him, "He is before you, with every person that belongs to him, all."

'There was sent down a Power of God from heaven, with the command, "Suffer not Neneferkaptah to come safe to Memphis, him and every person belonging to him, all."

'At a certain moment Merab the child came out from beneath the awning of the pleasure-boat of Pharaoh; he fell into the river, he fulfilled the will of Ra. All who were on board, all uttered a cry. Neneferkaptah came forth from under his awning; he spoke a written spell to him, he made him rise up, there being power of God in water, resting over him. He spoke a written spell to him, he caused him to relate all that had become of him, all, together with the accusation that Thoth had made before Ra.

'We returned to Coptos with him, we caused him to be taken to the Good House, we caused them to wait about him, we caused him to be embalmed after the manner of a prince and a noble, we caused him to rest in his sarcophagus in the necropolis-hill of Coptos.

'And Neneferkaptah, my brother, said "Let us go down stream, let us not delay; lest Pharaoh hear the things that have befallen us, and his heart be grieved because of it."

'We went up on board, we travelled down stream, we went without delay one schoenus to the north of Coptos, the place where Merab the child fell into the water. I came out from under the awning of the pleasure-boat of Pharaoh, I fell into the river, I accomplished the will of Ra. All they who were on board uttered a cry, all.

'It was told to Neneferkaptah, and he came forth from under the awning of the pleasure-boat of Pharaoh. He spoke a spell to me, he caused me to rise up, there being power of God resting in water above me. He caused me to be taken up, he spoke a spell to me, he caused me to tell before him all that had become of me, all, together with the accusation that Thoth had made before Ra.

He returned with me to Coptos, he caused me to be taken to the Good House, he caused them to wait about me, he caused me to be embalmed according to the embalmment of a prince and a great noble, he caused me to rest in the tomb in which Merab the child rested.

'He went on board, he travelled down stream, he went without delay one schoenus to the north of Coptos, to the place where we fell into the river.

'(And there) he spoke with his heart saying, "Can I go to Coptos and there abide? Otherwise, if I shall have gone to Memphis, when Pharaoh shall ask me of his children, what is it that I shall say to him? (How) can I say to him, 'I took your children to the Thebaid and, living, let them die; and I came to Memphis still alive?'"

'He caused to be brought to him a strip of royal linen and made it as a bandage. He bound the book, he put it on his body and made it firm. And coming forth from under the awning of the pleasure-boat of Pharaoh, he fell into the river, he accomplished the will of Ra. All they who were on board uttered a cry, all, saying, "Great woe! Grievous woe! has he returned, the good scribe and learned man whose equal there has not been?"

'The pleasure-boat of Pharaoh travelled down stream, none on earth knowing the place where Neneferkaptah was.

'And when they reached Memphis report of it was made before Pharaoh. And Pharaoh came down to meet the royal pleasure-boat wearing mourning apparel, the people of Memphis wearing mourning apparel, all; together with the priests of Ptah, the high priest of Ptah, and the council and the household of Pharaoh, all.

'And lo! they perceived Neneferkaptah grasping the rudders of the pleasure-boat of Pharaoh by his art of a good scribe.

They took him up, they saw the book on his body. Pharaoh said, "Let this book which is on his body be hidden away." And the council of Pharaoh, together with the priests of Ptah and the high priest of Ptah spoke before Pharaoh saying, "O our great lord, the king, may he accomplish the duration of Ra! Neneferkaptah was a good scribe and a learned man exceedingly."

'And Pharaoh caused to be given to him entry to the Good House of sixteen days, wrapping of thirty-five, coffining in seventy days, and he was laid to rest in his sarcophagus, in his house of rest.'

(*Here ends Ahure's tale*)

'I have told them, the evils that befell us because of this book whereof you have said "Let it be given to me!" You have no lot in it, whereas our term of life on earth was taken for it.'

But Setne said, 'Ahure, let there be given to me this book that I saw between you and Neneferkaptah, else will I take it by force.'

Neneferkaptah raised himself on the couch, he said, 'Are you Setne to whom this woman has spoken these vain words, and you have not hearkened to her words? The book named will you be able to take it by power of a good scribe or by prevailing over me in playing draughts? Let us play for it at the game of fifty-two points.'

And Setne said, 'I am ready.'

They set before them the gameboard with its pieces, they played at the game of fifty-two and Neneferkaptah won one game from Setne. He pronounced a spell to him, he supplemented it with the draftboard that was before him, he caused him to sink into the floor to his feet. He did the like by the second game, he won it from Setne; he caused him to sink into the floor as far as his middle. He did the like by the third game; he caused him to sink into the floor as far as his ears.

After these things Setne was in great straits at the hand of Neneferkaptah. Setne called to Anherru, his brother by Menkh-art, saying, 'Delay not to go up on earth and relate before Pharaoh all that is befalling me, and bring the amulets of Ptah my father, and my books of magic.'

Anherru delayed not to go up on earth and to relate before Pharaoh that which was befalling Setne. And Pharaoh said, 'Take to him the amulets of Ptah and his books of magic.'

Anherru delayed not to go down to the tomb; he put the amulets on the body of Setne, and immediately Setne sprang up high, and reaching forth his hand for the book he took it.

It came to pass that as Setne came up out of the tomb the light walked before him and the darkness walked behind him. And Ahure wept for it, saying, 'Hail King Darkness! Farewell King Light! Every power has gone that was in the tomb, all!'

But Neneferkaptah said to Ahure, 'Be not grieved in heart, I will cause him to bring this book here, a forked stick in his hand, and a censer of fire upon his head.'

Setne came up from the tomb, and fastened it behind him as it had been. He went into the presence of Pharaoh, he related before him what had befallen him concerning the book.

And Pharaoh said to Setne, 'Take this book to the tomb of Neneferkaptah like a learned man, otherwise he will cause you to take it, a forked stick in your hand, and a censer of fire upon your head.'

But Setne hearkened not to him. It came to pass that Setne did no other thing on earth but unroll the book that he might read from it before every one.

After these things, it fell on a day as Setne was walking on the dromos of the temple of Ptah that behold! he saw a woman beautiful exceedingly, no woman having been like to her for beauty. She was beautiful, and many ornaments of gold were upon her, damsels walked after her, and fifty-two household persons belonged to her. **V.** And when he beheld her Setne knew not where on earth he was. Setne called to his attendant slave saying, 'Delay not to go to the place where this woman is and learn what has come under her command.'

The attendant slave delayed not to go to the place in which the woman was; he called to the slave handmaid who was walking behind her, he questioned her saying, 'What person is this?'

She said to him, 'She is Ta-bubue, the daughter of the prophet of Bast, mistress of Ankh-taui; and behold! she has come hither to pray before Ptah the great God.'

The slave returned to Setne, he related to him everything that she had said to him, all.

And Setne said to the slave, 'Go and speak to the slave girl saying, "Setne Khamuas, the son of Pharaoh Usermara, he it is that sent me saying, I will give you ten pieces of gold: pass an hour with me; or, have you a complaint of wrong which I shall cause to be settled for you. I will cause you to be taken to a place well concealed, and no one on earth shall find you."'

The slave returned to the place in which Tabubue was, he called to her slave handmaid and spoke with her, but she answered him with railing as though it were blasphemy that he had spoken. And Tabubue said to the slave, 'Cease arguing with this foolish slave, come [here] and make speech with me.'

The slave hastened to the place where Tabubue was, and said to her, I will give ten pieces of gold: pass an hour with Setne Khamuas, the son of Pharaoh Usermara. Have you complaint of wrong? He will settle it besides. He will cause you to be taken to a place well concealed, and no one on earth shall find you.'

Said Tabubue, 'Go speak to Setne saying, "I am a priestess, no mean person am I. If it be that you seek to do that which you desire with me, you shall come to Per-Bast to my house. Therein are all things made ready, while you do that which you desire with me, and none on earth shall find me, while moreover I shall not do as does a mean woman in the face of the street."'

The slave returned to Setne, and related before him everything that she had said to him, all. Said he, 'That is well.'

Scandalized was every man that was about Setne.

Setne caused a boat to be brought to him; he went up on board it, he delayed not going to Per-Bast, he came to the west of the Qemy. And lo! he found a house exceeding high, an enclosure wall being round about it and a garden on the north, a bench being in front thereof. Setne asked, saying, 'This house, whose house is it?' They said to him, 'It is the house [of] Tabubue.'

Setne went inside the enclosure wall, and lo! he directed his attention (in wonder) to the garden kiosque. Report of it was made to Tabubue; she came down, she took the hand of Setne, She said to him, 'By the prosperity of the house of the prophet of Bast, mistress of Ankh-taui, at which you have arrived, I am exceedingly glad. Come up from where you are with me.'

Setne ascended the steps of the house with Tabubue. And lo! he found the upper story of the house swept and garnished, the floor thereof being adorned with true lapis lazuli and true turquoise. Many couches were there, furnished with royal linen, and upon the dresser cups of gold in large number.

A cup of gold was filled with wine and given into the hand of Setne. She said to him, 'Let it be that you eat.' He said to her, 'There is no (eating) that I could do.'

They put fragrant gums on the censer, and unguents of the kind that Pharaoh uses were brought before him. Setne made holiday with Tabubue, he had not seen her like ever before, ever.

Setne said to her, 'Let us accomplish that for which we came here.'

She said to him, 'You shall come to your house, that in which you are. I am a priestess, I am no mean person; if it be that you seek to do that which you desire with me, you shall make a writing of maintenance and a compensation in money with regard to everything and all goods that belong to you, all.'

He said to her, 'Let the scribe of the school be brought.' He was brought forthwith, and Setne caused to be made for her a writing of maintenance and a compensation in money, for everything and all goods belonging to him, all.

And at a certain hour it befell that announcement was made before Setne saying, 'Your children are below.' He said, 'Let them be brought up.'

Tabubue arose, she put a garment of royal linen upon her, Setne saw every part of her in it, while lo! his desire increased beyond what it was before. Setne said, 'Tabubue, let me accomplish that for which I came here.' She said to him, 'You shall reach your house, that in which you are. I am a priestess, I am no mean person if it be that you seek to do that which you desire with me you shall cause your children to write under my deed. Do not allow them to quarrel with my children concerning your goods.'

He caused his children to be brought, he caused them to write under the deed. He said to Tabubue, 'Let me accomplish that for which I have come here.' She said to him, 'You shall reach your house, that in which you are. I am a priestess, I am not a mean person; if it be that you seek to do that which you desire with me you shall cause your children to be slain; allow them not to make quarrel with my children concerning your goods.'

Setne said, 'Let there be done to them the abomination that has come to your heart.'

She caused his children to be slain before him, she caused them to be cast down from the window to the dogs and the cats. They ate their flesh, he hearing them, while he drank with Tabubue.

Setne said, 'Tabubue, let us accomplish that for which we came here. Everything that you have said I have done for you, all.'

Tabubue said to him, 'Come up from where you are to this chamber.' And Setne went to the chamber, he lay down upon a couch of ivory and ebony, his desire receiving gold.

Tabubue lay down by the side of Setne; he put forth his hand to touch her, but she opened her mouth wide in a great cry. And lo! Setne awaked being in a burning heat, his phallus being in a .... nor were there any clothes on earth upon him.

At a certain time it came to pass that Setne perceived a noble person riding in a litter, many men running at his feet, he being like a Pharaoh. And Setne was about to rise, but for shame he could not rise because there was no clothing upon him.

(The) Pharaoh said, 'Setne, what makes you in this guise in which you are?' He said, 'Neneferkaptah is he who has done these things to me, all.'

(The) Pharaoh said, 'Go to Memphis; as for your children they are seeking you, they are standing before Pharaoh in their due order.'

Setne said before (the) Pharaoh, 'My great lord the King, may he accomplish the duration of Ra! In what wise can I go to Memphis, there being no clothing on earth upon me?'

(The) Pharaoh called to a slave who was standing by and caused him to give clothing to Setne. (The) Pharaoh said, 'Setne, go to Memphis. Your children, they are alive, they are standing in their due order before Pharaoh.'

Setne came to Memphis, he embraced his children, he found them alive.

Pharaoh said, 'Is it drunken that you have been?' And Setne related everything that had befallen him with Tabubue and with Neneferkaptah, all. Pharaoh said, Setne, I did what I could for you before, saying, "They will slay you if you take not this book to the place where you brought it," and until this time you gave no heed. Let this book be taken to Neneferkaptah, a fork and stick in your hand, and a censer of fire on your head.'

Setne came out from the presence of Pharaoh, a fork and stick in his hand, a censer of fire on his head.

He went down to the tomb in which was Neneferkaptah. **VI.** Ahure said to him, 'Setne, the great god Ptah is he that has brought you safe.'

(But) Neneferkaptah laughed, saying, "This is that which I said to you before."

Setne made salutation to Neneferkaptah: he found it to be as though it were the Sun that was in the whole tomb, And Ahure and Neneferkaptah made salutation to Setne exceedingly.

Said Setne, 'Neneferkaptah, is there anything that is disgraceful?' Neneferkaptah said, Setne, you know that Ahure with Merab her child, they are in Coptos, (albeit, they are) also here in this tomb by the craft of a good scribe. Let it be laid upon you to undertake the task that you go to Coptos and that you bring them here.'

Setne came up from the tomb, he went into the presence of Pharaoh, he related before Pharaoh everything that Neneferkaptah said to him, all.

Pharaoh said, 'Setne, go to Coptos, bring Ahure with Merab her son.'

He said before Pharaoh, 'Let there be given to me the pleasure-boat of Pharaoh with its equipment.' The pleasure-boat of Pharaoh was given him with its equipment.

He went on board, he made sail, he delayed not, he reached Coptos. Announcement of it was made before the priests of Isis [of] Coptos and the high priest of Isis. They came down to meet him, they handed him to the shore. He went up from there, he went into the temple of Isis of Coptos and Harpochrates, he caused ox, goose, wine to be brought, he made offering and libation before Isis of Coptos and Harpochrates.

He went to the necropolis hill of Coptos with the priests of Isis and the high priest of Isis. They spent three days and three nights seeking in all the tombs which were on the necropolis hill of Coptos, turning over the stelae of the scribes of the House of Life, and reading the writings that were upon them. But they found not the resting-places in which were Ahure with Merab her son.

Neneferkaptah found that they had not found the resting-place of Ahure with Merab her son. He arose (from the dead) as an old man, a priest great of age exceedingly, and came to meet Setne.

Setne saw him; Setne said to the old man, 'You are in the likeness of a man that is great of age; do you know the resting-place in which are Ahure with Merab her child?'

The old man said to Setne, 'The father of the father of my father told it to the father of my father, saying, "the father (of the father) of my father told it to the father of my father, saying, The resting-place of Ahure and Merab her son is by the southern corner of the house of the .... priest ..."'

Said Setne to the old man, 'Perchance 'tis on account of cheating that the .... priest did to you, that you go about to cause his house to be pulled down.'

The old man said to Setne, 'Let a watch be placed over me, and let the house of the......priest be destroyed, and if it be that they find not Ahure with Merab her son under the south corner of his house, let abomination be done to me.'

They set a watch over the old man, they found the resting-place of Ahure with Merab her son under the south corner [of the] house of the ... priest. And Setne had them bring those great people on board the pleasure-boat of Pharaoh, and caused the house of the ... priest to be built according as it was at first.

And Neneferkaptah caused Setne to discover the fact that it was he that had come to Coptos to cause them to find the resting-place in which was Ahure with Merab her son.

Setne went up on board the pleasure-boat of Pharaoh, he went down-stream, he delayed not, he reached Memphis with the people that were with him, all.

Announcement of it was made before Pharaoh, he came down to meet the royal pleasure-boat. He had these great people brought to the tomb in which was Neneferkaptah, and so caused a filling to be made above them, in one manner.

Colophon.

A complete writing is this relating of Setne Khamuas and Neneferkaptah, and Ahure his wife, and Merab her child. This copy was written.....year 15, first month of winter (Tybi).......

119. THE TALE OF SETNE KHAEMWESET AND HIS SON SI-OSIRI

In this second demotic Setne story (often called "Setne 2"), Setne and his wife give birth to an unusual son with magical powers. The papyrus on which it was found (British Museum Papyrus 604) dates to the first century CE, but the tale was probably composed in the Ptolemaic period. The beginning is missing.

The Birth of Si-Osiri

[Setne Khamuas, the son of Pharaoh Usermara, took to wife his sister Meh-wesekht whom he loved extremely; but they had no child and their hearts were grieved because of it. It befell that one night as she slept she dreamed a] dream, they speaking with her [saying, 'Are] you Meh-wesekht [the wife] of Setne, who lies [in vain seeking] to obtain healing [for yourself and your husband. When the morning of tomorrow has] come, go to the entrance of the lavatory of Setne your husband; you shall find a melon-vine that grows there.....and its gourds, and you shall put it back. [It shall be to you] for medicine, and you shall give [of it to Setne your husband. You shall lie with him and you shall conceive seed] of him the same [night].'

Meh-wesekht awoke [from] the dream, this being what she had seen; she did according to all things [that had been told her by dream. She lay down by] the side of [Setne] her husband, and she conceived seed of him.

There came her [time of making purification, she made] the sign [of women who are pregnant. Setne made announcement of it before Pharaoh, his] heart [being glad] because of [it] exceedingly. He bound [on her] amulets, he read to her magic writing.

Setne laid [him] down one night [and dreamed a dream, they speaking] with him saying, 'Meh-wesekht your wife has con[ceived seed in the night]. The child that shall be born, he [shall be named] Si-Osiri; many [are the marvels that he shall do in the land of Egypt.'

Setne awoke] from the [dream], having seen these things. [His heart was glad] exceedingly.

[She] made [her months of] pregnancy, she divided ......

[There came her time of bearing], she bore a male child. It was made known to Setne, [and he named him] Si-Osiri, according to that which was said by dream .... and they nursed him.

It came to pass that when the child [Si-Osiri was in his first year, one] would have said, 'he is two years old,' and when he was in his second [year] one would have said, 'he is three years old.' ....

[And it came to pass that Setne never passed an hour] without looking at the child Si-Osiri, great being the love [that he had for him] exceedingly.

The child grew big, he grew strong, he was sent to the school .... He rivalled the scribe that had been appointed to teach him. The child [Si-Osiri] began to speak ...... with the scribes of the House of Life, in [the temple of Ptah; all who heard him were] lost in wonder at him.

Visit to Amenti

And it was Setne's delight to have him made ready and taken to the banquet before Pharaoh, that [the nobles might see his cleverness and their hearts be pleased thereat;] and that he should make for himself honour with them all. [And on a certain day it happened that] Setne [was] made ready for banquet according to [his custom in] his [own] dwellings ..... the child [Si-Osiri was brought for the] banquet (to be held) in [his] presence.

[At a] certain moment behold! Setne heard the voice of a wailing, ... and he looked [from the upper chambers] of his dwelling [and behold! he saw a rich man] whom they were carrying out to the desert-necropolis, the wailing being [loud exceedingly] ...... [his condition] being more glorious than his own. He gazed [again] he [looked] at his feet, behold! he saw [a poor man being carried out from Memphis to the cemetery] he being wrapped [in] a mat, there being ...... and [none] walking [after him.

Said] Setne, 'By [Ptah, the great god, how much better it shall be in Amenti for great men] for whom [they make glory with] the voice of [wailing] than for poor men whom they take to the desert-necropolis [without glory of funeral]!'

[But Si-Osiri said, 'There shall be done to you in Amenti] like [that which] shall be done to this poor man in Amenti; [there shall not be done to you that which shall be done to this rich man in Amenti]. You shall [go] into Amenti [and you shall see....

(*The scraps of the thirteen succeeding lines seem to show that Setne was much troubled at the prediction; some dialogue follows, Setne asking a question. Probably the banquet was set aside; at any rate we must suppose that in course of time Setne and his son go to the necropolis, where Si-Osiri leads his father to the mystic entrance of Te. Here they pass through three halls in succession. As to what they saw in them nothing can be discovered from these fragmentary lines, and subsequent parts of the tale contain no clear allusions to the lost paragraphs.*)

[They entered the fourth hall] [And Setne saw some men that were scattered and apart, they being also ravenous]; there being others whose food, water, and bread, were hung over them, and they were hastening to take it down, but others dug pits at their feet to prevent their reaching it.

They entered the fifth hall and behold! Setne saw the noble spirits standing in their places, and those who had charges of violence standing at the entrance praying; [and] one man in whose right eye the bolt of the door of the fifth hall was fixed, he praying, he uttering great lamentation.

They entered the sixth hall, and behold! Setne saw the gods of the [council] of the dwellers in Amenti, standing in their places, the attendants of Amenti standing and making proclamation. They entered the seventh hall, and behold! Setne saw the figure of Osiris the great god, seated upon his throne of fine gold, and crowned with the *atef* crown, Anubis the great god being on his left and the great god Thoth on his right; and the gods of the council of the dwellers in Amenti were standing to left and right of him. The balance was set in the midst before them, and they were weighing the evil deeds against the good deeds, the great god Thoth recording, and Anubis giving the word to his colleague. For he of whom it shall be found that his evil deeds are more numerous than his good deeds is delivered to Ama of the Lord of Amenti; his soul and his body are destroyed and she does not permit him to live again for ever. But as for him of whom it shall be found that his good deeds are more numerous than his evil deeds, he is taken among the gods of the council of the Lord of Amenti, his soul going to heaven with the noble spirits. And he of whom it shall be found that his good deeds are equal to his evil deeds, he is taken amongst the excellent spirits that serve Sokari-Osiris.

And Setne saw (there) a great man clothed in raiment of byssus, near to the place in which Osiris was, he being of exceeding high position.

Setne marvelled at those things which he saw in Amenti. And Si-Osiri walked out in front of him; and he said to him, 'My father Setne, do you not see this great man who is clothed in raiment of royal linen, standing near to the place in which Osiris is? He is that poor man whom you saw being carried out from Memphis, with no man following him, and wrapped in a mat. He was brought to the Te and his evil deeds were weighed against his good deeds that he did upon earth; and it was found that his good deeds were more numerous than his evil deeds, considering the life destiny which Thoth had written for him.....considering his magnanimity upon earth. And it was commanded before Osiris that the burial outfit of that rich man, whom you saw carried forth from Memphis with great laudation, should be given to this same poor man, and that he should be taken among the noble spirits as a man of God that follows Sokaris Osiris, his place being near to the person of Osiris. (But) that great man whom you did see, he was taken to the Te, his evil deeds were weighed against his good deeds, and his evil deeds were found more numerous than his good deeds that he did upon earth. It was commanded that he should be requited in Amenti, and he [is that man] whom [you did see], in whose right eye the pivot of the gate of Amenti was fixed, shutting and opening upon it, and whose mouth was open in great lamentation. By Osiris the great god, Lord of Amenti, behold! I spoke to you on earth [saying, "There shall be done] to you even as is done to this poor man; there shall not be done to you that which is done to that great man," for I knew that which would become of him.'

Said Setne, 'My son Si-Osiri, many are the marvels that I have seen in Amenti. In due time let me learn [what has happened] to these men which are scattered and apart, they being also gluttonous; there being others whose food, water, and bread is hung above them, they hastening to take it down while others are digging pits at their feet to prevent their reaching it.'

Said Si-Osiri, 'It is just, my father Setne. These men that you saw scattered and apart, they being also ravenous, they are the kind of men on earth who are under the curse of God, and do work night and day for their living, while moreover their women rob them and they find not bread to eat. They came to Amenti: their evil deeds were found to be more numerous than their good deeds; and they found that that which happened to them on earth happened to them in Amenti— both to them and to those other men whom you saw, whose food, water, and bread is hung over them, they running to take it down while others dig a pit at their feet to prevent them reaching it: they are the kind of men on earth whose life is before them, but God digs a pit at their feet to prevent them finding it. They came to Amenti and they found that that which befell them on earth befell them again [in Amenti]; behold! their souls were taken into the Te. Find it at your heart, my father Setne, that he who is good upon the earth they are good to him in Amenti, while he that is evil, they are evil to him. These things are established, [they shall not be changed] for ever. The things that you saw in the Te in Memphis, they happen in the forty-two nomes in which [are the assessors] of Osiris the great god, [whose seat is in] Abydos, the place of Oracle, the dwellings of princes,....Philae.'

Si-Osiri ended these words which he spoke before Setne [his father]; he [returned] up from the desert of Memphis, [his father Setne] embracing him, his hand being in his hand. Setne asked [him, saying, 'My] son Si-Osiri, is the place by which we descended different from the place from where we came up?' But Si-[Osiri made] answer to Setne never a word. And Setne marvelled at the experience in which he was, saying, 'He will be able to become even as the noble spirits and as a man of God, and I shall walk with him saying, "he is my son."' Setne pronounced a [writing from his] book of exorcising demons, being lost in wonder at [that which] he had seen in Amenti. And these things weighed [upon] him, for to [none on earth] could he reveal them.

Si-Osiri in Pharaoh's Court

Now when the boy Si-Osiri had attained twelve years it came to pass that there was no [good scribe or learned man] that rivalled him in Memphis in reading writing that compels.

After these things] on a certain day Pharaoh Usermara went to the court of the palace in Memphis, and [the council] of the princes, of the generals, and of the great men of Egypt [stood] according to their places of standing in the court. One came [to the palace saying], 'This is a communication that an *ate* of Ethiopia makes, on whose body a letter [is sealed].'

Announcement of it was made [before] Pharaoh. He was brought to the court, he made prayer [saying, 'Is there any to] read before Pharaoh this writing that I have brought to Egypt without spoiling its seal; to read in the writings that are on it without opening it? If it be that there [be no good scribe and learned man in] Egypt who is able to read it without opening it, I will take the humiliation of Egypt to the land of Nehes, my country.'

At hearing these words Pharaoh [with his princes knew not the place on] earth in which they were, saying, 'By Ptah, the great god, it is a feat for a good scribe and learned man to read writings of which he shall see [their] country! Truly exalted is it to read a letter [without opening it!'

Said] Pharaoh, 'Let there be summoned to me Setne Khamuas, my son.'

They ran, they brought him that instant. He bowed himself to the ground, he saluted [Pharaoh]; he [raised] himself, he stood on his feet making the blessings of the salutation of Pharaoh.

Said to him Pharaoh, 'My [son], Setne, have you heard the words that this *ate*[1] of Ethiopia has spoken before me, saying, "Is there a good scribe and learned man in Egypt who shall be able to read this letter that is in my hand without breaking its seal, and shall know what is written upon it without opening it?"'

At hearing these words Setne knew not where on earth he was, saying, 'My great lord, who is he that shall be able to read a writing without opening it? After a time let there be granted to me ten days of delay that I may see what I shall be able to do to prevent the humiliation of Egypt being taken to the land of Nehes, the country of eaters of gum.' Said Pharaoh, 'They are (granted) to my son Setne.'

Apartments for residence were given to the Ethiopian; there was made for him every wickedness after the manner of an Ethiopian. And Pharaoh arose from the court, his heart being grieved exceedingly; he lay down without drinking or eating.

Setne went to his apartments, not knowing whither on earth he was going. He gathered himself in his clothes from his head to his feet: he lay down without knowing where on earth he was. They informed Meh-wesekht, his wife, of it; she came to the place in which Setne was, she put her hand within his clothes and found no warmth; he lay still in his clothes.

She said to him, 'My brother, Setne, there is no warmth in the lap; a change for worse in the flesh, illness, sadness of heart.'

---

1   Meaning uncertain. It appears to be a foreign word.

Said he to her, 'Cease from me, my sister Meh-wesekht; the matter on account of which my heart is grieved is not a thing that it is right to reveal to a woman.'

The child Si-Osiri came in, he stood over Setne, his father; he said to him, 'My father Setne, why do you lie in grief of heart? The things that are in your heart, tell them to me that I may cause them to cease.'

Said he, 'Cease from me my son Si-Osiri. As for the things that are in my heart, you are little of age, you are not great; take heed to yourself.'

Said Si-Osiri, 'Tell it to me that I may cause your heart to be refreshed concerning them.'

Said Setne, 'My son Si-Osiri, it is an *ate* of Ethiopia who has come up to Egypt with a letter sealed on his body, and he says, "Is there he that will read it without opening it? If it be that there be no good scribe and learned man in Egypt who shall be able to read it, I will take the humiliation of Egypt to the land of Nehes, my country." Behold I lay down, my heart being grieved thereat, O my son Si-Osiri.'

When Si-Osiri heard these words he laughed long. Said to him Setne, 'Why do you laugh?' Said he, 'I laugh because you are lying your heart grieved because of such a thing as this small matter. Arise, my father Setne; I shall be able to read the letter that was brought to Egypt without opening it, and to find what is written upon it without breaking its seal.'

At hearing these words Setne arose suddenly, saying, 'What is the sign of the things that you say, my son Si-Osiri?' Said he to him, 'My father Setne, go to the cellars of your house: every book that you take out of the case I will tell you what book it is, I will read it without seeing it, standing above you in your cellars.'

Arose Setne, he stood on his feet, he did according to all that Si-Osiri had said to him, all. Setne (Si-Osiri) read every book that Setne his father brought up to him, without opening them. Setne came up from the cellars of his house in all gladness. He delayed not to come to the place in which Pharaoh was, he related before him all the things that the child Si-Osiri had said to him, all; his heart was glad of it exceedingly.

Pharaoh washed himself for banquet with Setne; he caused Si-Osiri to be brought to the banquet before him. They drank, they made a good day.

Came the morning of its morrow; Pharaoh came forth to the court between his great men. Pharaoh caused the *ate* of Ethiopia to be fetched; he was brought to the court, the letter sealed on his body, and he stood in the midst of the court. The child Si-Osiri came into the midst and stood with the *ate* of Ethiopia; he cried against him, saying, 'Woe! you wicked one of Ethiopia; may Amon, his god, smite him. You that have come up to Egypt, the beautiful pool of Osiris, the throne of Ra-Harakht, the beautiful horizon of the Spirit, saying "I will take its humiliation to the land of Nehes": by the inspiration of Amon, your god, which is cast upon you, the words which I shall narrate—which are those that are written in this letter —speak not falsehood of them before Pharaoh your sovereign.'

When the *ate* of Ethiopia saw the child Si-Osiri standing in the court, he held down his head, he spoke, saying, 'Every word that you shall say I will not speak falsehood of them.'

The Ethiopian's Letter

The beginning of the narrative made by Si-Osiri, which he related before Pharaoh and his nobles, the people of Egypt attending to his voice. He said, 'This is what is written on the letter of the *ate* of Ethiopia who stands in the midst:

'"It came to pass in the days of Pharaoh Menkh-pa-Ra Si-Amon,[2] he being the beneficent king of the whole land, that Egypt overflowed with all things in his time; he was lavish in giving expenditure and labour in the great temples of Egypt.

'"It befell on a day that the *Kwr*[3] of the land of Nehes was .... the fields of the land of Amon. Behold! he heard the voices of three *ate* of Ethiopia [in the] prison-house, one of them saying in a loud voice, after other words, "May Amon not find for me failure nor the *Kwr* of Egypt cause abomination to be done to me; for I would cast my magic up to Egypt and I would cause the people of Egypt to pass three days and three nights without seeing other light than that of *kiki*-oil."

'Another said, after other words, "May Amon not find for me failure nor the *Kwr* of Egypt cause abomination to be done to me; for I would cast my magic up to Egypt and cause Pharaoh of Egypt to be brought to the land of Nehes, and I would cause him to be beaten with five hundred blows of the stick in the midst before the Viceroy, and I would cause him to be brought back to Egypt in six hours there precisely."

'When the Viceroy heard these words from the voices of the three men of Ethiopia, he caused them to be brought before him; he said to them, "Which of you is he that said, 'I will cast my magic up to Egypt, I will not allow them to see the light for three days and three nights' ?"

'They said, "It is Hor, the son of the Sow."

'Said he, "Which is he that said, I will cast my magic up to Egypt, I will bring Pharaoh to the land of Nehes, I will cause him to be beaten with five hundred blows of the stick in the midst before the Viceroy, I will cause him to be taken back to Egypt in six hours there precisely?"

'Said they, "It is Hor, son of the Nubian Woman."

'Said he, "Which is he that said, I will cast my magic up to Egypt, I will not allow the land to be fertile for three years?"

'Said they, "It is Hor, son of the Princess."

'Said the Viceroy (to Hor son of the Nubian Woman), "Perform this your feat of magic-writing. By the life of Amon the bull of Meroe, my god, if the work of your hand succeed, I will do for you abundance of good things."

'Hor, the son of the Nubian Woman, made a litter of wax for four; runners; he read a writing to them, he gave them breath of respiration, he made them live. He commanded them saying, "You shall go up to Egypt, you shall bring Pharaoh of Egypt up to the place in which the Viceroy is, and he being beaten with five hundred blows of the stick in the midst before the Viceroy, you shall take him back up to, Egypt, all in six hours."

'Said they, "Yes truly; nor will we allow anything to fail."

'The sorceries of the Ethiopian proceeded up to Egypt by night, they seized Pharaoh Menkh-pa-Ra Si-Amon, they took him to the land of Nehes, to the place in which the Viceroy was. He was

---

2   Thutmose III.

3   Equivalent of the Meroitic word *Qore*, the title of the king of Kush.

beaten with five hundred blows of the stick in the midst before the Viceroy, and they returned him up to Egypt in six hours there precisely.'

Now when Si-Osiri had related these things in the midst before Pharaoh and his princes, the people of Egypt hearing his voice he said, 'The inspiration of Amon, your god, is cast upon you; the words which I am saying, are they those that are written according to the letter that is in your hand?'

Said the *ate* of Ethiopia, 'Read on as you have read; every word that you say is truth, all.'

Said Si-Osiri before Pharaoh: 'When these things had happened they returned Pharaoh Si-Amon up to Egypt, his hinder parts having been beaten with a very great beating. He lay down in the shrine of Per-Hor, his hinder parts having been beaten exceedingly.

'Came the morning of its morrow; said Pharaoh to the courtiers, "What is it that has come upon Egypt until I am made to depart from it? Shame on the thoughts of the hearts of the courtiers saying, 'Probably the thought of the heart of Pharaoh has gone.'"

'Said they, "You are in health, you are in health, O Pharaoh our great lord! Isis the great goddess will cause your troubles to cease. What manner of words are these which you have spoken before [us O Pharaoh] our great lord? You (are) lying down in the shrine of Per-Hor and the gods protect you."

'Pharaoh arose, he caused the courtiers to see his back, it having been beaten with a great beating exceedingly. He said, "By the life of Ptah the great god, some one took me to the land of Nehes in the night, some one beat me with five hundred blows of the stick in the midst before the Viceroy. They took me back to Egypt all within the space of six hours here."

'At seeing the hinder parts of Pharaoh that they had been beaten with a great beating exceedingly, they opened their mouths with great clamour.

'Now Menkh-pa-Ra Si-Amon had a librarian who was called Hor son of Pa-neshe by name, a learned man exceedingly. He came to the place in which he (Pharaoh) was, he uttered a great cry saying, "My great lord, these are the sorceries of the Ethiopians. By the life of your.....I will cause them to enter your house of torment and execution."

'Said to him Pharaoh, "Hasten to me; let me not be taken to the land of Nehes another night."

'The librarian, Hor son of Pa-neshe, straightway came forth; he brought his books and his amulets to the place in which Pharaoh was. He read to him writing, he bound amulets on him to prevent the sorceries of the Ethiopians from getting power over him.

'He came out from before Pharaoh, he took with him offerings and libations, he went on board a boat, he went straight to Khmun. He entered the temple of Khmun; he made his offerings and libations before Thoth, the eight times great, Lord of Khmun, the great god; he made prayer before him, saying, "Give heed to me, my lord Thoth. Let not the Ethiopians take the humiliation of Egypt to the land of Nehes. You are he that made magic in writing, you are he that hanged up the heaven, that establisheth the earth, the underworld, that places the gods with the........ Cause me to know how to save Pharaoh from the sorceries of the Ethiopians."

'Hor son of Pa-neshe lay down in the temple. And in that same night he dreamed a dream that the figure of the great god Thoth spoke with him, saying, "Are you Hor son of Pa-neshe, the librarian of Pharaoh Menkh-pa-Ra Si-Amon? When the morning of to-morrow has come, go into the library of the temple of Khmun. You shall find (there) a shrine closed and sealed: open it. You shall find a box in the shrine named, and in it a roll of papyrus written with mine own hand. Bring it up, take a copy thereof, and let it rest in its place again. The Book of Magic is its name; it made protection for me from the enemies, and this it is that shall make protection to Pharaoh that it may save him from the sorceries of the Ethiopians."

'Hor son of Pa-neshe awoke from the dream, these being the things which he had seen; he recognized that the thing that had befallen was divine. He did according to every word that had been said to him in the dream, he went straight to the place in which Pharaoh was, he made for him amulets against sorceries in writing.

'Came the second day. The sorceries of Hor the son of the Nubian Woman returned up to Egypt by night, to the place in which Pharaoh was; (but) they returned to the place in which the Viceroy was immediately, (for) they could not get power over Pharaoh because of the amulets and sorceries that the librarian, Hor son of Pa-neshe, had bound upon him.

'Came the morning of its morrow. Pharaoh told before the librarian, Hor son of Pa-neshe, of everything that he had seen by night, and of how the sorceries of the Ethiopians had returned, for that they were not able to get power over him.

'Hor son of Pa-neshe caused to be brought to him much wax and pure, he made a litter for four bearers, he pronounced writing upon them, he gave them breath of respiration, he made them live. He commanded them, saying, "You shall go to the land of Nehes this night; you shall bring the Viceroy up to Egypt, to the place in which Pharaoh is, he shall be beaten with five hundred blows of the stick in the midst before Pharaoh, and you shall return him to the land of Nehes again, all in six hours there."

'They said, "Yes truly, nor will we allow anything to fail."

'The sorceries of Hor son of Pa-neshe travelled under the clouds of heaven, they went straight to the land of Nehes by night. They mastered the Viceroy, they brought him up to Egypt, he was beaten with five hundred blows of the stick in the midst before Pharaoh, and they returned him to the land of Nehes, all in six hours there.'

These things are what Si-Osiri related in the midst before Pharaoh and his nobles, the people of Egypt hearing his voice.

He said, 'By the inspiration of Amon your god which is cast upon you, O enemy of Ethiopia, the words that I am speaking, are they what are written in this letter?'

Spoke the Ethiopian, his head being held toward the ground, saying, 'Read on that as you have read; every word that you say is written in this letter.'

Said Si-Osiri, 'All these things having happened, they having brought back the Viceroy to the land of Nehes, all in six hours there, they put him in his place and he lay down.

'He arose at morn, having been beaten exceedingly with blows that had been given him up in Egypt.

(*The scribe has omitted accidentally a part of the story which must have described the conditions in which the Viceroy was found by the princes of Ethiopia, and have contained the beginning of the account of what had happened.*)

'beat me with five hundred blows of the stick in the midst before Pharaoh of Egypt, and returned to the land of Nehes again."

'He turned his back to the princes; they opened their mouths with great clamour. The Viceroy sent for Hor the son of the Nubian Woman. Said he (to him), "May Amon, the bull of Meroe, my god, curse you! You who did go to the men of Egypt hasten to my help to see what you shall do to save me from the hand of Hor son of Pa-neshe!"

'He (Hor the son of the Nubian Woman) made his sorceries; he bound them on the Viceroy to save him from the sorceries of Hor son of Pa-neshe.

'Came the night of the second day. The sorceries of Hor son of Pa-neshe travelled to the land of Nehes; they carried the Viceroy up to Egypt, he was beaten with five hundred blows of the stick in the midst before Pharaoh, he was taken back to the land of Nehes all in six hours there.

'It happened on this wise to the Viceroy for three days; the sorceries of the Ethiopians were not able to save the Viceroy from the hand of Hor son of Pa-neshe. The Viceroy was in anguish exceedingly... He caused Hor the son of the Nubian Woman to be brought to him, he said to him, "Woe you wicked one of Ethiopia! You did cause me to be humiliated by the hand of the men of Egypt; you could not save me from their hands. By the life of Amon, the bull of Meroe, my god, if it be that you shall not be able to cause me to be saved from the aerial cars of the men of Egypt, I will cause you to suffer an evil death exceedingly."

'Said Hor the son of the Nubian Woman, "My master the Viceroy! let me be sent up to Egypt that I may see him that makes sorcery there, that I may strive against him, that I may cause him to find the scorn for his hand that is at my heart."

'Hor the son of the Nubian Woman was dispatched from before the Viceroy. He came to the place where his mother the Nubian Woman was.

(*The scribe appears to have omitted accidentally another section.*)

"'If you go up to Egypt to do sorcery therein, take heed for yourself with the men of Egypt. You will not be able to contend with them. Be not caught in their hands so that you will not return to the land of Nehes for ever."

'Said he, "There is nothing of them, these things that you say. I cannot avoid going up to Egypt and (instead) cast my sorceries up into it (from Ethiopia)."

'Said to him the Nubian Woman his mother, "Whereas it has come to pass that you are going up to Egypt, set some signs between me and you: be it that you fail, I will come to you that I may see whether I shall be able to save you."

'Said he to her, "If it be that I am overcome, when you shall drink [and eat], any kind of liquid shall turn colour of blood before you, the foods that are before you shall turn the colour of flesh, the heaven shall turn the colour of blood before you."

'Hor the son of the Nubian Woman set signs between himself and his mother. He went up to Egypt, being crammed with sorcery; he traversed from that which Amon made as far as Memphis, to the place in which Pharaoh was, hunting for him who was making sorcery in Egypt.

'He came to the court before Pharaoh, he spoke, his voice being loud, saying, "Hey you that make sorcery against me in the court, in the place in which Pharaoh is, in the sight of the people of Egypt, you two scribes of the House of Life, (or) you scribe of the House of Life that does sorcery to the Viceroy, bringing him up to Egypt in spite of me!"

'As he spoke these words Hor son of Pa-neshe stood in the court before Pharaoh saying, "Hey you impious Ethiopian, are you not Hor the son of the Nubian Woman whom I saved in the reeds of Ra, as well as your companion of Ethiopia that was with you, when you were drowning in the water, being cast down from upon the hill on the east of On? Did you not consider the freeing of Pharaoh your sovereign, you causing his hinder parts to be beaten in the place where the Viceroy was, you coming up to Egypt saying, 'Is there he that does sorcery against me?' By the life of Atum, lord of On, the gods of Egypt have put you on your back to requite you in their country! Entertain yourself; I have come to you."

'At what time Hor the son of Pa-neshe said these words, Hor the son of the Nubian Woman answered him saying, "Is it he to whom I taught jackal language that does sorcery against me?"

'The man of Ethiopia made an effort of written magic, he caused fire to come out in the court. Pharaoh and the princes of Egypt uttered a great cry, saying, "Hasten to us you librarian, Hor son of Pa-neshe."

'Hor son of Pa-neshe made a formula of writing, he caused the sky to make a southern rain upon the top of the flame; It was extinguished on the instant.

'The Ethiopian made another effort of magic in writing, he made a great darkness over the court, none saw his brother nor his companion.

'Hor son of Pa-neshe read a writing to the sky, he caused it to desist and to be calm from the evil wind which possessed it.

'Hor the son of the Nubian Woman made another effort of written magic. He created a great vault of stone 200 cubits in length by fifty cubits in width above Pharaoh and his princes, which threatened to make Egypt without a king, the world without a sovereign.

'Pharaoh looked at the sky, he saw the vault of stone above him, he opened his mouth with a great cry together with the people that were in the court Hor the son of Pa-neshe pronounced a formula of writing. He created an aerial boat of papyrus, he caused it to carry away the vault of stone. Behold! it flew with it towards the Mighty Pool, the Great Water of Egypt. (Then) the man of Ethiopia knew that he was not able to contend with (the Egyptian); he made an effort in written magic to prevent his seeing him in the court, that he might transport himself to the land of Nehes, his city.

'Hor son of Pa-neshe pronounced a writing at him, he caused the sorceries of the Ethiopian to be revealed, he made him visible to Pharaoh and the people of Egypt that were standing in the court, he being in the form of an evil fox-goose and about to flee away. Hor son of Pa-neshe pronounced a writing at him, he caused him to fall on his back, a fowler standing over him, the knife in his hand ready to pierce, he being about to do abomination to it.

'All these things having happened, the signs which Hor the son of the Nubian Woman had set between himself and his mother happened before her—all. She delayed not to go up to Egypt she being in the form of the female goose; she stopped over the palace of Pharaoh, she wailing with her voice to her son, he being in the form of an evil fox-goose, the fowler standing over him.

'Hor son of Pa-neshe looked at the sky, he saw the Nubian Woman in the guise in which she was, he knew her to be the Nubian Woman, the Ethiopian. He pronounced a writing to her, he caused her to fall on her back, there being a fowler standing over her, his knife being about to put her to death.

'She changed from the form in which she was, she made her (proper) guise as an Ethiopian woman, she praying, saying, "Make not an end of us, Hor son of Pa-neshe. Forgive us this evil attempt. If it be that you give to us an aerial boat we will not return to Egypt ever again."

'Hor son of Pa-neshe made an oath by Pharaoh and the gods of Egypt saying, "I will not [let go] my effort of sorcery until you have made to me oath not to return up to Egypt for any kind of purpose."

'The Nubian Woman raised her hand (in oath) not to come up to Egypt for ever eternally. Hor the son of the Nubian Woman made oath saying, "I will not come up to Egypt until fifteen hundred years."

'Hor son of Pa-neshe withdrew his hand from his feat of written magic, he gave an aerial boat to Hor the son of the Nubian Woman and the Nubian Woman his mother. They proceeded to the land of Nehes, their city.'

This was the story told by Si-Osiri before Pharaoh, the people of Egypt attending to his voice, Setne his father seeing everything, the head of the man of Ethiopia being held towards the ground. And he said, By the life of your face, my great lord, that man that stands before you is Hor the son of the Nubian Woman whose words I have been relating and who has not repented concerning those things which he did at first; for he has come up to Egypt at the end of fifteen hundred years to cast sorceries therein. By the life of Osiris, great god Lord of Amenti, in whose kingdom I repose, I am Hor son of Pa-neshe— this man—I who stand before Pharaoh; and I that was in Amenti found that the Ethiopian enemy would fling his sorceries up into Egypt, there being no good scribe or learned man in Egypt at the time that would be able to contend with him. I prayed before Osiris in Amenti to let me come forth to the world again, to prevent his taking the humiliation of Egypt to the land of Nehes. It was commanded before Osiris to let me forth into the world. I awoke, I flew right up to find Setne the son of Pharaoh upon the peak of On and the peak of Memphis. I grew as that melon-vine with the intent of returning to the body again that I might be born to the world to make sorcery against this enemy of Ethiopia that stands in the court.'

Hor son of Pa-neshe, he being in the shape of Si-Osiri, made an effort of written magic against the man of Ethiopia. He caused the fire to surround him, it consumed him in the midst of the court, Pharaoh beholding him with the nobles and the people of Egypt.

(But) Si-Osiri passed away as a shade out from the hand of Pharaoh and Setne his father, nor did they see him.

Pharaoh and his great men marvelled exceedingly at the things they saw upon the court, saying, 'There is not a good scribe and learned man like Hor son of Pa-neshe, there will not be his like after him again, ever.'

Setne opened his mouth with a great cry when Si-Osiri had passed away as a shade, he not having seen him.

Pharaoh rose from the court in trouble of heart at these things that he had seen. Pharaoh commanded that preparation should be made for Setne, to lodge him, because of Si-Osiri his son, to refresh his heart.

Came evening, Setne went to his apartments, his heart being sad exceedingly. Meh-wesekht lay at his side, she conceived seed of him in the night named. In due time she bore a male child, he was called by name Usy-ment-Hor.

It came to pass that Setne ceased not from making burnt offerings and libations before the genius of Hor son of Pa-neshe on every occasion.

This is the end of this book, written ... (blank).

120. THE ROSETTA STONE

This bilingual inscription was issued by Ptolemy V in 196 BCE to establish him as a new member of the divine ruler cult. It was inscribed on a large granodiorite stela erected in Memphis. Like the Canopus Decree, the same message appears in three scripts: hieroglyphics, demotic, and Greek. The stone was instrumental in the decipherment of hieroglyphics in the early nineteenth century.

On the twenty-fourty clay of the month Gorpiaios, which corresponds to the twenty-fourth day of the fourth month of the season Pert of the inhabitants of Ta-Mert (Egypt), in the twenty-third year of the reign of Honus-Ra the Child, who has risen as King upon the throne of his father, the lord of the shrines of Nekhebet and Uatchet, the mighty one of two-fold strength, the establisher of the Two Lands, the beautifier of Egypt, whose heart is perfect (or benevolent) towards the gods, the Horus of gold, who makes perfect the life of the *hamemet* beings, the lord of the thirty-year festivals like Ptah, the sovereign prince like Ra, the King of the South and North, Neterui-merui-atui-aua-setep-en-Ptah-usr-ka-Ra-ankh-sekhem-Amen, the Son of the Sun Ptolemy the ever-living, the beloved of Ptah, the god who makes himself manifest, the son of Ptolemy and Arsinoe, the Father-loving gods; when Ptolemy, the son of Pyrrhides, was priest of Alexander, and of the Saviour-Gods, and of the Brother-loving Gods, and of the Beneficent Gods, and of the Father-loving Gods, and who makes himself manifest; when Demetria, the daughter of Telemachus, was the Bearer of the prize of victory of Berenice, the Beneficent Goddess; and when Arsinoe, the daughter of Cadmus, was the Basket Bearer of Arsinoe, the Brother-loving Goddess; when Irene, the daughter of Ptolemy, was the Priestess of Arsinoe, the Father loving Goddess; on this day the superintendents of the temples, and the servants of the god, and those who are over the secret things of the god, and the libationers [who] go into the most holy place to array the gods in their apparel, and the scribes of the holy writings, and the sages of the Double House of Life, and the other libationers who] had come from the sanctuaries of the South and North to Memphis, on the day of the festival whereon His Majesty, the King of the South and North Ptolemy, the ever-living, the beloved of Ptah, the god who makes himself manifest, the lord of beauties, received the sovereignty from his father, entered into the Sehetch-Chamber wherein they were accustomed to assemble, in Maktly-taui, and behold, they declared thus:—

"Inasmuch as the King who is beloved by the gods, the King of the South and North, Neterui-merui-atui-aua-en-Ptah-setep-usr-en-Ra-ankh-sekhem-Amen, the Son of the Sun, Ptolemy, the ever-living, the beloved of Ptah, the Gods who have made themselves manifest, the lord of beauties, has given things of all kinds in very large quantities to the lands of Horus and to all those who dwell in them, and to each and every one who holds any dignity whatsoever in them,—now behold, he is similar to a God, being the son of a God, [and] he was given by a Goddess, for he is the counterpart of Horus, the son of Isis [and] the son of Osiris, the avenger of his father Osiris—and behold, His Majesty possessed a divine heart which was beneficent towards the gods; and he has given gold in large quantities, and grain in large quantities to the temples; and he has given very many lavish gifts in order to make Ta-mert [Egypt] prosperous, and to make stable [her] advancement; and he has given to the soldiers who are in his august service.....according to their rank; [and of the taxes] some of them he has cut off, and some of them [he has lightened], thus causing the soldiers and those who live in the country to be prosperous under his reign [and as regards the sums which were due to the royal house from the people of Egypt, and likewise those [which were due from every one who was in his august service, His Majesty remitted them altogether, however great they were; and he has forgiven the prisoners who were in prison, and ordered that every one among them should be released from [the punishment] which he had to undergo.

"And His Majesty made an order saying:—In respect of the things [which are to be given to] the gods, and the money and the grain which are to be given to the temples each year, and all the things [which are to be given to] the gods from the vineyards and from the corn-lands of the nome, all the things which were then due under the Majesty of his holy father shall be allowed to remain [in their amounts] to them as they were then; and he has ordered:—Behold, the treasury shall not be made more full of contributions by the hands of the priests than it was up to the first year of the reign of His Majesty, his holy father; and His Majesty has remitted to the priests who minister in the temples in courses the journey which they had been accustomed to make by river in boats to the city of Alexandria at the beginning of each year; and His Majesty commanded:—Behold, those who are boatmen [by trade] shall not be seized [and made to serve in the Navy]; and in respect of the cloths of byssus [which are] made in the temples for the royal house, he has commanded that two-thirds of them shall be returned [to the priests]; similarly, His Majesty has [re]-established all the things the performance of which had been set aside, and has restored them to their former condition, and he has taken the greatest care to cause everything which ought to be done in the service of the gods to be done in the same way in which it was done in former [days]; similarly, he has done [all things] in a right and proper manner; and he has taken care to administer justice to the people, even like Thoth, the great, great [God]; and he has, moreover, ordered in respect of those of the troops who come back, and the other people also, who during the strife of the revolution which took place had been ill-disposed [towards the Government], that when they return to their homes and lands they shall have the power to remain in possession of their property; and he has taken great care to send infantry, and cavalry, and ships to repulse those who were coming against Egypt by land as well as by sea; and he has in consequence expended a very large amount of money and of grain on them in order to make prosperous the lands of Horus and Egypt.

"And His Majesty marched against the town of Shekam, which is in front of the town of Uiset, which was in the possession of the enemy, and was provided with catapults, and was made ready for war with weapons of every kind by the rebels who were in it—now they had committed great acts of sacrilege in the land of Horus, and had done injury to those who dwelt in Egypt—His Majesty attacked them by making a road [to their town], and he raised mounds (or walls) against them, and he dug trenches, and whatever would lead [him] against them that he made; and he caused the canals which supplied the town with water to be blocked up, a thing which none of the kings who preceded him had ever been able to do before, and he expended a large amount of money on carrying out the work; and His Majesty stationed infantry at the mouths of the canals in order to watch and to guard them against the extraordinary rise of the waters [of the Nile], which took place in the eighth year [of his reign], in the aforesaid canals which watered the fields and were unusually deep in this spot; and His Majesty captured the town by assault in a very short time, and he cut to pieces the rebels who were therein, and he made an exceedingly great slaughter among them, even like to that which

Thoth and Horus, the son of Isis and [the son of Osiris], made among those who rebelled against them when they rebelled in this very place; and behold, those who had led on the soldiers and were at their head, and who had disturbed the borders [in the time of his father, and who had committed sacrilege in the temples, when His Majesty came to Memphis to avenge his father and his own sovereignty he punished, according to their deserts, when he came there to celebrate] the festival of the receiving of the sovereignty from his father; and [besides this], he has set aside [his claim to] the things which were due to His Majesty, and which were [then] in the temples, up to the eighth year [of his reign, which amounted to no small sum of] money and grain; and His Majesty has also set aside [his claim] to the cloths of byssus which ought to have been given to the royal house and were [then] in the temples, and also the tax which they (i.e. the priests) ought to have contributed for dividing the cloths into pieces, which was due up to this day; and he has also remitted to the temples the grain which was usually levied as a tax on the corn-lands of the gods, and likewise the measure of wine which was due as a tax on the vineyards [of the gods]; and he has done great things for Apis, and Mnevis, and for every shrine which contained a sacred animal, and he expended upon them more than did his ancestors; and his heart has entered into [the consideration of everything] which was right and proper for them at every moment; and he has given everything which was necessary for the embalming of their bodies, lavishly, and in magnificent abundance; and he has undertaken the cost of their maintenance in their temples, and the cost of their great festivals, and of their burnt offerings, and sacrifices, and libations; [and he has respected the privileges of the temples, and of Egypt, and has maintained them in a suitable manner according to what is customary and right; and he has spent] both money and grain to no small amount; and [has provided] everything in great abundance for the house wherein dwells the Living Apis; and His Majesty has decorated it with perfect and new ornamentations of the most beautiful character always; and he has made the Living Apis to rise [like the sun], and has founded temples, and shrines, and chapels [in his honour]; [and he has repaired the shrines which needed repairs, and in all matters appertaining to the service of the gods he has manifested the spirit of a beneficent god; and during his reign, having made careful inquiry, he has restored the temples which were held in the greatest honour, as was right]; and in return for these things the gods and goddesses have given him victory, and power, and life, and strength, and health, and every beautiful thing of every kind whatsoever, and in respect of his exalted rank, it shall be established to him and to his children for ever and ever, with happy results (or, life)."

And it has entered into the heart[s] of the priests of the temples of the South and of the North, and of each and every temple [that all the honours which are paid to the King of the South and North Ptolemy, the ever-living, the beloved of Ptah, the God who [makes himself manifest, whose deeds are beautiful, [and those which are paid to the Father-[loving Gods who begot him, and to the Beneficent [Gods who begot those who begot him, and to [the Brother-Gods who begot the begetters of his [begetters,] and to the Saviour-Gods, shall be [greatly increased]; and a statue of the King of the South and North Ptolemy, ever-living, beloved of Ptah, the God who makes himself manifest, the lord of beauties, shall be set up [in every temple, [in the most prominent place], and it shall be called by his name "Ptolemy, the Saviour of Egypt," the interpretation of which is "Ptolemy, the victorious one." And it [shall stand side by side with a statue of the Lord [of the gods, who give him the weapon of [victory, and it shall be fashioned after the manner [of the Egyptians, and a statue of this kind shall [be set up in] all the temples which are called by his name. And adoration shall be paid to these statues three times each day, and every rite and ceremony which it is proper to perform before them shall be performed, and whatsoever is prescribed, and is fitting for their doubles, shall be performed, even as it is performed for the gods of the Nomes during the festivals and on every sacred day, on the day of [his] coronation, and on his name-day.

And there shall likewise [be set up] a magnificent statue of the King of the South and North Ptolemy, ever-living, beloved of Ptah, the God who makes himself manifest, whose deeds are beautiful, the son of Ptolemy, and Arsinoe, the Father-loving gods, and with the statue there shall be a magnificent shrine, [made] of the finest copper and inlaid with real stones of every kind, in every temple which is called by his name; and this statue shall rest in the most holy place [in the temples] side by side with the shrines of the gods of the Nomes. And on the days of the great festivals, when the god [of the temple] comes forth from his holy habitation, according to his day, the holy shrine of the God who makes himself manifest, the lord of beauties, shall likewise be made to rise [like the Sun] with them. And in order to make this new shrine to be easily distinguishable [both at the present day, and in future times, they shall set] upon this shrine [ten royal double crowns, made of [gold, and upon each double crown there shall be [placed the serpent which it is right and proper to [make for the double crown of gold], instead of the two Uraei which are [placed] upon the tops of shrines, and the Sekhent Crown shall be in the middle of them, because it was in the Sekhent Crown in which His Majesty shone in the House of the Ka of Ptah (i.e., Memphis) at the time when the King entered into the temple, and performed the ceremonies which it was meet and right for him to perform on receiving the exalted rank of King. And on the upper surface of the square pedestal which is round about these crowns, and in the middle part thereof [which is immediately beneath] the double Crown [they shall engrave a papyrus plant and a plant of the south; and they shall set them in such a way that a vulture, upon *neb*, beneath which a plant of the south [shall be found, shall be affixed to the right-hand [upper corner of the golden shrine, and a serpent, under which is *neb*, placed upon] a papyrus plant, [shall be affixed] to the left-hand side [at the upper comer]; and the interpretation [of these signs is]:—"Lord of the shrine of Nekheret, and Lord of the shrine of Uatchet, who illumines the Land of the White Crown, and the Land of the Red Crown."

And inasmuch as the last day of the fourth month of the season Shemu (i.e., Mesore), which is the birthday of the beautiful, ever-living god, is already established as a feast day, and it has been observed as a day of festival in the lands of Horus (i.e., the temple-lands) from olden time; and moreover, the seventeenth day of the second month of the season Shat (i.e., Paopi), whereon [His Majesty] performed the ceremonies of royal accession, when he received the sovereignty from his father, [is also observed as a day of festival], and behold [these days] have been the source of all [good] things [wherein all men have participated]; these days, that is to say, the seventeenth and the last day of each month shall be kept as festivals in the temples of Egypt, in each and every one of them; and on these days burnt offerings shall be offered up, and meat offerings, and everything which it is right and customary to perform at the celebration of festivals shall be performed on these days every month, and on these festivals every man shall do (i.e., offer up) what he is accustomed to do on [other] festivals in the temples. [And the priests also decreed] that the things which [are brought to the temples] as offerings shall be given to the persons who [minister in the temples; and festivals and processions shall be established in the temples, and in all Egypt, in honour of] the King of the South and North, Ptolemy, ever-living beloved of Ptah, the God who makes himself manifest, whose deeds are beautiful, each year, beginning with the first day of the first month of the season Shat (i.e., Thoth) up to the fifth day thereof; [and on these days the people shall wear] garlands on their heads, and they shall make festal the altars, and shall offer up meat and drink offerings, and shall perform every thing which it is right and proper to perform.

And the priests of all the temples which are called after his name shall have, in addition to all the other priestly titles which they may possess, the title of "Servant of the God who makes himself manifest, whose deeds are beautiful, [and this title shall [be endorsed on all deeds and documents which are [laid up in the temples]; and they shall cause to be engraved on the rings which they wear on their hands, the title of "Libationer of the God who makes himself manifest, whose deeds are beautiful."

And behold, it shall be in the hands of those who live in the country, and those who desire [it], to establish a copy of the shrine of the God who makes himself manifest, whose deeds are beautiful, and set it up in their houses, and they shall be at liberty to keep festivals and make rejoicings [before it] each month and each year; and in order to make those who are in Egypt to know [why it is that the Egyptians [pay honour—as it is most right and proper to [do—to the God who makes himself beautiful, [whose deeds are beautiful, the priests have decreed] that this Decree shall [be inscribed] upon a stele of hard stone in the writing of the words of the gods, and the writing of the books, and in the writing of the Haui-nebui (i.e., Greeks), and it shall be set up in the sanctuaries in the temples which [are called by] his name, of the first, second, and third [class], near the statue of the Horus, the King of the South and North, Ptolemy, ever-living, beloved of Ptah, the God who makes himself manifest, whose deeds are beautiful.

121. THE LETTER OF ARISTEAS

The account of the translation of the Hebrew Bible into Greek is told in a lengthy letter written in Greek and addressed to a man named Philocrates by his brother Aristeas, who presumably was a courtier of Ptolemy II. Philological examination, however, has shown that the letter is a forgery and was written about a hundred years after the events it describes. The purpose of the work is to demonstrate the superiority of the Greek translation of the Bible over any other version. How much historical truth is in the story is unknown. Here are two excerpts from the lengthy letter.

The Occasion of the Translation and Preliminary Proceedings

As the story of our interview with Eleazar, the high priest of the Jews, is a remarkable one, and because you, Philocrates, have set your heart, as you are constantly reminding me, on learning the object and the occasion of our mission, I have endeavoured to give you a clear account of what took place. I know that love of learning of yours; and it is indeed man's highest task "ever to make addition to his store of learning and acquirements," either by the study of history or by actual experience of affairs. For in this way there is formed a pure disposition in the soul, which, assimilating what is best, and inclining towards that which is all-important, even piety, directs its course by the guidance of an unerring rule.

Having determined to make a close investigation into things divine, we offered our services for an embassy to the man above-named, who, owing to his virtuous character and exalted position, is held in high honour both by his countrymen and by the rest of the world, and is in possession of [documents of] the greatest service to his nation, whether at home or abroad. The object of our mission was the translation of the law of God, because in their country they have it inscribed on parchment in Hebrew letters. And the interest which we displayed, when an opportunity offered itself, in bringing before the king the case of the men who were removed to Egypt from Judaea by the king's father, who was the first possessor of the city [of Alexandria] and ruler of Egypt, this also it is worth while my telling you. For I am convinced that you above all men, with your leanings towards the holiness and the sentiments of the men who live in accordance with the holy law, will gladly listen to the story about them which we are proposing to narrate, having but recently come over from the island to us, and being anxious to gather any instructive information. On a former occasion I sent you a description of matters in my opinion worthy of record concerning the Jewish nation, which we obtained from the high priests, the most learned body in that most learned of countries, Egypt. It is right to communicate such things to you with your eagerness to learn what may benefit the mind; I would, if possible, impart them to all who are like-minded with you, but chiefly to you; so sincere are your principles, and not only does your conduct show you to be my brother by birth, but in your striving after goodness you are at one with us. For precious gold or any other of the objects that the vain-glorious hold in honour does not confer the same advantage as the training of culture and the study of these subjects. But, lest we become tedious by extending our introductory remarks to an inordinate length, we will come back to the thread of the narrative.

Demetrius of Phalerum, being keeper of the king's library, received large grants of public money with a view to his collecting, if possible, all the books in the world; and by purchases and transcriptions he to the best of his ability carried the king's purpose into execution. Being asked once in our presence, about how many thousands of books were already collected, he replied, "More than two hundred thousand, Sire: but I will before long make diligent search for the remainder, so that a total of half a million may be reached. And I am informed that the Jews also have certain laws which are deserving of transcription and a place in your library." "What is to hinder you, then," replied the king, "in this task? For all the necessary means are at your service." And Demetrius answered, "Translation is also required. For in the Jews' land they use a writing of their own (just as Egyptians have their system of letters) as well as a language peculiar to themselves. It is commonly thought that they use the Syrian language, but this is an error: it is another dialect." And when the king had learnt all the facts, he gave command that a letter should be written to the high priest of the Jews, in order that the proposal above-mentioned might be carried into effect.

And now thought I was the opportunity for introducing a matter about which I had often made request to Sosibius of Tarentum and Andreas, the heads of the body-guard, namely the liberation of the Jews who had been carried away from Judaea by the king's father. For he, after overrunning the whole of Coele-Syria and Phoenicia, assisted by good fortune and his own prowess, transplanted some and made prisoners of others, terrorizing and reducing the whole country to submission. It was on this occasion that he carried away more than a hundred thousand persons from the Jews' country into Egypt, of which number he armed about thirty thousand picked men and settled them in the fortresses in the country. Many Jews had already before this entered the country along with the Persian, and others had at a still earlier time been sent out as auxiliaries to fight in the army of Psammetichus against the king of the Ethiopians; but these immigrants were not so large a body as those whom Ptolemy, son of Lagus, introduced. Well, as we said before, he selected those who were best fitted by their age for service and the strongest, and armed them, but the rest of the multitude, old and young, and the women, he handed over [to the soldiers] as menials, not of his own free will, but rather compelled thereto by the soldiers, in return for the services which they had rendered on his campaigns. When, therefore, we found some pretext for their release, as has been already explained, we addressed the king somewhat as follows: "It would surely be unreasonable, O king, to let ourselves be placed in the wrong by the actual facts. For, as the laws which we are proposing not only to transcribe but also to translate are binding on all Jews, what reasonable ground shall we have for our mission, while large numbers of the race continue in slavery in your kingdom? No, with a perfect and bounteous heart release those who are held fast in miseries, since the same God who gave them the law directs your kingdom, as my careful investigations have taught me. For the God who sees and created all things, whom they worship, is he whom all men worship, and we too, O king, though we address him by other names as Zeus and Dis; and by these names they of old time not inappropriately signified that he through whom all things receive their life and being, is the director and lord of all. Outdo, then, all men in magnanimity, and set at liberty those who are held in bondage."

The king kept silence for a brief while, and we inwardly prayed to God to incline his mind to a general release. (For the human race, being God's creation, is subject to change and alteration under his hand; and therefore I called with many and divers prayers upon him that rules the heart, that he might be constrained to fulfill my desire. For I had a good hope, in bringing forward a proposal concerning the deliverance of men, that God would cause the fulfilment of my desires; for when men piously think that they are working for righteousness and the furtherance of good deeds, their actions and designs are directed by Almighty God.) But the king, raising his head and looking at me with a cheerful countenance, said, "How many thousands do you think there will be?" And Andreas, who was standing beside him, replied, "A little over a hundred thousand." "Of a truth," said he, "it is but a small request which Aristeas makes of us." But Sosibius and some of the bystanders said, "It is indeed an action worthy of your magnanimity to offer the release of these men as a thank-offering to the most High God. For, as you have been most highly honoured by the Almighty and exalted above your forefathers, so is it fitting that you should make the very highest of thank-offerings." And he, greatly elated, gave orders that [the redemption money] should be added to the soldiers' pay: for every slave the owner should receive twenty drachmas: a royal decree should be issued on the subject, and the lists should be drawn up forthwith. So magnificent was his zeal, and thus did God fulfill our whole desire, constraining him to liberate not only those who had entered the country with his father's army, but also any who were there before, or had since been introduced into the kingdom. It was pointed out that the donation would exceed four hundred talents. And I think that it will not be without use to set down here the copy of the royal decree. For the munificence of the king, who was enabled by God to be the means of deliverance to vast multitudes, will thus be made far clearer and more evident. It ran thus:—

"By the king's decree. All persons who took part in the expedition of our father into the regions of Syria and Phoenicia, and invaded the territory of the Jews, and became possessors of Jewish slaves, and have brought these over into the city and the country, or have sold them to others, likewise also if any such were beforetime [in the country] or have since been introduced, the possessors shall straightway release them. Compensation shall forthwith be paid for every slave twenty drachmas, to the soldiers with their pay, and to the rest at the royal bank. For we are of opinion that the making of these persons prisoners was contrary to the will of our father and to justice, and that the spoliation of their country and the transportation of the Jews into Egypt were due to the recklessness of the soldiery; for the spoil which accrued to the soldiers on the field of battle should have sufficed, and that, not content with this, they reduced these men to subjection is therefore wholly unreasonable. Forasmuch then as we undertake to award justice to all men, but chiefly to those who are without reason kept in subjection, and do in all things seek after what is right from motives of justice and piety towards all, we have decreed that the owners of all Jewish persons who are held in bondage anywhere in any manner within the kingdom, shall on receipt of the prescribed sum release them: and no one shall in any way be dilatory in arranging for these matters, but they shall within three days from the date of publication of this decree hand in their lists to those who are set over this business, and shall also forthwith exhibit the persons. For we are resolved that it is expedient for ourselves and for the realm that this matter be accomplished. And any who will may give information concerning defaulters, on condition that the informer shall become owner of the person if found guilty, but the property of such persons shall be confiscated to the royal purse."

When the decree was submitted to be read over to the king, containing all the rest with the exception of the words, "Also if any such were beforetime [in the country] or have since been introduced," the king himself out of his munificence and magnanimity appended this clause, and gave orders to assign a grant of the moneys in a lump sum to the regimental paymasters and the royal bankers. This decision being arrived at, the decree was confirmed within seven days: and the donation amounted to over six hundred and sixty talents. For many children at the breast were also liberated along with the mothers. And when the further question was referred, whether twenty drachmas should be given for these as well, the king ordered that this also should be done. So strictly to the letter did he carry out every detail of the resolution.

And when this business was ended, he ordered Demetrius to submit a statement concerning the transcription of the Jewish books. For all business used to be transacted by these kings by means of decrees and with great security, and nothing was done in an offhand or casual manner. And therefore have I set down here the copy of the memorial, and the copies of the letters, and the number of the presents sent, and the nature of each, for every one of these excelled in magnificence and technical skill. And the following is a copy of the memorial.

"To the great king [a statement submitted] by Demetrius. In obedience to your order, O king, concerning the books that are wanting to complete the library, that these should be added to the collection, and that those which have been lost should be duly replaced, after making careful inquiry into these matters, I refer the following statement to you.

"Certain books of the Jewish law with some few others are wanting; for these are composed in Hebrew letters and in the Hebrew tongue, but have been interpreted somewhat carelessly and not according to their true meaning, according to information supplied by the experts, because they have not up to now received the supervision of royalty. And it is necessary that these books should in an emended form find a place in your library, because these laws, in that they are divine, are most full of wisdom and faultless. For this reason the writers of prose and verse and the host of historians have avoided any mention of the books aforesaid, and of the men who have lived [and are living] their lives in accordance with them, because the views presented in them have a certain sanctity and holiness, as says Hecataeus of Abdera. Be it then your good pleasure, O king, that a letter be written to the high priest at Jerusalem, bidding him send such men as have lived the best of lives and are advanced in years, versed in their country's law, six from each tribe, in order that we may test wherein the more part agree, and so obtaining an accurate translation may deposit it in a conspicuous place in a manner worthy of the undertaking and of your gracious will. Fare ever well!"

And when this memorial had been presented, the king ordered that a letter should be written to Eleazar on these matters, informing him also of the liberation of the captives that had taken place. And he likewise presented towards the construction of bowls and vials and a table and cups for libations fifty talents' weight of gold and seventy talents of silver and of precious stones a great number (enjoining the treasurers to leave to the craftsmen the selection of such materials as they might desire), and of stamped money for sacrifices and other purposes as much as a hundred talents. And we will describe to you the construction [of these works of art], but must first set out the copies of the letters. The tenor of the king's letter was as follows:

"King Ptolemaeus to Eleazar the high priest greeting and health. Forasmuch as many of the Jews chance to have been forcibly removed from Jerusalem by the Persians at the time of their power and to have been settled in our country, and others have entered Egypt as captives in the train of our father—of these he enrolled many in the army, giving them higher pay, and in like manner from his confidence in those who were already in the country he placed under their charge the fortresses which he built, that the native Egyptians might be intimidated by them: and we too on inheriting the kingdom meet all men, but chiefly your countrymen, in a very friendly spirit—we, then, have given liberty to more than a hundred thousand captives, paying their owners the value in money which is right, and making good any wrong which they have suffered through the violence of the rabble. For we are resolved that in this we are doing a pious action, and we hereby dedicate a thank-offering to the most high God, who has preserved our kingdom in peace and in the highest esteem throughout the whole world. And we have further placed in the army those who are in the prime of their life, but to such as are qualified for attendance on our person, and deserving of confidential posts at court, have we assigned offices of state. And since we desire to confer a favour not on these only, but on all Jews throughout the world, and on future generations, it is our royal will that your law be translated from the Hebrew, as you call it, into Greek, that so these writings also may find a place in our library with the other royal volumes. You will therefore do well and will duly repay our zeal, if you look out men who have lived honourable lives, advanced in years, well versed in the law and able to translate, six out of each tribe, that we may discover wherein the more part agree: for the inquiry concerns matters of more than ordinary import. For we are of opinion that we shall through this achievement gain great renown. And we have sent on this business Andreas, of the chief of the body-guards, and Aristeas, who hold honoured places in our court, to confer with you. They bring with them dedicatory offerings for the temple, and for sacrifices and other purposes a hundred talents of silver. And should you also write to us concerning any desires of yours, you will be welcome and will be doing only what friendship requires: and be assured that your wishes will receive instant fulfilment. Farewell."

In reply to this letter Eleazar wrote much as follows: "Eleazar the High Priest to king Ptolemaeus, a sincere friend, greeting. Do fare well and the queen Arsinoe, your sister, and the children, so will it be well and we have our desire: we ourselves also are in good health. On receiving your letter we greatly rejoiced because of your royal purpose and noble resolve, and we collected the whole people and read it to them, in order that they might know your pious reverence for our God. And we also exhibited the vials which you sent, twenty of gold and thirty of silver, the five bowls, and a table as dedicatory offerings, and the hundred talents of silver for the offering of sacrifices and for such repairs as the temple may require —gifts which were brought by Andreas, who is of those who hold an honoured place at your court, and Aristeas, virtuous and cultivated men, who in all ways show themselves worthy of your high principles and righteousness. They have also imparted to us your commissions, and have heard from our lips such replies as befit what you have written. For in all things which are to your profit, even though they be contrary to our natural impulses, will we do your bidding: for this is a mark of friendship and affection. For you too have in diverse manners done great services to our countrymen which cannot pass out of mind. We therefore straightway offered sacrifices on your behalf and on behalf of your sister and your children and your 'friends', and the whole people prayed that your undertakings might ever prosper, and that Almighty God would preserve your kingdom in peace with honour, and that the transcription of the holy law might be to your profit and carefully executed. And in the presence of them all we selected virtuous men, advanced in years, six from each tribe, whom we are also sending with [the copy of] the law. You will therefore do well, O just king, if you give orders that, so soon as the transcription of the books be accomplished, the men may be restored to us again in safety. Farewell. And their names are, of the first tribe, Joseph, Ezekias, Zacharias, John, Ezekias, Elisha: of the second, Judas, Simon, Samuel, Adaius, Mattathias, Eschlemias: of the third, Nehemiah, Joseph, Theodosius, Baseas, Ornias, Dakis: of the fourth, Jonathas, Abraius, Elisha, Ananias, Zacharias, Chelkias: of the fifth, Isaac, Jacob, Jesus, SabbataiusSimon, Levi: of the sixth, Judas, Joseph, Simon, Zacharias, Samuel, Selemias: of the seventh, Sabbataius, Zedekiah, Jacob, Isaac, Iesias, Natthaius: of the eighth, Theodosius, Jason, Jesus, Theodotus, John, Jonathas: of the ninth, Theophilus, Abraham, Arsamus, Jason, Endemias, Daniel: of the tenth, Jeremiah, Eleazar, Zacharias, Baneas, Elisha, Dathaius: of the eleventh, Samuel, Joseph, Judas, Jonathes, Caleb, Dositheus: of the twelfth, Isaelus, John, Theodosius, Arsamus, Abietes, Ezekiel: in all seventy-two persons."

Such, then, was the reply which the king's letter met with at the hands of Eleazar. ...

Reception of the Translators at Alexandria

So Eleazar, when he had offered sacrifice and selected the men and made ready many gifts for the king, sent us on our way with a strong escort. And when we reached Alexandria, the king was informed of our arrival. And Andreas and I, being admitted to the court, gave friendly greetings to the king and delivered the letter from Eleazar. And, since he attached great importance to the reception of the delegates, he gave orders to dismiss all the other officials and to summon the men. And this proceeding excited universal surprise, because the custom is that those who come on official business gain access to the king's presence on the fifth day, while envoys from kings or eminent cities were hardly admitted to the court within thirty days. But since he considered the new comers worthy of higher honour, and rightly estimated the eminent position of him who sent them, he dismissed those whom he considered superfluous, and remained walking to and fro, waiting to greet them on their arrival. And when they entered with the gifts which had been sent and the precious parchments, whereon was inscribed the law in gold in the Jewish characters, the material being wonderfully prepared, and the joining of the several leaves being rendered imperceptible, the king, when he saw the men, made inquiry concerning the books. And when they had taken the rolls out of their coverings and unrolled the leaves, the king after pausing for a long while and making obeisance some seven times, said, "I thank you, friends, and him that sent you still more, but most of all do I thank God, whose oracles these are." And when all with one accord and with one voice, both the new comers and the bystanders, exclaimed, "Well spoken, O king," he was moved to tears out of the fullness of his joy. For the tension of mind and the exceeding greatness of the honour where our achievements are successful constrain to tears. And when he had ordered them to put the rolls back in their places, then at length did he greet the men and say, "It was right, O God-fearing men, first to pay due homage to those treasures, for the sake of which I sent for you, and thereafter to extend the right hand to you: for that reason have I done this first. But I have regarded this day of your arrival as a great day, and from year to year shall it be held in honour all our life long . Moreover it happens that our naval victory over Antigonus fell on the same day. And therefore also it shall be my pleasure to sup with you to-day. And all things (he added) of which your customs allow you to partake shall be duly prepared for you, and for me with you." And when they had expressed their gratitude, he ordered that the best chambers should be given to them in the neighbourhood of the citadel, and the banquet made ready.

So Nicanor, the lord high steward, summoned Dorotheus, who had the charge of guests from this nation, and ordered him to make preparation for everything. For such was the arrangement decreed by the king, and it may still be seen in operation. To every state which has its special usages in matters of drink and meat and in its mode of reclining, was there a corresponding official in charge: and then, whenever any persons visited the reigning king, preparations were made in accordance with their customs, in order that they might experience no discomfort but live at their ease. And this happened in the case of these men. For Dorotheus, the patron of visitors from this nation, was a most attentive man. He laid out all the coverings for the couches which were in his keeping and were set apart for receptions of this kind. And he placed the couches in two rows, according to the king's direction: for he had ordered him to make half of the men recline at his [right] hand, and the remainder behind his own couch, neglecting no means of showing them honour.

And when they had taken their places, he ordered Dorotheus to perform the customary rites of all his visitors from Judaea. So he dispensed with the services of the sacred heralds and ministers of the sacrifices and the others who usually offered the prayers, and requested one of our number, Elisha, a priest advanced in years, to offer a prayer. And he, upstanding, uttered this noteworthy prayer: "May the Almighty God give you your fill, O king, of all the good things which he has created, and may he grant you and your wife and children and them that live in harmony with you unfailing enjoyment of them all throughout life!" At these words there was a burst of applause with shouting and jubilation lasting for some while: and thereafter they betook themselves to the enjoyment of the feast spread out before them. All the attendance at table was undertaken by the staff of Dorotheus, among whom were royal pages and some of those who held places of honour at the king's court.

122. THE FAMINE STELA

Inscribed onto a rock face near Elephantine, this text purports to be a decree of Djoser (Dynasty 3) but in fact is of the same genre as the Bentresh Stela (reading #111) and is designed to glorify the local priesthood of Khnum. The reference to the seven-year famine is believed to have been borrowed from the biblical story of Joseph in the book of Genesis of the Hebrew Bible, which was translated into Greek in Egypt during the reign of Ptolemy II. The implication is that Imhotep and Joseph are one and the same person.

(1) Year 18 of Horus: *Neterkhet*; the King of Upper and Lower Egypt: Neterkhet; Two Ladies: Neterkhet; Gold-Horus: *Djoser*; under the Count, Prince, Governor of the domains of the South, Chief of the Nubians in Yebu, Mesir. There was brought to him this royal decree. To let you know:

I was in mourning on my throne,
Those of the palace were in grief,
My heart was in great affliction,
Because Hapy had failed to come in time
In a period of seven years.
Grain was scant,
Kernels were dried up,
Scarce was every kind of food.
Every man robbed (3) his twin,
Those who entered did not go.
Children cried,
Youngsters fell,
The hearts of the old were grieving;
Legs drawn up, they hugged the ground,
Their arms clasped about them.
Courtiers were needy,
Temples were shut,
Shrines covered with dust,
Everyone was in distress.

I directed my heart to turn to the past,
I consulted one of the staff of the Ibis,
The chief lector-priest of Imhotep,
Son of Ptah South-of-his-Wall:
"In which place is Hapy born?
Which is the town of the Sinuous one?
Which god dwells there?
That he might join with (5) me."

He stood: "I shall go to Mansion-of-the-Net,

It is designed to support a man in his deeds;
I shall enter the House of Life,
Unroll the Souls of Re,
I shall be guided by them."

He departed, he returned to me quickly,
He let me know the flow of Hapy,
[His shores] and all the things they contain.
He disclosed to me the hidden wonders,
To which the ancestors had made their way,
And no king had equaled them since.
He said to me:
"There is a town in the midst of the deep,
Surrounded by Hapy, (7) Yebu by name;
It is first of the first,
First nome to Wawat,
Earthly elevation, celestial hill,
Seat of Re when he prepares
To give life to every face.
Its temple's name is 'Joy-of-life,'
'Twin Caverns' is the water's name,
They are the breasts that nourish all.

It is the house of sleep of Hapy,
He grows young in it in [his time],
[It is the place whence] he brings the flood:
Bounding up he copulates,
As man copulates with woman,
Renewing his manhood with joy;
Coursing twenty-eight cubits high,
He passes Sema-behdet (9) at seven.
Khnum is the god [who rules] there,
[He is enthroned above the deep],
His sandals resting on the flood;
He holds the door bolt in his hand,
Opens the gate as he wishes.
He is eternal there as Shu,
Bounty-giver, Lord-of-fields,
So his name is called.
He has reckoned the land of the South and the North,
To give parts to every god;
It is he who governs barley, [emmer],
Fowl and fish and all one lives on.

Cord and scribal board are there,
The pole is there with its beam
....
(11) His temple opens southeastward,
Re rises in its face every day;
Its water rages on its south for an iter,
A wall against the Nubians each day.
There is a mountain massif in its eastern region,
With precious stones and quarry stones of all kinds,
All the things sought for building temples
In Egypt, South and North,
And stalls for sacred animals,
And palaces for kings,
All statues too that stand in temples and in shrines.

"Their gathered products are set before the face of Khnum and around him; likewise (13) tall plants and flowers of all kinds that exist between Yebu and Senmut,18 and are there on the east and the west.

"There is in the midst of the river—covered by water at its annual flood—a place of relaxation for every man who works the stones on its two sides.

"There is in the river, before this town of Yebu, a central elevation of difficult body which is called *grf-3bw*.

"Learn the names of the gods and goddesses of the temple of Khnum: Satis, Anukis, Hapy, Shu, Geb, Nut, Osiris, Horus, Isis, Nephthys.

"Learn the names of (15) the stones that are there, lying in the borderland:20 those that are in the east and the west, those [on the shores] of Yebu's canal, those in Yebu, those in the east and west, and those in the river: *bḫn, mt3y, mḥtbtb, r'gs, wtšy* in the east; *prdn* in the west; *tšy* in the west and in the river.

"The names of the precious stones of the quarries that are in the upper region—some among them at a distance of four *iter*—are: gold, silver, copper, iron, lapis lazuli, turquoise, *thnt*, red jasper, *k', mnw*, emerald, *tm-ikr*. In addition, *nšmt, t3-mḥy, ḥm3gt,* (17) *ibht, bks-'nḫ,* green eye-paint, black eye-paint, carnelian, *shrt, mm,* and ochre are within this township."

When I heard what was there my heart was guided. Having heard of the flood [I] opened the wrapped books. [I] made a purification; [I] conducted a procession of the hidden ones; [I] made a complete offering of bread, beer, oxen, and fowl, and all good things for the gods and goddesses in Yebu whose names had been pronounced.

As I slept in peace, I found the god standing before me. [I] propitiated him by adoring him and praying to him. He revealed himself to me with kindly face; he said:

"I am Khnum, your maker!
My arms are around you,
To steady your body,
To (19) safeguard your limbs.

I bestow on you stones upon stones,
[That were not found] before,
Of which no work was made,
For building temples,
Rebuilding ruins,
Inlaying statues' eyes.

For I am the master who makes,
I am he who made himself,
Exalted Nun, who first came forth,
Hapy who hurries at will;
Fashioner of everybody,
Guide of each man in his hour,
Tatenen, father of gods,
Great Shu, high in heaven!

The shrine I dwell in has two lips,
When I open up the well,
I know Hapy hugs the field,
A hug that fills each nose with life,
(21) For when hugged the field is reborn!
I shall make Hapy gush for you,
No year of lack and want anywhere,
Plants will grow weighed down by their fruit;
With Renutet ordering all,
All things are supplied in millions!
I shall let your people fill up,
They shall grasp together with you!
Gone will be the hunger years,
Ended the dearth in their bins.
Egypt's people will come striding,
Shores will shine in the excellent flood,
Hearts will be happier than ever before!"

The Donation

I awoke with speeding heart. Freed of fatigue I made (23) this decree on behalf of my father Khnum. A royal offering to Khnum, lord of the cataract region and chief of Nubia:

In return for what you have done for me, I offer you Manu as western border, Bakhu as eastern border, from Yebu to Kemsat, being twelve *iter* on the east and the west, consisting of fields and pastures, of the river, and of every place in these miles.

All tenants who cultivate the fields, and the vivifiers who irrigate the shores and all the new lands that are in these miles, their harvests shall be taken to your granary, in addition to (25) your share which is in Yebu.

All fishermen, all hunters, who catch fish and trap birds and all kinds of game, and all who trap lions in the desert—I exact from them one-tenth of the take of all of these, and all the young animals born of the females in these miles [in their totality].

One shall give the branded animals for all burnt offerings and daily sacrifices; and one shall give one-tenth of gold, ivory, ebony, carob wood, ochre, carnelian, *shrt*, *diw*-plants, *nfw*-plants, all kinds of timber, (being) all the things brought by the Nubians of Khent-hen-nefer <to> Egypt, and (by) every man (27) who comes with arrears from them.

No officials are to issue orders in these places or take anything from them, for everything is to be protected for your sanctuary.

I grant you this domain with (its) stones and good soil. No person there .... anything from it. But the scribes that belong to you and the overseers of the South shall dwell there as accountants, listing everything that the *kiry*-workers, and the smiths, and the master craftsmen, and the goldsmiths, and the … , (29) and the Nubians, and the crew of Apiru, and all corvee labor who fashion the stones, shall give of gold, silver, copper, lead, baskets of… , firewood, the things that every man who works with them shall give as dues, namely one-tenth of all these. And there shall be given one-tenth of the precious stones and quarrying stones that are brought from the mountain side, being the stones of the east.

And there shall be an overseer who measures the quantities of gold, silver, copper, and genuine precious stones, the things which the sculptors shall assign to the gold house, (31) <to> fashion the sacred images and to refit the statues that were damaged, and any implements lacking there. Everything shall be placed in the storehouse until one fashions anew, when one knows everything that is lacking in your temple, so that it shall be as it was in the beginning.

Engrave this decree on a stela of the sanctuary in writing, for it happened as said, (and) on a tablet, so that the divine writings shall be on them in the temple twice. He who spits (on it) deceitfully shall be given over to punishment.

The overseers of the priests and the chief of all the temple personnel shall make my name abide in the temple of Khnum-Re, lord of Yebu, ever-mighty.

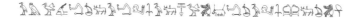

123. THIRD PETITION OF THE SERAPEUM TWINS

A papyrus document was discovered at Memphis (Papyrus Paris 26), which contains a petition by twin-sisters Thaues and Taous to the king Ptolemy VI and his queen Cleopatra II. The sisters were attendants of the Apis Bull at the Serapeum temple, who had been defrauded by their mother and her lover. The petition, which can confidently be dated to 163 BCE, is the third one sent to the king and queen, and it would seem the previous two had not been answered. This one was timed to their royal visit to Memphis. Once can only hope that justice was eventually done.

To King Ptolemy and Queen Cleopatra the sister, gods Philometores, greetings. We, Thaues and Taous, the twin-sisters who minister in the great Serapeum at Memphis, on a former occasion when you were in residence at Memphis and had gone up to the temple to sacrifice petitioned you, and gave in a petition, bringing before you our plea that we are not receiving the contribution of necessaries which it is fitting should be given to us both from the Serapeum and the Asclepeum. And having failed to receive them up to the present time in full, we have been compelled, under pressure of necessity, wasting away as we are through starvation, to petition you again, and in a few words to set before you the selfishness of those who are injuring us. For although you already from former times have proclaimed a contribution for the Serapeum and Asclepeum, and in consequence of this the twins who were there before us daily received what they required, to us also when we first went up to the temple straightway for a few days the impression was conveyed as if everything fitting would be done for us in good order, but for the remainder of the time this was not carried out. Wherefore we both sent repeatedly to the supervisors persons to petition on our behalf, and laid information on these matters before you, on the occasion of your visits to Memphis. And when those who had been appointed to the administration in the Serapeum and Asclepeum had insolently maltreated us, and were removing the privileges conferred on us by you, and were paying no regard to religious scruple, and when we were being crushed by our wants, we often made representations even to Achomarres the supervisor of the temple to give us (our rights). And we approached the son of Psintaes the supervisor of the sacrifices, when he went up to the temple the day before yesterday, and gave him detailed information. And having called Achomarres to him, he strictly commanded him to give what was owing to us. And he, being by nature the most unfeeling of all mankind, promised us that he would perform what he had been directed to do, but no sooner had the son of Psintaes departed from Memphis than he took no further account of the matter. And not only this man, but also others connected with the Serapeum, and others connected with the Asclepeum in the administration, from whom it is usual for us to receive what we need, are defrauding, whose names and obligations, because they are numerous, we have decided not to record.

We beg you therefore, having as our one hope the assistance that lies in your power, to send away our petition to Dionysius Privy Councillor and strategus, that he may write to Apollonius the supervisor to compel them to render to us (what is owing), when he has received from us the written list of the necessaries owing to us and what further debts are due us along with the periods for which they have been owing and the persons who owe them, so that, when we have everything in order, we may be much better able to perform our regular duties to Serapis and to Isis, both for your own sakes and for the sake of your children. May it be given you to hold fast all the territory you desire. Farewell.

124. POLYBIUS' *HISTORIES*

Polybius was an Arcadian Greek historian who moved to Rome and pledged loyalty to the Roman Republic. His work The Histories, *which is written in Greek and was completed shortly after 146 BCE, chronicles the rise of the power of Rome in the Mediterranean. Much of the work no longer exists, but these fragments provide some interesting details about the Ptolemy family.*

Book XXVII

19. When Antiochus[4] saw that the government of Alexandria was openly making preparations for a war of annexation in Coele-Syria, he sent Meleager at the head of an embassy to Rome, with instructions to inform the Senate of the fact, and to protest that Ptolemy (VI) was attacking him without the least justification. …

20. In all human affairs perhaps one ought to regulate every undertaking by considerations of time; but this is especially true in war, in which a moment makes all the difference between success and failure, and to miss this is the most fatal of errors. …

Many men desire honour, but it is only the few who venture to attempt it; and of those who do so, it is rare to find any that have the resolution to persevere to the end. …

Book XXVIII

1. When the war between the kings Antiochus and Ptolemy for the possession of Coele-Syria had just begun, Meleager, Sosiphanes, and Heracleides came as ambassadors from Antiochus, and Timotheos and Damon from Ptolemy. The one actually in possession of Coele-Syria and Phoenicia was Antiochus; for ever since his father's victory over the generals of Ptolemy at Panium all those districts had been subject to the Syrian kings. Antiochus, accordingly, regarding the right of conquest as the strongest and most honourable of all claims, was now eager to defend these places as unquestionably belonging to himself: while Ptolemy, conceiving that the late king Antiochus had unjustly taken advantage of his father's orphan condition to wrest the cities in Coele-Syria from him, was resolved not to acquiesce in his possession of them. Therefore Meleager and his colleagues came to Rome with instructions to protest before the Senate that Ptolemy had, in breach of all equity, attacked him first; while Timotheos and Damon came to renew their master's friendship with the Romans, and to offer their mediation for putting an end to the war with Perseus; but, above all, to watch the communications made by Meleager's embassy. As to putting an end to the war, by the advice of Marcus Aemilius they did not venture to speak of it; but after formally renewing the friendly relations between Ptolemy and Rome, and receiving a favourable answer, they returned to Alexandria. To Meleager and his colleagues the Senate answered that Quintus Marcius should be commissioned to write to Ptolemy on the subject, as he should think it most to the interest of Rome and his own honour. Thus was the business settled for the time. …

(A missing section described Ptolemy (VI) Philometer's unsuccessful war against Antiochus. Antiochus Epiphanes defeated the Egyptian troops at Pelusium, took young Ptolemy captive, and advanced as far as

---

4 Antiochus IV Epiphanes, ruler of the Seleucid Empire and uncle of Ptolemy VI.

Memphis. Thereupon Ptolemy Physcon, Ptolemy Philometer's brother, assumed the royal title at Alexandria as Euergetes II, and sent envoys to Antiochus at Memphis; Antiochus, however, treated Ptolemy Philometor with kindness, established him as king at Memphis, and advanced to Naucratis, and thence to Alexandria, which he besieged on the pretext of re-establishing Philometor.)

18. King Antiochus was a man of ability in the field and daring in design, and showed himself worthy of the royal name, except in regard to his manoeuvres at Pelusium. …

19. When Antiochus was actually in occupation of Egypt, Comanus and Cineas,[5] after consultation with king Ptolemy Physcon, determined upon summoning a conference of the most distinguished Egyptian nobles to consult about the danger which threatened them. The first resolution the conference came to was to send the Greek envoys who were then at Alexandria as envoys to Antiochus to conclude a pacification. There were at that time in the country two embassies from the Achaean league, one which had been sent to renew the alliance between the league and Egypt, and which was composed of Alcithus of Aegium, son of Xenephon, and Paslodes, and another sent to give notice of the festival of the Antigoneia. There was also an embassy from Athens led by Demaratus on the subject of some present, and two sacred embassies, one in connexion with the Panathenaea under the presidency of Callias the pancratiast, and the other on the subject of the mysteries, of which Cleostratus was the active member and spokesman. There were also there Eudemus and Hicesius from Miletus, and Apollonides and Apollonius from Clazomenae. The king also sent with them Tlepolemus and Ptolemy the rhetorician as envoys. These men accordingly sailed up the river to meet Antiochus. …

20. While Antiochus was occupying Egypt, he was visited by the Greek envoys sent to conclude terms of peace. He received them courteously, devoted the first day to giving them a splendid entertainment, and on the next granted them an interview, and bade them deliver their instructions. The first to speak were the Achaeans, the next the Athenian Demaratus, and after him Eudemus of Miletus. And as the occasion and subject of their speeches were the same, the substance of them was also nearly identical. They all laid the blame of what had occurred on Eulaeus, and referring to Ptolemy's youth and his relationship to himself, they intreated the king to lay aside his anger. Thereupon Antiochus, after acknowledging the general truth of their remarks, and even supporting them by additional arguments of his own, entered upon a defence of the justice of his original demands. He attempted to establish the claim of the king of Syria on Coele-Syria, "Insisting upon the fact that Antigonus, the founder of the Syrian kingdom, exercised authority in that country; and referring to the formal cession of it to Seleucus, after the death of Antigonus, by the sovereigns of Macedonia. Next he dwelt on the last conquest of it by his father Antiochus; and finally he denied that any such agreement was made between the late king Ptolemy and his father as the Alexandrian ministers asserted, to the effect that Ptolemy was to take Coele-Syria as a dowry when he married Cleopatra, the mother of the present king." Having by these arguments not only persuaded himself, but the envoys also, of the justice of his claim, he sailed down the river to Naucratis. There he treated the inhabitants with humanity, and gave each of the Greeks living there a gold piece, and then advanced towards Alexandria. He told the envoys that he would give them an answer on the return of Aristeides and Thesis, whom he had sent on a mission to Ptolemy; and he wished, he said, that the Greek envoys should all be cognisant and witnesses of their report. …

---

5   Ptolemy Physcon's ministers.

21. The eunuch Eulaeus persuaded Ptolemy to collect his money, give up his kingdom to his enemies, and retire to Samothrace. This will be to any one who reflects upon it a convincing proof of the supreme mischief done by evil companions of boyhood. That a monarch so entirely out of reach of personal danger and so far removed from his enemies, should not make one effort to save his honour, while in possession too of such abundant resources, and master over such wide territory and such numerous subjects, but should at once without a blow surrender a most splendid and wealthy kingdom—is not this the sign of a spirit utterly effeminate and corrupted? And if this had been Ptolemy's natural character, we must have laid the blame upon nature and not upon any external influence. But since by his subsequent achievements his natural character has vindicated itself, by proving Ptolemy to be sufficiently resolute and courageous in the hour of danger, we may clearly, without any improbability, attribute to this eunuch, and his companionship with the king in his boyhood, the ignoble spirit displayed by him on that occasion, and his idea of going to Samothrace. ...

22. After raising the siege of Alexandria, Antiochus sent envoys to Rome, whose names were Meleager, Sosiphanes, and Heracleides, agreeing to pay one hundred and fifty talents, fifty as a complimentary present to the Romans, and the rest as a gift to be divided among certain cities in Greece. ...

23. In the course of these same days envoys sailed in from Rhodes to Alexandria, headed by Pration, to negotiate a pacification; and a few days afterwards presented themselves at the camp of Antiochus. Admitted to an interview, they argued at considerable length, mentioning their own country's friendly feelings to both kingdoms, and the ties of blood existing between the two kings themselves, and the advantage which a peace would be to both. But the king interrupted the envoy in the middle of his speech by saying that there was no need of much talking, for the kingdom belonged to the elder Ptolemy, and with him lie had long ago made terms, and they were friends, and if the people wished now to recall him Antiochus would not prevent them. And he kept his word. ...

Book XXIX

2. The Senate being informed that Antiochus had become master of Egypt, and all but taken Alexandria, and conceiving that the aggrandisement of that king was a matter affecting themselves, appointed Gaius Popilius and others to go as ambassadors to put an end to the war, and generally to inspect the state of affairs. ...

(*After reigning in Memphis for a time Philometor made terms with his brother and sister, returned to Alexandria, and there all three were being besieged by Antiochus.*)

23. In the Peloponnesus a mission arrived before the end of the winter from the two kings, Ptolemy (Philometor) and Ptolemy (Physcon), asking for help. This gave rise to repeated and animated discussions. The party of Callicrates and Diophanes were against granting the help; while Archon, Lycortas, and Polybius were for sending it to the kings in accordance with the terms of their alliance. For by this time it had come to pass that the younger Ptolemy had been proclaimed king by the people (at Alexandria), owing to the danger which threatened them; and that the elder had subsequently returned from Memphis, and was reigning jointly with his sister. As they stood in need of every kind of assistance, they sent Eumenes and Dionysodorus to the Achaeans, asking a thousand foot and two hundred horse, with Lycortas to command the foot and Polybius the horse. They sent a message also to Theodoridas of Sicyon, urging him to hire them a thousand mercenaries.

For the kings chanced to have become intimately acquainted with these particular men, owing to the transactions I have related before. The ambassadors arrived when the Achaean congress was in session in Corinth. They therefore came forward, and after recalling the many evidences of friendship shown by the Achaeans to the kingdom of Egypt, and describing to them the danger in which the kings then were, they entreated them to send help. The Achaeans generally were ready enough to go to the help of the kings (for both now wore the diadem and exercised regal functions), and not only with a detachment, but with their full levy. Put Callicrates and his party spoke against it; alleging that they ought not to meddle in such affairs at all, and certainly not at that time, but should reserve their undivided forces for the service of Rome. For there was a general expectation just then of a decisive battle being fought, as Q. Philippus was wintering in Macedonia.

24. The people were alarmed lest they should be thought to fail the Romans in any way: and accordingly Lycortas and Polybius rose in their turn, and, among other advice which they impressed upon them, argued that "When in the previous year the Achaeans had voted to join the Roman army with their full levy, and sent Polybius to announce that resolution, Quintus Marcius, while accepting the kindness of their intention, had yet stated that the assistance was not needed, since he had won the pass into Macedonia. Their opponents therefore were manifestly using the need of helping the Romans merely as a pretext for preventing this aid being sent to Alexandria. They entreated the Achaeans, in view of the greatness of the danger surrounding the king of Egypt, not to neglect the right moment for acting; but keeping in mind their mutual agreement and good services, and above all their oaths, to fulfil the terms of their agreement."

The people were once more inclined to grant the aid when they heard this: but Callicrates and his party managed to prevent the decree being passed, by staggering the magistrates with the assertion that it was unconstitutional to discuss the question of sending help abroad in public assembly. But a short time afterwards a meeting was summoned at Sicyon, which was attended not only by the members of the council, but by all citizens over thirty years of age; and after a lengthened debate, Polybius especially dwelling on the fact that the Romans did not require assistance,—in which he was believed not to be speaking without good reason, as he had spent the previous summer in Macedonia at the headquarters of Marcius Philippus,—and also alleging that, even supposing the Romans did turn out to require their active support, the Achaeans would not be rendered incapable of furnishing it by the two hundred horse and one thousand foot which were to be despatched to Alexandria,—for they could, without any inconvenience, put thirty or forty thousand men into the field,— the majority of the meeting were convinced, and were inclined to the idea of sending the aid. Accordingly, on the second of the two days on which, according to the laws, those who wished to do so were bound to bring forward their motions, Lycortas and Polybius proposed that the aid should be sent. Callicrates, on the other hand, proposed to send ambassadors to reconcile the two Egyptian kings with Antiochus. So once more, on these two motions being put, there was an animated contest; in which, however, Lycortas and Polybius got a considerable majority on their side. For there was a very wide distinction between the claims of the two kingdoms. There were very few instances to be found in past times of any act of friendship on the part of Syria to the Greeks,—though the liberality of the present king was well known in Greece,—but from Egypt the acts of kindness in past times to the Achaeans had been as numerous and important as any one could possibly expect. By dwelling on this point Lycortas made a great impression, because the distinction between the two kingdoms in this respect was shown to be immense. For it was as difficult to count up all the benefactions of the Alexandrine kings, as it was impossible to find a single act of friendship done by the dynasty of Antiochus to the Achaeans. ...

25. For a time Andronidas and Callicrates kept on arguing in support of the plan of putting an end to the war: but as no one was persuaded by them, they employed a stratagem. A letter-carrier came into the theatre (where the meeting was being held), who had just arrived with a despatch from Quintus Marcius, urging those Achaeans who were of the pro-Roman party to reconcile the kings; for it was a fact that the Senate had sent a mission under T. Numisius to do so. But this really made against their argument: for Titus Numisius and his colleagues had been unable to effect the pacification, and had returned to Rome completely unsuccessful in the object of their mission. However, as Polybius and his party did not wish to speak against the despatch, from consideration for Marcius, they retired from the discussion: and it was thus that the proposal to send an aid to the kings fell through. The Achaeans voted to send ambassadors to effect the pacification: and Archon of Aegeira, and Arcesilaus and Ariston of Megalopolis were appointed to the duty. Whereupon the envoys of Ptolemy, being disappointed of obtaining the help, handed over to the magistrate the despatch from the kings, in which they asked that they would send Lycortas and Polybius to take part in the war. ...

26. Forgetful of all he had written and said Antiochus began preparing for a renewal of the war against Ptolemy. So true are the words of Simonides,—"Tis hard to be good." For to have certain impulses towards virtue, and even to hold to it up to a certain point, is easy; but to be uniformly consistent, and to allow no circumstances of danger to shake a resolute integrity, which regards honour and justice as the highest considerations, is indeed difficult. ...

27. When Antiochus had advanced to attack Ptolemy in order to possess himself of Pelusium, he was met by the Roman commander Gaius Popilius Laenas. Upon the king greeting him from some distance, and holding out his rirfit hand to him, Popilius, answered by holding out the tablets which contained the decree of the Senate, and bade Antiochus read that first: not thinking it right, I suppose, to give the usual sign of friendship until he knew the mind of the recipient, whether he were to be regarded as a friend or foe. On the king, after reading the despatch, saying that he desired to consult with his friends on the situation, Popilius did a thing which was looked upon as exceedingly overbearing and insolent. Happening to have a vine stick in his hand, he drew a circle round Antiochus with it, and ordered him to give his answer to the letter before he stepped out of that circumference. The king was taken aback by this haughty proceeding. After a brief interval of embarrassed silence, he replied that he would do whatever the Romans demanded. Then Popilius and his colleagues shook him by the hand, and one and all greeted him with warmth. The contents of the despatch was an order to put an end to the war with Ptolemy at once. Accordingly a stated number of days was allowed him, within which he withdrew his army into Syria, in high dudgeon indeed, and groaning in spirit, but yielding to the necessities of the time.

Popilius and his colleagues then restored order in Alexandria: and after exhorting the two kings to maintain peaceful relations with each other, and charging them at the same time to send Polyaratus to Rome they took ship and sailed towards Cyprus, with the intention of promptly ejecting from the island the forces that were also gathered there. When they arrived, they found that Ptolemy's generals had already sustained a defeat, and that the whole island was in a state of excitement. They promptly caused the invading army to evacuate the country, and remained there to keep watch until the forces had sailed away for Syria. Thus did the Romans save the kingdom of Ptolemy, when it was all but sinking under its disasters. Fortune indeed so disposed of the fate of Perseus and the Macedonians, that the restoration of Alexandria and the whole of Egypt was decided by it; that is to say, by the fate of Perseus being decided previously: for if that had not taken place, or had not been certain, I do not think that Antiochus would have obeyed these orders.

Book XXX

17. In Egypt the first thing the kings did after being relieved from the war with Antiochus was to send Numenius, one of their friends, as an envoy to Rome to return thanks for the favours received; and they next released the Lacedaemonian Menalcidas, who had made active use of the occasion against the kingdom for his own advantage; Gaius Popilius Laenas asked the king for his release as a favour to himself. ...

(*Ptolemy VI Philometor was expelled by Ptolemy Physcon Euergetes II, and took refuge in Cyprus, but had been restored by a popular outbreak in his favour, and under the authority of Commissioners sent from Rome. Fresh quarrels, however, broke out, in the course of which Physcon was much worsted by his brother, and at length it was arranged that one should reign in Egypt the other in Cyrene.*)

18. After the Ptolemies had made their partition of the kingdom, the younger brother arrived in Rome desiring to set aside the division made between himself and his brother, on the ground that he had not acceded to the arrangement voluntarily, but under compulsion, and yielding to the force circumstances. He therefore begged the Senate to assign Cyprus to his portion; for, even if that were done, he should still have a much poorer share than his brother. Canuleitis and Quintus supported Menyllus, the ambassador of the elder Ptolemy, by Protesting that "the younger Ptolemy owed his possession of Cyrene and his very life to them, so deep was the anger and hatred of the common people to him; and that, accordingly, he had been only too glad to receive the government of Cyrene, which he had not hoped for or expected; and had exchanged oaths with his brother with the customary sacrifices." To this Ptolemy gave a positive denial: and the Senate, seeing that the division was clearly an unequal one, and at the same time wishing that, as the brothers themselves were the authors of the division being made at all, it should be effected in a manner advantageous to Rome, granted the petition of the younger Ptolemy with a view to their own interest. Measures of this class are very frequent among the Romans, by which they avail themselves with profound policy of the mistakes of others to augment and strengthen their own empire, under the guise of granting favours and benefiting those who commit the errors. On this principle they acted now. They saw how great the power of the Egyptian kingdom was; and fearing lest, if it ever chanced to obtain a competent head, he would grow too proud, they appointed Titus Torquatus and Gnaeus Merula to establish Ptolemy Physcon in Cyprus, and thus to carry out their own policy while satisfying his. These commissioners were accordingly at once despatched with instructions to reconcile the brothers to each other, and to secure Cyprus to the younger. ...

26. After this the younger Ptolemy arrived in Greece with the Roman commissioners, and began collecting a formidable army of mercenaries, among whom he enlisted Damasippus the Macedonian, who, after murdering the members of the council at Phacus, fled with his wife and children from Macedonia, and after reaching Peraea, opposite Rhodes, and being entertained by the people there, determined to sail to Cyprus. But when Torquatus and his colleagues saw that Ptolemy had collected a formidable corps of mercenaries, they reminded him of their commission, which was to restore

him "without a war," and at last persuaded him to go as far as Side (in Pamphylia), and there disband his mercenaries, give up his idea of invading Cyprus, and meet them on the frontiers of Cyrene. Meanwhile, they said that they would sail to Alexandria, and induce the king to consent to their demands, and would meet him on the frontiers, bringing the other king with them. The younger Ptolemy was persuaded by these arguments, gave up the attack upon Cyprus, dismissed the mercenaries, and first sailed to Crete, accompanied by Damasippus and Gnaeus Merula, one of the commissioners; and, after enlisting about a thousand soldiers in Crete, put to sea and crossed to Libya, landing at Apis.

27. Meanwhile Torquatus had crossed to Alexandria and was trying to induce the elder Ptolemy to be reconciled to his brother, and yield Cyprus to him. But Ptolemy, by alternate promises and refusals and the like, managed to waste the time, while the younger king lay encamped with his thousand Cretans at Apis in Libya, according to his agreement. Becoming thoroughly irritated at receiving no intelligence, he first sent Gnaeus Merula to Alexandria, hoping by this means to bring Torquatus and those with him to the place of meeting. But Merula was like the others in protracting the business: forty days passed without a word of intelligence, and the king was in despair. The fact was that the elder king, by using every kind of flattery, had won the commissioners over, and was keeping them by him, rather against their will than with it. Moreover, at this time the younger Ptolemy was informed that the people of Cyrene had revolted, that the cities were conspiring with them, and that Ptolemy Sympetesis had also taken their side. This man was an Egyptian by birth, and had been left by the king in charge of his whole kingdom when he was going on his journey to Rome. When the king was informed of this, and learned presently that the Cyreneans were encamped in the open country, afraid lest, in his desire to add Cyprus to his dominions, he might lose Cyrene also, he threw everything else aside and marched towards Cyrene. When he came to what is called the Great Slope, he found the Libyans and Cyreneans occupying the pass. Ptolemy was alarmed at this: but, putting half his forces on board boats, he ordered them to sail beyond the difficult ground, and show themselves on the rear of the enemy; while with the other half he marched up in their front and tried to carry the pass. The Libyans being panic-stricken at this double attack on front and rear, and abandoning their position, Ptolemy not only got possession of the pass, but also of Tetrapyrgia, which lay immediately below it, in which there was an abundant supply of water. Thence he crossed the desert in seven days, the forces under Mochyrinus coasting along parallel to his line of march. The Cyreneans were encamped eight thousand five hundred strong, eight thousand infantry and five hundred cavalry: for having satisfied themselves as to the character of Ptolemy from his conduct at Alexandria, and seeing that his government and policy generally were those of a tyrant rather than a king, they could not endure the idea of becoming his subjects, but were determined to venture everything in their desire for freedom. And at last he was beaten. . .

28. At this time Gnaeus Merula also came from Alexandria, informing the king (Physcon) that his brother would consent to none of the proposals, but maintained that they ought to abide by the original agreements. On hearing this, Physcon selected the brothers Comanus and Ptolemy to go as ambassadors to Rome with Gnaeus, and inform the Senate of his brother's selfish and haughty behaviour. At the same time the elder Ptolemy sent away Titus Torquatus also without having attained the object of his mission. Such was the state of things in Alexandria and Cyrene. ...

Book XXXII

1. This year Comanus and his brother arrived at Rome on their mission from the younger Ptolemy, and Menyllus of Alabanda from the elder. Their interview with the Senate was the occasion of many mutual recriminations expressed with great Philometor, and bitterness; and when Titus Torquatus and Gnaeus Merula gave evidence in favour of the younger king, and supported him with great earnestness, the Senate voted that Menyllus and his colleagues should leave Rome within five days, and that the treaty of alliance with the elder Ptolemy should be annulled; but that they should send envoys to the younger to inform him of the decree of the Senate. Publius Apustius and Gains Lentulus were appointed to this service, who immediately sailed to Cyrene, and with great despatch announced to Physcon the decree of the Senate. Greatly elated by this, Ptolemy began collecting mercenaries, and devoted his whole attention and energies to the acquisition of Cyprus. This was what was going on in Italy. ...

Book XXXIII

8. At the same time as the Senate despatched Opimius to the war with the Oxybii, Ptolemy the younger arrived at Rome; and being admitted to the Senate brought an accusation against his brother, laying on him the blame of the attack against his life. He showed the scars of his wounds, and speaking with all the bitterness which they seemed to suggest, moved his hearers to pity him; and when Neolaidas and Andromachus also came on behalf of the elder Ptolemy, to answer the charges brought by his brother, the Senate refused even to listen to their pleas, having been entirely prepossessed by the accusations of the younger. They commanded them to leave Rome at once; while they assigned five commissioners to the younger, headed by Gnaeus Merula and Lucius Thernuis, with a quinquereme for each commissioner, and ordered them to restore Ptolemy (Physcon) to Cyprus; and at the same time sent a circular to their allies in Greece and Asia, granting permission to them to assist in the restoration of Ptolemy. ...

Book XXXIX

18. Ptolemy, king of Syria,[6] died from a wound received in the war: a man who, according to some, deserved great praise and abiding remembrance, and according to others the reverse. If any king before him ever was, he was mild and benevolent; a very strong proof of which is that he never put any of his own friends to death on any charge whatever; and I believe that not a single man at Alexandria either owed his death to him. Again, though he was notoriously ejected from his throne by his brother, in the first place, when he got a clear opportunity against him in Alexandria, he granted him a complete amnesty; and afterwards, when his brother once more made a plot against him to seize Cyprus, though he got him body and soul into his hands at Lapethus, he was so far from punishing him as an enemy, that he even made him grants in addition to those which formerly belonged to him in virtue of the treaty made between them, and moreover promised him his daughter.

---

6 Ptolemy Philometor, king of Egypt, is called, by way of distinction, "King of Syria," because that title was bestowed on him by the people of Antioch during his last expedition in Syria. This was undertaken in support of Alexander Balas, who repaid him by conniving at an attempt upon his life. Whereupon Ptolemy joined Demetrius, the son of Demetrius Soter, and supported his claim against Alexander Balas.

However, in the course of a series of successes and prosperity, his mind became corrupted; and he fell a prey to the dissoluteness and effeminacy characteristic of the Egyptians: and these vices brought him into serious disasters. …

𓈖𓏤 𓆑𓄿𓈖𓏏𓆑𓄿𓈖𓏏𓆑𓈖𓏏𓆑𓄿𓈖𓏏𓆑𓄿𓈖𓏏𓆑𓄿

125. THE DRYTON AND APOLLONIA ARCHIVE

Fragments of over 40 papyri, written in both Greek and demotic Egyptian, all from the household of a man named Dryton have been found. Dryton was a cavalry officer who lived in Ptolemais, a Greek city in Upper Egypt. Apollonia (also known by her Egyptian name Senmonthis) was his second wife, whom he married when she was in her teens and he in his fifties. They had five daughters. Here are two documents from the family archive, the first being Dryton's will, which is dated to the 44th year of Ptolemy VIII Euergetes II (126 BCE), and the second being a petition by Dryton's daughters to the strategos of Thebes concerning a property dispute some ten to fifteen years later, after Dryton has died.

The Will of Dryton, Son of Pamphilus

Year 44, Pauni the 9th, in Pathyris before Asclepiades, the agoranomus. Being in good health and of sound mind, Dryton, son of Pamphilus, Cretan, ranking as a Successor and Hipparch in the Troops of the Reserve.

So long as health remains to me I am to remain in control of my property; but in case of death, I hereby leave and bequeath the real estate and furniture and herds belonging to me and whatsoever else I may possess, as follows:

My war-horse and all my arms to Esthladas, the son born to me and Sarapias, daughter of Esthladas, son of Theon, citizeness, with whom I lived as my wife, in accordance with the laws and a will (deposited) at the record office in Diospolis Parva before Dionysius the agoranomus in the sixth year in the time of Philometer. This will makes the rest clear and has established …. And of the four household slaves Esthladas is to have the two whose names are Myrsine and …. The remaining two female slaves whose names are Irene and Ampelion, are to go to Apollonia and her four sisters, making five in all; likewise, the vineyard belonging to me in the (district of) Pathyris, and the well of burnt brick I and the other appurtenances, and the wagon with the cow, … one dove-cote and a second one unfinished, a yard, next to which on the south are waste fields of the beforementioned Esthladas, on the north a vaulted chamber of Apollonia the Younger, on the east a waste place belonging to Petrasis … son of Esthladas, on the west a waste field of Esthladas up to the open doorway upon the west. The house to the west and bowls ... and waste field up to the dove-cote stretching away below the doorway of Esthladas and to the left of the vaulted chamber, I give to Apollonia and Aristo and Aphrodisia and Nicarion and Apollonia the younger making five daughters born to me and Apollonia, also called Semmonthis, with whom I lived as legal wife. Let them share equally in the two female slaves and the cow and the houses, according as I have made the division. Let Esthladas have the waste field already given him, facing his doorway from east to west, four strips extending to the place of the earthen pot. Of the remaining buildings and empty lots in Diospolis Magna in the Ammonium and among the potters' shops let Esthladas have one half, and Apollonia and her sisters one half, and all my other belongings, contracts for loans in money or wheat, and furniture, let them share by halves. Let Esthladas and Apollonia with her sisters pay the expenditures for building the aforementioned dovecote, until it be completed.

And to Apollonia also called Semmonthis, my wife, let them pay for four years, if she remains at home and without reproach, for the support of herself and the second and third daughters, 2½ artabae of wheat, 1/12 artaba of croton, and 200 copper drachmae each month. And let them give the same amounts out of the common stock to the two youngest daughters for eleven years. And to Tachratis let them give out of the common stock 12 talents in copper as her dowry. Whatsoever additional income Semmonthis appears to have made while living with Dryton, of this she is to have absolute possession, and any one who starts action against her regarding this income ... (*will suffer such and such a penalty*). Year 44, Pauni 9th.

Petition of the Daughters of Dryton to Phommoutis the Strategos

To Phommoutis, the King's Cousin and Epistrategus and Strategus of the Thebaid.

From Apollonia also called Senmouthis, and Aphrodisia also called Tachratis, both daughters of Dryton dwelling in Pathyris. To us and to our sisters, Aristo also called Senmonthis, and Nicarion also called Thermouthis, and Apollonia the younger also called Senpelais, belongs a half share of our father's estates of which there are four in the Peri-Theban nome and the Pathyrite nome, likewise the household slaves. Included in these estates, in Cochlax on the Arabian side (eastern bank of the Nile) of the beforementioned Pathyrite nome, is a half share of a vineyard amounting 2½ arourae, or as much more as it may be, and the orchard to the east of this, and wells and buildings and ... and barren land and other land without the ... , and their appurtenances, all of which our father owned while he lived, and we, his relics, own sue his death... . Ariston, son of Athenodotus, living in Diospolis Magna has forcibly taken possession of the beforementioned vineyard and its appurtenances in the period when communication ceased (between the two banks of the Nile) and unjustly maintains possession of the half share belonging to us and has planted a certain part in vines, knowing that we are women and that ne dwell in another place and cannot easily take action against the possession above stated. Therefore we deem it right to appeal to you, if it seems best, to examine him, and if the matter be as we declare it, to compel him to leave the half share of the vineyard which clearly belongs to us and the vines planted upon it and the places belonging with it, and to pay back the produce which he has taken away from them, and in return for his violent behavior to arrest him as a rogue that we may receive satisfaction. Farewell.

126. THE INSTRUCTION OF ANKHSHESHONQY

Our last example from a work in the sebayt *genre comes from the 28-page long demotic British Museum Papyrus 10508. The teaching comes from the mouth of Ankhsheshonqy (sometimes spelled without the 'y'), a priest of Re at Heliopolis while he is visiting his friend Harsiese at Memphis. The teachings are down-to-earth and pragmatic, rather than idealistic and lofty, and they are addressed to the average man. There is even an element of humor. The text may have been composed earlier, but the scribe who made this copy was definitely from the late Ptolemaic period. The condition of the paprus deteriorates considerably after section 25, so sections 26 to 28 are not included here.*

(**1**,9) ... - - - - - - Pharaoh asked him many [things] and (10) he answered them all - - - - - - ... (11) of the chief physician; and the chief physician did nothing without consulting (12) Harsiese son of Ramose about it. A few days later it happened that the chief physician went (13) to his fathers. Harsiese son of Ramose was made chief physician, and he was given everything that belonged to the chief physician (14) entirely, and his brothers were made priests without fee. And Pharaoh did nothing without (15) consulting Harsiese son of Ramose about it.

After this it happened one (16) day that Ankhsheshonq son of Tjainufi - - - was in great trouble. He thought (17) to himself, saying:"What I should like to do is to go to Mem[phis] and stay with (18) Harsiese son of Ramose. I have been told he has been made chief physician [and has been given everything] that belonged to the chief physician (19) entirely, and his brothers have been made priests without fee. Perhaps the god will put it [in his heart] to do for me what is right."

He went away (20) from Heliopolis without [informing] any man on earth of his going. He found a ship which was sailing (**2**,x) - - - - - - (**2**,1) - - - - - (2) "- - - - - [stay] here in Memphis with me. (3) - - - - - - your people three times a month." (4) [Ankhsheshonq son of Tjainufi stayed with] Harsiese son of Ramose; and he (5) - - - - - - to Heliopolis (to) his people three times a month.

(6) - - - - - - consulting about an evil destiny (7) - - - - - - Harsiese son of Ramose, the chief physician, consulted (8) - - - - - - Ankhsheshonq son of Tjainufi about it. Then said (9) Ankh[sheshonq son of Tjainufi] to him: " - - - may your life prosper! Pharaoh is the image of Pre! (10) - - - - - - agree to the misfortune of Pharaoh? Pharaoh has done for you many good things, [more than to] all [the courtiers of] the palace. You were brought to the palace when you (12) had nothing in the world. He appointed you chief physician. He let you be given everything that belonged to the chief physician entirely. (13) He had your brothers made priests without fee. Is what you are doing in return to have him killed?" Said he: "Let go (14) of me, Ankhsheshonq son of Tjainufi. There is nothing to the words you have said. The councillors, the generals, (15) the grandees of the palace are all agreed to do it."

Now it happened that everything (16) Harsiese son of Ramose was saying to Ankhsheshonq son of Tjainufi, and that Ankhsheshonq said to him (17) in reply—there was a man of the household inside a [place] where he heard the voices of the two men who was called Wahibre-(18)makhy son of Ptahertais. It was the turn of this same man8 to lie down that night in the vestibule (19) of the private chamber where Pharaoh was. When [night] came he lay down in the vestibule of the (20) private chamber where Pharaoh was.

In the 8th hour of the night (21) Pharaoh awoke, uncovered his face, and called out, saying, "Who is outside?" Wahibre-makhy (22) son of Ptahertais answered him. Pharaoh said to him: "Woe - - - , woe at the hand of Pre and the gods who are (3,x) - - - - - - (3,1) - - - - - - (2) - - - - - - when he had said "- - - - - - , he said: "Shall I (3) be saved, shall I be saved, Wahibre-makhy son of Ptahertais, shall I be saved?" He said: "You will be saved by the hand of Pre and (4) the gods who are with him, and great Neith, the mother, the great goddess, shall place the peoples of the whole (5) earth beneath the feet of Pharaoh." He related to Pharaoh everything he had overheard (6) Harsiese son of [Ra] mose saying to Ankhsheshonq son of Tjainufi and what Ankhsheshonq had said to him (7) in reply, without altering a single word. Pharaoh was unable to sleep till morning.

When (8) the morning of the next day had come, Pharaoh took his seat in the hall of the palace in Memphis. (9) The magistrates stood in their station and the generals in their ranks. Pharaoh looked to the station (10) of Harsiese son of Ramose. Pharaoh said to him: "Harsiese son of Ramose, you were brought to the palace (11) when you had nothing in the world. I appointed you chief physician and let you be given everything that belonged to the chief physician (12) entirely; and I had your brothers made priests without fee. What have you done, conspiring against me to have me killed?"

(13) He said to Pharaoh: "My great lord! On the day on which Pre commanded to do good to me he put Pharaoh's good fortune (14) in my heart. On the day on which Pre commanded to do harm to me he put Pharaoh's misfortune (15) in my heart."

Pharaoh said to him: "The words, since they were said to us, did you say them to any man at all?" He said: "I said them (16) to Ankhsheshonq son of Tjainufi, a priest of Pre who is here in Memphis with me." Pharaoh said to him: "Ankh(17)sheshonq son of Tjainufi, what is he to you?" He said: "His father was the friend of my father. His heart (18) was much attached to him."

(19) Pharaoh said: "Let (20) Ankhsheshonq son of Tjainufi be brought!" They ran for (Ankhsheshonq son) of Tjainufi; they ran and returned bringing him (21) before Pharaoh at once.

Pharaoh said to him: "Ankhsheshonq son of Tjainufi, did you eat my bread and hear evil against me without coming to inform me of it, saying, 'They are conspiring against you to kill you'?" (4,x) - - - - - (4,1) - - - - - - 'Is what you are doing in return, to have him killed?' By your face, my great lord, I did all I could with him, but he did not give me (3) an answer. I knew that these matters would not be hidden from Pharaoh."

As soon as he had said this, Pharaoh (4) had an altar of earth built at the door of the palace. He had Harsiese son of Ramose placed in (5) the fire together with all his people and every man who had conspired in Pharaoh's doom. Pharaoh had (6) Ankhsheshonq son of Tjainufi taken to the houses of detention of Daphnae. A personal servant, a staff-(7)bearer, a man of Pharaoh's household, was assigned to him, and his food was brought from the palace (8) daily.

After this there occurred the accession-day of Pharaoh. Pharaoh released everyone who was (9) (in) the prisons at Daphnae except Ankhsheshonq son of Tjainufi. His heart sank (10) on account of it. He said to the staff-bearer who was assigned to him: "Let a favor be done to me by you. Let (11) a palette and a scroll be brought to me. For I have a boy whom I have not yet been able to instruct. (12) I shall write an Instruction for him and have it taken to Heliopolis to instruct him with it." The staff-bearer said: "I will (13) report it before Pharaoh first." The staff-bearer reported (14) it before Pharaoh first. Pharaoh commanded, saying: "Let a palette be taken to him; do not let a scroll be taken (15) to him." They took a palette to him; they did not take a scroll to him. He wrote on the sherds of jars the matters which he could (16) teach his son in writing.

(17) This is the Instruction which the divine father Ankhsheshonq, whose mother was - - - , wrote for his son on the sherds (18) of the jars that were brought in to him containing mixed wine, while he was imprisoned in the house of detention of Daphnae. He (19) said:

Mistreatment and misery, my great lord Pre! Imprisonment, mistreatment is what is done to me in return for not having killed a man! This is what you despise, my great lord Pre! Is this not how Pre is angry with a land? Oh (21) you people who shall find these potsherds, hear from me how Pre is angry with a land!

(5,x) - - - - - -

(5,1) [When Pre is angry] with a land he causes - - - - - -.

(2) [When] Pre is angry with a land its ruler neglects the law.

(3) When Pre is angry with a land he makes law cease in it.

(4) When Pre is angry with a land he makes sanctity cease in it.

(5) When Pre is angry with a land he makes justice cease in it.

(6) When Pre is angry with a land he makes value scarce in it.

(7) When Pre is angry with a land he does not let one be trusting in it.

(8) When Pre is angry with a land he does not let one receive ransom[1] [in] it.

(9) When Pre is angry with a land he makes great its humble people and humbles its great people.

(10) When Pre is angry with a land he sets the fools over the wise.

(11) When Pre is angry with a land he orders its ruler to mistreat its people.

(12) When Pre is angry with a land he appoints its scribe to rule it.

(13) When Pre is angry with a land he appoints its washerman as chief of police.

(14) Here follow the words that Ankhsheshonq son of Tjainufi wrote on (15) the sherds of the jars that were brought in to him containing mixed wine, so as to give them (16) as an Instruction to his son, and which were reported before Pharaoh and (17) his great men daily. Ankhsheshonq son of Tjainufi had realized (18) the fact that he was to linger in prison since they had not released him, (19) and he wrote on the sherds of the jars the matters that he could teach his son in writing.

(6,x) - - - - - -

(6,1) S[erve your] god, that he may guard you.

(2) Serve your brothers, that you may have good repute.

(3) Serve a wise man, that he may serve you.

(4) Serve him who serves you.

(5) Serve any man, that you may find profit.

(6) Serve your father and mother, that you may go and prosper.

(7) Examine every matter, that you may understand it.

(8) Be gentle and patient, then your heart will be beautiful.

(9) It is in maturity that instruction succeeds.

(10) Do not rely on the property of another, saying, "I will live on it"; acquire your own.

(11) Do not abuse when you fare well, lest you fare badly.

(12) Do not send a low woman on a business of yours; she will go after her own.

(13) Do not send a wise man in a small matter when a big matter is waiting.

(14) Do not send a fool in a big matter when there is a wise man whom you can send.

(15) Do not send into town when you may find trouble in it.

(16) Do not long for your home when you do an errand.

(17) Do not long for your home to drink beer in it in midday.

(18) Do not pamper your body, lest you become weak.

(19) Do not pamper yourself when you are young, lest you be weak when you are old.

(20) Do not hate a man to his face when you know nothing of him.

(21) Do not fret so long as you own something.

(22) Do not worry so long as you own something.

(23) Do not fret at all.

(24) Do not fret about your occupation.

(7,x) - - - - - -

(7,1) - - - - - -

(2) Force [your son], do not let your servant force him.

(3) Do not spare your son work when you can make him do it.

(4) Do not instruct a fool, lest he hate you.

(5) Do not instruct him who will not listen to you.

(6) Do not rely on a fool.

(7) Do not rely on the property of an idiot.

(8) Do not hide and then let yourself be found.

(9) Do not hide when you have no food.

(10) He who hides when he has no food is in the place of one who seeks it.

(11) Do not go away and then come back of your own accord.

(12) Do not run away after you have been beaten, lest your punishment be doubled.

(13) Do not insult your superior.

(14) Do not neglect to serve your god.

(15) Do not neglect to serve your master.

(16) Do not neglect to serve him who can serve you.

(17) Do not neglect to acquire a manservant and a maidservant when you are able to do so.

(18) A servant who is not beaten is full of curses in his heart.

(19) A small man with great wrath makes much stench.

(20) A great man with small wrath gets much praise.

(21) Do not say "young man" to one who is old.

(22) Do not belittle an old man in your heart.

(23) Do not speak hastily, lest you give offense.

(24) Do not say right away what comes out of your heart.

(8,x) - - - - - -

(8,1) - - - - - -

(2) Learning and foolishness belong to the people of your town; respect the people of your town.

(3) Do not say "I am learned"; set yourself to become wise.

(4) Do not do a thing that you have not first examined.

(5) Examining makes your good fortune.

(6) If you examine three wise man about a matter it is perfect;
    the outcome lies with the great god.

(7) Do well by your body in your days of well-being.

(8) There is no one who does not die.

(9) Do not withdraw from a scribe who is being taken to the house of detention.

(10) If you withdraw from him they will take him to his house of eternity.

(11) Do not go to court against your superior when you do not have protection [against] him.

(12) Do not take to yourself a woman whose husband is alive, lest he become your enemy.

(13) In strait times or happy times wealth grows because of spreading it.

(14) May your fate not be the fate of one who begs and is given.

(15) When you work the land do not pamper your body.

(16) Do not say "Here is my brother's acre"; look to your own.

(17) The wealth of a town is a lord who does justice.

(18) The wealth of a temple is the priest.

(19) The wealth of a field is the time when it is worked.

(20) The wealth of a storehouse is in stocking it.

(21) The wealth of a treasury is in (being in) a single hand.

(22) The wealth of property is a wise woman.

(23) The wealth of a wise man is his speech.

(9,x) - - - - - -

(9,1) The wealth - - - - - -

(2) The wealth of an army is its [leader].

(3) The wealth of a town is not taking sides.

(4) The wealth of a craftsman is his equipment.

(5) Do not scorn a document that has a claim on you.

(6) Do not scorn a remedy that you can use.

(7) Do not scorn Pharaoh's business.

(8) Do not scorn a matter that concerns a cow.

(9) He who scorns matters too often will die of it.

(10) Do not quarrel over a matter in which you are wrong.

(11) Do not say "My land thrives"; do not cease to inspect it.

(12) Do not dwell in a house with your in-laws.

(13) Do not be a neighbor to your master.

(14) Do not say "I have plowed the field but there has been no payment." Plow again,
    it is good to plow.

(15) More joyous is the face of him who rests above the field
    than of him who spends the day in town.

(16) Do not say "It is summer"; there is winter too.

(17) He who does not gather wood in summer will not be warm in winter.
(18) Do not dwell in a house in which you get no income.
(19) Do not entrust your wealth to a house of profit[1].
(20) Do not put your wealth into a house only.
(21) Do not put your wealth in a town to which you must send!
(22) Wealth takes hold of its owner.
(23) The owner of a cow gets to run.
(24) Do not spend before you have set up your storehouse.
(25) Spend according to the size of your means.

(**10**,x) - - - - - -
(**10**,1) Do not say - - - - - -
(2) Do not say "I am good at writing" - - - - - -
(3) A scribe (in) a shipyard, a craftsman (in) a . . .
(4) When the crocodile shows itself its reputation is measured.
(5) A crocodile does not die of worry, it does of hunger.
(6) "What they do insults me," says the fool when one instructs him.
(7) You may trip over your foot in the house of a great man; you should not trip over your tongue.
(8) If you are thrown out of the house of your master, be his doorkeeper.
(9) If your master is sitting by the river, do not (10) immerse your hands in front of him.
(10) May my brother be a groom! When he mounts I would boast.
(11) May my companion say "Thoth knows not."
(12) May he not die for whom I would rend my clothing!
(13) May the "elder brother" of the town be the one to whom it is entrusted!
(14) May the kindly brother of the family be the one who acts as "elder brother" for it!
(15) May I have something and my brother have something,
    that I may eat my own without abstaining!
(16) May the floodwater never fail to come!
(17) May the field never fail to flourish!
(18) May the poor plot of land be the one that grows fodder in abundance!
(19) May the cow receive her bull!
(20) May the son do honor to his father!
(21) May it be a master's son who becomes master!
(22) May my mother be my hairdresser, so as to do for me what is pleasant!
(23) May the moon follow the sun and not fail to rise!
(24) May existence always follow death!

(**11**,x) - - - - - -
(**11**,1) May I - - - - - -
(2) May I stretch out my hand to my - - - ...
(3) May I get to know my neighbor, that I may give him my goods.
(4) May I get to know my brother, that I may open my heart to him.
(5) Do not be a hindrance often, lest you be cursed.

(6) Do not get drunk often, lest you go mad.

(7) Take a wife when you are twenty years old, that you may have a son while you are young.

(8) Do not kill a snake and then leave its tail.

(9) Do not hurl a lance if you cannot hold its aim.

(10) He who sends spittle up to the sky will have it fall on him.

(11) A man's character is his family.

(12) A man's character is his destiny?

(13) A man's character is on his face.

(14) A man's character is one of his limbs.

(15) The fisherman throws on board without knowing that it is the god who sends to every house.

(16) Do not stay on the road till evening, saying "I am sure of the houses."
 You do not know the hearts of their inhabitants.

(17) A magistrate who steals, his son will be poor.

(18) Do not tie your donkey's foot to the palm tree lest he shake it.

(19) Do not laugh at your son in front of his mother, lest you learn the size of his father.

(20) It is not of a bull that a bull is born.

(21) Do not say "The enemy of the god is alive today"; look to the end.

(22) Say "Good fate" at the end of old age.

(23) Put your affairs in the hand of the god.

(**12**,x) - - - - - -

(**12**,1) Do not - - - - - -

(2) Do not - - - - - - suffer.

(3) Man does not know the days of his misfortune.

(4) Do not entrust your people to one who has not experienced distress.

(5) Do not delay to get yourself a tomb on the mountain; you do not know the length of your life.

(6) Do not do evil to a man and so cause another to do it to you.

(7) Do not be discouraged in a matter in which you can ask (advice).

(8) Happy is the heart of him who has made judgment before a wise man.

(9) A wise master who asks (advice), his house stands forever.

(10) Disdain ruins a great man.

(11) A great crime ..... is what one despises.

(12) The work of a fool does not succeed in a house where a wise man is.

(13) Let your wife see your wealth; do not trust her with it.

(14) Do not trust her with her provisions for one year.

(15) As long as my brother does not abstain from stealing, I do not abstain from restraining him.

(16) Do not retaliate; do not let one retaliate against you.

(17) Let your benefaction reach him who has need of it.

(18) Do not be stingy; wealth is no security.

(19) Even a kind master will kill to have peace.

(20) The prudent killer does not get killed.

(21) Do not undertake a matter if you cannot carry it out.

(22) Do not speak harshly to a man if you cannot make him yield by it.

(23) Loud is the voice of him who acts (or, has acted) because he has been commanded.

(24) Do not say something when it is not the time for it.

(**13**,x) - - - - - -
(**13**,1) - - - - - -
(2) A wise man seeks [a friend; a fool] seeks an enemy.
(3) He to whom a good deed was done in the past cannot repay it.
(4) - - - - - -
(5) Do not give your son to the wet nurse and so cause her to set aside her own.
(6) The friend of a fool is a fool; the friend of a wise man is a wise man.
(7) The friend of an idiot is an idiot.
(8) The mother makes a child, the way makes a companion.
(9) Every man acquires property; it is a wise man who knows how to protect it.
(10) Do not hand over your property to your younger brother
          and thereby make him act as your elder brother.
(11) Do not prefer one of your children to another; you do not know
          which one of them will be kind to you.
(12) If you find your wife with her lover get yourself a bride to suit you.
(13) Do not get a maidservant for your wife if you do not have a manservant.
(14) Do not speak in two voices.
(15) Speak truth to all men; let it cleave to your speech.
(16) Do not open your heart to your wife; what you have said to her goes to the street.
(17) Do not open your heart to your wife or to your servant.
(18) Open it to your mother; she is a woman of discretion!
(19) A woman knows her own business.
(20) Instructing a woman is like having a sack of sand whose side is split open.
(21) Her savings are stolen goods.
(22) What she does with her husband today she does with another man tomorrow.
(23) Do not sit down beside your superior.
(24) Do not take a youth for your companion.

(**14**,x) - - - - - -
(**14**,1) - - - - - -
(2) He will make him give - - - while the condemnation of the god is yet after him.
(3) Do not have a thief for a companion [lest] he cause you to be killed.
(4) Even a small concern has a man in its grip.
(5) Shut up a house and it will perish as a result.
(6) He who is patient in a bad situation will not be harmed by it.
(7) He who steals from the property of another will not profit by it.
(8) If you become the companion of a wise man
          whose heart you do not know, do not open your heart to him.
(9) If you do good to a hundred men and one of them acknowledges it, no part of it is lost.
(10) Make burnt offering and libation before the god; let the fear of him be great in your heart.
(11) A thief steals by night; he is found by day.

(12) Do not make many words.

(13) A house is open to him who has goods in his hand.

(14) He who is bitten of the bite of a snake is afraid of a coil of rope.

(15) The man who looks in front of him does not stumble and fall.

(16) Do not abandon a woman of your household when she has not conceived a child.

(17) Good fortune turns away destruction by a great god.

(18) Honor your (fellow)man . . . . . .

(19) Do not let your servant lack his food and clothing.

(20) Do not cast glances at another's property lest you become poor.

(21) Do not trespass on the territory of another.

(22) Do not put a house on farmland.

(23) Do not cause a man to sue you.

(**15**,x) - - - - - -

(**15**,1) Do not - - - - - -

(2) Do not - - - something which your - - - - - -

(3) There is no - - - reaches the sky.

(4) There is no - - - without crying.

(5) Do not say "- - - a good deed to this man but he did not acknowledge it to me."

(6) There is no good deed except a good deed which you have done for him who has need of it.

(7) If you have reached your prime and gained much property let your brothers be great with you.

(8) Need, if its condition becomes known in the street, is reckoned a disgrace.

(9) When a youth who has been taught thinks, thinking of wrong is what he does.

(10) When a man has earned his first money he spends it on drinking and eating.

(11) When a man smells of myrrh his wife is a cat before him.

(12) When a man is suffering his wife is a lioness before him.

(13) Do not be afraid to do that in which you are right.

(14) Do not commit theft; you will be found out.

(15) Do not let your son marry a woman from another town, lest he be taken from you.

(16) Muteness is better than a hasty tongue.

(17) Sitting still is better than doing a mean errand.

(18) Do not say "I undertook the matter," if you did not undertake it.

(19) Being evil will not provide for you.

(20) Gluttony will not give you food.

(21) If you are sent to get chaff and you find wheat, do not buy [it].

(22) If you trade in straw when it is wanted, you should not go around with wheat.

(23) Do not do to a man what you dislike, so as to cause another to do it to you.

(24) Do not consort with a man who is discouraged and
    who may say "I am discouraged right now."

(25) A hundred men are slain through one moment of discouragement.

(**16**,x) - - - - - -

(**16**,1) Do not - - - [lest you be] poor forever.

(2) Do not - - - - - -

(3) Do not let your schoolboy son go to the door of the storehouse in a lean year.

(4) Do not go to your brother when you are in distress; go to your friend.

(5) Do not drink water in the house of a merchant; he will charge you for it.

(6) Do not deliver a servant into the hand of his master.

(7) Do not say "My master dislikes me, I will not serve him."

(8) Zealous service removes dislike.

(9) Borrow money at interest and put it in farmland.

(10) Borrow money at interest and take a wife.

(11) Borrow money at interest and celebrate your birthday.

(12) Do not borrow money at interest in order to live well on it.

(13) Do not swear falsely when you are in distress, lest you become worse off than you are.

(14) Do not ask advice from the god and then neglect what he said.

(15) Do not laugh at a cat.

(16) Do not speak of Pharaoh's business when drinking beer.

(17) Do not make a judgment in which you are wrong.

(18) Do not be fainthearted in a bad situation.

(19) Do not conceal yourself from a stranger who comes from outside.

(20) If there is nothing in your hand there may be something in his.

(21) Do not lend money at interest without obtaining a security.

(22) Do not be too trusting lest you become poor.

(23) Do not dislike one who says to you "I am your brother."

(24) If my share in my father's house is small it will not increase.

(25) Do not disdain a small document, a small fire, a small soldier.

(**17**,x) - - - - - -

(**17**,1) - - - - - -.

(2) - - - - - -......

(3) [Do not] insult a woman whose husband is your subordinate.

(4) [Do not scorn] to do the work by which you can live.

(5) Do not acquire goods if you do not have a storehouse.

(6) Do not accept a gift if you are not going to make a contract.

(7) Do not say "My illness has passed, I will not use medication."

(8) Do not go away (from work) often, lest you become disliked.

(9) Do not cast a weary glance at the door bolt.

(10) Do not hasten when you speak before your master.

(11) Do not run too hard lest you must halt.

(12) Do not often clean yourself with water only.

(13) Water grinds the stone.

(14) Do not walk the road without a stick in your hand.

(15) Do not ... a man before his opponent at the trial.

(16) Do not walk alone at night.

(17) Do not scorn your master before an inferior.

(18) If you have grown up with a man and are faring well with him,
    do not abandon him when he fares badly.

(19) Let him attain his house of eternity.

(20) He who comes after him will support you.

(21) A woman who is loved, when one abandons her she is (truly) abandoned.

(22) Inspect your house at all times and you will find its thief.

(23) Teach your son to write, plow, fowl and trap against a year of low Nile,
    so that he will reap the profit of what he has done.

(24) Gather dung, gather clay, but do not make an occupation out of scavenging.

(25) Do not talk much before your master.

(26) Be gentle and your reputation will increase in the hearts of all men.

(**18**,x) - - - - - -

(**18**,1) - - - - - -.

(2) [If] a gardener becomes a fisherman his [trees] perish.

(3) If you have acquired - - - give one part of them for protection.

(4) [If you] work the land do not practice deception.

(5) Better an honorable failure than a half success.

(6) If you are powerful throw your documents into the river; if you are week throw them also.

(7) If an inferior says "I will kill you," he will surely kill you.

(8) If a superior says "I will kill you," lay your head on his doorstep.

(9) Give a hundred silver pieces to a prudent woman; do not accept
    two hundred from a foolish one.

(10) He who battles together with the people of his town will rejoice with them.

(11) The children of the fool wander in the street, those of the wise man stand before him?

(12) He who hides from his master will get a hundred masters.

(13) A man who has no town, his character is his family.

(14) A man who has no property, his wife is his partner.

(15) Do not rejoice in your wife's beauty; her heart is set on her lover.

(16) Do not say "I have this wealth, I will not serve god nor will I serve man."

(17) Wealth comes to an end; serving the god is what creates (it).

(18) Do not send to someone whom you do not know at all.

(19) He who loves his house so as to dwell in it warms it to its beams.

(20) He who hates it builds it and mortgages it.

(21) Do not be despondent when you are ill; your landing is not made yet.

(22) Do not say "I shall give this property to this man" if you are not going to give it to him.

(23) Take a superior to your house, take an inferior to your boat.

(24) When Hapy comes he sets limits for everyone.

(25) When the fish is brought up from the water it sends him who would eat it.

(**19**,x) - - - - - -

(**19**,1) - - - - - -.

(2) If you say - - - - - -.

(3) Sweeter is the water of him who has given it than the wine of him [who has received] it.

(4) If a cow is stolen from the field one - - - its owner to the town.

(5) If your enemy seeks you do not hide from him.

(6) If a bird flies to the place of another it will lose a feather.

(7) There is no son of Pharaoh at night.

(8) If a fool follows his heart he acts wisely.

(9) A man does not love what he hates.

(10) Do a good deed and throw it in the water; when it dries you will find it.

(11) When two brothers quarrel do not come between them.

(12) He who comes between two brothers when they quarrel
     will be placed between them when they are reconciled.

(13) If the daughter of the strong man is the one who eats, her rival is the daughter of the . . .

(14) If the son of the master were to act as master, the people would not worship before the god.

(15) Do not be impatient when you are suffering, so that you pray for death.

(16) He who is alive, his herb grows.

(17) There is none wretched except him who has died (or, is dying).

(18) With a thousand servants in the merchant's house the merchant is one of them.

(19) If your master speaks wise words to you, you should fear him.

(20) A wise man is one who knows what goes on before him.

(21) Give your words with your goods, and it will make two gifts.

(22) Beer matures only on its mash.

(23) Wine matures as long as one does not open it.

(24) A remedy is effective only through the hand of its physician.

(25) If you are given bread for being stupid you may despise instruction.

(**20**,x) - - - - - -

(**20**,1) - - - - - -.

(2) ... - - - - - -.

(3) ... - - - - - -.

(4) End by planting any tree, begin by planting a sycamore.

(5) The warp does not stray away from the woof.

(6) All good fortune is from the hand of the god.

(7) A single plowing does not produce . . .

(8) A single 'measuring' is not adequate.

(9) The hissing of the snake is more effective than the braying of the donkey.

(10) There is a running to which sitting is preferable.

(11) There is a sitting to which standing is preferable.

(12) Do not dwell in a house which is decaying; death does not say "I am coming."

(13) A snake that is eating has no venom.

(14) A window with a large opening gives more heat than coolness.

(15) All kinds of cattle are welcome in a house; a thief is not welcome.

(16) Coming close to a fool is to flee him.

(17) If you harness a big team you may lie down in its shade.

(18) Honor the old men in your heart, and you will be honored in the hearts of all men.

(19) A woman lets herself be loved according to the character of her husband.

(20) A man does not eat what is under his eyes.

(21) Even if filled with soap, a storehouse yields a profit.

(22) The waste of a house is not dwelling in it.

(23) The waste of a woman is not knowing her.

(24) The waste of a donkey is carrying bricks.

(25) The waste of a boat is carrying straw.

(**21**,x) - - - - - -

(**21**,1) There is no - - - - - -.

(2) There is no - - - - - -.

(3) There is no - - - - - -.

(4) There is no tooth that rots yet stays in place.

(5) There is no Nubian who leaves his skin.

(6) There is no friend who goes by alone.

(7) There is no wise man who comes to grief.

(8) There is no fool who finds profit.

(9) There is none who insults his superior who is not in turn insulted.

(10) There is none who abandons his traveling companion whom the god does not hold to account for it.

(11) There is none who deceives who is not deceived.

(12) There is none who sins yet goes and prospers.

(13) Do not hasten to reach a magistrate and then draw back from him.

(14) He who is ashamed to sleep with his wife will not have children.

(15) Do not be greedy, lest you be scolded.

(16) Do not be stingy, lest you be hated.

(17) Do not steal copper or cloth from the house of your master.

(18) Do not violate a married woman.

(19) He who violates a married woman on the bed will have his wife violated on the ground.

(20) Better a statue of stone than a foolish son.

(21) Better no brother than one who is evil.

(22) Better death than want.

(23) If you are thirsty at night let your mother give you to drink.

(24) Do not stay in a town in which you have no one.

(25) If you stay in a town in which you have no one, your character is your family.

(**22**,x) - - - - - -

(**22**,1) - - - - - -

(2) Do not - - - - - -

(3) Do not start [a fire if you] can[not put] it [out].

(4) Give your daughter in marriage to a goldsmith (or, gold dealer); [do not] give - - - [to] his daughter.

(5) He who shakes the stone will have it fall on his foot.

(6) He who makes love to a woman of the street will have his purse cut open on its side.

(7) One does not load a beam on a donkey.

(8) If a woman loves a crocodile she takes on its character.

(9) A woman at night, praise in midday.

(10) Do not slander a woman who is beloved.

(11) Do not praise a woman who is disliked.

(12) A fool wanting to go with a wise man is a goose wanting to go with its slaughter knife.

(13) A fool in a house is like fine clothes in a wine cellar.

(14) A decaying house does not get hold of a stranger.

(15) A crocodile does not get hold of a townsman.

(16) When you are hungry eat what you despise; when you are sated despise it.

(17) He who has not got his eye on the river should pay attention to the water jugs.

(18) If you come to say something to your master count on your fingers till ten.

(19) Give one loaf to your laborer, receive two from (the work of) his arms.

(20) Give one loaf to the one who labors, give two to the one who gives orders.

(21) Do not insult a common man.

(22) When insult occurs beating occurs.

(23) When beating occurs killing occurs.

(24) Killing does not occur without the god knowing.

(25) Nothing occurs except what the god ordains.

(23,x) - - - - - -

(23,1) - - - - - -.

(2) - - - - - -.

(3) - - - - - -.

(4) Silence conceals foolishness.

(5) One uses sunlight - - - - - -.

(6) Do not make love to a married woman.

(7) He who makes love to a married woman is killed on her doorstep.

(8) It is better to dwell in your own small house than to dwell in the large house of another.

(9) Better is small wealth which is kept together than large wealth which is dispersed.

(10) A slip of the tongue in the royal palace is a slip of the helm at sea.

(11) A bull does not bellow at a calf; a great stable is not destroyed.

(12) The way of the god is before all men (but) the fool cannot find it.

(13) "Am I going to live?" says the dying.

(14) Every hand is stretched out to the god (but) he accepts (only) the hand of his beloved.

(15) A cat that loves fruit hates him who eats it.

(16) "Your word is my word" says the weakling.

(17) Do not be active in all sorts of business and slack in your own.

(18) He who is not slack, his father will be active for him.

(19) The builders build houses, the musicians inaugurate them.

(20) The frogs praise Hapy, the mice eat the emmer.

(21) The oxen harvest the barley and emmer, the donkeys eat it.

(22) Do not grovel before a great man.

(23) Do not drink the water of a well and then throw the pitcher into it.

(24) Belly of woman, heart of horse.

(**24**,x) - - - - - -

(**24**,1) - - - - - -.

(2) - - - - - -.

(3) - - - - - -.

(4) If much wealth accrues to you - - - - - -.

(5) - - -...- - - you die.

(6) Do not marry an ailing woman.⁹⁰

(7) If a donkey goes with a horse it adopts its pace.

(8) If a crocodile loves a donkey it puts on a wig.⁹¹

(9) One uses a horse to go after a - - - one does not take a donkey to attain it.

(10) Man is even more eager to copulate than a donkey; his purse is what restrains him.⁹²

(11) One gives bread to the inspector for inspecting; if he does not inspect one cuts it off.

(12) Yesterday's drunkenness does not quench today's thirst.

(13) Better to - - - hunger than to die of want.

(14) Do not be ashamed to do your - - - without blaming it.

(15) If you quarrel with your - - - do not tell him you are patient.⁹³

(16) If a town comes to ... - - - - - -.

(17) If a town comes to ruin - - - - - -.

(18) He who does not carry his father's wheat will carry chaff to their storehouses.

(19) Do not take charge of a matter if you cannot take charge to its end.

(20) A woman is a stone quarry; the ... exploits her.

(21) A good woman of noble character is food that comes in time of hunger.

(22) My son is useless if I do not ... - - -.

(23) My servant is useless if he does not do my work.

(24) My brother is useless if he does not take care of me.

(**25**,x) - - - - - -

(**25**,1) - - - - - -.

(2) - - - - - -.

(3)- - - - - -.

(4) More nu[merous are the] - - - of the god - - - than the appearances of Pre in the great hall.

(5) If [a woman is at peace] with her husband it is the influences of the god.

(6) Do not sell your house and your income for the sake of one day and then be poor forever.

(7) Do not remove a common man⁹⁶ from the property of Pharaoh,
     lest he destroy you and your family.

(8) Do not take - - - of a woman to your heart.

(9) She is a harmful woman who does not leave a tree undamaged.

(10) Learn how to send (a report) to the palace of Pharaoh.

(11) Learn how to sit in the presence of Pharaoh.

(12) Learn the constitution of the sky.

(13) Learn the constitution of the earth.

(14) May the heart of a wife be the heart of her husband, that they may be free of strife.

(15) Choose a prudent husband for your daughter; do not choose for her a rich husband.

(16) Spend one year eating what you possess, so that you spend three years - - - the bank.

(17) Do not marry an impious woman, lest she give your children an impious upbringing.

(18) If a woman is at peace with her husband they will never fare badly.

(19) If a woman whispers about her husband [they will never] fare well.

(20) If a woman does not desire the property of her husband she has another man [in her] heart.

(21) A low woman does not have a life.

(22) A bad woman does not have a husband.

(23) The wife of a fool ... - - - - - -.

(24) - - - - - -.

127. THE WINGED DISK

This story is one of several appearing on the walls of the temple of Horus at Edfu, which was built between 237 and 57 BCE on the site of an earlier temple. The wall inscriptions are numerous and shed much light on Egyptian myth, religion and language during the Ptolemaic period.

XII 2. In the three hundred and sixty-third year of Ra-Heru-Khuti, who lives for ever and forever, His Majesty was in Ta-kens, and his soldiers were with him; [the enemy] did not conspire against their lord, and the land [is called] Uauatet to this day.

3. And Ra set out on an expedition in his boat, and his followers were with him, and he arrived at Uthes-heru, [which lay to] the west of this nome, and to the east of the canal Pakhennu, which is called [. . . . . to this day]. And Heru-Bebutet was in the boat of Ra, and he said to his father Ra-Heru-Khuti (i.e., Ra-Harmachis), "I see that the enemies are conspiring against their lord; let your fiery serpent gain the mastery . . . . . over them."

XIII. 1. Then the Majesty of Ra Harmachis said to your divine *ka*, O Heru-Behutet, O son of Ra, you exalted one, who did proceed from me, overthrow the enemies who are before you straightway." And Heru-Behutet flew up into the horizon in the form of the great Winged Disk, for which reason he is called "Great god, lord of heaven," to this day. And when he saw the enemies in the heights of heaven he set out to follow after them in the form of the great Winged Disk, and he attacked with such terrific force those who opposed him,

2. that they could neither see with their eyes nor hear with their ears, and each of them slew his fellow. In a moment of time there was not a single creature left alive. Then Heru Behutet, shining

with very many colours, came in the form of the great Winged Disk to the Boat of Ra-Harmachis, and Thoth said to Ra, "O Lord of the gods, Behutet has returned in the form of the great Winged Disk, shining [with many colours] . . . . . . children;"

3. for this reason he is called Heru-Behutet to this day. And Thoth said, "The city Teb shall be called the city of Heru-Behutet," and thus is it called to this day. And Ra embraced the . . . . . of Ra, and said to Heru-Behutet, "You put grapes into the water which comes forth from it, and tby heart rejoiced thereat;" and for this reason the water (or, canal) of Heru-Behutet is called "[Grape-Water]" to this day, and the . . . . to this day.

4. And Heru-Behutet said, "Advance, O Ra, and look upon your enemies who are lying under you on this land;" thereupon the Majesty of Ra set out on the way, and the goddess Asthertet ('Ashtoreth?) was with him, and he saw the enemies overthrown on the ground, each one of them being fettered. Then said Ra to Heru-Behutet,

5. "There is sweet life in this place," and for this reason the abode of the palace of Heru-Beutet is called "Sweet Life" to this day. And Ra, said to Thoth, "[Here was the slaughter] of my enemies;" and the place is called Teb to this day. And Thoth said to Heru-Behutet, "You are a great protector (*makaa*);" and

6. the Boat of Heru-Behutet is called Makaa to this day. Then said Ra to the gods who were in his following, "Behold now, let us sail in our boat upon the water, for our hearts are glad because our enemies have been overthrown on the earth;" and the water where the great god sailed is

7. called P-ken-nur to this day. And behold the enemies [of Ra] rushed into the water, and they took the forms of [crocodiles and] hippopotami, but nevertheless Ra-Heru-Khuti sailed over the waters in his boat, and when the crocodiles and the hippopotami had come near to him, they opened wide their jaws in order to destroy Ra-Heru-Khuti.

8. And when Heru-Behutet arrived and his followers who were behind him in the forms of workers in metal, each having in his hands an iron spear and a chain, according to his name, they struck the crocodiles and the hippopotami; and there were brought in there straightway six hundred and fifty-one crocodiles,

9. which had been slain before the city of Edfu. Then spoke Ra-Harmachis to Heru-Behutet, "My Image shall be [here] in the land of the South, (which is a house of victory (or, strength);" and the House of Heru-Behutet is called Nekht-het to this day.

XIV. 1. Then the god Thoth spoke, after he had looked upon the enemies lying upon the ground, saying, "Let your hearts rejoice, O you gods of heaven! Let your hearts rejoice, O you gods who are in the earth! Horus, the Youthful One, comes in peace, and he has made manifest on his journey deeds of very great might, which he has performed according to the Book of Slaying the Hippopotamus." And from that day figures of Heru-Behutet in metal have existed. Then Heru-Behutet took upon himself the form of the Winged Disk, and he placed himself upon the front of the Boat of Ea.

2. And he placed by his side the goddess Nekhebet and the goddess Uatchet, in the form of two serpents, that they might make the enemies to quake in [all] their limbs when they were in the forms of crocodiles and hippopotami in every place wherein be came in the Land of the South and in the Land of the North. Then those enemies rose up to make their escape from before him, and their face was towards the Land of the South. And their hearts were stricken down through fear of him. And Heru-Behutet was at the back (or, side) of them in the Boat of Ra, and there were in his hands a metal lance and a metal chain; and the metal workers who were with their lord were equipped

3. for fighting with lances and chains. And Heru-Behutet saw them to the south-east of the city of Uast (Thebes) some distance away. Then Ra said to Thoth, "Those enemies shall be smitten with blows that kill;" and Thoth said to Ra, "[That place] is called the city Tchetmet to this day." And Heru-Behutet made a great overthrow among them, and Ra said, "Stand still, O Heru-Behutet," and [that place] is called "Het-Ra" to this day, and the god who dwells therein is Heru-Behutet-Ra-imsu (or, Min).

4. Then those enemies rose up to make their escape from before him, and the face of the god was towards the Land of the North, and their hearts were stricken through fear of him. And Heru-Behutet was at the back (or, side) of them in the Boat of Ra, and those who were following him had spears of metal and chains of metal in their hands;

5. and the god himself was equipped for battle with the weapons of the metal workers which they had with them. And he passed a whole day before he saw them to the north-east of the nome of Tentyra (Dendera). Then Ra said to Thoth, "The enemies are resting . . . . . . their lord."

6. And the Majesty of Ra-Harmachis said to Heru-Behutet, "You are my exalted son who did proceed from Nut. The courage of the enemies has failed in a moment." And Heru-Behutet made great slaughter among them. And Thoth said "The Winged Disk shall be called. . . . . in the name of this Aat;"

7 and is called Heru-Behutet . . . . . its mistress. His name is to the South in the name of this god, and the acacia and the sycamore shall be the trees of the sanctuary. Then the enemies turned aside to flee from before him, and their faces were [towards the North, and they went] to

8. the swamps of Uatch-ur (i.e., the Mediterranean), and [their courage failed through fear of him]. And Heru-Behutet was at the back (or, side) of them in the Boat of Ra, and the metal spear was in his bands, and those who were in his following were equipped with the weapons for battle of the metal workers.

9. And the god spent four days and four nights in the water in pursuit of them, but he did not see one of the enemies, who fled from before him in the water in the forms of crocodiles and hippopotami. At length he found them and saw them. And Ra said to Horus of Heben, "O Winged Disk, you great god and lord of heaven,

10. seize them . . . . . . ;" and he hurled his lance after them, and he slew them, and worked a great overthrow of them. And he brought one hundred and forty-two enemies to the forepart of the Boat [of Ra], and with them was a male hippopotamus

11. which had been among those enemies. And he hacked them in pieces with his knife, and he gave their entrails to those who were in his following, and he gave their carcases to the gods and goddesses who were in the Boat of Ra on the river-bank of the city of Heben. Then Ra said to Thoth,

12. "See what mighty things Heru-Behutet has performed in his deeds against the enemies: truly he has smitten them! And of the male hippopotamus he has opened the mouth, and he has speared it, and he has mounted upon its back." Then said Thoth to Ra, "Horus shall be called 'Winged Disk, Great God,

13. Smiter of the enemies in the town of Heben' from this day forward, and he shall be called 'He who stands on the back' and 'prophet of this god,' from this day forward." These are the things which happened in the lands of the city of Heben, in a region which measured three hundred and forty-two measures on the south, and on the north, on the west, and on the east.

XV. 1. Then the enemies rose up before him by the Lake of the North, and their faces were set towards Uatch-ur which they desired to reach by sailing; but the god struck their hearts and they turned and fled in the water, and they directed their course to the water of the nome of Mertet-Ament, and they gathered themselves together in the water of Mertet in order to join themselves with the enemies [who serve] Set and who are in this region. And Heru-Behutet followed them, being equipped with all his weapons of war to fight against them.

2. And Heru-Behutet made a journey in the Boat of Ra, together with the great god who was in his boat with those who were his followers, and he pursued them on the Lake of the North twice, and passed one day and one night sailing down the river in pursuit of them before he perceived and overtook them, for he knew not the place where they were. Then he arrived at the city of Per-Rehu. And the Majesty of Ra said to Heru-Behutet, "What has happened to the enemies? They have gathered together themselves in the water to the west of the nome of Mertet in order to unite themselves with the enemies [who serve] Set, and who are in this region,

3. at the place where are our staff and sceptre." And Thoth said to Ra, "Uast in the nome of Mertet is called Uaseb because of this to this day, and the Lake which is in it is called Tempt." Then Heru-Behutet spoke in the presence of his father Ra, saying, I beseech you to set your boat against them, so that I may be able to perform against them that which Ra wills; "and this was done. Then he made an attack upon them on the Lake which was at the west of this district, and he perceived them on the bank of the city . . . . . . which belongs to the Lake of Mertet.

4. Then Heru-Behutet made an expedition against them, and his followers were with him, and they were provided with weapons of all kinds for battle, and he wrought a great overthrow among them, and he brought in three hundred and eighty-one enemies, and he slaughtered them in the forepart of the Boat of Ra,

5. and he gave one of them to each of those who were in his train. Then Set rose up and came forth, and raged loudly with words of cursing and abuse because of the things which Heru-behutet had done in respect of the slaughter of the enemies. And Ra said to Thoth, "This fiend Nehaha-hra utters words at the top of his voice because of the things which

6. Heru-Behutet has done to him; and Thoth said to Ra, "Cries of this kind shall be called Nehaha-hra to this day." And Heru-Behutet did battle with the Enemy for a period of time, and he hurled his iron lance at him, and he throw him down on the ground in this region,

7. which is called Pa-Rerehtu to this day. Then Heru-Behutet came and brought the Enemy with him, and his spear was in his neck, and his chain was round his hands and arms, and the weapon of Horus had fallen on his mouth and had closed it; and he went with him before his father Ra, who said, "O Horus, you Winged Disk,

8. twice great (Urui-Tenten) is the deed of valour which you have done, and you have cleansed the district." And Ra, said to Thoth, "The palace of Heru-Behutet shall be called, 'Lord of the district which is cleansed' because of this;" and [thus is it called] to this day. And the name of the priest thereof is called Ur-Tenten to this day.

9. And Ra said to Thoth, "Let the enemies and Set be given over to Isis and her son Horns, and let them work all their heart's desire upon them." And she and her son Horus set themselves in position with their spears in him at the time when there was storm (or, disaster) in the district, and the Lake of the god was

10. called She-en-aha from that day to this. Then Horus the son of Isis cut off the head of the Enemy [Set], and the heads of his fiends in the presence of father Ra and of the great company of the gods, and he dragged him by his feet through his district with his spear driven through his head and back. And Ra said to Thoth,

11. "Let the son of Osiris drag the being of disaster through his territory;" and Thoth said, "It shall be called Ateh," and this has been the name of the region from that day to this. And Isis, the divine lady, spoke before Ra, saying, "Let the exalted Winged Disk become the amulet of my son Horus, who has cut off the head of the Enemy and the heads of his fiends."

XVI. 1. Thus Heru-Behutet and Horus, the son of Isis, slaughtered that evil Enemy, and his fiends, and the inert foes, and came forth with them to the water on the west side of this district. And Heru-Behutet was in the form of a man of mighty strength, and he had the face of a hawk, and his head was crowned with the White Crown and the Red Crown, and with two plumes and two uraei, and he had the back of a hawk, and his spear and his chain were in his hands. And Horus, the son of Isis, transformed himself into a similar shape, even as Heru-Behutet had done before him.

2. And they slew the enemies all together on the west of Per-Rehu, on the edge of the stream, and this god has sailed over the water wherein the enemies had banded themselves together against him from that day to this. Now these things took place on the 7th day of the first month of the season Pert. And Thoth said, "This region shall be called Aat-shatet," and this has been the name of the region from that day to this; and the Lake which is close by it

3. has been called Temt from that day to this, and the 7th day of the first month of the season Pert has been called the Festival of Sailing from that day to this. Then Set took upon himself the form of a hissing serpent, and he entered into the earth in this district without being seen. And Ra said, "Set has taken upon himself the form of a hissing serpent. Let Horus, the son of Isis, in the form of a hawk-headed staff, set himself over the place where he is, so that the serpent may never more appear."

4. And Thoth said, "Let this district be called Hemhemet by name;" and thus has it been called from that day to this. And Horus, the son of Isis, in the form of a hawkheaded staff, took up his abode there with his mother Isis; in this manner did these things happen. Then the Boat of Ra arrived at the town of Het-Aha;

5. its forepart was made of palm wood, and the hind part was made of acacia wood; thus the palm tree and the acacia tree have been sacred trees from that day to this. Then Heru-Behutet embarked in the Boat of Ra, after he had made an end of fighting, and sailed; and Ra said to Thoth, "Let this Boat be called . . . . ;" and thus has it been called from that day to this,

6. and these things have been done in commemoration in this place from that day to this. And Ra said to Heru-Behutet, "Behold the fighting of the Smait fiend and his two-fold strength, and the Smai fiend Set, are upon the water of the North, and they will sail down stream upon . . . . [And] Heru-Behutet said, "Whatever you command shall take place,

7. O Ra, Lord of the gods. Grant, however, that this your Boat may pursue them into every place wherever they shall go, and I will do to them whatever pleases Ra." And everything was done according to what he had said. Then this Boat of Ra was brought by the winged Sun-disk upon the waters of the Lake of Meh, [and] Heru-Behutet took in his hands his weapons, his darts, and his harpoon, and all the chains [which he required] for the fight.

8. And Heru-Behutet looked and saw one [only] of these Sebau fiends there on the spot, and he was by himself. And he threw one metal dart, and brought (or, dragged) them along straightway, and

he slaughtered them in the presence of Ra. And he made an end [of them, and there were no more of the fiends] of Set in this place at [that] moment.

XVII 1. And Thoth said, "This place shall be called Ast-ab-heru," because Heru-Behutet wrought his desire upon them (i.e., the enemy); and he passed six days and six nights coming into port on the waters thereof and did not see one of them. And he saw them fall down in the watery depths, and he made ready the place of Ast-ab-Heru there. It was situated on the bank of the water, and the face (i.e., direction) thereof was full-front towards the South.

2. And all the rites and ceremonies of Heru-Behutet were performed on the first day of the first month of the season Akhet, and on the first day of the first month of the season Pert, and on the twenty-first and twenty-fourth days of the second month of the season Pert. These are the festivals in the town of Ast-ab, by the side of the South, in An-rut-f. And he came into port and went against them, keeping watch as for a king over the Great God in An-rut-f, in this place, in order to drive away the Enemy and his Smaiu fiends at his coming by night from the region of Mertet, to the west of this place.

3. And Heru-Behutet was in the form of a man who possessed great strength, with the face of a hawk; and he was crowned with the White Crown, and the Red Crown, and the two plumes, and the Urerit Crown, and there were two uraei upon his head. His hand grasped firmly his harpoon to slay the hippopotamus, which was [as hard] as the *khenem* stone in its mountain bed. And Ra said to Thoth, "Indeed [Heru-]Behutet is like a Master-fighter in the slaughter of his enemies . . . . . ." And Thoth said to Ra, "He shall be called 'Neb-Ahau '" (i.e., Master-fighter); and for this reason he has been thus called by the priest of this god to this day.

4. And Isis made incantations of every kind in order to drive away the fiend Ra from An-rut-f, and from the Great God in this place. And Thoth said [to Ra], "The priestess of this god shall be called by the name of 'Nebt-Heka' for this reason." And Thoth said to Ra, "Beautiful, beautiful is this place wherein you have taken up your seat, keeping watch, as for a king, over the Great God who is in An-rut-f in peace."

5. And Thoth said, "This Great House in this place shall therefore be called 'Ast-Nefert' from this day. It is situated to the south-west of the city of Nart, and [covereth] a space of four schoinoi." And Ra Heru-Behutet said to Thoth, "Have you not searched through this water for the enemy?" And Thoth said,

6. "The water of the God-house in this place shall be called by the name of 'Heh' (i.e., sought out)." And Ra said, "Your ship, O Heru-Behutet, is great upon Ant-mer . . . . . . And Thoth said, "The name of [your ship] shall be called 'Ur', and this stream shall be called 'Antmer.'"

7. As concerning (or, now) the place Ab-Bat is situated on the shore of the water. "Astnefert" is the name of the Great house, "Neb-Aha" [is the name of] the priest . . . . is the name of the priestess, "Heh" is the name of the lake . . . . , [is the name] of the water,

8. "Ain-her-net" is the name of the holy acacia tree, "Neter-het" is the name of the domain of the god, "Uru" is the name of the sacred boat, the gods therein are Heru-Behutet, the smiter of the lands, Horus, the son of Isis [and] Osiris . . . .

9. his blacksmiths are to him, and those who are in his following are to him in his territory, with his metal lance, with his [mace], with his dagger, and with all his chains (or, fetters) which are in the city of Heru-Behutet. [And when he had reached the land of the North with his followers, he found the enemy.]

10. Now as for the blacksmiths who were over the middle regions, they made a great slaughter of the enemy, and there were brought back one hundred and six of them. Now as for the blacksmiths of the West, they brought back one hundred and six of the enemy. Now as for the blacksmiths of the East, among whom was Heru-Behutet,

11. he slew them (i.e., the enemy) in the presence of Ra in the Middle Domains. And Ra, said to Thoth, "My heart [is satisfied] with the works of these blacksmiths of Heru-Behutet who are in his bodyguard. They shall dwell in sanctuaries, and libations and purifications and (offerings shall be made to their images, and

12. [there shall be appointed for them] priests who shall minister by the month, and priests who shall minister by the hour, in all their God-houses whatsoever, as their reward because they have slain the enemies of the god." And Thoth said, "The [Middle] Domains shall be called after the names of these blacksmiths from this day onwards,

13. and the god who dwells among them, Heru-Behutet, shall be called the 'Lord of Mesent' from this day onwards, and the domain shall be called 'Mesent of the West' from this day onwards." As concerning Mesent of the West, the face (or, front) thereof shall be towards [the East], towards the place where Ra rises, and this Mesent shall be called "Mesent of the East" from this day onwards.

14. As concerning the double town of Mesent, the work of these blacksmiths of the East, the face (or, front) thereof shall be towards the South, towards the city of Behutet, the hiding-place of Heru-Behutet. And there shall be performed therein all the rites and ceremonies of Heru-Bebutet on the second day of the first month of the season of Akhet, and on the twenty-fourth day of the fourth month of the season of Akhet, and on the seventh day of the first month of the season Pert, and on the twenty-first day of the second month of the season Pert, from this day onwards.

15. Their stream shall be called the name of their Great House shall be called "Abet," the [priest] shall be called "Qen-aha," and their domain shall be called "Kau-Mesent" from this day onwards."

XVIII. 1. And Ra said to Heru-Behutet, "These enemies have sailed up the river, to the country of Setet, to the end of the pillar-house of Hat, and they have sailed up the river to the east, to the country or Tchalt (or, Tchart), which is their region of swamps." And Heru-Behutet said, "Everything which you have commanded has come to pass, Ra, Lord of the gods; you are the lord of commands." And they untied the Boat of Ra, and they sailed up the river to the east. Then he looked upon those enemies whereof some of them had fallen into the sea (or, river), and the others had fallen headlong on the mountains.

2. And Heru-Behutet transformed himself into a lion which had the face of a man, and which was crowned with the triple crown. His paw was like to a flint knife, and he went round and round by the side of them, and brought back one hundred and forty-two [of the enemy], and be rent them in pieces with his claws. He tore out their tongues, and their blood flowed on the ridges of the land in this place; and he made them the property of those who were in his following [while] he was upon the mountains. And Ra said to Thoth, "Behold, Heru-Behutet is similar to a lion in his lair [when] he is on the back of the enemy who have given to him their tongues."

3. And Thoth said, "This domain shall be called 'Khent-abt,' and it shall [also] be called 'Tchalt' (or, Tchart) from this day onwards. And the bringing of the tongues from the remote places of Tchalt (or, Tchart) [shall -be commemorated] from this day onwards. And this god shall be called 'Heru-Behutet, Lord of Mesent,' from this day onwards." And Ra said to Heru-Behutet, "Let us

sail to the south up the river, and let us smite the enemies [who are] in the forms of crocodiles and hippopotami in the face of Egypt."

4. And Heru-Behutet said, "Your divine *ka*, O Ra, Lord of the gods! Let us sail up the river against the remainder -- one third -- of the enemies who are in the water (or, river)." Then Thoth recited the Chapters of protecting the Boat [of Ra] and the boats of the blacksmiths,

5. [which he used] for making tranquil the sea at the moment when a storm was raging on it. And Ra said to Thoth, "Have we not journeyed 'throughout the whole land? Shall we not journey over the whole sea in like manner?" And Thoth said, "This water shall be called the 'Sea of journeying,' from this day onward." And they sailed about over the water during the night,

6. and they did not see any of those enemies at all. Then they made a journey forth and arrived in the country of Ta-sti, at the town of Shas-hertet, and he perceived the most able of their enemies in the country of Uaua, and they were uttering treason against Horus their Lord.

7. And Heru-Behut changed his form into that of the Winged Disk, [and took his place] above the bow of the Boat of Ra. And he made the goddess Nekhebit and the goddess Uatchit to be with him in the form of serpents, so that they might make the Sebau fiends to quake in [all] their limbs (or, bodies). Their boldness (i.e., that of the fiends) subsided through the fear of him, they made no resistance whatsoever, and they died straightway.

8. Then the gods who were in the following of the Boat of Heru-khuti said, "Great, great is that which he has done among them by means of the two Serpent Goddesses, for he has overthrown the enemy by means of their fear of him." And Ra Heru-khuti said, "The great one of the two Serpent Goddesses of Heru-Bebutet shall be called 'Ur-Uatchti' from this day onwards."

XIX. 1. And Heru-khuti travelled on in his boat, and landed at the city of Thes-Heru (Apollinopolis Magna). And Thoth said, "The being of light who has come forth from the horizon has smitten the enemy in the form which he has made, and he shall be called Being of light who has come forth from the horizon from this day onwards." And Ra Heru-khuti (Ra Harmachis) said to Thoth, "You shall make this Winged Disk to be in every place wherein I seat myself (or, dwell), and in [all] the seats of the gods in the South, and in [all] the seats of the gods in the Land of the North ... in the Country of Horus,

2 that it may drive away the evil ones from their domains." Then Thoth made the image of the Winged Disk to be in every sanctuary and in every temple, where they now are, wherein are all the gods and all the goddesses from this day onwards. Now through the Winged Disk which is on the temple-buildings of all the gods and all the goddesses of the Land of the Lily, and the Land of the Papyrus, [these buildings] become shrines of Heru-Behutet. As concerning Heru-Behutet, the great god, the lord of heaven, the president of the Ater of the South, he it is who is made to be on the right hand. This is Heru-Behutet

3 on whom the goddess Nekhebit is placed in the form of a serpent (or, uraeus). As concerning Heru-Behutet, the great god, the lord of heaven, the lord of Mesent, the president of the Ater of the North, he it is who is made to be on the left hand. This Heru-Behutet on whom the goddess Uatebit is placed is in the form of a serpent.

As concerning Heru-Behutet, the great god, the lord of heaven, the lord of Mesent, the president of the two Aterti of the South and North, Ra Heru-khuti set it (i.e., the Winged Disk) in his every place, to overthrow the enemies in every place wherein they are. And he shall be called President of the two Aterti of the South and North because of this from this day onwards.

128. DIODORUS SICULUS, *BIBLIOTHECA HISTORICA*

The Bibliotheca historica *("Historical Library") is a lengthy history written at some time between 60 and 30 BCE by Diodorus Siculus, a Greek from Agyrium in Sicily. Out of an original forty books, only books 1–5 and 11–20 still exist. The history concerns the whole world (at least as Diodorus knew it), but here are some of his words on Egypt.*

Book I, Chapter 1

The Egyptians report, that, at the beginning of the world, the first men were created in Egypt, both by reason of the happy climate of the country, and the nature of the river Nile. For this river being very fruitful, and apt to bring forth many animals, yields, of itself, likewise food and nourishment for the things produced. For it yields the roots of canes, the fruit of the lote-tree, the Egyptian bean, that which they call Corseon, and such like rarities for man's food, always ready at hand.

And that all living creatures were first produced among them, they use this argument—that even at this day, about Thebes, at certain , times, such vast mice are bred, that it causes admiration to the beholders; some of which, to the breast and fore-feet, are animated, and begin to move, and the rest of the body (which yet retains the nature of the soil) appears without form. Whence it is manifest, that in the beginning of the world, through the fertileness of the oil, the first men were formed in Egypt, being that in no other parts of the world any of these creatures are produced only in Egypt these supernatural births may be seen.

And that we may sum up all in a word: if in the tune of Deucalion's flood, the greateat part only of all living creatures were destroyed, then of such as were so preserved, it is very probable that those in Egypt, especially, were of the number, whose inhabitants lie under the south pole, and the country for the most part without sain: or, if all that had life generally perished, (as some affirm), and that the earth produced animals anew, yet they say, that notwithstanding this the chief production of things animated is to be ascribed to this country. For they affirm, that if the showers which fell in any other places were warmed with the same heat that is in Egypt the air would be of that temperature, as that it would aptly conduce to the generation of animals, as at first, in the beginning of the world. For even at this day, such births may be seen (in the waters that have lain long) over all the watered country of Egypt. For they affirm, that when the river returns into its channel, and the sun dries the mud, living creatures are generated, some perfect, others half formed, even cleaving to the soil whence they are produced.

The first generation of men in Egypt, therefore, contemplating the beauty of the superior world, and admiring with astonishment the frame and order of the universe, supposed there were two chief gods that were eternal, that is to say, the sun and the moon, the first of which they called Osiris, and the other Isis. ...

And besides these, they say there are others that are terrestrial, which were begotten of these former gods, and were originally mortal men, but by reason of their wisdom and beneficence to all mankind, have obtained immortality, of which tome have been kings of Egypt: some of whom, by interpretation, have had the same names with the celestial gods, others have kept their own proper names. For they report that Sol, Saturn, Rhea, Jupiter, (surnamed by some Ammon), Juno, Vulcan, Vesta, and lastly, Mercury, reigned in Egypt; and that Sol was the first king of Egypt, whose name was the same with the celestial planet called Sol.

But there are some of the priests who affirm Vulcan to be the first of their kings, and that he was advanced to that dignity upon the account of being the first that found out the use of fire, which was so beneficial to all mankind. For a tree in the mountains happening to be set on fire by lightning, the wood next adjoining was presently all in a flame; and Vulcan thereupon coming to the place, was mightily refreshed by the heat of it, being then winter season; and when the fire began to fail, he added more combustible matter to it, and by that means preserving it, called in other men to enjoy tie benefit of that which be himself was the first inventor, as he gave out.

Afterwards they say Saturn reigned, and married his sister Rhea, and that he begat of her Osiris and Isis; but others say, Jupiter and Juno, who for their great virtues, ruled over all the world. That of Jupiter and Juno ware born five gods, one upon every day of the five Egyptian intercalary days. The names of these gods are Osiris, Isis, Typhon, Apollo, and Venus. That Osiris was interpreted Bacchus, and Isis plainly Ceres. That Osiris married Isis, and after he came to the kingdom, did mocb, and performed many things fog the common benefit and advantage of mankind. For he was the first that forbade men eating one another; and at the same time Ins found out the way of making of bread of wheat and barley, which before grew here and there in the fields, amongst other common herbs and grass, and the use of it unknown: and Osiris teaching the way and manner of tillage, and well management of the fruits of the earth, this change of food became grateful; both because it was naturally sweet and delicious, and men were thereby restrained from the mutual butcheries one of another: for an evidence of this first finding out the use of these fruits, they alledge an ancient custom among them: for even at this day, in the time of harvest, the inhabitants offer the first fruits of the ears of corn, bowling and wailing about the handfuls they offer, and invoking this goddess Isis: and this they do in return of due honour to her for that indention at the first. In some cities also, when they celebrate the feast of Isis, in a pompous procession, they carry about vessels of wheat and barley, in memory of the first invention, by the care and industry of this goddess. They say, likewise, that Isis made many laws for the good of human society, whereby men were restrained from lawless force and violence one upon another, out of fear of punishment. And therefore Ceres was called by the ancient Greeks, Themophorus, that is, lawgiver, being the princess that first constituted laws for the better government of her people.

Osiris moreover built Thebes, in Egypt, with an hundred gates, and called it after his mother's name; but in following times, it was called Diospolis, and Thebes; of whose first founder not only historians, but the priests of Egypt themselves, are much in doubt For some say that it was not built by Osiris, but many years after, by a king of Egypt, whose history we shall treat of hereafter, in its proper place. They report, likewise, that he built two magnificent temples, and dedicated them to his parents, Jupiter and Juno; and likewise two golden altars, the greater to the great god Jupiter; the other to his father Jupiter, who had formerly reigned there, whom they call Ammon. That he also erected golden altars to other gods, and instituted their several rites of worship, and appointed priests to have the oversight and care of the holy things. In the time of Osiris and Isis, projectors and ingenious artists were in great honour and esteem; awl therefore in Thebes there were then goldsmiths and braziers, who made arms and weapons for the killing of wild beasts, and other instruments for the husbanding of the ground, and improvement of tillage; besides images of the gods, and altars in gold. They say that Osiris was much given to husbandry, that he was the son of Jupiter, brought up in Nysa, a town of Arabia the happy, near to Egypt, called by the Greeks Dionysius, from his father, and the place of his education. The poet in his hymns makes mention of Nysa, as bordering upon Egypt, where he says.

Far off from Phenice stands the sacred Nyse,
Where streams of Egypt's Nile begin to rise,
On mountain high with pleasant woods adorn'd.

Here near onto Nysa, they say he found out the use of the vine, and there planting it, was the first that drank wine; and taught others how to plant it and use it, and to gather in their vintage, and to keep and preserve it. Above all others he most honoured Hermes, one of an admirable ingenuity, and quick invention, in finding out what might be useful to mankind. This Hermes was the first (as they report) that taught how to speak distinctly and articulately, and gave names to many things that had none before. He found out letters, and instituted the worship of the gods; and was the first that observed the motion of the stars, and invented music; and taught the manner of wrestling; and invented arithmetic, and the art of curious graving and cutting of statues. He first found out the harp with three strings, in resemblance of the three seasons of the year, causing three several sounds, the treble, base, and mean. The treble to represent the summer; the base, the winter; and the mean, the spring. He was the first that taught the Greeks eloquence; thence he is called Hermes, a speaker or interpreter. To conclude, he was Osiris's sacred scribe, to whom he communicated all his secrets, and was chiefly steered by his advice in every thing. He (not Minerva, as the Greeks affirm) found out the use of the olive-tree, for the making of oil. It is moreover reported, that Osiris being a prince of a public spirit, and very ambitious of glory, raised a great army, with which he resolved to go through all parts of the world that were inhabited, and to teach men how to plant vines, and to sow wheat and barley. For he hoped that if he could civilize men, and take them off from their rude and beast-like course of lives, by such a public good and advantage, he should raise a foundation amongst all mankind, for his immortal praise and honour, which happened accordingly. For not only that age, but posterity ever after honoured those among the chiefest of their gods, that first found out their proper and ordinary food. Having therefore settled his affairs in Egypt, and committed the government of his whole kingdom to his wife Isis, he joined with her Mercury, as her chief counsellor of state, because he far excelled all others in wisdom and prudence. But Hercules, his near kinsman, he left general of all his forces within his dominions, a man admired by all for his valour and strength of body. As to those parts which lay near Phoenicia, and upon the sea-coasts of them, he made Busiris lord lieutenant, and of Ethiopia and Lybia, Anteus.

Then marching out of Egypt, he began his expedition, taking along with him his brother, whom the Greeks called Apollo. This Apollo is reported to have discovered the laurel-tree, which all dedicate especially to this god. To Osiris they attribute the finding out of the ivy-tree, and dedicate it to him, as the Greeks do to Bacchus: and therefore in the Egyptian tongue, they call Ivy, Osiris's plant, which they prefer before the vine in all their sacrifices, because this loses its leaves, and the other always continues fresh and green: which rule the ancients have observed in other plants, that are always green, dedicating myrtle to Venus, laurel to Apollo, and the olive-tree to Pallas.

It is said that two of his sons accompanied their father Osiris in this expedition, one called Anubis, and the other Macedo, both valiant men: both of them wore coats of mail, that were extraordinary remarkable, covered with the skins of such creatures as resembled them in stoutness and valour. Anubis was covered with a dog's, and Macedo with the skin of a wolf; and for this reason these beasts are religiously adored by the Egyptians. He had likewise for his companion, Pan, whom the Egyptians have in great veneration; for they not only set up images and statues in every temple, but built a city in Thebides after his name, called by the inhabitants Chemmin, which by interpretation is Pan's city. There went along with them likewise, those that were skilful in husbandry, as Maro in the planting of vines, and Triptolemus in sowing of corn, and gathering in the harvest.

Book I, Chapter 2

All things being now prepared, Osiris having vowed to the gods to let his hair grow till he returned into Egypt, marched through Ethiopia; and for that very reason it is a piece of religion, and practised among the Egyptians at this day, that those that travel abroad, suffer their hair to grow, till they return home. As he passed through Ethiopia, a company of satyrs were presented to him, who (as it is reported) were all hairy down to their loins: for Osiris was a man given to mirth and jollity, and took great pleasure in music and dancing; and therefore carried along with him a train of musicians, of whom nine were virgins, most excellent singers, and expert in many other things, (whom the Greeks call muses), of whom Apollo was the captain; and thence called the Leader of the Muses: upon this account the satyrs, who are naturally inclined to skipping, dancing, and singing, and all other sorts of mirth, were taken in as part of the army: for Osiris was not for war, nor came to fight battles, and to decide controversies by the sword, every country receiving him for his merits and virtues, as a god. In Ethiopia, having instructed the inhabitants in husbandry, and tillage of the ground, and built several stately cities among them, he left there behind him some to be governors of the country, and others to be gatherers of his tribute.

While they were thus employed, it is said that the river Nile about the dog-days, (at which time it uses to he the highest), broke down its banks, and overflowed the greatest part of Egypt, and that part especially where Prometheus governed, insomuch as almost all the inhabitants were drowned; so that Prometheus was near to killing of himself for very grief of heart: and, from the sudden and violent eruption of the waters, the river was called Eagle.

After his death, Isis and Mercury celebrated his funeral with sacrifices and other divine honours, as to one of the gods, and instituted many sacred rites and mystical ceremonies, in memory of the mighty works wrought by this hero, now deified, Anciently the Egyptian priests kept the proper of the death of Osiris secret io their own registers among themselves; but in after-times it fell out, that some that could not hold, blurted it out, and so it came abroad. For they say that Osiris, while he governed in Egypt with all justice imaginable, was murdered by his wicked brother Typhon; and that he mangled his dead body into six-and-twenty pieces, and gave to each of his confederates in the treason a piece, by that means to bring them all within the same hybrid guilt, and thereby the more to engage them to advance him to the throne, and to defend and preserve him in the possession.

But Isis, the sister and wife likewise of Osiris, with the assistance of her son Orus, revenged his death upon Typbon and his accomplices, and possessed herself of the kingdom of Egypt. It is said the battle was fought near a river not far off a town now called Antaea in Arabia, so called from Anteus, whom Hercules slew in the time of Osiris. She found all the pieces of his body, save his privy members; and having a desire to conceal her husband's burial, yet to have him honoured as a God by all the Egyptians, she thus contrived it. She closed all the pieces together, cementing them with wax and aromatic spices, and so brought it to the shape of man of the bigness of Osiris; then she sent for the priests to her one by one, and swore them all that they should not discover what she should then intrust them with. Then she told them privately, that they only should have the burial of the king's body; and recounting the many good works he had done, charged them to bury the body in a proper place among themselves, and to pay to him all divine honour, as to a God. That they should dedicate to him one of the beasts bred among them, which of them they pleased, and that while it was alive, they should pay it the same veneration as they did before to Osiris himself; and when it was dead, that they should worship it with the same adoration and worship given to Osiris. But being willing to encourage the priests to these divine offices by profit and advantage, she gave them the third part of the country for the maintenance of the service of the Gods and their attendance at the altars.

In memory, therefore, of Osiris's good deeds, being incited thereunto by the commands of the queen, and in expectation of their own profit and advantage, the priests exactly performed every thing that Isis injoined them; and therefore every order of the priests at this day are of opinion that Osiris is buried among them. And they have those beasts in great veneration, that were so long since thus consecrated; and renew their mournings for Osiris over the graves of those beasts. There are two sacred bulls especially, the one called Apis, and the other Mnevis, that are consecrated to Osiris, and reputed as gods generally by all the Egyptians. For this creature of all others was extraordinarily serviceable to the first inventors of husbandry, both as to the sowing corn, and other advantages concerning tillage, of which all reaped the benefit. Lastly, they say, that after the death of Osiris, Isis made a vow never to marry any other man, and spent the rest of her days in an exact administration of justice among her subjects, excelling all other princes in her acts of grace and bounty towards her own people; and therefore, after her death, she was numbered among the gods, and, as such, had divine honour and veneration, and was buried at Memphis, where they shew her sepulchre at this day in the grove of Vulcan.

Yet there are some that deny that these gods are buried at Memphis; but near the mountains of Ethiopia, and Egypt, in the isle of Nile, lying near to a place called Philas, and upon that account also named the Holy Field. They confirm this by undoubted signs and marks left in this island, as by a sepulchre built and erected to Osiris, religiously reverenced by all the priests of Egypt, wherein are laid up three hundred and threescore bowls, which certain priests appointed for that purpose, fill every day with milk, and call upon the Gods by name, with mourning and lamentation. For that cause none go into the island but priests. The inhabitants of Thebes (which is the most ancient city of Egypt) account it a great oath, and by no means to be violated, if a man swear by Osiris that lies buried at Philas.

The several parts, therefore, of Osiris being found, they report were buried in this manner before related; but his privy-members (they say) were thrown into the river by Typhon, because none of his partners would receive them; and yet that they were divinely honoured by Isis; for she commanded an image of this very part to be set up in the temples, and to be religiously adored; and in all their ceremonies and sacrifices to this god, she ordered that part to be held in divine veneration and honour. And therefore the Grecians, after they had learned the rites and ceremonies of the feast of Bacchus, and the orgian solemnities from the Egyptians, in all their mysteries and sacrifices to this god, they adored that member by the name of Phallus.

From Osiris and Isis, to the reign of Alexander the Great, who built a city after his own name, the Egyptian priests reckon above ten thousand years, or (as some write) little less than three-and-twenty thousand years. ...

The Egyptians report that Isis found out many medicines for the recovery of men's health, being very expert in the art of physic, and contrived many remedies for that purpose; and therefore even now when she is advanced to an immortal state, she takes pleasure in curing men's bodies; and to those that desire her assistance, in their sleep she deafly manifests her presence, and affords ready and effectual relief to them that stand in need of it.

For clear proof of all this, they say, they have not only the usual fables of the Greeks, but the undoubted evidence of the fact to confirm it; and that almost the whole world bears testimony to this, by the respect and honour they pay to this goddess upon the account of her great fame in curing of diseases: for in sleep she is present with persons, and applies remedies to the sick, and wonderfully cures those that are her votaries. That many that have been given up by the physicians as incurable, have been restored by her; and that many that have been blind and lame, who have sought to her for help, have been perfectly restored to their former sight, and soundness of body.

They say she found out a medicine that would raise the dead to life, with which she not only raised her son Orus, that was killed by the Titans, and found dead in the water, but, by that application, made him immortal. This Orus was the last of the gods that reigned in Egypt, after the translation of Osiris his father. This Orus, they say, by interpretation is Apollo, who being taught by his mother Isis, the art of physic and divination, was very beneficial to mankind in these respects.

The Egyptian priests in their computation of time do reckon above three and twenty thousand years from the reign of Sol, to the passage of Alexander the Great into Asia.

In their fabulous stories they say, that the most ancient of their gods reigned twelve hundred years, and the latter no less than three hundred years a-piece. Whereas this great number of years seems incredible, some have not stuck to affirm that the motion of the sun not being then known, the year was reckoned according to the course of the moon; and therefore the solar year, consisting then but of three hundred days, some of them were sure to live twelve hundred lunary years; and even at this day now that there are twelve months in the year, many live a hundred solar years.

The like they say of them that reigned three hundred years: for in their time (they say) the year was made up of four months, every four applicable to each of the three seasons of the solar year, that is to say, spring, summer, and winter; which is the reason that some of the Grecians call years *Horas*, seasons; and historical annals, *Horography*.

The Egyptians moreover among their fables report, that in the time of Isis, there were men of vast bodies, whom the Grecians call Giants, and whom they place in their temples in prodigious shapes, who are whipt and scourged by them that sacrifice to Osiris. Some idly give forth, that they sprang from the earth, when at first it gave being to living creatures. Others report, that from many extraordinary things done by men of strong bodies, the fables and stories of giants arose. But in this most agree, that for the war they raised against the gods Jupiter and Osiris, they were all destroyed.

It was a law likewise (they say) in Egypt, against the custom of all other nations, that brothers and sisters might marry one with another, which accordingly was prosperous and successful in the marriage of Isis, who married her brother Osiris, and after his death made a vow never to marry any other man; and after she had revenged her husband's death upon his murderers, she governed the kingdom, and reigned justly all her days; and did good universally to all sorts of people, obliging them with many and extraordinary benefits and advantages. And for her sake it is a custom among them, that they honour a queen, and allow her more power and authority than a king: and in their contracts of marriage authority is given to the wife over her husband, at which time the husbands promise to be obedient to their wives in all things.

Isis was buried at Memphis, where at this day her shrine is to be seen in the grove of Vulcan: although some affirm, that these gods lie buried in the Isle of Nile, at Philas, as is before said. Neither am I ignorant that some writers say their sepulchres are at Nysa in Arabia; whence Dionysius is called Nysaeus; there they say is a pillar erected to each of the deities with inscriptions of sacred letters upon them; in one of which, that belonging to Isis, are these words: —"I am Isis, queen of all this country, the scholar of Mercury; what laws I have made, none ought to disannul. I am the eldest daughter of the youngest god, Saturn. I am the wife and sister of king Osiris. I am she that first found out corn for man's use. I am the mother of king Orus. I am she that arises in the dog-star. The city Bubastus was built in memory of me. Farewell, rejoice O Egypt that was my nurse, that brought me up."

Upon Osiris's pillar are these that follow:—"My father was Saturn, the youngest of all the gods. I am Osiris, that led an army through all the nations, as far as to the deserts of India, and in the countries lying to the north, as far as to the head springs of the river Ister; and to other parts, as far as to the ocean. I am the eldest son of Saturn, a branch of a famous noble stock, cousin german to the day. There is not a place in the world where I have not been; and what I have discovered, I have imparted to all."

So much of the inscriptions on the pillars (they say) may be read; the rest is defaced and worn out through length of time. Thus, therefore, many disagree concerning the sepulchres of these gods because the priests, who were secretly instructed in the perfect knowledge of these matters, would not suffer them to be spread abroad, out of fear of those punishments that such were liable to who revealed the secrets of the gods. ...

At the first, (as some of them, i.e. the priests have fabulously reported), the gods and demi-gods reigned in Egypt for the space almost of eighteen thousand years, the last of which was Orus, the son of Isis. Afterwards, they say, that men reigned there for the space of fifteen thousand years, to the hundred and eightieth Olympiad, at which time I myself came into Egypt in the reign of Ptolemy, who took upon him the name of Dionysius the younger. Most of their kings were natives of the country. There were a few in the mean time that were Ethiopians, Persians, and Macedonians. Four of them that were Ethiopians, reigned not in a continued line, but at several times, for the space of thirty-six years or thereabouts: from the time that Cambyses cotoquered the nation, the Persians reigned for the space of a hundred and thirty-five years, reckoning the defections of the Egyptians within the time occasioned by the intolerable cruelty of the governors, and their impiety against the Egyptian gods. Last of all, the Macedonians ruled there for the space of two hundred and seventy-six years. The rest of the princes were Egyptians, to the number of four hundred and seventy men, and five women. The Egyptian priests keep registers in their temples of all their kings successively, from many generations past; to what greatness and majesty every one of them arrived; what were their particular tempers and inclinations, and their actions in their several times. To write particularly of every one of them, as it would be tedious, so it would be altogether superfluous, inasmuch as many things concerning them are insignificant, and of no use; and therefore we have limited ourselves to treat only of those matters that are most remarkable and worthy of remembrance.

Book 1, Chapter 6

Since sufficient has been said of the Egyptian kings from the most ancient times, to the death of Amasis, (leaving for awhile what remains till a more proper time), we shall now give a brief account of those laws and customs of the Egyptians that are most to be admired, and may especially delight and profit the reader. For many of the ancient customs of the Egyptians were not only allowed, by the natural inhabitants, but were greatly admired by the Grecians, so that every learned man earnestly coveted to travel into Egypt to learn the knowledge of their laws and customs; as things of great weight and moment: and though the country anciently forbade all reception of strangers, (for the reasons before alledged), yet some of the ancients, as Orpheus and Homer, and many of later times, as Pythagoras the Samian, and Solon the lawgiver, ventured to travel hither. And therefore the Egyptians affirm that letters, astronomy, geometry, and many other arts were first found out by them; and that the best laws were made and instituted by them. To confirm which, they alledge this as an undeniable argument, that the native kings of Egypt have reigned there for the space of above four thousand and seven-hundred years, and that their country, for all that time has been the most prosperous and flourishing kingdom in the world, which could never have been so, if the inhabitants had not been civilized, and brought up under good laws, and liberal education in all sorts of arts and sciences. But we shall omit what Herodotus and other writers of the Egyptian history relate, who wilfully pursue and prefer prodigious stories before truth, and relate a company of fictions merely for sport and diversion sake, and shall give an account of such things as we have carefully perused and examined recorded in their books by the Egyptian priests.

The first kings of Egypt lived not after the way and manner of other monarchs, to do what they list, without controul; but in every thing conformed themselves to their laws, not only in the public administration of the government, but in their daily private conversation, and their very meals and diet. For among their attendants, they had neither slaves for servants, nor such as were born in their houses; but the sons of the chiefest of the priests, (after they attained to the age of twenty years), brought up and educated more nobly than any other of the rest of the Egyptians; that having such noble attendants upon his person, (of the best and highest rank in the kingdom) to be always with him night and day, he might not do any thing that was base and blame-worthy. For no prince is apt to be very wicked, except he have some ready at hand to encourage him in his lusts.

There were hours set apart in the night as well as the day, wherein the king was to do something enjoined him by the laws, and not to indulge himself in his pleasures.

When he rose in the morning, the first thing he was to do, was to peruse all the public letters and advices sent from all parts, that he might order his concerns the better, by having perfect knowledge of all the affairs of the kingdom. Then washing himself, and putting on his splendid robes, and the ensigns and badges of his royal authority, he went to sacrifice to the gods.

When the victims were brought to the altar, it was the custom for the high priest, in the presence of the king and people standing round about him, to pray with a loud voice for the health and prosperity of the king, who righteously ruled and governed his subjects, wherein he recounted all the virtues of the prince, his piety towards the gods, his kindness to his people; how continent, just, magnanimous and faithful he was; how bountiful, and what a master he was over all inordinate appetites and passions; how he was mild and gentle in inflicting punishments upon offenders, less than their deserts, and bountiful in distributing of his rewards. When the priest had uttered these and such like commendations, he at last pronounced a curse upon all such offences and miscarriages as had been ignorantly committed; yet withal, clearing the king, and laying all the blame and guilt upon his ministers and advisers. And this the priest did that he might thereby induce and persuade the king to an awe of the gods, and to live so as might be pleasing to them; and likewise by praise and commendation rather gently to win upon him than by harsh and rugged rebukes to drive him to the practice of virtuous actions. Afterwards, when the jcintf had viewed the entrails, and finished his sacrifices, the priest read out of the sacred records, the edicts, laws, and most useful and remarkable actions, of such as were most famous in their generation that the prince might seriously consider and ponder upon what was most commendable in those examples, and imitate them according to the rules there prescribed. For there were not only set times allotted for despatch of public business, and administration of justice, but likewise for taking the air, bathing, lying with the queen, and almost every action of their lives.

The custom was likewise for the kings to feed upon plain and ordinary meat, as veal and goose, and to drink wine according to a stinted measure, which might neither overcharge their stomachs, nor make them drunk. Such a moderate diet was prescribed, as that it seemed rather to be ordered by a skilful physician for health sake, than by a law-maker. It is indeed to be admired and very strange, that the king should not be left to his liberty for his daily food; but much more is it to be admired that he could not do any public business, condemn or punish any man to gratify his own humour or revenge, or for any other unjust cause; but was bound to do according as the laws had ordered in every particular case. The kings observing those rules according to the ancient custom, were so far from thinking it dishonourable, or being uneasy under it, that they looked upon themselves to live most desirable and happy lives; and judged that all other men who inconsiderately indulged their natural appetites, did many things that were attended with great losses, or apparent hazards at the least; yea, that some, though they know beforehand that what they were about (to do was ill and unjustifiable, yet, overcome either with love or hatred, or some other unruly passion, committed the wicked act notwithstanding; and therefore they were resolved to follow the rules of living, before approved of by wise and prudent men, and not to fall into the least irregularity. The kings, therefore, carrying this even hand towards all their subjects, were more beloved by them than by their own, kindred and relations: for not only all the orders of the priests, but the whole nation together, were more concerned for the health and prosperity of their kings, than they were for their wives and children, or their private interests in their goods and estates; and therefore, as long as these wholesome laws were observed amongst them, they preserved their government without stain or blemish for many ages under the king's before mentioned, living in the height of all worldly happiness: and besides all this, were conquerors of many nations, and grew exceeding rich, and their provinces were beautified with many stately magnificent works, and their cities adorned with many rich gifts of all sorts.

What the Egyptians performed after the deaths of every of their kings, clearly evidences the great love they bore to them. For honour done him that cannot possibly know it, (in a grateful return of a former benefit), carries along with it a testimony of sincerity without the least colour of dissimulation. For upon the death of every king, the Egyptians generally lament with an universal mourning, rend their garments, shut up their temples, inhibit sacrifices, and all feasts and solemnities for the space of seventy-two days; they cast dust likewise upon their heads, and gird themselves under their breasts with a linen girdle; and thus men and women, two hundred or three hundred sometimes in a company, twice a-day go about singing mournful songs in praise of the deceased king, recalling his virtues, (as it were), from the very grave. During that time, they neither eat flesh, nor any thing baked or heated by the fire, and abstain from wine and all sumptuous fare: neither dare any use baths or ointments, beds trimmed up, or indulge themselves with women. But every one, (as if they had lost their dearest beloved child), is in mourning and sadness, and spends all these days in lamentation. In the mean time all things are prepared in a stately manner for the funeral, and the last day the coffin, with the body enclosed, is set at the entrance into the sepulchre: and there, according to the law, in honour of the deceased, all the actions of his life are rehearsed, where every one that will, has free liberty to accuse him. But all the priests set forth his praise, mentioning all the noble actions of his life; and many thousands of people met together at the bringing forth of the body, (if the king have ruled well), second the priests with a tumultuous cry and noise of approbation: but if he have governed otherwise, they are hush and still: and therefore many of the kings, (through the dislike of the people), have not been honoured with any funeral pomp or solemn burial; upon which account the succeeding kings, (not only for the reasons before mentioned, but because they fear the abuse of their bodies after death, and everlasting disgrace and dishonour), have studied how to acquit themselves by just and virtuous actions. These are the most remarkable manners and customs of the ancient kings of Egypt.

The whole land of Egypt is divided into several parts, which the Greeks call Nomoi, over every one of which is appointed a lord lieutenant, or provincial governor, who is intrusted with the ad-ministration pf public affairs in the province. The whole country likewise is divided into three parts, whereof the first is allotted to the priests, who are highly reverenced, and are in great authority among the people, both for their piety towards the gods, and their great wisdom and learning wherein they instruct the people. And out of their revenues, they provide sacrifices throughout all Egypt, and maintain their families and servants, and procure all other things necessary for themselves; for they judge it not lawful by any means, that the worship of the gods should be altered, (but always performed by them after the same manner), nor that those who are the public ministers of state should want any thing that is necessary. For these are always at the king's elbow, as the chief of his privy counsel, who assist, advise, and instruct him upon all occasions. By the help of astrology, and viewing the entrails of the sacrifices, they divine and foretell future events, and out of the records in the sacred registers from things done in former times, they read profitable lectures for present use and practice. For it is not, (as among the Grecians), that one man or one woman only executes the priest's office, but in Egypt, many are employed in the sacrifices and worship of the gods, who teach the same way and manner of service to their children and posterity. They are free from all public taxes and impositions, and are in the second place to the king in honour and authority. The second portion belongs to the king, as his revenue to support his royal state and dignity, and maintain the charge of his wars, and to enable him to reward those that have been eminent for their virtue and public service, with gifts according to their deserts; and inasmuch as this portion brings in a plentiful provision for all these purposes, the people are not oppressed with taxes and heavy impositions. The last portion belongs to the soldiers, who at a word are ready at the king's commands for every expedition; that they who venture their lives in the wars, being endeared to their country by that plentiful share and proportion allotted them, may more cheerfully undergo the hazards of war. For it would be an irrational thing to intrust the safety and preservation of the whole, with them who have nothing in their country that is dear or valuable to them to fight for. And the chief reason why so large a share is allotted to them, is, that they might more readily marry, and by that means make the nation more populous; and so there might be no need of foreign aids and assistances. Besides, that children descended from soldiers, would be apt to imitate the valour of their ancestors, and, minding arms from their very childhood, would at length, (through their natural courage and skill in their arms), become unconquerable.

The nation likewise is distinguished into three other classes and orders of men, shepherds, husbandmen, and artificers. The husbandmen take the land, (fit for tillage and bearing of other fruits) of the king, the priests, and the swordmen, upon an easy rent, and take up all their time in this business; and because they are bred up from their very infancy in country affairs, they are the most skilful husbandmen of any other nation in the world. For they know exactly the nature of the land, the inundation of the waters, seed-time and harvest, and the gathering in of the other fruits of the earth, partly from the knowledge gained from their ancestors, and partly from their own particular experience.

The way and manner of the shepherds is the same, who being used to look after the floeks and herds from father to son, make it their whole employment to feed and pasture them. They have indeed learnt many things from their ancestors concerning the best way of governing and feeding their flocks, but not a few, by their own study and invention. And that which is chiefly to be admitted, is, that their industry is such in these matters, that they that keep poultry and geese, not content with the ordinary way of breeding these creatures (as amongst other people), but by their wit and ingenuity, cause them to increase to an infinite number, for they do not suffer them to hatch, but, to admiration, force out the young with their hands with so much art and skill, that it is done as effectually as by nature itself.

Arts and trades likewise, among the Egyptians, are greatly improved and brought to their highest perfection. For it is a rule only among the Egyptians, that no mechanic or other artificer is to be of any other trade or employment, or to be reckoned among any other order ot class of the commonwealth, than such as by the law is allowed, and taught them by their parents; to the end that neither envy attending magistracy, nor public business of the state, nor any thing else might interrupt them in the diligent improvement of their trades. In other places, we see artificers and tradesmen busied about many other things, and, (to gratify their covetousness), not to stick to any one employment. For some apply themselves to husbandry, others to merchandise, and some follow two or three trades at once. And many who ran to the public assemblies in cities, under a democratical government, by bribes and rewards enrich themselves, to the damage and prejudice of the commonwealth. But in Egypt, if any tradesman meddle in civil affairs, or exercise any more than one trade at once, he is grievously punished. And in this manner the ancient Egyptians divided their commonwealth, and every order took care to preserve themselves entire, as that which they had learnt, and had been handed down to them from their ancestors. They were likewise extraordinarily careful concerning their courts of justice, for they looked upon just sentences and decrees, pronounced from the seats of justice on both sides, to be of great weight and moment to the advancement of the public good. For they knew very well, that men's miscarriages would be best reformed, if offenders were duly punished, and the injured and oppressed relieved: and, on the contrary, they foresaw, that if the punishment due by the law to malefactors could be bought off for money, favour, or affection, then nothing but disorder and confusion would enter into all orders and societies of men among them: and therefore, to prevent this, (with good effect), they chose men of the greatest reputation out of the chiefest cities to be their judges: as out of Heliopolis, Thebes, and Memphis; which assembly of the judges was nothing inferior to the Areopagitae in Athens, or the senate at Sparta. Out of these, (being thirty in number), they chose one, the most eminent among them, to be president, and in his room the city sent another. The judges received their salaries from the king, but the president had the greatest allowance; about his neck be wore a golden chain, at which hung a picture representing truth, set with precious stones. When the president put on his chain, it was a sign that he was about to hear causes. And when the eight books wherein the laws were written were laid before the judges, it was the custom that the plaintiff should exhibit his complaint in writing, distinctly and particularly, setting forth wherein he was injured, and how, and the value of his damage sustained. On the other side the defendant or the party accused, after a copy had of his adversary's libel, answered in writing to every particular, either by denying or justifying, or pleading something in mitigation of damages. Then the plaintiff replied in writing, and the defendant rejoined. After the litigants had thus twice exhibited their libels, it was then the part of the thirty judges to consider amongst themselves of the judgment to be pronounced, and incumbent upon the president to turn the effigy of truth towards one of the litigants. And this was the usual manner of proceeding in the courts of justice among the Egyptians. For it was judged, that by the harangues of lawyers, a cloud was cast upon the truth and justice of the cause; inasmuch as the arts of rhetoricians, the juggling tricks of dissemblers, and the fears of them that are like to be overthrown in their cause, have wrought upon many to wave the strictness of the law, and to turn aside from the rule of justice and truth: and indeed it is often found by experience, that offenders, brought to the bar of justice, by the help of a cunning orator, or their own rhetorical flourishes, (either through a fallacy put upon the court, or taking insinuations, or melting compassions wrought by the speaker on the judge), have escaped: therefore the Egyptians concluded, that if all the accusation was put into writing, and consideration had barely of what was there set down, the sentence would be more exact and just. And so by that means crafty and ingenious fellows would be no more favoured than those that were more dull, nor the experienced artist more than those that were ignorant and unskilful, nor the audacious liar more than those that are modest and sincere; but all would have equal justice, in regard sufficient time was allowed by the law, both for the parties to answer each other, and for the judges to consider and give judgment upon the allegations of both sides.

And since now we are come to mention the laws, we conceive it will not be foreign from our history to give an account of such laws of the Egyptians as are either remarkable for their antiquity, or strange and different from all others, or that may be any way useful and profitable to the studious readers.

1. And, in the first place, those were to die who were guilty of perjury, being such as committed the two greatest crimes; that is, impiety towards the gods, and violation of faith and truth, the strongest bond of human society.
2. If any upon the road saw a man likely to be killed, or to be violently assaulted, and did not rescue him, if he were able, he was to die for it. And if in truth he were not able to defend him, yet he was bound to discover the thieves, and to prosecute them in a due course of law. If he neglected this, he was, according to the law, to be scourged with a certain number of stripes, and to be kept without food for three days together.
3. False accusers were to suffer the same punishment as those whom they falsely accused were to have undergone, if they had afterwards been convicted of the offence.

4. All the Egyptians were enjoined to give in their names in writing, to the governors of the provinces, shewing how and by what means they got their livelihood. He that gave a false account in such case, or if it appeared he lived by robbery, or any other unjust course, he was to die; which law it is said Solon brought over out of Egypt into Athens.

5. He that wilfully killed a free man; nay, a very bond slave, was by the law to die; thereby designing to restrain men from wicked actions, as having no respect to the state and condition of the person suffering, but to the advised act of the offender; and by this care of slaves, men learned that freemen were much less to be destroyed.

6. Parents that killed their children, were not to die, but were forced for three days and nights together to hug them continually in their arms, and had a guard all the while over them, to see they did it; for they thought it not fit that they should die, who gave life to their children; but rather that men should be deterred from such attempts by a punishment that seemed attended with sorrow and repentance.

7. But for parricides, they provided a most severe kind of punishment: for those that were convicted of this offence, were laid upon thorns, and burnt alive, after they had first mangled the members of their bodies with sharp canes, piecemeal, about the bigness of a man's thumb. For they counted it the most wicked act that man could be guilty of, to take away the lives of them from whom they had their own.

8. Those that were with child were not to be executed till they were delivered, which law was received by many of the Grecians, judging it very unjust for the innocent to suffer with the offender, and two to die for the offence of one only. Besides, inasmuch as the crime was maliciously and advisedly committed, it was unreasonable that the child that understood not what was done, should undergo the same punishment. And that which is of the greatest consideration, is, that it was altogether unjust, (being the mother was only accused and condemned as guilty), the child, (common both to father and mother), should lose its life; for that judge is as unjust that destroys the innocent, as he that spares him that is guilty of murder.

9. These are the capital laws which are chiefly worthy of praise and commendation; as to others, those concerning military affairs, provided that soldiers who ran away from their colours, or mutinied, though they should not die, yet should be otherwise punished with the utmost disgrace imaginable; but if they afterwards wipe off their disgrace by their valour, they are restored to their former post and trust. By thus inflicting of a punishment more grievous than death, the lawgiver designed that all should look upon disgrace and infamy as the greatest of evils; besides it was judged, that those who were put to death, could never be further serviceable to the commonwealth, but such as were degraded only, (through a desire to repair their reputation), might be very useful, and do much service in time to come.

10. Such as revealed the secrets of the army to the enemy, were to have their tongues cut out.

11. They that coined false and adulterated money, or contrived false weights, or counterfeited seals; and scriveners or clerks that forged deeds, or razed public records, or produced any forged contracts, were to have both their hands cut off, that every one might suffer in that part wherewith he had offended in such a manner as not to be repaired, during their life; and that others, warned by so severe a punishment, might be deterred from the commission of the like offence.

12. In relation to women, the laws were very severe: for he that committed a rape upon a free woman was to have his privy members cut off; for they judged that three most heinous offences were included in that one vile act, that is, wrong, defilement, and bastardy.

13. In case of adultery, the man was to have a thousand lashes with rods, and the woman her nose cut off. For it was looked upon very fit, that the adulteress that tricked up herself to allure men to wantonness, should be punished in that part where her charms chiefly lay.

14. They say that Bocchoris made the laws concerning merchandise. As to these, it was a law, that if a man borrowed money, and the lender had no writing to shew for it, and the other denied it upon, his oath, he should be quit of the debt; to that end, therefore, in the first place, they were to sacrifice to the gods, as men making conscience, and tender and scrupulous in taking of an oath. For it being clear and evident, that he that swears often again and again, at last loses his credit; every man to prevent that mischief, will be very cautious of being brought to an oath. Moreover, the lawgiver had this design, that by grounding a man's credit and reputation wholly upon the integrity of his life and conversation, every one would be induced to honest and virtuous actions, lest he should be despised as a man of no credit or worth. Besides, it was judged a most unjust thing, not to believe him upon his oath, in that matter relating to his contract, to whom credit was given in the self-same thing, without an oath before.

15. For those that lent money by contract in writing, it was not lawful to take usury above what would double the stock; and that payment should be made only out of the debtor's goods; but his body was not to be liable in any wise to imprisonment: and those were counted the debtor's goods, which he had either earned by his labour, or had been bestowed upon him by the just proprietors. But as for their bodies, they belonged to the cities where they inhabited, who had an interest in them for the public service, both in times of peace and war; for that it was an absurd thing for him who was to venture his life for his country, to be carried to jail for a debt by his creditor, (if it should so happen), and that the public safety should be hazarded, to gratify the covetousness of some private men. This law seems to have been established in Athens, by Solon, which he called Sisachthy, freeing all the citizens from being imprisoned by their creditors for debt. And some do justly blame many of the law-makers of Greece, that they forbade arms, plows, and other things absolutely necessary for labour, to be taken in pawn, and yet permitted them that should use them to be imprisoned.

16. There is a very remarkable law among the Egyptians, concerning theft. Those that enter into the list of thieves, are to give in their names to one who is their chief and head, and whatever they steal, they engage to bring to him. They that have lost any things are to set down in writing every particular, and bring it to him, and set forth the day, hour, and place, when and where they lost their goods. Every thing being thus readily found out, after the things stolen are valued, the true owner is to pay a fourth part of the value, and so receive his goods again. For being it was not possible to restrain all from thieving, the law-maker found out a way that all might be restored, except a small proportion for redemption.

The Egyptian priests only marry one wife, but all others may have as many wives as they please; and all are bound to bring up as many children as they can, for the further increase of the inhabitants, which tends much to the well-being either of a city or country. None of the sons are ever reputed bastards, though they be begotten of a bond-maid, for they conceive that the father only begets the child, and that the mother contributes nothing but place and nourishment. And they call trees that bear fruit males, and those that bear none, females; contrary to what the Grecians name them. They bring up their children with very little cost, and are sparing upon that account, to admiration: for they provide for them broth, made of any mean and poor stuff that may easily be had; and feed those that are of strength able to eat it, with the pith of bulrushes, roasted in the embers, and with roots and herbs got in the fens; sometimes raw, and sometimes boiled; and at other times fried and boiled. Most of their children go barefooted and naked, the climate is so warm and temperate. It costs not the parent to bring up a child to man's estate, above twenty drachmas; which is the chief reason why Egypt is so populous, and excels all other places in magnificent structures. The priests instruct the youth in two sorts of learning; that which they call sacred, and the other, which is more common and ordinary. In arithmetic and geometry, they keep them a long time: for in regard the river every year changes the face of the soil, the neighbouring inhabitants are at great difference among themselves concerning the boundaries of their land, which cannot be easily known but by the help of geometry. And as for arithmetic, as it is useful upon other occasions, so it is very helpful to the study of geometry, and no small advantage to the students of astrology; for the Egyptians, (as well as some others),are diligent observers of the course and motions of the stars; and preserve remarks of every one of them for an incredible number of years, being used to this study, and to endeavour to outvie one another therein, from the most ancient times. They have with great cost and care, observed the motions of the planets; their periodical motions, and their stated stops; and the influences of everyone of them, in the nativity of living creatures, and what good or ill they foreshew; and very often they so clearly discover what is to come in the course of men's lives, as if they pointed at the thing, with the point of a needle. They frequently presage both famine and plenty, grievous diseases likely to seize both upon man and beast; earthquakes, inundations, and comets; and through long experience, they I come to the foreknowledge of such things as are commonly judged impossible for the wit of man to attain to. They affirm, that the Chaldeans in Babylon are Egyptian colonies, and that their astrologers have attained to that degree of reputation, by the knowledge they have learned of the Egyptian priests.

The rest of the common people of Egypt, (as we have before declared), are trained up from their very childhood either by their parents or kindred, in all manner of arts and trades whereby to get their livelihood.

They teach but a very few to write and read; but tradesmen especially learn both. It is not the custom there to learn the art of wrestling or music; for they think that by the exercise of daily wrestling, tbe youth improve in their strength but for a little time, and that with a great deal of hazard, but gain no advantage at all as to the health of their bodies. And as for music, they look upon it not only unprofitable, but that it also makes men soft and effeminate.

To prevent diseases, they make use of elysters and purging potions, abstinence, and vomits; and this they repeat sometimes for several days together, and other times, every third or fourth day. For in all manner of food, (they say), the greatest part of it is superfluous, which breeds diseases, and therefore the aforesaid method, whereby the root of the disease is plucked up, (they say), is a mighty help both to the preservation and recovery of health. For the physicians have a public stipend, and make use of receipts prescribed by the law, made up by the ancient physicians; and if they cannot cure the patient by them, they are never blamed; but if they use other medicines, they are to suffer death, in as much a the law-maker appointed such receipts for care, as were approved by the most learned doctors, such as by long experience had been found effectual.

The adoration and worshipping of beasts among the Egyptians seems justly to many a most strange and unaccountable thing, and worthy of inquiry; for they worship some creatures even above measure, when they are dead, as well as when they are living; as cat, ichneumons, dogs, kites, the bird ibis, wolves, and crocodiles, and many other such like. The cause of which 1 shall endeavour to give, having first premised something briefly concerning them. And first of all, they dedicate a piece of land to every kind of creature they adore, assigning the profits for feeding and taking care of them. To some of these deities, the Egyptians give thanks for recovering their children from sickness, as by shaving their heads, and weighing the hair, with the like weight of gold or silver; and then giving that money to them that have the care of the beasts. To the kites, while they are flying, they cry out with a loud voice, and throw pieces of flesh for them upon the ground, till such time as they take it. To the cats and ichneumons, they give bread soaked in milk, stroaking and making much of them; or feed them with pieces of fish, taken in the river Nile. In the same manner they provide for the other beasts food according to their several kinds. They are so far from not paying this homage to their creatures, or being ashamed of them, that on the contrary, they glory in them, as in the highest adoration of the gods, and carry about special marks and ensigns of honour for them through city and country; upon which account, those that have the care of the beasts, (being seen afar off), are honoured and worshipped by all by falling down upon their knees. When any one of them die, they wrap it in fine linen, and with howling, beat upon their breasts, and so carry it forth to be salted; and then, after having anointed it with the oil of cedar and other things, which both give the body a fragrant smell, and preserve it a long time from putrefaction, they bury it in a secret place. He that wilfully kills any of these beasts, is to suffer death; but if any kill a cat, or the bird ibis, whether wilfully, or otherwise, he is certainly dragged away to death by the multitude, and sometimes most cruelly, without any formal trial or judgment of law. For fear of this, if any by chance find any of these creatures dead, they stand aloof, and with lamentable cries and protestations, tell every body that they found it dead. And such is the religious veneration impressed upon the hearts of men towards these creatures, and so obstinately is every one bent to adore and worship them, that even at the time when the Romans were about making a league with Ptolemy, and all the people made it their great business to caress and shew all civility and kindness imaginable to them that came out of Italy, and through fear strove all they could that no occasion might in the least be given to disoblige them, or be the cause of a war; yet it so happened, that upon a cat being killed by a Roman, the people in a tumult ran to his lodging, and neither the princes sent by the king to dissuade them, nor the fear of the Romans, could deliver the person from the rage of the people, though he did it against his will; and this I relate not by hearsay, but was myself an eye-witness of it, at the time of my travels into Egypt. If these things seem incredible and like to fables, those that we shall hereafter relate, will look more strange. For it is reported, that at a time when there was a famine in Egypt, many were driven to that strait, that by turns they fed one upon another; but not a man was accused to have in the least tasted of any of these sacred creatures. Nay, if a dog be found dead in a house, the whole family shave their bodies all over, and make great lamentation; and that which is most wonderful is, that if any wine, bread, or any other victuals be in the house, where any of these creatures die, it is a part of their superstition, not to make use of any of them for any purpose whatsoever. And when they have been abroad in the wars in foreign countries, they have with great lamentation brought with them dead cats, and kites into Egypt; when in the mean time, they have been ready to starve for want of provision. Moreover, what acts of religious worship they performed towards Apis in Memphis, Mnevis in Heliopolis, the goat in Mendes, the crocodile in the lake of Meris, and the lion kept in Leontopolis; and many other such like, is easy to describe, but very difficult to believe, except a man saw it. For these creatures are kept and fed in consecrated ground enclosed, and many great men provide food for them at great cost and charge; for they constantly give them fine wheat flour, frumenty, sweet-meats of all sorts, made up with honey, and geese, sometimes roasted, and sometimes boiled; and for such as fed upon raw flesh, they provide birds. To say no more, they are excessive in their costs and charges in feeding of these creatures; and forbear not to wash them in hot baths, to anoint them with the most precious unguents, and perfume them with the sweetest odours. They provide likewise for them most rich beds to lie upon, with decent furniture; and are extraordinarily careful about their generating, and coition one with another, according to the laws of nature. They breed up for every one of the males, (according to their kinds), the most beautiful she mate, and call them their concubines or sweet-hearts, and are at great costs and charges in looking to them.

When any of them die, they are as much concerned as at the death of their own children, and lay out in burying them as much as all their goods are worth, and far more. For when Apis, through old age, died at Memphis, after the death of Alexander, and in the reign of Ptolemy Legus, his keeper not only spent all that vast provision he had made, in burying of him, but borrowed of Ptolemy fifty talents of silver, for the same purpose. And in our time, some of the keepers of these creatures have lavished away no less than a hundred talents in the maintaining of them. To this may be further added, what is in use among them concerning the sacred ox, which they call Apis. After the splendid funeral of Apis is over, those priests that have the charge of the business, seek out another calf, as like the former as possibly they can find; and when they have found one, an end is put to all further mourning and lamentation; and such priests as are appointed for that purpose, lead the young, ox through the city of Nile, and feed him forty days. Then they put him into a barge, wherein is a golden cabin, and so transport him as a god to Memphis and place him in Vulcan's grove. During the forty days before mentioned, none but women are admitted to see him, who being placed full in his view, pluck up their coats, and shew their privy parts. Afterwards, they are forbid to come into the sight of this new god. For the adoration of this ox, they give this reason. They say, that the soul of Osiris passed into an ox; and therefore, whenever the ox is dedicated, to this very day, the spirit of Osiris is infused into one ox after another, to posterity. But some say, that the members of Osiris, (who was killed by Typhon), were thrown by Isis into an ox made of wood, covered with ox-hides, and from thence the city Busiris was so called. Many other things they fabulously report of Apis, which would be too tedious particularly to relate.

But in as much as all that relate to this adoration of beasts are wonderful, and indeed incredible, it is very difficult to find out the true causes and grounds of this superstition. We have before related, that the priests have a private and secret account of these things, in the history of the gods; but the common people give these three reasons for what they do. The first of which is altogether fabulous, and agrees with the old dotage: for they say, that the first gods were so very few, and men so many above them in number, and so wicked and impious, that they were too weak for them, and therefore transformed themselves into beasts, and by that means avoided their assaults and cruelty. But afterwards, they say, that the kings, and princes of the earth, (in gratitude to them that were the first authors of their well-being, directed how carefully those creatures, whose shapes they had assumed), should be fed while they were alive, and how they were to be buried when they were dead. Another reason they give is this: the ancient Egyptians, they say, being often defeated by the neighbouring nations, by reason of the disorder and confusion that was among them in drawing up of their battalions, found out at last the way of carrying standards or ensigns before their several regiments; and therefore, they painted the images of these beasts, which now they adore, and fixed them at the head of a spear, which the officers carried before them, and by this means, every man perfectly knew the regiment he belonged to; and being that by the observation of this good order aud discipline, they were often victorious, they ascribed their deliverance to these creatures; and to make to them a grateful return, it was ordained for a law, that none of these creatures, whose representations were formerly thus carried, should be killed, but religiously and carefully adored, as is before related. The third reason alledged by them, is the profit and advantage these creatures bring to the common support and maintenance of human life. For the cow is both serviceable to the plow, and for breeding others for the same use. The sheep yeans twice a-year, and yields wool for clothing and ornament, and of her milk and cream are made large and pleasant cheeses. The dog is useful both for the guard of the house, and the pleasure of hunting in the field, and therefore their god whom they call Anubis, they represent with a dog's head, signifying thereby, that a dog was the guard both to Osiris and Isis. Others say, that when they sought for Osiris, dogs guided Isis, and by their barking and yelling, (as kind and faithful associates with the inquisitors), drove away the wild beasts, and diverted others that were in their way; and therefore in celebrating the feast of Isis, dogs lead the way in the procession. Those that first instituted this custom, signifying thereby the ancient kindness and good service of this creature. Tlie cat likewise is very serviceable against the venemous stings of serpents, and the deadly bite of the asp. The ichneumon secretly watches where the crocodile lays her eggs, and breaks them in pieces, and that he does with a great deal of eagerness, by natural instinct, without any necessity for his own support; and if this creature were not thus serviceable, crocodiles would abound to that degree, that there would be no sailing in the Nile: yea, the crocodiles themselves are destroyed by this creature in a wonderful and incredible manner. For the ichneumon rolls himself in the mud, and then observing the crocodile sleeping upon the bank of the river with his mouth wide open, suddenly whips down through his throat into his very bowels, and presently gnaws his way through his belly, and so escapes himself, with the death of his enemy. Among the birds, the ibis is serviceable for the destroying of snakes, locusts, and the palmer worm. The kite is an enemy to the scorpions, horned serpents, and other little creatures, that both bite and sting men to death. Others say, that this bird is deified, because the augurs make use of the swift flight of these birds in their divinations. Others say, that in ancient time, a book bound about with a scarlet thread (wherein were written all the rites and customs of worshipping of the gods), was carried by a kite, and brought to the priests at Thebes: for which reason the sacred scribes wore a red cap, with a kite's feather in it.

The Thebans worship the eagle, because she seems to be a royal bird, and to deserve the adoration due to Jupiter himself. They say, the goat was accounted amongst the number of the gods, for the sake of his genitals, as Priapus is honoured among the Grecians: for this creature is exceeding lustful, and therefore they say that member, (the instrument of generation), is to be highly honoured, as that from which all living creatures derive their original. They say that these privy parts are not only accounted sacred among the Egyptians, but among many others are religiously adored in the time of their solemn rites of religious worship, as those parts that are the causes of generation. And the priests, who succeed in the office, descended to them from their fathers in Egypt, are first initiated into the service of this God. For this reason the Pans and Satyrs are greatly adored among them, and therefore they have images of them set up in their temples, with their privy parts erected like to the goat, which they say, is the most lustful creature in the world. By this representation they would signify their gratitude to the gods, for the populousness of their country.

The sacred bulls Apis and Mnevis, (they say), they honour as gods by the command of Osiris, both for their usefulness in husbandry, and likewise to keep up an honourable and lasting memory, of those that first found out bread-corn and other fruits of the earth.

But however, it is lawful to sacrifice red oxen, because Typhon seemed to be of that colour, who treacherously murdered Osiris, and was himself put to death by Isis, for the murder of her husband. They report likewise, that anciently men that had red hair, like Typhon, were sacrificed by the kings at the sepulchre of Osiris. And indeed, there are very few Egyptians that are red, but many that are strangers: and hence arose the fable of Busiris's cruelty towards strangers amongst the Greeks, not that there ever was any king called Busiris; but Osiris's sepulchre was so called in the Egyptian language. They say, they pay divine honour to wolves, because they come so near in their nature to dogs, for they are very little different, and mutually engender and bring forth whelps.

They give likewise another reason for their adoration, but most fabulous of all other; for they say, that when Isis and her son Orus' were ready to join battle with Typhon, Osiris came up from the shades below in the form of a wolf, and assisted them; and therefore when Typhon was killed, the conquerors commanded that beast to be worshipped, because the day was won presently upon his appearing.

Some affirm, that at the time of the irruption of the Ethiopians into Egypt, a great number of wolves flocked together, and drove the invading enemy beyond the city Elephantine, and therefore that province is called Lycopolitana; and for these reasons came these beasts before mentioned, to be thus adored and worshipped.

Book I, Chapter 7

Now it remains, that we speak of the deifying the crocodile, of which many have inquired what might be the reason; being that these beasts devour men, and yet are adored as gods, who in the mean time are pernicious instruments of many cruel accidents. To this they answer, that their country is not only defended by the river, but much more by the crocodiles; and therefore the thieves out of Arabia and Africa, being afraid of the great number of these creatures, dare not pass over the river Nile, which protection they should be deprived of, if these beasts should be fallen upon and utterly destroyed by the hunters.

But there is another account given of these things: for one of the ancient kings, called Menas, being set upon and pursued by his own dogs, was forced into the lake of Meris, where a crocodile, (a wonder to be told), took him up and carried him over to the other side, where, in gratitude to the beast, he built a city, and called it Crocodile; and commanded crocodiles to be adored as gods, and dedicated the lake to them for a place to feed and breed in. Where he built a sepulchre for himself with a four-square pyramid, and a labyrinth greatly admired by every body. In the same manner they relate stories of other things, which would be too tedious here to recite. For some conceive it to be very clear and evident, (by several of them not eating many of the fruits of the earth), that gain and profit by sparing has infected them with this superstition: for some never taste lentils, nor other beans; and some never eat either cheese, or onions, or such like food, although Egypt abounds with these things. Thereby signifying, that all should learn to be temperate; and whatsoever any feed upon, they should not give themselves to gluttony. But others give another reason; for they say that in the time of the ancient kings, the people being prone to sedition, and plotting to rebel, one of their wise and prudent princes divided Egypt into several parts, and appointed the worship of some beast or other in every part, or forbade some sort of food, that by that means every one adoring their own creature, and slighting that which was worshipped in another province, the Egyptians might never agree amongst themselves. And this is evident from the effects; for when one country despises and contemns the religious rites and customs of their neighbours, this always begets heart burnings among them. But some give this reason for deifying of these creatures: they say, that in the beginning, men that were of a fierce and beastly nature, herded together and devoured one another; and being in perpetual war and discord, the stronger always destroyed the weaker. In process of time, those that were too weak for the other, (taught at length by experience), got in bodies together, and had the representations of those beasts, (which were afterwards worshipped), in their standards, to which they ran together when they were in a fright, upon every occasion, and so made up a considerable force against them that attempted to assault them. This was imitated by the rest, and so the whole multitude got into a body; and hence it was that that creature, which every one supposed was the cause of his safety, was honoured as a god, as justly deserving that adoration. And therefore, at this day, the people of Egypt differ in their religion, every one worshipping that beast that their ancestors did in the beginning. To conclude, they say, that the Egyptians, of all other people, are the most grateful for favours done them, judging gratitude to be the safest guard of their lives, inasmuch as it is evident, that all are most ready to do good to them, with whom are laid up the treasures of a grateful mind to make a suitable return. And for these reasons, the Egyptians seem to honour and adore their kings, no less than as if they were very gods. For they hold that without a divine providence, they never could be advanced to the throne; and being they can confer the greatest rewards at their will and pleasure, they judge them partakers of the divine nature. Now, though we have said perhaps more than is needful of their sacred creatures, yet with this, we have set forth the laws of the Egyptians, which are very remarkable. But, when a man comes to understand their rites and ceremonies in burying their dead, he will be struck with much greater admiration.

For after the death of any of them, all the friends and kindred of the deceased throw dirt upon their heads, and run about through the city, mourning, and lamenting, till such time as the body be interred, and abstain from baths, wine, and all pleasant meats in the mean time, and forbear to clothe themselves with any rich attire. They have three sorts of funerals: the stately and magnificent, the moderate, and the meanest. In the first, they spend a talent of silver; in the second, twenty punas; in the last, they at very small charges. They that have the charge of wrapping up, and burying the body, are such as have been taught the art by their ancestors. These give in a writing to the family of every thing that is to be laid out in the funeral, and inquire of them after what manner they would have the body interred. When every thing is agreed qpon, they take up the body, and deliver it to them whose office it is to take care of it. Then the chief among them, (who is called the scribe), having the body laid upon the ground, marks out how much of the left side towards the bowels is to be incised and opened, upon which the Parasohistes, (so by them called), with an Ethiopian stone, dissects so much of the flesh, as by the law is justifiable, and having done it, he forthwith runs away, might and main, and all there present pursue him with execrations, and pelt him with stones, as if he were guilty of some horrid offence, for they look upon him as an hateful person, who wounds and offers violence to the body in that kind, or does it any prejudice whatsoever. But as for those whom they call the Taricheutae, they highly honour them, for they are the priest's companions, and, as sacred persons, are admitted into the temple. As soon as they come to the dissected body, one of tho Taricheutae thrusts up his hand through the wound, into the breast of the dead, and draws out all the intestines, but the reius and the heart. Another cleanses all the bowels, and washes them in Phoenician wine, mixed with diverse aromatic spices. Having at last washed the body, they first anoint it all over with the oil of cedar and other precious ointments for the space of forty days together; that done, they rub it well with myrrh, cinnamon, and such like things, not only apt and effectual for long preservation, but for sweet-scenting of the body also, and so deliver it to the kindred of the dead, with every member so whole and entire, that no part of the body seems to be altered, till it come to the very hairs of the eye-lids, and the eye-brows, insomuch as the beauty and shape of the face seems just as it was before. By which means, many of the Egyptians laying up the bodies of their ancestors in stately monuments, perfectly see the true visage and countenance of those that were buried, many ages before they themselves were born. So that in viewing the proportion of every one of their bodies, and the lineaments of their faces, they take exceeding great delight, even as much as they were still living among them. Moreover, the friends and nearest relations of the dead acquaint the judges and the rest of their friends with the time prefixed for the funeral of such a one by name, declaring, that such a day he is to pass the lake. At which time forty judges appear and sit together in a semicircle, in a place beyond the lake; where a ship, (before provided by such as have the care of the business), is haled up to the shore, governed by a pilot, whom the Egyptians call Charon. And therefore they say, that Orpheus seeing this ceremony when he was in Egypt, invented the fable of hell, partly imitating them in Egypt, and partly adding something of his own; of which we shall speak particularly hereafter. The ship being now in the lake, every one is at liberty by the law, to accuse the dead before the coffin be put aboard; and if any accuser appears, and makes good his accusation, that he lived an ill life, then the judges give sentence, and the body is debarred from being buried after the usual manner; but if the informer be convicted of a scandalous and malicious accusation, he is very severely punished. If no informer appear, or that the information prove false, all the kindred of the deceased leave off mourning, and begin to set forth his praises; but say nothing of his birth, (as is the custom among the Greeks), because they account all in Egypt to be equally noble. But they recount how the deceased was educated from a child, his breeding till he came to man's estate, his piety towards the gods, and his justice towards men, his chastity and other virtues, wherein he excelled; and they pray and call upon the infernal deities to receive the deceased into the society of the just. The common people take it from the other, and approve of all that is said in his praise with a loud shout, and set forth likewise his virtues with the highest praises and strains of commendation, as he that is to live for ever with the just in the kingdom of Jove. Then they (that have tombs of their own) inter the corpse in places appointed for that purpose; they that have none of their own, build a small apartment in their own houses, and rear up the coffin to the sides of the strongest wall of the building. Such as are denied common burial; either because they are in debt, or convicted of some horrid crime, they bury in their own houses; and in after times it often happens, that some of their kindred growing rich, pay off the debts of the deceased, or get him absolved, and then bury their ancestor with state and splendour. For amongst the Egyptians, it is a sacred constitution, that they should at their greatest costs honour their parents and ancestors, who are translated to an eternal habitation. It is a custom likewise among them, to give the bodies of their parents in pawn to their creditors, and they that do not presently redeem them, fall under the greatest disgrace imaginable, and are denied burial after their deaths. One may justly wonder at the authors of this excellent constitution, who both by what we see practised among the living, and by the decent burial of the dead, did, (as much as possibly lay within the power of men), endeavour to promote honesty and faithful dealing one with another. For the Greeks, (as to what concerned the rewards of the just, and the punishment of the impious), had nothing amongst them but invented fables, and poetical fictions, which never wrought upon men for the amendment of their lives; but on the contrary, were despised and laughed at by the lewder sort. But among the Egyptians, the punishment of the bad, and the rewards of the good, being not told as idle tales, but every day seen with their own eyes, all sorts were warned of their duties, and by this means was wrought and continued a most exact reformation of manners and orderly conversation among them. For those certainly are the best laws that advance virtue and honesty, and instruct men in a prudent converse in the world, rather than those that tend only to the heaping up of wealth, and teach men to be rich.

And now it is necessary for us to speak of the legislators of Egypt, who established such laws as are both unusual elsewhere, and admirable in themselves. After the ancient way of living in Egypt, which was, (according to their own stories), in the reigns of the gods and demigods; they say that Mnevis, a man of an heroic spirit, and famous in his generation for a commendable life, was the first that instituted written laws, feigning that he received them from Mercury, and that from them would accrue great benefit and advantage to the public. The same device Minos used among the Grecians in Crete, and Lycurgus among the Lacedaemonians: the first pretending be had them from Jupiter, and the other from Apollo. This contrivance, it is said, has been made use of amongst divers other nations, who have reaped much advantage by observing such laws. For it is reported, that among the Aramaspi, Zathraustes pretended he received his laws from a good genius; and that Zamolxis, amongst the people called the Getes, patronised his by Vesta; and among the Jews, that Moses alleged the god called Jao, to be the author of his. And this they did either because they judged such an invention (which brought about so much good to mankind) was wonderfully commendable, and of a divine stamp; or that they concluded the people would be more observant, out of a reverend regard to the majesty and authority of those who were said to be the law-makers.

The second lawmaker of Egypt, they say, was Sasyches, a very wise and prudent prince, who added to the former, and made excellent laws also relating to the honour and worship of the gods. He is reported to have found out geometry, and to have taught the art of astronomy.

The third whom they cry up, is Sesostris; who not only excelled all the kings of Egypt in his warlike achievements, but framed laws military discipline among the Egyptians, and put every thing in due order relating to military affairs.

The fourth law-maker they say was king Bocchoris, a wise prudent man; he established every thing that concerned the kings and prescribed exact rules and laws for the making of contracts. He was so wise and of so piercing a judgment in his decisions, that many of his sentences, for their excellency, are kept in memory to this very day. He was, they say, of a very weak constitution of body and extraordinarily covetous.

After him, king Amasis employed himself in the framing of laws for the direction of the Nomarchi, in their several governments, which reduced all the provinces of Egypt into due order. It is said he was a most wise, just, and good man, for which he was advanced to the throne by the Egyptians, though be was not of the blood-royal. It is reported, that when the Eleans were about to celebrate the Olympic games, and sent their ambassadors to him to advise them how they might manage those sports most justly, he answered, "That the way to do that, was for none of the Eleans to be parties in the contest." Polycrates, the petty king of Samos, entered into a league of friendship with him: but when he heard how Polycrates oppressed his subjects, and injured strangers that came into his country, he sent ambassadors to him to advise to moderation; but not being able to persuade him, he at length sent a letter to him, to let him know he dissolved and renounced the league that was betwixt them; saying, "He was not willing forthwith to be involved in grief and sorrow, for that he perfectly foresaw the miserable fall that would presently overtake one who governed so tyrannically." He was greatly admired, they say, by the Grecians, both for his kind and gentle disposition, and for that which he said having shortly after befell Polycrates.

Darius, the father of Xerxes, is said to be the sixth who made laws for the government of the Egyptians. For, with hatred and abhorrence of the impiety of Cambyses his predecessor, for his profaning the temples in Egypt, he made it his business to approve his reverend regard towards the gods, and his kindness towards men; for he familiarly conversed with the Egyptian priests, and learned their theology, and acquainted himself with the things and transactions recorded in their sacred registers, whereby be came to understand the heroic spirit of the ancient kings, and their kindness towards their subjects, which caused him to imitate them in the like; and upon that account he was so highly honoured amongst them, that, while he was alive, he gained the title of a god, which none of the other kings ever did; and when he was dead, the people allowed him all those ancient honours due and accustomed to be done to the former kings of Egypt after their deaths.

And these are the men, (they say), who composed the laws of Egypt, that are so celebrated and cried up amongst other people. But in after times, (they say), many of their excellent laws were abrogated by the Macedonians, who came to be lords and kings of Egypt.

Having now given an account of these things, it remains we should declare how many wise and learned men among the Grecians journied into Egypt in ancient times, to understand the laws and sciences of the country. For the Egyptian priests, out of their sacred records relate, that Orpheus, Musaeus, Melampodes, Daedalus, Homer the poet, Lycurgus the Spartan, Solon the Athenian, Plato the philosopher, Pythagoras the Samian, Eudoxus the mathematician, Democritus the Abderite, and Oenopides the Chian, all came to them in Egypt, and they shew certain marks and signs of all these being there. Of some, by their pictures; and of others, by the names of places, or pieces of work that have been called after their names. And they bring arguments from every trade that is used, to prove that every thing wherein the Grecians excel, and for which they are admired, was brought over from Egypt into Greece. For they say, that Orpheus brought over most of the religious rites and ceremonies, both as to what concerns the celebration of the Orgia, and relating to his wandering up and down, and the whole entire fable of hell; for that the ceremonies and rites of Osiris agree in every thing with those of Bacchus, and that those of Isis and Ceres are one and the same, differing iu nothing but the name. And whereas he introduces the wicked tormented in hell, the Elysian fields for the pious and just, and the fictitious appearances of ghosts, (commonly noised abroad), they say he has done nothing but imitated the Egyptian funerals. And that the feigning of Mercury to be the conductor of souls, as derived from the old Egyptian custom, that he who brought back the dead body of Apis, (when he came to the place), delivered it to him who represented Cerberus, which being communicated by Orpheus to the Greeks, Homer, in imitation of him, inserted it in his poem,

Cyllenius leads to the infernal strand.

The hero's ghost, arm'd with his golden wand.

And then he adds.

They reach th' effluxes or the swelling seas,

Then Leuca's rock; thence on their course they keep

To the sun's portals, and the land of sleep;
When straight they come into a flow'ry mead,
Where, after death, departed souls reside.

The name, (they say), of Oceanus here mentioned, is attributed to the river Nile, for so the Egyptians in their own language call it; by the sun's portals is meant Heliopolis; the meadow feigned to be the habitation of the dead, (they say), is the place bordering upon the lake called Acherusia, near to Memphis, surrounded with pleasant ponds and meadows, with woods and groves of lotus and sweet canes; and that therefore he feigned those places to be inhabited by the dead, because that many of the Egyptian funerals, and such as were the most considerable were there; the dead bodies being carried over the river and the lake Acherusia, and there interred. And that other fictions among the Grecians concerning hell agree with those things that are done in Egypt even at this day. For the ship which transports the dead bodies is called Baris, and that for the fare an halfpenny is paid to the ferryman, who is called in their own country language, Charon. They say likewise, that near to these places is the temple of black Hecates, and the gates of Cocytus and Lethe, made up with brazen bars; and besides these, there is another gate of truth, next to which stands the headless image of justice. There are many others of these Grecian fictions remaining still in Egypt, which both in name and practice continue there to this day. For in the city of Acanthus, beyond the Nile, towards Libya, about an hundred and twenty furlongs from Memphis, stands an hogshead full of holes, into which, (they say), three hundred priests every day pour in water carried out of the river Nile. The fable likewise of the ass is acted at a solemn festival not far from thence, where a man is twisting a long rope, and many that follow him are as fast undoing what he had before wrought.

The Egyptians further say, that Melampodes brought into Greece the rites and solemnities of Bacchus, and the fabulous story of Saturn and the Titans, and the entire history of the sufferings of the gods out of Egypt. And they say that Dredalus imitated the labyrinth there, which remains to this very day, built at first by Mendes, or, (as some report), by king Marus, many years before the reign of Minos. They affirm likewise, that the ancient statues of Egypt are of the same size and proportion with those set up by Daedalus in Greece; and that the stately porch of Vulcan in Memphis, was the handy-work of Daedalus, and that he was in such high esteem among them, that they placed his statue of wood, (made by his own hands), in the temple; whom at length, for his ingenuity and excellent inventions, they honoured as a god; for in one of the islands belonging to Memphis, a temple dedicated to Daedalus is resorted to by the inhabitants at this day.

That Homer came into Egypt, amongst other arguments, they endeavour to prove it especially by the potion Helen gave Telemachus, (in the story of Menelaus), to cause him to forget all his sorrows past. For the poet seems to have made an exact experiment of the potion Nepenthes, which he says Helen received from Polymnestes, the wife of Thonus, and brought it from Thebes in Egypt; and indeed in that city, even at this day, the women use this medicine with good success: and they say, that in ancient times, the medicine for the cure of anger and sorrow, was only to be found among the Diospolitans; Thebes and Diospolis being by them affirmed to be one and the same city. And that Venus, from an ancient tradition, is called by the inhabitants, Golden Venus; and that there is a field so called, within the liberties of Memphis: and that Homer derived from Egypt his story of the embraces between Jupiter and Juno, and their travelling into Ethiopia; because the Egyptians every year carry Jupiter's tabernacle over the river into Africa, and a few days after bring it back again, as if the god had returned out of Ethiopia: and that the fiction of the nuptials of these two deities was taken from the solemnization of their festivals, at which time both their tabernacles, adorned with all sorts of flowers, are carried by the priests to the top of a mountain. To these they add, that Lycurgus, Solon, and Plato, borrowed from Egypt many of those laws which they established in their several commonwealths. And that Pythagoras learnt his mysterious and sacred expressions, the art of geometry, arithmetic, and transmigration of souls, in Egypt. They are of opinion likewise, that Democrates was five years in Egypt, and in that time much improved himself in the art of astrology. So they say, that Oenopides by his familiar converse with the priests and astrologers, amongst other advantages, gained especially the knowledge of the periodical motion of the sun; and came to know that his course is contrary to that of the stars: and that Eudoxus likewise, by studying astrology in Egypt, left many useful monuments of his art behind him in Greece, for which his name was famous. Lastly, they say, that the most famous statuaries of ancient time lived amongst them for some time, as Telecles and Theodoras, the sons of Rhecus, who made the statue of Apollo Pythius in Samos; for it is said, that one half of this statue was made by Telecles in Samos, and the other part was finished by Theodoras in Ephesus; and that there was such an exact symmetry of parts, that the whole seemed to be the work of one and the same hand: which art, (they say), the Grecians were not at all acquainted with, but that it was in frequent use among the Egyptians. For with them the exact cut of a statue is not judged of by the eye and fancy, (as it is by the Greeks), but after that they have cut out the stone, and wrought every part by itself, then they measure the exact proportion of the whole, from the least stone to the greatest. For they divide the whole body into twenty-one parts, and one-fourth, which makes up the symmetry and entire proportion. Upon which, after the workmen have agreed among themselves as to the bigness of the statue, they go away, and every one of them carve their several parts so exactly, according to their just proportions, that the singular skill of these workmen is wonderful and amazing. And thus the statue in Samos, which, (according to the art and skill in Egypt), was cut in two from the head to the privities, exactly in the middle, yet notwithstanding was equally proportioned in every part. And they say, that it exactly resembles the statues in Egypt, having its hands stretched out, and its thighs in a walking posture.

But we have now said enough of such things as are remarkable and worthy of memory in Egypt.

CREDITS

Image: Copyright © Kallerna (CC BY-SA 3.0) at http://commons.wikimedia.org/wiki/ File:Great_Sphinx_of_Giza_and_Pyramid_of_Cheops.jpg.

1. James H. Breasted, Ancient Records of Egypt, vol. I, pp. 86. University of Chicago Press, 1906. Copyright in the Public Domain.
2. Nigel Strudwick, Texts from the Pyramid Age, pp. 381. Copyright © 2005 by Society of Biblical Literature. Reprinted with permission.
3. James H. Breasted, Ancient Records of Egypt, vol. I, pp. 108-109. University of Chicago Press, 1906. Copyright in the Public Domain.
4. James H. Breasted, Ancient Records of Egypt, vol. I, pp. 115. University of Chicago Press, 1906. Copyright in the Public Domain.
5. Nigel Strudwick, Texts from the Pyramid Age, pp. 181. Copyright © 2005 by Society of Biblical Literature. Reprinted with permission.
6. Nigel Strudwick, Texts from the Pyramid Age, pp. 311-312. Copyright © 2005 by Society of Biblical Literature. Reprinted with permission.
7. The Pyramid Texts, trans. Samuel A. B. Mercer, pp. 92-95. Longmans, Green and Co., 1952. Copyright in the Public Domain.
8. James H. Breasted, Ancient Records of Egypt, vol. I, pp. 126-127. University of Chicago Press, 1906. Copyright in the Public Domain.
9. Nigel Strudwick, Texts from the Pyramid Age, pp. 219-220. Copyright © 2005 by Society of Biblical Literature. Reprinted with permission.
10. The Pyramid Texts, trans. Samuel A. B. Mercer, pp. 118-120, 123-124. Longmans, Green and Co., 1952. Copyright in the Public Domain.
11. Nigel Strudwick, Texts from the Pyramid Age, pp. 276-277. Copyright © 2005 by Society of Biblical Literature. Reprinted with permission.
12. Nigel Strudwick, Texts from the Pyramid Age, pp. 265-269. Copyright © 2005 by Society of Biblical Literature. Reprinted with permission.
13. The Pyramid Texts, trans. Samuel A. B. Mercer, pp. 144-145, 163-165, 192-195, 210-211, 257-259. Longmans, Green and Co., 1952. Copyright in the Public Domain.
14. Nigel Strudwick, Texts from the Pyramid Age, pp. 182-183. Copyright © 2005 by Society of Biblical Literature. Reprinted with permission.
15. "Inscription of Uni," Records of the Past, 2nd series, vol. II, ed. A. H. Sayce, trans. Gaston Maspero, pp.

4-10. Samuel Bagster and Sons, Ltd, 1888. Copyright in the Public Domain.
16. James H. Breasted, Ancient Records of Egypt, vol. I, pp. 151-154, 160-161. University of Chicago Press, 1906. Copyright in the Public Domain.
17. James H. Breasted, Ancient Records of Egypt, vol. I, pp. 162-163. University of Chicago Press, 1906. Copyright in the Public Domain.
18. Nigel Strudwick, Texts from the Pyramid Age, pp. 186-187. Copyright © 2005 by Society of Biblical Literature. Reprinted with permission.
19. "The Precepts of Ptah-hotep," Records of the Past, 2nd series, vol. III, ed. A.H. Sayce, trans. M. Philippe Virey, pp. 16-35. Samuel Bagster and Sons, Ltd, 1890. Copyright in the Public Domain.
    Image: Copyright © David Liam Moran (CC BY-SA 3.0) at http://commons.wikimedia.org/wiki/ File:Funerary_stele_of_Intef_II.jpg.
20. Nigel Strudwick, Texts from the Pyramid Age, pp. 391-392. Copyright © 2005 by Society of Biblical Literature. Reprinted with permission.
21. Miriam Lichtheim, Ancient Egyptian Literature, vol. I: The Old and Middle Kingdoms, pp. 85-86. Copyright © 1973 by University of California Press. Reprinted with permission.
22. James H. Breasted, Ancient Records of Egypt, vol. I, pp. 185-187. University of Chicago Press, 1906. Copyright in the Public Domain.
23. Alan H. Gardiner, Excerpt from: "New Literary Works from Ancient Egypt," Journal of Egyptian Archaeology, vol. 1, no. 1, pp. 22-35. Egypt Exploration Society, 1914. Copyright in the Public Domain.
24. Edward F. Wente, Letters from Ancient Egypt, pp. 215. Copyright © 1990 by Society of Biblical Literature. Reprinted with permission.
25. James H. Breasted, Ancient Records of Egypt, vol. I, pp. 201-203. University of Chicago Press, 1906. Copyright in the Public Domain.
26. Miriam Lichtheim, Excerpts from: "The Songs of the Harpers," Journal of Near Eastern Studies, vol. 4, no. 3, pp. 192-194. Copyright © 1945 by University of Chicago Press. Reprinted with permission.
    Copyright © Keith Schengili-Roberts (CC BY-SA 2.5) at http://commons.wikimedia.org/ wiki/File:Mentuhotep-OsirideStatue-CloseUp_ MuseumOfFineArtsBoston.png.
27. James H. Breasted, Ancient Records of Egypt, vol. I, pp. 208-210. University of Chicago Press, 1906. Copyright in the Public Domain.

28. Edward F. Wente, Letters from Ancient Egypt, pp. 60-62. Copyright © 1990 by Society of Biblical Literature. Reprinted with permission.

29. James H. Breasted, Ancient Records of Egypt, vol. I, pp. 214-215. University of Chicago Press, 1906. Copyright in the Public Domain.

30. Alan H. Gardiner, Excerpt from: "New Literary Works from Ancient Egypt: II," Journal of Egyptian Archaeology, vol. 1, no. 2, pp. 101-105. Egypt Exploration Society, 1914. Copyright in the Public Domain.

31. "The Foundation of the Temple of the Sun at Heliopolis," Records of the Past, vol. XII, trans. Ludwig Stern pp. 53-55. Samuel Bagster and Sons, Ltd, 1881. Copyright in the Public Domain.

32. James H. Breasted, Ancient Records of Egypt, vol. I, pp. 250-253. University of Chicago Press, 1906. Copyright in the Public Domain.

33. Alan H. Gardiner, Notes on The Story of Sinuhe, pp. 168-176. Librairie Honoré Champion, 1916. Copyright in the Public Domain.

34. The Instruction of Ptah-hotep and the Instruction of Ke'gemni: The Oldest Books in the World, trans. Battiscombe Gunn, pp. 67-71. John Murray Publishers Limited, 1912. Copyright in the Public Domain.

35. Adolf Erman, The Literature of the Ancient Egyptians, trans. Aylward M. Blackman, pp. 86-92. Copyright © 1927 by Taylor & Francis Group LLC. Reprinted with permission.

36. James H. Breasted, Ancient Records of Egypt, vol. I, pp. 267-269. University of Chicago Press, 1906. Copyright in the Public Domain.

37. James H. Breasted, Ancient Records of Egypt, vol. I, pp. 282-289. University of Chicago Press, 1906. Copyright in the Public Domain.

38. Miriam Lichtheim, Ancient Egyptian Literature, vol. I: The Old and Middle Kingdoms, pp. 131-133. Copyright © 1973 by University of California Press. Reprinted with permission.

39. James H. Breasted, Ancient Records of Egypt, vol. I, pp. 295-297. University of Chicago Press, 1906. Copyright in the Public Domain.

40. Adolf Erman, The Literature of the Ancient Egyptians, trans. Aylward M. Blackman, pp. 134-137. Copyright © 1927 by Taylor & Francis Group LLC. Reprinted with permission.

41. James H. Breasted, Ancient Records of Egypt, vol. I, pp. 298-300. University of Chicago Press, 1906. Copyright in the Public Domain.

42. T. Eric Peet, The Stela of Sebek-khu: The Earliest Record of an Egyptian Campaign in Asia, pp. 4-5. Longmans, Green and Co., 1914. Copyright in the Public Domain.

43. Adolf Erman, The Literature of the Ancient Egyptians, trans. Aylward M. Blackman, pp. 36-47. Copyright © 1927 by Taylor & Francis Group LLC. Reprinted with permission.

44. Alan H. Gardiner, Excerpt from: "The Eloquent Peasant," Journal of Egyptian Archaeology, vol. 9, no. 1/2, pp. 7-22. Copyright © 1923 by Egypt Exploration Society. Reprinted with permission.

45. Adolf Erman, The Literature of the Ancient Egyptians, trans. Aylward M. Blackman, pp. 30-35. Copyright © 1927 by Taylor & Francis Group LLC. Reprinted with permission.

46. Adolf Erman, The Literature of the Ancient Egyptians, trans. Aylward M. Blackman, pp. 68-72. Copyright © 1927 by Taylor & Francis Group LLC. Reprinted with permission.

47. Hieratic Papyri in the British Museum, vol. 1: Text, ed. Alan H. Gardiner, pp. 38-39, 41, 43. British Museum, 1935. Copyright in the Public Domain.

48. Legends of the Gods: The Egyptian Texts, ed. E. A. Wallis Budge, pp. 15, 17, 19, 21, 23, 25, 27, 29, 31, 33, 35, 37, 39, 41. Kegan Paul, Trench, Trübner & Company, 1912. Copyright in the Public Domain.

49. James H. Breasted, Ancient Records of Egypt, vol. I, pp. 326-327. University of Chicago Press, 1906. Copyright in the Public Domain.

50. Edward F. Wente, Letters from Ancient Egypt, pp. 86. Copyright © 1990 by Society of Biblical Literature. Reprinted with permission.
image: Copyright © Walters Art Museum (CC BY-SA 3.0) at http://commons.wikimedia.org/wiki/File:Canaanite_-_Scarab_with_Cartouche_of_King_Sheshi_-_Walters_4217_-_Bottom_%282%29.jpg.

51. James H. Breasted, Ancient Records of Egypt, vol. I, pp. 333-337. University of Chicago Press, 1906. Copyright in the Public Domain.

52. Alan H. Gardiner, The Admonitions of an Egyptian Sage, pp. 109-110. J. C. Hinrichs, 1909. Copyright in the Public Domain.

53. The Edwin Smith Surgical Papyrus, vol. 1, trans. James H. Breasted, pp. 439, 504-507. Copyright © 1930 by The Oriental Institute of the University of Chicago. Reprinted with permission.

54. James H. Breasted, Ancient Records of Egypt, vol. I, pp. 340-341. University of Chicago Press, 1906. Copyright in the Public Domain.

55. Battiscombe Gunn and Alan H. Gardiner, Excerpt from: "New Renderings of Egyptian Texts: II (The Expulsion of the Hyksos)," Journal of Egyptian Archaeology, vol. 5, no. 1, pp. 45-46. Egypt Exploration Society, 1918. Copyright in the Public Domain.
image: Copyright © Roberto Venturini (CC BY 2.0) at http://commons.wikimedia.org/wiki/File:Ramesses_II_in_the_Turin_Museum24.jpg.

56. Battiscombe Gunn and Alan H. Gardiner, Excerpt from: "New Renderings of Egyptian Texts: II (The Expulsion of the Hyksos)," Journal of Egyptian

Archaeology, vol. 5, no. 1, pp. 48-52. Egypt Exploration Society, 1918. Copyright in the Public Domain.

57. J. J. Tylor and F. Ll. Griffith, The Tomb of Paheri at El Kab, pp. 29-31. Egypt Exploration Society, 1894. Copyright in the Public Domain.

58. T. Eric Peet, Excerpt from: "Two Eighteenth Dynasty Letters," Journal of Egyptian Archaeology, vol. 12, no. 1/2, pp. 71-72. Copyright © 1926 by Egypt Exploration Society. Reprinted with permission.

59. James H. Breasted, Ancient Records of Egypt, vol. II, pp. 96-99. University of Chicago Press, 1906. Copyright in the Public Domain.

60. James H. Breasted, Ancient Records of Egypt, vol. II, pp. 180-187. University of Chicago Press, 1906. Copyright in the Public Domain.

61. James H. Breasted, Ancient Records of Egypt, vol. II, pp. 268-270. University of Chicago Press, 1906. Copyright in the Public Domain.

62. James H. Breasted, Ancient Records of Egypt, vol. II, pp. 321-324. University of Chicago Press, 1906. Copyright in the Public Domain.

63. Adolf Erman, The Literature of the Ancient Egyptians, trans. Aylward M. Blackman, pp. 235-242. Copyright © 1927 by Taylor & Francis Group LLC. Reprinted with permission.

64. Legends of the Gods: The Egyptian Texts, ed. E. A. Wallis Budge, pp. 97, 99, 101, 103, 105. Kegan Paul, Trench, Trübner & Company, 1912. Copyright in the Public Domain.

65. Harry A. Hoffner, Jr., Letters from the Hittite Kingdom, pp. 269-270, 275-276. Copyright © 2009 by Society of Biblical Literature. Reprinted with permission.

66. "Letters to Egypt from Babylonia, Assyria, and Syria in the Fifteenth Century B.C.," Records of the Past, 2nd series, vol. III, ed. A. H. Sayce, pp. 84-89. Samuel Bagster and Sons, Ltd, 1890. Copyright in the Public Domain.

67. Harry A. Hoffner, Jr., Letters from the Hittite Kingdom, pp. 277-279. Copyright © 2009 by Society of Biblical Literature. Reprinted with permission.

68. E. A. Wallis Budge, Tutankhamen: Amenism, Atenism and Egyptian Monotheism, ed. David Miano, pp. 122-135. Martin Hopkinson and Company Ltd, 1923. Copyright in the Public Domain.

69. The Tell Amarna Tablets, trans. C. R. Conder, pp. 102-103. Macmillan, 1893. Copyright in the Public Domain.

70. The Tell Amarna Tablets, trans. C. R. Conder, pp. 122-123, 126-128. Macmillan, 1893. Copyright in the Public Domain.

71. The Tell Amarna Tablets, trans. C. R. Conder, pp. 140-143. Macmillan, 1893. Copyright in the Public Domain.

72. James H. Breasted, Ancient Records of Egypt, vol. III, pp. 25-33. University of Chicago Press, 1906. Copyright in the Public Domain.

73. Battiscombe Gunn and Alan H. Gardiner, Excerpt from: "New Renderings of Egyptian Texts," Journal of Egyptian Archaeology, vol. 4, no. 4, pp. 244-245. Egypt Exploration Society, 1917. Copyright in the Public Domain.

74. Edward F. Wente, Letters from Ancient Egypt, pp. 114-115. Copyright © 1990 by Society of Biblical Literature. Reprinted with permission.

75. Alan H. Gardiner and Kurt Sethe, Egyptian Letters to the Dead, pp. 8-9. Copyright © 1928 by Egypt Exploration Society. Reprinted with permission.

76. James H. Breasted, Ancient Records of Egypt, vol. III, pp. 113-117. University of Chicago Press, 1906. Copyright in the Public Domain.

77. James H. Breasted, Ancient Records of Egypt, vol. III, pp. 143-147, 153-155. University of Chicago Press, 1906. Copyright in the Public Domain.

78. S. Langdon and Alan H. Gardiner, Excerpts from: "The Treaty of Alliance between Hattusili, King of the Hittites, and the Pharaoh Ramesses II of Egypt," Journal of Egyptian Archaeology, vol. 6, no. 3, pp. 185-194, 197-198. Egypt Exploration Society, 1920. Copyright in the Public Domain.

79. James H. Breasted, Ancient Records of Egypt, vol. III, pp. 259-264. University of Chicago Press, 1906. Copyright in the Public Domain.

80. Edward F. Wente, Letters from Ancient Egypt, pp. 124-126. Copyright © 1990 by Society of Biblical Literature. Reprinted with permission.

81. Edward F. Wente, Letters from Ancient Egypt, pp. 141-142. Copyright © 1990 by Society of Biblical Literature. Reprinted with permission.

82. Peter Le Page Renouf, "The Tale of Two Brothers," Records of the Past, vol. II, pp. 139-152. Samuel Bagster and Sons, Ltd, 1874. Copyright in the Public Domain.

83. Miriam Lichtheim, Ancient Egyptian Literature, vol. II: The New Kingdom, pp. 211-214. Copyright © 1976 by University of California Press. Reprinted with permission.

84. F. Ll. Griffith, Excerpt from: "The Teaching of Amenophis the Son of Kanakht," Journal of Egyptian Archaeology, vol. 12, no. 3/4, pp. 195-225. Copyright © 1926 by Egypt Exploration Society. Reprinted with permission.

85. Battiscombe Gunn and Alan H. Gardiner, Excerpt from: "New Renderings of Egyptian Texts: II (The Expulsion of the Hyksos)," Journal of Egyptian Archaeology, vol. 5, no. 1, pp. 40-42. Egypt Exploration Society, 1918. Copyright in the Public Domain.

86. T. Eric Peet, Excerpt from: "The Legend of the Capture of Joppa and the Story of the Foredoomed Prince," Journal of Egyptian Archaeology, vol. 11, no. 3/4, pp. 227-229. Copyright © 1925 by Egypt Exploration Society. Reprinted with permission.

87. Alan H. Gardiner, The Library of A. Chester Beatty: The Chester Beatty Papyri, no. 1, pp. 30-38. Copyright

© 1931 by Chester Beatty Library. Reprinted with permission.

88. James H. Breasted, Ancient Records of Egypt, vol. IV, pp. 36-40. University of Chicago Press, 1906. Copyright in the Public Domain.

89. James H. Breasted, Ancient Records of Egypt, vol. IV, pp. 212-221. University of Chicago Press, 1906. Copyright in the Public Domain.

90. James H. Breasted, Ancient Records of Egypt, vol. IV, pp. 198-206. University of Chicago Press, 1906. Copyright in the Public Domain.

91. Edward F. Wente, Letters from Ancient Egypt, pp. 150-151. Copyright © 1990 by Society of Biblical Literature. Reprinted with permission.

92. Yakov Rabinovich, Isle of Fire: A Tour of the Egyptian Further World, Volume One, pp. 170, 172, 174, 176, 178, 180, 182, 184, 186, 188, 190, 192, 194, 196, 198, 200, 202, 204, 206, 208, 210, 212, 214, 216, 218, 220, 222, 224, 226, 228, 230, 232, 234. Copyright © 2004 by Yakov Rabinovich. Reprinted with permission.

93. Edward F. Wente, Letters from Ancient Egypt, pp. 129-130. Copyright © 1990 by Society of Biblical Literature. Reprinted with permission.

94. James H. Breasted, Ancient Records of Egypt, vol. IV, pp. 252-264, 268-271. University of Chicago Press, 1906. Copyright in the Public Domain.

95. The Egyptian Book of the Dead: Translation and Commentary, trans. Peter Le Page Renouf and Edouard Naville, pp. 15-16, 21, 60-64, 66-67, 69, 157-161, 175, 212-220, 314, 322-323. The Society of Biblical Archaeology, 1904. Copyright in the Public Domain.

96. James H. Breasted, Ancient Records of Egypt, vol. IV, pp. 278-287. University of Chicago Press, 1906. Copyright in the Public Domain.

97. Edward F. Wente, Letters from Ancient Egypt, pp. 180-181. Copyright © 1990 by Society of Biblical Literature. Reprinted with permission.

98. Edward F. Wente, Letters from Ancient Egypt, pp. 203. Copyright © 1990 by Society of Biblical Literature. Reprinted with permission.
image: Copyright © David Liam Moran (CC BY-SA 3.0) at http://commons.wikimedia.org/wiki/File:Shabti_of_King_Taharqa.jpg.

99. James H. Breasted, Ancient Records of Egypt, vol. IV, pp. 317-320. University of Chicago Press, 1906. Copyright in the Public Domain.

100. James H. Breasted, Ancient Records of Egypt, vol. IV, pp. 329-330. University of Chicago Press, 1906. Copyright in the Public Domain.

101. James H. Breasted, Ancient Records of Egypt, vol. IV, pp. 356-357. University of Chicago Press, 1906. Copyright in the Public Domain.

102. James H. Breasted, Ancient Records of Egypt, vol. IV, pp. 418-444. University of Chicago Press, 1906. Copyright in the Public Domain.

103. James H. Breasted, "The First Philosopher," The Monist, vol. XII, no. 3, pp. 333-336. Open Court, 1902. Copyright in the Public Domain.

104. James H. Breasted, Ancient Records of Egypt, vol. IV, pp. 468-473. University of Chicago Press, 1906. Copyright in the Public Domain.
image: Copyright © Walters Art Museum (CC BY-SA 3.0) at http://commons.wikimedia.org/wiki/File:Egyptian_-_Iret-horru_with_Osiris_-_Walters_22215_-_Three_Quarter_Right.jpg.

105. James H. Breasted, Ancient Records of Egypt, vol. III, pp. 481-484. University of Chicago Press, 1906. Copyright in the Public Domain.

106. Original translation.

107. Original translation.

108. Original translation.
image: Copyright © Institute for the Study of the Ancient World (CC BY 2.0) at http://commons.wikimedia.org/wiki/File:Flickr_-_isawnyu_-_Hibis,_Temple_Decorations_%28III%29.jpg.

109. Excerpt from: "The Pastophorus of the Vatican," Records of the Past, vol. X, trans. P. Le Page Renouf. pp. 49-54. Samuel Bagster and Sons, Ltd, 1878. Copyright in the Public Domain.

110. Catalogue of the Demotic Papyri in the John Rylands Library, vol. III, trans. F. Ll. Griffith, pp. 77-92, 95-105. Manchester University Press, 1909. Copyright in the Public Domain.

111. The History of Herodotus, vol. 2, trans. George Rawlinson, pp. 2-6, 53-67, 136-146, 163-184, 191-202, 205-210, 214-224, 228, 233-237, 239, 242-251. J.M. Dent & Sons Limited, 1858. Copyright in the Public Domain.

112. James H. Breasted, Ancient Records of Egypt, vol. III, pp. 190-195. University of Chicago Press, 1906. Copyright in the Public Domain.

113. Legends of the Gods: The Egyptian Texts, ed. E. A. Wallis Budge, pp. 157, 159, 161, 163, 165, 167, 169, 171, 173, 175, 177, 179, 181, 183, 185, 187, 189, 191, 193, 195, 197. Kegan Paul, Trench, Trübner & Company, 1912. Copyright in the Public Domain.
image: Source: http://commons.wikimedia.org/wiki/File:Cleopatra_VII_statue_fragment,_69-30_BC_-_Royal_Ontario_Museum_-_DSC09761.JPG. Copyright in the Public Domain.

114. "Decree of Ptolemy Lagides, the Satrap," Records of the Past, vol. X, ed. S. Birch, trans. S. M. Drach, pp. 69-74. Samuel Bagster and Sons, Ltd, 1878. Copyright in the Public Domain.

115. Selections from the Greek Papyri, ed. George Milligan, pp. 2-4. Cambridge University Press, 1912. Copyright in the Public Domain.

116. The Works of Flavius Josephus, vol. IV, trans. William Whiston, pp. 275-278. Khull, Blackie, & Co., 1825. Copyright in the Public Domain.

117. E . A. Wallis Budge, The Decrees of Memphis and Canopus, vol. III: The Decree of Canopus, pp. 17-22, 25-26, 29-35. Oxford University Press, 1904. Copyright in the Public Domain.

118. F. Ll. Griffith, Stories of the High Priests of Memphis, pp. 16-40. Clarendon Press, 1900. Copyright in the Public Domain.

119. F. Ll. Griffith, Stories of the High Priests of Memphis, pp. 42-66. Clarendon Press, 1900. Copyright in the Public Domain.

120. E. A. Wallis Budge, The Decrees of Memphis and Canopus, vol. 1: The Rosetta Stone, pp. 169-183. Oxford University Press, 1904. Copyright in the Public Domain.

121. H. St. J. Thackery, Excerpts from: "Translation of the Letter of Aristeas," Jewish Quarterly Review, vol. 15, pp. 341-352, 370-372. Dropsie College for Hebrew and Cognate Learning, 1903. Copyright in the Public Domain.

122. Miriam Lichtheim, Ancient Egyptian Literature, vol. III: The Late Period, pp. 95-100. Copyright © 1980 by University of California Press. Reprinted with permission.

123. Selections from the Greek Papyri, ed. George Milligan, pp. 13-18. Cambridge University Press, 1912. Copyright in the Public Domain.

124. The Histories of Polybius, vol. II, trans. Evelyn S. Shuckburgh, pp. 370-372, 385-388, 401-406, 419-420, 437-438, 444-446, 471-473, 540. Macmillan, 1889. Copyright in the Public Domain.

125. Hellenic Civilization, ed. G. W. Botsford and E. G. Sihler, trans. William L. Westermann, pp. 603-606. Columbia University Press, 1915. Copyright in the Public Domain.

126. Miriam Lichtheim, Ancient Egyptian Literature, vol. III: The Late Period, pp. 161-179. Copyright © 1980 by University of California Press. Reprinted with permission.

127. Legends of the Gods: The Egyptian Texts, ed. E. A. Wallis Budge, pp. 57, 59, 61, 63, 65, 67, 69, 71, 73. 75, 77, 79, 81, 83, 85, 87, 89, 91, 93, 95. Kegan Paul, Trench, Trübner & Company, 1912. Copyright in the Public Domain.

128. The Historical Library of Diodorus the Sicilian, vol. 1, trans. G. Booth, pp. 18-19, 21-25, 27-29, 31-33, 50-51, 72-98. W. McDowell, 1814. Copyright in the Public Domain.

CPSIA information can be obtained
at www.ICGtesting.com
Printed in the USA
LVHW02s1527181018
594041LV00010B/512/P